The recent att... ...logy ou... the laboratory makes autobiographical m... ...stic ...one while maintaining empirical rig... ...e ...biographical memory,
such as eyewit... ...hi... there is memory
loss or distortio... ...extends beyond psychol... ...sociology, and
literature.

   Work on autobiographical memory has matured ...aphical Memory appeared in 1986, and the time is right for a ...ur
Past presents innovative research chapters and ge... ...p-
ment emotions, eyewitness memory, the false ill
appeal to graduate students and researchers in ...

Remembering our past

Remembering our past

Studies in autobiographical memory

Edited by

DAVID C. RUBIN
Duke University

CAMBRIDGE
UNIVERSITY PRESS

PUBLISHED BY THE PRESS SYNDICATE OF THE UNIVERSITY OF CAMBRIDGE
The Pitt Building, Trumpington Street, Cambridge

CAMBRIDGE UNIVERSITY PRESS
The Edinburgh Building, Cambridge, United Kingdom
40 West 20th Street, New York, NY 10011-4211, USA
10 Stamford Road, Oakleigh, Melbourne 3166, Australia

First published 1995
First paperback edition 1999

Printed in the United States of America

Library of Congress Cataloging-in-Publication Data is available.

A catalog record for this book is available from the British Library.

ISBN 0 521 46145 6 hardback
ISBN 0 521 65723 7 paperback

Contents

Part IV   Social functions

Part V   Development and disruption

List of contributors

Alan D. Baddeley
Medical Research Center
Applied Psychology Unit
Cambridge

Craig R. Barclay
Graduate School of Education and
    Human Development
University of Rochester

Robert F. Belli
Institute for Social Research
Survey Methodology Program
University of Michigan, Ann Arbor

William F. Brewer
Department of Psychology
University of Illinois at
    Urbana-Champaign

Jerome Bruner
New York University

Sven-Åke Christianson
Department of Psychology
University of Stockholm

Siew Eng Chua
Fulbourn Hospital
Cambridge

Martin A. Conway
Department of Psychology
University of Bristol

Carol Fleisher Feldman
New York University

Joseph M. Fitzgerald
Department of Psychology
Wayne State University

Robyn Fivush
Department of Psychology
Emory University

Catherine Haden
Department of Psychology
Emory University

Tia Hansen
Institute of Psychology
University of Aarhus

William Hirst
Department of Psychology
New School for Social Research

Steen F. Larsen
Institute of Psychology
University of Aarhus

Anneliesa Beebe Law
Department of Psychology
Wellesley College

Elizabeth F. Loftus
Department of Psychology
University of Washington

David Manier
Department of Psychology
New School for Social Research

Peter McKenna
Fulbourn Hospital
Cambridge

Martha L. Picariello
Department of Psychology
Brandeis University

David B. Pillemer
Department of Psychology
Wellesley College

Elaine Reese
University of Otago

Jill S. Reichman
Human Development
University of Chicago

John A. Robinson
Department of Psychology
University of Louisville

David C. Rubin
Department of Experimental Psychology
Duke University

Martin A. Safer
Department of Psychology
The Catholic University of America

Charles P. Thompson
Department of Psychology
Kansas State University

Andrew Thornton
Fulbourn Hospital
Cambridge

Willem A. Wagenaar
Unit of Experimental and Theoretical
   Psychology
Leiden University

J. M. G. Williams
Department of Psychology
University of Wales, Bangor

1   Introduction

David C. Rubin

Just about ten years ago I wrote the introduction to another collection of essays. *Autobiographical Memory* was the first edited book dedicated to a topic that has become an expanding area of study: an area that mixes rigorous, controlled, laboratory methods and theory with everyday questions. The time has come to ask what we have learned and what are we likely to learn, and the chapters of this book do that.

Autobiographical memory is one of the oldest and most complex areas of psychological inquiry. It is the presenting problem in most reports of Alzheimer's disease, closed head injury, and memory loss in general. It is the data base of talking-cure psychotherapies. It involves storytelling, group communication, and concepts like the self (Neisser, 1993; Neisser & Fivush, 1994; Srull & Wyer, 1993). It is what we usually mean by the term *memory* in everyday usage and thus is the basis of many of psychologists' ideas and intuitions about memory in general. Autobiographical memory therefore requires the integration of ideas and data from neuropsychology, clinical psychology, personality theory, social psychology, the study of narrative, folk psychology, and laboratory memory research. Because so many aspects of psychology, as well as other fields, are involved it should have been one of the least tractable areas to study. Nonetheless, in recent years, in large part because of these varied and rich sources of data and theory, cognitive psychology has made surprising advances understanding autobiographical memory. We have learned much thanks to solid findings and theorizing and to critical debates about basic concepts. In addition, much of what we have learned is of practical value.

Ten years ago (Rubin, 1986) and even four years ago (Rubin, 1992), I resisted attempts to define formally the term *autobiographical memory*. I believed that definitions should not be set a priori, but should reflect the natural cleavages that researchers found in nature. Others were more courageous. One of Baddeley's definitions is that "autobiographical memory is concerned with the capacity of people to recollect their lives" (1992, p. 26). Brewer defined an individual autobiographical memory (which he initially called a *personal memory* and in this volume calls a *recollective memory*) as "a recollection of a particular episode from an individual's past" (1986, p. 34). Characteristics include a "reliving" of the individual's phenomenal experience of the original event, reports of visual imagery and less frequently of other forms of imagery, a belief

1

that the remembered episode was personally experienced, and a belief that the remembered episode is a veridical record of the original event. I will not try to improve. Rather, based on Baddeley's and Brewer's definitions, I will look at the minimal components that go into the notion of autobiographical memory as used in cognitive psychology and in English.

One component of autobiographical memory is verbal narrative. Autobiographical memories are usually recalled as words, often as stories. The verbal structure of an autobiographical memory is the structure of the genre of narrative that it is. The extent to which autobiographical memories are stored as narratives is an open question (Barclay, this volume; Conway, this volume), but whether told to oneself or to another, autobiographical memories are usually told. Thus the structure of discourse affects the structure of recall, which in turn affects the structure of later recall (Barclay, this volume; Barclay & Smith, 1992; Bruner & Feldman, this volume; Fitzgerald, 1988; Fivush, Haden, & Reese, this volume; Freeman, 1993; Hirst & Manier, this volume; Labov & Waletzky, 1967; Robinson, 1981; Sarbin, 1986; Schank & Abelson, in press). Autobiographical memories usually take the form of stories or newspaper reports rather than fragmentary lists of attributes. Flashbulb memories may have canonical categories of who, what, and where because all news reports do (Neisser, 1982), and the inability to form coherent stories of one's memories can lead to difficulties (Barclay, this volume). Moreover, this narrative structure must be learned (Fivush, Haden, & Reese, this volume; Miller & Sperry, 1988; Nelson, 1993).

The narrative structure of autobiographical memory seems similar to the narrative structure of other social communication, and the recall of autobiographical memories is usually a social act (Hirst & Manier, this volume) that can define the social group (Bruner & Feldman, this volume). This social nature of autobiographical memory, to which I will return when considering imagery, links autobiographical memory research with the growing concern of cognitive psychology with socially distributed knowledge (Lave & Wenger, 1991; Middleton & Edwards, 1990). Parents teach their children the culturally appropriate genre for telling their memories in a socially interesting and informative way, one that gives them and their parents both a sense of the importance of sharing their memories and access to their personal histories (Fivush, Haden, & Reese, this volume).

Imagery is another major component of autobiographical memory. As Brewer notes (1986, this volume), autobiographical memories consist in part of images and this is one way to separate them from facts about one's life that are not autobiographical memories. Thus, I know that I received a program at the Cognitive Science Meetings in Boulder, Colorado, but I have no autobiographical memory for this event. I say this because I have the program and remember carrying it home, but I have no image or other sense of personally receiving the program, nor can I relive the event. In contrast, I have an autobiographical memory for having lunch with Bill Brewer at those meetings, prompted by reading Brewer's chapter. I have an image of the surroundings. Without the image, I doubt that I would claim a "reliving" or a belief that the lunch was "personally experienced," although if I had no image after reading Brewer's recollection, I would still have a nonautobiographical memory of the lunch from Brewer's point of view. Brewer's claim for the importance of imagery in autobiographical memory comes from his and others' phenomenological reports, from the analyses of philosophers, and from psychology.

Imagery is also a part of the metaphor of taking a picture that was used to name the flashbulb memory phenomenon (Brown & Kulik, 1977) and is noted throughout the flashbulb memory literature as an important component of what makes vivid memories vivid (see Winograd and Neisser, 1992, for a recent review). In addition there is literature on field versus observer point of view in autobiographical memory (that is, on whether one sees oneself in the memory or sees it from the original observer's viewpoint) that goes back at least to Freud (see Robinson & Swanson, 1993, for a recent review). Central to the current discussion is the role of imagery in increasing the specific, relived, personally experienced aspect of autobiographical memory (also see Rubin, 1995, for the implications of the same issue for oral traditions).

Imagery leads to the specific, concrete details that make memories seem more accurate, thoughtful, and believable (Pillemer, 1992; Pillemer, et al., this volume). People act as if memory for details implies that the central points are remembered correctly. For instance, an eyewitness's testimony is more effective, that is more believable, if details are included, even if they are irrelevant to the case (Bell & Loftus, 1989), and sensory details make people likely to judge that they did an action rather than just thought about it (Johnson & Raye, 1981). In addition, as Pillemer (1992) notes, specific details increase the sense of emotionality, intimacy, and immediacy of a communication when compared to abstract statements that remove the events described from particular situations. Thus, like a common narrative structure, imagery adds to the social nature of autobiographical memory by increasing the likelihood of communication and by making that communication more believable. Thus evidence that the rememberer has an image is routinely taken as evidence for a relived, personally experienced, that is autobiographical, memory.

Emotions are another main component of autobiographical memory. Like narrative and imagery, emotions have functions beyond their contributions to autobiographical memory. Unlike narrative and imagery, emotions are traditionally seen as outside cognition rather than as an aspect of it. As seen in the work of Christianson and Safer (this volume) and of Williams (this volume), emotions have profound effects on autobiographical memory. They can focus attention on one aspect of a scene and they can reduce the ability to retrieve specific, as opposed to generic, autobiographical memories of generalized categories of events.

The effects noted by Christianson and Safer and by Williams can both be seen as interactions with the imagery component. Christianson and Safer compare the focusing of memory on emotionally salient objects in an event to the focusing of attention in vision, allowing the focusing to be mediated by imagery. The inability of depressed individuals to retrieve specific, single-occurrence autobiographical memories, documented by Williams, may be related to the inability of abstract versus concrete, imageable memories to produce specific details (Chase & Ericsson, 1981, pp. 161–163;

Schwanenflugel, Akin, & Luh, 1992). In addition, Robinson (this volume) observes that changes in the viewer's perspective of an image affects the intensity of emotion.

The accuracy of memory is a general issue, but one that has been especially well studied in autobiographical memory because of its implications for the legal system and the validity of survey research. A brief review of the accuracy of memory in laboratory situations can set the stage for its consideration in autobiographical memory (Baddeley, Thornton, Chua, & McKenna, this volume; Belli & Loftus, this volume; Larsen, Thompson, & Hansen, this volume; Wagenaar, this volume; Winograd & Neisser, 1992).

People are very accurate in the laboratory-free recall of lists of isolated words. They omit words, but there are few intrusions. One technique to produce intrusions, that is inaccurate recall, is to use lists of organized words in which one word in the organization is missing and so is likely to be recalled although it was not on the list. Thus a list of animal names including *cat* but not *dog* will often have *dog* as an intrusion. A second way of producing intrusions is to give people many lists to remember with little in the way of temporal or context cues to make them distinctive. Under these conditions, words from one list will intrude into another. A third technique is to replace free recall with a forced-choice recognition test among alternatives. Every error in recognition then becomes an inaccurate choice, not just an omission. Similar effects can be found in prose, as well as lists, where schema theory is often invoked to account for them, though both schema and instance theories can provide explanations (Hintzman, 1986).

In autobiographical memory, the same basic mechanisms seem to be at work. People distort instances toward the generic or schematic occurrence. Events from nearby times intrude into the requested time both in the dating of events (Rubin & Baddeley, 1989) and in the "wrong time slice errors" noted by Brewer in the recall of random events (Brewer, 1988) and present in flashbulb memories (Winograd & Neisser, 1992). When forced to choose among alternatives, people often make the wrong choice. In autobiographical memory, however, there is the added question of what accurate memory means (Robinson, this volume). Scoring a word for verbatim recall or a proposition for content is much simpler than deciding whether one person's account of an event accurately reflects the event that occurred.

One theme that occurs throughout this book is that autobiographical memories are constructed. This does not mean that they are either accurate or inaccurate, but that they are not encoded, stored, and retrieved as wholes but rather are created at retrieval using components like the narrative, imagery, emotion division used in this introduction or the components of a model as in Conway (this volume). However, to the extent that the construction is guided by the person's goals at the time of retrieval, as well as by the goals at the time of encoding, changes in what is remembered should be expected (see both Conway and Robinson, this volume).

The question of accuracy also involves one of the most interesting paradoxes in autobiographical memory. Autobiographical memories are not always accurate, but as Brewer (this volume) notes, we do believe that our own autobiographical memories are true even in cases when we know from independent evidence that they are not. Imagery may be one cause of this paradox. Autobiographical memories are accompanied by images that provide specific details of the same kind that can lead us to judge that a remembered event occurred as opposed to just being thought about (Johnson & Raye, 1981).

The use of components to describe autobiographical memory was undertaken to show the full breadth of the topic (Rubin, in press) and how these components might interact with the issue of accuracy, but it also can relate the behavioral studies undertaken in this volume to the neural systems supporting them. The brain imaging techniques of cognitive neuroscience are being used to map the locations, timing, and interactions of brain systems involved in cognition. Experimental and cognitive psychologists are considering how behavioral and human imaging studies can inform each other. Autobiographical memory is a good place to start because this interplay of brain and behavior has been of interest since people began studying organic amnesia, and because recent behavioral and neuropsychological work has shown with more precision what will be needed. The neural pathways for various memory systems, language behavior including narrative, imagery, and emotions are under study. Their integration in autobiographical memory may provide a tractable area of research. Rather than exclude patients with imagery or emotional problems or with language deficits that affect narrative from autobiographical memory studies in order to obtain "pure" memory disorders, the integration of these deficits needs to be studied. In any case, if we are to get involved in the modern magic of mind reading, it might as well be in search of the soul or at least the sense of self.

The definition of autobiographical memory given earlier accurately considered autobiographical memory as a subset of memory. However, the thrust of this essay has been that in the history of psychological research on memory, autobiographical memory is better considered as an expansion of memory as normally studied to include new components and fields of study. To make progress by simplifying its domain of interest, mainstream cognitive psychology at its inception accepted a machine, the computer, as its model. It thereby made marginal to its domain of interest most considerations of the physiology and neural substrates of cognition, of the social and cultural supports for cognition, and of motivation and emotion. Progress has been made and in recent years we have begun bringing these aspects of cognition back from the margins into central positions in our collective definition of cognitive psychology. This book is part of that effort.

The book is divided into five sections, each with its own topic. But in reality the book is more integrated than that. The division is intended only to provide a convenient grouping. The introductory section of the book, titled "Approaches," is the most general and ambitious. Brewer, Conway, and Barclay each attempt to provide a framework for all of autobiographical memory, each in their own ways. Later chapters, for the most part, have more clearly defined limits and databases.

It is not my intention to scare the reader expecting more traditional experimental psychology by placing these chapters first. Rather the time has come to examine some of the difficult questions that the more cautious of us (including myself) have avoided. We need to try to integrate with experimental techniques ideas that have remained marginal. Cognitive psychology has recently welcomed neuroscience into its attempt at understanding, but much of the clinical, anthropological, and philosophical work still tends to be excluded. The authors of the three first chapters make such data and ideas central without abandoning the aims and methods of cognitive psychology.

Brewer begins the book by providing a broad definition of autobiographical memory, or as he now names it, "recollective memory." He then proceeds to examine the arguments and introspections of philosophers, the theory and data collected by psychologists to study autobiographical memory directly, and the theory and data collected in more traditional laboratory settings. Triangulating from these three perspectives he refines his definition of recollective memory and describes its properties. This is Brewer's fourth attempt (Brewer 1982, 1986; Brewer & Pani, 1983) and progress is evident.

Like the other two chapters in the first section and like most chapters throughout the book, at least one field outside mainstream cognitive psychology is read seriously, and integrated into the chapter. Philosophy of mind is a natural source for Brewer because he takes phenomenological reports as data on an equal footing with reaction times and amount recalled, making the phenomenological analysis of philosophers primary data.

One example of the usefulness of this approach comes in his treatment of Tulving's (1972) initial semantic-episodic memory distinctions and its later expansions. He credits Tulving with reintroducing recollective memory, in the form of episodic memory, back into psychology after it had been ignored by the dominant behaviorist approach. However, by using a combination of Ebbinghaus's and philosophical writings he faults the initial binary semantic-episodic formulation on two grounds. The first is for the choice of the list-learning laboratory techniques used to study it, which distorts much that was held to be central to recollective memory. The second is for proposing semantic memory, as opposed to the more classic skill or habit memory as the concept contrasted with episodic-recollective memory. This nonclassical opposition leaves much in episodic memory that Brewer would like to exclude from recollective memory. Brewer's integration of ideas from philosophy, list-learning experiments, and studies of autobiographical memory provides a broader base than the one we had to decide the most useful way to divide memory into its parts.

Conway formulates an "outline sketch" of a model of autobiographical memory in the cognitive science tradition. It is an account of the processes of encoding, retaining, and retrieving autobiographical memories in both normal adult and amnesic populations. To arrive at a full model Conway needs to use a broad range of data and theory and still he has to be speculative in places. He therefore notes where sufficient data or theories are lacking to support his assumptions, helping to find our areas of knowledge and ignorance.

Central to Conway's model is the idea that autobiographical memories, except highly rehearsed ones, are not stored and retrieved, but are constructed anew from stored information and the immediate situation. This is an extreme constructivist position and one that Barclay also adopts in the chapter that follows Conway's. Autobiographical memories are formed from a hierarchical knowledge base that has no autobiographical memories but rather levels for lifetime periods, general events, and event-specific knowledge. Conway's model uses cyclic retrieval in which the recall from a cue becomes the cue for the next cycle. Dynamic, changing themes of the self, which are a person's active set of goals and plans, organize knowledge bases at the time of encoding. Later, when these themes may have changed, they guide processing at retrieval. The emphasis on goals in the themes of the self makes discrepancies between what is and what is desired especially salient.

Barclay covers many of the same issues as Conway, but from a very different perspective that can be described as more literary, more social, and more anthropological. Besides the familiar terms of cognitive science and experimental psychology, such as context, framing, and instantiation, his model includes terms like objectification, subjectification, and contextual restructuring. Through instantiation, reconstructive activities become autobiographical memories or objectifications available to others.

Through consensus building and subjectification these objectifications become the social contexts that frame further reconstructive activities. But the model is not linear; it is a circle that can be traversed in either direction. Through subjectification the publicly available objectifications produce reconstructive activities. Through contextual restructuring these reconstructive activities affect the context. The language is at first difficult, but it describes a process by which individuals in social settings offer their memories to others. The inability to find a social context in which to express one's memories inhibits a coherent sense of self.

In parallel with his model of the social construction of memories, Barclay proposes a model of coherent personal narratives. Autobiographical memories are told; the narrative structure of their genre informs others who know the genre what to expect and how to interpret the memories. The inability to find a shared narrative structure inhibits a coherent sense of self. Barclay applies his models to the recollections of a man he knows well and to those of concentration camp survivors.

The second section of the book is concerned with the issue of accuracy, of how well memories correspond to the events they report. As argued in the first section, the truthfulness of and belief in autobiographical memories are important independent of their accuracy. Nonetheless, the relationship of autobiographical memories to the events reported in them is of theoretical importance and is often of practical importance. Accuracy is often impossible to decide. It assumes a neutral observer who knows what really happened in a way that is correct for all other observers. Nonetheless, in survey research, legal systems, and everyday life, accuracy is important and psychological experiments can be devised in which the accuracy of recall can be judged. An object was either present or absent from a scene. An event either occurred on one day or another.

Time is an ideal topic to study accuracy in autobiographical memory and an important issue in its own right. First, as Larsen, Thompson, and Hansen (this volume) note, time is central to what we mean by autobiographical memory; autobiographical memories without a sense of temporal order would be marginal autobiographical memories at best. Second, errors lie on a physical continuum that is easy to measure. Third, time appears to function differently than other cues and thus requires individual study. Each time uniquely defines a location and activity for a person, which should make time an effective cue, but it is not in earlier studies by Wagenaar and by Brewer (see Brewer, this volume, for a review). Time is central to the concept of autobiographical memory, but it is not an inherent part of most memories (Brewer, this volume). Fourth, although time is a basic and simple dimension to define operationally in the physical world, it is a deceptively complex term theoretically for philosophers and empirical scientists alike. In psychology it has proven especially difficult for models of both standard laboratory memory and autobiographical memory. The regular ticks of a clock accumulated from an arbitrarily chosen zero point are not what matters for most human behavior. Time appears as cycles within cycles; for Larsen et al., days within weeks within years. Unraveling the mystery of what aspects of time matter for autobiographical memory occupies most of the Larsen et al. chapter. The chapter argues against several simple models of time and settles on a constructed temporal dimension.

Belli and Loftus review what could be a dull technical debate in cognitive psychology. Experiment is pitted against experiment, control group against control group, in the best tradition of experimental psychology. But the debate is exciting. It is about central theoretical issues, about how well we can trust our own memories, and about how well courts can. Moreover, the debate does not lead to a yes or no conclusion, but by an evaluation of mechanisms and of what conditions that are most and least likely to produce accurate remembering. Like all such debates, this one is not going to be resolved in a single chapter, but the reader is given the history, brought up to date, and made aware of the subtleties of the arguments.

The basic issue Belli and Loftus address is how various sources combine to produce autobiographical memories. In their earlier work, the sources were a target event that was witnessed and postevent information usually introduced in misleading questions. The person remembering the original target event would in many situations often report postevent information as part of the event. This work was couched in terms of the legal system in which the target event would be a crime and the postevent questions would be out-of-court questions by lawyers and police. Since then there has been a rise in the reporting by adults of sexual abuse and satanic rituals that occurred when the adults were children. The question now becomes whether the events occurred as reported or were introduced or heavily influenced, not by police or lawyers investigating a crime, but by therapists probing the causes of current symptoms. The evidence reviewed demonstrates that such influence is possible and indicates conditions under which it is most likely to occur.

Wagenaar's chapter can be viewed as the other side of the Belli and Loftus chapter. Instead of starting with a theoretical question about memory, which Wagenaar does at times, here he begins as a psychologist who is asked practical, important questions by a court. To what extent can a particular part of a particular person's testimony be trusted? Which of two conflicting testimonies are more likely to reflect the original events? Such questions need to be answered every day by people trying to understand their worlds as well as by courts. The results of Wagenaar's search are sobering and provide one measure of the limits of our field. Whereas Belli and Loftus can give general principles, Wagenaar cannot apply them in a particular situation with the certainty and precision needed to say whether an autobiographical memory is from the target event of the purported crime or from a different source.

Wagenaar presents the case of Yolanda who "accused her parents and a considerable number of other people of continual sexual abuse, 23 illegal abortions, the murder of at least six babies, and the sexual abuse of her children." The case resulted in convictions. More recently her accusations have expanded to include satanic rituals. Wagenaar reports on his efforts as a memory expert to sort though testimony and documents to answer particular questions set to him by the courts. To return to relatively mild questions of dating reviewed by Larsen et al., Wagenaar had to try to determine the exact date of a purported event. If a satanic ritual occurred when the fetus was younger than 24 weeks then by Dutch law it was an illegal abortion. If the ritual occurred when the baby was older than 24 weeks then it was a murder.

Robinson provides a broad, thoughtful bridge from the second section on accuracy to the third section on emotions. Taking a difficult middle ground he argues that meaning must be decided both from the first-person perspective of the experiencer and from the third-person perspective of a privileged, sanctioned, neutral observer. From these perspectives he wants to "understand when and why meaning changes or remains stable over time." Robinson notes that in most of cognitive psychology meaning is a characteristic of the stimulus, but in fact, the situation is more complex leading him to four propositions about meaning. First, there are multiple meanings because meanings also involve characteristics of the person and the choices the person makes. Second, meanings are not always clear when an event occurs but often must be categorized and elaborated later. Third, the meaning of an experience can change over time. Though different meanings from different times cannot all be accurate from a third-person perspective, they all can be authentic from a first-person perspective. Fourth, as argued earlier in the book by Barclay and later in the book by Bruner and Feldman and by Hirst and Manier, meanings need to be negotiated among groups.

In this context, Robinson examines memory for feelings and reasons. In the chapter that follows Robinson's, Christianson and Safer also review the literature on how accurately people recall their past feelings, concluding from a third-person perspective that people are so inaccurate as to require those who use questionnaires about past emotional states to be exceedingly cautious about their conclusions. In contrast, Robinson reviews the same literature and concludes from a first-person perspective that people recall past emotions in an authentic way that reflects their current emotional state. Present emotion affects the way a past experience is integrated and remembered.

As in the Conway chapter, Robinson notes the importance of the people's goals and also of their reasons or explanations of those goals. Again, as with the recall of emotions, changes in explanation are seen as revisionism only if the rewriting of history from a third-person perspective is taken. If memory is constructive, conditions at the time of construction will affect recall.

Christianson and Safer review the complex literature on emotion and memory as it applies to autobiographical memory, making sense of data that often has appeared contradictory. Although extremely strong traumatic emotions can be detrimental to conscious recall of an event, in most cases even a high level of emotional stress increases rather than decreases recall of an event. In both real-world observation and laboratory experiments the increase is strongest for details directly associated with the information that elicits the emotion. Moreover, in both the real world and the laboratory, things not initially recalled, which are often peripheral to the information eliciting the emotion, are often recalled later with either the passage of time, the reinstatement of cues, or repeated testing. Christianson and Safer propose the concept of tunnel memory to account for the existing literature, which suggests a focusing of attention both spatially and temporarily on critical details related to the source of arousal. This tunnel memory is helped by the inherent congruence between the details causing the emotion and the emotion being experienced. They note that even weak mood-state dependent effects are strengthened when mood is integrated with the information to be remembered. Christianson and Safer then review memory for emotions per se rather than the effect of emotions on the memory of events. Examples are given to demonstrate conditions under which such recall exists and its possible neural basis is discussed.

Williams reviews an impressive body of literature that depressed people recall general as opposed to specific events. In terms of Conway's model they lack an ability to retrieve event-specific knowledge. Williams, like Conway, notes that this phenomenon occurs in many clinical syndromes, but unlike Conway, Williams suggests specific hypotheses as to why this occurs in depression. Searching for specific events fails in a specific way. It produces other general events that belong to the same general category; it does not produce events that are general because they extend in time. Thus successive recall attempts do not lead to specific memories, but to other related general memories. As might be expected, such a failure to be able to reach event specific knowledge has detrimental effects for general problem-solving abilities.

Williams terms this process "mnemonic interlock." He hypothesizes that such a process can occur in any population with an impaired central executive capacity of working memory. Depressed people in particular are impaired because they lack a retrieval strategy that at times would result in the discovery of painful memories. Following this reasoning, Williams hypothesizes that distinctive cues will help overcome this deficit and that more self-focused questions will make it worse.

At a more general level Williams' chapter demonstrates an integration of cognitive and clinical psychology that extends both. To do so he has looked not only at the number of memories and the reaction times to produce memories in various conditions but also to the qualities of the memories themselves.

The three chapters in the next section of the book look at functions of autobiographical memories, especially the social functions. The chapters by Hirst and Manier and by Bruner and Feldman both study the recall of groups, but in different ways and from different perspectives. Hirst and Manier collect autobiographical memories about the same set of events from the four members of a family individually and then in a group. In this way they can see how each individual's recalls are affected by their social context, and they can see what aspects of each of the four individual's stories become part of the group story. Hirst and Manier's analysis yields three narrative roles: the narrator, who assumes the function of telling the story and maintaining its continuity; the mentor, who guides the narrative by providing retrieval cues, criticisms, and directions to the narrator; and the monitor, who does not take personal responsibility for the telling, but who explicitly evaluates the telling as to whether it is complete and correct in his or her view. These roles tend to be assigned repeatedly to the same family members, though the role of the narrator often shifts to the character who is central in the story being discussed.

Like Barclay, Hirst and Manier view autobiographical memories as acts of communication. Remembering an event is telling a story. Like both Barclay and Conway, autobiographical memories are constructions that come into being as they are told. In practice they need not reside in one person's memory, but as both Barclay and Robinson stress can be the negotiated product of a group.

Bruner and Feldman compare the autobiographical memories of members of three theater groups about their group's history. Unlike Hirst and Manier's study, individuals are interviewed without other group members, but the influence of the group is still important. Using a mix of quantitative frequency counts and qualitative analyses, Bruner and Feldman examine how autobiographical memories are told and how the differences in the tellings are influenced by and help define each group. That is, the members of a group define themselves and their group by recalling autobiographical memories. If the group is important it should help shape those memories.

Bruner and Feldman describe three theater groups that were all founded by New York University students interested in experimental theater shortly after the students left school. The three groups were similar in their success with finding space and audiences. Nonetheless, the autobiographical memories of the members of each of the three groups differ qualitatively in ways that can also be seen quantitatively in the words they, as compared to members of the other two groups, most frequently use to describe themselves and their actions. Each group develops its own genre, which reflects and shapes its experience. Thus one group with a closed membership and a common teacher and set of acting principles uses *we* as its most common personal pronoun, whereas a group that accepts new members and emphasizes the personal growth of the members uses *I* and *they* most frequently. Bruner and Feldman's analyses of the autobiographical memories of three comparable groups demonstrate some ways in which the values, beliefs, and experiences of local cultures shape the recall of individuals in both general and detailed ways.

Pillemer, Picariello, Law, and Reichman report on the autobiographical memories of undergraduates and alumnae who recalled events that occurred during their four years at Wellesley. Like Bruner and Feldman, they use a mix of quantitative and qualitative analyses. Following their emphasis on the importance of specific autobiographical memories, Pillemer et al. examine the contents of the autobiographical memories to infer the function they serve. College is a time of changes for undergraduates and many of the memories served a directive function. Some were implicit or explicit prescriptions for future behavior; others were of originating events, which told of a life course change, such as how the choice of a career came about; and others were anchoring events, which made concrete and helped to validate the student's beliefs. Pillemer et al. suggest that such memories tell about undergraduates' education in a way that more standardly used information about education does not and suggest using such autobiographical memories in the way case studies are used in business schools. Professors could benefit from a systematic study of such memories that shows the importance of the emotional content of a communication, of the communication's timing in the life of the student, and of the role of personal communications in which the professors go beyond their more usual impersonal roles.

In a more quantitative vein, Pillemer et al. support their qualitative analysis by examining the temporal distribution of influential memories over the freshman year for undergraduates and over the entire college period for alumnae. Like their previous studies of Wellesley students that asked for autobiographical memories of any kind, here there were a large proportion of influential memories coming from September of the freshman year and to a lesser extent from the end of the senior year. The increase of such memories from transition points, supports the idea that autobiographical memories in general and influential memories in particular occur in response to changes in the student's life and serve as directives for future action.

The three chapters of the final section examine the development and disruption of autobiographical memory. If, as many of the authors of this book claim, narrative structure is central to autobiographical remembering and if the narrative structures of local cultures vary, then such structures must be learned, much as are the words and grammar of the language or a literary genre. Fivush, Haden, and Reese examine how this is done by studying a parent and child reminiscing about shared events over the course of the child's development from 40 to 70 months old. In the beginning of this period, parents do most of the remembering, but by the end children have learned to participate much more fully. Some parents are more elaborative than others. That is, they work to elicit and maintain their child's contribution to the conversation by providing new information on the same topic even when the child recalls little. Fivush et al. argue that this is a parental style, not a response to the child's style or ability, and that it has consequences for the child's development. Over the course of longitudinal testing, parents are consistent in using this style, but children are not consistent in their behavior. In addition, the parent's elaborative style when the child is 40 months old predicts the child's behavior at 70 months.

Fivush et al. use these and similar observations to explore broader issues such as the relation of language development to memory development and thereby of language to memory. They argue that the child not only learns to remember but also learns to value the social interaction of sharing experiences. Thus the Fivush et al. chapter plots the development of some of the social interactions studied in adult families and groups in the previous two chapters.

Fitzgerald concentrates on the other end of the lifespan. He notes that for a time, based on laboratory tasks, developmental psychologists viewed both children and older adults as barely competent. However, work on autobiographical memory and other tasks more central to everyday functioning has revealed a different picture. People develop expertise, not only about chess and physics, but also "self-expertise" involving their autobiographical memories. Fitzgerald synthesizes and evaluates the work on reminiscence in the two separate senses in which the term has appeared in the literature. First, reminiscence is an increase in the number of autobiographical memories that come from between ages 15 and 25 relative to memories from surrounding periods, and second, reminiscence is a behavior engaged in by older adults.

As Fitzgerald notes, the increase in memories from late adolescence by older adults has become a well-replicated phenomena over the last decade, but its explanation remains open. Initially, differential encoding from age 15 to 25 was discarded as an explanation because there was no increase in memories in that period for younger adults and because there was no evidence for the cognitive difference on which such an explanation would depend. Fitzgerald challenges both objections. An increase in memories in younger adults could be overshadowed by recent memories; an increase in memories from age 15 to 25 may not be seen in 35-year-olds because their routine memories from 25 to 35 may mask it. Using new data from vivid memories he shows this to be the case. People in the 15-to-25-year-old range need not have markedly superior memories, Fitzgerald notes that there are noncognitive factors, such as identity formation, that would cause the cognitive factors to be used more and thus to result in differential encoding. Fitzgerald is less optimistic about telling a clear story about the existing literature on reminiscence as an everyday behavior in older adults, but he has suggestions for improving the situation and for merging the two senses of reminiscence that now appear in their own separate literatures.

In earlier work Baddeley and Wilson (1986) viewed the confabulations of frontal lobe patients as a problem in autobiographical memory. This novel approach raised questions both about the behavior and underlying neurology of confabulation as well as about the accuracy and belief in autobiographical memories of patients and of non-injured controls. Here Baddeley, Thornton, Chua, and McKenna take a similar approach with the delusions of schizophrenics. Delusions are like confabulations in that they consist of information about personal experiences that is not factual, that may be fantastic in nature, but that is held with firm conviction. The two differ in that confabulations are false episodic memories that often change on repeated telling, whereas delusions tend to be stable and are often more semantic in nature.

Transcripts of interviews with five delusional schizophrenics are presented and analyzed. The results of neuropsychological tests on these five patients compared to those of five schizophrenics who do not show as many delusions usually did not differ. When they did differ, as they did on several autobiographical memory measures, the delusional subjects act more like nonschizophrenics. Baddeley et al. search for possible neuropsychological deficits that would lead to such delusional memories only to conclude that the causes are probably widespread, and though there may be a single underlying cause, such as a deficiency in one neurotransmitter, there is no likely single function or location in the nervous system that is mainly responsible for the delusions or for the host of other schizophrenic symptoms. One suggestion that does come from the collections of autobiographical memories and neuropsychological testing is that the delusions are often clearer, more specific, and more vivid than usual nondelusional memories. Thus, returning full circle to Brewer's first chapter, delusional memories may be an extreme case of autobiographical memories that have even clearer images.

References

Baddeley, A. D. (1992). What is autobiographical memory? In M. A. Conway, D. C. Rubin, H. Spinnler, & W. A. Wagenaar (Eds.). *Theoretical perspectives on autobiographical memory* (pp. 13–29). Dordrecht, The Netherlands: Kluwer Academic Publishers.

Baddeley, A., & Wilson, B. (1986). Amnesia, autobiographical memory, and confabulation. In D. C. Rubin (Ed.), *Autobiographical memory* (pp. 225–252). Cambridge, UK: Cambridge University Press.

Barclay, C. R., & Smith, T. S. (1992). Autobiographical remembering: Creating personal culture. In M. A. Conway, D. C. Rubin, H. Spinnler, & W. A. Wagenaar (Eds.), *Theoretical Perspectives on Autobiographical Memory* (pp. 75–97). Dordrecht, The Netherlands: Kluwer Academic.

Bell, B. E., & Loftus, E. F. (1989). Trivial persuasion in the courtroom: The power of (a few) minor details. *Journal of Personality and Social Psychology, 56*, 669–679.

Brewer, W. F. (1982). Personal memory, generic memory, and skill: A reanalysis of the episodic-semantic distinction. In *Proceedings of the Fourth Annual Conference of the Cognitive Science Society* (pp. 112–113). Ann Arbor, MI.

—— (1986). What is autobiographical memory? In D. C. Rubin (Ed.), *Autobiographical Memory* (pp. 25–49). Cambridge, UK: Cambridge University Press.

—— (1988). Memory for randomly sampled autobiographical events. In U. Neisser & E. Winograd (Eds.), *Remembering reconsidered: Ecological and traditional approaches to the study of memory* (pp. 21–90). Cambridge, UK: Cambridge University Press.

Brewer, W. J., & Pani, J. R. (1983). The structure of human memory. In G. H. Bower (Ed.), *The psychology of learning and motivation: Advances in research and theory* (Vol. 17, pp. 1–38). New York: Academic Press.

Brown, R., & Kulik, J. (1977). Flashbulb memories. *Cognition, 5*, 73–99.

Chase, W. G., & Ericsson, K. A. (1981). Skilled memory. In J. R. Anderson (Ed.), *Cognitive skills and their acquisition* (pp. 141–189). Hillsdale, NJ: Lawrence Erlbaum.

Fitzgerald, J. M. (1988). Vivid memories and the reminiscence phenomenon: The role of a self-narrative. *Human Development, 31*, 261–273.

Freeman, M. (1993). *Rewriting the self: History, memory, narrative*. London: Routledge.

Hintzman, D. L. (1986). "Schema abstraction" in a multiple-trace memory model. *Psychological Review, 93*, 411–428.

Johnson, M. K., & Raye, C. L. (1981). Reality monitoring. *Psychological Review, 88*, 67–85.

Labov, W., & Waletzky, J. (1967). Narrative analysis: Oral versions of personal experience. In J. Helm (Ed.), *Essays on the verbal and visual arts: Proceedings of the 1966 Annual Spring Meeting of the American Ethnological Society* (pp. 12–44). Seattle, WA: University of Washington Press.

Lave, J., & Wenger, E. (1991). *Situated learning: Legitimate peripheral participation*. Cambridge, UK: Cambridge University Press.

Middleton, D., & Edwards, D. (Eds.). (1990). *Collective remembering*. London: Sage Publications.

Miller, P. J., & Sperry, L. L. (1988). Early talk about the past: The origins of conversational stories of personal experiences. *Journal of Child Language, 15*, 293–315.

Neisser, U. (1982). Snapshots or benchmarks. In U. Neisser (Ed.), *Memory observed*. San Francisco: W. H. Freeman.

—— (Ed.). (1993). *The perceived self: Ecological and interpersonal sources of self-knowledge*. Cambridge, UK: Cambridge University Press.

Neisser, U., & Fivush, R. (Eds.). (1994). *The remembering self: Construction and accuracy in the self-narrative*. Cambridge, UK: Cambridge University Press.

Nelson, K. (1993). The psychological and social origins of autobiographical memory. *Psychological Science*, *4*, 7–14.

Pillemer, D. B. (1992). Remembering personal circumstances: A functional analysis. In E. Winograd & U. Neisser (Eds.), *Affect and accuracy in recall: Studies of "flashbulb" memories* (pp. 236–264). Cambridge, UK: Cambridge University Press.

Robinson, J. A. (1981). Personal narratives reconsidered. *Journal of American Folklore*, *94*, 58–85.

Robinson, J. A., & Swanson, K. L. (1993). Field and observer modes of remembering. *Memory*, *1*, 169–184.

Rubin, D. C. (Ed.). (1986). *Autobiographical Memory*. Cambridge, UK: Cambridge University Press.

—— (1992). Definitions of autobiographical memory. In M. A. Conway, D. C. Rubin, H. Spinnler, & W. A. Wagenaar (Eds.), *Theoretical perspectives on autobiographical memory* (pp. 495–499). Dordrecht, The Netherlands: Kluwer Academic.

—— (1995). *Memory in oral traditions: The cognitive psychology of epic, ballads, and counting-out rhymes*. New York: Oxford University Press.

—— (In press). Stories about Stories. In R. S. Wyer, Jr. (Ed.), *Knowledge and memory: The real story*. Hillsdale, NJ: Lawrence Erlbaum.

Rubin, D. C., & Baddeley, A. D. (1989). Telescoping is not time compression: A model of dating autobiographical events. *Memory and Cognition*, *17*, 653–661.

Sarbin, T. R. (Ed.). (1986). *Narrative psychology: The storied nature of human conduct*. New York: Praeger.

Schank, R. C., & Abelson, R. P. (In press). Knowledge and memory: The real story. In R. S. Wyer, Jr. (Ed.), *Knowledge and memory: The real story*. Hillsdale, NJ: Lawrence Erlbaum.

Schwanenflugel, P. J., Akin, C., & Luh, W. M. (1992). Context availability and the recall of abstract and concrete words. *Memory and Cognition*, *20*, 96–104.

Srull, T. K., & Wyer, R. S. (Eds.). (1993). *The mental representation of trait and autobiographical knowledge about the self*. Hillsdale, NJ: Lawrence Erlbaum.

Tulving, E. (1972). Episodic and semantic memory. In E. Tulving & W. Donaldson (Eds.), *Organization of memory*. New York: Academic Press.

Winograd, E., & Neisser, U. (Eds.). (1992). *Affect and accuracy in recall: Studies of "flashbulb" memories*. New York: Cambridge University Press.

Part I

Approaches

2   What is recollective memory?

William F. Brewer

The goal of this chapter is to describe recollective memory and give an account of some of the characteristics of this form of human memory. I take recollective memory to be the type of memory that occurs when an individual recalls a specific episode from their past experience. I start with this very loose definition because a large part of this chapter consists of an attempt to work out a more detailed and analytic description of this form of memory.

In an earlier chapter (Brewer, 1986), I attempted to describe the types of memory involved in the study of autobiographical memory. I argued that autobiographical memory was memory for information related to the self and that there were four basic forms of autobiographical memory. I organized these forms of memory in terms of their acquisition conditions (single instance versus repeated) and their form of representation (imaginal versus nonimaginal). I concluded that the phenomenally experienced product of a single episode is a *personal memory* (e.g., I can picture David Rubin sitting across from me at lunch in a cafe in Boulder, Colorado, last summer). The nonphenomenally experienced product of a single episode is an *autobiographical fact* (e.g., I can recall *that* I had lunch with David Rubin at the Meetings of the Cognitive Science Society last summer). The phenomenally experienced product of multiple episodes is a *generic personal memory* (e.g., I have a general image of myself standing in an [unspecified] hotel lobby in an [unspecified] city talking with David Rubin). The nonphenomenally experienced product of multiple episodes contributes to one's *self schema* (e.g., I am a person who frequently talks with David Rubin at conferences).

In essence the present chapter is a discussion of what I called "personal memory" in my earlier chapter. As will become obvious, terminology in this area is a real problem. Even though the *construct* of personal memory/recollective memory is relatively clear, there is no consistent lexical form used for this concept in ordinary English or in the technical vocabulary of psychology or philosophy. In my previous work on this topic (Brewer, 1986, 1988, 1992b; Brewer & Pani, 1983), I have used the term "personal

I would like to thank Ellen Brewer, Clark Chinn, and David Lockhart for comments on an earlier draft of this chapter.

memory" for this form of memory. I adopted the term from the technical usage by certain philosophers (e.g., D. Locke, 1971). However, given the total lack of agreement concerning the technical terminology in this area, I have, after some agonizing, decided that we might be better off by adopting the closest ordinary language term, "recollecting," for our technical term. Therefore I will use "recollective memory" as the technical term for this form of memory.

Throughout this chapter, data derived from reports of phenomenal experience are given equal treatment with data derived from behavior. Even though many writers in recent years have argued for the acceptability of data from phenomenal experience (Ericsson & Simon, 1980; Hilgard, 1980; Natsoulas, 1970), most researchers still avoid this type of data. My position on this issue can be seen in the following analogy from the physical sciences: If in the early stages of the development of chemistry an investigator notices that one sample of material is yellow in color (e.g., gold) and another sample of material is white (e.g., silver), it seems reasonable to assume that these two substances might be different and to try to capture that difference in some form of theory. In psychology it is obvious that different forms of mental activity have different phenomenological correlates (cf. Brewer & Pani, 1983), and thus it seems to me that one ought to adopt the same strategy as that outlined in the chemistry example. We accept the phenomenological differences as possible guides to differences in the nature of the mental activity and try to capture them in our theories. The core assumption here is that a comprehensive psychology cannot be based exclusively on phenomenal experiences as in early introspective psychology (Boring, 1950), nor can it be based exclusively on behavior as in behaviorist psychology (Watson, 1913). Even though I feel strongly about the inclusion of phenomenal experience as data, I do not think it has any "privileged" status. Its eventual status will be determined by its role in our mature scientific theories. It might turn out that phenomenological similarities in two mental operations will not play a crucial role in our mature theories, in the same way that it turns out that the fact that both gold and iron pyrite have similar colors is not a good guide to concluding that they are similar substances. On the other hand, it may turn out that phenomenological differences in two mental operations are a good sign that the two should be treated differently in psychological theory, in the same way that the colors of gold and silver reflect an important difference between these substances in chemical theory. Given that we do not yet possess mature scientific theories in the area of human memory, it seems to me that our best research strategy is to include both the data from phenomenal experience and the data from behavior in our current attempts at theory development in this area.

There are three fairly independent scholarly traditions that have contributed to the topic of recollective memory: philosophy, psychological studies of autobiographical memory, and psychological studies of memory in the laboratory. This chapter examines each of these areas in an attempt to understand the nature and characteristics of recollective memory. The first section of the chapter is devoted to philosophy, the second section to psychological studies of autobiographical memory, and the final section to laboratory studies of memory.

Philosophy

The study of memory by philosophers has been more sophisticated than that of psychologists on the issues of types of memory and the description of these different types. Philosophical discussions of functional relationships involving recollective memory (e.g., variables related to successful recall) have not been as successful. These differences presumably reflect the strengths and weaknesses of the armchair method used by philosophers.

Terminology

The number of different terms used by philosophers to refer to recollective memory is truly impressive: "memory" (Bradley, 1899; Earle, 1956; Harrod, 1956); "memory par excellence" (Bergson, 1896/1911); "true memory" (Russell, 1921); "perceptual memory" (Broad, 1925; Malcolm, 1963); "reminiscence" (Stout, 1930); "retrospective memory" (Furlong, 1948); "memory of events" (Ayer, 1956); "remembering$_2$" (Strawson, 1957); "recollection" (Von Leyden, 1961); "suddenly remembering" (Munsat, 1967); "personal memory" (D. Locke, 1971); "occurrent memory" (Ayer, 1972); "occurrent retrospective memory" (Salmon, 1974); "conscious recall" (Brockelman, 1975); and "picture memory" (Lacey, 1989). Many of these lexical items were attempts to establish a new technical term for this form of memory, but the total lack of convergence of usage over time shows that all these attempts were failures, making it very difficult for an outsider to follow this literature.

Types of memory and forms of representation

Over the last century philosophers have distinguished a number of types of memory and have dramatically reevaluated the importance of the different types of memory. In traditional philosophy (e.g., the British Empiricists) memory was effectively equated with recollective memory. In modern philosophy the first major differentiation of the forms of memory was Bergson's (1896/1911) distinction between recollective memory and "habit memory" (i.e., memory for skilled actions). Bertrand Russell (1921) followed Bergson in making this fundamental distinction. However, both Bergson and Russell continued the traditional emphasis on recollective memory as the crucial form of memory, as can be seen in the terms they used to refer to it: "memory par excellence" and "true memory." This extreme focus on recollective memory led to some strange positions. For example, Carr stated that recognition was not memory (1916, p. 225).

Broad (1925, p. 221) made an important contribution by distinguishing three basic forms of memory: recollective memory, skill/rote memory, and propositional memory. He was very clear about distinguishing the last two and noted that "memory of propositions . . . cannot be identified with a mere power to repeat the sentences in which these propositions were expressed" (p. 272). Note that on this issue the philosophers were running over 40 years ahead of the psychologists (e.g., Anderson & Bower, 1973; Sachs, 1967; Tulving, 1972). The distinction between recollective memory and propositional memory was continued by philosophers such as Furlong (1948). Even though

Broad and Furlong discussed propositional memory, they still felt that recollective memory was the crucial form of memory for philosophy because of its role in the acquisition of knowledge.

However, as some philosophers became more behavioristic and more interested in providing linguistic explanations for philosophical problems, recollective memory lost status. Ryle (1949, p. 272) argued that propositional memory and rote memory were "by far the most important and the least discussed." Holland (1954) argued that all forms of memory, including recollective memory, might be reduced to forms of knowledge in memory. Ayer (1956) described habit memory, propositional memory, and recollective memory. However, he finally suggested that propositional memory might be reduced to habit memory and then recollective memory could be reduced to propositional memory (the reasoning is complex, but at one point [p. 142] he states that a habit is performed by displaying a skill, while a recollection is simply performed by reliving a past experience).

This reevaluation of recollective memory continued in a powerful paper by Malcolm (1963). Malcolm noted that one can have a propositional memory of something without a recollective memory (e.g., I recall that the platypus is a monotreme). In addition, he argued that if one has a recollective memory of an event one also has a propositional memory of the same event. Thus (to use my earlier example), if I can *recollect* having lunch with David Rubin, I can also recall *that* I had lunch with him. Malcolm (p. 212) also argued that an individual without propositional memory would be less than human, whereas an individual without recollective memory would show only minor impairment. On the basis of this type of evidence Malcolm concluded that propositional memory was more "primitive" and more "fundamental" than recollective memory (p. 214).

In more recent work most philosophers accept the distinctions between skill, propositional memory, and recollective memory. However, those with a behaviorist or ordinary language orientation (e.g., Munsat, 1967; Zemach, 1968) try to play down the role of imagery in recollective memory and propose that propositional memory may be the core for all forms of memory. Some (e.g., D. Locke, 1971) take a middle-of-the-road position, assuming that there are three basic types of memory and that they have different attributes and serve different functions. Finally, there are philosophers (e.g., Brockelman, 1975) who accept the three forms of memory but still maintain that recollective memory is the essence of memory of the past.

In looking at the philosophical work on memory over the past century one sees an initial extreme focus on recollective memory to the exclusion of other forms of memory. Then propositional memory was recognized as a form of memory and came to be seen as either the most important form of memory or as the core for all other forms of memory. Throughout this whole period most philosophers considered skill, and particularly rote memory, to be a minor component of human memory. In this respect the position of philosophers has been very different from that taken by psychologists during most of the history of the experimental study of memory. In the next sections of this chapter we will examine in some detail philosophical discussions of recollective memory.

Phenomenological descriptions of recollective memory

Occurrence of imagery. Essentially all the philosophical treatments of recollective memory assume that imagery occurs during the recollective process. This assumption can be seen in the use of terms such as "picture memory" and "perceptual memory" as the technical terms for recollective memory. Many philosophers made imagery a defining feature of recollective memory. For example, Russell (1921, p. 186) stated that recollective memory "demands . . . an image." Malcolm (1963, p. 207) stated, "Therefore [recollective memory] involves mental imagery." B. Smith (1966, p. 171) stated, "imagery is indispensable for [recollective memory]." D. Locke (1971, p. 80) noted that "the recollection of particular items essentially involves mental imagery." Finally, Brockelman (1975, p. 316) stated, "[recollective memory] is essentially and necessarily tied up with 'images'."

Characteristics of memory imagery. A number of philosophers have carried out armchair phenomenological descriptions of recollective memory imagery, and there is considerable agreement on its attributes:

1. Compared to perception, memory imagery is *dim* (not vivid) (Furlong, 1951 p. 97; D. Locke, 1971, p. 2; Price, 1936, p. 26; Von Leyden, 1961, p. 73). B. Smith (1966, p. 83) suggested that it is like visual perception with poor illumination.

2. Compared to perception, memory imagery is *unclear* (D. Locke, 1971, p. 2). B. Smith (1966, p. 83) suggested that memory imagery is like seeing something through frosted glass and Furlong (1951, p. 74) stated that the quality of memory imagery is such that one cannot read the time off the memory image of a watch.

3. Compared to perception, memory imagery is *sketchy, simplified,* and *schematic* (Ayer, 1956, p. 141; Furlong, 1948, p. 22; Price, 1936, p. 26; B. Smith, 1966, p. 86; Von Leyden, 1961, p. 75). However, several scholars have also argued that the memory image often contains *irrelevant detail* (Bradley, 1899, p. 159; B. Smith, 1966, p. 142).

4. Frequently memory images are *not in color* (B. Smith, 1966, pp. 180–181). When there are colors they are often *washed out* (less saturated) (Price, 1936, p. 26).

5. B. Smith (1966, p. 180) argued that the *size* of memory images in the visual field is frequently the same size as they would have been in perception. Thus, he suggested that a recollective image of a snapshot will be seen to be as if it were being viewed from normal viewing distance.

6. B. Smith (1966, p. 180) suggested that a recollective memory image is perceived as if there were a *blank area* surrounding the focal point of the image.

7. The issue of the *point of view* of visual recollective mental images has come up implicitly and explicitly in discussions of the veridicality of recollective memory. Many philosophers (e.g., Bergson, 1896/1911; Brockelman, 1975; Earle, 1956; Furlong,

1951; B. Smith, 1966) assumed that memory imagery displays the original experience; therefore, it appears that they would have to hold that visual memory images are perceived from the same point of view as the original experience. However, Von Leyden (1961, p. 78) and D. Locke (1971, pp. 88–89) noted that at least some visual memory images represent the scene (including the recollecting individual) as it would have been seen by an outside observer.

8. An issue that has rarely been discussed is whether the *ego* (cf. Brewer, 1986, p. 27) that experienced the past episode is part of the current memory image. Earle (1972), one of the few people to treat this problem, gave an ambivalent answer. He stated that in recollecting an occasion when he saw a burning building, "I now remember (myself looking at) a burning building. Now this is obviously a *reflexive* conscious act . . . insofar as I am now aware of a past awareness of an object" (p. 155). However, he also stated that when one has a recollective memory of a past event, attention is focused on the event and not the (past) ego observing the event (p. 154).

9. The overall memory image is *unsteady* (D. Locke, 1971, p. 2; Price, 1936, p. 26; B. Smith, 1966, p. 83). Price and Smith refer to it as "flickering."

Essentially all of the descriptions of recollective memory imagery use examples of visual imagery. However, many philosophers have noted that memory imagery is not restricted to the visual domain (e.g., Broad, 1925, p. 227; Brockelman, 1975, p. 317), but it is not clear to what degree the descriptions of memory imagery given above can be extended to other forms of imagery.

Suddenly remembering

Several philosophers have stated that one of the characteristics of recollective memory images is that they are "suddenly remembered" (cf. Ayer, 1956, p. 146; Munsat, 1967, chap. 3). It is not completely clear to me what psychological claim they are making here. It seems likely that retrieval speed for propositional information is faster than that for image information (e.g., Moore, 1915; Paivio, 1966), so I do not think retrieval speed can be what they are getting at. However, there is a sudden change of mental state when one shifts from the (largely unconscious) recollective search process to the successful retrieval of a recollective memory, and perhaps this is what they were trying to highlight with the "suddenly remembering" observation.

Sensation, uninterpreted perception, interpreted perception

Another issue that has been discussed by the philosophers is the degree to which the memory image is an interpreted representation (in other words, the issue that was raised during the analog/propositional debates in psychology in a powerful paper by Zenon Pylyshyn, 1973). In traditional philosophy some theorists (e.g., Hobbes, 1651/1952) considered the memory image to be a decaying sensation. Given this position, it would appear that during recollection one should be able to read information off the memory image (just as one can look at a photograph) and perhaps locate information that was not even noticed during the original event. B. Smith and D. Locke appear to adopt the view that memory images are images of the original perceptions, but that they can be reinterpreted during recollection (B. Smith, 1966, p. 54, 121) or later used to retrieve information not noticed during the original episode (D. Locke, 1971, p. 54). A number of philosophers have taken the view that memory images are images of one's perception at the time of the original event and that one cannot reinterpret the image (Von Leyden, 1961, p. 61) or later extract information that was not noticed while perceiving the original event (Furlong, 1951, p. 38). Clearly, this is one topic for which the techniques used by the philosophers have not been successful in achieving consensus.

Limits on recollective memory

Ayer (1956, p. 140) noted that there are limits on recollective memory and that one cannot have a recollective memory representation for a conversation. He argued that one can have memory for the content of the conversation, but not an auditory image of the words in a (long?) conversation.

Propositional components of recollective memory

Several philosophers have argued that the recollective memory experience is considerably broader than a simple visual image (Brockelman, 1975; Earle, 1956; Furlong, 1951) and includes the individual's "whole state of mind" at the moment of the original episode (Furlong, 1951, p. 83) or the whole "event as experienced" (Earle, 1956, p. 11). Furlong suggested that a recollective memory includes nonvisual information such as the remembering person's earlier feelings of happiness or pain. He also stated that recollections include the individual's thoughts at the moment of the original episode. Note that Furlong means something different by this than the fact that one can have propositional memory *that* some event occurred. In the context of my earlier Colorado example what Furlong is proposing is that in addition to my knowing *that* I had lunch with David Rubin, my recollective memory also includes my memory of being concerned that if we did not get waited on soon I would be late for a session I wanted to attend. It is not exactly clear how this nonsensory information is to be represented. Furlong (1948, p. 40) explicitly stated that propositional beliefs/thoughts can be part of the memory image. However, Price (1952, p. 355) argued that this cannot be correct. B. Smith (1966) agreed that recollective memories usually include propositional information (p. 197) but seemed to think that the propositional information is represented in nonimage form (p. 92). Furlong (1951) stated that even though we place ourselves in the past during a recollective experience, the current memory contains propositional attitudes that distinguish past perceptions from current memories. He stated, "we note that we did believe them on the past occasion, even though we do not believe them now" (p. 81).

Metamemory – confidence

Many philosophers have noted that individuals have very strong confidence in the accuracy of recollective memories (ignoring for the moment, the degree to which they are actually accurate). Russell (1921, p. 163) argued that mental images that have both "feelings of familiarity" and "feelings of pastness" give rise to a belief in the accuracy of the memory. Furlong (1951, p. 83) proposed that the confidence in recollective memories is based on the "spontaneity and vividness of the imagery." A number of other philosophers (B. Smith, 1966, pp. 197–198; Von Leyden, 1961, p. 91) have agreed that recollective memories are accompanied by strong beliefs in their accuracy (without committing themselves to Russell's or Furlong's particular psychological proposals).

Earle (1956, p. 4) has made a somewhat similar point by suggesting that recollective memories are accompanied by the belief that the events contained in the recollective memories happened in the past of the individual.

Veridicality of recollective memories

The basic reason why philosophers have been interested in the psychological topic of human memory is that they want to know if recollective memories provide certain knowledge (i.e., justified true belief). Given my biases as a psychologist, this seems to me to be an empirical issue to be answered by experimentation. Nevertheless, the answers provided by philosophers, using their own methods, have spanned a wide range of answers. A few philosophers have asserted that recollective memories are completely veridical – Earle (1956, p. 10) stated that recollective memory is "a direct vision of the genuine past, and veridical to the extent that it is clear." Other philosophers have stated that certain types of recollective memories are veridical. For example, Russell (1912, p. 115) argued that recollective memories of events that occurred in the last 30 seconds are veridical. Furlong (1953/1954, p. 138) made a similar argument for memories of events that occurred within the last 5 minutes.

B. Smith (1966, p. 94) noted that if recollective memory is memory for perceptions, then if one misperceives some event and later recalls the event, one can have an accurate memory that is not veridical with respect to the original event.

Many philosophers have argued that recollective memories are frequently not veridical. They have used two lines of evidence to support this position – reports of false recollective memories and point-of-view shifts in memory imagery.

Von Leyden (1961, p. 40) argued that all theorists who believe that recollective memories are veridical have to deal with what he calls the "childhood test case." He defines this as the case where person A is told by another person about some event from person A's childhood and person A comes to have a constructed recollective memory of the event that they believe to be an authentic recollection. B. Smith (1966, p. 23) states that there is frequent evidence for errors in childhood memories that can be observed when an individual, who has a vivid memory of some location, revisits it, and finds that it is quite different from their recollected memory representation. Smith states that in these cases the errors are in the actual recollective imagery, not in some propositional tag. D. Locke (1971, p. 103) agrees that correct memories and memory errors ("imagination") can give rise to identical phenomenological experiences. Salmon (1974, pp. 143–144) gives a personal example of this type of phenomenon. He describes a false childhood memory in which he recalled his father "frisking" a garage mechanic for a gun. Broad (1925, p. 231) reported that England's King George IV falsely recalled leading a charge at the battle of Waterloo.

Von Leyden (1961, p. 78) developed an interesting attack on the position that recollective memories are accurate copies of the original experience. He reported that he had a vivid childhood memory of being carried out of class during an attack of appendicitis. However, he noted that his current recollective memory was *not* from the viewpoint of someone being carried out of class, but that he saw himself being carried out of class as an observer would have viewed the scene. Von Leyden (1961, p. 82) appears to suggest that the viewpoint shifts may occur more frequently as the retention interval increases. D. Locke (1971, pp. 88–89) made a similar argument and gave the example of someone recollecting an event of falling down stairs and "seeing" themselves falling down the stairs from the viewpoint of an observer.

Phenomenal experience and memory accuracy

The British Empiricists had a rather simple imagistic theory of the mind. Within this framework, recollective memory posed two troublesome problems that have continued to be a major concern of philosophers since that time. J. Locke (1690/1959) was concerned with how one can distinguish recollective memory images from current perceptions. Hume (1739/1978) was concerned with how one can distinguish recollective memory images from images of imagination. The attempts to answer these questions have led to an extensive set of observations and proposals about recollective memory, such as those discussed in the next sections.

Vividness and accuracy. Hume (1739/1978) argued that there were characteristics of the memory image itself that allow one to distinguish recollective memories from imagined events. He stated, "the ideas of the memory are much more lively and strong than those of the imagination" (p. 9). These issues were reintroduced into modern cognitive psychology through the important work of Johnson and Raye (1981). The vast majority of philosophers following Hume have rejected his observation and asserted that the criterion does not work because some images of imagination are more vivid than some memory images (Holland, 1954, p. 466; O'Connor & Carr, 1982, p. 123; Salmon, 1974, pp. 148–151; Shoemaker, 1967, p. 267; Woozley, 1949, p. 40).

Irrelevant detail. Bradley (1899) suggested that the occurrence of irrelevant detail in a recollective memory was a possible criterion for distinguishing between memory and imagination. He stated, "The character of the detail is, however, a sign to be noticed. If the particulars are many and yet appear as an accidental conjunction, not depending upon any general idea but all seeming irrelevant, that, so far as it goes, is a mark of genuine memory" (p. 159). B. Smith (1966, pp. 140–143) was another theorist who did not want to give up the position that there are characteristics of the memory images that allow one to distinguish them from images of imagination. Thus, he also suggested that memory images may be distinguished from images of imagination because they bring along irrelevant detail (e.g., in trying to recollect a person riding a bicycle, one also gets an image of the trees and buildings in the background).

Munsat (1967) has used memory for details to justify a quite different claim. Munsat was attempting to apply the ordinary language approach to the analysis of memory and did not want to use imagery in his criteria for recollective memory. He argued that "the claim that I remember doing such and such, as opposed to merely remembering that I did it . . . is the claim that I remember the event in detail, or remember a lot of details about the event" (p. 108).

Lack of control. Hume (1739/1978, p. 9) proposed a second possible difference between memory and imagination. He argued that memory images tend to preserve the original order imposed by the nature of the original episode, whereas images of imagination can be arranged in any order. However, he thought that there was no phenomenological correlate of this difference that one could use to distinguish imagination from memory (p. 85). Both Furlong (1956, p. 545) and B. Smith (1966, p. 141) have argued that memory and imagination differ along the lines suggested by Hume, but have also concluded that one actually experiences recollective memory images as being less under one's control.

Feelings of familiarity. J. Locke (1690/1959, p. 109) attempted to solve the problem of how one distinguishes perception from memory by stating that "to remember is to perceive anything with memory, or with a consciousness that it was perceived or known before." Russell (1921, pp. 160–163) disagreed with Hume's view that there was some "pictorial" quality of memory images that allowed one to distinguish them from imagination. However, he agreed with Locke that there was a phenomenally experienced characteristic that allowed one to distinguish memory images from imaginations. Russell referred to this memory indicator as a "feeling of familiarity." Woozley (1949, pp. 46–47) noted that you do frequently have a feeling of familiarity on those occasions when you see an individual who seems "familiar" but you are unable to retrieve any propositional or recollective memory information about that person. However, Woozley went on to argue that recollective memory images do not give rise to this particular "feeling of familiarity." Hamlyn (1970, p. 192) also did not accept the feeling of familiarity as an attribute of recollective memory images, noting that the feeling of familiarity that occurs in the déjà vu experience does not occur during recollective recall.

Other phenomenal properties. Several philosophers have rejected the proposal that recollective memory images are experienced as being "familiar," but have suggested that memory images *do* have some other unique phenomenological attribute. Ayer (1956, p. 147) stated that a recollective memory simply "feels different." Woozley (1949, p. 47) stated they are accompanied by a "feeling of rightness"; whereas Earle (1956, p. 18) stated that "[m]emory declares itself to be memory by its own intrinsic character . . . and imagination declares itself to be such by the accompanying awareness that indeed its bogus, memory-like appearance is the product of our own will."

Point of view. As discussed earlier, Von Leyden (1961) and D. Locke (1971) have used evidence from the point of view of recollective memories to attack strict copy theories of recollective memory. It seems likely that they would argue that individuals could use the occurrence of observer point of view in their recollective memory images as an indication that a particular memory was not accurate.

Mental intention. A number of philosophers (Brockelman, 1975, p. 318; Furlong, 1953/1954, p. 138; Holland, 1954, p. 486; D. Locke, 1971, p. 16, 103; Urmson, 1967, p. 86) have rejected the whole approach of finding an attribute of the memory image that will distinguish memory images from images of imagination. They suggest that memory is distinguished from imagination by the individual's awareness that they are intending to recollect in one case and are intending to imagine something in the other case.

Schema-based distortions of recollective memories

Several philosophers have speculated on what factors lead to errors in recollective memory. Price (1958, p. 447) noted that, in addition to the episodic images that occur in recollective memory, one can also have generic visual images based on repeated past exposure to some object (cf. Brewer, 1986, p. 31). He proposed that when one experiences a recollective memory for a person or a place that one is very familiar with, the recollective memory image may be distorted in the direction of the generic information. Von Leyden (1961, pp. 74–75) made a similar point, stating that recollective memory images are more like paintings than like pictures, and that we fill in missing aspects of the memory with other types of information. Salmon (1974, p. 155) also argued that individuals' current beliefs can distort their current recollections of a past event.

Forgetting

Studies of forgetting have been the major focus of experimental effort by psychologists studying memory. Yet forgetting has received remarkably little treatment by philosophers. In fact D. Locke (1971, p. 96) explicitly says that issues of forgetting should be treated by psychologists or physiologists, not by philosophers. However, it is clear that some claims by philosophers are explicit or implicit proposals about forgetting. For example, Russell's (1912, p. 115) assertion that recent recollective memories are veridical is an implicit proposal about accuracy and forgetting. Another implicit proposal about forgetting can be found in Furlong's suggestion (1951, p. 6) that recollective memories turn into propositional memories as the imagery associated with recollective memory fades over time.

Variables influencing recall

One of the major lines of research in experimental studies of human memory has been the investigation of factors that influence memory performance (e.g., rehearsal, uniqueness, emotion, etc.). Within the framework of philosophical approaches to memory this topic appears to be of little interest, and there have been few, if any, discussions in the philosophical literature.

Organization of recollective memories

One of the core concerns of modern cognitive approaches to human memory has been theoretical and empirical work on the nature of the organization of the information stored in long-term memory. This has also been an important issue for researchers in autobiographical memory (cf. Conway, 1990, chap. 6), though perhaps not as central as it has been for many other areas of human memory. This aspect of memory organization was discussed in Bergson's (1896/1911) early work. He hypothesized that "consciousness . . . retains the image of the situations through which it has successively travelled, and lays them side by side in the order in which they took place" (p. 96). In essence, he was proposing that recollective memory was organized along a strict time line. After Bergson there have been almost no discussions of this issue in the philosophical literature on memory. Apparently this is one of those topics that is not seen as important within the theoretical framework of philosophical approaches to memory, but is considered to be a central problem within the theoretical framework of modern cognitive psychology.

Dating recollective memories

Several philosophers have speculated about how we date specific recollective memories. Furlong (1951) suggested that there are several different ways one can date memories. He proposed that one can use the vividness of the image (p. 99) to give an indication of its "temporal distance." He also noted that one can recall explicit temporal propositional information (p. 94) such as "that event occurred on a Thursday" and then work out a date by inference (p. 95). B. Smith (1966, p. 209) agreed that for recent memories one can use the vividness of the image. He also argued that one can date a recollective memory by its relations to "temporal markers" (p. 210), such as knowing which house one lived in at a particular time in one's life.

Rote memory and recollective memory

In this last section I will examine what philosophers have said about rote memory. This has not been a topic of much interest to philosophers, but given the emphasis on this issue by laboratory psychologists, it will be important for our later discussions to try to work out the relevance of the investigations of recollective memory for standard laboratory research on recall.

Bergson (1896/1911) stated that rote memory is a form of habit memory. It requires repetitions to acquire, and after it is acquired it is some form of procedural knowledge ("it is no longer a representation, it is an action . . . it is lived and acted, rather than represented" [p. 91]). He thought of rote memory as a minor form of memory, and stated that "memories which we acquire voluntarily by repetition are rare and exceptional" (p. 94). Broad (1925) noted that when someone learns something by rote, the material is learned just as a parrot might learn it. He stated that "[w]hat has really been acquired and retained is a certain motor-capacity in the throat and tongue or in the fingers" (p. 269), which he wished to distinguish from memory for the propositions that might be expressed by the surface linguistic information that had been learned in rote fashion (p. 272). Price (1936) distinguished rote memory from other forms of memory and used the distinction to make a professorial joke. He stated that with rote memory "we merely behave as if we remembered, without having even an image before our mind, still less a proposition. This might be called 'memory in the Behavouristic sense.'

It is perfectly compatible with the utterance of long and complicated concatenations of noises, and with the production of large masses of handwriting, as for instance in an examination" (p. 24). B. Smith (1966), like Broad, distinguished memory for propositions from memory for words and then stated that "to remember words is either to have visual or auditory or kinaesthetic images, or else to remember propositions about the words themselves" (p. 66). Brockelman (1975) argued that in memorizing a poem, "I don't so much picture the poem as train my body, i.e., my tongue and lips and mouth, to repeat it. Given this sound, the tongue forms the next syllable, seemingly automatically. The whole thing can be carried out with no reference to an image" (p. 315). Ayer (1956, p. 135) noted that habits ("having the power to reproduce a certain performance") are independent of recollection, but stated that performance of a skill is sometimes facilitated by the occurrence of a recollection of a particular instance of learning (cf. Ross, 1984, for a similar argument by a psychologist). Thus, it appears that there are two basic positions on how to treat rote memory for linguistic material. Some philosophers wish to see this as learning a motor skill, and others as recollecting (visual or auditory) images of the surface form of the linguistic material.

This discussion of rote memory concludes the review of philosophical work on memory. I will now turn to the research on the issue of recollective memory carried out by psychologists who work in the area of autobiographical memory.

Psychological studies of autobiographical memory

Types of memory and forms of representation

In my earlier chapter on autobiographical memory (Brewer, 1986), I concluded that there was considerable confusion about the subject matter being investigated in the field of autobiographical memory, but that, overall, the research in this area did cover a natural domain – memory for information relating to the self. For memories involving a specific episode from an individual's life, I distinguished between personal memories and autobiographical facts. I used the term *personal memory* to refer to the phenomenally experienced aspect of such memories and the term *autobiographical facts* to refer to the nonphenomenally experienced aspect of these types of memories. As discussed earlier, I now prefer to use the term *recollective memory* to refer to a memory of a particular episode in an individual's life.

There has been considerable discussion of these issues by researchers in the area of autobiographical memory, and the core distinction between recollection and autobiographical facts has continued to be reflected in most recent theoretical discussions of the nature of autobiographical memory (e.g., Baddeley, 1992; Conway, 1990, this volume; Larsen, 1992; Robinson & Swanson, 1990).

One important issue in the study of recollective memory is whether *flashbulb memories* are to be considered to be a form of recollective memory or are to be classified as a separate form of memory. In an important paper in 1977, Brown and Kulik initiated the modern study of flashbulb memories. Flashbulb memories are memories for the *circumstances* of learning about a surprising and consequential event, such as the assassination of John F. Kennedy. These memories were said to be like photographs, to show little forgetting, and to be produced by a special-purpose biological mechanism. It seems clear that Brown and Kulik intended flashbulb memories to be a unique type of memory. However, several researchers (e.g., Brewer, 1986, pp. 35–36; Rubin & Kozin, 1984, p. 94) have suggested that, as a type of memory, flashbulb memories showed few qualitative differences from ordinary recollective memory and so might better be thought of as instances of recollective memory that appear to show a reduced rate of forgetting. In a recent paper (Brewer, 1992b) I have carried out an intensive analysis of the flashbulb memory literature, and found strong support for the view that flashbulb memories are examples of recollective memory; therefore, in this section I will discuss the literature on flashbulb memories along with the literature on autobiographical memory.

Terminology

In some ways the issues of terminology are worse in psychology than those in philosophy. In philosophy there has been fairly general agreement about the basic characteristics of recollective memory (with disagreement about the role of recollective memory in acquiring knowledge). The terminological problem in the philosophical literature has been that each scholar writing about recollective memory has developed their own technical term for the same construct.

In psychology there has also been a wide divergence of terms used for recollective memory, but in addition there has also been considerable disagreement and imprecision about what memory phenomena the terms are intended to cover. Examples (in chronological order) of technical terms that appear to have been used to refer to recollective memory are "memories" (M. E. Smith, 1952); "episodic memory" (Crovitz & Schiffman, 1974); "memory for real-world events" (Linton, 1975); "autobiographical memory" (Robinson, 1976); "personal memory" (Franklin & Holding, 1977); "personal real-world episodic memory" (Linton, 1978); "personal recollections" (Linton, 1979); "autobiographical memory" (Rubin, 1982); "memory for unique personal events" (Thompson, 1982); "memory for personal events" (White, 1982); "personal memory" (Brewer & Pani, 1983); "personal memory" (Nigro & Neisser, 1983); "autobiographical memory" (Barclay & Wellman, 1986); "autobiographical memory" (Wagenaar, 1986); "personal memory" (Brewer, 1986); "autobiographical memory" (Barclay, 1986); "personal memory" (Brewer, 1988); and "autobiographical memory" (Barsalou, 1988).

It seems to me that there are two different terminological problems represented in this list. A number of the terms are long definite descriptions (e.g., "personal real-world episodic memory"; "memory for unique personal events"). These are relatively precise, but probably too long and awkward to become our technical term. A number of the other terms are too general (e.g., "memories"; "episodic memory"). When terms such as these are used in an experimental study, one has to read the methods section of the paper to find out if the author is actually referring to recollective memory.

The term "autobiographical memory" has probably become the most frequently used term to refer to recollective memory. However, it appears to me that the use of this term leads to a serious problem of ambiguity. Some authors clearly intend the term to refer to recollective memory. For example, in Robinson's (1976) early paper he presented the subjects with a word and instructed them to "think of an experience from your own life which the word reminds you of" (p. 581). If the subject responded with an autobiographical fact or some generic information they were told "to continue thinking until a specific incident associated with the word came to mind" (p. 581). Thus, it is clear that Robinson intended the term "autobiographical memory" to refer to recollective memory. In a recent paper discussing the problems of terminology in this area, Larsen (1992) explicitly proposes that we use the term "autobiographical memory" to cover recollective memory and states that this technical usage has the advantage that it conforms to current usage.

The problem with using "autobiographical memory" as the term for recollection is that many authors (cf. Rubin's 1986 book) use the term "autobiographical memory" to refer to the larger class of memories relating to the self or, in some cases, to factual knowledge about a person's life. If a memory theorist believes that memories relating to the self should be distinguished from other forms of memory, but does not believe there are any differences between recollective memory and autobiographical facts, then use of the term "autobiographical memory" is perhaps appropriate, and, for that theorist, has no ambiguity. However, for theorists such as myself (e.g., Brewer, 1986) who have argued that recollective memory appears to be a mental "natural kind," then the use of the term "autobiographical memory" makes more sense as the lexical item to refer to the larger set of memories relating to the self, and a more specific term is needed for the subclass of recollective memories. In a recent paper discussing these problems of terminology, Baddeley (1992) has used a very similar line of reasoning to reject the adoption of the term "autobiographical memory" as the lexical form to refer to recollective memory.

The term "personal memory" has been used fairly consistently by researchers in this area to refer specifically to recollective memory. However, despite the efforts of several of us, the field as a whole has not chosen to adopt this as the technical term for recollective memory. I think part of the reason may be that it sounds a bit "soft-headed." Therefore, I have decided to adopt the ordinary language term "recollective memory" as my technical term for this specific form of memory, and I recommend this usage to other researchers in this area. Note that this technical usage is consistent with the implicit use of the term "recollection" in many discussions of the area of autobiographical memory. Even some of the earliest studies that adopted other technical terms used "recollection" in their actual discussion of this type of memory (e.g., Crovitz & Quina-Holland, 1976, p. 62; Robinson, 1976, p. 578). A close reading of Baddeley (1992) will show that he systematically uses the term "recollection" when he wants to distinguish this type of memory from other forms of memory. For example, he describes a patient who only has access to factual/propositional memory about his life history and states that this patient's recall of past events is not a true case of "recollection" (pp. 15–16).

In the area of flashbulb memory there has been little problem of terminology. Almost all authors have found Brown and Kulik's (1977) term "flashbulb memory" to be a felicitous term for recollective memories of the circumstances of hearing about very emotional or surprising events, and there has been considerable consistency in the adoption of the term "flashbulb memory" for these types of memories (Pillemer, 1992, and Rubin & Kozin, 1984, are exceptions). While it seems to me that usage has locked this technical term into place, it should be noted that the term "flashbulb memory" is not a neutral term, and is strongly biased in favor of Brown and Kulik's biological "Now Print!" theory. To be fair to those who do not accept Brown and Kulik's particular theory, we should be clear that "flashbulb memory" is to be used as a theory-neutral term for the class of memories relating to the circumstances of hearing about an emotional or surprising event.

Methods for the study of recollective memory

Life event recall. The history of empirical studies of recollective memory by psychologists is a curious one. Sir Francis Galton (1880) carried out the first experimental study of recollective memory with his "breakfast technique." In this study Galton distributed questionnaires to different groups of individuals asking them to recall the appearance of their breakfast table from that morning's breakfast. The questionnaire asked them to describe the phenomenological properties of the resulting memory along certain dimensions (e.g., "Is the image dim or fairly clear?"). There is a nice cross-check that reassures one that psychologists carrying out empirical studies of recollection, and the philosophers discussed earlier, are talking about the same phenomena – in his 1921 book Bertrand Russell discusses "true memory" (defined as "the recollection of a unique event") and gives remembering what he had to eat for breakfast as an example of this type of memory (pp. 166–167).

The Galton study became a classic and is mentioned in many history books as one of the first studies of individual differences for a higher psychological process (i.e., imagery). However, his study has not been seen as a study of memory (see Brewer, 1986, pp. 36–39, for a discussion) and so has had little direct influence on the study of recollective memory. The technique of studying human memory by directing the subject to recall a specific episode from their personal lives was reintroduced into psychology through Linton's (1975) innovative study of events from her own life and Brown and Kulik's (1977) study of individuals' recall of the personal circumstances of hearing of a traumatic public event.

Galton's word technique. The line of research carried out by Galton that *did* have a direct impact on the study of recollective memory was his study of his own memory using the word technique. Galton (1879a, 1879b) was interested in a procedure that would allow him to sample the total contents of his memory. The technique he developed was to display a word to himself and then allow the word to elicit some type of association. As might be expected, this open-ended technique sampled a number of different forms of memory, such as rote linguistic responses (e.g., verses of poetry) and generic perceptual memories (e.g., generic images of landscapes from his youth). While it seems likely that this open-ended probing did produce some recollective memories, ironically, none of the actual examples he gives are clear cases of this type of memory.

The Crovitz technique. After a pause of almost a century, Crovitz and Schiffman (1974) modified Galton's word technique so that it became an explicit method for studying recollective memory. In the Crovitz and Schiffman experiment, the subjects received a list of words. The instructions to the subjects stated that the experiment "was a study of their personal memories" (1974, p. 517) and told them to "think of a specific memory associated with each word" (Crovitz & Quina-Holland, 1976, p. 61). Later researchers used even more specific instructions. For example, as mentioned earlier, when Robinson (1976) obtained a nonrecollective response to a word he asked the subject "to continue thinking until a specific incident associated with the word came to mind" (p. 581). The Crovitz technique has become one of the major methods used by psychologists to study recollective memory (see reviews by Conway, 1990, chap. 3; Fitzgerald, this volume; Rubin, Wetzler & Nebes, 1986).

Now I will shift to an examination of some the findings about recollective memory that psychologists have uncovered using these various techniques.

Phenomenological descriptions of recollective memory

Given the central role that the philosophers attribute to mental imagery in their descriptions of recollective memory, one might think that this would have been a major focus of research by psychologists interested in autobiographical memory. However, except for Galton's early work, this has not been the case. It appears that even though researchers in the areas of autobiographical memory and flashbulb memory have parted from mainstream laboratory memory research on the grounds of ecological validity (cf. Conway, 1991; Neisser, 1978), they have remained relatively conservative with respect to the empirical study of mental imagery (cf. Brewer, 1992b, pp. 284–285), and most studies have not gathered data on this issue.

Occurrence of imagery. The results from Galton's (1880, 1883) breakfast questionnaire for schoolchildren and for adults showed almost universal reports of visual imagery while these individuals were recollecting what they had for breakfast. Secondary sources (e.g., James, 1890, Vol. 2, p. 53; Posner, 1973, p. 154; Woodworth & Schlosberg, 1954, p. 721) state that Galton found that scientists show little or no visual imagery during recollective memory tasks. However, Brewer and Schommer (1991) have reanalyzed Galton's data and have shown that this is an incorrect interpretation of the data.

Somewhat over a century later, Galton's work on the occurrence of mental imagery in recollective memory was followed up by my study of memory for randomly selected events from the lives of undergraduate subjects (Brewer, 1988) and Johnson, Foley, Suengas, and Raye's (1988) study of actual and imagined autobiographical events. The subjects in my 1988 experiment carried random alarm devices and recorded the event that was occurring when the alarm went off. At different time delays, the subjects were asked to rate their phenomenal experience while attempting to retrieve the episodes from their lives that they had recorded weeks to months earlier. The data from this experiment showed that most recollective memory retrievals gave rise to reports of visual imagery. Accurate recollections tended to show stronger imagery than inaccurate recollections, and memories with very high confidence ratings showed very strong imagery reports.

Johnson et al. (1988) asked subjects to recall past actual events and past imagined events. They found that the recollective memories for actual events showed higher ratings than imaginary recollections on "involves visual detail" and also showed higher ratings for location and the spatial arangement of objects in the recalled event.

Those studies in the area of flashbulb memory that have gathered data on the issue have also shown the strong role of imagery in the recollective memory experience. The paper by Brown and Kulik (1977) that initiated the modern study of flashbulb memories does not overtly discuss the issue of mental imagery. However, in their description of flashbulb memory they state that these memories have a "primary, 'live' quality that is almost perceptual" (p. 74). It seems to me that this is an oblique reference to mental imagery by authors who do not want to actually use the term "mental image."

Rubin and Kozin's (1984) study of flashbulb memory also tends to avoid the term "mental imagery," but the instructions to the subjects for the scale of memory "vividness" stated that "1 means no image at all and 7 means as vivid as normal vision" (p. 86), so in practice this article provides data on mental imagery. Rubin and Kozin gave their subjects examples of flashbulb memories and asked them to retrieve memories of this type. They found that over half of the subjects rated their flashbulb memories as falling in the top two imagery categories and that no subject reported having a total lack of imagery while retrieving a flashbulb memory.

Pillemer (1984) carried out a study of flashbulb memories among faculty members for the attempted assassination of president Reagan. He found that roughly 73% of the respondents reported visual imagery while retrieving memories about the Reagan assassination attempt (it is not clear that all of these memories would be classified as flashbulb memories). While this is a fairly impressive rate of imagery, it is still lower than the other studies of recollective and flashbulb memory, and one wonders if the faculty sample had particular theoretical beliefs about visual imagery that may have made them interpret the question differently than the usual undergraduate subjects.

Neisser and Harsch (1992) studied flashbulb memories for the *Challenger* explosion. Some 3 years after the event they asked subjects to recollect how they had heard the news. Over 97% of the subjects reported the occurrence of imagery during the recollective task (Neisser, personal communication, May 17, 1994).

Thus, overall there is strong agreement that visual imagery occurs during the recollective memory process. The imagery is rated as quite strong on scales of visual imagery, and the frequency of occurrence of imagery is frequently close to 100% when undergraduate subjects are asked if any imagery occurred.

Characteristics of memory imagery. While the philosophers have given quite detailed accounts of the phenomenology of the mental imagery that occurs during recollective memory, there has been relatively little empirical work on this issue by psychologists studying autobiographical memory. Research on point of view of recollective visual images has been a notable exception. The study of the point of view of the visual images involved in recollective memory is another area with a rather long gap between the initial studies and the modern research. In a study of adults' early childhood memories, Henri and Henri (1897, pp. 192–193) noted that a number of their subjects stated that in their visual image they could see themselves as part of the image (i.e., their image represented the overall scene as it would have appeared to an external observer). Freud (1899/1953) used the point-of-view data from Henri and Henri to argue that many childhood memories cannot be copies of the original event because in memory the scene is not viewed from the same perspective as was the original event.

Over 80 years later Nigro and Neisser (1983) took up the issue again in a very impressive paper. This study reports only phenomenological data (no reaction time or number correct data). Nigro and Neisser asked subjects to "recall some specific occasion" of an activity such as swimming and found that most of their recollective images could be classified as: (1) "field memories" – recollective memory images that represented the original scene from the viewpoint from which it was originally experienced; or (2) "observer memories" – recollective memory images that represented the original scene as an external observer might have seen it. Nigro and Neisser found a tendency for recent memories to show a higher proportion of field memories than did older memories. This finding has been replicated by Robinson and Swanson (1993); also see Robinson (this volume).

Irrelevant detail. In my 1986 paper I proposed a partially reconstructive view of recollective memory. I asserted that recollective memory images frequently contained irrelevant detail and argued that this was evidence that recollective memory included a copy component that encoded relatively veridical episodic information about the original perceptual experience (p. 43). While this still seems to me to be a reasonable argument, it would have stronger force if there were a theory-motivated criterion for "irrelevant detail" and if there were data showing the occurrence of such irrelevant detail in recollective memories.

Brown and Kulik (1977) used irrelevant detail to argue for the uniqueness of flashbulb memories and for a special-purpose biological memory mechanism. They noted that in many of their subjects' flashbulb memory reports there was "completely idiosyncratic content" such as the statement, "I was carrying a carton of Viceroy cigarettes" (p. 80). Brown and Kulik claimed that the occurrence of such "accidental" information was strong evidence for their biological "Now Print!" theory. A few later studies of flashbulb memory (Bohannon, 1988; Christianson, 1989) have included questions designed to study memory for irrelevant detail (e.g., questions about the clothing worn by the subjects when the flashbulb memory occurred).

However, in my analysis of the flashbulb memory literature (Brewer, 1992b, p. 286), I noted that my study of ordinary recollective memory (Brewer, 1988) also found evidence for "irrelevant detail"; therefore, without data from nonflashbulb control events, Brown and Kulik's flashbulb memory data provide no support for the special nature of flashbulb memories or the special nature of the hypothesized biological memory mechanism.

Sensation, uninterpreted perception, interpreted perception

The issue of whether recollective memory images are interpreted or uninterpreted representations has rarely been discussed by researchers in the area of autobiographical memory. An exception is my 1986 paper on autobiographical memory in which I asserted that recollective memories had to be interpreted memory representations (p. 43). One might be tempted to say that Brown and Kulik's (1977) "Now Print!" mechanism for flashbulb memories implicitly assumes an uninterpreted mental representation for these types of memories. However, I do not think this is the case. Their theory is clearly a copy theory of memory, but they are not explicit enough about what is being copied for one to know if they assume the copy to be an uninterpreted sensation or an interpreted perception of the original event.

Limits on recollective memory

There has been little discussion in the literature on autobiographical memory on the range of occurrence of recollective memory. Most studies obtain recollective memories by asking subjects to retrieve a specific memory from their lives and do not discuss the issue of the generality of the phenomenon. I once asserted (Brewer, 1986, p. 42) that one could not have a recollective memory for a long conversation, but did not provide any evidence to support this claim. Clearly we need theoretical and empirical work on the place of recollective memory in the overall context of human memory.

Propositional components of recollective memory

The psychological literature on recollective memory contains few discussions of the issue of the relationships between images and propositional information. My analysis in 1986 seems to me to be inconsistent and to suffer from many of the same problems I pointed out in my discussion of this topic in the philosophical literature earlier in this chapter. In the 1986 paper I made a separation between personal memory and autobiographical fact (pp. 29–30). The way I made the distinction seems to require that personal memory be represented in image form. Yet, in my later discussion I stated that a naturalistic description of personal memory includes "occurrent thoughts and felt affects" (p. 34). If one assumes that thought and emotion can be represented in image form, then there is no problem. However, if one assumes that these forms of information are not well represented in image form, then it appears to me that my definition restricting personal memory to imaginal forms of representation is in disagreement with my more descriptive account of personal memory as it occurs naturally. Clearly we need conceptual clarification of the representation issue and empirical study of the problem.

Metamemory beliefs about accuracy

In the same way that people have knowledge about phenomena in the external world, they have beliefs about the operation of their own mental processes. Thus, it is interesting to examine people's beliefs about the characteristics of recollective memory and the accuracy of those beliefs.

One somewhat indirect form of evidence on the issue of metamemory comes from the behavior of psychologists studying human memory. In many studies of recognition memory the only dependent measure used is a scale of recognition confidence. Clearly, if experimental psychologists did not have very strong metamemory beliefs about the usefulness of recognition confidence as an index of the subject's memory accuracy they would not use such a scale as their only dependent measure!

Experimental investigation shows that people exhibit metamemory ability at many different stages of the memory process. Thus, on standard laboratory memory tasks, subjects can reliably predict, at the time of exposure, which items they will remember on a later memory test (Maki & Swett, 1987; Underwood, 1966). The "feeling of knowing" phenomenon shows that, after a recall failure, subjects can reliably predict whether they will be able to recognize an item they have been unable to recall (Hart, 1965; Nelson, 1990).

Autobiographical memory. One type of evidence that suggests that people believe recollective memories to be particularly accurate is that, in debates about inconsistent memories for the same event, one form of argument often used is the statement, "but, you must be wrong, I can *see* [the event] as it occurred." Another form of evidence can be found in the positions of the philosophers reviewed earlier who argued that recollective memories were a form of justified true belief. Given that they had not collected any data on this issue, they must have been expressing a metamemory judgment that recollective memories are highly accurate (as in Russell's statement that recollective memories that occurred in the last 30 seconds could be assumed to be completely accurate). Thus, to the degree that one is willing to take Bertrand Russell as a reasonable sample of human opinion, there is additional evidence for the view that recollective memories are considered to be highly accurate.

My 1988 study of randomly selected events from the lives of undergraduates provides evidence about the relationship of memory confidence and visual imagery at time of recall. The data showed that every memory response that received the highest memory confidence score ("certain that remember the event") also received a visual image rating in one of the highest two categories (on a 1–7 scale). These data provide direct evidence that confidence is related to imagery in memory for life events. Given that the high imagery responses in this data are almost certainly canonical recollective memories, then the data also suggest that recollective memory events are assigned high confidence.

Flashbulb memory. The evidence from popular culture provides strong evidence that people's beliefs about their memories include the belief that one never forgets the circumstances of hearing about a flashbulb memory event. At each decade anniversary of traumatic public events, such as the Kennedy assassination, popular magazines run stories containing the personal recollections of famous people describing the circumstances of their hearing about the flashbulb event. A clear example of the pervasive nature of this belief is provided by a 1993 "Far Side" cartoon in which a group of forest animals are sitting around talking about where they were (i.e., the circumstances of a flashbulb memory) when they heard the traumatic news about Bambi's mother being shot (e.g., snake: "I was under a rock, getting ready to shed").

Another form of evidence about this metamemory belief can be found in discussions of flashbulb memory by memory researchers. In the flashbulb memory literature there are a number of reports of researchers (e.g., Linton, 1975, p. 387; Neisser, 1982, p. 45) being surprised to find out that a particular flashbulb memory was, in fact, incorrect. Obviously, an individual would not be surprised to find out that their flashbulb memory from many years in the past was in error, unless they had a strong prior belief that it was veridical. In fact, in an earlier paper (1986, p. 41) I suggested that the strong belief in the accuracy of recollective memories is one factor that has led memory theorists to propose copy theories of memory (e.g., Brown & Kulik, 1977) even though there was little available evidence to support this theoretical position.

Weaver (1993) examined flashbulb memories of the bombing of Iraq. He noted that in a comparison of flashbulb and nonflashbulb events, the flashbulb events show higher absolute levels of confidence (.4 units on a 1–3 scale) for the same levels of accuracy, and concluded that one of the special properties of flashbulb memories is their high (absolute) level of confidence. This data is thus consistent with the view that some aspects of flashbulb memory (e.g., imagery, metamemory beliefs) lead to high levels of memory confidence. In the next section I will shift from the issue of the *believed* accuracy of recollective memory to the *actual* accuracy of these memories.

Veridicality of recollective memories

Autobiographical memory. The researchers who carried out the initial studies of recollective memory with the Crovitz technique had no way to verify the memories they obtained, so they had very little to say about the accuracy issues (see Rubin, 1982, Exp. 5, for an attempt to verify memories obtained with the Crovitz technique). However, Neisser (1981) and Barclay (1986; Barclay & Wellman, 1986) opened up a vigorous attack on the view that recollective memories were copies of the original experience. For a continuation of the debate from various perspectives, see Baddeley, Thornton, Chua, & McKenna; Barclay; Belli & Loftus; Bruner & Feldman; Christianson & Safer; Robinson; and Wagenaar, all this volume). Neisser (1981) carried out an ingenious study of John Dean's testimony at the Watergate hearing. (Neisser was able to study the accuracy issue, because of the secret taping of all conversations in the Oval Office.) On the basis of his analysis of the errors in Dean's testimony, Neisser concluded that many single clear recollective memories are actually "screen memory" representations for repeated actions that did actually occur. Barclay and Wellman (1986) had subjects record events from their lives and then carried out recognition testing several months later with actual events and foil events. They found that subjects made false recognition responses to the foils. In a chapter summarizing his strong reconstructive view, Barclay (1986) stated, "Memories for most everyday life events are, therefore, transformed, distorted, or forgotten" (p. 89).

In my 1986 paper I argued for a more moderate "partially reconstructive" view. First, I noted that the data about Dean's testimony was predominately memory for conversations and not recollective memory, and so it was not directly relevant to the issue. Secondly, I argued that it was difficult to interpret Barclay and Wellman's (1986) data on false recognitions of foils because the number of false recognition errors could be dramatically shifted by the type of foils chosen. For example, subjects in a typical autobiographical memory study could easily reject foils such as, "I carried a platypus to the top of the Eiffel Tower," but would have trouble rejecting a foil such as, "I opened the front door."

My 1988 experiment on recollective memory provides some direct evidence on the issue of accuracy of recollective memory. In Experiment 2 of that paper subjects carried a random alarm device for several weeks. When the alarm went off they wrote down the events that were occurring (e.g., actions, thoughts) and other descriptive information (e.g., location, time). At several periods over the next few months they were given a cued-recall test (using different probes such as actions, location, time) for the events they had recorded previously. A qualitative analysis of these recalls showed that they made many errors (roughly 50%). However, almost all of these errors were retrieval errors (the subjects appeared to be recalling the wrong event to the probe). In only 1.5% of the cases did the subjects make true reconstructive errors in which they appeared to be recalling the original event but recalled information that was in conflict with what they had originally recorded about the event. I argued that this relatively low rate of reconstructive memory errors for ordinary events was in fair agreement with my earlier partially reconstructive view "that recent (days to weeks) personal memories are, in fact, reasonably accurate copies of the individual's original phenomenal experience" (1986, p. 43) "but that with time, or under strong schema-based processes, the original experience can be reconstructed to produce a new nonveridical personal memory" (1986, p. 44).

Flashbulb memory. The initial studies of flashbulb memory (e.g., Brown & Kulik, 1977) strongly implied that flashbulb memories were accurate copies of the original event. For example, Brown and Kulik stated that a flashbulb memory "is very like a photograph that indiscriminately preserves the scene" (p. 74). However, these studies gathered data many years after the original flashbulb event and so could not provide evidence relevant to the accuracy issue.

Neisser, who has a long record as a strong opponent of copy theories of memory (Neisser, 1967, pp. 279–286), led the attack on copy theories of flashbulb memory (Neisser, 1982). He pointed out that the flashbulb studies did not provide the type of data needed to support the copy theory of memory and gave some evidence against the copy theory in the form of several anecdotal examples of flashbulb memories that were apparently in error. Unfortunately for his argument, his personal erroneous flashbulb memory for hearing about the bombing of Pearl Harbor turned out to be more accurate than he thought it was (cf. Thompson & Cowan, 1986).

The first round of empirical studies after Brown and Kulik's initial study typically obtained the subjects' first recall weeks after the flashbulb event and then obtained a second recall some months after the event (e.g., Christianson, 1989; Pillemer, 1984). The data analysis in these studies focused on the percent of items from the first recall that were also included in the second recall and so do not directly address the veridicality issue which requires that recall *errors* be distinguished from recall *omissions*.

Later studies have been better designed to address the veridicality issue. McCloskey, Wible, & Cohen (1988) found about an 8% error rate between the initial recall and the second recall some 9 months later. They note that none of these errors were "grossly incongruent" (p. 175).

Neisser and Harsch's (1992) study of memories of the *Challenger* explosion is one of the most careful and most complete of the recent studies of flashbulb memory. These researchers gathered data within 24 hours of the flashbulb event (presumably at some cost to the experimenters' sleep the night of the event!) and carried out recalls 2 to 3 years later. They found that 25% of their subjects' recalls were completely in error and that only 7% of the subjects were totally correct. They interpret this data as strong evidence against copy theories of flashbulb memory.

However, in my review of the flashbulb literature (1992b, pp. 290–291) I conclude that the Neisser and Harsch data is not as strongly reconstructive as it appears to be. My basic line of attack was to argue that most of the errors in their data are retrieval errors and not reconstructive errors. For example, Neisser and Harsch report data from a subject who heard, in class, that something had happened. She rushed back to her room and then watched the accounts on her TV. When she carried out her recall several years later she recalled that she *initially* found out about the explosion from watching TV. I suggested that in her second recall she may have been accurately recalling the wrong event (the strongly emotional circumstances of watching the replay of the explosion on TV). In support of my argument I noted that when I carried out a qualitative analysis of the recalls of randomly selected events from the lives of undergraduates (Brewer, 1988), I found that 97% of the total errors were retrieval errors and only 3% of the errors were true reconstructive errors. However, I go on to note that there *is* clear evidence of true reconstruction occurring in the Neisser and Harsch data (e.g., the subject discussed above needed some account of how she came to know about the *Challenger* explosion, and appears to have reconstructed the information that she learned of it through a news flash on her TV). Therefore, on the issue of the veridicality of flashbulb memories I once again take the position that the data support a moderate reconstructive view.

Phenomenal experience and memory accuracy

The earlier discussion of the philosophical literature showed that one of the main themes in that tradition was an attempt to find a property of memory images that would allow them to be distinguished from nonmemory images with complete accuracy. Experimental psychologists accept the possibility of memory error, and so they have not been as interested in searching for a crucial defining attribute.

The few studies in this area have tended to focus on the phenomenal properties of memory errors. This approach leads to a rather interesting bias in this research. If one examines recollective errors and finds differences in their phenomenal properties versus those of correct recollections, then one is examining the subset of cases where the subjects, for one reason or another, were not able to use the phenomenal evidence to correctly classify the incorrect instances as incorrect recollections. The typical designs and procedures in the study of autobiographical memory do not examine those cases in which the individual entertains a representation for a nonaccurate memory and (correctly) rejects it. However, see the work of Johnson et al. (1988) for an interesting attempt to deal with this topic.

Memory image vividness and accuracy.   One approach to this issue is simply to look at the overall relation of levels of imagery and memory accuracy. Given that there are a variety of mental processes (some involving imagery and some not) that can lead to memory accuracy, it is a little unclear how to interpret this type of data. However, if one believed that recollective memory imagery tends to be veridical, then one might predict a positive correlation between memory imagery and memory accuracy.

The Neisser and Harsch (1992) study of flashbulb memories of the *Challenger* explosion provides data on this issue. These authors found that ratings of auditory imagery vividness were reliably related to memory accuracy.

In my study of randomly selected events from the lives of undergraduates I provide a table that breaks down the recall data into seven qualitative types of recall and the strength of imagery associated with each of these recall types (1988, p. 68). The data show much variability, but there is an overall tendency for the correct responses to show stronger imagery than the errors.

The imagery data for the individual recall types in that study provides a more analytic account of the relation of imagery and accuracy. The correct recalls demonstrating a very complete representation ("correct with detail") show extremely strong imagery reports (with 50% of the responses reported as being a "complete reexperiencing of the particular visual experience"). One of the recall types included responses in which the subject reported the correct event, but appeared to be recalling an aspect of the event that was offset in time ("wrong time slice"). If one thinks of these as retrieval errors (of the wrong recollective memory), then one would expect them to show high imagery, and they do. My analysis of the responses that appear to be recalls of the totally wrong event ("wrong event") suggests that they should also be treated as retrieval errors and should show strong imagery. However, the data show these responses to have relatively weak imagery ratings, so there is a problem here. Perhaps many of these responses were simply inferences and not retrieval errors as I had thought in my classification.

Reconstructed memory images.   If one believes that memory reports are derived from a number of different mental processes (e.g., inferences, metamemory processes, imagery), then there is an interesting issue about the mental representation of errors in recollective memory tasks. For example, in the Brewer and Treyens (1981) study of memory for rooms, the subjects frequently reported the occurrence of books in the "graduate student office," when there were no books. One can imagine two possible representations for the information about the room: (1) The subjects might have a more or less complete image of the room plus a nonimage, schema-based belief that there were books in the room; or (2) The schema-based processes might have become incorporated into the image so that the inferred books are part of the overall recollective memory image.

Brewer and Pani (1983, p. 32) carried out a limited examination of these two positions. We replicated the Brewer and Treyens (1981) study, but included a questionnaire asking the subjects about their imagery during the recall trials. We found that correct items (objects present in the room) and schema-based errors (expected objects not actually in the room) showed roughly equivalent levels of imagery. This suggests that the schema-based information was typically incorporated into the subject's recollective memory image of the room.

However, the data from Brewer (1988) can be interpreted as supporting the nonimage inference view. In that study there were a group of items that appeared to be generated from the subjects' generic knowledge of their lives ("inferences"). These items showed moderate to weak imagery, suggesting that the inferences were not incorporated into a strong generic image. Schooler, Gerhard, and Loftus (1986) carried out a study of misleading postevent information that can be interpreted as being relevant to this issue. They showed subjects slides, and asked some of the subjects questions that presupposed the presence of a nonoccurring object. They do not refer to imagery in this study, but do analyze the frequency of "sensory details" in the recalls. They found that the recalls of the nonpresent items showed fewer sensory details than those of the actually present items. These data can be interpreted as supporting the view that, for some recalls, the suggested information was not incorporated into the subjects' recollective memory images. Thus, these very different studies give a variety of possible answers to the issue of reconstructed recollective memory images. Clearly this is an area in need of additional study.

Irrelevant detail. It is difficult to find data that directly address the hypothesis that the occurrence of irrelevant detail in recollective memory images is related to memory accuracy. As discussed earlier, Brown and Kulik (1977) emphasized that the flashbulb memory recalls that they obtained contained "utterly idiosyncratic and, in a sense, accidental content" (p. 95). They argued that this provided direct support for their copy theory of flashbulb memory. However, since they had no data on the accuracy of their subjects' flashbulb memory reports, it is not clear how their data provide evidence relevant to the accuracy issue. Bell and Loftus (1989) report data showing that *observers* (mock jurors) use the occurrence of irrelevant details in the reports of witnesses as evidence for memory accuracy. However, this is evidence about metamemory beliefs, not about the actual relation of details to memory accuracy. There is considerable internal evidence in my 1988 study of randomly selected autobiographical events that recalls containing extra details ("correct with detail") are particularly strong and accurate memories. However, this evidence does not directly address the basic issue. It is clear from the earlier discussion of the views of the philosophers and from the studies just discussed that many scholars believe that the occurrence of irrelevant detail is related to memory accuracy, but there appears to be little evidence to support those views.

Point of view. As discussed earlier, Freud (1899/1953, p. 68) used the evidence for the occurrence of memory images from an observer's point of view as evidence against copy theories of memory. Nigro and Neisser (1983) and Robinson and Swanson (1993) provide some evidence that there is a higher proportion of field memories in recent memories. These findings can be taken to support the view that the field memories are the more recent and more veridical memories. However, this is a complex issue. First, note that evidence showing that a memory image is not a copy of the original experience does not necessarily show that the information that is in the memory image is incorrect (i.e., essentially correct information could just be portrayed from a different perspective). A second and even more troubling problem is that the phenomenally experienced point of view of a memory image may not reflect its form of storage in long-term memory. This may appear to be such a general criticism that it is unfair to use it for this specific issue. However, Nigro and Neisser (1983) provide considerable evidence that subjects are capable of varying the point of view of particular memory images. Clearly, as a start in working out these complex issues, we need some direct evidence about the empirical relation of recollective point of view and memory accuracy.

Schema-based distortions of recollective memories

It seems likely that schema-based processes are a major source of errors in recollective memory, just as they are in other forms of memory (cf. Brewer & Nakamura, 1984). Barclay's (1986) chapter elaborates this argument (in a rather extreme form). However, the empirical evidence for this claim is relatively weak. For example, in my 1988 study of randomly selected events I provide a qualitative analysis of the four overt errors (p. 80) and note that two of the original event descriptions contain negative statements (e.g., "Not sitting next to D. whom I usually sit next to"). I argued that these negative statements were evidence that the original events violated the subjects' schema-based expectations, and that the errors occurred when the subjects' recalls were reconstructed to be consistent with the original schema-based expectations (e.g., "I was next to D. taking notes on lecture"). The example I discussed earlier from Neisser and Harsch's (1992) study of *Challenger* flashbulb memories seems to be another possible example of schema-based reconstruction (i.e., the student's recall of hearing about the *Challenger* contained the plausible, but false, information that she had initially heard about the explosion on TV). Neisser's (1981) analysis of John Dean's Watergate testimony suggests that, in addition to the normal schema-based processes, autobiographical memories may show a considerable degree of distortion in the direction of portraying the individual's actions in a more favorable light than occurred in the actual events. While I find these arguments for schema-based recollective memory errors fairly persuasive, it is obvious that they are based on a very limited set of data.

Validity of memory confidence at retrieval

Confidence is a measure of an individual's degree of belief about some state of affairs. Recollective memory is just one type of evidence that can be used in arriving at an overall judgment of confidence. For example, most of us are quite confident about when and where we were born, yet we have no recollective memory of the event.

Given the theoretical interest in memory errors, there has been much discussion of memory situations in which erroneous responses are given with high confidence (Brewer & Treyens, 1981; Franks & Bransford, 1971; Loftus, Miller, & Burns, 1978). In general, it appears that when unconscious schema-based reconstructive memory processes operate, they cause subjects to be confident about erroneous recalls and thus produce a breakdown between confidence and accuracy (cf. Leippe, 1980). However, I think that a more striking fact about human memory is that frequently individuals show that they *do* have reliable information about the accuracy of their memory performance.

Validity. There is considerable evidence that after making memory responses on a standard laboratory memory task, the subjects' confidence in their memory responses is reliably related to their memory accuracy (Hollingworth, 1913; Murdock, 1965, 1966; Strong, 1913; Tulving & Thomson, 1971; Wagenaar, 1988). Retrieval of information from nonepisodic memory (knowledge) shows the same relation – subjects' confidence judgments are reliably related to their memory accuracy (Fischoff, Slovic, & Lichtenstein, 1977; Gigerenzer, Hoffrage, & Kleinbölting, 1991). The relationship between confidence and accuracy can be quite strong. Murdock (1974, p. 27, 33) presents data showing, in a standard laboratory word-recognition task, that when a subject gives the highest confidence rating ("sure old" on a 3-point scale) their memory accuracy scores can be as high as 99%.

I will refer to the relation between measures of memory confidence (taken after memory retrieval) and memory accuracy as confidence *validity*. The evidence that subjects frequently show strong validity in their memory confidence demonstrates a remarkable aspect of human memory – human beings have direct access to aspects of their own memory processes that allow them to judge the accuracy of these mental processes against an external criterion. It is not clear what gives rise to the validity of confidence judgments, but two types of information seem most likely to be involved: phenomenological evidence from the memory retrieval process itself and information derived from metamemory reasoning processes (cf. Ross & Buehler, in press).

The phenomenological sources of evidence could include almost any of the forms discussed by the philosophers in the earlier sections of this chapter, for example, occurrence of (vivid?) imagery, occurrence of irrelevant detail in images, feelings of familiarity, etc.

The metamemory processes that lead to confidence could be simple, such as being confident of your answer about where you were born, because you believe that you thoroughly know all the basic facts about your life, so your answer must be correct. Or the confidence could be based on more complex chains of reasoning. For example, in the Brewer and Treyens (1981) study of memory for places, subjects were asked to make confidence judgments about their recognition memory for objects from a room that they had previously seen. The data from this experiment showed that subjects were quite confident in rejecting highly salient foils. Presumably this confidence was based on the following metamemory reasoning process: When asked about a highly salient object that had not actually been in the room (e.g., a rat in a cage), they reasoned that if the rat had been in the room they would have noticed it. If they had noticed it, they would recall it, and since they did not recall it, they were confident that the object must not have been in the room. Johnson, Hashtroudi, and Lindsay (1993) provide an insightful account of some of these issues.

One last general point about confidence and memory error: It seems highly likely that in evolutionary terms there would have been selection for accurate memory of past states of the world. Having the ability to make valid confidence judgments would be an important refinement of human memory. Therefore, when the memory system in human beings developed the capacity to have access to its own workings, there would be selection pressure for the confidence judgments to be valid reflections of the state of the external world. If one accepts this line of reasoning, then it seems likely that situations that lead to a breakdown between confidence and accuracy are a by-product of some memory process that more typically gives rise to accurate memory. For similar arguments with respect to errors of human reasoning see Einhorn and Hogarth (1978) and Gigerenzer, Hoffrage, and Kleinbölting (1991). Now I will turn to an examination of the confidence and memory issue for recollective memory.

Autobiographical memory. My 1988 study of memory for randomly selected events provides direct data on the validity of subjects' confidence in their memories for events from their lives. In Experiment 2, I had the subjects' initial descriptions of the experienced events and the subjects' recall of those events months later. In addition, for each event, I had the subjects' confidence ratings ("Overall memory") made at the time of recall. I assigned each recall to one of seven categories without knowledge of the subjects' confidence scores. For those responses I classified as highly correct ("correct with detail"), the mean confidence score was 6.0, while the mean confidence score for those that I classified as complete failures ("omits") was 1.3. Thus, for the two extreme categories in terms of memory accuracy, the subjects' mean confidence scores span almost the complete range of the 1–7 scale. Clearly the subjects' confidence scores for their own memories were highly predictive of memory accuracy. Those items that I classified as ordinary correct recalls ("correct") received a mean score of 4.5 on the confidence scale, while those items I classified as retrieval of totally the wrong episode ("wrong event") received a mean score of 3.1. Apparently, when the subjects retrieved an event from their lives, they had access to information that frequently allowed them to distinguish correct events from incorrect events. Thus, the data from this study provide clear evidence that confidence judgments are valid indicators of memory accuracy for randomly selected events from the lives of undergraduates.

Flashbulb memory. As noted above, the initial studies of flashbulb memory did not obtain data that allowed one to examine memory accuracy and so could not provide evidence relevant to the confidence validity issue.

However, a number of recent investigations have obtained appropriate data. Many of these studies have focused on memory errors and have emphasized the breakdown of the confidence/accuracy relation for flashbulb memory (e.g., Harsch & Neisser, 1989). I would like to argue that the data are not quite as bad as they have been portrayed.

First, before reviewing the evidence, it is important to note that the nature of the experimental designs typically used in flashbulb memory experiments would be *expected* to lead to a reduced confidence/accuracy relationship. In a typical flashbulb memory experiment there is only one flashbulb memory, and thus one confidence judgment for each subject. Therefore, the use of the confidence scale is a between-subject comparison and includes variability due to individual differences in confidence and in the use of the scales. The studies that have found strong relations between confidence and accuracy (e.g., Brewer, 1988; Murdock, 1974) have often involved within-subject designs in which the subjects made hundreds of memory confidence judgments that were then related to the corresponding memory performance to derive a measure of memory accuracy. See Gruneberg and Sykes (1993) and Peterson and Pitz (1988) for similar arguments.

McCloskey, Wible, & Cohen (1988) studied flashbulb memories of the explosion of the space shuttle *Challenger*. They point out that 3 of their 9 inconsistent recalls were given the maximum confidence rating and suggest that there has been a breakdown of the confidence/accuracy relation. However, examination of the confidence data for all 9 inconsistent recalls shows that they were rated about one scale unit (on a 1–7 scale) below the correct recalls on the confidence scale. This suggests that, overall, there was some relationship between the subjects' confidence and their recall accuracy. Weaver's (1993) study of flashbulb memory emphasized the high absolute levels of confidence given to flashbulb memory items. However, examination of his data shows that there was a relatively strong relation between memory confidence and memory accuracy. Events given the lowest confidence rating (1 on a 1–3 scale) show about 30% correct recalls, whereas events given the highest confidence rating show about 90% correct recalls.

Neisser and Harsch (1992) present evidence on memory and confidence for a flashbulb event and argue that their data show an almost complete breakdown of the confidence/accuracy relation. They point to a high level of confidence for some completely inaccurate recalls and to a low correlation between confidence and accuracy (.29). Examination of their data suggests that at the extremes the confidence judgments may show some modest validity. The recalls with confidence scores below about 3 (on a 1–7 scale) have memory accuracy scores of 7%, whereas those with confidence scores above about 5 have accuracy scores of 44%. In addition, in my analysis of their paper (Brewer, 1992b, pp. 289–291), I argued that there is internal evidence ("TV priority") in their data to suggest that a number of their subjects were recalling a vivid event that occurred that day, but not the initial reception event that Neisser and Harsch were scoring against. If this is true, then it would produce high confidence for these "erroneous" recalls and would necessarily reduce the obtained correlation between confidence and accuracy.

What conclusion are we to draw from this analysis of memory confidence in the flashbulb memory literature? It seems to me that if one considers the problem of the between-subject confidence judgments that derive from the typical designs used in flashbulb memory studies, one can hold that the flashbulb memory studies are in essential agreement with the other studies in showing a robust relation between memory confidence and memory accuracy.

Although this is a defensible position given the current state of the evidence, I actually tend to think that there may be some unique aspects of flashbulb memories that do tend to lead to higher absolute confidence and to a reduction in the confidence/accuracy relationship. In particular, it seems to me that the occurrence of strong imagery and strong metamemory beliefs about the accuracy of flashbulb memories might well contribute to high confidence beliefs and reduced confidence validity for flashbulb memories.

Validity of memory confidence at input

Another interesting type of metamemory is the ability of individuals to predict, *at the time of exposure*, how successful they will be at remembering the information on a later memory test. Laboratory studies have shown that subjects can reliably predict their later memory performance for materials ranging from nonsense syllables (Underwood, 1966) to narrative text (Maki & Swett, 1987).

Wagenaar's (1986) study of events from his own life provides data on his ability to predict his later recall at the time he recorded the original events. The results show that his recall predictions had very high validity. For example, those he assigned the lowest estimated probabilities showed less than 5% correct recalls; whereas, those he assigned the highest estimated probabilities showed about 85% correct recalls. Thompson's (1982) study of events from lives of undergraduates and their roommates showed that a subject's memorability ratings of these events, made at the time they were recorded, predicted later recognition memory ratings for both that subject's events and their roommate's events.

My 1988 study of randomly selected events from the lives of undergraduates also provided evidence on the ability of subjects to predict later memory performance. In that study subjects were asked to record the most memorable event of the day. The data showed that subjects' recognition memory for these items was considerably better than their memory for the randomly selected events. Comparison of the attributes of the memorable events with those of the random events suggested that the criteria that the subjects had been using to select the memorable events were the rareness of the action and degree of affect associated with the action.

Rate of forgetting

Autobiographical memory. Studies of probed recall for recollective memories show relatively impressive rates of recall over long time intervals. Wagenaar (1986) showed about 70% recall of events from his life after 6 months, dropping to 29% after 5 years. The subjects in my study of the recall of randomly selected events showed about 46% recall of actions after 2 months. While it is hard to know exactly what would be a fair comparison, it is clear that recollective recall shows much lower rates of forgetting than does standard laboratory memory tasks of verbal material.

Recognition memory for recollective memories is, as would be expected, even better. Both Linton (1978) and Wagenaar (1986) appear to show 99% recognition of events from their lives after 1 year. White's (1982) study of events from his life shows about 60% recognition after 1 year, whereas my (1988) study of random events showed about 70% recognition of events after 5 months. These levels of recognition seem strong; however, it is a little difficult to know how to compare these findings with other memory tasks. None of these studies of autobiographical memory have used foils (nonexperienced life events) due to the conceptual difficulty in developing foils for autobiographical events. In addition, it is known that laboratory studies of recognition memory for pictures (Nickerson, 1968; Shepard, 1967) can show levels of performance similar to those for autobiographical events reported above.

Flashbulb memory. The core assumption in the flashbulb memory literature, from the time of the original work of Brown and Kulik (1977), has been that memory for the circumstances of a flashbulb event shows little or no forgetting. The methodological issues and data in this area are quite complex (cf. Brewer, 1992b, pp. 293–302); however, a number of the flashbulb memory studies (e.g., Christianson, 1989; McCloskey, Wible, & Cohen, 1988; Weaver, 1993) show strong recall for the circumstances of hearing about a flashbulb event for long periods of time.

There is some additional information about rate of forgetting that is implicit in flashbulb memory experiments. For theoretical reasons the studies in this area focus on memory for the circumstances of hearing about a flashbulb event (cf. Larsen, 1992, p. 64, for a similar observation). Yet, note that these experimenters uniformly assume that the subjects recall the flashbulb event itself (otherwise how could one ask them if they recalled the circumstances for the events). It would appear that the recall for the flashbulb event is even better than that for the circumstances. For public flashbulb events (i.e., those learned about through the media) it is not clear that the memory for the flashbulb event is a true recollective memory; however, for private flashbulb events (i.e., those personally experienced) the event itself should produce a classic recollective memory, and one would think that they would show an extremely low level of forgetting.

Variables influencing recall

Autobiographical memory. A large number of studies have investigated the characteristics of events that lead to successful memory performance. These studies consistently find that low-frequency events show better memory (Brewer, 1988, p. 38, 48; Linton, 1982, p. 86; M. E. Smith, 1952, p. 166; Wagenaar, 1986, p. 238; White, 1982, p. 176). There is also a weaker finding that overall level of emotionality (deviation from neutrality in either pleasant or unpleasant directions) is associated with better memory performance (Brewer, 1988, p. 38; Linton, 1982, p. 87; M. E. Smith, 1952, p. 168; Wagenaar, 1986, p. 238; White, 1982, p. 176; see also Christianson & Safer, this volume). However, there is a problem in interpreting these data because highly emotional events also tend to be infrequent events. In the two studies (Brewer, 1988; White, 1982) to use regression techniques to examine this issue, only event frequency was reliably associated with memory performance.

These correlational findings take on even more significance because there is a theoretical account of memory distinctiveness that predicts the correlation with event frequency. Both Linton (1982, pp. 79–81) and I (1986, p. 45) have argued for what I have come to call a "dual-process theory of repetition" (1988, p. 76). My initial formulation of the theory stated, "repetition of events leads to the development of generic personal memories at the expense of the individual personal memories that were repeated" (1986, p. 45). In essence, this theory proposes that one has to consider sets of events as potentially having a generic representation and a set of unique episodic representations; and that repetition of the episodic events leads to interference in memory for these representations, while at the same time leading to improved memory for the generic aspects of the events. Clearly the dual-process theory of repetition would predict better retention of recollective memories of low-frequency events and poorer retention of recollective memories of high-frequency events.

Flashbulb memory. A number of studies of flashbulb memory have correlated event variables with flashbulb memory strength. For theoretical reasons (e.g., the hypotheses proposed by Brown & Kulik, 1977) these studies have typically examined variables such as surprisingness, consequentiality, and emotionality. The results are quite inconsistent (see Brewer, 1988, pp. 286–287, for a review). However, it seems to me that for flashbulb memories, this type of correlational analysis is not the technique of choice. Flashbulb memories are an extraordinarily select class of recollective memories (perhaps 1 in 10,000 or 1 in 100,000). Given this extreme selection there should be an considerable restriction in the range of the variables being measured, so the standard correlational analysis is probably not appropriate. Variables related to the apparently low rate of forgetting of flashbulb memories would probably be better explored by comparing the characteristics of flashbulb events with nonflashbulb events.

Organization of recollective memories

A number of psychologists have developed accounts of how recollective memory is organized in long-term memory. This issue is somewhat separate from the core issue of the present chapter and so will receive only limited treatment here. See Conway (1990, chap. 6) and Friedman (1993) for reviews of this topic.

Koffka (1935, pp. 446–451) appears to have suggested that recollective memories are organized in a temporal "trace column" from first to last (i.e., along a time line). Given any plausible values for the time of mental operations, it seems to me that this approach would have to predict impossibly long retrieval times for old memories, so I think it is unlikely to be a successful account.

In more recent times, with the development of theories of semantic networks (e.g., Collins & Quillian, 1969), Robinson (1976) appears to have suggested that recollective memories are organized in terms of semantic categories. Conway and Bekerian (1987) carried out a priming experiment that attempted to test the hypothesis that recollective memories are organized in semantic categories. They interpret their data as showing that recollective memories are not organized into semantic categories. The most sophisticated model of the organization of recollective memory is the recent work of Conway (1992, this volume). He has argued that individual recollective memories are independently represented and retrieved by "thematic" knowledge structures such as "lifetime periods" and "general events," and has used this model to account for certain classes of data dealing with retrieval time for recollective memories. However, recent evidence (Friedman, 1993) suggests that the organization of autobiographical memory is likely to be very complex, so it is clear that much additional work is needed on this topic.

Dating recollective memories

Many researchers in the area of autobiographical memory have thought that absolute time must somehow be a part of the memory representation (see Friedman, 1993; and Larsen, Thompson, & Hansen, this volume, for thoughtful reviews of these positions). However, in my recent papers on recollective memory (1986, 1988) I have argued that the analysis of the recollective memory experience as an apparent "reliving" of the original experience tends to exclude absolute time information for most events. To be more specific, a typical recollection will include information about location, actions, people, and thoughts. If this position is correct, then information about absolute dates must be derived from the other information available in a typical recollective memory. Thus, if the recollective memory content happened to be about a birthday party, then it could provide direct date information. In the more typical case, the recollective memory might contain information about eating dinner at home and so provide reliable information about time of day, but not about the date.

There is considerable evidence to support this view. Wagenaar's study of his own memories (1986) and my study of randomly selected events (1988) show that date information is a very poor retrieval cue for recollective memories. This is as would be expected from my position about the content of recollective memories, whereas theories that postulate that absolute date information is typically encoded in memories should predict that dates would be excellent cues for memory retrieval.

Both White (1982, 1989) and Friedman (1987) have shown that subjects are much better at providing information about time of day than they are about providing information about dates. Once again, this finding derives nicely from the view about the content of recollective memories.

There is an extensive literature suggesting that subjects provide date information by inferential processes based on such things as physical location (M. E. Smith, 1952; White, 1982, 1989) and "landmark" events (Baddeley, Lewis, & Nimmo-Smith, 1978; Thompson, 1982). Once again this is what one would expect if subjects typically had recollective memory information but no absolute date information.

Laboratory tasks and recollective memory

Attempting to specify the relationship between autobiographical memory tasks and laboratory memory tasks has proved very difficult. Larsen (1992) and Conway (1992, chap. 1) provide recent accounts from the point of view of autobiographical memory researchers. In the next section of this chapter I turn to this complex problem.

Laboratory studies of memory

The issue of the role of recollective memory in standard laboratory tasks is a demanding topic and one that requires independent treatment. Therefore, all I will be able to do here is to give a light sketch of some of the issues and findings.

Types of memory and forms of representation

Ebbinghaus. Ebbinghaus's great monograph (1885/1964) initiated laboratory studies of memory and raised theoretical issues about the nature of human memory that have yet to be resolved. Ebbinghaus recognized two basic forms of memory: recollection and skill/implicit memory. He described recollective memory as the form of memory in which we "can call back into consciousness by an exertion of the will directed to this purpose the seemingly lost states (or, indeed, in case these consisted in immediate sense-perceptions, we can recall their true memory images)" (p. 1). For skill/implicit memory he stated that the "vanished mental states give indubitable proof of their continuing existence even if they themselves do not return to consciousness at all" (p. 2). Ebbinghaus did not see how it was possible to bring recollective memory under strict laboratory control and so invented the method of savings (i.e., the improvement in the speed of learning a task that results from previous trials) to study rote/implicit memory. Ebbinghaus's view seems clear and straightforward. However, soon after his initial work the researchers in the Ebbinghaus Empire found the savings method too restrictive and began using various types of recall tasks. This decision opens the way for recollective memory to occur and gives rise to conceptual and empirical problems that are still with us.

At the time Ebbinghaus carried out his research almost all psychologists conceived psychology to be the science that investigated the phenomena of the conscious mind (Boring, 1950). I think it seemed clear to all concerned that Ebbinghaus's research was a major contribution to the study of memory. However, how could an introspective psychologist deal with this work? One solution was simply to ignore the conceptual conflict. For example, Calkins' (1905) textbook defined memory as recollection ("reproductive imagination") and then proceeded to describe Ebbinghaus's experiments and data.

Recollective memory versus skill. However, the more frequent solution, particularly among American functional psychologists, was to make a distinction between two fundamentally different forms of memory – recollection and skill. For example, Stratton (1903, p. 190) stated that "we must distinguish between the mere persistence of influences from the past, and conscious recall of the past." Bentley (1924, p. 251) argued that "[t]o apprehend something as belonging to my past is very different from using the past experiences of the organism as a means to present recital or as an acquirement which aids thinking, perceiving, or acting."

In a fascinating and forgotten study, Smith and McDougall (1920) actually carried out an experiment designed to provide empirical support for the two forms of memory. They formulated their experiment as a test of Bergson's distinction between true memory and habit memory. They described one of the forms of memory as "recollections which in their very nature are unique experiences" (p. 199) and the other as "the power of forming mechanical associations" (p. 199). Smith and McDougall gave subjects two tasks that they thought were examples of recollective memory (picture recall after a single exposure and form recognition after a single exposure). In addition, they gave the subjects two tasks that they thought were examples of skill memory (CVC learning with multiple trials and a motor skill task with multiple trials). They found that the two recollective memory tasks were highly correlated and the two skill tasks were highly correlated, and yet the recollective memory tasks were not correlated with the skill tasks. They also gave subjects a prose memory task and found that it was moderately correlated with both the recollective tasks and the skill tasks, and so they suggested that this type of task involved both types of memory.

Only skill. Recollective memory was clearly incompatible with behaviorism, and so as behaviorism came to dominate American psychology, the construct of recollective memory was abandoned. Watson (1926) directly attacked recollective memory in one of his behaviorist polemics. He noted that some introspective psychologists had argued that his behavioristic approach could not deal with the recollective memory experience. His reply was to say that "the behaviorist having made a clean sweep of all the rubbish called consciousness, comes back at you: 'Prove to me,' he says, 'that you have auditory images, visual images, or any other kind of disembodied processes. So far I have only your unverified and unsupported word that you have them.' Science must have objective evidence to base its theories upon" (p. 248).

Semantic versus episodic memory. Given the framework of this paper it is now obvious that Tulving's (1972) classic paper on semantic and episodic memory reintroduced the construct of recollective memory into laboratory psychology and juxtaposed it to what the philosophers had called memory for propositions. It is no wonder that this is one of the landmark papers in the history of the study of memory.

However, some time ago, John Pani and I (Brewer & Pani, 1983) argued that there was a problem with Tulving's treatment of episodic memory. Tulving's *definition* of episodic memory was clearly intended to refer to recollective memory. He stated that episodic memory "stores information about temporally dated episodes or events and temporal-spatial relations among these events" (p. 385) and stated that instances of episodic memory refer "to a personal experience that is remembered in its temporal-spatial relation to other such experiences" (p. 387). Yet, in the paper he explicitly asserted that traditional verbal learning experiments were examples of episodic memory (p. 402). In the 1983 paper we argued that most traditional laboratory task procedures are antithetical to the ordinary operation of recollective memory (p. 12). In the context of the current paper it is clear what was concerning us. Tulving defined episodic memory in agreement with the construct of recollective memory, but his actual application of the term (and that of most laboratory investigators following him) included the construct of memory skills. Thus, when Tulving proposed that there were two primary forms of memory he did not adopt the two forms of memory that had been proposed by the functional psychologists at the beginning of the century. Instead, Tulving introduced a new form of memory (semantic) that they had not considered, and in his actual usage, combined the two forms they had discussed under the single term *episodic memory*.

Since the original 1972 paper, Tulving has continued to discuss the types of memory. For example, Tulving (1985a) suggested that there are three basic forms of memory: procedural, semantic, and episodic. More recently, Tulving (1991) has suggested that there are five forms of memory: procedural, perceptual, short-term memory, semantic, and episodic. It seems to me that some of the nonepisodic aspects of memory discussed by the philosophers and by the introspective psychologists are captured by the new formulations. However, it is not clear to me that any of them capture the essential skill involved in many verbal learning tasks (what Brewer & Pani [1983] referred to as "rote linguistic skill").

The issue of forms of memory remains highly controversial. Some researchers simply deny that there is a conflict between the Ebbinghaus paradigm and recollective memory. For example, Banaji and Crowder (1989, p. 1185) state "every study conducted on episodic memory since, and including specifically, those of Ebbinghaus (1885/1964), has concerned memory for personally experienced, and therefore autobiographical, information." I believe the present chapter provides considerable evidence for recollective memory as a unique form of memory and thus stands in strong opposition to positions such as that of Banaji and Crowder.

Methods for the study of recollective memory

The procedures used in laboratory memory tasks have typically not been designed with the intent of studying recollective memory. It is not completely clear how one should design such tasks to focus on recollective memory, but if one operates by analogy from the typical, nonlaboratory, recollective memory situation, then one might use tasks that involved the recall of single stimuli (preferably nonlinguistic) with techniques designed to gather evidence on the subject's phenomenal experience during the recall. Given that most laboratory tasks do not fit this description, evidence about recollective memory derived from laboratory tasks is relatively limited.

Most of the relevant data comes from two sets of studies separated by a gap of about 75 years. The earlier line of research consists of experiments carried out in the first few decades of this century when introspective reports were still gathered in laboratory tasks (e.g., Kuhlmann, 1906, 1907; Strong 1913; Woods, 1915). The second line of studies follow from Tulving's (1985b) innovative work on "know" and "remember" responses in laboratory tasks (e.g., Gardiner, 1988; Gardiner & Java, 1991; Rajaram, 1993), plus some preliminary studies by Brewer (1982) and Brewer and Pani (1983).

Methodology in this area has been driven by the experimenters' theoretical beliefs about the nature of memory and about the acceptability of phenomenal data. Ebbinghaus's approach quickly became the standard method of studying memory, and this led to many complaints from those interested in the phenomenal aspects of memory

(Bentley, 1899, p. 7, 11, 13; Kennedy, 1898, p. 494; Kuhlmann, 1906, p. 317, 1907, p. 390; Titchener, 1910, p. 414). Titchener (1910, p. 414) said the use of the Ebbinghaus methodology had "forced into the background of current interest the more immediately psychological problem of a description of the memory consciousness." Bentley (1899, p. 13) complained that the Ebbinghaus researchers "have measured the volume of the stream and the pressure at given points, to a neglect of the contents."

However, these arguments failed, and the behaviorist position (cf. the earlier quote from Watson [1913]) won the day, and laboratory memory researchers ceased gathering data about the phenomenological experiences of their subjects. With the advent of cognitive psychology in the 1960s, one might have thought that this methodological position would have shifted, but it did not. On the issue of the use of phenomenal reports as data, information-processing approaches differed little from behaviorist approaches. Therefore, there was another round of arguments from those who believed that reports of phenomenological states are acceptable data in the study of human memory. Brewer and Pani (1983, p. 5) noted that "the focus on unconscious mental processes within the information-processing tradition has led to remarkably little serious use of data from phenomenal experience." (In taking this position Brewer also notes an interesting coincidence – he is following a University of Illinois tradition because Bentley and Kuhlmann, two of the strongest earlier advocates of the use of phenomenal data, both taught at the University of Illinois.) Tulving (1989, p. 4) stated "the bulk of research within the general framework of cognitive psychology has not been greatly different from earlier work on verbal learning in its concentration on memory performance and its neglect of conscious experience." It is too soon to be sure, but it appears that the use of phenomenal data may once again become one of the tools of the laboratory scientist studying human memory.

Phenomenological descriptions of recollective memory

Occurrence of imagery. There was wide agreement in the textbooks in the first few decades of this century that recollective memory involves phenomenally experienced imagery (Angell, 1909, p. 222; Bentley, 1924, p. 253; Warren & Carmichael, 1930, p. 201). Kuhlmann carried out two studies that gathered introspective reports in laboratory recall tasks. One looked at the recall of visual geometric forms seen once (1906), and the other at the recall of pictures seen once (1907). Both studies found very high rates of imagery in the reports of the subjects after their recalls.

Tulving (1985b) carried out the first modern study of recollection in a laboratory recall task. Subjects were given a word recall task with varying degrees of cues. For each item recalled, the subjects were asked to indicate if they "actually 'remembered' its occurrence in the list" (p. 8) or "whether they simply 'knew' on some other basis that the item was a member of the study list" (p. 8). Tulving found that the number of "remember" responses (recollective responses) declined with the specificity of the cue.

Characteristics of memory imagery. A number of the early introspective studies gave scattered reports about the characteristics of memory images. Boring, Langfeld, and Weld (1939, pp. 356–357) summarized the findings as showing that compared to perception, memory images are (1) less detailed, (2) unstable, (3) less clear (more blurred), (4) less intense, and (5) colors are less saturated.

Several studies (Crosland, 1921; Philippe, 1897) had subjects give phenomenal reports over varying time intervals. These studies found that the memory images tend to become more vague and indistinct. Crosland (1921) also reports that they tend to become more decontextualized (i.e., lose their recollective context).

Point of view. There are few discussions of point of view in this literature. Kuhlmann (1907, p. 414) reported that his subjects' recollections frequently included instances where objects were seen from a different point of view than in the original pictures. Warren and Carmichael (1930, p. 218) made the somewhat unusual assertion that the "composite image of [someone's] face usually includes both profile and full front views." They provide no evidence for this assertion.

Repetition and recollection

Slaughter (1902, p. 529) argued that when one has repeated exposure to members of a class, a general image develops "whose location in space and time has been lost." Warren and Carmichael (1930) made a similar argument and called the product of this type of abstraction a "general image." They also asserted that if one has repeated exposure to essentially the same object, the resulting "composite image" "shows the object without any definite location in time and space and with no fixed surroundings or background" (p. 217). See Brewer (1993) for a discussion of these image abstraction views as they occur in theories about the nature of concepts.

Woods (1915) reported an important study of the role of repetition in recognition memory. She obtained introspections from subjects who were exposed to initially unfamiliar stimuli (e.g., smells, music) and then observed them over repeated recognition trials. She found that on the first recognition trial the subjects reported large amounts of recollective imagery, but that this imagery showed a sharp drop over trials, so that the stimuli were eventually recognized directly without recollection.

Sensation, uninterpreted perception, interpreted perception

Washburn (1916/1973, p. 65) argued that memory images are interpreted. She stated, "We cannot recall a memory image several hours after an experience, and hope by examining it to note peculiarities which we overlooked when the experience was first received." Woodworth (1938, p. 47) made essentially the same claim.

Recollective memory during recognition tasks

Very early in the laboratory study of memory, Kulpe (1895) proposed that recollection is involved in recognition memory tasks. Kulpe stated, "Recognition may take place in two very different ways: either in the form of a judgment . . . expressive of familiarity with an object or an occurrence, without a reproduction of the sensations involved in its previous perception; or by the intermediation of reproduced sensations, which connect with the object of present perception or ideation and repeat certain circumstances of the original situation. The first is *direct*, the second *indirect* recognition" (p. 171). This position surfaces in modern laboratory research in Mandler's (1980) dual-process model of recognition, which included reference to evidence from phenomenal experience.

Strong (1913) and Strong and Strong (1916) carried out very important empirical studies of the role of recollection in laboratory recognition tasks. In these studies the subjects (often the Strongs themselves) learned lists of words and then carried out recognition after various time intervals. After the recognition responses the subjects gave introspective reports about the phenomenal experiences involved in making the response. These studies supported Kulpe's view and found that some recognition responses were made directly and some through recollection. For example, Strong and Strong (1916, p. 349) report that on one occasion "a word called up a kitchen utensil and we remembered that we had been in the kitchen while reading the list, hence the word belonged to the list read on that day." Strong (1913, p. 368) stated that for the indirect recognitions, "[t]he introspections had the same relation to the words as the occasion of meeting someone has to the recognition of that one again. The recognition is confirmed as the occasion comes to mind." A more detailed account of these early recognition experiments is given in Brewer (1992a).

Once again Tulving (1985b) was the first modern investigator to study recollection in laboratory recognition tasks. He carried out a word recognition task and asked subjects to make "know" or "remember" judgments for each response. He found that "remember" responses (recollective responses) showed a sharper rate of forgetting than did "know" responses.

Gardiner (1988) followed up the original Tulving study with a more formal experiment. His instructions to the subjects defined "remember" responses as "the ability to become consciously aware again of some aspect of what happened or what was experienced at the time the word was presented (e.g., aspects of the physical appearance of the word, or of something that happened in the room, or of what one was thinking or doing at that time)" (p. 311). Clearly "remember" responses were intended to index recollective memory. In this experiment and others (e.g., Gardiner & Java, 1991), Gardiner has been systematically investigating variables that are known to have an impact on recognition memory to find out how these variables affect "know" versus "remember" responses. This is very important work for it shows a functional relation between phenomenal data and memory performance – a finding that is hard for those in the Ebbingaus Empire to ignore. The literature on "know" versus "remember" responses is growing rapidly. For example, Rajaram (1993) has shown that subjects give more recollective responses to picture stimuli than to words. Clearly, we are beginning to uncover the role of recollection in laboratory recognition tasks.

Metamemory beliefs about accuracy

Tulving's (1985b) innovative study also included data on confidence judgments. He found that subjects showed more confidence for "remember" judgments than for "know" judgments.

Veridicality of recollective memories

Philippe (1897) and Kuhlmann (1906, 1907) have given extensive accounts of qualitative errors that occur in laboratory tasks involving recollective memory. The data will be discussed later, in the section on the role of schemata in recollective memory.

Phenomenal experience and memory accuracy

Kuhlmann (1907) gave a very insightful analysis of the criteria subjects used to judge the correctness of their recollections in a picture recall task. He stated that his subjects' reports reveal the use of four basic processes: (1) direct feeling that the image was correct, (2) use of the vividness and spontaneity of the image, (3) absence of rival imagery, and (4) inferences from other remembered or known facts.

Schema-based distortions of recollective memories

Philippe (1897) carried out an important early experiment investigating the changes over time in memory images for objects. He reported two basic types of qualitative changes. The most common types were shifts away from representations of the original stimulus object toward more canonical representations of that *type* of object. He also reported shifts in the direction of geometric simplification. Kuhlmann's (1906) study of the recall of geometric forms produced data very similar to that of Philippe. He found that the memory images for figures that were not quite vertical or horizontal tended to become more precisely vertical or horizontal over time. Kuhlmann's (1907) study of picture memory found that the memory images took "on characteristics that belong to the object, which are not represented in the picture" (p. 411) and "the imagery of the picture tends to the imagery of the object represented by the picture" (p. 415). Thus, the laboratory studies of recollective memory appear to show powerful schema effects.

Rate of forgetting

Both Tulving (1985b) and Gardiner and Java (1991) have reported that "remember" responses show a higher rate of forgetting than do "know" responses.

Laboratory tasks and recollective memory

In general, it seems to me that most laboratory paradigms for the study of memory are heterogeneous in the types of memory that are involved. John Pani and I give extensive arguments on this point in our paper on the structure of human memory (Brewer & Pani, 1983).

Task restrictions. The classic verbal learning paradigm developed by Ebbinghaus involves the repeated presentation of nonsense materials. Pani and I argued that these procedures were essentially "antithetical to the development of personal memory" (Brewer & Pani, 1983, p. 12). Note that this is not an accident – Ebbinghaus believed that recollective memory was too complex to study and was attempting to develop conditions to remove it from the experimental task. In addition, Ebbinghaus chose not to gather data on the phenomenological experiences of his subjects. In a real sense he was a pre-

Watsonian methodological behaviorist. He was also very successful – after over 100 years of research we have very limited data on the phenomenological experience of subjects in the classic Ebbinghaus task. In an early study (Brewer & Pani, 1982), we indirectly explored the issue of types of tasks involved in laboratory experiments. In this study we asked subjects to carry out different types of retrievals from long-term memory. We found that an autobiographical recollective memory task generated a much higher proportion of image responses than did motor skill tasks (type the word "truth") or rote tasks (give your phone number). However, this study focused on material from long-term memory and not on information learned in the laboratory, and so it is not strictly comparable to the Ebbinghaus paradigm.

Meaningless materials. The use of "meaningless" stimuli tends to force the subject to rely on "rote skill" (Brewer & Pani, 1983). The discussion of these issues by the philosophers that was summarized earlier expands some of the arguments we made. However, note that one of the few introspective studies of the learning of meaningless material (Kuhlmann, 1906) suggested that the subjects' "effort after meaning" (Bartlett, 1932) makes the task heterogeneous. Kuhlmann (1906) investigated memory for geometric forms and found that the subjects reported working very hard to find associations for the forms and that these associations were frequently recollected during recall.

Repetition. Many laboratory tasks involve repetition of stimuli. The earlier review of the impact of repetition on recollective memory suggests that repetition tends to lead to the decontexualization of the memory, and thus a shift from recollective memory to some form of generic memory (cf. Brewer & Pani, 1983).

Content focus. Both Tulving (1983, p. 143) and Larsen (1992) have argued that the demands of laboratory tasks tend to focus the subjects' attention on the content of the task. In the terms of Brewer (1986), the experiencing "ego" tends to fade from consciousness.

Overall it appears that many aspects of traditional rote learning paradigms are designed to reduce recollective memory. Laboratory tasks with meaningful stimuli and single presentation should show more involvement of recollective memory. Clearly this is a topic in need of additional data.

Conclusions

It seems to me that the evidence reviewed in this paper provides strong support for the view that recollective memory is a mental "natural kind." I take the following description of recollective memory to be an example of "cutting nature at her joints."

Recollective memory is memory for a specific episode from an individual's past. It typically appears to be a "reliving" of the individual's phenomenal experience during that earlier moment. Thus, these memories typically contain information about place, actions, persons, objects, thoughts, and affect. They do not contain any direct representation of time. The information in this form of memory is expressed as a mental image. Compared to visual perception, recollective memory images are dim, unclear, sketchy, and unsteady. The point of view of recollective memory images can be from the original perspective or from an observer's point of view. The image may contain irrelevant detail. Recollective memories also appear to include propositional (nonimage) information. They are accompanied by a belief that the remembered episode was personally experienced by the individual in that individual's past. Recent recollective memories tend to be fairly veridical unless they are influenced by strong schema-based processes. Recollective memories give rise to high confidence in the accuracy of their content and that confidence can frequently predict objective memory accuracy.

References

Anderson, J. R., & Bower, G. H. (1973). *Human associative memory*. Washington, DC: V. H. Winston.

Angell, J. R. (1909). *Psychology* (revised, 4th ed.). New York: Henry Holt.

Ayer, A. J. (1956). *The problem of knowledge*. Baltimore, MD: Penguin.

—— (1972). *Bertrand Russell*. New York: Viking Press.

Baddeley, A. (1992). What is autobiographical memory? In M. A. Conway, D. C. Rubin, H. Spinnler, & W. A. Wagenaar (Eds.), *Theoretical perspectives on autobiographical memory* (pp. 13–29). NATO ASI Series D: Behavioural and Social Sciences, Vol. 65. Dordrecht, The Netherlands: Kluwer Academic.

Baddeley, A. D., Lewis, V., & Nimmo-Smith, I. (1978). When did you last . . . ? In M. M. Gruneberg, P. E. Morris, & R. N. Sykes (Eds.), *Practical aspects of memory* (pp. 77–83). London: Academic Press.

Banaji, M. R., & Crowder, R. G. (1989). The bankruptcy of everyday memory. *American Psychologist, 44*, 1185–1193.

Barclay, C. R. (1986). Schematization of autobiographical memory. In D. C. Rubin (Ed.), *Autobiographical memory* (pp. 82–99). Cambridge, UK: Cambridge University Press.

Barclay, C. R., & Wellman, H. M. (1986). Accuracies and inaccuracies in autobiographical memories. *Journal of Memory and Language, 25*, 93–103.

Barsalou, L. W. (1988). The content and organization of autobiographical memories. In U. Neisser & E. Winograd (Eds.), *Remembering reconsidered: Ecological and traditional approaches to the study of memory* (pp. 193–243). Cambridge, UK: Cambridge University Press.

Bartlett, F. C. (1932). *Remembering*. Cambridge, UK: Cambridge University Press.

Bell, B. E., & Loftus, E. F. (1989). Trivial persuasion in the courtroom: The power of (a few) minor details. *Journal of Personality and Social Psychology, 56*, 669–679.

Bentley, I. M. (1899). The memory image and its qualitative fidelity. *American Journal of Psychology, 11*, 1–48.

Bentley, M. (1924). *The field of psychology*. New York: D. Appleton.

Bergson, H. (1896/1911). *Matter and memory*. London: Allen & Unwin.

Bohannon, J. N., III. (1988). Flashbulb memories for the Space Shuttle disaster: A tale of two theories. *Cognition, 29*, 179–196.

Boring, E. G. (1950). *A history of experimental psychology* (2nd ed.). New York: Appleton-Century-Crofts.

Boring, E. G., Langfeld, H. S., & Weld, H. P. (1939). *Introduction to psychology*. New York: Wiley.

Bradley, F. H. (1899). Some remarks on memory and inference. *Mind, 8*, 145–166.

Brewer, W. F. (1982, August). Personal memory, generic memory, and skill: A re-analysis of the episodic-semantic distinction. In *Proceedings of the Fourth Annual Conference of the Cognitive Science Society* (pp. 112–113). Ann Arbor, MI: Cognitive Science Society.

—— (1986). What is autobiographical memory? In D. C. Rubin (Ed.), *Autobiographical memory* (pp. 25–49). Cambridge, UK: Cambridge University Press.

—— (1988). Memory for randomly sampled autobiographical events. In U. Neisser & E. Winograd (Eds.), *Remembering reconsidered: Ecological and traditional approaches to the study of memory* (pp. 21–90). Cambridge, UK: Cambridge University Press.

—— (1992a). Phenomenal experience in laboratory and autobiographical memory. In M. A. Conway, D. C. Rubin, H. Spinnler, & W. A. Wagenaar (Eds.), *Theoretical perspectives on autobiographical memory* (pp. 31–51). NATO ASI Series D: Behavioural and Social Sciences, Vol. 65. Dordrecht, The Netherlands: Kluwer Academic.

—— (1992b). The theoretical and empirical status of the flashbulb memory hypothesis. In E. Winograd & U. Neisser (Eds.), *Affect and accuracy in recall: Studies of "flashbulb" memories* (pp. 274–305). New York: Cambridge University Press.

—— (1993). What are concepts? Issues of representation and ontology. In G. V. Nakamura, R. Taraban, & D. L. Medin (Eds.), *The psychology of learning and motivation: Categorization by humans and machines* (Vol. 29, pp. 495–533). San Diego: Academic Press.

Brewer, W. F., & Nakamura, G. V. (1984). The nature and functions of schemas. In R. S. Wyer, Jr., & T. K. Srull (Eds.), *Handbook of social cognition* (Vol. 1, pp. 119–160). Hillsdale, NJ: Lawrence Erlbaum.

Brewer, W. F., & Pani, J. R. (1982, November). *Personal memory, generic memory, and skill: An empirical study*. Paper presented at the Twenty-Third Annual Meeting of the Psychonomic Society. Minneapolis, MN.

—— (1983). The structure of human memory. In G. H. Bower (Ed.), *The psychology of learning and motivation* (Vol. 17, pp. 1–38). New York: Academic Press.

Brewer, W. F., & Schommer, M. (1991, July). *Imagery reports in scientists and nonscientists on an autobiographical memory task: Galton's breakfast questionnaire revisited*. Paper presented at the International Conference on Memory. Lancaster, UK: Lancaster University.

Brewer, W. F., & Treyens, J. C. (1981). Role of schemata in memory for places. *Cognitive Psychology, 13*, 207–230.

Broad, C. D. (1925). *The mind and its place in nature*. London: Routledge & Kegan Paul.

Brockelman, P. (1975). Of memory and things past. *International Philosophical Quarterly, 15*, 309–325.

Brown, R., & Kulik, J. (1977). Flashbulb memories. *Cognition, 5*, 73–99.

Calkins, M. W. (1905). *An introduction to psychology* (2nd ed.). New York: Macmillan.

Carr, H. W. (1916). Symposium: The implications of recognition. *Proceedings of the Aristotelian Society, 16*, 224–233.

Christianson, S.-A. (1989). Flashbulb memories: Special, but not so special. *Memory & Cognition, 17*, 435–443.

Collins, A. M., & Quillian, M. R. (1969). Retrieval time from semantic memory. *Journal of Verbal Learning and Verbal Behavior, 8*, 240–247.

Conway, M. A. (1990). *Autobiographical memory: An introduction*. Milton Keynes, UK: Open University Press.

—— (1991). In defense of everyday memory. *American Psychologist, 46*, 19–26.

—— (1992). A structural model of autobiographical memory. In M. A. Conway, D. C. Rubin, H. Spinnler, & W. A. Wagenaar (Eds.), *Theoretical perspectives on autobiographical memory* (pp. 167–193). NATO ASI Series D: Behavioural and Social Sciences, Vol. 65. Dordrecht, The Netherlands: Kluwer Academic.

Conway, M. A., & Bekerian, D. A. (1987). Organization in autobiographical memory. *Memory & Cognition, 15*, 119–132.

Crosland, H. R. (1921). A qualitative analysis of the process of forgetting. *Psychological Monographs, 29* (1, Whole No. 130).

Crovitz, H. F., & Quina-Holland, K. (1976). Proportion of episodic memories from early childhood by years of age. *Bulletin of the Psychonomic Society, 7*, 61–62.

Crovitz, H. F., & Schiffman, H. (1974). Frequency of episodic memories as a function of their age. *Bulletin of the Psychonomic Society, 4*, 517–518.

Earle, W. (1956). Memory. *Review of Metaphysics, 10*, 3–27.

—— (1972). *The autobiographical consciousness*. Chicago: Quadrangle Books.

Ebbinghaus, H. (1885/1964). *Memory*. New York: Dover.

Einhorn, H. J., & Hogarth, R. M. (1978). Confidence in judgment: Persistence of the illusion of validity. *Psychological Review, 85*, 395–416.

Ericsson, K. A., & Simon, H. A. (1980). Verbal reports as data. *Psychological Review, 87*, 215–251.

Fischhoff, B., Slovic, P., & Lichtenstein, S. (1977). Knowing with certainty: The appropriateness of extreme confidence. *Journal of Experimental Psychology: Human Perception and Performance, 3*, 552–564.

Franklin, H. C., & Holding, D. H. (1977). Personal memories at different ages. *Quarterly Journal of Experimental Psychology, 29*, 527–532.

Franks, J. J., & Bransford, J. D. (1971). Abstraction of visual patterns. *Journal of Experimental Psychology, 90*, 65–74.

Freud, S. (1899/1953). Screen memories. In J. Strachey (Ed.), *Sigmund Freud: Collected papers* (Vol. 5, pp. 47–69). London: Hogarth Press.

Friedman, W. J. (1987). A follow-up to "Scale effects in memory for the time of events": The earthquake study. *Memory & Cognition, 15*, 518–520.

—— (1993). Memory for the time of past events. *Psychological Bulletin, 113*, 44–66.

Furlong, E. J. (1948). Memory. *Mind, 57*, 16–44.

—— (1951). *A study in memory.* London: Thomas Nelson.

—— (1953/1954). Memory and the argument from illusion. *Proceedings of the Aristotelian Society, 54*, 131–144.

—— (1956). The empiricist theory of memory. *Mind, 65*, 542–547.

Galton, F. (1879a). Psychometric experiments. *Brain, 2*, 149–162.

—— (1879b, March). Psychometric facts. *The Nineteenth Century, 5*, 425–433.

—— (1880). Statistics of mental imagery. *Mind, 5*, 301–318.

—— (1883). *Inquiries into human faculty and its development.* London: Macmillan.

Gardiner, J. M. (1988). Functional aspects of recollective experience. *Memory & Cognition, 16*, 309–313.

Gardiner, J. M., & Java, R. I. (1991). Forgetting in recognition memory with and without recollective experience. *Memory & Cognition, 19*, 617–623.

Gigerenzer, G., Hoffrage, U., & Kleinbölting, H. (1991). Probabilistic mental models: A Brunswikian theory of confidence. *Psychological Review, 98*, 506–528.

Gruneberg, M. M., & Sykes, R. N. (1993). The generalisability of confidence – accuracy studies in eyewitnessing. *Memory, 1*, 185–189.

Hamlyn, D. W. (1970). *The theory of knowledge.* Garden City, NY: Anchor.

Harrod, R. (1956). *Foundations of inductive logic.* London: Macmillan.

Harsch, N. & Neisser, U. (1989, November). *Substantial and irreversible errors in flashbulb memories of the Challenger explosion.* Paper presented at the Thirtieth Annual Meeting of the Psychonomic Society. Atlanta, GA.

Hart, J. T. (1965). Memory and the feeling-of-knowing experience. *Journal of Educational Psychology, 56*, 208–216.

Henri, V., & Henri, C. (1897). Enquête sur les premiers souvenirs de l'enfance. *L'Année Psychologique, 3*, 184–198.

Hilgard, E. R. (1980). Consciousness in contemporary psychology. *Annual Review of Psychology, 31*, 1–26.

Hobbes, T. (1651/1952). *Leviathan.* In Great Books of the Western World (Vol. 23). Chicago: Encyclopaedia Britannica.

Holland, R. F. (1954). The empiricist theory of memory. *Mind, 63*, 464–486.

Hollingworth, H. L. (1913). Characteristic differences between recall and recognition. *American Journal of Psychology, 24*, 532–544.

Hume, D. (1739/1978). *A treatise of human nature* (2nd ed.). L. A. Selby-Bigge (Ed.). Oxford: Clarendon Press.

James, W. (1890). *The principles of psychology* (2 Vols.). New York: Henry Holt.

Johnson, M. K., & Raye, C. L. (1981). Reality monitoring. *Psychological Review, 88*, 67 85.

Johnson, M. K., Foley, M. A., Suengas, A. G., & Raye, C. L. (1988). Phenomenal characteristics of memories for perceived and imagined autobiographical events. *Journal of Experimental Psychology: General, 117*, 371–376.

Johnson, M. K., Hashtroudi, S., & Lindsay, D. S. (1993). Source monitoring. *Psychological Review, 114*, 3–28.

Kennedy, F. (1898). On the experimental investigation of memory. *Psychological Review, 5*, 477–499.

Koffka, K. (1935). *Principles of Gestalt psychology.* London: Routledge & Kegan Paul.

Kuhlmann, F. (1906). On the analysis of the memory consciousness: A study in the mental imagery and memory of meaningless visual forms. *Psychological Review, 13,* 316–348.

—— (1907). On the analysis of the memory consciousness for pictures of familiar objects. *American Journal of Psychology, 18,* 389–420.

Kulpe, O. (1895). *Outlines of psychology.* London: Swan Sonnenschein.

Lacey, A. R. (1989). *Bergson.* London: Routledge.

Larsen, S. F. (1992). Personal context in autobiographical and narrative memories. In M. A. Conway, D. C. Rubin, H. Spinnler, & W. A. Wagenaar (Eds.), *Theoretical perspectives on autobiographical memory* (pp. 53–71). NATO ASI Series D: Behavioural and Social Sciences, Vol. 65. Dordrecht, The Netherlands: Kluwer Academic.

Leippe, M. R. (1980). Effects of integrative memorial and cognitive processes on the correspondence of eyewitness accuracy and confidence. *Law and Human Behavior, 4,* 261–274.

Linton, M. (1975). Memory for real-world events. In D. A. Norman & D. E. Rumelhart (Eds.), *Explorations in cognition* (pp. 376–404). San Francisco: W. H. Freeman.

—— (1978). Real world memory after six years: An *in vivo* study of very long term memory. In M. M. Gruneberg, P. E. Morris, & R. N. Sykes (Eds.), *Practical aspects of memory* (pp. 69–76). New York: Academic Press.

—— (1979, July). I remember it well. *Psychology Today,* 80–82, 85–86.

—— (1982). Transformations of memory in everyday life. In U. Neisser (Ed.), *Memory observed: Remembering in natural contexts* (pp. 77–91). San Francisco: W.H. Freeman.

Locke, D. (1971). *Memory.* Garden City, NY: Doubleday (Anchor Books).

Locke, J. (1690/1959). *An essay concerning human understanding* (2 Vols.). A. C. Fraser (Ed.). New York: Dover.

Loftus, E. F., Miller, D. G., & Burns, H. J. (1978). Semantic integration of verbal information into a visual memory. *Journal of Experimental Psychology: Human Learning and Memory, 4,* 19–31.

Maki, R. H., & Swett, S. (1987). Metamemory for narrative text. *Memory & Cognition, 15,* 72–83.

Malcolm, N. (1963). *Knowledge and certainty.* Englewood Cliffs, NJ: Prentice-Hall.

Mandler, G. (1980). Recognizing: The judgment of previous occurrence. *Psychological Review, 87,* 252–271.

McCloskey, M., Wible, C. G., & Cohen, N. J. (1988). Is there a special flashbulb-memory mechanism? *Journal of Experimental Psychology: General, 117,* 171–181.

Moore, T. V. (1915). The temporal relations of meaning and imagery. *Psychological Review, 22,* 177–225.

Munsat, S. (1967). *The concept of memory.* New York: Random House.

Murdock, B. B., Jr. (1965). Signal-detection theory and short-term memory. *Journal of Experimental Psychology, 70,* 443–447.

—— (1966). The criterion problem in short-term memory. *Journal of Experimental Psychology, 72,* 317–324.

—— (1974). *Human memory: Theory and data.* New York: Wiley.

Natsoulas, T. (1970). Concerning introspective "knowledge." *Psychological Bulletin, 73,* 89–111.

Neisser, U. (1967). *Cognitive psychology.* New York: Appleton-Century-Crofts.

—— (1978). Memory: What are the important questions? In M. M. Gruneberg, P. E. Morris, & R. N. Sykes (Eds.), *Practical aspects of memory* (pp. 3–14). London: Academic Press.

—— (1981). John Dean's memory: A case study. *Cognition, 9,* 1–22.

—— (1982). Snapshots or benchmarks? In U. Neisser (Ed.), *Memory observed: Remembering in natural contexts* (pp. 43–48). San Francisco: W. H. Freeman.

Neisser, U., & Harsch, N. (1992). Phantom flashbulbs: False recollections of hearing the news about *Challenger.* In E. Winograd & U. Neisser (Eds.), *Affect and accuracy in recall: Studies of "flashbulb" memories* (pp. 9–31). Cambridge, UK: Cambridge University Press.

Nelson, T. O. (1990). Metamemory: A theoretical framework and new findings. In G. H. Bower (Ed.), *The psychology of learning and motivation* (Vol. 26, pp. 125–173). San Diego: Academic Press.

Nickerson, R. (1968). A note on long-term recognition memory for pictorial material. *Psychonomic Science, 11,* 58.

Nigro, G., & Neisser, U. (1983). Point of view in personal memories. *Cognitive Psychology, 15*, 467–482.

O'Connor, D. J., & Carr, B. (1982). *Introduction to the theory of knowledge.* Minneapolis: University of Minnesota Press.

Paivio, A. (1966). Latency of verbal associations and imagery to noun stimuli as a function of abstractness and generality. *Canadian Journal of Psychology, 20*, 378–387.

Peterson, D. K., & Pitz, G. F. (1988). Confidence, uncertainty, and the use of information. *Journal of Experimental Psychology: Learning, Memory, and Cognition, 14*, 85–92.

Philippe, J. (1897). Sur les transformations de nos images mentales. *Review Philosophique, 43*, 481–493.

Pillemer, D. B. (1984). Flashbulb memories of the assassination attempt on President Reagan. *Cognition, 16*, 63–80.

—— (1992). Remembering personal circumstances: A functional analysis. In E. Winograd & U. Neisser (Eds.), *Affect and accuracy in recall: Studies of "flashbulb" memories* (pp. 236–264). Cambridge, UK: Cambridge University Press.

Posner, M. I. (1973). *Cognition: An introduction.* Glenview, IL: Scott, Foresman.

Price, H. H. (1936). Memory-knowledge. *Proceedings of the Aristotelian Society* (supplementary volume), *15*, 16–33.

—— (1952). Memory. *Philosophical Quarterly, 2*, 350–355.

—— (1958). Professor Ayer on the problem of knowledge. *Mind, 67*, 433–464.

Pylyshyn, Z. W. (1973). What the mind's eye tells the mind's brain: A critique of mental imagery. *Psychological Bulletin, 80*, 1–24.

Rajaram, S. (1993). Remembering and knowing: Two means of access to the personal past. *Memory & Cognition, 21*, 89–102.

Robinson, J. A. (1976). Sampling autobiographical memory. *Cognitive Psychology, 8*, 578–595.

Robinson, J. A., & Swanson, K. L. (1990). Autobiographical memory: The next phase. *Applied Cognitive Psychology, 4*, 321–335.

—— (1993). Field and observer modes of remembering. *Memory, 1*, 169–184.

Ross, B. H. (1984). Remindings and their effects in learning a cognitive skill. *Cognitive Psychology, 16*, 371–416.

Ross, M., & Buehler, R. (In press). Creative remembering. In U. Neisser & R. Fivush (Eds.), *The remembering self.* New York: Cambridge University Press.

Rubin, D. C. (1982). On the retention function for autobiographical memory. *Journal of Verbal Learning and Verbal Behavior, 21*, 21–38.

—— (Ed.). (1986). *Autobiographical memory.* Cambridge, UK: Cambridge University Press.

Rubin, D. C., Wetzler, S. E., & Nebes, R. D. (1986). Autobiographical memory across the lifespan. In D. C. Rubin (Ed.), *Autobiographical memory* (pp. 202–221). Cambridge, UK: Cambridge University Press.

Rubin, D. C., & Kozin, M. (1984). Vivid memories. *Cognition, 16*, 81–95.

Russell, B. (1912). *The problems of philosophy.* London: Oxford University Press.

—— (1921). *The analysis of mind.* London: Allen & Unwin.

Ryle, G. (1949). *The concept of mind.* London: Hutchinson.

Sachs, J. S. (1967). Recognition memory for syntactic and semantic aspects of connected discourse. *Perception & Psychophysics, 2*, 437–442.

Salmon, W. C. (1974). *Memory and perception in human knowledge.* In G. Nakhnikian (Ed.), *Bertrand Russell's philosophy* (pp. 139–167). New York: Barnes & Noble.

Schooler, J. W., Gerhard, D., & Loftus, E. F. (1986). Qualities of the unreal. *Journal of Experimental Psychology: Learning, Memory, and Cognition, 12*, 171–181.

Shepard, R. N. (1967). Recognition memory for words, sentences, and pictures. *Journal of Verbal Learning and Verbal Behavior, 6*, 156–163.

Shoemaker, S. (1967). Memory. In P. Edwards (Ed.), *Encyclopedia of philosophy* (pp. 265–274). New York: Macmillan.

Slaughter, J. W. (1902). A preliminary study of the behavior of mental images. *American Journal of Psychology, 13*, 526–549.

Smith, B. (1966). *Memory.* London: Allen & Unwin.

Smith, M., & McDougall, W. (1920). Some experiments in learning and retention. *British Journal of Psychology*, *10*, 199–209.

Smith, M. E. (1952). Childhood memories compared with those of adult life. *Journal of Genetic Psychology*, *80*, 151–182.

Stout, G. F. (1930). In what way is memory-knowledge immediate? In G. F. Stout (Ed.), *Studies in philosophy and psychology* (pp. 166–181). London: Macmillan.

Stratton, G. M. (1903). *Experimental psychology*. New York: Macmillan.

Strawson, P. F. (1957). Professor Ayer's "The problem of knowledge." *Philosophy*, *32*, 302–314.

Strong, E. K. J. (1913). The effect of time-interval upon recognition memory. *Psychological Review*, *20*, 339–372.

Strong, M. H., & Strong, E. K. J. (1916). The nature of recognition memory and of the localization of recognitions. *American Journal of Psychology*, *27*, 341–362.

Thompson, C. P. (1982). Memory for unique personal events: The roommate study. *Memory & Cognition*, *10*, 324–332.

Thompson, C. P., & Cowan, T. (1986). Flashbulb memories: A nicer interpretation of a Neisser recollection. *Cognition*, *22*, 199–200.

Titchener, E. B. (1910). *A text-book of psychology*. New York: Macmillan.

Tulving, E. (1972). Episodic and semantic memory. In E. Tulving & W. Donaldson (Eds.), *Organization of memory* (pp. 381–403). New York: Academic Press.

—— (1983). *Elements of episodic memory*. Oxford, UK: Oxford University Press.

—— (1985a). How many memory systems are there? *American Psychologist*, *40*, 385–398.

—— (1985b). Memory and consciousness. *Canadian Psychology*, *26*, 1–12.

—— (1989). Memory: Performance, knowledge, and experience. *European Journal of Cognitive Psychology*, *1*, 3–26.

—— (1991). Concepts of human memory. In L. R. Squire, N. M. Weinberger, G. Lynch, & J. L. McGaugh (Eds.), *Memory: Organization and locus of change* (pp. 3–32). New York: Oxford University Press.

Tulving, E., & Thomson, D. M. (1971). Retrieval processes in recognition memory: Effects of associative context. *Journal of Experimental Psychology*, *87*, 116–124.

Underwood, B. J. (1966). Individual and group predictions of item difficulty for free learning. *Journal of Experimental Psychology*, *71*, 673–679.

Urmson, J. O. (1967). Memory and imagination. *Mind*, *76*, 83–91.

Von Leyden, W. (1961). *Remembering*. New York: Philosophical Library.

Wagenaar, W. A. (1986). My memory: A study of autobiographical memory over six years. *Cognitive Psychology*, *18*, 225–252.

—— (1988). Calibration and the effects of knowledge and reconstruction in retrieval from memory. *Cognition*, *28*, 277–296.

Warren, H. C., & Carmichael, L. (1930). *Elements of human psychology* (rev. and enlarged ed.). Boston: Houghton Mifflin.

Washburn, M. F. (1916/1973). *Movement and mental imagery*. New York: Arno Press.

Watson, J. B. (1913). Psychology as the behaviorist views it. *Psychological Review*, *20*, 158–177.

—— (1926). Memory as the behaviorist sees it. *Harper's Magazine*, *153* (July), 244–250.

Weaver, C. A., III. (1993). Do you need a "flash" to form a flashbulb memory? *Journal of Experimental Psychology: General*, *122*, 39–46.

White, R. T. (1982). Memory for personal events. *Human Learning*, *1*, 171–183.

—— (1989). Recall of autobiographical events. *Applied Cognitive Psychology*, *3*, 127–135.

Woods, E. L. (1915). An experimental analysis of the process of recognizing. *American Journal of Psychology*, *26*, 313–387.

Woodworth, R. S. (1938). *Experimental psychology*. New York: Henry Holt.

Woodworth, R. S., & Schlosberg, H. (1954). *Experimental psychology* (rev. ed.). New York: Henry Holt.

Woozley, A. D. (1949). *Theory of knowledge*. London: Hutchinson's University Library.

Zemach, E. M. (1968). A definition of memory. *Mind*, *77*, 526–536.

3   Autobiographical knowledge and autobiographical memories

Martin A. Conway

The central argument of this chapter is that there are no such things as autobiographical memories at least in the sense of discrete, holistic, units in long-term memory. Rather, autobiographical memories are conceived as temporary mental representations constructed and maintained by a set of central processes such as the central executive of working memory (Baddeley, 1986; Norman & Shallice, 1980). Although the view that memory is constructive or reconstructive is not new (Bartlett, 1932; Neisser, 1976, 1981; Schank, 1982) there have been relatively few attempts to specify processes involved in memory construction (but see Kolodner, 1983). One aim of the present chapter is to provide at least an outline sketch of the types of knowledge, processes, and constraints mediating the construction of autobiographical memories. In order to achieve this outline sketch, a synthesis of a number of extant theoretical proposals is required, and in the sections that follow I summarize what is known of autobiographical knowledge, how this can be constructed into memories, and how this whole process may become disrupted in neurological disorders of memory. Finally, I briefly consider the encoding of autobiographical memories and the types of recollective experience characteristic of autobiographical remembering.

Autobiographical knowledge

Conway and Rubin (1993) in their review of the area described at least three types of autobiographical knowledge identified in recent research. *Lifetime periods* are the most general, most abstract, or most inclusive type of knowledge and denote time periods typically measured in units of years; *general events* represent more specific types of event knowledge typically measured in units of months, weeks, and days; and finally, *event specific knowledge* refers to memory for highly specific knowledge unique to a single event and typically measured in units of seconds, minutes, or, possibly, hours. These types of knowledge are organized into knowledge structures within the autobiographical memory knowledge base, and indices between different levels of a knowledge structure mediate the construction of patterns of activated knowledge that consti-

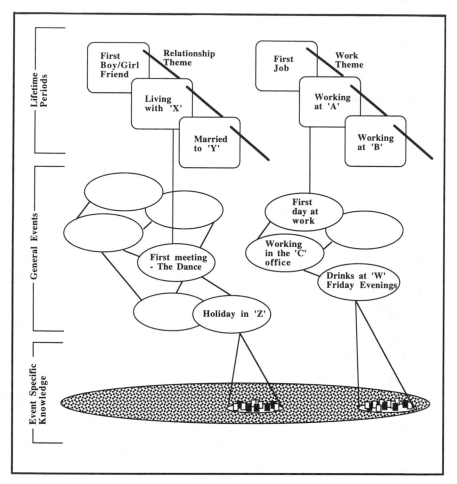

Figure 3.1 Hierarchical knowledge structures in the autobiographical knowledge base.

tute autobiographical memories. Figure 3.1 illustrates this putative scheme for two thematically organized sets of lifetime periods, a work theme and a relationship theme.

Lifetime periods have been independently identified in a number of studies using different experimental paradigms (Barsalou, 1988; Brown, Shevell, & Rips, 1986; Conway, 1992; Conway & Bekerian, 1987; Linton, 1986; Schooler & Herrmann, 1992; Treadway, McCloskey, Gordon, & Cohen, 1992). Lifetime periods, such as when I was at school, when I was at University, working for company X, when the the children were little, when I lived with Y, and so forth, contain general knowledge about significant others, common locations, actions, activities, plans, and goals characteristic of a period. Lifetime periods also name distinct periods of time with identifiable beginnings and endings, although these, of course, may be fuzzy rather than discrete. The content of a lifetime period represents what I shall call *thematic knowledge* about common features of that period, as well as temporal knowledge about the duration of a period. For any given period of time there may, however, be a number of lifetime periods. For instance, when I lived with Y may overlap in time with when I worked at X, but the thematic knowledge of the two time periods may index different parts of the autobiographical knowledge base (Barsalou, 1988; Conway & Bekerian, 1987; Linton, 1986). Moreover, lifetime periods may themselves be thematically linked together (as shown in Figure 3.1) to form higher order themes (Conway, 1992; Linton, 1986).

General events, shown in ellipses in Figure 3.1, are more specific and at the same time more heterogeneous than lifetime periods. Barsalou (1988) found that general events encompass both repeated events, for example, evening hikes to meadows, and single events. In this later case a general event such as sharing a bottle of wine with a friend in a cafe in Paris is a summary of a whole sequence of more minor events of which the general event is comprised. Robinson (1992) pointed out that general events may also represent sets of associated events and so encompass a series of memories linked together by a theme. For example, Robinson (1992) studied what he called "mini-histories" for activities such as learning to drive a car and a first romantic relationship. Initial findings suggested that these were organized around individual memories representing events featuring goal-attainment knowledge (both positive and negative) that appeared to convey significant information for the self, for example, about how easily a skill was acquired, and about success and failure in intimate interpersonal relations. Interestingly, both types of mini-history featured highly vivid memories for critical moments of goal attainment. Virtually all Robinson's (1992) subjects had vivid memories of the first time they drove a car alone and of a first kiss. Indeed, Robinson proposed that these first-time memories were a particularly important category of general event and served to determine the nature of the self. Thus, Robinson's work suggests that there may be local organization within the overall class of general events such that small groups of memories that are thematically related and which refer to a relatively proscribed period of time form distinct knowledge structures at this level in the autobiographical knowledge base. Obviously, other types of events may also lead to local organization, for example, a holiday, a period performing some particular piece of work, a period of illness, and so on. Organization of general-event knowledge has yet to be extensively investigated and the variety, structures, and frequency of mini-histories is currently unknown. Nonetheless, one prominent feature of these general-event structures is that they feature vivid memories of goal attainment (Conway 1992; Robinson, 1992).

Recently we (Anderson, in preparation; Anderson & Conway, 1993; Anderson & Conway, submitted) have investigated the organization of knowledge of general events for specific, rather than extended, episodes. One technique we employed was to have subjects recall memories to cue words and then list memory details in a timed production task featuring different types of listing schedules. For example, subjects on some trials might be required to list memory details in a free-recall order, whereas on other trials the instruction might be to list details in forward order, reverse order, or according to how central or interesting each detail was to a memory. The main finding across a series of memory detail production experiments was that forward order provided fastest access to memory details (Anderson & Conway, 1993). We had expected that the listing schedule that led to fastest memory detail production (forward order) would be sponta-neously used in the free-recall control condition, but this was not the case. Forward-or-der listing was spontaneously used, but only for approximately 60% of memories. Often subjects recalled memory details clustered around the detail they subsequently judged to be the most distinctive detail of the memory. Other retrieval time studies confirmed that distinctive thematic information played an important role in accessing memory de-tails. Anderson and Conway (1993) concluded that although the details of a specific event may be organized in memory in terms of forward temporal order, access to the set of details was by way of thematic knowledge represented as distinctive memory de-tails. Figure 3.2 illustrates this proposal. The main idea conveyed in Figure 3.2 is that a set of memory details are usually accessed by some distinctive cue or index held in a more general structure. Thus, the general event "meeting Angela" is accessed by way of the distinctive detail "dancing with Angela." We assume, however, that fast access to other memory details is only achieved if the head of the memory can be located and a sequential search made through the remaining details, and this is because although details are accessed by distinctive/thematic knowledge, they are actually organized in memory in terms of forward temporal order.

One interesting feature of memory details is they themselves can be further decom-posed into what might be termed "microdetails." Consider the *talking with friends* de-tail in Figure 3.2. This microevent would have featured turn taking in conversation, per-haps a number of different topics were covered, possibly people left and joined the group during the discussion, and so on. Anderson (in preparation) found that subjects generally could not list many microdetails of a memory detail. In fact, for most details little knowledge appeared to be available, although distinctive details were found to be associated with sensory information, vivid images, affect, and occasionally a highly specific "fact," for example, "I remember that X said. . . ." This event-specific knowl-edge (ESK) forms the lowest level in hierarchical autobiographical memory knowledge structures. Although ESK has not been directly investigated there are a number of stud-ies that have demonstrated the importance of this type of knowledge in autobiographi-cal memory. Johnson, Foley, Suengas, and Raye (1988) found that sensory (perceptual) knowledge was the key feature that distinguished memory for experienced events from memory for imagined events. Brewer (1988) observed that the more sensory detail available at recall, the more accurate an autobiographical memory was likely to be, and Ross (1984) found that subjects learning to use a word processor over a number of training sessions were often reminded of the exact words they had edited in a previous session. These findings all suggest that ESK is central to autobiographical memories, and may play a critical role in convincing a rememberer that they have in fact "remem-bered" an event (see below).

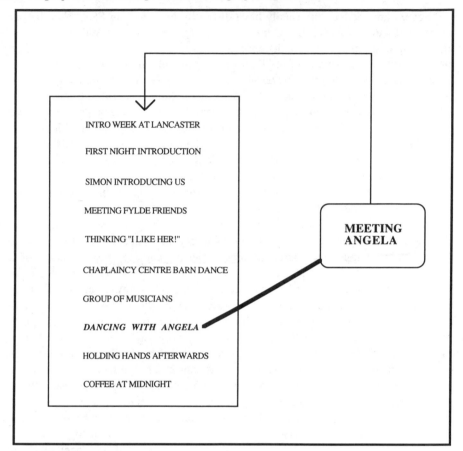

Note: Memory details are listed in forwards chronological order from top to bottom of the figure.The italicised memory detail is the distinctive detail. Taken from Anderson & Conway (1993) Figure 2.

Figure 3.2 Memory details from a specific autobiographical memory.

One intriguing possibility is that ESK, although indexed by structures in the autobiographical knowledge base, is not itself part of that knowledge base. This is illustrated in Figure 3.1 where ESK is depicted as an undifferentiated pool of event-specific details accessed by cues held at the general-event level. According to this scheme, the part of the autobiographical knowledge base that comprises lifetime periods and general events is a relatively distinct part of a much larger general-purpose knowledge base (Anderson & Conway, 1993; Conway, 1990a, 1990b, 1992), whereas ESK is part of a separate memory system. Certainly it is notable that patients suffering from retrograde amnesia often appear to have some preserved access to lifetime periods and, to some extent, general-event knowledge, but usually have difficulty in retrieving ESK from the periods covered by their amnesia (see Conway [1993] for a review; see Williams [this volume] for a similar phenomenon in depression). Moreover, this proposal is at least partly compatible with recent studies of implicit memory that clearly demonstrate that highly specific sensory knowledge can be retained and influence subsequent behavior (Roedigger & McDermott, in press; Schacter, 1987). Indeed, Tulving and Schacter (1990) proposed that implicit memory effects may be mediated by a presemantic perceptual memory system. Such a system, when indexed by cues from autobiographical memory knowledge structures, might give rise to the recall of sensory details, vivid images, and so forth, that appear to characterize ESK.

The proposal that ESK is represented in a separate memory system remains a conjecture, although, as we shall see later, evidence from the study of amnesia lends some support to the suggestion. Moreover, postulating a separate nonconceptual memory system indexed by conceptual knowledge in the form autobiographical memory knowledge structures provides a plausible account of forgetting in autobiographical memory. Consider the following. Autobiographical memories typically refer to sequences of activities that often feature multiple actors and may feature multiple locations (see Figure 3.2). General events rarely seem to be forgotten, although information from a general event may be lost. Thus, the subject who provided us with the memory shown in Figure 3.2 may remember, for many years, that he met Angela at an introductory undergraduate dance at Lancaster University. He may, however, forget that he had been talking to friends prior to dancing with her; he may even forget that he did dance with her or that they had coffee together later that evening. In the shorter term perhaps, these details are preserved, but over time the indices to ESK become degraded or lost so that although the subject knows that, for example, they danced, more specific details cannot be recalled. In general it would be unusual for individuals to forget the general events of their lives. For instance, if a person could remember that they went to school X, or worked for company Y, for protracted periods of time but could no longer recall *any* general events from these times, then we might suspect some abnormality of memory. In contrast, if the individual could recall general events and some memory details but could not bring to mind ESK, then it might be concluded that some "natural" process of forgetting had occurred. Assuming that the most vulnerable aspect of the autobiographical memory knowledge base are the indices from general events, ESK provides a way in which the common experience of forgetting in autobiographical memories might occur.

Themes and the self

The notion that indices in the autobiographical knowledge base represent personally meaningful and self-relevant themes has been used to suggest how diverse types of autobiographical knowledge might be searched and organized. But what are themes and where do they come from? I assume that at any given time there are some active set of plans and goals and these reflect the current themes of the self (Conway, 1992). Themes arise in response to discrepancies between the current or "working" self concept and some desired or even feared self, and as such, are the affect-laden central meaning constructs of the self. This characterization of themes is based, in part, on Higgins's (1987) self-discrepancy theory, which proposes that discrepancies between different self states, for example, the actual self and and the ideal self, generate motives and affective experience. However, the concept of themes as used here is also closely related to Oatley's (1992) account of the plan-based structure of emotions. Briefly, in Oatley's model a plan consists of a goal, for example, some set of constraints or preconditions, a set of actions, and a set of effects. Obviously, few plans are this simple and most plans in human cognition take multiple goals, are structured (hierarchically or in some other way), and are dynamic in the sense that plan implementation is conditional on the outcome of subgoals within the whole plan structure (see Oatley, 1992, pp. 24–36; Oatley & Johnson-Laird, 1987). Emotions arise at junctures in plans, when goals are achieved, or when a plan is frustrated. According to the plan-based model of affect, emotions signal the need for the reevaluation of goals and plans, and facilitate processes that mediate such reevaluations. Within this general view, themes are generated in response to self-discrepancies and, when active, are instantiated in complex dynamic plan structures that have evolved to effect changes to the (current) self – in a sense themes might be thought of as the content of emotions. Themes directly influence the encoding of autobiographical memories, and when a theme becomes inactive (i.e., it is no longer associated with currently active self-discrepancies) it is then primarily represented by the autobiographical memories with which it was originally associated. Indeed, Strauman (1990) has found that cues based on self-discrepancies are particularly potent in eliciting related childhood memories.

Undoubtedly the area where thematic aspects of memory have been of most concern is in psychotherapy, and particularly in psychoanalysis. Indeed, Freud's (1914) account of repression assumes that one of the aims of analysis is to bring to consciousness memories of events and fantasies that, due to their affective qualities, are no longer directly accessible. Traumatic memories were thought to be "screened" by other nonthreatening memories, and part of the process of psychoanalysis involved "piercing" this screen to gain access to the repressed memories. Whether one agrees with this account of the role of memory in psychogenic disorders or not, the key point for the present discussion is that thematically associated sets of memories often emerge during the process of psychoanalysis and detailed accounts can be found in the case studies reported by Freud. Often these sets of memories were found to be affect laden and appeared to attenuate access to more traumatic memories. One interesting example of this was reported by Kris (1956/1975) who described what he called the "personal myth." Kris found that some of his patients could provide very detailed and fluent accounts of their lives, almost as though they had, as it were, carefully rehearsed their life story. During the process of therapy Kris discovered that often these personal myths were, in fact, incorrect and contained carefully edited sections in which whole lifetime periods had been omitted. For instance, for one of his patients who claimed to have left home at age 16, it later transpired that he had, in fact, left when he was 18 years old, the missing 2 years representing a period during which traumatic events from childhood were repeated. Thus, the personal myth acted to repress a lifetime period. Interestingly, Treadway et al. (1992) have recently reported two case studies of amnesics with lifetime period impairments similar to those described by Kris. The two patients studied by Treadway et al. were virtually totally amnesic for all memories and skills acquired during a lengthy period in adulthood. In both cases there was some indication of traumatic events occurring around the time the amnesias dated back to, and there appeared to be no other reasons, such as neurological injury, for the onset of the memory loss. Treadway et al. interpret these deficits in terms of loss of what they call "life contexts," and these appear to approximate to the present notion of thematic lifetime periods. Thus, one possibility is that Treadway et al.'s patients, like those studied by Kris, were operating a personal myth to protect the self from a set of traumatic memories.

A fixed and rigid personal myth may be characteristic of certain psychopathological disorders. However, for the nonpathological individual Kris proposed that the personal myth was subject to fairly constant change and updating in the normal course of everyday experience. Moreover, there may be periods for nontraumatised individuals when changes to the personal myth are rapid, far-reaching, and profound. One such period was identified by Erikson (1978) as the "identity period of late adolescence" when the self is in flux and new themes emerge and are discarded or elaborated. Kris argued that this was the period when the emerging individual attempted to answer the question, "how did it all come about?" Conway and Rubin (1993) suggest that evidence of the late adolescent period of stabilization of the themes of the self can be found in studies of the distribution of memories recalled across the lifespan. In these studies older subjects, but not younger subjects, showed an unexpected increase in recall of memories of events that occurred during the ages of 10 to 25 years.

The emergence of life themes in childhood has also been identified by Csikszentmihalkyi and Beattie (1979) who investigated a group of individuals who had in common extremely deprived childhoods. Some of this group became exceptionally successful in adult life, whereas others although surviving their impoverished upbringing did not achieve high-status professional occupations. Csikszentmihalkyi and Beattie found that all the individuals they examined had what they termed "life themes." Life themes were developed in response to existential problems facing the individuals in their childhood, such as extreme poverty, social injustice, etc. The critical determining factor for later occupational success was the conceptualization of the problem and its solution. For instance, subjects who conceptualized their existential problem as one of poverty and its solution as ensuring a constant supply of money, tended not to attain high-status occupations. Indeed, one of their subjects who by thrift and careful investment had become a millionaire, nevertheless continued as a blue-collar worker in the factory where he had always worked. Other individuals who generated a more abstract conceptualization of the existential problems of childhood, such as poverty is the result of social injustice therefore one must fight against social injustice, achieved professional occupations that provided the opportunity to implement, at least to some degree, solutions to their earlier universalist abstract conceptualization. From the point of view of the present discussion, all the individuals in the Csikszentmihalkyi and Beattie

(1979) study were able to provide highly detailed and vivid memories of critical moments in the evolution and attainment of their solutions to the life problems they had identified. Indeed, many memories were spontaneously produced and even corroborated by independent evidence the individuals (spontaneously) provided.

Aspects of memory that suggest life themes and personal myths are perhaps most strikingly evident in individuals who have suffered traumatic and stressful childhoods. However, consequences for memory, although apparently extreme in these cases, may nonetheless reflect the normal operation of memory adapting to unusual circumstances. More typically, in the nontraumatized and not abnormally stressed individual, each lifetime period may present its own existential problems and, consequently, its own life themes specific to that period. Cantor and Kihlstrom (1985) developed the notion of "life tasks" that encompass lifetime period-specific problems to which an individual allocates problem solving resources. According to these authors life tasks are most clearly evident during a period of transition and they report a study of first-year college students making the transition from high school to college (Cantor, Brower, & Korn, 1984, cited in Cantor & Kihlstrom, 1985). The life tasks identified by the students centered around issues of identity, intimacy, achievement, and power, and were focused on the two broad themes of social and academic tasks and how to prioritize and manage tasks within the two domains. Although in these abstract terms the life tasks appear general to all students, at the level of the individual specific tasks they were highly idiosyncratic and reflected personal projects. Thus, Cantor and Kihlstrom (1985, p. 25) comment that "one student considered living without family to involve learning to handle the stress of personal failure without dad's hugs," whereas another concentrated on the practical side of independence – "managing money, doing laundry, eating well." It is also notable that Pillemer and his colleagues (Pillemer, Goldsmith, Panter, & White, 1988; Pillemer, Rinehart, & White, 1986) in studies of the recall of autobiographical memories from the first year at college, found most memories to be recalled from the first term (perhaps the most intense phase of the transition period) and to be emotionally charged – as the plan-based theory of emotions predicts. Finally, the types of events recalled from the first year at university mirrored the life tasks identified by Cantor and Kihlstrom in their students.

The themes that appear to preoccupy first-year university students are, then, often associated with the attainment of highly specific "possible selves" (Markus & Nurius, 1986), and are associated with such possible selves as the good student, competent individual living alone, socially attractive person, and so forth. These themes represent solutions to existential problems of the period, such as how to overcome social isolation and how to achieve academic success, and are implemented by dynamic plans with complex subgoal structures. It is through this network of currently active themes of the self that knowledge of specific events comes to be encoded and indices created that form the structure of the autobiographical knowledge base. According to this account autobiographical knowledge is a record of past selves in the sense that retained knowledge, and the particular organization of that knowledge, reflect the operation at encoding of the themes of a (past) active or working self. For example, themes associated with the "good student" possible self might facilitate and prioritize the encoding of events carrying goal-attainment knowledge for thematic aspects of that self. After a retention interval the individual may no longer recall the themes that characterized that period, although they retain access to the autobiographical memory knowledge structures created by the themes of the past "good student" possible self. Of course, some themes may be explicitly retained in the form of a declarative representation or perhaps by a highly discrete and distinct knowledge structure representing a single or some few episodes (as in the case of Robinson's (1992) mini-histories). One implication of this view is that there may be differences in memories associated with explicitly retained themes compared to memories only indirectly associated with a theme or set of themes. However, the retention of themes in autobiographical memory has, as yet, to be formally investigated (but see Strauman, 1990).

Autobiographical memories

Unlike autobiographical knowledge autobiographical memories are not stored in long-term memory, but rather are constructed on the basis of knowledge sampled from the autobiographical knowledge base. By this view, memories are temporary or transitory mental representations that only exist in the context of some specific processing episode (Anderson & Conway, 1993; Conway, 1992; Norman & Bobrow, 1979; Williams & Hollan, 1981). According to Williams and Hollan (1981) memories are accessed by a process of "cyclic" retrieval. A retrieval cycle commences with a cue or memory description (Norman & Bobrow, 1979) that is used to search long-term memory. Knowledge accessed by the cue is then evaluated and a decision made whether to terminate the retrieval process. When the accessed knowledge does not satisfy the constraints of the evaluation phase then a new retrieval cycle is initiated with a new memory description. The new memory description will be some modification of the previous cue in the light of the knowledge most recently accessed. Thus, target information in long-term memory is located by a series of retrieval cycles that successively fine-tune memory descriptions until an effective description that accesses the sought-for knowledge is generated and the retrieval process can terminate.

Williams and Hollan's (1981) model of cyclic retrieval assumes that retrieval terminates once a memory has been located. However, another way in which cyclic retrieval may effect long-term knowledge is by activating (J. R. Anderson, 1983; Collins & Loftus, 1975) accessed knowledge during a memory search. The evaluation phase of cyclic retrieval may then act to inhibit or maintain activation resulting from a search, and the whole retrieval cycle terminates once the pattern of activated knowledge satisfies constraints imposed on memory retrieval in that particular processing episode. Consider a subject taking part in a cue-word experiment (Conway & Bekerian, 1987; Crovitz & Schiffman, 1974; Galton, 1883; Robinson, 1976; Rubin, 1982). The subject is presented with common words one at a time and is required to retrieve a memory to each word. Usually subjects are instructed to retrieve a memory, as quickly as possible, of a specific event that they themselves experienced, and which lasted for a period of minutes or hours. Subjects are explicitly instructed that responses such as when I was

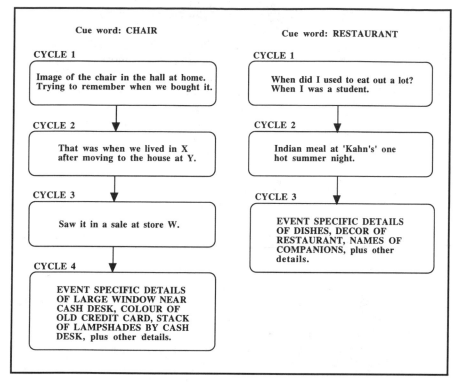

Figure 3.3 Memory retrieval protocols.

at school, during the summer, and so forth are not acceptable responses. We have used the cue-word procedure to collect memory retrieval protocols. In these (unpublished) studies subjects are required to "think aloud" while retrieving a memory to a cue word. In particular they are instructed to describe any thought they are conscious of while retrieving a memory. Figure 3.3 shows two sets of complete retrieval cycles to two separate cue words abstracted from verbal protocols supplied by a 38-year-old female subject.

Perhaps the main point concerning Figure 3.3 is that a memory is considered to be all the knowledge accessed in the whole set of retrieval cycles. So, for example, the autobiographical memory retrieved to the cue word *chair* is a compilation of the knowledge accessed in each of the four retrieval cycles shown in Figure 3.3. Similarly, the memory retrieved to *restaurant* is a composite of all the knowledge accessed in the three retrieval cycles depicted in Figure 3.3. Note also that the two examples in Figure 3.3 feature lifetime periods, general events, and ESK, and that this is a common feature of autobiographical memories (cf. Conway, 1992; Conway & Bekerian, 1987), which rarely seem to consist of only lifetime period knowledge, only general-event knowledge, or only ESK.

Obviously a critical question for this model of autobiographical memory is, how does the cyclic retrieval process terminate? In order to answer this question an account of control processes is required (Conway, 1992). One view, developed by Norman and Shallice (1980) and Shallice (1988), is that a supervisory attentional system (SAS) modulates the operation of more automatic or routine process, such as cyclic retrieval. Norman and Shallice argue that the SAS intervenes in routine processing sequences by activating or inhibiting specific schema featuring in a currently active processing sequence. The SAS is assumed to have access to models of the environment and of the cognitive system itself (Johnson-Laird, 1983), including knowledge of capacities and intentions. One important aspect of the SAS for the present discussion is that this putative system also has access to, or incorporates, the current self concept and the active themes, goals, and plans of that self. With these resources the SAS would be able to generate mental models featuring effective constraints for the termination of memory construction.

Consider again a subject retrieving autobiographical memories to cue words. One of the first steps will be to set constraints on exactly which types of knowledge can be accepted as autobiographical memories. This is not as difficult as it may appear, because much information is actually provided in the experimental instructions specifying that the memory must be highly specific, and that the recalled event must have been experienced by the subject. In addition, more general constraints on what a memory is may be specified within a culture and transmitted during the process of socialization (e.g., Edwards & Middleton, 1988; Fivush & Reese, 1992). Thus, cues specific to the experiment itself and the beliefs a subject brings to the memory retrieval task may be sufficient to generate effective constraints on what will cognitively constitute a memory in that processing task. These constraints will be used by the SAS in the evaluation phase of cyclic retrieval to assess whether or not appropriate knowledge has been activated in long-term memory. Only when these and other constraints have been satisfied can the retrieval process terminate.

Before an evaluation can take place, however, knowledge in long-term memory must be accessed. Elaboration of a cue into a memory description is the first step in initiating a memory search, and this process of elaboration is apparent in Figure 3.3, is present in by far the majority of protocols we have collected, and is also evident in the protocols reported by Williams and Hollan (1981) and Reiser, Black, and Kalamarides (1986). If it is accepted that the SAS or some other control process has access to a model of the cognitive system that includes the current dynamic self concept, then the process of memory description generation can be readily envisaged. For instance, the current themes of the self may provide comparatively fast access to cues in long-term memory that can be used to search autobiographical knowledge structures. In the two examples in Figure 3.3 it appears that memory descriptions capitalized on the structure of autobiographical knowledge and entered the system at the level of lifetime periods. It is assumed that this search phase is automatic, with activation spreading out from cues accessed in lifetime periods to associated general events and from there to ESK. During the search process the SAS monitors activated knowledge, evaluates it in terms of the constraints specified in the mental model of the task, and, according to the outcome of each evaluation phase, inhibits or increases activation. In this way new memory descriptions are created at different points in the search phase as the spread of activation through autobiographical memory knowledge structures is directed by the SAS.

When it is judged that the currently active range of knowledge satisfies the constraints of the task model, then retrieval is terminated. The resulting pattern of activated knowledge *plus* the task model, and perhaps some history of the processing sequences, constitute an autobiographical memory. It is important to note that in this model activation of knowledge has, at least in part, been influenced by the current self concept; during memory description generation and, possibly, in the evaluation phase. The influence of the dynamic self concept in the evaluation of output from long-term memory might be most evident in the personal meaning attached to the memory. For instance, events that were once judged meaningful may be reconceptualized as relatively trivial by the current self, whereas other events initially judged low in personal relevance may take on a new significance given the current plans and goals of the self.

Once a stable pattern of activation has been established in long-term memory and a memory has been "constructed" then this knowledge can be further manipulated and edited. If a task requires memory retrieval for a particular purpose, perhaps a revealing self-disclosure is called for, a denial, verification of some sequence of actions, etc., then activated knowledge can be used to satisfy the additional constraints imposed by a complete model of the task demands. Such constraints might arise from narrative conventions, impression management strategies, or other sets of rules and heuristics secondary to the process of memory construction.

A strong prediction of this constructive view of autobiographical memories is that such mental representations are inherently unstable. Instability arises in two ways. First, memory construction is effortful – memory retrieval times are measured in seconds rather than milliseconds (Conway, 1990a) – and once a memory has been constructed then that pattern must be actively maintained. There appear to have been no studies on the short-term maintenance of autobiographical memories, although one possibility is that the process of memory maintenance is similar to the maintenance of other types of temporary and transitory mental representations. For instance, images once generated start to fragment and "fade," and parts of an image must be actively refreshed if they are to be retained in the image (Kosslyn, 1980). Perhaps something like this also occurs in the construction of autobiographical memories, and unless the stable pattern of activation representing a memory is quickly used in the task for which it was created, then activation may start to decay and the pattern of activated knowledge become unstable. Obviously some central control mechanism such as the SAS could intervene to maintain the pattern of activation in long-term memory, but this presumably would entail a cost in terms of the allocation of additional processing resources.

A second way in which autobiographical memories can be unstable is across repeated retrievals of the same memory. In the constructivist model I have outlined, the critical component in establishing a memory is the incremental development of an effective memory description. However, development of a description is dependent on many fac-

80   MARTIN A. CONWAY

tors that are dynamic and, therefore, change over time, rendering the generation of similar descriptions progressively more unlikely as time between retrievals increases. So, for example, if the subject who retrieved the memory to the cue word *chair* shown in Figure 3.3 were asked to retrieve that memory again, then they would necessarily have to start the memory search with a different memory description: one which, at a minimum, included the knowledge that they had retrieved the memory before. Of course, the initial and subsequent memory descriptions would also differ in that the constraints of the task model would also be different due to changes to the self, the subject's developing understanding of the cue-word retrieval task, and other perhaps purely endogenous and local factors such as motivation or time of day and so on (see Mullin, Herrmann, & Searleman, 1993).

Counteracting these variations in the construction process are the structures of the autobiographical knowledge base in which stored indices between different representations constrain knowledge access and, ultimately, determine what patterns of activation can, in fact, be established in the knowledge base. However, it would be erroneous to assume that the constraints imposed by the organization of autobiographical knowledge are homogeneous, that is, that they are all equally strong or all equally weak. Rather, the strength of the constraints imposed by organization in the autobiographical knowledge base are themselves likely to be variable. Consider the indices between general events and ESK. As shown in Figure 3.1 the specific fragments of ESK activated during retrieval are critically dependent on the general-event cues used to probe associated ESK. Thus, the exact content of a memory will vary with the actual cues used when indexing different parts of the knowledge base. More generally it can be assumed that there will be variations, at all levels, in which cues are selected to act as indices, and consequently there will be multiple "routes" through even tightly structured sets of autobiographical knowledge.

Despite this potential for very marked variation in the construction of memories there still remain strong constraints. One constraint is in the hierarchical nature of autobiographical memory knowledge structures. For instance, once lifetime period knowledge is accessed then the range of cues available to probe other parts of the knowledge base becomes proscribed. In Figure 3.3 access of the lifetime period "when I was a student" – in the restaurant memory protocol – makes available a set of cues that channel the search process into knowledge structures associated with that lifetime period. Accessing the general event "Indian meal at Kahn's" further constrains the cues available for further search and evaluation. Thus, there should be some constancy as well as variation in the construction of the same memory in different retrieval episodes. Indeed, we (Anderson & Conway, submitted) have found evidence for both stability and instability in repeated recall of the same autobiographical memories. In our experiments subjects first recalled memories to cue words and listed the details of each memory. They also provided various ratings of the each memory, marked the memory's distinctive detail, and ordered the memory details in forward order. Some weeks later subjects returned and were presented with lists of details from a subset of the original memories. Each list was in a random order and subjects were required to sort the details in forward order and mark the distinctive detail. Subjects were able to reliably reinstate forward order (r = .64) and correctly identified 52% of distinctive details. In a second experiment subjects were presented with two complete sets of memory details intermingled and in a random order. The task was to sort the details into their separate memories, list the details in forward order, and identify the distinctive detail. Memory details proved to be highly discriminable and 91% were correctly assigned to their original memories. Details were reliably sorted into forward order (r = .68) and 57% of distinctive details were correctly identified. From these results it seems clear that people can accurately discriminate memory details and are able, to some extent, to order these consistently. But this stability is by no means perfect, and even in these comparatively undemanding memory experiments, in which subjects are provided with many highly specific cues in the form of memory details, the organization of those details and their distinctiveness was found to vary across different episodes of retrieval.

In a final experiment a group of subjects listed memory details as in the earlier experiments and returned to the laboratory after a few days. Subjects then recalled the same memories and details to each of the original cue words. A comparison of the memory details recalled on each occasion indicated moderate agreement across the two testing sessions with 61% of the same memory details recalled on the second retrieval and 76% of distinctive details accurately remembered. Despite the fact that the recall task is less constrained and more demanding than the earlier sorting tasks, performance remains at about the same level and subjects reliably recall many of the same memory details. However, new details are recalled in the second testing session, and distinctive details also change, clearly demonstrating marked differences in the construction of the same event across different episodes of retrieval.

In this section I have outlined a model of the construction of autobiographical memories in which a complex retrieval process modulated by central control processes initiates and coordinates the establishment of a pattern of activation in the autobiographical knowledge base. It is this pattern of activation and the various constraints of control processes that constitute a memory. According to this model the process of memory construction is dynamic and unfolds over time. It might be concluded that memory construction is somewhat unwieldy in that it is effortful and may make extensive demands on processing resources. Undoubtedly this is the case on at least some occasions, and everyone has experienced the effort required to recall general events and ESK. However, the autobiographical knowledge base may be exquisitely sensitive to cues, and patterns of activation may be continually stabilizing and dissipating within the knowledge base. Central control processes may turn to other tasks having initiated a memory search and switch rapidly back and forth between coordinating memory construction and modulating other processing sequences. Moreover, it is not assumed that the retrieval process requires conscious mediation, although this may often be the case. Rather, memories may be constructed, as it were, in the background, and only emerge into conscious awareness at some appropriate moment or when other tasks have been completed. In this way memories may spontaneously "pop" into mind (Salaman, 1970) or a person may be unexpectedly reminded of a previously experienced event (Schank, 1982).

Disruptions of autobiographical remembering

Studies of impairments to autobiographical memory in amnesia and in psychogenic disorders (Baddeley, Thornton, Chua, & McKenna, this volume; Conway, 1993; Kopelman, Guinan, & Lewis, 1995; also see Williams, this volume) lend further support to a constructivist account of autobiographical remembering. One group of patients with very dense retrograde amnesias (e.g., Cermak & O'Connor, 1983; Stuss & Benson, 1988; Tulving, Schacter, McLachlan, & Moscovitch, 1988) show a general inability to retrieve memories. These patients do, however, have access to more general knowledge of their lives and can report some lifetime period information, and in the case of Cermak and O'Connor's patient S.S., can provide accounts of well-established stories or narratives of events. Despite these preserved abilities the patients cannot retrieve memories, and perform at floor on autobiographical memory cue-word retrieval tests. Given that these amnesics can access the autobiographical knowledge base and appear to be able to search lifetime periods and general events, to at least some extent, their problem relates to an inability to access ESK. This may arise because brain injury has led to a disconnection of ESK from the autobiographical knowledge base (e.g., Warrington & Weiskrantz, 1982) or because of some malfunction of the retrieval process. Perhaps the brain injury has reduced the processing resources available to central control processes, and so a sustained search of autobiographical knowledge cannot be made and a stable pattern of activation established in long-term memory.

Other patients suffering from impaired autobiographical memory following brain injury do not show such dense retrograde amnesia. For instance, McCarthy and Warrington's (1992) patient R. F. R. was able to access knowledge about famous individuals, family members, and friends. So, for example, under certain circumstances he could discriminate famous faces and the faces of people he personally knew. He could access knowledge about occupations of the famous and his friends as well as accessing other types of knowledge. However, R. F. R. could not recall events in which the famous had been involved, even when a single event was the sole basis for an individual's fame. Moreover, he could recall virtually none of the events of his life, despite having preserved access to lifetime periods and some general-event knowledge. Thus, it would seem that R. F. R.'s autobiographical memory problem specifically related to the ability to construct memories and, in particular, to integrate schematic knowledge of people with other more episodic types of autobiographical knowledge, that is, general events and ESK. Ellis, Young, and Critchley (1989) report an interesting counterpoint to R. F. R. in a study of their patient K. S. This patient, although apparently unimpaired on standard laboratory memory tests after a right anterior temporal lobectomy, complained about the "mundane" quality of her memory. K. S. could recall specific autobiographical memories and appeared to have normal access to lifetime period and general-event knowledge for most of her life, but showed some problems with recent memories. In particular, K. S. could remember events in which she had been involved but could not access knowledge about other people who had been with her when a recent event had been experienced. She provided a full account of a lengthy trip to visit a consultant in another city and was able to give a detailed description of the consulting room and her conversations with the consultant, but was unable to provide any details about the appearance of the consultant. She had a detailed memory for a recent holiday but could not recall people she had met on holiday. K. S. then, unlike R. F. R., could recall event knowledge but could not access knowledge of people. Again, it seems possible that the memory problem here might arise from an impaired ability to construct a memory and to integrate knowledge of people with general events and ESK.

Perhaps the most striking evidence of a disrupted ability to construct autobiographical memories comes from a recent study of patient P. S. by Hodges and McCarthy (1993). P. S. suffered a stroke featuring a bilateral paramedian thalamic infarction. The result of this was a dense retrograde amnesia in which P. S. was amnesic for most of his adult life, and he believed himself to currently be on active service in the Navy during World War II. Extensive testing of his autobiographical memory revealed that he had some fairly consistent and accurate lifetime period and general-event knowledge of his life during and prior to his Navy service – which covered the period 1941–1946. He had some access to knowledge of his life after his Navy service, although this appeared to be intermittent and was associated with confabulatory reports of significant events, such as the dates of birth of his children, wedding day, and so on. However, on no occasion was P. S. able to retrieve a specific and detailed autobiographical memory. Hodges and McCarthy argue that the neurological damage to P. S.'s thalamus led to a partial disconnection of autobiographical knowledge from central retrieval processes, and this was compounded by P. S.'s regression to a set of themes associated with a lifetime period from early adulthood. Because P. S. is using the themes of his Navy lifetime period it is difficult for the retrieval process to accurately verify outputs from long-term memory which, in any case, are degraded by the partial disconnection. P. S., then, confabulates by inappropriately interpreting accessed knowledge in terms of his Navy lifetime period.

Finally, consider the case of patients who have suffered damage to the frontal lobes but not to other areas. The frontal lobes have often been identified as a possible site of central control processes (cf. Shallice, 1988), and so damage to these areas should feature disruption of the retrieval process more than impaired abilities to access knowledge. This is often the case, and frontal lobe amnesia is characterized by confabulations and what Baddeley and Wilson (1986) call a "clouding" of autobiographical memory. In the series of frontal patients studied by Baddeley and Wilson (1986) some showed striking confabulations and described long series of events that had not in fact occurred. For example, one patient related a long sequence of events concerning his brother's death in a road accident, but, it later transpired, his brother had been visiting him during his stay in the hospital. When confronted with this information the patient denied that he had related the earlier account. From our present perspective one of the most interesting features of such confabulations is that they are not delusional in the sense that they feature fantastic knowledge (although some confabulations can take this form). The knowledge drawn upon is part of the individual's autobiographical knowledge base and is not imaginary, rather it is the events into which this knowledge is compiled that are incorrect and confabulatory.

Many confabulations by patients with frontal lobe injuries are, however, rather less complex although equally striking. For instance, Dalla Barba, Cipolotti, and Denes (1990) describe their patient C. A. who could relate detailed autobiographical memories, many of which were verified, but who frequently assigned a recalled memory to an incorrect time. These dating errors were usually extreme, that is, C. A. dated her wedding day to 1964 when, in fact, she had married in 1943, but C. A. was both confident and persistent in her errors. Shallice (1988) describes a confabulation by his patient R.W. who related a recent memory of his wife trying on a feather boa in a shop, when, in fact, she had originally worn the boa at their home rather than a shop. The interesting feature of this memory was that R.W. accurately recalled the shop that had been visited and others who had been present, but was unaware that the shopping trip had taken place prior to the day his wife had tried on the feather boa. More recently Dalla Barba (1993) has describe a patient M. B. who, following brain injury, showed persistent and consistent confabulations featuring people, locations, and actions from his own autobiographical knowledge configured in events that did not occur or in events that occurred but not as described. The fascinating aspect of M. B.'s recall was that when he was asked to judge whether he actually remembered these events – that is to say, whether recall was accompanied by the experience of remembering (Gardiner, 1988; Gardiner & Java, 1993; Tulving, 1985) – he indicated that all his memories (correct and confabulated) were associated with the conscious experience of remembering.

In summary, disruptions of autobiographical remembering following frontal lobe injuries appear to primarily involve some sort of impairment of the retrieval process. It would seem that as patients can access the autobiographical knowledge base, and in most cases can construct bona fide autobiographical memories, then the disruption is intermittent and relates to the verification or evaluation stage of memory construction. It is thought that the evaluation stage is unable to appropriately prioritize the way in which knowledge is indexed, and items that receive only weak activation by a cue come to be closely linked to that cue at the expense of items that are more directly activated or indexed by the cue. So in the earlier case of R. W., (Shallice, 1988) the cue *feather boa*, which presumably directly indexes ESK relating to the event that took place at R. W.'s home, becomes inappropriately linked to ESK for a shopping trip occurring around the same time. Related to this Baddeley and Wilson (1986) also found that many of their frontal lobe patients showed a "clouding" of autobiographical memories such that, although they were able to recall specific episodes, these lacked the full range of detail usually observed in autobiographical remembering and the patients seemed unable to establish full and elaborate memories. This, perhaps, suggests that the retrieval cycle operates normally but terminates too rapidly. Taken together, the confabulatory responses and clouded autobiographical memories both implicate a failure in the retrieval cycle that may be related to the evaluation phase. Perhaps one consequence of injury to those parts of the frontal lobes that support cyclic retrieval is that processing resources become reduced, and this reduction leads to a degradation of the monitoring and modulating functions of the SAS on the complex retrieval cycle.

In this section I have provided limited coverage of the extensive literature on amnesia and have mainly focused on illustrative single case studies. These studies, and others like them (Conway, 1993), provide a growing body of evidence converging on the view that autobiographical remembering is a constructive process involving a complex retrieval cycle sampling an extensive knowledge base.

Encoding

One of the main concerns of researchers has been to establish how autobiographical memories are retrieved, that is, what knowledge is drawn upon and how the retrieval processes operate. This has led to the view that autobiographical memories are constructed rather than retrieved. However, this focus on the nature of autobiographical knowledge and construction processes has tended to deemphasize research into encoding and how autobiographical knowledge is acquired in the first place. Clearly, this is an important issue, particularly from a developmental perspective (Conway, 1990a; Fitzgerald, this volume; Fivush, this volume; Nelson, 1993), although here I will confine the discussion to adult autobiographical memories.

One possibility is that some or all of the processes involved in memory construction are also involved in memory encoding. For example, some type of description of the to-be-encoded (TBE) event must be created and this will entail accessing stored knowledge in long-term memory. Perhaps an event description is constructed by a series of successive evaluations of the event features in terms of stored knowledge and, if so, there may be a cyclic component to encoding. In addition to this, the TBE knowledge must be integrated with existing long-term memory knowledge structures and this will involve consolidation processes. There is, however, compelling evidence that encoding and retrieval processes cannot be simply equated in this way. For instance, in anterograde amnesia patients either cannot encode new information into long-term memory or the ability to encode is severely and drastically reduced. But this impairment in encoding is not inevitably reflected in a similarly severe impairment in memory retrieval, and anterograde amnesics may show only mild impairments in memory retrieval often limited to short and proscribed periods from their lives (cf. Mayes, 1988; McCarthy & Warrington, 1990; Parkin, 1987). Given that autobiographical memory construction in these patients appears unimpaired for memories formed before their brain injury, the proposal of a simple equivalence between encoding and retrieval processes is not tenable.

Nevertheless, anterograde amnesics do apparently encode some event features and many studies have now shown that in tasks that do not require the explicit consciously initiated retrieval of knowledge, amnesics can perform at levels similar to those achieved by nonbrain-damaged subjects (see Richardson-Klavehn & Bjork, 1988; Schacter, 1987, for reviews). Interestingly, it seems that this knowledge which is detected in implicit memory tasks (see Roedigger & McDermott, in press, for a recent review of implicit memory tasks) is similar in nature to ESK, and like ESK is highly event specific and nonconceptual or presemantic. By way of illustration of this point consider latter studies by Cermak and his colleagues of the amnesic patient S.S. (Cermak, Blackford, O'Connor, & Bleich, 1988). S.S. performed comparatively well on implicit memory tasks that drew upon past knowledge he had acquired prior to his illness, but performed poorly on implicit tasks that required conceptual learning. Indeed, when provided with a technical paper that reported new developments in his area of expertise, S.S. showed an excellent comprehension of the article but retained no knowledge of it.

As Cermak et al. (1988) point out, and as others have proposed (cf. Warrington & Weiskrantz, 1982), one problem in anterograde amnesia relates to disruptions of the ability to reconfigure parts of the memory system and integrate new knowledge with extant long-term memory knowledge structures. Clearly, integration is a central and general feature in the encoding of experienced events and may itself consist of a number of component processes. Consider the problem of segmentation of ongoing experience. In a classic series of studies Newtson (1976) found that subjects viewing a short video, and instructed to press a button when they considered one *meaningful* action sequence had ended, showed strong agreement on the main action sequences. In other experiments it was found that the unit of meaningful action sequences varied with the aims of the observer, that short action sequences could be chunked into larger sequences, and that the breakpoints in a sequence were defined by changes in salient event features. In everyday events the features selected as salient may be chiefly idiosyncratic to individuals, reflecting personally relevant themes and goals, and the sequences that comprise an event may then be established by monitoring changes in these self-salient event features (see also Conway, 1992; Conway & Bekerian, 1988). Possibly such sequences correspond to the memory details sampled in Anderson and Conway's (1993) experiments and, if so, the event sequences themselves may index ESK, and a set of sequences may be linked together to form a general event.

Given that an experience can be segmented and the local structure of that experience represented in memory, then the next phase in encoding might be that of integrating the newly processed knowledge with existing long-term knowledge. Conway, Anderson, Larsen, Donnelly, McDaniel, McClelland, Rawles, and Logie (1994) in a recent cross-national study of flashbulb and nonflashbulb memories (Brown & Kulik, 1977) found that prior knowledge, personal importance, and affect were central components in memory formation. For nonflashbulb memories the processes underlying these components acted relatively independently in memory formation, with prior knowledge, personal importance, and affect making separate contributions to memory consolidation. In contrast, the same processes operated more cohesively in the formation of flashbulb memories, where the effects of prior knowledge, personal importance, and affect were found to be integrated rather separate. One possibility here is that when an event is judged to be highly self-relevant then encoding processes coordinate to rapidly integrate a general event and its memory details in long-term memory. Events lower in self-relevance may not promote such coordination of encoding processes, and integration may then be less extensive and, as a further consequence of lack of integration of encoding process, the resulting memory less complete in terms of event details. In both cases, however, it is assumed that integration and consolidation are contemporaneous with the actual event being encoded and continue to operate for some period after the event has terminated.

This relatively "fast" integration and consolidation of an event stands in contrast to an intriguing finding relating to integration suggested by Linton (1986) in a study of her own memory. Linton recorded events from her life on a daily basis for a period of 6 years. Later she used her diary records to probe her memory for the recorded events. In one test she attempted to recall as many memories as possible and noted the strategies she employed in searching for memories. She found that for memories of events that had occurred 1 to 2 years before she tended to use temporally based searches, such as searching backward from one memory to the next, or starting with an older memory and searching forward. For memories of events older than about 2 years, she found that she tended to use personally relevant thematic knowledge. An implication of this finding is that there may be a slow process of consolidation during which temporal cues used to access and order memories gradually become less available. As the loss of temporal cues increases with time so the thematic structure of autobiographical memory gradually emerges as a second source of cues, and it is this knowledge that comes to provide the main indices that support memory construction.

In this section I have speculated that there are two broad classes of processes that mediate memory consolidation and integration. The first set of processes support the segmentation of experience into action sequences and general events on the basis of personally salient event features. The second set of processes integrate a general-event structure with knowledge structures in the autobiographical knowledge base, and this integration may occur rapidly or more gradually depending on the personal relevance of the event. Finally, integration into the lifetime period – general event structure of the autobiographical knowledge base may take place very slowly and only become apparent once the influence of certain temporal cues has diminished. As Ribot (1882) pointed out, the main temporal cue is the present, and perhaps it is not until the present is sufficiently different from the past that the organization of autobiographical knowledge is used in memory construction.

Memory completeness

The encoding of autobiographical memories is a complex process that must be influenced by the personal interpretation developed during an experience, changes in attention, and the integration of event knowledge with structures in the autobiographical knowledge base (cf. Kahneman & Miller, 1986). One implication of this view is that knowledge is only selectively encoded and, consequently, autobiographical memories are never "complete" accounts of an event. Moreover, it would seem likely that not only is event knowledge incompletely encoded, but some events may barely register in long-term memory at all. Events that do not impinge upon the current themes, plans, and goals of the self, and that do not correspond to existing autobiographical knowledge structures, may simply not be encoded in long-term memory. Thus, event knowledge is only incompletely retained and events themselves are only retained to the extent that they are self-relevant and/or compatible with and relevant to preexisting long-term knowledge.

One striking illustration of the incompleteness of autobiographical memories comes from studies we conducted to examine the nature of memory details (Anderson, in preparation). In these experiments subjects listed details of the "microevents" (Anderson & Conway, 1993) denoted by memory details. For example, the subject who provided the memory shown in Figure 3.2 might be asked to list details of the microevent "meeting Fylde friends." Our main finding was that subjects were comparatively poor at providing details of microevents and only occasionally were able to provide a list of microevent details. Instead, subjects claimed to have images of microevent details, usually of how other people looked, of the objects featured in the microevent, the layout of a room, and/or some nonimaginal but very specific item of knowledge such as a person's name. This incompleteness of ESK is not so surprising, yet, even at the level of general-event knowledge it seems clear that a whole set of memory details hardly cover all of the knowledge of an event. Instead, general-event memory details constitute a personal summary of an episode rather than a complete, literal, and objective record.

Despite this incompleteness of autobiographical knowledge as a record of experience it does not follow that autobiographical knowledge, or autobiographical knowledge when configured as a memory, is a necessarily inadequate and inaccurate account of an event. The adequacy of autobiographical knowledge presumably depends on its ability to support and promote continuity and developments of the self. As Robinson (1986) pointed out, autobiographical knowledge is a resource of the self and the richness of the resource may contribute to, for example, the resilience of the self in adverse conditions, the ability to bring about changes to the self and generate new themes, plans, and goals. However, although these may represent some of the potential functions of autobiographical memory, it does not follow that autobiographical knowledge is neutral as regards veridicality. If one function of autobiographical memory it to provide some sort of record of the actions of previous versions of the self, then a certain level of accuracy must be attained, otherwise the resulting record would be of little use. I suggest that the level of accuracy in autobiographical remembering reflects the need for summary accounts of episodes of self-relevance, such as memories for events featuring goal-attainment knowledge. At this level autobiographical knowledge is an accurate but incomplete record.

Autobiographical memory and recollective experience

Tulving (1985) pointed out that remembering is sometimes, but not always, accompanied by the "experience" of remembering. When this occurs the rememberer may have in mind images, feelings, highly specific knowledge of a previous event, and a sense of "pastness." Indeed, retrograde amnesics who have been retaught events from their own lives, usually by their spouses or parents, although then able to relate such events, for example, wedding day, etc., often claim that these memories have no sense of self, that they are simply stories that they have been told (e.g., Stuss & Benson, 1988). In contrast, remembering not accompanied by recollective experience does not feature imagery, sensory details, and a sense of pastness. Remembering in this case may be characterized by a sense of familiarity or a belief that the recalled information is simply "known." Consider a person recalling the name of a school they attended as a child. On some occasions recall may feature the construction of autobiographical memories and recollective experience. On other occasions the person may simply recall the name of the school and there may be no recollective experience other than a strong sense of familiarity and knowing. Again, it is interesting to note that in retrograde amnesia patients may retain factual knowledge of their lives and so presumably can experience a sense of familiarity when remembering autobiographical "facts" (cf. Conway, 1987, for further comment on factual autobiographical knowledge) but are unable to attain the experience of remembering. The nature of recollective experience in autobiographical remembering may, then, arise from the actual nature of the knowledge accessed in the construction of a memory. One possibility is that recollective experience is most powerfully felt when a memory extensively features ESK, and when ESK does not feature in the access of autobiographical knowledge then remembering is characterised by a feeling of knowing rather than an experience of remembering (Conway, 1992).

The phenomenology of autobiographical remembering can be fractionated further and Nigro and Neisser (1983) investigated what they called "field" and "observer" memories (see also Robinson, 1993). Field memories preserve the original point of view of the rememberer. For instance, a person may recall watching the mid-evening news on television and have in mind an image of their television, they may "feel" themselves to be seated in their habitual armchair, and, in short, the rememberer experiences their original point of view. In observer memories the original point of view is not preserved and the rememberer "sees" her/his self in images associated with the memory. Nigro and Neisser found that events comparatively low in emotional experience were often constructed as field memories, whereas events higher in emotion were more likely to be constructed as observer memories. More recently, Robinson & Swanson (1993) found that for most types of memories subjects could switch views from field to observer or vice versa.

The field/observer and remembering/knowing distinctions appear to be orthogonal, and presumably all memories whether field or observer are accompanied by recollective experience (remembering) as long as the constructed memories feature ESK. Yet, it may be the case that observer memories also represent a transitional state in the recoding of autobiographical knowledge. Consider an event that a rememberer recalls very frequently. One problem is that the instability of retrieval and the incompleteness of knowledge lead to slightly or even radically different memories on each occasion of construction. In order to stabilize the memory and provide consistent information on each episode of retrieval a fully integrated and declarative account of the memory may be developed, with creation of an observer perspective as a first step in this process. The final construct may be a narrative that includes ESK, but in the form of declarative knowledge rather than sensory/perceptual knowledge. Accessing such a narrative may not entail the extended process of cyclic retrieval outlined earlier, and remembering may not feature recollective experience – memories that have been narrativized are known rather than recollected, and accessed rather than constructed. Perhaps this is why amnesics such as S. S. can still relate such narratives even though they cannot construct memories. Studies of the phenomenology of autobiographical remembering remain few in total, and the relation between memory experience, cyclic retrieval, and the autobiographical knowledge base is obscure. Nevertheless, a complete theory of autobiographical memory will also have to account for the phenomenology of autobiographical remembering.

Summary: constructing autobiographical memories

In this chapter I have outlined a constructivist account of autobiographical remembering. This account assumes a structured and layered knowledge base that indexes sensory/perceptual event-specific knowledge. The knowledge base is accessed by a complex cyclic retrieval process controlled by central processes and a cognitive model of task demands. Memories are patterns of activation in the knowledge base temporally created and briefly maintained by central control processes and, especially, the self. Evidence from experimental investigations and neuropsychological case studies corroborate the proposed model, at least in broad outline. Yet, as emphasized above, many aspects of autobiographical memory remain uninvestigated and as the findings of further research become available it is certain that the constructivist view proposed here will change. But, given the current convergence of evidence from disparate fields, it seems unlikely that the general framework of structured knowledge base plus complex retrieval process will be subject to radical revision. However, as the findings of further research accrue it will become possible to propose models that place far stronger constraints on the proposed nature of autobiographical knowledge and on how this knowledge can be manipulated to form autobiographical memories.

References

Anderson, J. R. (1983). *The Architecture of Cognition.* Hillsdale, NJ: Lawrence Erlbaum.
—— (1993). *Organization of Specific Autobiographical Memories.* Doctoral dissertation, Lancaster University.
Anderson, S. J., & Conway, M. A. (1993). Investigating the structure of specific autobiographical memories. *Journal of Experimental Psychology: Learning, Memory, and Cognition, 19(5),* 1–19.
—— (submitted). *Are Autobiographical Memories Stable?*
Baddeley, A. D. (1986). *Working Memory.* Oxford: Clarendon Press.
Baddeley, A. D., & Wilson, B. (1986). Amnesia, autobiographical memory, confabulation. In D. C. Rubin (Ed.), *Autobiographical Memory* (pp. 225–252). Cambridge, UK: Cambridge University Press.
Barsalou, L. W. (1988). The content and organization of autobiographical memories. In U. Neisser & E. Winograd (Eds.), *Remembering Reconsidered: Ecological and Traditional Approaches to the Study of Memory* (pp. 193–243). Cambridge, UK: Cambridge University Press.
Bartlett, F. C. (1932). *Remembering: A Study in Experimental and Social Psychology.* Cambridge, UK: Cambridge University Press.
Brewer, W. F. (1988). Memory for randomly sampled autobiographical events. In U. Neisser & E. Winograd (Eds.), *Remembering Reconsidered: Ecological and Traditional Approaches to the Study of Memory* (pp. 21–90). Cambridge, UK: Cambridge University Press.

Brown, N. R., Shevell, S. K., & Rips L. J. (1986). Public memories and their personal context. In D.C. Rubin (Ed.) *Autobiographical Memory* (pp. 137–158). Cambridge, UK: Cambridge University Press.

Brown, R., & Kulik, J. (1977). Flashbulb memories. *Cognition, 5,* 73–99.

Cantor, N., Brower, A., & Korn, H. (1984). Cognitive basis of personality in a life transition. Paper presented at the 23rd International Congress of Psychology, Acapulco, Mexico.

Cantor, N., & Kihlstrom, J. F. (1985). Social intelligence: The cogntive basis of personality. In P. Shaver (Ed.), *Self, Situations, and Social Behaviour: Review of Personality and Social Psychology,* (Vol. 6, pp. 15–34). Beverly Hills, CA: Sage.

Cermak, L. S., Blackford, S. P., O'Connor, M., & Bleich, R. P. (1988). The implicit memory ability of a patient with amnesia due to encephalitis. *Brain and Cognition, 7,* 145–156.

Cermak, L. S., & O'Connor, M. (1983). The anterograde and retrograde retrieval ability of a patient with amnesia due to encephalitis. *Neuropsychologia, 21,* 213–234.

Collins, A. M., & Loftus, E. F., (1975). A spreading activation theory of semantic processing. *Psychological Review, 82,* 407–428.

Conway, M. A. (1987). Verifying autobiographical facts. *Cognition, 25,* 39–58.

—— (1990a). *Autobiographical Memory: An Introduction.* Buckingham, UK: Open University Press.

—— (1990b). Autobiographical memory and conceptual representation. *Journal of Experimental Psychology: Learning, Memory, and Cognition,* 16(5), 799–812.

—— (1992). A structural model of autobiographical memory. In M. A. Conway, D. C. Rubin, H. Spinnler, W. A. Wagenaar (Eds.), *Theoretical Perspectives on Autobiographical Memory* (pp. 167–194). Dordrecht, The Netherlands: Kluwer Academic.

—— (1993). Impairments of autobiographical memory. In F. Boller & J. Grafman (Eds.), *Handbook of Neuropsychology* (Vol. 8, pp. 175–191). The Netherlands: Elsevier.

Conway, M. A., Anderson. S. J., Larsen, S. F., Donnelly, C. M., McDaniel, M. A., McClelland, A. G. R., Rawles, R. E., & Logie, R. H. (1994). The formation of flashbulb memories. *Memory & Cognition,* 22(3), 326–343.

Conway, M. A., & Bekerian, D. A. (1987). Organization in autobiographical memory. *Memory & Cognition,* 15(2), 119–132.

—— (1988). Characteristics of vivid memories. In M. M. Gruneberg, P. Morris, R. N. Sykes (Eds.), *Practical Aspects of Memory: Current Research and Issues,* (Vol. 1, pp. 519–524). Chichester, UK: Wiley.

Conway, M. A., & Rubin, D. C. (1993). The structure of autobiographical memory. In A. E. Collins, S. E. Gathercole, M. A. Conway, & P. E. M. Morris (Eds.), *Theories of Memory* (pp. 103–137) Hove, Sussex: Lawrence Erlbaum.

Crovitz, H. F., & Schiffman, H. (1974). Frequency of episodic memories as a function of their age. *Bulletin of the Psychonomic Society, 4,* 517–518.

Csikszentmihalkyi, M., & Beattie, O. V. (1979). Life themes: A theoretical and empirical exploration of their origins and effects. *Journal of Humanistic Psychology, 19,* 45–63.

Dalla Barba, G. (1993). Confabulation: Knowledge and recollective experience. *Cognitive Neuropsychology,* 10(1), 1–20.

Dalla Barba, G., Cipolotti, L., Denes, G. (1990). Autobiographical memory loss and confabulation in Korsakoff's syndrome: A case report. *Cortex, 26,* 525–534.

Edwards, D., & Middleton, D. (1988). Conversational and remembering and family relationships: How children learn to remember. *Journal of Social and Personal Relationships, 5,* 3–25.

Ellis, A. W., Young, A. W., & Critchley, E. M. R. (1989). Loss of memory for people following temporal lobe damage. *Brain, 112,* 1469–1483.

Erikson, E. (1978). *Adulthood.* New York: W.W. Norton.

Fivush, R., & Reese, E. (1992). The social construction of autobiographical memory. In M. A. Conway, D. C. Rubin, H. Spinnler, W. A. Wagenaar (Eds.), *Theoretical Perspectives on Autobiographical Memory* (pp. 115–134). Dordrecht, The Netherlands: Kluwer Academic.

Freud, S. (1914). Remembering, repeating, and working through. *Standard Edition, Vol.12,* p. 145.

Galton, F. (1883). *Inquiries into Human Faculty and its Development* (1st ed.) London: Macmillan.

Gardiner, J. M. (1988). Functional aspects of recollective experience. *Memory & Cognition, 16,* 309–313.

Gardiner, J. M., & Java, R. I. (1993). Recognizing and remembering. In A. E. Collins, S. E. Gathercole, M. A. Conway, & P. E. Morris (Eds.), *Theories of Memory* (pp. 163–188). Hove, Sussex: Lawrence Erlbaum.

Higgins, E. T. (1987). Self-discrepancy: A theory relating self and affect. *Psychological Review, 94,* 319–340.

Hodges, J. R., & McCarthy, R. A. (1993). Autobiographical amnesia resulting from bilateral paramedian thalamic infarction. *Brain,* 116, 921–940.

Johnson, M. K., Foley, M. A., Suengas, A. G., & Raye, C. L. (1988). Phenomenal characteristics of memories for perceived and imagined autobiographical events. *Journal of Experimental Psychology: General, 117,* 371–376.

Johnson-Laird, P. N. (1983). *Mental Models.* Cambridge, MA: Havard University Press.

Kahneman, D., & Miller, D. T. (1986). Norm theory: Comparing reality to its alternatives. *Psychological Review, 93,* 136–153.

Kolodner, J. L. (1983). Maintaining memory organization in a dynamic long-term memory. *Cognitive Science, 7,* 243–280.

Kopelman, M. D., Guinan, E. M., & Lewis, P. D. R. (1995). Delusional memory, confabulation and frontal lobe dysfunction. In R. Campbell & M. A. Conwayt (Eds.). *Broken Memories: Case Studies in Memory Impairment* (pp. 137–154). Oxford: Basil Blackwell.

Kosslyn, S. M. (1980). *Image and Mind.* Cambridge, MA: Harvard University Press.

Kris, E. (1956/1975). The personal myth: A problem in psychoanalytic technique. In *The Selected Papers of Ernst Kris.* New Haven: Yale University Press.

Linton, M. (1986). Ways of searching and the contents of memory. In D. C. Rubin, *Autobiographical Memory* (pp. 50–67). Cambridge, UK: Cambridge University Press.

Markus, H., & Nurius, P. (1986). Possible selves. *American Psychologist, 41,* 954–969.

Mayes, A. R. (1988). *Human Organic Memory Disorders.* Cambridge, UK: Cambridge University Press.

McCarthy, R. A., & Warrington, E. K. (1990). *Cognitive Neuropsychology: A Clinical Introduction.* London: Academic Press.

—— (1992). Actors but not scripts: The dissociation of people and events in retrograde amnesia. *Neuropsychologia,* 30(7), 633–644.

Mullin, P. A., Herrmann, D. J., Searleman, A. (1993). Forgotten variables in memory theory and research. *Memory, 1,* 43–64.

Neisser, U. (1976). *Cognition and Reality.* New York: W. H. Freeman.

—— (1981). John Dean's memory: A case study. *Cognition, 9,* 1–22.

Nelson, K. (1993). Explaining the emergence of autobiographical memory in early childhood. In A. E. Collins, S. E. Gathercole, M. A. Conway, & P. E. Morris (Eds.), *Theories of Memory* (pp. 255–386). Hove, Sussex: Lawrence Erlbaum.

Newtson, D. (1976). Foundations of attribution: The perception of ongoing behavior. In J. H. Harvey, W. J. Ickes, & R. F. Kidd (Eds.), *New Directions in Attribution Research,* (Vol.1). Hillsdale, N.J.: Lawrence Erlbaum.

Nigro, G., & Neisser, U. (1983). Point of view in personal memories. *Cognitive Psychology, 15,* 467–482.

Norman, D. A., & Bobrow, D. G. (1979). Descriptions and intermediate stage in memory retrieval. *Cognitive Psychology, 11,* 107–123.

Norman, D. A., & Shallice, T. (1980). Attention to action: Willed and automatic control of behavior. San Diego, University of California: Technical Report No. 99.

Oatley, K. (1992). *Best Laid Schemes: The Psychology of Emotions.* Cambridge, UK: Cambridge University Press.

Oatley, K., & Johnson-Laird, P. N. (1987). Towards a cognitive theory of emotions. *Cognition and Emotion, 1,* 29–50.

Parkin, A. J. (1987). *Memory and Amnesia: An Introduction.* Oxford, UK: Basil Blackwell.

Pillemer, D. B., Goldsmith, L. R., Panter, A. T., & White, S. H. (1988). Very long-term memories of the first year in college. *Journal of Experimental Psychology: Learning, Memory, and Cognition, 14,* 709–715.

Pillemer, D. B., Rinehart, E. D., & White, S. H. (1986). Memories of life transitions: The first year in college. *Human Learning, 5,* 109–123.

Reiser, B. J., Black, J. B., & Kalamarides, P. (1986). Strategic memory search processes. In D. C. Rubin (Ed.), *Autobiographical Memory* (pp. 100–121). Cambridge, UK: Cambridge University Press.

Ribot, T. (1882). *Diseases of Memory: An Essay in the Positive Psychology.* W. H. Smith (trans.). New York: Appelton.

Richardson-Klavehn, A., & Bjork, R. A. (1988). Measures of memory. *Annual Review of Psychology, 39,* 475–543.

Robinson, J. A. (1976). Sampling autobiographical memory. *Cognitive Psychology, 8,* 578–595.

—— (1986). Autobiographical memory: A historical prologue. In D. C. Rubin (Ed.), *Autobiographical Memory* (pp. 19–24). Cambridge, UK: Cambridge University Press.

—— (1992). First experience memories: Contexts and function in personal histories. In M. A. Conway, D. C. Rubin, H. Spinnler, & W. Wagenaar (Eds.), *Theoretical Perspectives on Autobiographical Memory* (pp. 223–239). Dordrecht, The Netherlands: Kluwer Academic.

Robinson, J. A., & Swanson, K. L. (1993). Field and observer modes of remembering. *Memory, 1*(3), 169–184.

Roedigger, H. L., III, & McDermott, K. B. (1993). Implicit memory in normal human subjects. In F. Boller & J. Grafman (Eds.), *Handbook of Neuropsychology,* (Vol. 8, pp. 63–132). Amsterdam: Elsevier Science Publishers.

Ross, B. H. (1984). Remindings and their effects in learning a cognitive skill. *Cognitive Psychology, 16,* 371–416.

Rubin, D. C. (1982). On the retention function for autobiographical memory. *Journal of Verbal Learning and Verbal Behavior, 21,* 21–38.

Salaman, E. (1970). *A Collection of Moments: A Study of Involuntary Memories.* London: Longman.

Schacter, D. L. (1987). Implicit memory: History and current status. *Journal of Experimental Psychology: Learning, Memory, and Cognition, 13,* 501–518.

Schank, R. C. (1982). *Dynamic Memory.* New York: Cambridge University Press.

Schooler, J. W., & Herrmann, D. J. (1992). There is more to episodic memory than just episodes. In M. A. Conway, D. C. Rubin, H. Spinnler, & W. A. Wagenaar, (Eds.), *Theoretical Perspectives on Autobiographical Memory* (pp. 241–262). Dordrecht, The Netherlands: Kluwer Academic.

Shallice, T. (1988). *From Neuropsychology to Mental Structure.* New York: Cambridge University Press.

Strauman, T. J. (1990). Self-guides and emotionally significant childhood memories: A study of retrieval efficiency and incidental negative emotional content. *Journal of Personality and Social Psychology, 59,* 869–880.

Stuss, D. T., & Benson, D. F. (1984). Neuropsychological studies of the frontal lobes. *Psychological Bulletin, 95,* 3–28.

Treadway, M., McCloskey, M., Gordon, B., & Cohen, N. J. (1992). Landmark life events and the organization of memory: Evidence from functional retrograde amnesia. In S. Christianson (Ed.), *The Handook of Emotion and Memory: Research and Theory* (pp. 389–410). Hillsdale, NJ: Lawrence Erlbaum.

Tulving, E. (1985). Memory and consciousness. *Canadian Psychologist, 26,* 1–12.

Tulving, E., & Schacter, D. L. (1990). Priming and human memory systems. *Science, 247,* 301–305.

Tulving, E., Schacter, D. L., McLachlan, D. R., & Moscovitch, M. (1988). Priming of semantic autobiographical knowledge: A case study of retrograde amnesia. *Brain and Cognition, 8,* 3–20.

Warrington, E. K., & Weiskrantz, L. (1982). Amnesia: A disconnection syndrome. *Neuropsychologia, 16,* 233–249.

Williams, D. M., & Hollan, J. D. (1981). The process of retrieval from very long-term memory. *Cognitive Science, 5,* 87–119.

4 Autobiographical remembering: Narrative constraints on objectified selves

Craig R. Barclay

The general purposes of this essay are as follows: First, to outline an ecological model of autobiographical remembering by examining the purposes, processes, and products of reconstructing meaningful memories. Second, to argue that autobiographical remembering is embedded in affective, interpersonal, sociocultural, and historical contexts. Improvized selves are created in present contexts to serve psychosocial, cultural, and historical purposes, and third, to demonstrate essential constraints on the construction of coherent personal narratives that give meaning and purpose to our everyday lives.

The specific aim of this essay is to illustrate that the subjective experiences of trauma and atrocity often lack the essential narrative elements needed to give coherence to those experiences as well as affectively grounded evaluative information. Evaluations of experiences give meaning to our lives. Evaluative information leads to culturally recognized coherent stories structured by known canonical narrative forms because affect conveys how subjective experiences should be interpreted and understood. On this view, autobiographical memories that are the essence of one's personal history can appear as coherent or incoherent to others to the extent others are familiar with the narrative structure used to reconstruct the past and the coherence inherent in autobiographical memories associated with the temporal and evaluative structure of those recollections.

I claim that autobiographical experiences that cannot be reconstructed and shared through spoken or written language, music, movement (e.g., dance), art, literature, or science precipitate feelings of existential stress because articulated deep motivations cannot be related intimately to others. Objective symptoms of this kind of stress can be

This paper is dedicated to those who were murdered during the Nazi Holocaust and especially to those who lived through it. I am deeply grateful to A. S., H. S., T. M., S. A., J. K., and G. G. for their trust and courage in sharing their horrible knowledge with me.

This research would not have been possible without the help of Sandra Kinel who introduced me to A. S. and mediated my entry into the survivors community. My colleague Tom Smith was both intellectually and personally supportive throughout the past three years during the conduct of this project. I am personally grateful to Charlotte Pantall who inspired me to complete this work.

94

manifested in psychological and physical states of hypervigilence, psychological containment or "numbing," and intrusive ideation and images that signify the loss or inaccessibility of affective and psychological strengths. In the extreme, existential stress can produce the deconstruction of self, namely, "divided selves" (Delbo, 1985; Langer, 1982, 1991) that are described in the clinical psychology literature as dissociative disorders like multiple personalities, fugue states, posttraumatic stress disorders (PTSD), and functional amnesia (Baddeley, 1991; Ganaway, 1989; Nemiah, 1979).

The root metaphor underlying my thinking about the nature, functions, and dysfunctions of autobiographical remembering and self-composition is "a moment of being ("selfness") is a product of *improvisational* reconstructive remembering activities" (Barclay, 1993a). The key element of this metaphor is that improvisational activities constantly create and elaborate "protomemories" and "protoselves" (Barclay, 1993a) to fit contemporary contextualizing structures (e.g., audience expectations, justification of emerging feelings). Autobiographical remembering is one important means mediating "moments of being" (Woolf, 1976) with the world and others (Ryan, 1990), and while alone. Under this view, autobiographical remembering is an improvisational activity that forms emergent selves which give us a sense of needed comfort and a culturally valued sense of personal coherence over time. One conclusion following from this line of argument is that losing or lacking the generative abilities to improvise selves through the functional reconstruction of autobiographical memories results in the subjective experience of alienation from others and society. In addition, one comes to a sense of self-fragmentation. Under such circumstances it becomes increasingly difficult to ground oneself in the past, to make sense out of present experiences or imagine possible adaptive futures.

Improvisation as in music and dance, according to Pressing (1984), is a productive activity referenced to " . . . an underlying formal scheme or guiding image (e.g., image schemata [Johnson, 1987] or intrusive images [Herman, 1992]) used by the improvisor to facilitate the generation and editing of improvised behavior." The implication of this view is that improvisation is not a random activity, but an organized and grounded activity connected to referents (e.g., movements, sounds, memories, or feelings). Understanding the nature and functions of improvisation in the reconstruction of autobiographical remembering clearly involves specifying the referents from which memories are reconstructed and extrapolated.

It was not surprising to me to find that my conception of how improvisation functions is strikingly similar to Lakoff's (1986) conception of idealized cognitive models (represented as propositions and image schemata). Image schemata are mental representations that are not as abstract as propositions (i.e., subject-verb clauses) or as concrete as mental images. Idealized cognitive models are objectified through the "mapping" processes of image schematic projections and the creation of meaning in metaphor and metonymy. Idealized cognitive models are one important kind of mental referent acquired through embodied experiences (Johnson, 1987). The generative mapping activities associated with idealized cognitive models mediate the improvised creation of new knowledge (Lakoff, 1986).

This line of reasoning assumes that knowledge is created mostly by comparison (McCauley, 1992). Comparison, or metaphor usage, for instance, appears to be done through a finite number of – perhaps universally shared – embodied image schemata. These image schemata serve as foundational referents or source domains (e.g., "containers") from which knowledge about unknown target domains (e.g., memory) can be constructed. For instance, consider the image schemata *container*: the origins of this image schemata appear to be universal and associated with the physical experiences of being "inside" and "outside" of objects (e.g., houses) that are bounded by some kind of dividing structure. The metaphoric use of "container," as Lakoff (1986) has shown, has been used to conceptualize the nature of many unknown information domains. In my opinion, the discipline of psychology has used this metaphor to structure knowledge about such diverse domains as mind-body dualism, intrinsic-extrinsic motivation, internal-external locus of control, attribution theory (i.e., individual successes or failures are attributed to the abilities of the person, powerful others, effort, or luck, and the deconstruction of person and environment as if the individual stands separated from an ecological context), and theories of self as a property of the person above.

The embodiment of traumatic experiences provides a unique source of evidence consistent with the position outlined thus far. Specifically, the subjective experience of dissociation or "divided selves," that is, knowing and living two lives by a single person, is the case in point. Dissociative experiences result from exposure to short- and long-term trauma like living through the European Holocaust in work, slave labor, and concentration camps between 1939 and 1945. In order to capture the meaning of divided selves, I have appropriated two terms. The first, *momentary selves*, means selves composed in the present through autobiographical remembering that are unbounded by temporal-spatial and causal-conditional structures, and associated with a paucity of affective, evaluative information that would inform a witness about the meaning of traumatic experiences to the victim. The second, *narrative selves*, means selves composed in known story forms used to capture the phenomonology of prototypic lifespan developmental trajectories. The notion of divided selves comes from published accounts of survivors of the Holocaust during and after World War II (Delbo, 1985; Langer, 1975, 1982, 1991; Levi, 1958, and my own research on the personal histories and autobiographical memories of Holocaust victims, Barclay, 1993b, 1993c; Barclay & Smith 1992; March, personal communication, 1993).

The examination of memories of the Holocaust, coupled with documentary historical evidence (Browning, 1992) demonstrates the limits of our skills to conceptualize and articulate through metaphoric mappings certain kinds of acts and experiences. I propose that embodied experiences of atrocities do not yield a set of image schemata that lend themselves to a metaphoric language of extermination. There are no known narrative structures that can be used as referents from which to reconstruct traumatic experiences like those associated with the daily experience of seeing others selected and exterminated (murdered), especially when a witness to such atrocities does not know the basis upon which one might be "selected" from moment to moment and day to day.

In terms of improvisational activities used to reconstruct traumatic experiences, any referent for being is missing when one is a victim. The experiences of certain kinds of trauma lack consistent causal-explanatory systems (Linde, 1987); therefore, canonical narrative forms cannot be objectified within a coherent narrative system. The consequences of being unable to reconstruct meaningful interpretations, understandings, and explanations for why one experiences trauma include the construction of fragmented personal histories, and isolated moments of horrible and unspeakable knowledge. This fragmentation, in turn, may underly feelings of anxiety associated with perceptions of a lack of self-coherence in feeling, thought, self-concept, and interpersonal relatedness.

My major claim is that the experience of self-incoherence is associated with the loss of ability to use improvisational skills in a generative manner to construct meanings and explanations for one's experiences. The person becomes unable to compose an emergent self while alone and in relationship with others. Similar to other mediums affording improvisation, the perspective offered here is that autobiographical remembering is grounded in embodied experiences directly perceived and felt that cannot be narrated coherently (Johnson, 1987; Lakoff, 1986; Neisser, 1988). In brief, certain kinds of victimization – those lacking temporal organization and evaluative systems – cannot be narrated in a way that communicates the victimizing experience.

Many forms of victimization other than living through the Holocaust, like rape or traumatic violence, do not conform to widely known narrative systems (e.g., romantic sagas) or emotional scenarios that become the emotional context (e.g., depression, anger) in need of narrative justification (Gergen & Gergen, 1988). Nevertheless, the Holocaust has become a metaphor for victimization in contemporary world culture, and may well represent a unique narrative structure if a rhetoric for extermination can be created by the victims of the Holocaust. (From the perspective of the Nazi resettlement, ghettoization, and "final solution" policies developed between 1939 and 1941, there is a clear racist narrative structure – to make Europe "Jew free" was the theme – regardless of whether one takes an "intentionalist" or "functionalist" explanatory position [Browning, 1992].)

This essay is organized in four major sections: Section one outlines and defines an idealized model of autobiographical remembering. Section two specifies in detail, and defines, a model of coherent narrative structure. In section three, a case study is presented to demonstrate the usefulness of the models presented in section two. In section four, the models of autobiographical remembering and narrated structure developed previously are applied to the special case of victimization in an attempt to explain the development of and recovery from experiences of trauma. The primary purpose here is to demonstrate the limits of narrative structures in constructing highly coherent subjective experiences and a coherent sense of self.

An idealized ecological model of autobiographical remembering

An idealized ecological model of autobiographical remembering can be organized by examining the purpose, process, and products of remembering. The need for such a

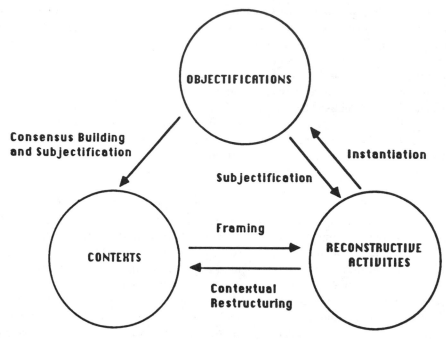

Figure 4.1 An idealized model of autobiographical remembering.

model comes from an ecological perspective that behavior and subjective experience are contextualized.

Purpose is considered first because an underlying assumption of ecological approaches is that behavior and experience have reasons for being used (e.g., adaptive or survival purposes). Next, the process of autobiographical remembering is examined in some detail within a conceptual model that specifies the mechanisms of remembering as a process of affect justification. The products of autobiographical remembering are discussed last because these products not only represent the "savings" of remembering but also indicate the nature of "protoselves" and "protocultures" (Barclay, 1993a).

Discussing the purposes, processes, and products of autobiographical remembering provides the context within which dysfunctional reconstructions of personal histories can then be understood.

Figure 4.1 represents my most recent thinking about the purposes (implied from the model), processes, and products of autobiographical remembering. A simple examination of the structure of this model indicates the interrelatedness of purpose, process, and product. Any changes in the structural elements of the model (i.e., reconstructive activities, objectifications, or context – defined below) influences not only the various process aspects of the model, but the actual structures themselves. My intention is to represent a model within which emergent memories, constructs, and affect justifications can be conceived. The model is not intended to represent a linear input–processing output conception of autobiographical remembering but, instead, a recursive, dynamic system.

Purpose

There are many purposes for reconstructing autobiographical information. Perhaps the most important purpose is to adapt to the present by conveying authentic meanings instead of simply preserving the past in an accurate fashion. In the model depicted in Figure 4.1, the purposes of autobiographical remembering are embedded in the structures and processes of the model. As I have proposed elsewhere (Barclay, 1993a, 1993b, 1993c), there are at least two major purposes: The first is to preserve a sense of being a coherent *person* over time, especially during times of anxiety and boredom. This purpose is referred to as the "intrapsychic function" of autobiographical remembering. The other purpose is to establish and maintain intimate relationships as we attempt to meet our need for meaningful relationships with others. This purpose is referred to as the "interpsychic function," and it is clearly perceptual and sociopsychological in nature, and may be associated with neurological functioning (e.g., limbic functions [Neisser, 1988]).

In addition to these purposes, the model suggests that autobiographical remembering can be used to establish "protoselves" (Barclay, 1993a) as well as "protocultures" (Obeyesekere, 1981). These can be established through two processes. The first is instantiation, defined as making public and explicit reconstructed past events (e.g., through rituals) that are objectified within some context. The other is subjectification, defined as returning to consciousness the meanings of contextualized objectifications of public idioms, or meanings that convey personal perspectives and cultural values and norms. The notion of context presented here includes both private and public contexts. Society and culture are two important contexts within which autobiographical remembering occurs. Societies and cultures are changed by the activities associated with reconstructive remembering activities, especially if those activities occur among collectives working together for some common purpose (Middleton & Edwards, 1990).

The intrapsychic, interpsychic functions, and social-cultural functions are related to a fourth important purpose: the construction and reconstruction, production and reproduction of "history." History viewed here is the story we wish to be known that justifies our being, culture, or way of life. History provides a context within which local, national, and world events are interpreted and understood. A conceptualization of history justifies certain actions for specific reasons, such as "national security." This view of history implies that the construction of history is not "objective." Instead histories are written and based largely on documents created by individuals and groups with certain motives in mind. History justifies these motives. Accordingly, like the personal histories of individuals, histories of societies, cultures, and events are reconstructions objectified over time, taking a particular form in the present to serve some contemporary purpose. However, like the construction of personal histories, history cannot be constructed without constrictions; there are certain "facts" to be accounted for and events to be "explained" that are socially legitimated. Unfortunately, as with the reconstruction of personal histories, the reconstruction of public histories are built upon fragments of information. These fragments require inferences in order to fill in the gaps until there is a "narrative fit" (Barclay, 1986, Spence 1982) between what is known and what is inferred.

Process

Five processes are identified in the model illustrated in Figure 4.1. These processes are framing, instantiation, subjectification and consensus building, and contextual restructuring, in reference to contexts, and subjectification, in reference to reconstructive activities.

Framing is considered first because this process brings context to consciousness and because context often provides the initial setting stimulus array for remembering. Framing thus refers to the instantiation of context that includes social, physical, cultural, historical, psychological, and collective awareness, as well as interpersonal intersubjectivities (Trevarthen, 1983). Framing contexts represents private and shared knowledge and the possibilities for emergent reconstructive activities to occur. Without framing, reconstructive activities would not be meaningful or possible because there would be no reference against which to judge the meaning of objectified autobiographical memories.

Instantiation is the process that leads to the objectification of reconstructed autobiographical memories (Barclay, 1993a). It is a process characterized by metaphoric mappings of image schemata (Johnson, 1987) such that embodied experiences are used to convey meaning to others in commonly shared idioms, images, and comparisons. Instantiations can take many forms: language, including American Sign Language, artistic images, film, music, or dance. Accordingly, instantiation is a mediational process like that described in the developmental literature regarding rehearsal, organization, directed forgetting, or categorization (Kail & Hagen, 1977). Perhaps the most common and effective forms of instantiation are evidenced through the use of metaphor and metonymy (Lakoff, 1986). I make this claim because it seems that the mappings associated with metaphor and metonymy are more likely to be universal in nature than culturally specific (school-related) mediational devices. This proposition suggests that the use of these mappings could lead to similarities in the objectifications found in reconstructed autobiographical memories across cultures. Common meanings of experiences may be shared cross-culturally, and the structures representing personal histories may take on similar forms (e.g., romantic sagas associated with "hero myths").

Subjectification and consensus building, in reference to contexts, refers to the processes through which common knowledge comes to be shared and accepted. This knowledge is thus returned to the contexts that form the ground within which autobiographical remembering occurs (context is viewed here as sets of physical, social, and psychological systems [see below]). Consensus building requires the construction of common meanings associated with objectifications of autobiographical memories by "cultural experts" (Barclay, 1993a). The process of consensus building is similar to the process of forming a common judgement among knowledgeable people (e.g., consensus among Supreme Court justices regarding First Amendment rights in a specific court case). This implies that consensus building is based on majority informed opinion that allows for legitimate minority opinions as well. Nevertheless, what becomes a consensus guides judgments and decisions made within some knowledge domain until new knowledge is created that is assimilated into what is already known.

Contextual restructuring is a bidirectional process associated with framing. That is, as contexts frame reconstructive activities, those activities can change the contexts that ground productive thinking. Claiming that contexts change as a function of reconstructive activities needs to be understood within the entire dynamics of the model. That is, not only do reconstructive activities (potentially) restructure contexts, but those activities lead to objectifications that are represented mentally through a process of subjectification (Obeyesekere, 1981).

Subjectification is the reverse of objectification: cultural ideas are used to justify the introduction of innovative acts and meanings. Subjective imagery is to subjectification what personal symbols are to objectification. The former help externalize . . . internal psychic states, yet such subjective externalization do not, and cannot, constitute a part of the publicly accepted culture (pp. 123–124). Subjectification . . . is the process whereby cultural patterns and symbols are put back into the melting pot of consciousness and refashioned to create a culturally tolerated set of images that I designated subjective imagery. Subjective imagery is often protocultural, or culture in the making (p. 169).

Subjectifications, in turn, influence contextual restructuring as those "patterns and symbols" are mediated by reconstructive remembering activities. It is noteworthy that Obeyesekere's description of subjectification is not wholly unlike Vygotsky's (1978) notion of "internalization." For Vygotsky, internalization begins in social speech acts between cultural novices and more knowledgeable others. These speech acts are internalized from the "social plain" to the "psychological plain" through the development of language. Subsequently, language comes to control and regulate a person's actions, as well as the actions of others.

Taken as a whole, the model represented in Figure 4.1 suggests that autobiographical remembering is a contextualized activity, and not one that occurs independent of sociocultural and historical factors. The dynamics of this model help explain how autobiographical memories are emergents of factors other than mental processes alone.

Products

Three products are proposed: contexts, reconstructive activities (which are processes as well), and objectifications. Consider contexts first. Here context refers to sociocultural, historical, psychological, and interpersonal "frames-of-reference" (see Dannefer, 1992). Given the focus of the current essay, narrative forms (see section on narrative structures below), and affective emotional states are perhaps the two most important contexts to discuss in detail. I will deal only with narrative structure here because such a discussion includes a consideration of many of the other aspects of context mentioned above.

Narratives are intellectual, sociocultural, and historical techniques constructed and refined over time. They are used for the purpose of telling different kinds of "stories."

It is clear that storytelling in oral and literate cultures preserves collective knowledge and leads to the creation of new knowledge through variations upon the themes and formula that constitute the underpinnings of narration (e.g., see Lord, 1960).

As with most stories known in Western cultures, narratives have beginnings, middles, and ends; they often present "problems" to be solved or overcome, or some kind of "trouble" that needs to be resolved. The solutions to problems and resolution of trouble lead to a coda or allegorical message that frequently summarizes some socioculture value. According to Gergen and Gergen (1988) narratives are shaped around canonical emotional schemata that are shared by members of some culture (e.g., anger, love, betrayal). Narratives take typical forms as justifications, explanations, and understandings of individual and group relationships. According to Gergen and Gergen, there are three basic narrative forms: progressive, regressive, and stable. Progressive narratives provide the structure for telling stories that begin with negative affective evaluations of events and proceed over time to positive evaluations. Regressive forms, like progressive forms, occur over time; however, instead of stories that begin with negative evaluations of events, regressive forms begin with positive event evaluations that become progressively negative over time. Stable narratives can be either positive or negative in affective tone but do not change evaluative valence over time.

The various combinations of the basic narrative structures form the scaffolding of most familiar stories. For instance, tragic stories are regressive, whereas comedy-romance begins with positive event evaluations that become negative, but resolve in positive outcomes. Comedy-romance is perhaps one of the most common narrative structures found in the public media today since it shapes the typical 30-minute situational comedy seen on television. More complex narratives can also be shaped by combining progressive, regressive, and stable forms; for example, following the typical romantic saga (e.g., "soap opera") over time shows repeated progressive and regressive evaluative changes.

Given the third purpose of this essay, there are two important aspects of each of the narrative structures available to us: One is the temporal-spatial structure and the other is the evaluative component. All narrative episodes take place over time; they have a temporal and spatial structure that includes the linking of events within episodes by some explanatory system (e.g, first X happened, then Y happened because of Z). The temporal organization and explanatory system found in narrative forms makes stories make sense. The other essential aspect is the evaluation of events within episodes. These evaluations, which vary along a positive-to-negative continuum, give narratives meaning because the evaluations tell the reader or listener how events should be understood and interpreted. Without each of these aspects, narratives would be meaningless and senseless (Labov & Waletzky, 1967; see Ricoeur [1983] for a discussion of relationships between the temporal structure of narratives and meaning).

Reconstructive activities are viewed also as a process yielding a significant product (the second product in the series which also includes contexts and objectives) – namely, autobiographical memories. As a process they involve the justification of affect and feelings for the purpose of reconstructing the past in the present as a means of adaptation. Common examples of reconstructive activities include the use of written or spoken language, or any semiotic system conveying meaning. This notion of reconstruction presented here differs from Bartlett (1932) in that I have chosen to exclude the notion of "reproductions" across individuals; instead I concentrated on reconstructions by the same person as a conventionalization process used to justify emotions, attitudes, and beliefs. My position is based on the argument that emotions, attitudes, and beliefs are cultural (cognitive) constructions or artifacts that serve certain purposes: Each of these constructions are concepts composed of more or less typical functions. Emotions, attitudes, and beliefs are considered here as "fuzzy concepts." They vary with culture, whereas reconstructive activities such as the justification of feelings are more universally adaptive processes that use the past to meet a current goal. Reconstructive activities as a product assume that people remember and these memories provide referential bases. When combined with contextual variables, these memories, including perceptions and feelings, lead to the objectification of autobiographical recollections. Examples of reconstructive activities in everyday life include the telling of family stories, personal histories or parts thereof, and the use of metaphor or examples as embodied autobiographical experiences to convey information to others.

According to Obeyesekere (1981, p. 77), Objectification "is the expression (projection and externalization) of private emotions in a public idiom." This suggests that objectified emotions are understood by people in a given culture through the interpretation of spoken language; however, what is actually said cannot be understood through the common meanings of the actual words spoken (e.g., to say something is "cool" does not always imply temperature alone). This implies that public idioms carry shared meanings that are constructed over time within a culture or subculture that can be used to create protocultures and transfer cultural meanings to less knowledgeable others (i.e., children). They externalize "deep motivations" (e.g., relatedness [Connell, 1990; Obeyesekere, 1990] in emotional terms that are themselves culturally sensitive [Lutz, 1982, 1987]).

The importance of the process of objectification as a structural element of the model cannot be overestimated. Obeyesekere (1990, p. 285) argues,

A striking feature of contemporary cultural anthropology is its failure to bring in the idea of human agency, intentionality, or motivation to the study of culture. As much as Cartesian thought made a radical distinction between mind and body, contemporary anthropologists make a parallel distinction between mind and culture, motivation and symbolic forms, even though many are willing to recognize that culture is generated out of the minds of people. Agency, motivation, and the idea of man making himself within the context of a preexistent tradition have been nearly eliminated in British social anthropology, in structuralist thought including the structural Marxism of Althusser, and even in the work of such scholars as Schneider and Geertz .

The only clarification and distinction I would add to this quote is that the term "emotion" needs to be formulated in more specific terms and differentiated from the concept of feelings. More specifically, "feelings" are states of consciousness that afford us the abilities to create and react to emotions, and are often undifferentiated as specific emotions, whereas the term "emotion" implies a strong subjective response (e.g., "hate" or "love") that is well formed and expressed through conventional means. Unlike emotions, feelings, being nonspecific, require elaboration, interpretative "false starts," and muddling-through processes that often characterize reconstructive activities. This said, reconstructive activities should be viewed as processes that construct and reconstruct the past as feelings are clarified and justified. Reconstructions are not reproductions of past events. Reproductions would be associated more with clear, well-formed, and commonly shared emotional subjective experiences.

Taken as a whole, the model illustrated in Figure 4.1 is intended to represent an empirically testable framework for the study of autobiographical remembering. My intention is to expand the notion of autobiographical remembering beyond an individual process or product, and introduce the collective nature of autobiographical remembering as a contextualized set of purposeful activities that involve, at times, collective efforts that lead to the creation of protocultures and protoselves.

A model of coherent narrative structures: Applications to analyzing personal histories

A model of coherent narrative structures is presented in Figure 4.2. One model using formative information for identifying and analyzing personal history narratives is illustrated in Figure 4.3.

These figures are presented together to illustrate the need to analyze narrative texts and discourse within a coherent and, as proposed here, hierarchical structure that gives order and meaning to narrative accounts. Figure 4.3 demonstrates how a narrative approach to understanding personal histories can provide insights into an individual's views of him/herself as a person over time, enmeshed in sociocultural, historical, and psychological contexts. These figures are only two examples of a host of other systems for analyzing narratives and are not to be taken as definitives. They were derived from work taken from many sources as well as my own work on the analysis of personal histories (especially Figure 4.3). I have found them useful in my work on the analysis of personal histories of people who have lived "conventional" lives and those who have experienced various kinds of traumatic experiences that take place over short (e.g., rape victims) and long periods of time (e.g., Holocaust survivors).

Figure 4.2 is a model of "coherent personal narratives." It is derived mainly from the work of Labov and Waletzky (1967), and the developmental research on the origins and structure of children's conversations with adults (Fivush, 1991; Fivush & Fromhoff, 1988; Hudson & Shapiro, 1991; Middleton & Edwards, 1990) as the children learn what and how to remember past experiences.

Coherent narratives appear to include two essential types of structures: amount of information and narrative organization. The amount of information included in any narrative account typically identifies main and supporting characters, locations where events occur, the kinds of activities that are being engaged in and the attributes of characters (e.g., "chatty," "introverted"), locations, and activities (e.g., group or individual activities, quiet or loud). The attributes of characters, locations, and activities provide important information regarding the setting within which events occur. Amount of in-

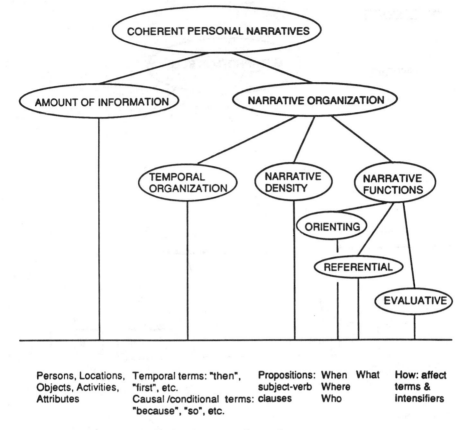

Figure 4.2 A model of coherent personal narratives.

formation can increase or decrease the vividness of a narrative. For example, consider the typical detailed descriptions of the environment offered by Thomas Hardy (1920) compared to those of Virginia Woolf (1927, 1929).

The other essential element to a coherent personal narrative is narrative organization. Narrative organization provides information regarding temporal structure, density, and narrative functions. Temporal structure is composed of two important parts that make narrative accounts sensible. These parts are the kind and amount of temporal-spatial and causal-conditional terms used. Temporal-spatial terms locate events within a linear temporal dimension so that the narrative consumer can follow the unfolding of events and experiences, whereas causal/conditional terms tell the reader or listener why events occur in the narrative. The use of causal-conditional words offer explanations for the sequence of unfolding events and afford an interpretation and understanding of narrative actions associated with characters, locations, and activities.

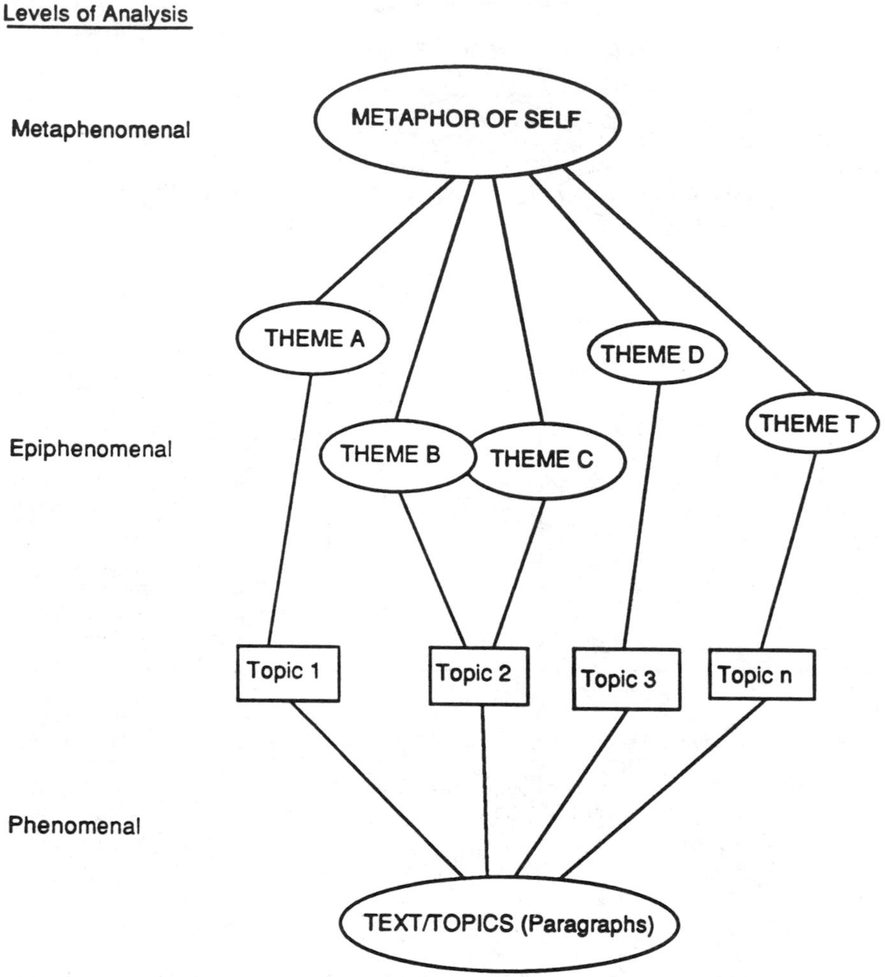

Levels of Analysis

Figure 4.3 A hierarchical model of metaphors of self.

Narrative density is taken as the frequency of propositions (defined as subject-verb clauses or some distinct stipulation of provisional information) found within a narrative. The higher the number of propositions, the greater the narrative density. The challenge to the writer or orator is to build a coherent personal narrative using a sufficient and necessary number of propositions to keep the narrative "flowing," interesting, and informative. Too many propositional statements tend to make narrative accounts confusing, whereas too few tend to lead to misunderstandings and the need for the consumer to fill in necessary gaps in the narrative. An abundance or paucity of propositions can also bore the reader or listener.

Three narrative functions are typically found in coherent narratives. These include an orienting, referential, and evaluative function. The orienting function sets the context within which events occur: this function is closely related to the amount of information given in a narrative account. The use of the term "context" here is broadened, however, to include the elements of context (including the framing and contextual restructuring processes) identified in the idealized model of autobiographical remembering in Figure 4.1. In canonical narratives, the orienting function provides information regarding when events occur, where they occur, and who is involved. When events occur can include the sociocultural and historical time period as well as a psychological time frame. The orienting narrative function is closely tied to the temporal organization of a narrative account because it gives the reader or listener information about why and how some events could possibly take place.

The referential function specifies what events or experiences occur. It addresses the question of what happened in the narrative. Part of the referential function makes up the plot in a story because it specifies a series of events that set the boundaries of a narrative account. Clearly the plot of a narrative is interdependent with temporal organization because events unfold over time and are interrelated through the use of causal-conditional statements.

Examples of the referential function are most transparent in Sir Arthur Conan Doyle's (1984) stories about the exploits of Sherlock Holmes. For example, consider the brief description of "The Red-Headed League" (published in *The Strand* between July 1891 and June 1892). The plot of this short story revolves around a bank robbery masterminded by Professor Moriarty. The key to the story is that a red-headed man, Mr. Jabez Wilson, owned a pawnshop in close proximity to a bank. Mr. Wilson had an assistant working with him (who was also employed by Professor Moriarty to carry out a bank robbery). This assistant informed Mr. Wilson that there was a newspaper advertisement announcing a vacancy in the "League of the Red-headed Men." Mr. Wilson was encouraged, and in fact, taken to the interview by his assistant to apply for selection into the League. Not surprisingly, among the many applicants, Mr. Wilson was selected and put to the task of copying the "Encyclopedia Britannica" between the hours of 10:00 A.M. and 2:00 P.M. He was also paid well ("four pounds a week," p. 17) for his work. Of course, this left the care of his business to his assistant who spent his days digging a tunnel from Mr. Wilson's shop to the vault beneath the bank containing an unusually large deposit of gold. As in most of Doyle's work, Mr. Holmes deduces the plot without revealing his methods or any specific information, yet is found at the scene of the crime as it is being committed. A policeman often accompanies Mr. Holmes who arrests the criminal(s) involved (and Dr. Watson seems ever present). Reading across the "Adventures of Sherlock Holmes" it becomes obvious that the plot structure (i.e., referential narrative function) described above is repeated in most all of Doyle's stories with minor changes in detail and level of ambiguity in the amount of information given, the temporal organization of events, as well as variability in the other elements of narrative organization.

Now consider the evaluative function of coherent narratives. Together with the temporal organization of a narrative, the evaluation (i.e., the person's subjective experiences of affective valence as positive-to-negative) of events lets the reader or listener know how reported events are to be understood. Affective, evaluative terms carry the greatest amount of information regarding the meaning of events and experiences to the characters in a story. I would argue that no narrative would be meaningful without some evaluation of events. What does it mean to the narrative consumer if I describe my latest trip to New Orleans and include only descriptive information without telling the reasons why I went (i.e., to visit a sick relative) and how I felt about my visit (i.e., concerned, worried, sad, and helpless to change the course of events that eventually lead to the death of my uncle). The meaning of this narrative would be quite different if I had gone to the Mardi Gras or a wedding. The point here is that no narrative makes sense or is meaningful without knowing how one feels about events that occur over time and for certain reasons. The amount of information given, propositional density, orienting, and referential functions are less important in determining the meaning of some experience to an individual relative to the amount and kind of affect terms used to evaluate an experience.

A brief example of a coherent personal narrative illustrates the elements of coherence described above. The example comes from Sartre (1964, p. 9),

Around 1850, in Alsance, a schoolteacher with more children than he could afford was willing to become a grocer. This unfrocked clerk wanted compensation. Since he was giving up the schooling of minds, one of his sons would school souls. There would be a minister in the family; it would be Charles.

Here Sartre is setting up the context with detailed descriptive information about his grandfather with whom he would eventually live. It seems that Sartre is also locating his family within an existing class structure in France during the nineteenth century. All of this information is designed as background for why Sartre sought solace in reading and writing, or as Eakin (1985, p. 126) has suggested, why Sartre was "the boy who wanted to be a book." Later in the text Sartre begins to explain his motives and feelings regarding the meaning of his life course at the time. He writes,

I keep creating myself; I am the giver and the gift! If my father were alive, I would know my rights and duties. He is dead, and I am unaware of them. I have no rights, since love heaps blessings upon me; I have no duties, since I give out of love. Only one mandate: to please; everything to show. What a riot of generosity in our family! My grandfather supports me and I make him happy; my mother devotes herself to all of us. When I think of it now, only that devotion seems true to me, but we tended to overlook it. No matter: our life is only a succession of ceremonies, and we spend our time showering each other with tribute. I respect adults on the condition that they idolize me. I am frank, open, gentle as a girl. My thoughts are quite proper. I trust people. Everyone is good since everybody is content. (pp. 32–33)

Later on in the text, in the section on "Writing," Sartre reveals his existential stress associated with not being original in his work. He writes, "Writing, my grim labor, had no reference to anything and was thus an end in itself: I wrote in order to write"

(p. 182). He continues, "In the beginning, I was sound as an apple: a little faker who knew enough to stop in time. But I worked hard; even when it came to bluffing, I remained a plugger. I now regard my tricks and jugglings as spiritual exercises and my insincerity as the caricature of an utter sincerity that was constantly grazing me and always eluding me. I had not *chosen* my vocation; it had been imposed on me by others" (p. 207). He subsequently resolves this stress by moving away from elaborating and extending plots and characters he learned about through his reading.

Sartre began to recognize the ingenuousness in writing as "labor" at an early age, around 9 or 10 years old. The following excerpt illustrates the kind of transitions Sartre experienced as he gained his own voice through his writing.

I have changed . . . I served my apprenticeship to violence and discovered my ugliness – which for a long time was my negative principle, the quicklime in which the wonderful child was dissolved; I shall also explain the reason why I came to think systematically against myself, to the extent of measuring the obvious truth of an idea by the displeasure it caused. I collared the Holy Ghost in the cellar and threw him out; atheism is a cruel and long-range affair: I think I've carried it through. I see clearly, I've lost my illusions, I know what my real jobs are. I still write. What else can I do? . . . It's a habit, and besides, it's my profession. For a long time, I took my pen for a sword; I now know we are powerless. No matter. I write and will keep writing books; they're needed; all the same, they do serve some purpose. Without equipment, without tools, I set all of me to work in order to save all of me. If I relegate impossible Salvation to the proproom, what remains? A whole man, composed of all me and as good as all of them and no better than any. (pp. 252–255)

What makes Sartre's autobiography compelling in my view is that it contains all of the elements of a coherent personal narrative. We know about his background and upbringing, where he lived, what he did, who the significant people and events were during his early life. In addition, Sartre reveals his personal struggle to become a "person." He experiences the existential anxiety of being unauthentic, a player carrying out a role, a nonperson without a generative voice. In the end he resolves his anxiety by accepting his existence, what he does – write – and the fact that he is no better or worse than any other person responsible for his or her own actions. Throughout, he also gives us dense descriptions of how he feels about his existence. It becomes clear early on in the text that he evaluates his existence in a positive (progressive) way, then becomes dissatisfied through the recognition of himself as a kind of intellectual fraud, and then resolves these regressive evaluations through a stable sense of who he is through what he does, and that his writing has an important purpose; namely, it preserves culture – a relatively positive evaluation of his life. In terms of a canonical narrative pattern (Gergen & Gergen, 1988), Sartre's autobiography may best be described as an unfinished romantic saga with the regressive aspects of his life being given greater emphasis than the progressive ones. For Sarte, he is what he does, he exists when he writes and reads. In a sense his self emerges through the activities of writing and reading, and vaporizes thereafter.

My point is that through an analysis of a coherent personal history, it is possible to construct a theory of a person and the deep motivations that give him or her a sense of meaningful being and a sense of groundedness in the present time and space. The following examples are illustrations of how the reporting of specific life events can be interpreted to shape the construction of a self-theory. Reference to Figure 4.3 will show the empirical and interpretative techniques used here for constructing an overall metaphor capturing an essential meaning or organizing perspective on the life of a single individual. The examples are taken from the work of Barclay and Hodges (1990) and were used to inductively construct the "Metaphors of Self" model. Consider the four examples that, in pairs, demonstrate the construction of thematic units which can be interpreted together to manufacture a metaphor of self from the narrative text.

Constructing metaphors of self: A case history

Barclay and Hodges (1990) examined an extensive personal history gathered during three 1-1/2-hour interviews. A "willing listener" paradigm was used. The interviewer simply asked the subject to tell his personal history in any way he chose but to include as much detail as possible. No questions were asked by the interviewer. A week prior to the first interview the subject was recruited and asked if he would be willing to tell his personal history. At that time, personal history was defined as autobiographical memories – memories from your life. Each session was tape recorded and transcribed.

The first analytic level (phenomenal level) was to identify topics taken as paragraphs because paragraphs represent the formal grammatical structures that direct topic changes. In addition, this was done to break the total narrative history into manageable analytic units. A paragraph was defined as "a distinct division of a written (or oral) work of composition that expresses a thought or point relevant to the whole but is complete in itself, and may consist of a single sentence or several sentences" (*The American Heritage Dictionary*, 1985, Second College Edition, p. 900).

The identification of thematic narrative units (creating a layer of epiphenomena or interpretative hypothetical constructs) was done independently by two judges who reached 100% agreement on the structure of the personal history and the themes found therein. Themes were not topics, although themes were located within topics, and more than one theme could be found within the same topic. A theme was identified as an existential problem the subject worked to solve and the means used to work toward a solution (Csikszentmihaly & Beattie, 1979). Themes were the subject's points of view on a variety of issues and activities that he had engaged in over his lifetime. A total of eight themes were identified. Since the first author had known the subject, R. F., for 15 years at the time of the interview, the final writeup, and interpretation, and because the interview was read and verified as "truthful" by both R. F. and his wife (who had known him for approximately 25 years), the information contained in the interview was considered valid, truthful, and interpreted correctly.

The two themes are presented in the four examples that follow.

Theme 1

(1a) . . . Bell Park Gardens . . .was a postwar Jewish garden apartment, middle-class ghetto . . . one of my many fond recollections . . . in the summer . . . after supper a hoard of . . . kids would descend on these grass court areas . . . and . . . play punchball . . . just big loud chaos.

It was great – lot of fun . . . I hit it side-arm . . . never generate a lot of power but I was a dependable fielder, not a liability, not a star.
(1b) When I was ten years . . . we had a pack of good friends and our basic mission in life . . . was playing ball. And I was always average to lousy . . . But I learned to live with my limitations 'cause that's something you just can't deceive yourself about . . . I wasn't a good hitter and I was slow – was a good fielder and . . . we would play ball . . . in the summer from four to five to six . . . after school in the early summer – in New York up to June thirteenth when school was out and after that we would play thirteen hours a day. . . .

Theme 2

(2a) D. R. and I were the co-founders . . . of the Trouble-makers Club when I was about seven years old. The Trouble-makers Club was devoted to making trouble . . . we used to let the air out of bicycle tires down in the communal basement; but the Trouble-makers Club was busted by my mother who . . . saw us returning bikes that weren't ours to the communal basement and she knew right away we were up to no good. . . .
(2b) I had my little group of friends and we all came from the fringe part of town . . . W. and F. and a guy named B., and a couple of others of lesser importance and we just were always on the fringe of things in junior high and high school. And we developed a kind of deviant little subculture . . . and . . . we got old enough, we'd just hang out . . . we'd drive around, we'd put on 300 miles on a Friday night doing nothing . . . we'd go from burger place to burger place and we'd just kind of see what little kind of trouble we could get in; we had a lot of funny funny escapades, we were so bored, we were do desperate for somethin' to do, we would do anything for a little stimulation. Once we, when Sergeant Berry Saddler's great hit the "Ballad of the Green Beret" was hot, they had it on the juke box . . . at White Castle . . . We went in there – you could preprogram that thing . . . we played Sergeant Berry's tune something like . . . eighty times and then we went and stood on the opposite corner outside the White Castle and watched. It was one of the funniest things I've ever seen. People go nuts. After like ten minutes . . . and we laughed so hard we couldn't breathe. . . .

It is clear that each of these examples contain the elements of a coherent narrative, especially the functional elements. The first two examples were labeled "Not a liability, not a star" and the second pair "The Trouble-makers Club." These were descriptive titles spontaneously offered by R. F. himself. In our view both themes symbolically represent a need to be related to others through enjoyable and, at times, risky activities.

Our interpretation of the "Not a liability, not a star" theme was that baseball was an activity that allowed R. F. to place himself socially and physically within a collective society of youngsters. Sports, school grades, etc. are often used for this purpose. They provide a subjective scale used to estimate one's worth and place in some important activities involving others. While R. F. clearly sees baseball as a central part of his youth (he is still an avid sports fan), and evaluates it in very positive terms (it represents a progressive narrative theme), he also uses baseball to demonstrate his limitations. He knows he is not an outstanding ballplayer, yet he sees himself as able to play and contribute to the game. In fact, he elaborates upon his abilities to a greater degree than his liabilities, indicating that he is closer to being a star than a liability – even though his self-characterization is that of a fringe kind of star close to some galaxy boundary.

What is interesting about "The Trouble-makers Club" is that it represents many of R. F.'s current activities as well! He still forms offbeat subcultures gathered together for certain kinds of activities (i.e, gambling on football, the horses, even curling, or forming a basketball team of middle-aged men to play in a league composed of younger and more capable players). His purpose for doing so seems to be participating in the postgame activities at local bars.

Our interpretation of this thematic unit is that R. F. is trying to simultaneously identify himself with certain kinds of different groups, yet at the same time struggle for an independent identity. Although not stated in the examples above, R. F. went on to elaborate that his mother was convinced he was a victim of D. R.'s bad influence, while R. F. describes himself as the president and D. R. as the vice-president of the club. Again, as in the earlier discussed theme, "The Trouble-makers Club" is composed of a group of individuals who form their identities around activities they consider unusual (even though if you examine the personal histories across individuals you discover that men in particular conceive of themselves as "different"), activities that place them on the fringe of mainstream social life.

Overall, we concluded that the common strand linking these themes (a metaphenomenal level or theory level), as well as six others identified (e.g., "inadequacy"), was that R. F. saw himself as the "King of the Fringe." This metaphor of self suggests a person in a leadership role (e.g., president of the "Trouble-makers Club") but clothed in the tattered dress of an "average person," aging in ungraceful ways, watching life pass in the third person, participating to a point, but always being the social critic that separates him from the mundane existence of "everyman."

As a gift we presented R. F. with a red tee shirt with large yellow letters announcing him as "The King of the Fringe." Even though this work was completed in the late 1980s, R. F. still wears his tee shirt with pride and explains to anyone who asks what the metaphor means to him at this point in his life.

In sum, Figures 4.2 and 4.3 illustrate the nature of a coherent personal history. Figure 4.2 offers a structural analysis, whereas Figure 4.3 puts that analysis to work to make sense out of the text of a single individual's reporting of his personal history. Taken together, this two-part analysis of the structure and meaning of personal histories promises to be a useful empirical method for evaluating narrative information and studying the nature of autobiographical memories and their uses. A model of coherent personal histories and metaphors of self offer explanatory systems (i.e, "a system of beliefs and relations among beliefs that provide the environment in which one statement may or may not be taken as a cause for another statement" [Linde, 1987, p. 343]) within which lives can be understood. One type of explanatory system is the "coherent life story" and as Linde (p. 346) argues, "An important property of the life story, both linguistically and psychologically, is that it must be coherent. Its coherence is not a property of life but rather an achievement of the speaker in constructing the story."

More importantly, the kinds of analyses just offered, when considered in relationship to the incoherent narrative accounts to be given, make it possible to offer partial explanations for errors in eyewitness testimonies (Langer, 1991; Loftus, 1979; Wagenaar, 1988; Wagenaar & Groeneweg; 1990). Eyewitnesses, like trauma victims, frequently attempt to infer and construct an explanatory system that creates cause-effect relationships and spatial-temporal sequences, giving coherence and credibility to their narrative accounts.

Narrative constraints on objectified selves

She stands mute before the emptiness of evil, feeling the insufficiency of any known system of explanation. Survivors of atrocity of every age and every culture come to a point in their testimony where all questions are reduced to one, spoken more in bewilderment than in outrage. Why? The answer is beyond human understanding. (Herman, 1992, p. 178)

All of the information described thus far forms a backdrop for understanding how narrative and a metaphors-of-self approach to interpreting, explaining, and understanding lives can be incomplete and misleading in certain cases. The cases in point are associated with individuals who have experienced traumatic events that lead to errors and fabrications in memory, the construction of partial or inaccurate life themes, amnesia, and, at times psychopathology.

My strong claim is that traumatic events have these effects on people because they lack the temporal organization of coherent narratives, that is, people who are traumatized often lose a sense of the order and location of the traumatic experience and the evaluative narrative function, or information, to explain what the traumatic events mean. Often, traumatic events are reported in a matter-of-fact way, without any evaluative information. As one Holocaust survivor put it, "there is no language of extermination." Furthermore, the inabilities of trauma victims to articulate in any medium what happened to them and why leads to a sense of isolation and often depression: no one understands because they have not lived the traumatic experience from the subjective perspective of the victim. In some cases (e.g., Holocaust survivors,[1] Poles, the infirmed and mentally handicapped), I would argue that even the survivors do not understand fully what happened to them and why, other than the knowledge that the Nazis were committed to making Europe Jew-free because they "hated the Jews."

The Jews, as a group, were mostly unaware of the specific reasons for eastward deportations. Deportation of the Poles, for example, "could provide the needed farms, businesses, and housing for the incoming *Volksdeutsche*" (Browning, 1992, p. 32). This was also the proposal made by Franz Rademacher in June 1940, and ordered by Himmler to deport all Jews to Madagascar (Browning, 1992, p. 18). The rationale behind the policy to create Jewish ghettos to locate Jews in a confined area, and to sell them their food and other daily necessities in order to drain the Jews of their wealth, was also not clear to most Jews. The Nazis also built slave labor camps to work and starve the Jews to death, and the rationale behind the "Final Solution to the Jewish Problem" (i.e., to gas and cremate them in death camps like Auschwitz, was developed and decided upon at the Wannsee Conference, held just outside Berlin, January 20, 1942) was not widely known to the Jews for some time.

In sum, the Jews were aware, in my opinion, that the Nazi tactics and those of others regarding their fate grew out of a racist philosophy even though they were unaware of the reasons behind these tactics. In concrete terms, for instance, the interned Jews could

---

[1] Even though the examples here are taken from Jews, it should not be forgotten that at least six million others were also systematically murdered, for example, Gypsies [at least 200,000 out of approximately 700,000].

not explain on a day-to-day basis the reasons why some were selected for extermination while others were not. One survivor of Auschwitz told me they were taken from their barracks one morning for the endless counting of prisoners; then, in a single line, walked past Gestapo officers who decided which prisoners would die and which would live that day. The reason for the selection, which was never told to inmates – but was discovered later – was that the camp commander had been given orders that no one with any type of handicapping condition (e.g., even wearing eyeglasses) was worthy to work for the German army. The woman who told this story wore glasses, and for some unknown reason, one of the rank-and-file soldiers knocked her glasses off and stepped on them before she reached the selection point, thereby saving her life.[2]

The examples used here to illustrate the limits of narrative in objectifying metaphors of self come mainly from my own work with Holocaust survivors over the past 3 years. The works of Browning (1992), Gilbert (1978, 1993), Langer (1975, 1982, 1991), and Yahil (1987) were used extensively to add explanatory notes, background, and support-ing evidence for my analysis of narrative incoherence in the autobiographical memories of Holocaust survivors.

In my work, I chose to interview only those survivors who were identified by other survivors as "nonprofessional survivors." This idiom meant that the survivors I was in-terviewing were people who did not give public lectures or write books about their ex-periences during the Holocaust. I selected nonprofessionals because I felt it would il-lustrate more clearly the incoherence of narrative structures that lack temporal organization and evaluative functions because these people had not been asked to tell their Holocaust stories before. In fact, I recorded the "story" of a "professional" survi-vor of Auschwitz as told to a class of Jewish children studying the Holocaust at a local temple. In evaluating that story, it was clear that explanation and evaluations occurred frequently, and the spatial-temporal organization of her "survival story" was clearly stated and similar to the storied nature of memories from other "professional" survivors. In addition, in closing her story, she questioned the class about the meaning of her ex-periences and what they had learned from her story (i.e., it was their responsibility and duty as Jews to "never forget" and "never let it happen again").

---

[2]The "Final Solution to the Jewish Problem" was to systematically exterminate all European Jews in the gas chambers of the concentration camps (e.g., Chelmno, Treblinka, Auschwitz, Sobibor) or to work them to death in the slave labor camps (e.g., Boghari and Djelfa in Algeria, Skarzysko-Kamienna, Sandomierz, Koldyczewo, Trawniki, and Krychow), combined with existing policies (e.g., forced death marches like the march across Austria from Koszeg to Ebensee during March-April 1945, or from Mauthausen to Gun-skirchen, May 1–5, 1945) or the use of *Einsatzgruppe* A, B, C, and D to mass murder Jews and other "undesirables" during and after the invasion of Russia. The plans for the *Einsatazgruppen* activities were formulated June 22, 1941, even before the Wannsee Conference, during and after the invasion of Russia. Each of these partial solutions to the "Jewish question" was linked directly and indirectly to the conduct of the war and the successes and failures of the German Army on three fronts. For example, the loss of the Battle of Britain, the failure of the Barbarossa Plan to conquer Russia, and the loss of the war in North Africa each created a context that forced the German high command to deal functionally with the self-im-posed "Jewish problem." However, these functional policies were developed within the context of an intention, articulated by Hitler in a speech given in the mid-1920s to make Europe Jew free (Browning, 1992).

Consider, first, an example from one survivor I interviewed during the summer of 1993. This survivor was an 83-year-old woman I call A. S. (her age is an estimate because she refused to give me her exact birthdate). A. S. lived in Tarnow, Poland, when the Germans invaded Poland in 1939. Two sources of materials were used: One was a letter A. S. wrote to the Archives Administration of Yad Vashem (the memorial museum in Jerusalem, Israel, dedicated to remembering the Holocaust), August 11, 1980; the other was the transcription of her personal history taken in the manner described earlier for R. F.

A. S. did ask me if I wanted her to tell me about her whole life, including her childhood and present autobiographical memories. I said yes; however, A. S. was reluctant to talk about her childhood and she said very little about her present life. I decided to include excerpts from the letter she wrote to the Archives Administration of Yad Vashem because I believe it gives a reflective context, information, and evaluative statements regarding her war experiences in a concise narrative form. In selecting the examples from A. S.'s personal history transcript I attempted to include information that contained the greatest amount of coherent narrative information as well as statements indicating incoherence. Contained in the 35-page transcript, approximately 85% of her autobiographical memories were incomplete relative to what would be expected given the model of a coherent personal narrative presented in Figure 4.2. In particular, most of her memories lacked an evaluation of her experiences as well as a paucity of causal-conditional terms.

Eleven thousand people were killed in Tarnow during a 2-day period. A. S. spent the war in at least five different locations where Jews were confined by the Nazis. These locations included work outside the Tarnow ghetto, a labor camp, slave labor camps, and a concentration camp. During the interview she provided copies of maps taken from Gilbert (1978) to orient me as she explained where she had been when certain experiences occurred. The use of these maps tended to increase the temporal organization of her testimony in my view, since when she reported her experiences without reference to the maps the temporal organization broke down.

She was first kept in the Tarnow ghetto – Tarnow was her hometown – for a nonspecific period of time, but it can be inferred from the date of closing the ghetto in September 1942 or 1943 (A. S. could not remember the year) that she was held there 3 to 4 years (the Tarnow ghetto was one of the last to be closed). During this time she was required to work each day outside of the ghetto. When the ghetto was closed she was deported in railroad cattle cars to the labor camp in Cycow, then to another camp she "can't remember exactly." The camp was probably K(C)rakow-Plaszow, just a few miles southeast of Auschwitz, and from there to the slave labor camp at Skarzysko-Kamienna, where she worked in the mines. From Skarzysko-Kamienna she was deported with only the women in Skarzysko-Kamienna to Leipzig, where she worked in a German munitions factory. In 1945, as the Allies were closing in on Leipzig, A. S. and the other prisoners were taken on a death march that lasted 2 weeks. It was during this march that the Germans abandoned the prisoners one night, and A. S. found her way to a Red Cross station where she stayed for approximately 6 weeks before going to the Jewish Committee in Munich instead of a displaced person (DP) camp. She eventually emigrated to the United States around 1946 and currently lives alone (her husband, who she married after the war and who was also a survivor, died about 11 years ago) in the countryside of upstate New York close to her only daughter and grandchildren. A. S. writes,

Gentlemen:
In 1978, during my trip to Israel, I visited Yad Vashem. I was shocked when I did not find on the map the camp Skarzysko- Kamienna in Poland, especially the part called "Werk C" which I describe as the "Valley of Ghosts and Dead."
I am a survivor of the camp, and if not for the fact that the camp was liquidated and the women / 100 in one sealed cattle car for approximately 8 to 10 days / were transferred to Leipzig without knowing of the destiny I would not be alive to write this letter.
I would like to share with you some of my experiences and feelings so that the martyrs of that camp would not be completely forgotten. I was also a prisoner in that terrible camp Krakow-Plaszow but in my opinion nothing supersedes Skarzysko "Werk C."
I witnessed the hanging of two boys and one man. One of the boys fell to the ground with the rope around his neck choking because the branch of the tree was so weak that it gave in. He was screaming "Schma Israel." To our greater horror, the hanging had to be executed by Jewish men from the camp who were forced to tie and pull the rope while murderers were staying behind their backs with machine guns. All this took place in the presence of all the inmates who were assembled before the execution. We were watched by the Nazis who were walking with the machine guns to make sure that everybody's eyes were open all the time. The other two victims were hanging quite a time till the[y] gave out their last breath. One could here some words that sounded like the "Vidah."
Sick people who could not leave the bunks were dragged by their feet out of the barrack into a pile of garbage without even being checked whether they are alive or dead. I witnessed two such cases in my barrack. One of the victims was the wife of a rabbi.
Many inmates were working in the plants where dynamite powder so called "picryna" and "trotyl" in Polish, was handle it. Some of them became affected by it so morbidly that their yellow skin color they looked like living ghosts. Since they were no longer productive they were deprived even that scarce inedible food given the inmates. To still their enormous hunger they licked the barrels empties after the distribution of the soup. There were incidents that while bending their upper body into the barrel they were not strong enough to get out of it and as a result they chocked to dead with their legs protruding in the air, a sight which gives me nightmares very often.
These are only a few examples of the horror of Skarzysko "WERK C." I believe that my survival of this place was a miracle. I also believe that I was destined to live.

The letter finished with closing remarks asking that her letter be given consideration. She states, "I feel very strongly that the martyrs of Skarzysko deserve this kind of memorial."

This letter has a coherent, but limited, narrative structure. For instance, A. S. sets the temporal organization of her comments in two locations, her visit to Vad Vashem in 1978 and Skarzysko-Kamienna, Werk C. The first temporal structure presented gives a time and place but no explicit reasons for her visit to Yad Vashem. We are left to our own imagination to explain why she made the visit. In the case of the second temporal structure, a location is given, however, no time or causal-conditional statements are made available. It may seem unimportant to A. S. to include causal-conditional statements explaining why she was an inmate at Skarzysko-Kamienna because she may assume that everyone already knows. Yet, while there is general knowledge why the Nazis interned Jews in slave labor camps, there is a need to know why A. S. was sent to Skarzysko-Kamienna and not some other camp. It is my contention that A. S. does not know why.

In her description of some of her experiences in Skarzysko- Kamienna the amount of information given is limited, which, in turn, makes it somewhat difficult to identify a clear orienting function in the text. Nevertheless, her letter is narratively dense and presents generalized evaluative statements, that is, "shocked," "martyrs," "horror" (used twice), "morbidly," "enormous," and "a sight which gives me nightmares very often." Surprisingly, in her description of sick people being taken from their bunks and piled as garbage, no specific evaluative statements are given; perhaps again none are needed. In addition, she makes two attributions for surviving the Holocaust. It was a "miracle" and "I also believe I was destined to live." Each of these attributions seems to imply that metaphysical forces were responsible for her survival. She makes no explicit statements that she may have survived because she was able to work. She was not sick and within the age range of people most capable of doing work for the German army. There were not attributions to luck, powerful others, or her own determination to live by using survival tactics well documented in the Holocaust literature (Langer, 1975).

In evaluating the coherence of the narrative structure and content of this letter it is necessary to consider that A. S. is writing in English and not her native language, Polish. In addition, the letter was written in 1980, 35 years after her "liberation." It is not an uncommon phenomenon to find the emergence of more coherence in narrative accounts over time as individuals construct meaning and attempt to make sense out of their traumatic experiences (Herman, 1992).

The body of her lengthy transcript is organized in much the same way as the letter presented above. My sense is that she used the letter during the interview to maintain some sense of coherence between what she wrote and told. The major difference is that she includes more details and one story from childhood in her oral testimony. Here childhood memory begins, "For one reason, that the Holocaust, my experiences after going through such a tragedy, that one by one, in the end I was left alone, to talk about my family, I didn't want to." She goes on, however, with the following childhood memory:

(1a) What I remember from, during the war is one thing, the only thing I can tell you that might very interest you, this you can take on . . . my oldest sister was on a very high position in a firm that time was ummm making all kinds of ummm undergarments for like ummm . . . women, when the Germans came to our hometown, they took all of the nice, the biggest businesses and of course, they let her stay there because she was running the whole place and they needed the people, they could take away the business from you but they needed the people. And she was, she got passes, she could go out of the ghetto because the place was, the ghetto was very small, they put only a few streets and so on. One day she brought home some butter. My mother was a very deep believer in God and she believed everything what was in the Jewish tradition, the Kosher and so on, she let the kids have the butter, she didn't want to eat it. Once morning because . . . because she liked to bring this over there, the fence, you know what happened the same day. Three hour later the Germans came and going from house to . . . and they took my parents away. And it's haunting me until today, you know how many years?, that she probably thought because she ate the nonKosher butter, that probably God punished her. [This part of her narrative is coherent in many ways, containing information and a degree of narrative organization. The continuation of the thoughts triggered by this memory told in the paragraph following represent a less coherent narrative.] (1b) And I can't even thought it is very tough, besides everything else, there are certain moments, that you know it is very hard to take. You don't talk about this everyday, maybe you don't even think but it's there and when you have to bring it out, it's hard. It is hard. I only know one thing. That is very, very hard, and I am sure that 80% of the people who miracles are still around or were around and died . . . after the war . . . and I am sure that everybody has the guilt feeling.

In the second paragraph she is trying to explain the feelings of "survivor guilt" even though she does so in a less than explicit manner. While the coherence of this narrative structure is weak, except for the evaluative narrative function, A. S. is largely unable to convey the total meaning of her experiences. For instance, she states elsewhere in the narrative that she does not talk about her experiences with her grandchildren. One possible explanation for why she finds it difficult to talk about the Holocaust is because of her feelings of guilt for surviving and a sense that they could not understand.

In the two last examples presented below, the first was selected because it is high in narrative coherence relative to the second example, which is considered low in coherence. In the first example A. S. is talking about the German invasion, occupation, and ghettoization of Tarnow; in the second, she is trying to set the context for her transfer with 99 other women from Skarzysko-Kimenna to Liepzig.

(2a) Now, speaking of the camps, what stays in my head one day, in September 1939, a very famous day, we found out there was a railroad was . . . the Germans were already very close, there, they had according what we found out later, a very easy coming to Poland to southwest border. When you look at them, lets say, in Europe, Germany is to the west of Poland, Russia was to the east, because . . . were a lot of German and Polish too, a lot of German people and a lot of people of German, German born parents . . . and they were, and they felt German, lived like Germans, according what we found out later, they came through Chrzanow[3] village, the man to the richest towns, almost to the border, on the red carpet. And from Cracow [a Polish town located just to the southwest of Tarnow where 2000 Jews were murdered June 1, 1942, and a railhead that was used to deport Jews to the concentration camp at Belzec, Poland] in village to Tarnow, there first is Cracow and then Tarnow, maybe two hours train ride at the time. All of a sudden a day later they came in, Storm Troopers, they came in like a, how do you call the insects, very vengeance insect, because the . . . they came with the motorcycles, these black uniforms, with the star hats, and with the heavy, the heavy guns, they came with tanks through the streets, and there was a shooting both ways, unexpected, whoever went was right away killed. There is only one expression, a mob, that's what they were. Right away it started the killings, the first day limited where you could go, on which side you could go, and then they said you were on the wrong side in order to kill, that you should go on that side [here A. S. is referring to which side of the street people were allowed to walk on from day to day]. There were a lot of restrictions, they were catching people on the street just like that into all kinds of work . . . to work, meantime they were catching them to take them somewhere to be corpses. Their life got a little bit stabilized when they got settled already what they are go-

[3]Chrzanow is a German town just west of Poland and northwest of Tarnow. Four thousand Jews were murdered in Chrzanow in 1942 even though many of them facilitated the German approach to the Polish border prior to the invasion.

ing to do. So they closed, we had to go out of our homes to a certain area and they closed the ghetto.

(2b) They are taking us out from Skarzysko we did not know where they are taking us out. One day the Gestapo came from . . . the town, the city there on the camp, and they called us out, were sitting outside, and they, in the night, we were sitting there, we did not know where we are going, what they are going to do with us, they didn't let us go back to the barracks, and were walking around, the Ukrainians, in black uniforms, calling us names, and I am talking "My God," they are all killed by Germans too, what, I couldn't understand, to be on your own free will, I can't I always, when people were complaining or criticizing somebody after the war, I used to say "I don't know what I would do in a certain situation." I can understand the saying that the skin is closer or dearer than everything else! But to volunteer, I could excuse certain things, I don't know what I would do, there is such a thing that you can never say I would do because you don't know what you would do it. But to volunteer is a different story. [In this excerpt A. S. is dealing with two issues simultaneously: one the selection during the night, and the other, how the Ukrainians could volunteer to work for the Germans even though they too were murdered.]

Upon closer narrative analysis of each of the examples it is seen that for the first example (1a: total number of words = 348) the proportions (number of relevant narrative terms/total number of words per paragraph) of temporal terms was 6/348 = .02; location terms, 6/348 =. 02; causal-conditional terms, 3/348 = .009; and evaluative terms, 9/348 = .03. For the second paragraph (1b: total number of words = 198, or 57% of the total number of words in the first example thereby leading to fewer numbers of each narrative term) the comparative proportions are temporal terms, 2/198 = .01; location terms, 2/198 = .01; causal-conditional terms, 0/198 = 0; and evaluative terms, 3/198 = .02. The proportion of relevant terms from both examples indicates that there is little difference between the making of sense of A. S.'s war experiences and the meaning of those experiences to her.

The corresponding data from the second example, paragraphs 2a and 2b, are for (2a: total number of words = 248; temporal terms, 6/248 = .02; location terms, 6/248 = .02; causal-conditional terms, 3/248 = .01; and evaluative terms, 9/248 = .04; and for paragraph 2b (total number of words = 198) are .01, .01, .00, .02. These data show clearly that the first example is more coherent narratively than the second example, especially in the use of causal-conditional and evaluative terms.

Compare these proportions with those found in the four examples (two thematic units) reported above for R. F. (R. F. is taken for comparison because his personal history was taken using the same methodology used for A. S.). Theme 1, "Not a liability, not a star," paragraph 1a (total number of words = 75); temporal terms, 2/75 = .03; location terms, 2/75 = .03; causal-conditional terms, 1/75 = .01; and evaluative terms, 8/75 = .12; for paragraph 1b (total number of words − 100), the corresponding proportions were .03, .02, .02, and .07, respectively. Theme 2, "Trouble-Makers Club," paragraph 2a total number of words = 68; temporal terms, 1/68 = .02; location terms, 2/68 = .03; causal-conditional terms, 2/68 = .03; and evaluative terms, 2/68 = .03. The corresponding proportions for paragraph 2b (total number of words = 220) were .03, .03, .02, .06.

Now consider the average proportions of narrative terms found in the examples from A. S. and R. F. These averages are given in Table 4.1.

Table 4.1 *Average proportion of Temporal, Location, Causal-Conditional and Evaluative terms found in R. F. and A. S.'s examples taken from their personal histories.*

	Narrative terms			
	Temporal	Location	Causal-conditional	Evaluative
Person				
A. S.	.015	.015	.01	.03
R. F.*	.027	.027	.02	.07

*Note: Unlike A. S.'s examples, R. F.'s examples were not chosen to demonstrate high versus low narrative coherence.

In comparisons of the average percentages of each term counted as an index of narrative coherence, R. F.'s average percentages of narrative terms used is nearly 100% greater overall than those found for A. S. The largest differences were found in the use of evaluative and causal-conditional terms by R. F. Even though the proportions are low, it is clear from the evidence that R. F. was able to explain why he did what he did in his life and what those experiences meant to him to a much greater degree than A. S. This was especially true in conveying the meaning of his life experiences. These kinds of data lend support to my claim that people who do not experience trauma (i.e., R. F.) are able to construct more coherent personal histories than people who have been traumatized. This conclusion was also reached by Barclay (1993b, 1993c) in the analysis of oral testimony taken from Langer (1991).

The explanation offered for the kinds of findings reported here and by Barclay (1993b, 1993c), and supported by Delbo (1985) and Herman (1992), is that experiences that lack temporal organization and clear evaluative functions lead to a sense of self-doubling. That is, the person develops a sense of two selves, one is coherent, the other not. As one survivor put it,

I feel my head is filled with garbage; all these images, you know, and sounds, and my nostrils are filled with the stench of burning flesh. And its . . . you can't excise it, it's like – like there's another skin beneath this skin and that skin is called Auschwitz, and you cannot shed it. . . . And it's a constant accompaniment. And though a lot of survivors will deny this, they too felt the way I do, but they won't give expression to it. I mean I will tell you that it's harder in many ways because . . . because we carry this. I am not like you. You have one version of life and I have two. (Langer, 1991, pp. 54–55)

When some survivors of the Holocaust claim that "you can't understand," they speak the truth because the nature of their experiences lacks an explanatory system as well as a clear temporal-spatial system. They were mostly unaware of where they were when deported to concentration camps, and in many camps (e.g., Auschwitz) they did not know what events were occurring outside of their own block of barracks in other parts of the camp. I suspect that many of those who survived the trauma of the Holocaust do not understand either; however, they do have the embodied experiences of atrocities that cannot be conveyed to others in a descriptive language. This claim may generalize other victims of trauma, who lack a coherent autobiographical narrative of the traumatic experiences. They, too, experience anxiety and hypervigilence, as well as a sense of "doubling," because they cannot explain why they were traumatized and frequently lack the language to describe what happened to them – a language of victimization.

Conclusions

The aims of this paper were to present an idealized model of autobiographical remembering by specifying the purposes, processes, and products of reconstructive memory. In outlining this model, the concept of "context" was introduced, and it was argued that context interacts with reconstructive activities and the objectification of autobiographical memories. Context was the connecting link to the model of coherent personal histories as well as the analysis of metaphors of self. In narrative terms, context is specified by the amount of information given as well as the orienting narrative function. Context provides a frame of reference within which events are recounted, explained, evaluated, and understood. This aim extends a theory of autobiographical remembering to include context, and extends the idea that reconstructive remembering activities include more than the justification of feeling as a purely individual set of mental processes.

The model of coherent personal narratives outlined both a model and an empirical method for analyzing narrative accounts that is only beginning to be used by developmental psychologists. Most importantly, this model provides an explanation for why certain memories make sense and have autobiographical significance (meaning) to the individual. In providing this explanation, it is possible to analyze reasons why certain autobiographical accounts (e.g., those associated with traumatic experiences that lack temporal organization and affect) are incoherent and difficult to understand. The metaphors of self-illustration demonstrate how personal histories can be analyzed and interpreted and integrated with empirical narrative methodology to build a systematic approach to the analysis of lives and their many meanings.

In application, the methods and examples outlined in this essay offer explanations for why memories are sensitive to suggestive questions, especially when there is no coherent narrative system working at the time or an incorrect system is being used when leading questions are asked. Interestingly, the analyses given above help explain why victims of the Holocaust have been shown to have accuracies and inaccuracies in their eyewitness testimonies (e.g, Wagenaar & Groeneweg, 1990); namely, their narratives do not often have well-formed temporal-spatial, causal-conditional, and evaluative elements that would tend to increase memory accuracy. This is not to argue that Holocaust survivors are not telling the truth about what happened to them. The argument is that, as with everyday memories and "flashbulb memories" (Neisser & Harsch, 1991), the accuracy of autobiographical recollections are remembered with high confidence because they are in fidelity with the person's present sense of self, and plausible given the narrative systems being used at the time past events are reconstructed. Other phenomena the approach taken here may help to explain are childhood memories of ritualistic Satanic trauma (Neisser, 1993), recovered memories of child abuse as an adult, fabrications of personal experiences to make certain actual events sensible and meaningful, and certain psychopathologies (e.g., anxiety disorders [panic] and dysfunctions such as functional amnesia or multiple personalities).

A narrative approach to the study of the development and explanation of autobiographical remembering and self-construction is limited. Most narrative accounts do not conform closely to known canonical forms. Narrative structures are constantly changing as new idioms emerge within and across cultures. Narrative "text" analysis alone cannot offer a full explanation or understanding of autobiographical memories because much of the meaning of narratives is constructed by the consumer as is the case in understanding the meaning of public idioms. Prior knowledge of both the creator and consumer of narrative functions is used to transmit much of the meaning and understanding of narrative beyond the actual words used. The last limitation mentioned may best explain the relative lack of perceived coherence in narrative accounts of trauma victims by nonvictims. People experiencing similar kinds of trauma may create idioms that are meaningless to others who have not been so traumatized.

In the special case of Holocaust survivors we may be witnessing a narrative genre that is constructed through idiomatic expressions, including movements and assumed shared knowledge, that has not been recognized to date. That is, within groups of individuals who share common traumatic experiences, the temporal organization and evaluative narrative function are not articulated because of known or assumed shared atrocities.

In many ways, Holocaust survivors and other victims of trauma have been "silenced" by the unwillingness of others to listen, without judgement, to the victims' experiences. Others do not believe what the traumatized person is telling them because it seems so fantastic, or the meanings are carried in the victims' voices because there are no affect terms to describe the kinds of experiences they have had. There appears to be a collective denial by many, or functional amnesia, that events like the Holocaust could not happen because most of us have not experienced or even imagined the kinds of human atrocities that have occurred historically and in the present. At best, we can only be witnesses to the autobiographical testimonies of victims and legitimate their voices by not denying the authenticity of their first-hand personal accounts.

The Holocaust, like other "crimes against humanity," did and still occur. It is less important that accurate details of those atrocities are remembered than it is to acknowledge the truthfulness of the victims' testimony. The idealized model of autobiographical remembering outlined in this essay is an attempt to acknowledge the authenticity of autobiographical memories by including contextualizing structures and processes to a reconstructive theory of autobiographical memory.

In closing, I argue that personal histories and selves are revised over time, especially in situations where remembered lives need framing in the narrative sense. Reconstructive activities can lead to objectifications and subjectifications used to justify unspeakable feelings, as is found in the emerging stories of many trauma victims. In this way, one's personal history and the meaning of that history change over time. Even given the limitations of narrative accounts of life experiences, the utility of narrative analyses provides a useful but incomplete methodology for explaining the creation, use, and meaning of autobiographical memories in the construction of self. I suspect that the study of selected special populations who have experienced various kinds of trauma (e.g., Holocaust survivors, rape victims, cancer survivors, or people who have lost loved ones to accident or disease) will provide the evidence needed to validate the arguments made here. Life is meaningful when experiences can be tied to functional affects and emotions, and one's self is sensed as coherent when there is a useful temporal-spatial system for organizing, interpreting, and explaining life events.

References

Baddeley, A. D. (1991). What is autobiographical memory? *Proceedings of the NATO Advanced Research Workshop on Theoretical Aspects on Autobiographical Memory.* In M. A. Conway, D. C. Rubin, H. Spinnler, & W. A. Wagenaar (Eds.), *Theoretical Perspectives on Autobiographical Memory* (pp. 13–29). Dordrecht, The Netherlands: Kluwer Academic.

Barclay, C. R. (1986). Schematization of autobiographical memory. In D. C. Rubin (Ed.), *Autobiographical Memory* (pp. 82–99). New York: Cambridge University Press.

—— (1993a). Composing protoselves through improvisation. In U. Neisser & R. Fivush (Eds.), *The Remembered Self: Construction and Accuracy in the Self-Narrative.* New York: Cambridge University Press.

—— (1993b). Remembering ourselves. In G. M. Davies & R. H. Logie (Eds.), *Memory in Everyday Life* (pp. 285–309). North Holland: Elsevier Science.

—— (1993c). Autobiographical remembering and self-knowledge. In V. S. Ramachandran (Ed.), *Encyclopedia of Human Behavior.* San Diego: Academic Press.

Barclay, C. R., & Hodges, R. M. (1990). La composition de soi dans les souvenirs autogiographiques. *Psychologie Francaise, 35,* 59–65.

Barclay, C. R., & Smith, T. (1992). Autobiographical remembering: Creating personal culture. In M. A. Conway, D. C. Rubin, H. Spinnler, & W. Wagenaar (Eds.), *Theoretical Perspectives on Autobiographical Memory* (pp. 1–28). Dordrecht, The Netherlands: Kluwer Academic.

Bartlett, F. C. (1932). *Remembering: A Study in Experimental and Social Psychology.* New York: Cambridge University Press.

Browning, C. R. (1992). *The Path to Genocide: Essays on Launching the Final Solution.* New York: Cambridge University Press.

Connell, J. P. (1990). Context, self and action: A motivational analysis of self-system processes across the life span. In D. Cicchetti and M. Beeghly (Eds.), *The Self in Transition: Infancy to Childhood* (pp. 61–97). Chicago: University of Chicago Press.

Csikszentmihalyi, M., & Beattie, O. (1979). Life themes: a theoretical and empirical exploitation of their origins and effects. *Journal of Humanistic Psychology, 19,* 45–63.

Dannefer, D. (1992). On the conceptualization of context in developmental discourse: Four meanings of context and their implications. In (Eds.) David L. Featherman, Richard H. Lerner, and Marion Perlmuter, *Life-Span Development and Behavior,* (Vol. 11, pp. 83–110). Hillsdale, NJ: Lawrence Erlbaum.

Delbo, C. (1985). *La memorie it les jouns.* Paris: Benz International.

Doyle, A.C. (1984). *The Illustrated Sherlock Holmes Treasury.* New York: Avenel Books.

Eakin, P. J. (1985). *Fictions in autobiography: Studies in the Art of Self-Invention.* Princeton, NJ: Princeton University Press.

Fivush, R. (1991). The social construction of personal narratives. *Merrill-Palmer Quarterly, 37,* 59–82.

Fivush, R., & Fromhoff. F. A., (1988). Style and structure in mother-child conservations about the past. *Discourse Processes, 11,* 337–355.

Ganaway, G. F. (1989). Historical truth versus narrative truth: Clarifying the role of exogenous traumas in the etiology of multiple personality disorder and its variants. *Dissociation, 2,* 205–220.

Gergen, K. J., & Gergen, M. M. (1988). Narrative and self as relationship. *Advances in Experimental Social Psychology, 21,* 17–56.

Gilbert, M. (1978). *The Holocaust.* New York: Hill & Wang.

—— (1993). *Atlas of the Holocaust.* New York: William Morrow and Company, Inc.

Hardy, T. (1920). *Under the Greenwood Tree.* Garden City, NY: Garden City Publications.

Herman, J. L. (1992). *Traumas and Recovery: The Aftermath of Violence – From Domestic Abuse to Political Terror.* New York: Basic Books.

Hudson, J. A., & Shapiro, L. R. (1991). Effects of task and topics on children's narratives. In A. McCabe & C. Peterson (Eds.), *New Directions in Developing Narrative Structure* (pp. 89–136). Hillsdale, NJ: Lawrence Erlbaum.

Johnson, M. (1987). *The Body in the Mind: The Bodily Basis of Meaning, Imagination, and Reason.* Chicago: University of Chicago Press.

Kail, R., & Hagen. J. (Eds.). (1977). *Perspective on the Development of Memory.* Hillsdale, NJ: Lawrence Erlbaum.

Labov, W., & Waletzky, J. (1967). Narrative analysis: oral versions of personal experience. In J. H. (Ed.)., *Essays on the Verbal and Visual Arts* (pp. 12–44). Seattle: University of Washington Press.

Lakoff, G. (1986). *Women, Fire and Dangerous Things: What Categories Reveal about the Mind.* Chicago: University of Chicago Press.

Langer, L. L. (1975). *The Holocaust and the Literary Imagination.* New Haven, CT: Yale University Press.

—— (1982). *Versions of Survival: The Holocaust and the Human Spirit.* Albany, NY: State University of New York Press.

—— (1991) *Holocaust Testimonies: The Ruins of Memory.* New Haven, CT: Yale University Press.

Levi, P. (1958). *Survival in Auschwitz: The Nazi Assault on Humanity.* Stuart Woolf (trans.) New York: Collier Books.

Linde, C. (1987). Explanatory systems in oral life stories. In D. Holland and N. Quinn (Eds.), *Cultural Models in Language and Thought* (pp. 343–366). New York: Cambridge University Press.

Loftus, E. F. (1979). *Eyewitness Testimony.* Cambridge, MA: Harvard University Press.

Lord, A. B. (1960). *The Singer of Tales.* Cambridge, MA: Harvard University Press.

Lutz, C. (1982). The domain of emotion words in Ifaluk. *American Ethnologist, 9,* 113–128.

—— (1987). Goals, events, and understanding in Ifaluk emotion theory. In D. Holland & N. Quinn (Eds.), *Cultural Models in Language and Thought* (pp. 290–312). New York: Cambridge University Press.

March, T. (1993). Personal communication.

McCauley, R. N. (1992). *Models of Knowing and Their Relations to Our Understanding of Liberal Education.* Atlanta, GA: Emory University.

Middleton, D., & Edwards, D. (Eds.). (1990a). *Collective Remembering.* London: Sage.

Middleton, D., & Edwards, D. (1990b). Conversational remembering: A social psychological approach. In D. Middleton & D. Edwards (Eds.), *Collective Remembering* (pp. 23–45). London: Sage.

Neisser, U. (1988). Five kinds of self-knowledge. *Philosophical Psychology, 1,* 35–59.

—— (1993). *Memory with a Grain of Salt.* Invited address at the Conference on Memory and Reality, Valley Forge, PA.

Neisser, U., & Harsch, N. (1991). Phantom flashbulbs: False recollections of hearing the news about *Challenger.* In E. Winograd and U. Neisser (Eds.), *Affect and Accuracy: Studies of "Flashbulb Memories."* New York: Cambridge University Press.

Nemiah, J. C. (1979). Dissociative amnesia: A clinical and theoretical reconsideration. In J. F. Kihlstrom & F. J. Evans (Eds.), *Functional Disorders of Memory* (pp. 303–323). Hillsdale, NJ: Lawrence Erlbaum.

Obeyesekere, G. (1981). *Medusa's Hair: An Essay on Personal Symbols and Religious Experiences.* Chicago: University of Chicago Press.

—— (1990). *The Working of Culture: Symbolic Transformation in Psychoanalysis and Anthropology.* Chicago: University of Chicago Press.

Pressing, J. (1984). Cognitive processes in improvisation. In W. R. Crozier and A. J. Chapman (Eds.), *Cognitive Processes in the Perception of Art* (pp. 345–363). North Holland: Elsevier Science.

Ricoeur, P. (1983). *Time and Narrative* (Vol. 1). Chicago: University of Chicago Press.

—— (1984). *Time and Narrative* (Vol. 2). Chicago: University of Chicago Press.

Ryan, R. (1990). The nature of the self in autonomy and relatedness. In J. Strauss and G. R. Goethals (Eds.), *Multidisciplinary Perspectives on the Self* (pp. 208–238). New York: Springer-Verlag.

Sartre, J. P. (1964). *The Words: The Autobiography of Jean-Paul Sartre*. New York: Vintage Books.

Spence, D. P. (1982). *Narrative Truth and Historical Truth: Meaning and Interpretation in Psychoanalysis*. New York: Norton.

Trevarthen, C. (1983). Emotions in infancy: Regulators of contact and relationships with persons. In K. Scherer & P. Eckman (Eds.), *Approaches to Emotion* (pp. 129–157). Hillsdale, NJ: Lawrence Erlbaum.

Vygotsky, L. S. (1978). *Mind in Society: The Development of Higher Psychological Processes*. Cambridge, MA: Harvard University Press.

Wagenaar, W. A. (1988). *Identifying Ivan: A Case Study in Legal Psychology*. Cambridge, MA: Harvard University Press.

Wagenaar, W. A., & Groeneweg, J. (1990). The memory of concentration camp survivors. *Applied Cognitive Psychology, 4*, 77–87.

Woolf, V. (1927). *To the Lighthouse*. New York: Harcourt, Brace and Company.

—— (1929). *A Room of One's Own*. London: Rosewood Associates, LTD.

—— (1976). *Moments of Being*. New York: Harcourt, Brace, Jovanovich.

Yahil, L. (1987). *The Holocaust*. New York: Oxford University Press.

Part II
Accuracy

---

5   Time in autobiographical memory

Steen F. Larsen, Charles P. Thompson, and Tia Hansen

Introduction

Nothing appears more fundamental to a biography than time. Life is a succession of events that are intricately related, causally and intentionally. But however complicated the relations may be, the events occur in a chronological sequence. Many events are repeated with minor variations from day to day, from week to week, and from year to year, and therefore merge to become general knowledge. No matter how small the variations may be, however, any two events in a person's life can in principle be distinguished by the unique times when they occurred. Accordingly, in the art of biography that flourished in the eighteenth century, the description of the life of the subject was fastidiously chronological, as seen in Boswell's famous "Life of Johnson" (1791/1980).

Autobiographical memory (i.e., memories of events experienced by the individual) is likewise unthinkable without reference to time. Though we do not recall the time of events precisely, the memories appear to our present consciousness as representing – more or less completely – a chronologically ordered, continuous past reality. Indeed, a person whose past was lacking temporal organization could not have the awareness of a history, of a course of development that is a defining part of the experience of a self; she/he would be not only a disorderly person, but a severely disordered personality (cf. Melges, 1982). Thus, if this temporal quality were missing entirely, the person's memories of the past would hardly be considered autobiographical in the everyday usage of the word.

Granted that time is important in principle, how much do we care about time in the practice of everyday life? When future plans and actions have to be coordinated with other people, timing is decisive; in so-called prospective memory, the psychology of time must be taken very seriously. But determining the time of past experiences is also very important. In the courtroom, at the doctor's, or in the bank, knowing the precise time of past events may be critical. Indeed, proper memory of time is also desirable in many mundane situations, like when to discard food in the freezer, when it is reasonable

This study was partially supported by the Danish Research Council for the Humanities under the Cognitive Science Program.

129

to buy a new dress, when to invite the neighbors for dinner, and so on. More generally, coordination of times in the past is a frequent part of the interpersonal use of autobiographical memory; agreement on the time of events confirms a common history.

Memory for time: An overview

Given the importance of remembering the time of events in everyday life, we need to examine three issues: First, we need to know how accurate people are when they attempt to place events in time. As we shall see, people are quite accurate (on average) in judging the time of events, that is, temporal judgments are normally unbiased estimates of actual time in the past. Furthermore, errors of judgment appear to obey the simple psychophysical law of being a constant fraction of the temporal distance that is judged (Weber's law). Second, we need to know how and on which basis events are placed in time. Four alternatives are considered: theories based on event order, on the strength of the memory trace, on special time tags added to the trace, and on generic knowledge of temporal patterns (schemata). To anticipate again, the evidence is overwhelming that the primary process for dating events is reconstruction based on schemata for time. Finally, we need to know the nature of the information used in the process of dating. Given that the process of dating consists of reconstruction from temporal schemata, we need to specify the characteristics of those schemata. We shall consider cyclic schemata for the hours of the day, the days of the week, and the months and seasons of the year, as well as linear schemata extending across the life span.

The accuracy of reconstructing time

Dating accuracy and the Weber function

A number of studies have been published on the dating of autobiographical memories in which the actual dates of the events were available to assess the accuracy of the datings. Usually, a diary method has been employed (e.g., Larsen & Thompson, in press; Linton, 1986; Thompson, 1982, 1985; Thompson, Skowronski, & Betz, 1993; Wagenaar, 1986). Subjects write a diary of events for a period and then date the events from the diary descriptions after some delay. Every study, extending across intervals up to 6 years back in time, has found the surprising result that the datings are, on the average, almost exactly correct (see the review by Rubin and Baddeley, 1989). The datings cluster symmetrically around the true date of the event so that forward and backward errors cancel out, that is, the average dating error is close to zero. To illustrate the robustness of the result, consider a study by Larsen and Thompson (in press, Exp. 1). The average dating error for autobiographical events from a 4-month period of diary writing was a meager 0.25 days immediately after the period had ended, and after a delay of 5 months, the error was still only 0.19 days.

This overall precision of event dating despite the passage of time is remarkable, but it does not necessarily mean that memory for dates is immune to forgetting. Several investigators (see the review by Rubin and Baddeley, 1989) have shown that the absolute magnitude of errors (i.e., error size irrespective of the direction of the error) increases over time. As pointed out by Thompson (1982), errors increase by about 1 day for each week that has passed since the event occurred. Rubin and Baddeley (1989) showed that this function holds for retention intervals up to 6 years. Thus, the growth of errors appears to be linear, conforming to Weber's classic psychophysical law that the error of a judgment is a constant proportion of the magnitude of the property being judged.

If the similarity to Weber's law is interpreted literally, it means that remembered time is analogous to a simple, one-dimensional perceptual property, like distance, weight, brightness, etc. This implies that information about distance in time from the present (i.e., event age) is somehow available in memory, as information about distance in space is available in the environment. Furthermore, it implies that the increase of errors with time does not reflect forgetting in the ordinary sense. The information in memory is not decaying or disturbed by interference; small differences just become less noticeable at a larger distance in time. Rubin and Baddeley (1989) did not draw these implications, however. Actually, they proposed no account of how the impressive dating accuracy is achieved and what information it might be based on (except for noting that "normal dating" of events is done by relating them to "reference points" [p. 659]). Their exposition was purely descriptive. Nevertheless, their observation that the linear function first described by Thompson (1982) holds over long retention intervals provides an important constraint on theories of memory for time; any theory has to be able to account for both accuracy and systematic errors.

Telescoping and boundary effects

There are characteristics other than the passage of time that affect the accuracy of dating autobiographical events. Starting with Gray (1955), a number of investigators (e.g., Bradburn, Rips, & Shevell, 1987; Loftus & Marburger, 1983; Neter & Waksberg, 1964; Thompson, Skowronski, & Lee, 1988) have looked at systematic errors of a kind known as telescoping, that is, estimates of dates being moved from the actual date of events forward toward the present so that time seems to be compressed as if viewed in a telescope. For example, Thompson et al. (1988) found that the telescoping occurred for older events in the 3-month period covered by their diary experiments, whereas very recent events tended to be displaced backwards in time – reverse telescoping, or time expansion.

Rubin and Baddeley (1989) showed that some biasing of datings will occur when the interval from which the events are drawn is known to have boundaries at the ends (e.g., a 3-month diary period). Because the boundaries prevent dating errors from moving outside the interval, but do not affect errors toward the middle of the interval, the result will be to move the average away from the boundaries. Moreover, since errors are larger for more remote events (the Weber function), movements from the far boundary toward the present (telescoping) will be larger than movements backward from the near boundary (reverse telescoping). Rubin and Baddeley (1989) demonstrated that these processes are sufficient to produce the telescoping effects that have been reported. Huttenlocher, Hedges, and Prohaska (1988) proposed a similar, formal model of boundary effects. They used the model to account also for apparent telescoping created by having a reference point or subboundary within a period; for instance, a semester boundary within the academic year.

The lesson of the telescoping discussion is that datings of events may be distorted, not because memory (and thus the apprehension of time in the past) is biased, but because the subject's knowledge of the temporal boundaries of the interval to which the events belong allows selective elimination of errors beyond the interval. The basic overall accuracy of memory for time is thus not invalidated.

The accessibility principle

Brown, Rips, and Shevell (1985) reported that well-remembered events were dated as more recent than events that were less accessible in memory. Brown et al. proposed an "accessibility principle" to explain this finding, claiming that memory for time is, to some significant extent, based on how easily or vividly events are remembered. This principle challenges the accuracy of temporal memory by predicting telescoping of vivid events and reverse telescoping (at least relatively speaking) of less vivid ones. However, the study by Brown et al. required subjects to give dates of news events that were not in some way tied to their personal life. As Rubin and Baddeley (1989) observed, a similar pattern has never been found in the datings of autobiographical events (e.g., Thompson et al., 1988). In the Larsen and Thompson study (in press, Exp. 1), autobiographical and news events were directly compared. The news was clearly less well remembered, which was indicated by much larger dating errors as well as by cued recall measures. The accessibility principle would therefore imply less forward telescoping of news than of personal events, but the reverse was found: somewhat greater telescoping of news. For the news, however, telescoping did decrease slightly when retention time was increased, as predicted by the accessibility principle because memories are eroded by forgetting. The average error was 4 days forward telescoping in an immediate test and only 1.9 days in a test 5 months later.

The impact of the accessibility principle may therefore be limited, and it may only apply when the person has no more precise information available from which to make the judgment of time. The difference between autobiographical events and news in this respect suggests that important temporal information is inherent to the activities of the person's life. We shall return to discuss the structure of temporal information later in the chapter. However, let us first consider arguments for claiming that this very accurate, unbiased assessment of time in the past is achieved mainly by a process of cognitive reconstruction.

The process of reconstructing time

In a comprehensive review, Friedman (1993) noted that among the many theories of memory for time that could be culled from the scientific literature, none were well developed. He attempted to explicate even those that were "little more than vague metaphors" (p. 45) in order to assess their ability to account for the empirical evidence. The conclusion he reached was that remembered events are not specifically coded for time (as already argued by Gibson, 1975). Instead, time in the past is actively reconstructed, mainly by reference to general knowledge of temporal patterns. Let us briefly consider the main alternatives to this reconstructive view.

Event succession theories

"Order code theory" rests on the very simple notion that the occurrence of an event may remind one of an earlier event and thus create a link between the two events that encodes their before-after relation. For instance, hearing of the Chernobyl nuclear power disaster might bring the Three Mile Island accident to mind. This mechanism has been demonstrated in the laboratory (e.g., Winograd & Soloway, 1985) by showing that the order of two items can be judged with greater success if they are meaningfully related. In autobiographical memory, however, order codes would need to be supplemented by information about the duration of the interval between the events and the temporal location of at least one of the events.

Some theories propose a more extensive, and possibly automatic, coding of event succession in memory. In one version, events are assumed to be linked in an associative chain. This view, which is implicit in classical associationist theory (Ebbinghaus, 1885/1964), again lacks definite temporal information, and it has difficulty accounting for recall that jumps around in time.

A more sophisticated version of the event succession notion maintains that events are somehow associated with their position in a sequence of events receding into the past like bags on a moving conveyer belt (Murdock, 1974). Friedman (1993) calls this a "chronological organization theory." To the extent that a temporal metric is assumed to be provided by a steady flow of events, or by coding the steady movement of time in memory (the "conveyer belt"), this theory incorporates duration, not just event order. The theory is consistent with a common tendency to recall events in chronological order (either forward or backward) and to be reminded of events that are close in time to a target event one is trying to put a date to. Furthermore, the spatial metaphor of judging distance into the past along the moving belt is compatible with the seemingly perceptual nature of memory for time that was implied by the Weber function for error magnitude. However, no detailed account has been proposed of how the temporal aspects of such an organization would be represented in memory; for instance, is an underlying dimension of absolute time assumed, independently of whether events are remembered or forgotten?

Trace strength theories

Strength theories are also concerned with duration. These theories hypothesize that the time since an event occurred is gauged from the "strength" of its memory trace; because the strength is assumed to decline across time, a stronger trace indicates a more recent event. Strength may be assessed by the vividness of the memory, ease of retrieving it, confidence in its correctness, or amount of detail recalled. Strength theories were proposed very early (by Guyau in 1890, see Michon, Pouthas, & Jackson, 1988) and exist in a number of forms (e.g., Hinrichs, 1970). We already encountered a modern and modest – version above in the accessibility principle of Brown et al. (1985) that might have some limited validity for explaining biases in dating nonpersonal events (news). But as a general account of memory for time, strength theory fails seriously. Thus, high-strength events do not tend to be telescoped forward as the theory predicts, but are rather dated more accurately than low-strength events. The Weber function analyzed above is also a case in point. Indeed, we noted that if recent, and therefore high-strength, events are affected by temporal bias, it is backward telescoping rather than forward. Moreover, as Friedman (1993) points out, subjects rarely mention vividness or other supposed aspects of strength when they are asked how they judge the time of events.

Time-tag theories

Time-tag theories provide the simplest form of theory in which the location of events in time is specified explicitly. Time-tag theories are equally as common as strength theories (e.g., Glenberg, 1987; Yntema & Trask, 1963). The core of time-tag theory is the assumption that time information is added on to the memory trace at encoding, analogous to a date stamp. This tag can then be retrieved later along with the memory trace. Friedman (1993) abstains from evaluating the time-tag idea as such because the nature of the time tags and the tagging process has never been spelled out. Under the conditions of ordinary life in an industrialized society, conventional calendar and clock labels might seem an obvious way to time-tag memories. Thompson et al. (1988) found that subjects who dated diary events sometimes indicated that they simply knew the exact date and retrieved it directly from memory. Such answers were given for about 10% of the datings. Thus, though acquisition of the exact date does appear to happen, it seems quite rare. Another finding suggesting that dates usually are not explicitly represented in memory is that time is invariably the worst possible cue for recalling events (Barsalou, 1988; Brewer, 1988; Wagenaar, 1986). Friedman (1993) notes that occasional representation of dates does not require a general time-tagging model; we only need to assume that dates can be learned and remembered just like any other information if they are attended and processed.

Reconstructive theories

Reconstructive theories propose that memory for time is primarily accomplished by using fragments of information remembered about the event ("temporal cues") to draw inferences from general knowledge about time patterns ("temporal schemata") and thus constrain the likely time of the event (e.g., Friedman & Wilkins, 1985; Lieury, Aiello, Lepreux, & Mellet, 1980; Linton, 1986; Thompson et al., 1993). To anchor these relative datings to the conventional time scales, it is presumed, in addition, that people have learned the precise calendar time of a few events that are used as reference points ("landmarks").

Friedman (1993) shows that reconstructive theories can in principle accommodate all the extant empirical findings, whether from naturalistic or laboratory studies and whether personal or public events are concerned. He finds no contradictory evidence. Thus, the high dating accuracy of well-remembered events is explained by the abundance of cues for accessing temporal schemata, which also accounts for the improvement of dating by procedures that improve memory of the event itself. Also, subjects' reports of their strategy as well as think-aloud protocols show the constructive use of regular time patterns and reference events. So-called scale effects provide particularly strong support for reconstructive theories. Experimental results have shown that temporal accuracy for an event can be high at one level of scale (e.g., the hour it happened) while it is low on others (e.g., the week it was); and scale differences are not correlated with the grain of the scales (Bruce & van Pelt, 1989; Friedman, 1987; Friedman & Wilkins, 1985; White, 1982). If a strictly linear view of time held true, memory should by necessity be more accurate at higher and more coarse-grained scale levels. In a reconstructive account, scale effects are readily explained by the use of independent schemata at each level.

The power of reconstructive theories is in large part due to their amorphous nature. First, any kind of information that can constrain temporal estimates is acknowledged. Though location in a cyclic, temporal schema is considered the main basis for temporal memory, the use of landmark events with specifically known dates is also assumed. There is no principled reason to stop here, however. To the extent that order codes and duration information exist, even though the evidence suggests that it is limited, it can be used in the reconstructive process to narrow the possible time of the event further. Accordingly, Friedman (1993) includes both order and duration as auxiliary factors in his proposal for a reconstructive theory. Second, critical parts of the theory are only loosely specified, in particular the properties of temporal schemata and the question of what information is employed to access the schemata and place events within them. It is symptomatic of this vagueness that Friedman (1993) excludes research on the internal structure of temporal schemata from his review. It therefore remains a postulate that reconstruction can achieve the degree of accuracy found in temporal estimates and that it will produce the error patterns that are observed. For instance, if the forgetting of information about the event levels off, as in the Ebbinghaus curve, how can it be explained that dating errors apparently continue to increase in a linear fashion?

In the following sections we shall analyze the nature and function of temporal schemata in more detail. The general points we shall suggest are (1) that, to understand memory for time, it is useful to consider the ecological origins of temporal schemata; (2) that converging applications of schemata at different levels can indeed account for both the accuracy and the error patterns of temporal memory; and (3) that it might be fruitful to augment the notion of landmark events by considering the linear temporal structure of the individual's life history in which they are embedded (e.g., events that mark transitions between periods of life).

The cognitive topology of time

Time, of course, is basic to the conception of the universe in the physical sciences. However, the common expression that time is "the fourth dimension" glosses over a number of difficult problems concerning the relation between the three spatial dimensions and the temporal one, which have occupied philosophers and physicists for centuries (cf. Whitrow, 1975). Let us just briefly note two questions from the philosophical discussion of the topology of time. First, is the structure of time linear or cyclic? In the modern philosophical and scientific view, there is no question that time is linear and unidirectional. Cyclic notions of time – for example, that history repeats itself – were entertained among some philosophers in ancient Greece. But such views were fought by the Christian church with the claim that the world has an absolute beginning (Creation) and end (Doomsday), and with the institutionalization of the calendar. Newton's theory of physics and Darwin's theory of evolution finally established the linear view of time in natural science. Cyclic processes in the micro- and macrophysical world are necessary to measure time, but they are held to carry no ontological implications. Second, is time objective or subjective? The answer is both. It has been found logically necessary to distinguish between objective time (also called static time), which is the time of physics and can be described logically with before/after relations, and subjective time (or dynamic time), in which the concepts past, present, and future have meaning. The ontological status of subjective/dynamic time is disputed, however; it is often claimed to be a pure mental construction, either independent from or only partly constrained by the objective time of the material world.

We take as a basic assumption that a topology of time exists as an objective structure among the things, events, and states of the world; we do not believe that time is entirely a subjective construction. However, the cognitive topology of time is intended to refer to the way that this temporal structure is reflected or represented mentally, that is, the functional structure of time that can be observed in behavior, language, thinking – and memory.

Temporal schemata

We employ the term temporal schemata when referring to a person's general knowledge about time patterns. It is important to realize that temporal schemata are not primarily temporal; they are not formed in response to the task of keeping track of time in the abstract, but rather to manage the activities of one's life whose regular patterns they represent. "Everyday life is dominated by routines" (Robinson, 1986, p. 159), and any extended routine may serve as an indicator of time, with more or less precision. Self-reports obtained in several different studies suggest that relating an event to such routines is a frequent means of time estimation (Baddeley, Lewis, & Nimmo-Smith, 1978; Brown, 1990; Friedman, 1987; Thompson et al., 1993). Temporal schemata is thus a shorthand expression for the temporal aspect built into many everyday schemata; they are not a different type of schema and do not have to exist in addition to and separate from "nontemporal schemata." Analysis of the cognitive topology of time must therefore begin with analyzing the life activities that are the basis of temporal schemata – an ecological (Neisser, 1986) or sociological/anthropological (Robinson, 1986) analysis.

Given that such regularities of activity are picked up perceptually, how do the schemata they establish become associated with our conventional time measures, the clock and the calendar? These measures form a multilevel structure, including seconds, minutes, hours, days, weeks, months, years, decades, and centuries. Probably, distinctions as fine as seconds and as gross as centuries are only occasionally relevant to the life of human individuals. But the intermediate seven levels seem to be used regularly for planning, coordinating, and describing the temporal aspects of people's activities. Our personal schemata become infused with calendar time because the things we do are in large part enabled and constrained by social patterns as well as by patterns of the natural environment. To coordinate our life with others, we have to schedule and describe activities in terms of the culturally accepted time scales. We use this common currency to check and rehearse our present status in relation to our schedule and to those of other people with whom we deal (cf. Robinson, 1986). Explicit associations to various levels of calendar time thus become part of many schemata. Separate "calendar schemata," representing the hours of the day and days of the week, for instance (cf. Friedman, 1989), are probably abstractions from the events that are known to ordinarily take place at particular points of that scale. Certainly, without events that occur on specific days of the week, the names of those days would have little practical meaning.

Origins of cyclic schemata. The temporal schemata most commonly mentioned are cyclic – schemata like the year, the week, the day. Friedman (1993) proposes a principled, functional-adaptive argument for the importance of cyclic schemata in cognition. He contends that through most of history human activity has been closely tied to recurrent patterns of the natural environment: day and night, the lunar cycle, the seasons of the year. It has been necessary to adapt to these cyclic variations and useful to pick up and retain information about their course. In contrast, the distance of events in linear time was often irrelevant to activity. Cognitive mechanisms have therefore been developed to support the apprehension of cyclic time, and anthropological studies suggest that cyclic time still governs much of temporal thinking in traditional societies.

The structure of a person's temporal schemata originates from a mixture of natural, cultural-societal, and personal regularities. But the mixture is different for the different temporal scales, with a number of implications for temporal memory. The astronomical cycles of the day (change of light from night to day) and the year (change of climate across the seasons) are, of course, inescapable, natural conditions of human activity. Thus, we will argue that the cycles of the day and the year are the common denominators of all temporal schemata. Independently of the cycles of nature, cultural habits and conventions have made the days of the week (e.g, workday versus weekend) a significant component of temporal schemata in contemporary Western society.

The months of the year represent the underlying year cycle. This division of the year is a cultural convention that is partly coordinated with natural, seasonal variations (at least in most calendars, such as the Gregorian calendar of present Western culture). The impact of the year cycle on individual life is strong for most people, although it differs considerably according to geographical localization, vocation (farmer, teacher and student, office clerk), personal interests (skiing, tennis, opera), and so forth (cf. Robinson, 1986). Thus, in addition to natural changes, social requirements and personal routines will tend to coincide, creating a richly patterned schema of the year. Though its content is partly idiosyncratic, the year schema can therefore be expected to correlate highly with the months of the Gregorian calendar.

The lunar cycle was also important for humans in the past (e.g., it determined whether one could travel at night), but in industrialized countries it has now lost all impact. We therefore expect it to play a negligible role in temporal schemata. Likewise, the internal structure of the calendar months – the 28 to 31 numbered days – has comparatively little influence on daily life, perhaps excepting some economic undertakings (payment of salaries, interest, and bills). An articulated day-of-the-month schema is therefore unlikely to exist. If the exact day of an event is remembered, it must either be retained verbatim or reconstructed by the use of other schemata.

Like the months, the division of the day into hours is a cultural convention largely coordinated with a natural cycle: day-night. The activities of the day cycle are strongly patterned by modern society, through prescribed working hours, school hours, shopping and restaurant hours, television programming, and so on. Although there is still much room for variation at the individual level, according to taste and habits, the activities of most individuals probably adhere pretty closely to a routine schedule of hours (on ordinary days, at least). We can therefore expect that the location of events in the day schema will frequently be specified with some precision by remembered information that is not inherently due to a temporal sense.

The cycle of days of the week is purely cultural; unlike the year and the day, it has no natural counterpart. The week structure differs somewhat between cultures and religions (e.g., the location of the days of rest), and in most industrialized countries it has changed slowly during the past few decades with the decrease of working hours. The week places strong constraints on people's activities, in particular the difference between work days and days of rest. Even people who do not work, or who work on changing days, will have to respect the week structure because a large part of regular social events – classes, sports events, cultural events, and so on – are scheduled on a weekly basis. The circumstances of remembered events may bear perceptual evidence of this social regularity: the streets and the parks of a Western city simply look different on a Sunday. As with the seasons and the times of the day, individuals fill in the slots in the structure very differently and therefore have quite idiosyncratic schemata. To the extent that they take part in social life, however, the general outline of the week should be reflected in people's activities.

Stability of cyclic schemata. The origin of our temporal schemata is interesting from the perspective of memory of time because it affects the kind and amount of information that we can expect to be useful for reconstructing the time of past events. It has implications for forgetting, too. The natural cycles are unchangeable, despite the considerable variations in climate that may occur from year to year and from day to day. Information referring to natural cycles therefore retains its validity as a temporal indicator across the individual's lifetime. Social cycles are also very stable, for instance, the difference between work days and weekend; but they do change across decades (e.g., changes in working hours and mass media programming) and, more importantly, with changes in the person's social situation (e.g., from school to job periods, birth of children in the family, retirement). Information referring to social cycles will lose its temporal validity if the corresponding schema has been modified or replaced and the old schema is no longer accessible. Personal cycles are probably the most variable. The private activities that are chosen within the natural and social constraints often vary from one year to the next – either slight variations in the timing of activities (e.g., hours and days of classes and sports) or larger changes in the type of activities performed (e.g., changing jobs or joining a new club).

It is important, however, that such changes of schemata, and the corresponding loss of veridicality of one's present temporal framework, cannot be assumed to obey the common forgetting function. Many, and perhaps most, changes of activity pattern are sudden shifts, but descriptions of the overall effect on the accuracy of reconstructions from memory have not yet been attempted.

Temporal cues. In order to take advantage of the general knowledge in a temporal schema, pieces of information must be available to invoke the schema and to decide the location of the event within it. Schema-based reconstruction presupposes that memory of the particular event contains sufficient detail to furnish such temporal cues. But what is the nature of these temporal cues? Contextual association theories developed in laboratory research assume that subjects acquire information about the context of to-be-remembered items (e.g., properties of the list of items, of the surrounding situation, or of their own internal state while learning it) that is used later to reconstruct the position of an item in the experimental session.

This notion of contextual cues is echoed in Friedman's (1993) repeated emphasis that it is contextual information that "happens to be associated with a memory" (p. 58) that is the basis for inferring when the event occurred. However, why should the context be an especially useful source of temporal cues? Friedman gives the example that "by remembering that there was snow on a path leading up to the dormitory, a subject could infer that some event must have been during the winter and in the particular year that the subject lived in that dormitory" (p. 47). If the event were that the subject broke a window in his dorm with a snowball, the same inference could be drawn from memory of this event itself, irrespective of the particular context. The point is that the distinction between the event and the context is not what matters in dating events, it is the presence of cues relevant to the subject's temporal schemata.

The emphasis on context is justified in research using laboratory events or public news events. Words in a list or dramatic news, like assassinations and natural disasters, have no temporal regularity that is known by the subjects. Under these conditions, the context (i.e., taking part in the experiment, hearing the news) becomes the major source of temporal cues because it provides connections to other personal activities of the subject (cf. Brown, 1990; Larsen, 1988). For this reason, caution must be exercised when results are generalized from laboratory studies or from studies of news events to the dating of autobiographical memories.

Landmarks and linear temporal structures

Landmark events. Temporal cycles only enable datings to be accurate up to a point. For instance, knowing the hour of the day, the day of the week, and the part of the year for a certain trip to the beach is still very imprecise. Which of the summer months was it, and which week in the month? Moreover, which year was it? There is no obvious cyclic schema longer than the year. The years may differ a great deal (climatic differences, different jobs or homes, changes to the family, different friends and hobbies, travels and vacations, etc.), but the changes are not cyclic. How, then, can the particular cycles of a schema be identified so that the relative times they provide may be pinpointed with sufficient accuracy on the linear time scale of our lives? The standard solution to this problem (cf. Friedman, 1993) is an appeal to a "small minority" of landmark events for which exact dates are learned by rote – a few narrow bridges linking the domains of personal/subjective and social/objective time. Thus, a certain picnic at the beach took place "just before I got married" or "the year I graduated from college."

The assumption that cyclic schemata are anchored to calendar time by landmark events with known calendar dates is intuitively appealing, but solid evidence is scarce: Are the landmarks only a small minority – how small? How are they acquired and forgotten? How accurately are they dated? Are they sufficient to account for the overall accuracy of temporal judgments? What constitutes a suitable landmark event in the first place? The use of landmark events has received some support from think-aloud protocols and subjects' reports of the methods they use in dating (Brown, 1990; Friedman, 1987; Lieury et al., 1980; Thompson et al., 1988). Similarly, the results of Loftus and Marburger (1983) suggest that both public and personal landmarks (the eruption of the volcano Mount St. Helens; one's birthday) reduce dating errors of personal events, provided the landmarks are distinctive ones and are exactly dated. On the other hand, Robinson (1986) found no effect of a personal landmark (the subject's birthday) on the accuracy of dating public events. To be useful in dating, it appears that the landmark event must bear some meaningful relation to the target event.

The dates of landmarks are commonly assumed to be exact and to be acquired by rote learning (e.g., Friedman, 1993), like one's own birthdate which everyone has had to recite innumerable times. Auriat (1992) made a similar point when discussing the year of a child's birth as an aid for parents' dating of events long past. The different places in which a person has lived and worked constitute periods of the past with imprecisely remembered dates, but Auriat shows that if a child's birth can be used as a landmark, the year of a migration is given accurately. The year of the birth serves as an absolute time marker. In addition, the date serves as an annual, cyclic time marker. Every year when celebrating the birthday, the parents consider the passage of linear as well as cyclic time, and the position of the birthday as an absolute as well as a cyclic marker is rehearsed.

As noted above, Thompson et al. (1988) also suggested that the dates of some everyday events are known exactly. However, only a portion of those dates seem to be directly retrieved from memory, and the number decreases substantially across the first year after the events occurred (Larsen & Thompson, in press). When more than a year has passed, it is likely that the dates even of dramatic events such as a volcano eruption or an earthquake (Friedman, 1987) must be reconstructed. Moreover, the reference events found in think-aloud protocols are not regularly accompanied by exact dates. The extent of learning dates by rote repetition may thus be more limited than presupposed by the temporal landmark notion.

Linear structure of the life span. Powerful though they are, the cyclic schemata appear to require more additional information than a few scattered landmarks to achieve a reasonable level of temporal accuracy across the memory of a lifetime. Even if the hour, the day of the week, and the season of events of the past were precisely remembered, they would still be far from making a coherent autobiographical history. Moreover, it is a common observation that people show a strong tendency to recall events in chronological order, or sometimes, for recent periods, in backward order (Linton, 1986). Chronological recall dominates whether the chain of events is contained in a single episode (see Conway, this volume), a short period like a summer (Barsalou, 1988), or even a full life story (Cohen & Faulkner, 1987; Fromholt & Larsen, 1991). Even if it is true that direct representation of time in memory is a "chronological illusion" (Friedman, 1993), it is therefore also true that memories bear strong witness to the temporal order of experience – something for which theories must account.

Friedman (1993) assumes that memory for unique event sequences related by meaning can be accounted for by simple event-to-event order codes that are established when a later event reminds the person of its predecessors (Winograd & Soloway, 1985). We believe that theoretical reliance on such order codes underestimates the importance of linear structure in memory for the time of autobiographical events. Most importantly, it is necessary to be able to distinguish and identify the particular years of the past, that is, memory for time above the level of cyclic schemata.

The common expression "life cycle" might suggest higher-order temporal cycles. However, this metaphor views the structure of life from an external, physical perspective – the material that makes up an individual returns to its original state when the individual has died. The idea of a life cycle may also express a religious view: freeing of the soul and reincarnation. But psychologically – in terms of the individual's experiences and memories – life is not a cycle. Rather, life is linear, it has a definite beginning and a definite end.

The linear structure of life is produced by both natural, biological processes and social-historical influences. Some linear changes such as the increase of capacities in early life, the ability to have offspring in mid-life, and weakening in late life are facts of nature. The definition of stages of life and the conditions they impose on the individual's activities are culturally variable, but constitute a linear progression that is almost equally hard to escape. It is becoming common to describe the structure of the individual life course as a narrative, as the story of the person or the self (e.g., Bruner, 1990; Fitzgerald, this volume). This suggests a coherent structure of one or more settings and a number of episodes of complication and resolution, all ending up in the present situation. There might even be an overriding theme or morale. Some conceive the structure as a dynamic set of narratives that are constantly changing and context dependent (Barclay, 1993, this volume). However, the narrative metaphor may not do justice to the temporal stability and detailed accuracy of knowledge concerning one's life (Larsen, 1993), nor to the gaps and quite unrelated, parallel courses of events that may exist in different domains of one's activities.

Nested levels and extended events. Linear structures are, in fact, central to a number of theories of autobiographical memory, although these theories have been concerned with the issue of hierarchical memory organization rather than with memory for time (see also Conway, this volume). Neisser (1986) presented a general argument for viewing autobiographical memory as a multilevel structure. Building on Gibson's (1979) notion of "nesting," Neisser argued that events are objectively nested within more molar, extended events at numerous higher levels; at the same time, they have more molecular events nested within them at lower tiers. Writing a certain paper, for instance, will be part of a longer-term research effort that is again part of a career, and so on; and the actual writing of the paper includes writing sections, sentences, even single letters at subordinate levels. Moreover, Neisser pointed out that events (at any level) need not be continuous – work on the paper will be interwoven with activities belonging to other superordinate events.

Barsalou (1988) also proposed a hierarchical structure with *extended events* (defined as events that last longer than a day and may be discontinuous) at the upper levels. However, he made the linear organization explicit by using the term "extended-event time line" to refer to the high-level units. "School" is an extended-event time line that may have "kindergarten," "elementary school," "high school," and "university" as ordered parts, each with different extended events as ordered subparts. At some point down the hierarchy, the parts are specific events of less than a day, with even more specific events as subparts.

Extended-event time lines may run in parallel or overlap, for instance, school, relationships, and work (similar to the "domains of action" described by Robinson, 1986). If they are temporally continuous and defined by a common life theme, by a persistent preoccupation, by typical activities, or by stable conditions (e.g., place of living, partner, job, children), we consider *period* a more natural term than extended event (cf. Robinson, 1986; Schooler & Herrmann, 1992).

Linear structure and memory for time. A linear-hierarchical event structure is, of course, inherently temporal since any event occurs in physical time. The temporal relations of an event reside primarily in the various higher-order periods and extended events of which it is a part. Since memory of extended events is assumed to be more durable and accessible than single events, memory for time should be relatively stable. Serious problems of dating may be expected with events that occur repeatedly, including the aggregated "repisodes" identified by Neisser (1981) in the testimony of John Dean in the Watergate trial. But to the extent that single events can be located at one or more higher-order levels, their location in conventional time can be reconstructed – provided that the linear schemata are linked to the calendar.

The linking of linear structures to the calendar has not been systematically studied. It would be useful to investigate, for example, to what extent people know the time of the boundaries between the periods into which they divide their life. Transition events between major life periods have been identified in research on the life span distribution of memories (e.g., Fitzgerald, 1988; Fromholt & Larsen, 1991). Transition events appear to be remembered distinctively and vividly, but there is not much evidence on the dating of them. Research by Auriat (1992) suggests that events of moving from one place to another, which define periods of geographical location, are dated quite well, though often indirectly by reference to other events. Similarly, Robinson (1992) presented results to suggest that memories of events that initiate some personally important period or theme in life (first experience memories) are often distinctive, rich in contextual information, and frequently rehearsed and retold. Distinctiveness, vividness, personal involvement, and rehearsal should increase the chances of recalling at least an approximate date.

It appears obvious that a number of important transition events can be dated with great accuracy. For example, people usually know the exact dates for their marriage and the birth of their children; such events enjoy rehearsal regularly by being celebrated annually. People can also specify, to within a few weeks, the dates of their graduation from high school, entrance into college, or entrance into the military. Transition events should be useful landmarks for dating other life events because they signify location at higher-order levels of the nested event structure. Accurate dating of the transitions could be relatively unimportant because information specific to the target event may serve to place it in temporal schemata at the lower, more fine-grained levels.

Using temporal schemata to date events

In this section, we examine evidence on the internal structure and the use of cyclic, temporal schemata at the three major levels of the day, the week, and the year. The level of the week is considered first because it has received most attention by researchers. An important theoretical question we discuss is whether a specific temporal memory trace for each level must be assumed, represented (with some imprecision) on a scale of time particular to that level, or whether reconstruction based on richly patterned temporal schemata is sufficient to account for the accuracy and the error patterns observed in memory for time.

The week schema

In order to provide evidence regarding the internal structure of the week schema, we shall focus on the ability to localize events on the correct day of the week. As we will see, events must be personal and predictable for accurate location to take place. The essence of a schema is predictability. That is, a schema suggests that certain events will happen and that those events will happen in a certain order or at a certain time. Thus, it is not surprising that unpredictable personal events and news events (for which, generally, the time cannot be predicted) cannot be placed accurately on the correct day of week. Friedman & Wilkins (1985) found that people estimated the weekday of news no better than chance and Friedman (1987) reported a similar result for a personally experienced earthquake, after a delay of only 9 months.

By contrast, personal events are generally placed on or near the correct day of the week. To use some of our recent data for illustration (from two different studies conducted in Aarhus, Denmark, and Manhattan, Kansas), we found errors of dating to be systematic in a way that strongly suggests the use of information concerning the week schema. Briefly stated, errors that are multiples of 7 days (positive or negative) are severely overrepresented. The frequency of errors from the two studies is shown in Figure 5.1.

These data show that people are often able to correctly localize an event with respect to day of the week, even when they are wrong about the absolute date of the event. Furthermore, when they are wrong about the day of the week, they tend to pick days adjacent to the correct day. This is shown clearly in Figure 5.2 where the errors are transformed into day-of-week errors with the peak value at zero indicating that the participants correctly identified the day of the week (even though they may have put it in the wrong week).

The increased frequency of selecting days adjoining the correct one might be regarded as reflecting the uncertainty distribution of an underlying, inexact memory representation of the original day of the week. Huttenlocher, Hedges, and Prohaska (1992) put forward exactly this interpretation to explain similar findings. They collected data by asking more than 800 participants to recall the day of the week of a specific personal event, namely, an interview for a national survey that had been performed 1 to 11 weeks earlier. The responses were tabulated as a confusion matrix of the frequencies with which each original day was placed on each estimated day. An account solely based on an inexact memory trace would predict symmetrical error distributions around each actual day. Contrary to that prediction, Huttenlocher et al. found skewed distributions, for example, Monday events were more often displaced to a Tuesday than to a Sunday.

To explain such irregularities, Huttenlocher et al. (1992) proposed that the dating estimates derived from the underlying memory representation (which they assumed to be dispersed according to an exponential function) were modified and biased by boundary effects produced by a week schema. Thus, the week schema might indicate that the event happened during a certain subcategory of days of the week. The boundary effect arises because, for instance, with the workdays (Monday to Friday) as a subcategory, Mondays and Fridays cannot readily be displaced in more than one direction. Huttenlocher et al. considered just the workdays and the weekend as possible subcategories. After fitting various versions of a 22-parameter mathematical formulation of the model to the confusion matrix frequencies, Huttenlocher et al. concluded that only the workdays function as a unit within the week schema that creates boundary effects, whereas the two weekend days are separate entities in the schema. This may be described as a 5 + 1 + 1 structure of the week.

A workdays category was also suggested by Thompson et al. (1993). Their subjects used a blank calendar to date personal episodes recorded in structured diaries up to 14 weeks before the test. However, they assumed no underlying, temporal memory trace

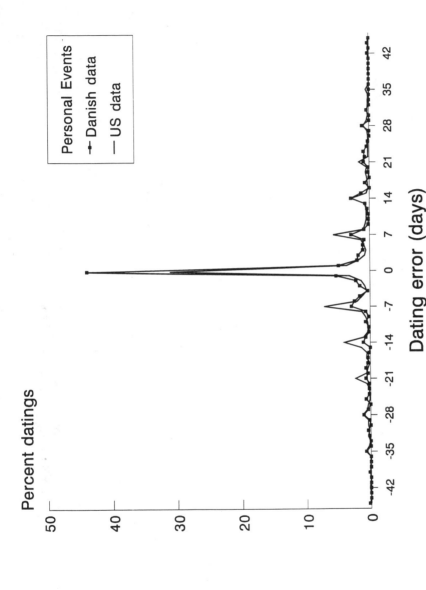

Figure 5.1 Difference between remembered and actual dates of personal events, tested 1 week after a 3- to 4-month diary period. Percent of total responses are plotted. (Data from Larsen and Thompson [in press], Exp. 1, Test 1 [Danish data] and Exp. 2 [US data]).

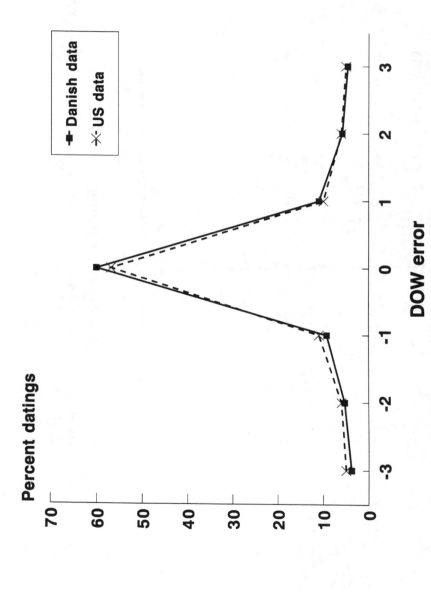

Figure 5.2 Day-of-week (DOW) errors calculated from the data in Figure 5.1 by totalling across 7-day intervals, each interval centered at an error magnitude that is a multiple of 7 (0 modulo 7, that is, 0, ±7, ±14, . . .).

corresponding to the day of the week. Rather, it was supposed that subjects possessed (or could deduce from schematic knowledge) information for each event about which part of the week it was likely to have occurred in. Thompson et al. suggested that this information could be more or less precise – pointing to either the workdays or the weekend, or to a subpart of the workdays ("mid-week"), or even to a specific day. If more than one day was indicated, the subject was assumed to select among these days by random guessing. Thompson et al. demonstrated that a mixture of such partial information at different levels of precision could generate the error pattern found empirically (the seemingly exponential function shown in Figure 5.2).

The subdivisions of the week schema considered by Huttenlocher et al. (1992) and by Thompson et al. (1993) were entirely intuitive. What subdivisions actually enter into the subjects' temporal estimation process? This question was investigated in the study by Larsen and Thompson (in press, Exp. 1). Ten months after the diary writing period, participants were each asked to localize a random sample of their personal events on the day-of-week scale by choosing freely which days, and how many days, to include for each event. A similar task was also completed on separate scales for the months, the day of the month, and the hour of the day (this will be discussed below).

A large number of different groupings of days of the week were used by the subjects, thus supporting the idea of a multilevel schema. The most common response (61%) was to pick a single day. The frequency with which single days were chosen ranged from 13% (Friday) to 5% (Monday). The five weekdays constituted the most frequently used multiple-day category (14%). Monday to Thursday formed the next most frequent category (4% of choices). The weekend category was also found (3% of choices), but other groups of two neighboring days were equally frequent (e.g., Thursday-Friday). In only 1% of the cases, participants felt completely unable to constrain the range days. For all sizes of day groups, the proportion of choices that were veridical (i.e., included the correct day) exceeded chance level.

The diaries included news items as well as personal events, and memory for the day of the week that the news was heard was tested by the same procedure. The overall pattern of day-of-week estimates was very similar to that found for personal events; however, it differed in two respects: (1) the proportion of estimates that included the correct day was only 60%, as opposed to 75% for personal events, and (2) participants made fewer single-day choices and more often left all 7 days open. Both differences reveal a greater level of uncertainty about the day of the week of news, reflecting an indistinctive schematic structure of the week scale. Instead, news events are to a large extent dated by reference to the personal component of news stories, that is, the reception context (as shown in Larsen & Thompson, in press). This is in accordance with the theory of memory for public events proposed by N. R. Brown and his associates (Brown et al., 1985; Brown, 1990).

To summarize, the schema for the week of these modern Western individuals seems to consist of one relatively frequent category of days (the workweek) and a number of less frequently occurring categories, most of which are subcategories of the work week. The variety of day groups occurring in the choices suggests that the week schema is quite flexible. Thus, it appears inappropriate to reduce the week schema to include only one or two predefined groups of days. A model that allows flexibility and still offers precision can be formulated by ignoring the individual days and considering only the size of day groups. Larsen and Thompson (in press) used the day group frequencies cited above in such a model, and demonstrated that it provided a remarkably close fit to the actual dating errors obtained under different conditions. Judging from this evidence at the level of the week schema, dating accuracy and dating errors may be explained without making elaborate assumptions about separate memory traces at each level of the temporal scale or about particular distributions to describe the uncertainty of memory traces in the temporal dimension.

It may appear a surprising claim that the degree of accuracy observed in day-of-week memory can be explained by a reconstructive theory. But note that even when a particular instance of a weekly routine becomes indistinguishable from other episodes of the same kind (e.g., another tennis match), it can still be correctly localized in time with respect to the day-of-week scale. If a person is asked about a tennis episode, and he always plays tennis on Mondays, he does not have to remember the specific episode in question to know that it happened on a Monday. On the other hand, when trying to estimate the time of an episode that has nothing to do with tennis, the person may still find that the regular tennis date helps to constrain the possible range of days. For example, a golf game would be unlikely to have occured on a Monday, whereas having a beer at the local pub in the company of a tennis partner might be very likely.

In short, all temporal structures can be used for assessing the time of episodes in either of two ways: By rendering it likely that the episode occurred during a certain day or period, or, less precisely, by rendering it unlikely. Furthermore, several pieces of partial information can be combined to narrow the plausible part of the week. A target event that contains properties associated with the workweek and, at the same time, properties associated with activities normally conducted on Fridays and Saturdays – an example could be an episode of working late and going directly to a party – is temporally constrained from two directions and thus will receive a single-day estimate (Friday).

The day schema

The day cycle is an even more obvious candidate for a hierarchical temporal schema than the week. The measuring units of conventional time (the hours) are completely arbitrary; but socially and biologically determined units exist that are more meaningful. The 24-hour day is divided into day and night, and the day is further split into morning, afternoon, and evening. The empirical evidence concerning the day schema is limited, however. Memory for the time of day has been found to be remarkably accurate for personal events as well as for news events up to 20 years old – at least as accurate as memory for the day of the week (Baddeley et al., 1978; Bruce & van Pelt, 1989; Friedman, 1987; Friedman & Wilkins, 1985). Time of day is reported more often in free recall of temporal information than day of week or day of month (Robinson, 1976), and with higher confidence (Friedman & Wilkins, 1985). Furthermore, Friedman (1991)

Table 5.1 *Accuracy of hour-of-day groups chosen by subjects*

Size of group (hours)	Frequency	Expected accuracy	Observed accuracy
3	68	.17	.81
4	90	.22	.70
5	51	.28	.78
6	28	.33	.79
7	19	.39	.89

Note: Since only 2% of events took place during the night (12–6 A.M.), expected accuracy is calculated as the chance of hitting the correct time in a day of 18 hours.

found that even children of 4 years were able, under some conditions, to point to the correct time of day of an event that took place more than 2 months earlier; in contrast, correct month judgments were not established until 6 years of age and day-of-week judgments not even at 8 years. To our knowledge, this study by Friedman (1991) is the first to specifically address the role of schematic knowledge in memory for the time of day. We shall briefly describe some unpublished data from adults that elucidate the functional structure of the day schema.

If the linguistic divisions of the day are actually the units of a functional day schema, they should be reflected in people's estimates of the time of day of past events. In the day group study described in the previous section, the participants also indicated the starting time of each event by choosing a group of hours from the 24 hours of the day (this part of Exp. 1 in Larsen & Thompson [in press] was carried out by Hansen [1993]). All the chosen groups of hours were continuous intervals with a modal interval size of 4 hours (ranging from 2 to 11 hours). There were no single-hour groups, suggesting that the functional units of the day schema are less fine grained than the scale of hours. If the divisions between morning, afternoon, evening, and night are set at midnight, noon, and 6 o'clock (A.M. and P.M.), only 25% of the chosen time intervals crossed the boundaries of these temporal chunks, whereas 50% would be expected by chance. Thus, there seems to exist a reasonably stable structure of the day schema at this level. Moreover, this structure seems to provide for veridical memory. The frequency of groups that included the correct hour was very high. For every interval size from 3 to 7 hours, which accounted for 93% of the responses, correct estimates were found at least twice as often as predicted by chance (see Table 5.1).

These results confirm the accurate reconstruction of time of day reported by previous studies, and they imply that people often possess schematic time information at a level more precise than the four conventional parts of day. With a retention interval of about 1 year, this precision is quite impressive, most likely reflecting the abundance of natural cues to time of day in the environment. However, it is not clear whether the quantitative distribution of hour-of-day estimates can be explained by reconstruction to the same extent as day-of-week estimates. As a first step toward understanding the role of the day cycle in memory, the study raises more questions than it answers.

The year schema

The year is conventionally divided into months that are further roughly subdivided into weeks. But what are the functional units of the year cycle? On intuitive grounds, the 52 weeks are a much too fine-grained and arbitrary scale for cognitively representing the year. Accordingly, most of the scant research available has considered memory of the month of events. Friedman (1987) and Friedman and Wilkins (1985) have found estimates of the month to be better than chance for children down to 6 years of age (Friedman, 1991). Evidence of memory for the month was also obtained by Auriat (1992) who interviewed Belgian couples about their migration and employment history. Comparison of their responses to records in the population register revealed that the month of a migration was often correctly recalled, even when the estimated year was wrong. This accumulation of errors that are multiples of 12 months is shown in Figure 5.3. A similar error systematicity was reported by Rubin (1982, Exp. 5), who asked diary keepers to recall personal events, date them, and finally control the datings against their diaries. Finally, consistencies when events are dated twice support the accuracy of memory for month; Robinson (1976) reported that redatings to a different year most often did not change the month.

Clearly, the memory of many events contains information that allows accurate judgment of the month of the year. Is memory for months the result of a temporal memory trace on the scale of the year – perhaps modulated by a year schema – or can it be explained by the application of higher-level units in the year schema to constrain the judgments? Robinson (1986) has begun to address the possible structure of the year schema. Robinson considered the cyclic pattern of semesters and vacations that is inescapable for students and teachers. He found that in students' free recall of everyday memories, the number of events were unevenly distributed over the year according to this pattern. This study did not include information about the original time of the events that would be required to investigate the accuracy of temporal memory. However, Huttenlocher et al. (1988) showed that memory for the months of on-campus movies was indeed affected by the boundaries of academic quarters.

We can thus glimpse some of the internal structure that may reside in people's year schema. The utility of this information for reconstructing the time of past events is still uncertain. Further research will be demanding because memory confusions between different cycles of the year schema can only be observed if the time window spanned by the study includes multiple cycles, that is, at least 2 years.

Are the scale levels independent?

We have argued that temporal information is usually deduced by relating an event to a number of cyclic schemata, and that for each of these schemata, the information can either point to a single unit or to a period within the schema. This may seem to imply that we are dealing with separate pieces of information linking the event to each schema, which is also suggested by the scale effects (i.e., independence of performance at different levels of temporal scale) reported by Friedman and Wilkins (1985). Like-

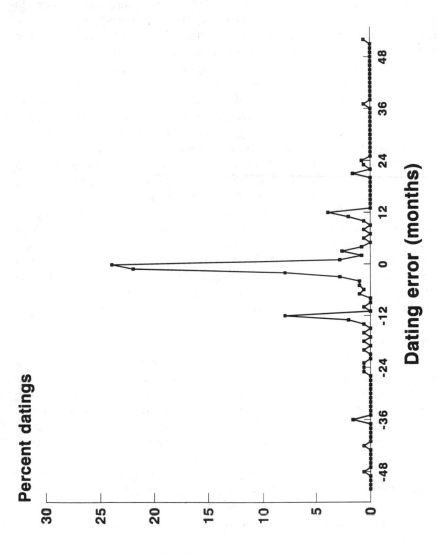

Figure 5.3 Deviation of remembered month and year of moving to a new home from the actual time of the move. (Data from Auriat, 1992).

wise, an account of temporal memory in terms of scale-specific tagging of episodes would predict such independent performance.

However, independent performance is not a necessary consequence of independent schematic reconstructions at each level. The three major levels of cyclic schemata (time of day, day of week, and time of year) often interact in determining what happens in everyday life. Thus, the structure of the day is usually different on workdays and on the weekend; some events occur only in the early evening, only on workdays, and not in the summer, like evening classes. Similarly, the semester and vacation categories proposed by Robinson (1986) as parts of the year schema for many people affect the activities that are possible and likely to occur during the cycles of days and hours in the different periods. The consequence is that a single piece of information about an event may constrain the time of its occurrence at several levels. Though the frequency of such multilevel constraints cannot easily be predicted, we must expect that the accuracy of temporal judgments at the various levels will not be entirely independent.

Scattered evidence of such points of convergence between different scale levels is found in the reports of the subjects of Baddeley et al. (1978) and Friedman (1987). More formally, in the study by Larsen and Thompson (in press, Exp. 1) a significant concordance was detected between hitting the correct day of the week and hitting the correct week when events were dated. This was the case for personal events as well as for news events; the z-values aggregated across the χ^2 of 11 subjects were 6.93 for personal events, 5.56 for news. This result clearly demonstrates that temporal judgments at the level of the week schema are not entirely independent of judgments at some higher level. It is tempting to interpret the superordinate level as a semester schema because the 14-week diary period of the study almost coincided with the semester.

Schema updating and forgetting

For most people, temporal schemata such as the seasons of the year, portions of the day cycle (e.g., meal times), and the distinction between the workday and weekend remain constant over their lifetime. At the same time, the importance of those schemata may change over time; for example, the distinction between weekend and workdays may be less clear-cut during college years than it is during later years in the workplace. A good example of the changing salience of schemata can be seen in the academic year. Through all the years of school until college graduation, the academic year is very salient and a good tool to use as an aid in estimating when events occurred during the year. For most people, the salience of the academic year is reduced markedly after graduation from college, but it reappears when one has children of school age. It remains salient until one's children have finished school and then, once more, becomes relatively unimportant.

To remain calibrated to current conditions, schemata need to be updated from time to time with the frequency of updating depending on the changing activities of the individual. One might play bridge on Monday evenings while in college and continue that activity later in life with a Thursday evening bridge group. College students have a workweek schema that has to be updated each semester (e.g., course X meets on Monday, Wednesday, and Friday at 10 A.M.; mathematics club meets on the second Thursday of each month). As a schemata is updated, the previous schema will probably be forgotten unless it is rehearsed as part of the narrative of one's life. For example, it is likely that many college students cannot remember which courses were taken 1 year ago. It is even less likely that the student could recall the time when those courses met. On the other hand, the student may remember the meeting time of a social club for many years because it was tied to an important event that is well-rehearsed (e.g., I met my husband at the bridge club which met every Wednesday evening).

We assume that the accuracy of reconstructing dates of events depends mainly on the degree to which people can bring relevant temporal schemata to bear. Thus, the implication that updating of schematic information has for reconstructing the dates of events is clear: dating accuracy will decrease as relevant temporal schemata are forgotten or overwritten. In this perspective, the linear, Weberian growth of dating errors that was discussed at the beginning of the chapter is an indirect and quite complex phenomenon, not an indication of a unitary temporal dimension in memory. First, as events recede in time higher-order schemata must be invoked that provide more coarse-grained estimates. However, errors at a more fine-grained level, for example, day of the week, may increase at a slower rate than the overall magnitude of dating errors. Second, the gradual accumulation of schema changes will continue to increase error magnitude. This should occur at all levels of time, though again not necessarily at the same rate; for example, time of year and time of day should be the most resistant. Third, loss of information about the individual event, which may occur in a negatively accelerated fashion, as in the Ebbinghaus (1885/1964) forgetting function, will impoverish the cues that are available for accessing the temporal schemata.

The impact of cue forgetting might normally not be noticeable because other cues can substitute, and, generally, higher levels of schemata are not affected by lower-level errors. However, massive forgetting of event details, as in Alzheimer's dementia (Fromholt & Larsen, 1991) and the source amnesia observed in other amnesic conditions (Schacter, Harbluk, & McLachlan, 1984), may prevent access to temporal schemata. If there are few schemata to rely upon, as in the period of early childhood (Rubin, 1982), even slight cue forgetting could be damaging to temporal estimates and thus to the preservation of a coherent sense of history. In the domain of public news, schemata are similarly poor, suggesting an interesting parallel between childhood amnesia and the common "amnesia" for public news events among adult citizens (Larsen, 1992).

Conclusion

The time of past events is, on the average, remembered quite accurately and with little systematic bias. But errors are frequent; they increase with increasing distance into the past; they are larger for events that are distant from the person's own life than for events closely related to it; and they often occur independently at different levels of the conventional time scale.

We have argued that time in the past is largely reconstructed rather than just retrieved from memory. Friedman (1993) showed that considerable evidence favors this theory over alternative theories, such as associative order theories, strength theories, and time-tag theories. Nevertheless, reconstructive theory is only loosely specified. The theory postulates two main sources of information for temporal judgments, namely, temporal schemata and landmark events. The general accuracy of temporal judgments requires that temporal schemata are developed to agree extremely well with the temporal structure of real life, as it is lived by the particular person. Research on the origin, organization, and function of these temporal schemata is scarce, however. We suggested that natural and sociocultural constraints render it likely that three levels of temporal schemata will be prominent: the day, the week (at least in Western societies), and the year.

Recent studies have shown the effectiveness of the week schema for dating autobiographical events at intervals close to 1 year into the past. This research also provides some understanding of the structure of the week schema that does not seem to reduce to a simple subdivision into workdays and weekend. The periodicity of errors when people judge the day of the week of events can be accounted for by a process of constrained guessing within the boundaries of parts of the week schema. Similar investigations at other levels of the time scale are called for to explicate the reconstructive view of memory for time.

It is commonly assumed that the temporal estimates reconstructed from these cyclic schemata are anchored to the conventional linear calendar time by reference to a few explicitly dated landmark events. In particular, to distinguish between the individual years of one's life, temporal reference points that are long-lived and noncyclic must exist. There is even less solid knowledge about the properties and incidence of landmark events than about temporal schemata. However, we suggest that memory of the approximate time of events that occupy important points in the linear structure of a person's autobiography (e.g., transition points and first experience memories [cf. Robinson, 1992]) may be sufficient to reconstruct time with reasonable accuracy even over intervals commensurate with the human life span.

References

Auriat, N. (1992). Autobiographical memory and survey methodology: Furthering the bridge between two disciplines. In M. A. Conway, D. C. Rubin, H. Spinnler, & W. A. Wagenaar (Eds.), *Theoretical perspectives on autobiographical memory* (pp. 295–312). Dordrecht, The Netherlands: Kluwer Academic.

Baddeley, A. D., Lewis, V., & Nimmo-Smith, I. (1978). When did you last . . . ? In M. M. Gruneberg & R. N. Sykes (Eds.), *Practical aspects of memory* (pp. 77–83). San Diego: Academic Press.

Barsalou, L. W. (1988). The content and organization of autobiographical memories. In U. Neisser & E. Winograd (Eds.), *Remembering reconsidered: Ecological and traditional approaches to the study of memory* (pp. 193–243). New York: Cambridge University Press.

Barclay, C. R. (1993). Remembering ourselves. In G. M. Davies & R. H. Logie (Eds.), *Memory in everyday life* (pp. 285–309). Amsterdam: North-Holland.

Boswell, J. (1791/1980). *Life of Johnson.* Harmondsworth: Penguin.

Bradburn, N. M., Rips, L. J., & Shevell, S. K. (1987). Answering autobiographical questions: The impact of memory and inference on surveys. *Science, 236,* 158–161.

Brewer, W. F. (1988). Memory for randomly sampled autobiographical events. In U. Neisser & E. Winograd (Eds.), *Remembering reconsidered: Ecological and traditional approaches to the study of memory* (pp. 21–90). New York: Cambridge University Press.

Brown, N. R. (1990). Organization of public events in long-term memory. *Journal of Experimental Psychology: General, 119,* 297–314.

Brown, N. R., Rips, L. J., and Shevell, S. K. (1985). The subjective dates of natural events in very-long-term memory. *Cognitive Psychology, 17,* 139–177.

Bruce, D., & van Pelt, M. (1989). Memories of a bicycle tour. *Applied Cognitive Psychology, 3,* 137–156.

Bruner, J. (1990). *Acts of meaning.* Cambridge, MA: Harvard University Press.

Cohen, G., & Faulkner, D. (1987). Life span changes in autobiographical memory. In M. M. Gruneberg, P. E. Morris, & R. N. Sykes (Eds.), *Practical aspects of memory: Current research and issues* (Vol. 1, pp. 277–282). Chichester, UK: Wiley.

Ebbinghaus, H. (1885/1964). *Memory: A contribution to experimental psychology.* New York: Dover.

Fitzgerald, J. M. (1988). Vivid memories and the reminiscence phenomenon: The role of self narrative. *Human Development, 31,* 261–273.

Friedman, W. J. (1987). A follow-up to "Scale effects in memory for the time of events": The earthquake study. *Memory and Cognition, 15,* 518–520.

—— (1989). The representation of temporal structure in children, adolescents, and adults. In I. Levin & D. Zakay (Eds.), *Time and human cognition: A life span perspective* (pp. 259–304). Amsterdam: North-Holland.

—— (1991). The development of children's memory for the time of past events. *Child Development, 62,* 139–155.

—— (1993). Memory for the time of past events. *Psychological Bulletin, 113,* 44–66.

Friedman, W. J., & Wilkins, A. J. (1985). Scale effects in memory for the time of past events. *Memory and Cognition, 13,* 168–175.

Fromholt, P., & Larsen, S. F. (1991). Autobiographical memory in normal aging and primary degenerative dementia (dementia of Alzheimer type). *Journal of Gerontology: Psychological Sciences, 46,* 85–91.

Gibson, J. J. (1975). Events are perceivable but time is not. In J. T. Fraser & N. Lawrence (Eds.), *The study of time II* (pp. 295–301). Berlin: Springer-Verlag.

—— (1979). *The ecological approach to visual perception.* Boston: Houghton Mifflin.

Glenberg, A. M. (1987). Temporal context and recency. In D. S. Gorfein & R. R. Hoffman (Eds.), *Memory and learning: The Ebbinghaus Centennial Conference* (pp. 173–190). Hillsdale, NJ: Lawrence Erlbaum.

Gray, P. G. (1955). The memory factor in social surveys. *Journal of the American Statistical Association, 50,* 344–363.

Hansen, T. (1993). *Day of week and hour of day in memory for everyday events.* Unpublished master's thesis, University of Aarhus, Denmark.

Hinrichs, J. V. (1970). A two-process memory-strength theory for judgments of recency. *Psychological Review, 77,* 223–233.

Huttenlocher, J., Hedges, L., & Prohaska, V. (1988). Hierarchical organization in ordered domains: Estimating the dates of events. *Psychological Review, 95,* 471–484.

—— (1992). Memory for day of the week: A 5 + 2 day cycle. *Journal of Experimental Psychology: General, 121,* 313–325.

Larsen, S. F. (1988). Remembering without experiencing: Memory for reported events. In U. Neisser & E. Winograd (Eds.), *Remembering reconsidered: Ecological and traditional approaches to the study of memory* (pp. 326–355). New York: Cambridge University Press.

—— (1992). Potential flashbulbs: Memories of ordinary news as the baseline. In E. Winograd & U. Neisser (Eds.), *Affect and accuracy in recall. Studies of "flashbulb" memories* (pp. 32–64). New York: Cambridge University Press.

—— (1993). Memory of schemata, details, and selves. In G. M. Davies & R. H. Logie (Eds.), *Memory in everyday life* (pp. 310–315). Amsterdam: North-Holland.

Larsen, S. F., & Thompson, C. P. (in press). Reconstructive memory in the dating of personal and public events. *Memory and Cognition.*

Lieury, A., Aiello, B., Lepreux, D., & Mellet, M. (1980). Le rôle des rèperes dans la récuperation et la datation des souvenirs. *Année Psychologique, 80,* 149–167.

Linton, M. (1986). Ways of searching and the contents of memory. In D. C. Rubin (Ed.), *Autobiographical memory* (pp. 51–67). New York: Cambridge University Press.

Loftus, E. F., & Marburger, W. (1983). Since the eruption of Mt. St. Helens, has anyone beaten you up? Improving the accuracy of retrospective reports with landmark events. *Memory and Cognition, 11,* 114–120.

Melges, F. T. (1982). *Time and the inner future: A temporal approach to psychiatric disorders.* New York: Wiley.

Michon, J. A., Pouthas, V., & Jackson, J. L. (1988). *Guyau and the idea of time.* Amsterdam: North-Holland.

Murdock, B. B. (1974). *Human Memory: Theory and data.* Potomac, MD: Lawrence Erlbaum.

Neisser, U. (1981). John Dean's memory: A case study. *Cognition, 9,* 1–22.

—— (1986). Nested structure in autobiographical memory. In D. C. Rubin (Ed.), *Autobiographical memory* (pp. 71–81). New York: Cambridge University Press.

Neter, J., & Waksberg, J. (1964). A study of response errors in expenditures data from household interviews. *Journal of the American Statistical Association, 59,* 17–55.

Robinson, J. A. (1976). Sampling autobiographical memory. *Cognitive Psychology, 8,* 578–595.

—— (1986). Temporal reference systems and autobiographical memory. In D. C. Rubin (Ed.), *Autobiographical memory* (pp. 159–188). New York: Cambridge University Press.

—— (1992). First experience memories: Contexts and functions in personal histories. In M. A. Conway, D. C. Rubin, H. Spinnler, & W. A. Wagenaar (Eds.), *Theoretical perspectives on autobiographical memory* (pp. 223–240). Dordrecht, The Netherlands: Kluwer Academic.

Rubin, D. C. (1982). On the retention function for autobiographical memory. *Journal of Verbal Learning and Verbal Behavior, 21,* 21–38.

Rubin, D. C., & Baddeley, A. (1989). Telescoping is not time compression: A model of the dating of autobiographical events. *Memory and Cognition, 17,* 653–661.

Schacter, D. L., Harbluk, J. L., & McLachlan, D. R. (1984). Retrieval without recollection: An experimental analysis of source amnesia. *Journal of Verbal Learning and Verbal Behavior, 23,* 593–611.

Schooler, J., & Herrmann, D. J. (1992). There is more to episodic memory than just episodes. In M. A. Conway, D. C. Rubin, H. Spinnler, & W. A. Wagenaar (Eds.), *Theoretical perspectives on autobiographical memory* (pp. 241–262). Dordrecht, The Netherlands: Kluwer Academic.

Thompson, C. P. (1982). Memory for unique personal events: The roommate study. *Memory and Cognition, 10,* 324–332.

—— (1985). Memory for unique personal events: Effects of pleasantness. *Motivation and Emotion, 9,* 277–289.

Thompson, C. P., Skowronski, J. J., & Betz, A. L. (1993). The use of partial temporal information in dating personal events. *Memory and Cognition, 21,* 352–360.

Thompson, C. P., Skowronski, J. J., & Lee, D. J. (1988). Telescoping in dating naturally occurring events. *Memory and Cognition, 16,* 461–468.

Wagenaar, W. A. (1986). My memory: A study of autobiographical memory over six years. *Cognitive Psychology, 18,* 225–252.

White, R. T. (1982). Memory for personal events. *Human Learning, 1,* 171–183.

Whitrow, G. J. (1975). *The nature of time.* Harmondsworth, UK: Penguin.

Winograd, E., & Soloway, R. M. (1985). Reminding as a basis for temporal judgment. *Journal of Experimental Psychology: Learning, Memory, and Cognition, 11,* 65–74.

Yntema, D. B., & Trask, F. P. (1963). Recall as a search process. *Journal of Verbal Learning and Verbal Behavior, 2,* 65–74.

6   The pliability of autobiographical memory: Misinformation and the false memory problem

Robert F. Belli and Elizabeth F. Loftus

One aspect of autobiographical memory that has received considerable attention during the past two decades deals with the psychological mechanisms that underlie the memory and report of eyewitnesses. The *misinformation effect* is particularly concerned with what happens to people when they witness an event, such as a crime or accident, and are later misinformed about some aspect of the original event (Loftus, 1992). As is well known, eyewitnesses are not secluded after witnessing an event. Rather, they may discuss the event with other witnesses, and they are usually extensively questioned by criminal justice personnel both before and during any criminal or civil court appearance (Loftus, 1975, 1979). Such interactions provide ripe opportunities for the introduction of misinformation.

Recent experimental work supports the view that misinformation affects memory, and therefore, that actual eyewitnesses may be susceptible to making unintentional false reports. In fact, false reports have been relatively easy to induce in the laboratory. After exposure to misinformation, subjects have been induced to report having seen a variety of nonexistent objects, such as yield signs (Loftus, Miller, & Burns, 1978), hammers (McCloskey & Zaragoza, 1985a), eggs (Ceci, Ross, & Toglia, 1987), mustaches (Gibling & Davies, 1988), broken glass (Loftus & Palmer, 1974) and even something as large as a barn (Loftus, 1975). This research shows that misinformation can be dangerously robust in compromising the accuracy of the memory and report of actual eyewitnesses.

Although we are convinced of the dangers of misinformation, the precise psychological mechanisms responsible for false reports are not completely understood and continue to be investigated. Early experimental work (see especially Loftus, 1975; Loftus et al., 1978; Loftus & Palmer, 1974) appeared to support the existence of *memory impairment*, that is, that misinformation can either alter or make less accessible the original memory representation of the event. Although it is universally accepted that misinformation will exacerbate inaccurate reports in experimental contexts, the role that memory impairment plays has been the subject of a lively, and sometimes heated, debate (see Belli, 1989; Loftus & Hoffman, 1989; Loftus, Schooler, & Wagenaar, 1985;

157

McCloskey & Zaragoza, 1985a, 1985b; Tversky & Tuchin, 1989; Zaragoza & McCloskey, 1989). This debate has not only led to challenges regarding the memory impairment hypothesis, but as will be made clearer, has led some to question whether exposure to misinformation in real life can color the quality of eyewitness reports.

In addressing this debate, our thinking regarding the psychological processes responsible for the misinformation effect has become much more sophisticated and complex. In particular, the memory impairment hypothesis is but one of several hypotheses that we believe are responsible for the effect. For instance, an alternative way to view misinformation effects is in terms of the source misattribution hypothesis: the exploration of whether people genuinely, but incorrectly, remember that the misinformation occurred at the original event (Ackil & Zaragoza, 1992; Belli, Lindsay, Gales, & McCarthy, 1994; Carris, Zaragoza, & Lane, 1992; Lindsay, 1990, 1994; Lindsay & Johnson, 1989; Loftus, Donders, Hoffman, & Schooler, 1989; Loftus & Hoffman, 1989; Weingardt, Toland, & Loftus, 1994; Zaragoza & Lane, 1991, 1994; Zaragoza & Moore, 1990).

In a variety of contexts, people have been noted to misattribute the sources of actual events, such that the exact origin of experiences are misremembered. As an example, Neisser and Harsch (1992) found, in their study of people's memory of the *Challenger* explosion, that a number of individuals were unable to accurately remember the setting in which they initially had heard about the explosion; they tended to misremember a later setting in which they had received additional information about the incident as the original setting. Brewer (1988) found that these "mislocations" of events occurred with mundane experiences as well. Although these source misattributions involve the remembering of a real event in the "wrong time slice" (Brewer, 1988), the misinformation effect more dramatically points to occasions in which people may misremember an event as real, when in fact, it never had occurred. Further, such source misattributions are not confined to situations in which people are witnesses to an external event, as there is evidence that people can at times remember having themselves performed actions that in actuality never took place (see Johnson, Hashtroudi, & Lindsay [1993] for a comprehensive review). In other words, people may misattribute the source of a memory of their own behavior to reality, when in actuality the source lay elsewhere, perhaps in imagination or suggestion.

In this chapter, we describe some of these subtle issues that have been uncovered in exploring the misinformation effect. In order to do this, we review a number of major experimental studies that are particularly insightful in elucidating the memory mechanisms that are involved. Following this discussion, we derive several implications of having a memory system that has difficulty determining what has occurred. There is no doubt that the misinformation effect has provided tremendous understanding, and has broad implications, in a number of areas that involve autobiographical memory. In particular, one area in which we pay particularly close attention is how the misinformation effect may have devastating consequences concerning people who report being the victims of childhood abuse. There has been a recent upsurge of claims by adults, in the course of therapy or through reading self-help books, of having recovered repressed memories of having been victimized (Loftus, 1993). As will be detailed below, we illustrate how it is possible for adults to honestly but falsely remember being victims of childhood abuse. That is, we have become concerned that some of these reports are honest fabrications due to suggestions introduced during treatment (see also Belli & Loftus, 1994; Lindsay & Read, 1994; Loftus, 1993).

The memory impairment debate

To appreciate current thinking regarding the misinformation effect, it is helpful to review the debate on whether misinformation leads to memory impairment. This debate has led to proposals of several impairment and nonimpairment hypotheses as being responsible for the misinformation effect, and the introduction of a number of different test procedures to examine these hypotheses.[1] To help the reader navigate through this web of experimental research, Table 6.1 presents an outline of the representative studies, tests, and hypotheses that will be discussed.

Our story begins with two critical experimental studies (Loftus et al., 1978; McCloskey & Zaragoza, 1985a) that not only set the stage for the memory impairment debate but also frame many of the issues that motivate current work. Loftus et al. introduced the standard methodology for exploring the misinformation effect, and provided evidence, accepted by many experimental psychologists at the time, that memory impairment was likely to result from exposure to misinformation. In direct contrast, McCloskey and Zaragoza provided evidence that misinformation does not lead to memory impairment, and by implication, that misinformation will not bias the accuracy of real-world eyewitness reports.

The methodology introduced by Loftus et al. (1978) to explore the misinformation effect involved three phases. In the first phase, subjects were shown a series of slides that depicted an event, such as a traffic accident. During this phase, subjects were shown a critical event item, such as a Coke can.[2] In the second phase, half the subjects were verbally misled with a postevent item, for example, they may have been told that

---

[1] In many ways, the exploration of the misinformation effect is reminiscent of an earlier generation's exploration of retroactive interference (for discussion on parallels, see Bekerian & Bowers, 1983; Chandler, 1989; Lindsay & Johnson, 1989; Loftus & Hoffman, 1989; Tversky & Tuchin, 1989; Zaragoza, McCloskey, & Jamis, 1987). Explorations of both the misinformation effect and of retroactive interference involve examining the influence of later information on the ability to remember earlier information. Both explorations have led to several hypotheses being introduced to explain the effects. We will consider "retrieval-based impairment," "storage-based impairment," and "source misattribution" as explanations of the misinformation effect; these hypotheses are analogous to the earlier proposals of "response competition" (e.g., McGeoch, 1942), "unlearning" (e.g., Melton & Irwin, 1940), and "list differentiation" (e.g., Winograd, 1968) as being responsible for retroactive interference. Finally, both research programs have found the need to introduce a great many different memory tests to help differentiate among hypotheses, including a peculiar tendency to introduce "modified" tests (e.g., Barnes & Underwood, 1959; McCloskey & Zaragoza, 1985a)!

[2] Loftus et al. (1978) actually presented either stop or yield signs as critical items. For ease of exposition with later experiments, we will illustrate our points using varieties of soda cans as our critical items.

Table 6.1 *Outline of representative studies, memory tests used, and hypotheses explored in experiments conducted on the misinformation effect*

Representative studies	Type of test	Hypotheses Explored			
		Memory impairment		Source misattribution	Misinformation acceptance
		Retrieval-based	Storage-based		
Loftus et al. (1978)	Standard; event vs. postevent items	Suggested	Suggested		
McCloskey & Zaragoza (1985a)	Modified; event vs. novel items	Unsupported	Unsupported		Suggested
Belli (1989); Zaragoza & McCloskey (1989)	Novel item yes/no				Supported
Lindsay & Johnson (1989); Zaragoza & Lane (1992)	Source monitoring; specify any saw and/or read sources			Supported	Supported
Lindsay (1990)	Logic of opposition recall			Strongly supported	
Belli (1989)	Event vs. novel items yes/no				
Belli et al. (1994)	Informed cued recall	Preclusion supported	Partial-degradation suggested		
Loftus et al. (1989)	Modified with response time				
Belli et al. (1992); Ceci et al. (1987)	Long retention modified	Blocking suggested	Some form suggested		
Lindsay (1990)	Long retention Logic of opposition				
Belli (1993); Schooler et al. (1988); Schreiber (1989)	Interpolated response with final modified	Some form suggested; blocking unsupported	Some form suggested		

they were shown a 7-Up can.[3] The other half were not misinformed during the second phase and served as the control condition. Finally in the third phase, following a short (20 minute) retention interval, subjects were given a *standard* forced-choice test in which they had to select, between event and postevent items (the Coke and 7-Up cans), which item they had been shown originally in the slides. Loftus et al. discovered a robust misinformation effect with the standard test. Whereas control subjects selected the event item 75% of the time, misled subjects were correct only 41% of the time.

Loftus et al. (1978) offered the memory impairment hypothesis to explain these results. In the 8 years following the Loftus et al. study, virtually no researchers questioned this hypothesis. Instead, attention was devoted to determining whether impairment was retrieval-based, in which both event and postevent items exist in memory but that the postevent item renders the event item to be less accessible (see especially Bekerian & Bowers, 1983; Christiaansen & Ochalek, 1983), or storage-based, in which the trace of the event item in memory has been altered or disintegrated by the misinformation (see especially Loftus & Loftus, 1980). Then, in 1985, McCloskey and Zaragoza published a critique of the memory impairment hypothesis that was so profound that reactions to their critique altered the course and direction of later explorations of the misinformation effect.

According to McCloskey and Zaragoza (1985a), the misinformation effect observed by Loftus at al. (1978) and subsequent researchers (e.g., Bekerian & Bowers, 1983; Christiaansen & Ochalek, 1983) could be largely explained as being due to a guessing artifact; simply, the control condition has an advantage over the misled condition to correctly guess the event item. As argued by McCloskey and Zaragoza, assume that misinformation does *not* impair memory. Then, the same proportion of responses in both control and misled conditions on the standard test, let's say 40%, ought to be based on those subjects who actually remember the event item, and will be correct. The remaining 60% of responses in both conditions are made by subjects who don't remember the event item, either because the item was not originally encoded or because the item became forgotten through ordinary (i.e., non impairment) mechanisms, and these responses are essentially guesses. Since there are two responses on the standard test, subjects in the control condition who have no memory for the event item ought to be correct by chance half the time. Altogether then, in the control condition, 70% of the responses will be correct, the 40% of responses that were based on remembering the event item plus half of the 60% (30%) of those responses that were guesses. On the other hand, in the misled condition, guessing is much more complicated because of exposure to the postevent item. Subjects who have no memory for the event item may remember the postevent item, and thus may opt to select the postevent item on the standard test because they accept the possibility that the postevent item may have been

---

[3] The versions of critical items were counterbalanced to ensure that each version served as event and postevent items equally often. Counterbalancing of critical items is a standard and necessary technique used in experiments that explore the misinformation effect.

shown during the event, a process known as "misinformation acceptance" (Belli, 1989). The net result is that guessing correctly is no longer at 50% chance in the misled condition, but much lower, depending on the number of responses affected by misinformation acceptance. Overall then, even if misinformation does not lead to impairment, correct performance in the misled condition will be considerably lower (perhaps slightly above the 40% of those responses that were based on remembering the event item) than the 70% found in the control condition.[4]

In order to control for misinformation acceptance, and to provide an adequate test of the memory impairment hypothesis, McCloskey and Zaragoza (1985a) devised the modified test procedure. If you will remember, the standard test required subjects to choose between the event and postevent items (e.g., Coke and 7-Up). The only change with the modified test was to eliminate the postevent item as a response choice and replace it with a novel item (e.g., a Sunkist can), that is, an item that was neither originally shown nor introduced as postevent misinformation. Thus, the modified test was a forced-choice test in which subjects had to choose between event and novel items (e.g., Coke and Sunkist). All other aspects of McCloskey and Zaragoza's experimental procedure were essentially the same as developed by Loftus et al. (1978).

McCloskey and Zaragoza (1985a) reasoned that if the misinformation impaired the ability to remember the event item, the modified test would detect a misinformation effect, that is, there would be fewer selections of the event item in the misled than control conditions. Since impairment essentially involves an inability to gain access to the event item that is accessible when not misinformed (either because the misinformation either rendered the event item inaccessible or actually disintegrated the event item trace), then subjects in the misled condition who suffer impairment would need to guess on the modified test and be correct on average 50% of the time. In comparison, subjects in the control condition who remember the event item would not suffer impairment and would be correct 100% of the time. Also, importantly, the modified test rules out misinformation acceptance. As the postevent item is not an option on the modified test, subjects in the misled condition who remember only the postevent item have the same 50% chance of guessing correctly as control subjects who don't remember any items.

McCloskey and Zaragoza (1985a) found no differences in the performance of control and misled conditions on the modified test, providing evidence against the memory impairment hypothesis. Consequently, they argued that the misinformation effect found

---

[4]Misinformation acceptance was not the only nonimpairment process hypothesized by McCloskey and Zaragoza (1985a) that could lead to a misinformation effect on the standard test. The deliberation hypothesis asserts that some misled subjects may remember having seen the event item and having read the postevent item, but become unsure of the accuracy of their memory and deliberate that the postevent item must have been shown in the event since the postevent information was constructed by the experimenter who must have known what was shown. In fairness, it should also be noted that Loftus et al. (1978) were aware of both the misinformation acceptance and deliberation hypotheses and took steps to rule them out. In retrospect, however, their efforts were insufficient, especially in light of McCloskey and Zaragoza's critique.

on the standard test was likely the result of misinformation acceptance. Although McCloskey and Zaragoza found support for misinformation acceptance only by default, that is, by failing to find evidence for memory impairment, later research provided positive empirical support for misinformation acceptance. Belli (1989) and Zaragoza and McCloskey (1989) had subjects in control and misled conditions respond only to the novel item and to respond either yes or no as to whether the item appeared in the slides. In these experiments, subjects in the control condition more often said yes to the novel item than subjects in the misled condition, ostensibly because of misinformation acceptance. By remembering the postevent item, misled subjects tend to reject the novel item because they accept that the postevent item had instead been presented at the event.

By ruling out memory impairment, McCloskey and Zaragoza (1985b) argued that experimental research on the misinformation effect had little bearing on the issue of whether actual eyewitnesses provide less accurate reports due to being misinformed. Granted, the experimental evidence did show that misled subjects were less accurate in their reports than control subjects, but one had to wonder whether such effects were confined to the laboratory. If the misinformation effects were largely due to misinformation acceptance, then subjects could possibly be remembering that they had only read about the postevent item and were responding with the item during the test only because of an inference that the item possibly could have been shown. On the other hand, actual eyewitnesses may be much more critical in reporting having seen something that they specifically remembered having been introduced to them after the event.

Despite McCloskey and Zaragoza (1985a, 1985b), a compelling argument that real-world eyewitnesses would similarly experience misinformation effects could be made if it could be shown that actual memory is influenced by exposure to misinformation. An even stronger argument could be made if one could show that the presented misinformation is not even detected by those who are afflicted.

Misinformation acceptance versus source misattribution

By definition, misinformation acceptance is a process that does not involve memory impairment (Belli, 1989). For memory impairment to occur, there must be a memory for the original event that would be accessible if misinformation had not been presented. On the other hand, misinformation acceptance can occur only if there is no accessible memory of the original event due to processes other than the introduction of misinformation, either because the information was never encoded originally or because the memory was rendered inaccessible due to ordinary forgetting processes. Despite the fact that misinformation acceptance is independent of any memory impairment process, the exact mechanisms that lead to misinformation acceptance are ambiguous (Loftus & Hoffman, 1989). Instead of subjects remembering that they had only read the misinformation, perhaps subjects actually remember having seen the misinformation at the original event. After all, with the standard test, subjects are asked to report those items they remember seeing in the slides. Thus, perhaps misinformation acceptance involves a mechanism that leads to "the creation of new memories" (Loftus & Hoffman, 1989, p. 103).

Recent work has explored whether the source of misinformation is remembered as having occurred at the original event, a process that has become known as "source misattribution." The evidence does support the occurrence of genuine misattributions of source. One procedure involves the use of the source monitoring test (Lindsay & Johnson, 1989), in which subjects are informed that some (unspecified) items were presented only after the event; subjects are then specifically asked to evaluate the sources of remembered items by responding whether they only saw, only read, both saw and read, or did not experience certain event and postevent items. Although fewer subjects claim to have seen postevent items with the source monitoring test in comparison to other tests (such as the standard test) that do not require such close scrutiny of source (Lindsay & Johnson, 1989; Zaragoza & Koshmider, 1989), several experiments have found robust source misattributions even with the source monitoring test (Ackil & Zaragoza, 1992; Carris et al., 1992; Zaragoza & Lane, 1991, 1994; Zaragoza & Moore, 1990).[5] Importantly, many of the experiments conducted by Zaragoza and colleagues have used as postevent items only items that were not in direct contradiction with any event items originally presented. Thus, the source misattributions found in these studies are suggestive of a memory alteration process, in the sense of the creation of new memories for nonexistent items, that is independent of memory impairment (since there was no available original memory to impair). Taken together, these studies suggest that some subjects on the standard test may respond with postevent items by accepting the misinformation, that is, while actually having a memory of these items being presented only after the original event, whereas other subjects respond with a newly created memory of seeing items that they had actually only read.

Additional work highlights the extent to which subjects genuinely but falsely remember seeing postevent items. Subjects have been found to respond as quickly and confidently to seeing postevent items as they do to event items, and they are willing to bet nearly as much money on the authenticity of postevent items as they are on event items (Loftus et al., 1989; Weingardt et al., 1994). Also, subjects continue to claim to remember seeing postevent items despite strong warnings that there were items that *only* came from the verbal postevent information and not from the original visual event (Belli et al., 1994; Zaragoza & Lane, 1994).

Even more striking evidence has been presented by Lindsay (1990) with the use of logic of opposition instructions. In Lindsay's study, subjects were correctly informed that there was no question on the test for which a correct answer was an item that came from the verbal postevent information. Thus, if subjects remembered having read about an item, they were instructed not to report that item at test because none of the items that were presented in verbal form were ever actually originally shown. Despite these logic of opposition instructions, 27% of all reports (in a recall test) of items in the mis-

---

[5]Source misattributions are assessed when subjects either claim to have only seen, or to both having seen and read, postevent items, which of course they had only read.

led condition were postevent items, compared to a 9% guessing rate of postevent items found in the control condition. This finding provides cogent evidence that postevent details may become incorporated into people's memories of eyewitnessed events.

In summary, despite the possibility that our ability to remember some original memory is not impaired by misinformation (McCloskey & Zaragoza, 1985a), it is still the case that misinformation can alter memory by creating new visual memories for details that were presented only verbally. Actual eyewitnesses, then, may inaccurately report seeing things that never originally occurred, even though they may be able to accurately report those details that did occur. But this is not the whole story, as recent evidence has also shown that misinformation can lead to memory impairment.

Memory impairment revisited

The crux of McCloskey and Zaragoza's (1985a, 1985b; Zaragoza & McCloskey, 1989) suggestion that failure to obtain a misinformation effect on the modified test provides evidence against the memory impairment hypothesis rests on the assumption that the modified test is sensitive to detecting memory impairment. Certainly the modified test is sensitive to, and thus does rule out with null results, strong forms of the memory impairment hypothesis. For example, any form that presumed that the original event information would become totally inaccessible either through retrieval- or storage-based mechanisms is ruled out (Zaragoza & McCloskey, 1989). However, the modified test is not sensitive to all forms of the memory impairment hypothesis (Zaragoza et al., 1987). Since the modified test presents a choice between the event item and a novel item, and thus prevents subjects from responding with the postevent item, the modified test is not sensitive to detecting forms of memory impairment that require the postevent items to be a potential alternative on the test.

The preclusion hypothesis. For example, one retrieval-based impairment hypothesis (see Bekerian & Bowers, 1983; Belli, 1989; Belli et al., 1994; Belli et al., 1992; Johnson & Lindsay, 1986; Lindsay & Johnson, 1989; Loftus et al., 1989) that would not be detected with the modified test asserts that misled subjects preferentially gain access to the postevent item in comparison to the event item (which is stored in memory) because the postevent item was either more recently experienced or encoded more thoroughly. On tests (such as the standard test) that permit subjects to respond with the postevent item, misled subjects who gain access to the postevent item will make a postevent item response that precludes the ability to otherwise gain access to the event item. On tests (such as the modified test) that do not permit subjects to respond with the postevent item, misled subjects who gain access to the postevent item will find that the item is not an acceptable response and will continue their search of memory, eventually gaining access to the event item.

One prediction of this preclusion hypothesis asserts that having received misinformation forces a more prolonged and time-consuming search of memory in order to gain access to the event item on the modified test. In fact, Loftus et al. (1989) have found that subjects in the misled condition, in comparison to the control condition, do take significantly longer to make an event item response on the modified test. Other evidence favoring the preclusion hypothesis has been found with studies that have used memory tests that do not rule out making a postevent response and yet control for nonimpairment processes such as misinformation acceptance.

For example, consider Belli's (1989) study that used a yes/no testing procedure. As mentioned above, Belli (1989) with a yes/no novel item test found that subjects in the misled condition more often said no to the novel item in comparison to the control condition. Ostensibly, this result was due to misinformation acceptance of remembering the postevent item led to rejections of the novel item. Importantly, Belli also compared the novel item test performances with event item responses gathered in misled and control conditions given a yes/no event item test. To understand the logic of this procedure, note that for any subjects who do not remember the event item, the item presented on the event item test will appear novel and ought to be treated exactly like the item presented on the novel item test. Thus, misled subjects, who remember the postevent item, but who do not remember the event item due to ordinary (nonimpairment) mechanisms, ought to have the same level of rejections to event and novel items on the respective tests as a result of misinformation acceptance. Yet, Belli found significantly more rejections of event items than novel items in the misled condition (see also Tversky & Tuchin [1989] for replication experiments) in support of memory impairment. On the novel item test, impairment is not expected to influence responses between control and misled conditions: remembering either the event item (in the control condition) or the postevent item (due to impairment in the misled condition) ought to lead to the same level of rejections of the novel item. On the other hand, with the event item test, the inability to remember the event item due to impairment will lead to more rejections in the misled than control conditions, and this is apparently what happened.

Additional evidence in support of the preclusion hypothesis comes from experiments conducted by Belli et al. (1994) with the use of a recall test. During this test, subjects were informed that some of the verbal postevent information contradicted items that were originally shown, and they were then instructed to write down all of the items that they remembered having experienced during the experiment. More precisely, subjects were told to write down both event and postevent items if that was what they remembered. Note that misinformation acceptance, which by definition can occur only when there is no event item in memory to impair, will not bias the misled condition to respond with event items less frequently than the control condition on this recall test: subjects in the misled condition will respond with the postevent item, whereas subjects in the control condition will respond with nothing.[6] On the other hand, if remembering and responding with a postevent item prevents gaining access to the event item, then such

---

[6]There is the problem of guessing, however. Subjects in the control condition may be able to guess the event item more frequently than those in the misled condition, since misled subjects have the opportunity to provide a postevent item response, whereas those in the control condition do not. Belli et al. (1994) took great care to eliminate this potential guessing bias as being responsible for the misinformation effects that were observed.

impairment will lead to fewer event item responses in the misled condition. In fact, in one experiment, Belli et al. found that subjects in the control condition reported event items 43% of the time compared to 27% in the misled condition, supporting the presence of substantive impairment.

Thus, in nearly identical conditions, impairment is found with test procedures that permit the postevent item response, but impairment is not detected with test procedures (such as the modified test) that exclude the postevent item response. Such evidence strongly supports the claim that memory impairment partly adds to the misinformation effect as found with any test procedure that permits the postevent item response, such as the standard test developed by Loftus et al. (1978), although other nonimpairment processes, such as misinformation acceptance and source misattribution, also appear to contribute to the standard test effect. There can be no doubt, then, that real-world eyewitnesses are susceptible to memory impairment.

But how damaging is impairment likely to be with real-world eyewitnesses? The preclusion hypothesis is a fairly mild form of impairment. According to the preclusion hypothesis, in the right conditions, persons are able to gain access to event information that is stored intact in memory. There is hope then, that real-world eyewitnesses may be encouraged, through appropriate techniques, to overcome any impairment that they may suffer. However, the preclusion hypothesis is not the only form of memory impairment that may not be detected by the modified test. In fact, certain storage-based impairment mechanisms are potentially viable and would result in an impairment that is more entrenched.

Partial degradation hypotheses. Certainly failure to obtain a misinformation effect on the modified test rules out one storage-based hypothesis proposed by Loftus and Loftus (1980), namely, the possibility that the misinformation erases any original memory for the event item (Zaragoza & McCloskey, 1989). But what about storage-based hypotheses that assert that the original memory is only partially degraded or destroyed (Brainerd & Reyna, 1988; Chandler, 1989; Johnson & Lindsay, 1986; Toglia, Ross, Ceci, & Hembrooke, 1992; Tversky & Tuchin, 1989)? These forms of memory impairment may not be detected by the modified test, not so much because of the exclusion of the postevent response, but because the modified test sets up a situation in which a correct response becomes possible by the rejection of the novel item. That is, any lingering amount of event information in memory that survives the impairing influences of misinformation may be sufficient to reject a novel item because the item is entirely new. Yet, such impairment may lead subjects to be unable to respond correctly in test conditions, such as the standard test, the yes/no event item test, and the recall test, that do not automatically lead to a correct response by the rejection of something novel.

Zaragoza and McCloskey (1989) have provided arguments against the notion that the modified test is insensitive to forms of memory impairment that involve a partial storage-based impairment. According to their argument, such partial degradation is synonymous with the notion that misinformation weakens the ability to remember the original event, leading to the memory trace of event information having less strength than it would otherwise have. Given that control performance is not perfect in most studies that have used a modified test, then original traces, when uninfluenced by misinformation, must already vary in their strength with only the strongest traces leading to correct responses on the modified test. In other words, the modified test must be sensitive to trace strength (if trace strength affects memorability) for some subjects to be correct on the basis of remembering the event item and others to be incorrect because they were unable to remember the event item sufficiently. Thus, any additional weakening of event traces due to misinformation would result in a misinformation effect whether the probability of correct responses 1) continuously decreases with decreases in trace strength, or 2) is perfect above some strength threshold but at chance below this threshold. Therefore, according to Zaragoza and McCloskey, partial degradation forms of memory impairment are not viable faced with the failure to obtain misinformation effects on the modified test.

Yet partial degradation forms may remain viable. Zaragoza and McCloskey's (1989) argument hinges on the assumption that a memory for event information can be represented by a single unimodal strength distribution. Chandler (1989) and Johnson and Lindsay (1986) suggest that memories are not aptly represented by a single distribution of strength, but are better considered as multidimensional, with any particular memory consisting of a number of features. In addition, each feature is seen as being represented by its own independent strength distributions. Misinformation, then, may weaken only some of these features. Success on the modified test is possible despite this impairment if enough features remain intact to reject a novel item. On the other hand, such impairment may lead to greater inabilities to remember the event item in tests that do not provide the novel item distractor.

In any event, the status of partial degradation forms of memory impairment is perhaps one aspect of the misinformation effect that is still open to controversy and debate. A definitive resolution to this issue is still in the making and can only be resolved by well-designed empirical evidence that isolates the various possibilities.

Misinformation effects with the modified test. To this point we have focused on versions of memory impairment to which the modified test is not sensitive. Yet the evidence favoring memory impairment is not limited to only these forms because there have also been studies that have found misinformation effects with the modified test (Belli, Windschitl, McCarthy, & Winfrey, 1992; Ceci et al., 1987; Chandler, 1989, 1991; Delamothe & Taplin, 1992; Toglia et al., 1992). Given that the modified test is particularly stringent in yielding misinformation effects, finding the effects suggests an impairment that is particularly profound. Yet since other studies have failed to find misinformation effects with the modified test, the equivocal research findings have shown that the factors that promote impairment on the modified test are not completely understood.

In 1992, Belli et al. documented that out of 22 published modified test experiments (see Bonto & Payne, 1991; Ceci et al., 1987; Loftus et al., 1989; McCloskey & Zaragoza, 1985a; Toglia et al., 1992; Zaragoza, 1987, 1991; Zaragoza, Dahlgren, & Muench, 1992) that explored the misinformation effect (and which also used the typical paradigm of visual event and verbal postevent information), only 4 found significantly poorer memory for event details in the misled than control conditions. Importantly, all 4 of the experiments that found significant results used preschool children as subjects (out of 13 experiments), whereas all of the remaining 9 experiments that used adult subjects failed to find a misinformation effect. This evidence suggests that children are more susceptible to impairment than are adults, consistent with other evidence favoring age differences in suggestibility (Ceci & Bruck, 1993; Loftus, Levidow, & Duensing, 1992). Nevertheless, with experimental materials considerably different than those traditionally used to explore the misinformation effect,[7] Chandler (1989, 1991) has provided evidence that adult subjects also can be susceptible to impairment as revealed on a modified test. Thus, the picture is not clear regarding what role, if any, age differences may play in susceptibility to misinformation.

One factor noted by Belli et al. (1992), that differentiated whether a misinformation effect was found with the modified test with children as subjects, involved the length of the retention interval. All six experiments (Zaragoza, 1987, 1991) that used short retention intervals (< 30 min) did not find an effect, whereas four out of seven experiments (Ceci et al., 1987; Toglia et al., 1992; Zaragoza, 1991; Zaragoza et al., 1992) that used long retention intervals (2 to 3 days) did find an effect. Importantly, with adult subjects, all but one of the nine studies used short retention intervals, and the one study that used a long retention interval produced a ceiling effect and therefore was not a good test of impairment. Perhaps, with the traditional experimental procedure, finding a misinformation effect with the modified test relies on a long retention interval.

In fact, Belli et al. (1992) found that impairment can be produced on the modified test with long (5 to 7 days) but not with short (15 min) retention intervals with adult subjects (cf. Lindsay, 1990). Thus, although age differences may yet be found to be an important factor moderating memory impairment, the results of Belli et al. suggest that long retention intervals promote certain processes that make impairment more likely. Perhaps there is an interaction between the forgetting of original event information and the susceptibility to impairment via postevent misinformation (Brainerd & Reyna, 1988), such that increasing the retention interval encourages a certain degree of forgetting of event information that may be necessary for impairment to occur.

More specifically, speculation reveals that both retrieval- and storage-based impairment mechanisms may be possible. One particularly attractive retrieval-based mechanism is the blocking hypothesis (see especially Belli, 1993; Chandler, 1989, 1991, 1993), in which gaining access to the postevent item actually blocks or totally prevents the ability to gain access to the event item that remains stored in memory. Another way to think of the blocking hypothesis is that it represents a more entrenched form of impairment as depicted by the preclusion hypotheses. Both hypotheses depend on the

---

[7]Chandler's (1989, 1991) materials involved visually presenting subjects with holistic nature scenes. The postevent misinformation consisted of similar visual scenes. It's not clear how generalizable the effects obtained with Chandler's materials are with the effects found in experiments more typical of those used to explore the misinformation effect.

postevent item being more accessible than the event item (and thus the postevent item is preferentially accessed), the only difference is that the degree of impairment represented by preclusion is sufficiently mild to be overcome by the modified test, whereas blocking represents an impairment so profound that it survives the modified test.

Evidence favoring blocking comes from analyzing the experimental procedures used by Belli et al. (1992, cf. Lindsay, 1990) in finding impairment with long retention intervals. In these experiments, the postevent misinformation is presented at the end of the long retention interval and right before the final modified test, which in all likelihood led to the postevent information being much more accessible than the original event. On the other hand, the experiments by Ceci et al. (1987) and Toglia et al. (1992) found impairment on the modified test with the misinformation being presented midway during the 3-day retention interval. Blocking is less supported by these latter experiments because it is less clear whether the misinformation would have much of an accessibility advantage over the event information as required by the blocking hypothesis.

Finally, there is evidence that is unfavorable to the blocking hypothesis, lending support to retrieval-based mechanisms. As Chandler's work (1993) has shown, blocking does not depend on long retention intervals, but can be produced in short retention intervals that encourage the postevent information to be more accessible than the event information. Thus, if blocking is responsible for the impairment found with typical misinformation effect studies that have used the modified test, then enhancing the accessibility of the postevent information ought to lead to blocking even with experiments that use short retention intervals. Interestingly, there are several such experiments (McCloskey & Zaragoza, 1985a, Exp. 3–6; Zaragoza, 1991, Exp. 1–2) that have presented postevent items on two occasions, ostensibly increasing the accessibility of misinformation, and yet have not found a misinformation effect. Even more directly, Belli (1993) presented subjects with either an interpolated recall or a yes/no postevent item test before a final modified test. The interpolated tests were designed to encourage subjects to gain access to the postevent item and thus enhance the postevent item's later accessibility on the modified test. Misled subjects did indeed gain access to the postevent item during the interpolated test phase as revealed by substantive misinformation effects on these tests. Moreover, we can speculate that some of the postevent item responses during interpolated testing were the result of the preclusion mechanism, given the similarity between these tests and tests that have found support for the preclusion hypothesis (see above). Nevertheless, no misinformation effects were obtained on the final modified test. Although there cannot be much doubt that the accessibility of postevent items was enhanced by the interpolating testing, such accessibility did not promote blocking.

Belli's (1993) finding that interpolated tests will fail to induce memory impairment with a modified test directly contrasts with the work of others who have found that interpolating testing will induce misinformation effects on a final modified test. Schooler et al. (1988) and Schreiber (1989) used conditions almost identical to those of Belli, with one exception: their interpolated tests forced subjects into making an incorrect response, whereas Belli permitted subjects to be correct during interpolated testing. Although on the surface it may appear that by forcing the incorrect response, Schooler et al. and Schreiber were sufficiently enhancing the accessibility of the postevent items so as to lead to later blocking, further analysis reveals that their results are not supportive of the blocking hypothesis. In Belli's interpolated tests, the misled subjects who are less likely to be correct are those who have a lesser accessibility to the event item, and the ones more likely to be correct are those with greater accessibility to the event item. The blocking hypothesis depends on postevent items being more accessible than event items, thus, those subjects who have lesser accessibility to event items ought be more vulnerable to blocking. Yet, as suggested by the results of Schooler et al. and Schreiber, interpolated testing is successful in inducing impairment on a final modified test by forcing those with greater accessibility to the event item to make an incorrect interpolated response. It appears that Schooler et al. and Schreiber achieved their results by encouraging misled subjects to actively reject the event item that had been accessed during interpolated testing. This rejection may have led to another form of retrieval-based impairment, or may have led to some form of storage-based impairment, but is clearly not in accord with the blocking hypothesis (Belli, 1993).

As noted above, the blocking hypothesis appears as the most viable form of retrieval-based impairment that is possibly responsible for the misinformation effects found with experiments that have used the modified test and long retention intervals. Yet Belli's (1993) results illustrate the difficulty associated with attempts to find direct evidence for the blocking hypothesis. Given that the status of the blocking hypothesis is somewhat tarnished, the status of storage-based impairments as being responsible for these observed misinformation effects becomes enhanced. More precisely, what mechanisms may induce storage-based impairment? One mechanism conceives of memory as consisting of a bundle of features that are held together more or less well by bonds that "glue" the features together (Belli et al., 1992; Brainerd, Reyna, Howe, & Kingma, 1990). Successful remembering requires having a stored trace with enough features. Over time, these bonds loosen. Once a bond has sufficiently loosened, that feature becomes "lost" and is no longer readily available in memory; forgetting occurs when a trace no longer has sufficient features to make remembering feasible.[8] Given this basic memory model, storage-based impairment mechanisms are easy to conceive. Misinformation may act to either speed the loosening process or may simply loosen the bonds a certain amount upon its presentation. In any event, the role of misinformation is to further degrade the memory trace so that remembering becomes more difficult.

---

[8] Our claim is not that remembering becomes impossible, because such a claim would insist that the features are never recoverable under any circumstances. Clearly we don't have the ability to observe all circumstances. However, perhaps in the future, by invading the physiological structure of organisms, we may find that memories can become so disintegrated that they may be considered forever gone.

The aftermath of the debate

Since McCloskey and Zaragoza (1985a) raised serious questions about whether misinformation affects the ability to accurately remember a past event, a collection of new research findings supports the proposition that memory can be altered by postevent misinformation. The misinformation can be remembered as having occurred at the event, a process known as *source misattribution*, and misinformation can hinder the ability to remember what occurred at the event, a process known as *memory impairment*. Source misattribution and memory impairment are processes that depict how misinformation affects memory per se. People suffer these memory alterations because, like the classic Trojan Horse, misinformation invades memory so successfully that people are unaware of its influence.

Given that misinformation can alter memory, recent scientific attention has focused on enhancing our understanding of the various mechanisms. Is memory impairment retrieval- or storage-based? What conditions exacerbate or lessen the severity of the memory alteration processes? Are there individual differences in susceptibility, and if so, what characterizes these differences? In a word, attention is now being devoted to determining more precisely the different forms that memory alteration can assume and the factors that influence its magnitude.

The implications of research into the misinformation effect are staggering. Subjects have shown a high degree of confidence in their altered memories, and these memories are apparently virtually indistinguishable from unaltered memories. Misinformation affects memory in myriad settings. Obviously there is the legal field (see Wagenaar, this volume), but the potential role of misinformation in advertising, political persuasion, and psychotherapy is also considerable.

The false memory debate

One particular area in which the misinformation effect is implicated involves the false or illusory memory debate (Belli & Loftus, 1994; Lindsay & Read, 1994; Loftus, 1993). An increasing number of adults are claiming, often during therapy, that they have recovered autobiographical memories of being sexually abused as children. In some cases, such as the case of Yolanda presented by Wagenaar (this volume), there are "recovered" memories of being abused many (even hundreds and thousands of) times over many years, and the memories may involve satanic rituals of torture and murder. Although many clinicians believe that these reports are authentic, given what we know about the power of suggestive postevent information, some scholars have worried that some of these reports may not be veridical, but rather may be the product of suggestion. Put another way, misinformation may be affecting memory in the form of suggestions introduced during the course of therapy. If false claims are being made, then the accused, the accusers, and genuine victims of abuse are suffering. Accused and accusers suffer as family relationships are damaged, reputations are ruined, extensive financial loss often occurs, and autobiographical memories of childhood are scarred.[9] Genuine victims of abuse suffer if for no other reason than the fact that limited resources are being drained away from their care.

The consequences of these claims of abuse are severe. Although we do not deny that some reports may be true, our fear is that many reports are also false. In this section, we will expose how it is possible to induce false memories of childhood abuse in adults. Our hope is that by exposing the possibility of false reports, greater care will be devoted to reduce the likelihood of false reports. Ultimately, such care will help reduce human suffering (cf. Lindsay & Read, 1994).

The potential role of misinformation

As we have shown, misinformation can lead people to remember things that never really happened or to remember seeing things differently than the way they actually were. To what extent may clients be exposed to misinformation during therapy? In regard to the issue of sexual abuse, a theme that emerges among some therapists is that there are a number of symptoms in adults that signal the presence of childhood sexual abuse (Bass & Davis, 1988; Blume, 1990; Fredrickson, 1992). The symptoms mentioned are rather broad (e.g., depression, anxiety, relationship problems, sexual dysfunction, eating disorders), and although sexual abuse may contribute to their onset, there may be other causes as well. Nevertheless, convinced that sexual abuse was likely to have occurred, therapists may use a variety of techniques that are believed to encourage the recovery of abuse memories in order to promote the healing process. Although these techniques may be helpful toward revealing authentic memories of abuse, they may also be, if there was actually no history of abuse, a potent source of misinformation (Lindsay & Read, 1994).[10]

An initial technique may involve informing the client that their symptoms are indicative of a history of childhood sexual abuse and asking if there are any memories of such abuse (Belli & Loftus, 1994; Forward & Buck, 1988; Fredrickson, 1992; Loftus, 1993). Clients may be asked questions such as, "Your symptoms sound like you've been abused when you were a child. What can you tell me about that?" (Trott, 1991, p. 18). Although such questions may seem harmless, for clients who weren't abused, they serve as misleading suggestions. These questions, at the very least, raise suspicions in clients that they may have been abused, and thus can set the stage for techniques that are more potentially dangerous in leading to false memories.

[9] Testifying to the number and burdensome nature of these reports, the False Memory Syndrome Foundation was created by members of the lay public in March 1992 to support the interests of the accused. Although we believe that false memories are possible, we also assert that it is too premature to claim the existence of an identifiable "syndrome."

[10] If we are correct that the techniques used by some therapists may lead to false memories, then if an individual actually was abused, there still can be no guarantee that the memories "recovered" in the course of therapy are of events that actually did occur. In addition, the generation of false memories may impair the ability to remember actual abuse incidents, or if there was no history of abuse, impair the ability to remember innocuous or pleasant childhood events.

Many of the techniques, including the use of leading questions, encourage clients to visualize abuse incidents. Visualization seems to be a key factor in leading people to remember imagined or suggested events as real. For example, the implicit or explicit visualization of postevent misinformation has been shown to enhance the likelihood of source misattribution with the misinformation effect (Carris et al., 1992; Zaragoza & Lane, 1994). Ostensibly, visualization leads subjects to enrich the suggested information with perceptual detail enhancing the likelihood that the misinformation appears to be "real."

Source monitoring. The source monitoring framework developed by Johnson et al. (1993) and other colleagues (e.g., Johnson, Foley, Suengas, & Raye, 1988; Johnson & Raye, 1981) has been particularly helpful toward understanding the psychological mechanisms responsible for misremembering suggested or imagined events as real. According to this framework, the source of one's memories, say between reality and imagination, is inferred partly on the basis of the characteristics of the remembered information. Memories that are rich in perceptual information (e.g., sights, sounds, smells) tend to be inferred as having had as their source real external perceptual experience, whereas memories that contain a great deal of information on cognitive operations (e.g., reflection, thought) tend to be inferred as having had as their source internal generation. Although such inferences are often correct, at times, they are incorrect and lead to source misattribution, that is, remembering some experience as having really happened when, in fact, it did not.

Experiments that are successful in leading to source misattributions largely do so by increasing the amount of perceptual information in an event that was merely imagined or suggested (Johnson et al., 1993). Unlike most work with the misinformation effect which has concentrated on relatively small details, some of these experiments have led to illusory memories of complex holistic events that may involve self-activity. Intraub and Hoffman (1992) found that subjects will remember having seen photographs of holistic scenes that were only verbally described, and may actually draw what they had misremembered seeing. Other research has shown that subjects will misremember having performed actions that they had only imagined themselves as performing (Anderson, 1984; Foley & Johnson, 1985; Lindsay, Johnson, & Kwon, 1991). Thus, people can misremember experiencing complex events that never did happen.

Because the techniques employed by some therapists to dislodge repressed memories also tend to increase the perceptual detail in clients' "recall" of abuse incidents, they may be inadvertently encouraging clients to misattribute the images of abuse to reality, when in actuality, no abuse had occurred. For example, one technique is to use family photographs as aids to recall (Bass & Davis, 1988; Fredrickson, 1992). Photographs contain many perceptual details (such as style of clothing; home furnishings) that can later embellish the visualizations of abuse incidents, making them appear quite real. Another technique, reported by Wagenaar (this volume), encourages clients to visualize scenes from a third-person perspective. The use of third person is likely to dissociate the remembering process from those characterisitics of the memories that are rich in information of internal cognitive operations, and instead, encourage a focusing on perceptual information that can color a reconstruction of these events as appearing more real.

Some therapists have also used hypnosis to dredge up repressed memories. Yet the suggestive nature of hypnosis can be quite potent in encouraging the creation of false memories (see Gordon, 1991; Laurence & Perry, 1983; Nash, 1987; Smith, 1983). Another technique involves clients writing and rewriting their memories of abuse. Loftus and Coan (in press) used this technique to implant an extensive autobiographical memory of a childhood event (being lost in a shopping center) that was known to the experimenters to never have occurred. Apparently, in recounting events, people will begin to visualize perceptual details and to embellish their memories with those additional details. For example, in the Loftus and Coan study, one individual remembered the color of a flannel shirt that a stranger wore.

Another technique involves dream interpretation, and there are reports of dreams that contain abuse content (Loftus, 1993). The difficulty resides in correctly attributing the source of this content. Dreams by their nature are internally generated, as revealed by their delusional character (see Baddeley, Thornton, Chua, & McKenna, this volume). Yet because they are unconsciously generated, they are lacking in information on cognitive operations that typify imagined events (Johnson, Kahan, & Raye, 1984). On the other hand, they are also often perceptually vivid. Thus, people are particularly vulnerable to misattribute the source of their dreams to reality.[11] Moreover, it is well known that dreams often contain day residue, that is, they reflect what is happening in daily life (Hall & Van deCastle, 1966; Nielsen & Powell, 1992). Given that clients may be thinking of the possibility of past abuse in their waking hours, their dreams of abuse may simply be reflecting day residue rather than being an authentic memory of actual events.

Childhood memories. One important aspect of adults remembering abuse incidents that occurred during childhood is that these recovered memories are for long-ago events. For adults, childhood memories are particularly vulnerable to source misattribution because the amount of perceptual information in an event that happened a long time ago is likely to be relatively small (Johnson et al., 1988). Thus, the amount of perceptual detail needed to accept a memory of a long-ago event as having really happened is considerably less than the amount needed for a recent event (Johnson et al., 1993). As we have seen, there are a number of experiments that have induced source misattributions for very recent events; trying to accurately determine the source of long-ago memories would likely be even more difficult.

Perhaps because of the relative lack of perceptual detail, clients sometimes express the nebulous character of their recovered memories, and thus may begin to doubt their authenticity (Bass & Davis, 1988; Petersen, 1991). Some therapists then encourage

---

[11] All of us have probably had the uncanny experience of waking up from a particularly vivid and bizarre dream and wondering, at least momentarily, whether the dream events are true.

their clients to consider that the abuse is consistent with other evidence, such as a strained relationship with one's parents. Additionally, the difficulty that clients may have in developing clear abuse memories may be interpreted by therapists and accepted by clients as a function of repression (Blume, 1990). Consistent with the ideas explored by Barclay (this volume), Robinson (this volume), and Hirst and Manier (this volume), the therapeutic context can be viewed as a unique conversational interchange in which past and present events can be (re)interpreted to bolster the belief that abuse has taken place.

The end result may be clients who are quite confident in their false memories of abuse. We have seen that subjects can be as confident in the authenticity of misinformation as they are in actual event information (Loftus et al., 1989). In controlled conditions, some subjects have been so confident in their false memories that they actually resist the truth when it is presented to them (Neisser & Harsch, 1992). Once people become confident in their false memories, it can be very difficult to persuade them that their memories are not of real events.

The problem of false memories

We have shown that there is a real danger that some recovered memories of abuse may be honest fabrications that may be created during the course of therapy. Although we do not deny the possibility of authentic repressed memories, given the attributional nature of determining the source of memories, there is no apparent means by which to accurately determine the authenticity of these recovered memories (especially since most claims lack any firm corroborating evidence). In addition to the trauma that the accusers and accused suffer when claims are false, genuine abuse victims suffer too. They may find themselves unable to get timely help because valuable but limited resources are being diverted. Even worse, the exposing of proven false claims, sadly, makes people wonder about the genuine victim – Is this case also false?

References

Ackil, J., & Zaragoza, M. S. (1992, November). *Developmental differences in source monitoring and eyewitness suggestibility*. Poster presented at the meeting of the Psychonomic Society, St. Louis, MO.

Anderson, R. E. (1984). Did I do it or did I only imagine doing it? *Journal of Experimental Psychology: General, 113*, 594–613.

Barnes, J. M., & Underwood, B. J. (1959). "Fate" of first-list associations in transfer theory. *Journal of Experimental Psychology, 58*, 97–105.

Bass, E., & Davis, L. (1988). *The courage to heal*. New York: Harper & Row.

Bekerian, D. A., & Bowers, J. M. (1983). Eyewitness testimony: Were we misled? *Journal of Experimental Psychology: Learning, Memory, & Cognition, 9*, 139–145.

Belli, R. F. (1989). Influences of misleading postevent information: Misinformation interference and acceptance. *Journal of Experimental Psychology: General, 118*, 72–85.

—— (1993). Failure of interpolated tests in inducing memory impairment with final modified tests: Evidence unfavorable to the blocking hypothesis. *American Journal of Psychology, 106*, 407–427.

Belli, R. F., Lindsay, D. S., Gales, M. S., & McCarthy, T. T. (1994). Memory impairment and source misattribution in postevent misinformation experiments with short retention intervals. *Memory & Cognition, 22*, 40–54.

Belli, R. F., & Loftus, E. F. (1994). Recovered memories of childhood abuse: A source monitoring perspective. In S. J. Lynn & J. Rhue (Eds.), *Dissociation: Theory, clinical, and research perspectives*, pp. 415–433. New York: Guilford Press.

Belli, R. F., Windschitl, P. D., McCarthy, T. T., & Winfrey, S. E. (1992). Detecting memory impairment with a modified test procedure: Manipulating retention interval with centrally presented event items. *Journal of Experimental Psychology: Learning, Memory, and Cognition, 18*, 356–367.

Blume, E. S. (1990). *Secret survivors: Uncovering incest and its aftereffects in women.* New York: Ballantine.

Bonto, M. A., & Payne, D. G. (1991). Role of environmental context in eyewitness memory. *American Journal of Psychology, 104*, 117–134.

Brainerd, C. J., & Reyna, V. F. (1988). Memory loci of suggestibility development: Comment on Ceci, Ross, and Toglia (1987). *Journal of Experimental Psychology: General, 117*, 197–200.

Brainerd, C. J., Reyna, V. F., Howe, M. L., & Kingma, J. (1990). The development of forgetting and reminiscence. *Monographs of the Society for Research in Child Development, 55*(3, Whole No. 222).

Brewer, W. F. (1988). Memory for randomly sampled autobiographical events. In U. Neisser & E. Winograd (Eds.), *Remembering reconsidered: Ecological and traditional approaches to the study of memory.* New York: Cambridge University Press.

Carris, M., Zaragoza, M. S., & Lane, S. (1992, May). *The role of visual imagery in source misattribution errors.* Paper presented at the meeting of the Midwestern Psychological Association, Chicago, IL.

Ceci, S. J., & Bruck, M. (1993). Suggestibility and the child witness: A historical review and synthesis. *Psychological Bulletin, 113*, 403–439.

Ceci, S. J., Ross, D. F., & Toglia, M. P. (1987). Suggestibility in children's memory: Psycholegal implications. *Journal of Experimental Psychology: General, 116*, 38–49.

Chandler, C. C. (1989). Specific retroactive interference in modified recognition tests: Evidence for an unknown cause of interference. *Journal of Experimental Psychology: Learning, Memory, and Cognition, 15*, 256–265.

—— (1991). How memory for an event is influenced by related events: Interference in modified recognition tests. *Journal of Experimental Psychology: Learning, Memory, and Cognition, 17*, 115–125.

—— (1993). Accessing related events increases retroactive interference in a matching recognition test. *Journal of Experimental Psychology: Learning, Memory, and Cognition, 19*, 967–974.

Christiaansen, R. E., & Ochalek, K. (1983). Editing misleading information from memory: Evidence for the coexistence of original and post-event information. *Memory & Cognition, 11*, 467–475.

Delamothe, K., & Taplin, J. E. (1992, November). *The effect of suggestibility on children's recognition memory.* Paper presented at the meeting of the Psychonomic Society, St. Louis, MO.

Foley, M. A., & Johnson, M. K. (1985). Confusions between memories for performed and imagined actions. *Child Development, 56*, 1145–1155.

Forward, S., & Buck, C. (1988). *Betrayal of innocence: Incest and its devastation.* New York: Penguin Books.

Fredrickson, R. (1992). *Repressed memories: A journey to recovery from sexual abuse.* New York: Simon & Shuster.

Gibling, F., & Davies, G. (1988). Reinstatement of context following exposure to postevent information. *British Journal of Psychology, 79*, 129–141.

Gordon, J. S. (1991). The UFO experience. *The Atlantic Monthly, 268*, 82–92.

Hall, C. S., & Van deCastle, R. L. (1966). *The content analysis of dreams.* New York: Appleton-Century-Crofts.

Intraub, H., & Hoffman, J. E. (1992). Reading and visual memory: Remembering scenes that were never seen. *American Journal of Psychology, 105*, 101–114.

Johnson, M. K., Foley, M. A., Suengas, A. G., & Raye, C. L. (1988). Phenomenal characteristics of memories for perceived and imagined autobiographical events. *Journal of Experimental Psychology: General, 117*, 371–376.

Johnson, M. K., Hashtroudi, S., & Lindsay, D. S. (1993). Source monitoring. *Psychological Bulletin, 114*, 3–28.

Johnson, M. K., Kahan, T. L., & Raye, C. L. (1984). Dreams and reality monitoring. *Journal of Experimental Psychology: General, 113*, 329–343.

Johnson, M. K., & Lindsay, D. S. (1986). *Despite McCloskey and Zaragoza, suggestibility effects may reflect memory impairment.* Unpublished manuscript, Princeton University, Department of Psychology.

Johnson, M. K., & Raye, C. L. (1981). Reality monitoring. *Psychological Review, 88,* 67–85.

Laurence, J. R., & Perry, C. (1983). Hypnotically created memory among highly hypnotizable subjects. *Science, 222,* 523–524.

Lindsay, D. S. (1990). Misleading suggestions can impair eyewitnesses' ability to remember event details. *Journal of Experimental Psychology: Learning, Memory, and Cognition, 16,* 1077–1083.

—— (1994). Memory source monitoring and eyewitness testimony. In D. F. Ross, J. D. Read, & M. P. Toglia (Eds.), *Adult eyewitness testimony: Current trends and developments* (pp. 27–55). New York: Cambridge University Press.

Lindsay, D. S., & Johnson, M. K. (1989). The eyewitness suggestibility effect and memory for source. *Memory and Cognition, 17,* 349–358.

Lindsay, D. S., Johnson, M. K., & Kwon, P. (1991). Developmental changes in memory source monitoring. *Journal of Experimental Child Psychology, 52,* 297–318.

Lindsay, D. S., & Read, J. D. (1994). Psychotherapy and memories of childhood sexual abuse: A cognitive perspective. *Applied Cognitive Psychology, 8,* 281–338.

Loftus, E. F. (1975). Leading questions and the eyewitness report. *Cognitive Psychology, 7,* 560–572.

—— (1979). *Eyewitness testimony.* Cambridge, MA: Harvard University Press.

—— (1992). When a lie becomes memory's truth: Memory distortion after exposure to misinformation. *Current Directions in Psychological Science, 1,* 121–123.

—— (1993). The reality of repressed memories. *American Psychologist, 48,* 518–537.

Loftus, E. F., & Coan, J. (In press). The construction of childhood memories. In D. Peters (Ed.), *The child witness in context: Cognitive, social, and legal perspectives.* New York: Kluwer Academic.

Loftus, E. F., Donders, K., Hoffman, H. G., & Schooler, J. W. (1989). Creating new memories that are quickly accessed and confidently held. *Memory & Cognition, 17,* 607–616.

Loftus, E. F., & Hoffman, H. G. (1989). Misinformation and memory: The creation of new memories. *Journal of Experimental Psychology: General, 118,* 100–104.

Loftus, E. F., Levidow, B., & Duensing, S. (1992). Who remembers best? Individual differences in memory for events that occurred in a science museum. *Applied Cognitive Psychology, 6,* 93–107.

Loftus, E. F., & Loftus, G. R. (1980). On the permanence of stored information in the human brain. *American Psychologist, 35,* 409–420.

Loftus, E. F., Miller, D. G., & Burns, H. J. (1978). Semantic integration of verbal information into a visual memory. *Journal of Experimental Psychology: Human Learning and Memory, 4,* 19–31.

Loftus, E. F., & Palmer, J. C. (1974). Reconstruction of automobile destruction: An example of the interaction between language and memory. *Journal of Verbal Learning and Verbal Behavior, 13,* 585–589.

Loftus, E. F., Schooler, J. W., & Wagenaar, W. A. (1985). The fate of memory: Comment on McCloskey and Zaragoza. *Journal of Experimental Psychology: General, 114,* 375–380.

McCloskey, M., & Zaragoza, M. (1985a). Misleading postevent information and memory for events: Arguments and evidence against memory impairment hypotheses. *Journal of Experimental Psychology: General, 114,* 1–16.

—— (1985b). Postevent information and memory: Reply to Loftus, Schooler, and Wagenaar. *Journal of Experimental Psychology: General, 114,* 381–387.

McGeoch, J. A. (1942). *The psychology of human learning.* New York: Longmans, Green.

Melton, A. W., & Irwin, J. M. (1940). The influence of degree of interpolated learning on retroactive inhibition and the overt transfer of specific responses. *American Journal of Psychology, 53,* 173–203.

Nash, M. (1987). What, if anything, is regressed about hypnotic age regression? A review of the empirical literature. *Psychological Bulletin, 102,* 42–52.

Neisser, U., & Harsch, N. (1992). Phantom flashbulbs: False recollections of hearing the news about *Challenger.* In E. Winograd & U. Neisser (Eds.), *Affect and accuracy in recall: Studies of "flashbulb" memories.* New York: Cambridge University Press.

Nielsen, T. A., & Powell, R. A. (1992). The day-residue and dream-lag effects: A literature review and limited replication of two temporal effects in dream formation. *Dreaming Journal of the Association for the Study of Dreams, 2,* 67–77.

Petersen, B. (1991). *Dancing with Daddy: A childhood lost and a life regained.* New York: Bantam.

Schooler, J. W., Foster, R. A., & Loftus, E. F. (1988). Some deleterious consequences of the act of recollection. *Memory & Cognition, 16,* 243–251.

Schreiber, T. A. (1989). *The effects of misleading postevent information: Evidence for memory impairment using the modified testing procedure.* Unpublished master's thesis, University of South Florida, Tampa.

Smith, M. (1983). Hypnotic memory enhancement of witnesses: Does it work? *Psychological Bulletin, 94,* 387–407.

Toglia, M. P., Ross, D. F., Ceci, S. J., & Hembrooke, H. (1992). The suggestibility of children's memory: A social-psychological and cognitive interpretation. In M. L. Howe, C. J. Brainerd, and V. F. Reyna (Eds.), *Development of long-term retention* (pp. 217–241). New York: Springer-Verlag.

Trott, J. (1991). The grade five syndrome. *Cornerstone, 20,* 16–18.

Tversky, B., & Tuchin, M. (1989). A reconciliation of the evidence on eyewitness testimony: Comments on McCloskey and Zaragoza. *Journal of Experimental Psychology: General, 118,* 86–91.

Weingardt, K. R., Toland, H. K., & Loftus, E. F. (1994). Reports of suggested memories: Do people truly believe them? In D. F. Ross, J. D. Read, & M. P. Toglia (Eds.), *Adult eyewitness testimony: Current trends and developments* (pp. 3–26). New York: Cambridge University Press.

Winograd, E. (1968). List differentiation as a function of frequency and retention interval. *Journal of Experimental Psychology Monographs, 76*(2), Pt. 2.

Zaragoza, M. S. (1987). Memory, suggestibility, and eyewitness testimony in children and adults. In S. J. Ceci, M. P. Toglia, & D. F. Ross (Eds.), *Children's eyewitness memory* (pp. 53–78). New York: Springer-Verlag.

—— (1991). Preschool children's susceptibility to memory impairment. In J. Doris (Ed.), *The suggestibility of children's recollections* (pp. 27–39). Washington, DC: American Psychological Association.

Zaragoza, M. S., Dahlgren, D., & Muench, J. (1992). The role of memory impairment in children's suggestibility. In M. L. Howe, C. J. Brainerd, and V. F. Reyna (Eds.), *Development of long-term retention* (pp. 184–213). New York: Springer-Verlag.

Zaragoza, M. S., & Koshmider, J. W., III. (1989). Misled subjects may know more than their performance implies. *Journal of Experimental Psychology: Learning, Memory, and Cognition, 15,* 246–255.

Zaragoza, M. S., & Lane, S. (1991, November). The role of attentional resources in suggestibility. Paper presented at the meeting of the Psychonomic Society, San Francisco, CA.

Zaragoza, M. S., & Lane, S. (1994). *Source misattributions and the suggestibility of eyewitness memory. Journal of Experimental Psychology: Learning, Memory, and Cognition, 20,* 934–945.

Zaragoza, M. S., & McCloskey, M. (1989). Misleading postevent information and the memory impairment hypothesis: Comment on Belli and reply to Tversky and Tuchin. *Journal of Experimental Psychology: General, 118,* 92–99.

Zaragoza, M. S., McCloskey, M., & Jamis, M. (1987). Misleading postevent information and recall of the original event: Further evidence against the memory impairment hypothesis. *Journal of Experimental Psychology: Learning, Memory, and Cognition, 13,* 36–44.

Zaragoza, M. S., & Moore, K. (1990, November). Source misattributions in eyewitness memory. Poster presented at the meeting of the Psychonomic Society, New Orleans, LA.

7   Autobiographical memory in court

Willem A. Wagenaar

Without falling into the trap of portraying autobiographical memory as a wholly inadequate device, we can safely say that it is not precise. Every chapter in this book can be used as a reference to support this statement. The fact is so obvious that no legal system in the world is based upon an absolute trust in witness memory. An exception is the absolute trust in the memory of a police officer, enshrined in Dutch criminal law. For other witnesses the relevant question is not whether their memories are precise, but whether they are sufficiently precise to answer the questions asked in the courtroom. These questions can be detailed, like the exact times at which things happened; the exact wording of a statement made a long time ago; the voice of a person met only once; the face of a person seen driving a car at high speed in the middle of the night. To psychologists such questions may seem stupid, because obviously they cannot be answered with complete precision. To the lawyer, however, it is obvious that without answers to such questions there can be no criminal justice, and hence no safety in our society. There is no alternative to getting the best possible answers from witnesses, even though it is realized that these answers can be wrong.

The legal solution to this problem has taken several forms. One is the development of rules of evidence, which specify conditions that must be met before evidence can be admitted. For instance, English law has a "fleeting glance" rule, which specifies that witnesses who saw only a fleeting glance of a criminal are not allowed to take part in an identification test. The exact physical definition of a fleeting glance may be a matter of debate, but here experimental psychologists may be of assistance, because we know about the conditions in which face recognitions tend to deteriorate (cf. Wagenaar & van de Schrier, 1994). In some of the American states there is a law preventing abuse victims from giving testimony if the police used some form of suggestive questioning, such as hypnosis. Presumably the legislator reasoned that suggestion may affect autobiographical memory.

The Anglo-Saxon legal tradition has put more emphasis on laws of evidence than the continental European tradition, which emerged in the age of Rationalism, and which is based on the assumption that the evidentiary value of witness testimony is immediately obvious to any rational human being. As a consequence, the Dutch legal system has no rules that relate to the quality of evidence. Almost anything is acceptible when the court says so. Hence in The Netherlands court decisions are often based on hearsay evidence; witnesses rarely make live appearances in the courtroom. The worst example is the statement by a baby of eight months that she was raped by her babysitter in the middle of the night while nobody was present. The statement was related through her sister of two and a half, who told her mother, who told a police officer, who wrote a deposition that was given to the court. The court, the appeals court, and finally the supreme court ruled on the basis of this document, without ever questioning the police officer, the mother, the sister, or the baby (cf. Wagenaar, Van Koppen, & Crombag, 1993). Thus we have a quadruple hearsay situation with a baby as the original source. One might think that such evidence is not reliable, but the assumption that judges are rational gives them the freedom to accept such evidence as an accurate report of the baby's autobiographical memory.

An alternative solution is to request a certain *amount* of evidence, instead of specifying the quality. Many countries have endorsed the old Roman unis testis rule, which says that the testimony of one witness is never enough to warrant a conviction. There must be corroboration by another witness or by other facts. This rule causes serious problems in cases of rape or sexual abuse of children, where often the testimony of the victim is the only available evidence. The consequence to acquit because the victim cannot be sufficiently believed is almost unacceptable, which may lead courts to accept flimsy additional information as corroboration. In a quite notorious case (Supreme Court nr. 83887, see Van Bavel & Verbunt, 1990), the accusation of incest was made by a young woman who had left her parental home and now lived with her boyfriend. The proof consisted of the testimony by the purported victim, supported by two additional facts: the woman was not a virgin anymore, and the father had admitted that occasionally he had been alone in the house with his daughter. Logically these two facts have no evidentiary value because any woman who lives with a man can be expected to have lost her virginity, and any normal father has been in the house alone with his daughter. The addition of these facts is to satisfy the formal requirement of the unis testis rule; the court was obviously convinced by the daughter's testimony alone.

From this short discussion it is evident that doubt about the reliability of autobiographical memory has shaped all legal systems, no matter which system is ultimately adopted. Is the result satisfactory, in the sense that problems of reliability are sufficiently met by legal provisions? I think not, and I would like to illustrate my point of view by comparing the amount of precision required for legal applications to the amount of precision that is to be expected from witnesses in all sorts of situations. Such an enterprise requires a whole book, however, which is not what the editors of this volume had in mind. Therefore I will limit the presentation by focusing on a single case that happened recently in the small village of Epe, The Netherlands, and that has caused a tremendous uproar for all sorts of reasons. I will demonstrate in what respect the autobiographical memories of witnesses appeared to be highly inadequate for use in the criminal trial, even though, maybe, the quality of these memories was not abnormal.

The case of Yolanda

Yolanda accused her parents and a considerable number of other people of continual sexual abuse, 23 illegal abortions, the murders of at least six babies, and the sexual abuse of her children. The story started as a complaint about incest and sexual abuse, for which Yolanda's parents and her husband were convicted in 1991. But the story grew during the years and has not yet come to an end. The latest addition is that she seems to remember a monthly cycle in the violence, possibly connected to the phases of the moon, and some vague images of satanic rituals. Two trials, in 1991 and 1994, have resulted in the convictions of four and six defendants; a third trial against seven suspects is now in preparation. I was asked, together with my colleague Herman Soppe, to analyze the reliability of all statements in the 1994 trial made by Yolanda, other witnesses, and the defendants; our analysis should take into account the context of all other legal documents in the file. Clearly, the idea was that we should assess the extent to which these statements could be accepted as accurate autobiographical memories. The task was baffling; the file contained some 3,000 pages, but much of the necessary information was lacking. The degree of precision demanded by the legal logic was high, as will be explained later. The amount of material caused a problem because no file of that size allows a single coherent reconstruction of the facts. Most suspects were questioned 20 to 30 times. The changes in their statements ranged from total denial to the confession of numerous violent but sometimes physically impossible crimes. What criteria would enable us to find the intermediary account that is most reliable among the many obvious lies and fantasies? The lack of material was even more troublesome, because the particular selection made by the police tended to create a misleading impression of coherence among memories.

The precision of recall demanded by the court, the central issue in this paper, can be easily understood when it is realized that the law makes a distinction between abortion and murder of a live baby. Abortion is defined as the termination of a pregnancy that has lasted less than 24 weeks. The termination of a pregnancy that lasted over 24 weeks is technically a murder. The distinction is important, because different sentences are given for the two crimes. Yolanda's story was that deliveries were started forcefully, in a somewhat ritual ceremony with four to six naked people around her. The babies were born alive, and almost immediately skinned or cut into pieces with butcher's knifes and chainsaws. Gruesome as these stories might be, the legal question is not only whether such details are true, but also how long the pregnancy had lasted. How can we know this, when the first pregnancies were supposed to have occurred around 1980?

Sjon and Sanne

As an example I will analyse the alleged murders of Sjon and Sanne, twin babies murdered, according to the charge, "in the period between January 1984 and December 1985." From this definition of a 2-year period it is already clear that a precision of a few weeks will be almost impossible. If the prosecutor cannot specify with the precision of a year when the babies were killed, how can a judge determine the duration of the pregnancy with the precision of a week? Interestingly we have argued in this case that an error of a full year is quite possible, but an error of 1 day is unlikely.

Yolanda's story is that she became pregnant in October, and first became aware of it in November. In December she bought two stuffed monkeys for the babies, because at that time she knew already that she would have twins. In April she left school, because being pregnant with twins, she did not fit into the school desks anymore. On May 4 the delivery started spontaneously. She saw that the children were fully developed and she heard them cry. Then, in her presence, they were slowly cut into pieces. Yolanda was absolutely certain about May 4 as the exact date, because in The Netherlands that day is War Memorial Day, the day on which victims of World War II are commemorated. The association between war victims and her murdered babies was easy to remember. From then on, May 4 had been the day of Sjon and Sanne. She was in doubt about the exact year, which is not surprising when the association is not to a unique milestone, but to an event that returns every year. In her first deposition she had stated that the pregnancy lasted from October 1984 until May 1985. But when it transpired that she had left school in 1984, she claimed that an earlier version of the deposition situated the pregnancy between October 1983 and May 1984. Police officer Deelman, who took the deposition, had convinced Yolanda that 1984–1985 fit the facts better, and hence she had changed the dates. The benevolent interpretation of this incident is that Yolanda had a precise recall of the day and month, not of the year. Literature about the dating of events in memory (cf. Wagenaar, 1986, Larsen, Thompson, & Hansen, this volume; Rubin & Baddeley, 1989) suggests that it is indeed possible to err a full year. Deelman may have been aware of this phenomenon, which is why he saw no harm in changing Yolanda's account without mentioning it. The worst interpretation is that Deelman and Yolanda conjured a fitting story in the full awareness of its falsehood. Is it possible that Yolanda believed Deelman's reconstruction more than her own recollection? The choice between the wide variety of interpretations is closely related to what kind of errors we believe autobiographical memory may produce.

Diaries

A complicating factor was Yolanda's diary of the relevant period. She submitted the diary to the police, who noted that it looked genuine, because the notebook was old. The diary said that the murders had occurred on May 4, 1985. Surprisingly the dropout from school was also situated in 1985, whereas we know from various records that it occurred in 1984. That year is also more likely, because Yolanda then reached the age of 16, which is the official end of compulsory education. Given her moderate success in school, it is quite likely that she would leave school as soon as possible, instead of staying until the age of 17 in a class that normally has girls aged 13 or 14. Confronted with this anomaly, Yolanda admitted that the diary was a copy. She stated that the copy was accurate with the exception of the dates, which she had shifted a full year at the suggestion of police officer Deelman. She has refused to reveal the original diary, so we do not know whether there is a diary, whether the copy was accurate, and whether the original situates the murder of Sjon and Sanne on May 4, 1984.

Again, the benevolent interpretation of this chain of events is that Yolanda had a diary and that she was convinced by Deelman that through the years she had systematically used the wrong dates. But is it possible that an adult woman can be induced to doubt all dates in her own diary? Since the only alternative interpretation is that Yolanda consciously submitted a false diary, the question is of the utmost importance. In the public debate, defenders of Yolanda have argued that she was honest and sane, but suffered from a diffused time notion. In the study of my own autobiographical memory I have reported that even after a few years events can be totally forgotten, to the extent that the recordings in my own handwriting looked like fakes inserted by a practical joker. Would it not be possible, then, for a traumatized victim of violent crimes to doubt her own diaries? If she moved the memories of the period 1983–1984 forward across a full year, what happened to the real memories of 1984–1985? Were they also advanced, were they destroyed, or were the periods swapped? Did she have a complete void for the now missing period 1983–1984? Nobody tried to answer these questions, even though they are clearly relevant. If we can establish that memory does not allow such a drastic shift, we must conclude that Yolanda tried to mislead the court; which does not mean that the murders did not happen, but only that she fabricated the evidence to prove it.

It is also relevant to ask whether dates in a diary can be a full year off. Was Deelman right when he induced Yolanda to change the dates, maybe in the belief that she had suffered from a diffused time notion in 1984? Or should he have assumed that a diary cannot be wrong in this respect, and that Yolanda's willingness to change the dates only signified her *present* confusion? This would make Deelman's act a criminal attempt to influence a witness and to mislead the court.

Is it important to establish the authenticity of Yolanda's diaries? Even if she fabricated the diary about Sjon and Sanne, might it not contain a truthful report of the events? Is it possible for a woman to forget the rough details of how her children were murdered? What if some sort of "Othello complex" induced Yolanda to produce the evidence that was needed to convict the perpetrators of a crime that she knew could not be proved after 9 years? Why would her representation be wrong, even though the record is not a diary but a recall after 9 years? There are several answers to this question. One answer is that a record made on the same day is more likely to be correct than a recall after 9 years. A date recorded immediately affords more certainty than a date reported after 9 years. The required precision of 1 week can be obtained from a diary, and maybe not from a recall after 9 years. A second answer is that the existence of a diary proves that the story of the murders was not recently produced, for instance, in order to increase the sentences given in 1991. It would support the notion that the incremental nature of Yolanda's stories was a matter of deliberate choice, not of an ever-growing fantasy. The third answer is that an independent diary may corroborate Yolanda's testimony, whereas an account written after her deposition has no corroborative value whatsoever. The fourth answer is that Yolanda's credibility as a witness is greatly diminished when it is shown that she fabricated complete diaries with the explicit intention of misleading the court. The fifth answer is that, even when Yolanda's account was an honest attempt to recall the distant past, we should realize that in 1993 she was under the influence of police officer Deelman and a hypnotherapist by the name of Dori King. Deelman had at least 30 talks with Yolanda before she reported the murders, and he had been quite successful in making her change the dates in her report of the murders of Sjon and Sanne. The nature of Dori King's therapy remained largely unknown, but it is clear that it involved some form of hypnosis.

There is at least one authentic diary, which Yolanda wrote in January and February of 1991, when the first trial against her parents and husband was on. The diary was confiscated in February 1991, so we know it was not written after that date. The style of this diary is totally different, with entries for each day instead of one or two entries per month and coherent descriptions of daily events instead of exclamations with no clear structure. In this diary she mentioned the murders of Sjon and Sanne, but the details do not make much sense. She wrote: "I can say that Sjon and Sanne were quite healthy babies, 1,100 gram and 1,000 gram." How did Yolanda know their weight? Were they weighed before they were murdered? Why would anyone do that? The weights mentioned do not indicate full-grown, healthy babies, but rather fetuses aborted in an early stage of their development.

The bottom line of the diary analysis is that we cannot accept the diaries as accurate autobiographies, but there is also no clear indication that they are entirely devoid of information. But since the autobiographical memories in the diaries have an unknown degree of precision, they are quite useless for legal purposes.

Dropping out of school

As was said before, one anchor for the correct dating of the murders of Sjon and Sanne was the date Yolanda left school. It is not unusual in studies on autobiographical memory to assess the amount of accuracy with the help of official records. In a legal case the official record can be used as corroboration of testimony based on memory. Here is an example of how confusing such corroboration can be. The official school record mentioned that Yolanda left school on April 1, 1984. But the list of class attendance showed that she was present until July 1984. There is a letter to one of her teachers, which shows that Yolanda left school on March 29, 1984. But her diary, for what it is worth, mentions leaving school in November 1983, the beginning of March 1984, and the first of April 1984. The teacher did not remember that pregnancy was the reason for her dropping out. Four school friends, Miranda, Madelon, Maureen, and Audrey, remembered the pregnancy, but these memories are questionable for several reasons. First, they knew that Yolanda had an officially documented abortion in 1983. Second, none of the four produced the information about the pregnancy spontaneously. Third, after her interview Maureen called some of her friends who were still to be questioned to ask them whether they remembered a pregnancy. Fourth, Yolanda had apparently talked a lot about pregnancies, but none of the women reported a visible pregnancy. Fifth, none of the women was able to date the event to April 1984. Miranda said May

1985; Madelon said end of 1983; Maureen did not produce any date; Audrey said 1985/1986. Two other friends, Linda and Helen, did not remember any pregnancy.

It is astounding that official records and the memories of six witnesses are so confused that they allow no conclusion about such a simple fact as dropping out of school, let alone the question of whether Yolanda was pregnant or not. Insights into autobiographical memory would help here, if only we can safely say that not remembering a school friend carrying twins, which must have been a highly significant event in a small village like Epe, means that there simply was no pregnancy. But we cannot make such a claim with any degree of certainty; we simply don't know how much can be forgotten.

Monkeys

A similar confusion arose when we tried to establish when Yolanda bought her two stuffed monkeys. In her final version of the story, Yolanda said December 1983. She gave the monkeys to herself, as a Santaklaus present (Santaklaus is intensely celebrated in The Netherlands, on December 5th). The importer said that the monkeys were produced for the Apeldoorn Zoo in September 1992. They were made by putting monkey heads on the bodies of teddy bears. They were sold to the public after January 1993. The shop owners in the Apeldoorn Zoo did not recognize the monkeys and denied that they were ever sold in their shop. Whose memory was defective: the importer's, when he recognized the monkeys, or the shopowners', when they failed to recognize them? Later when the police returned to the shop; the owners then stated that they had sold such monkeys recently, and also that they had *never* sold such monkeys. Despite the confusion there seems to be some agreement that the monkeys were not bought in 1983, as claimed by Yolanda. Does this mean that the diary of 1983 (or 1984), in which the acquisition is mentioned, was false? No, it does not, because the file also contains statements about two stone monkeys with colored bows which had been in Yolanda's room. The diary of 1991 also mentions two monkeys, thus antedating the marketing of the stuffed monkeys by 2 years. Is it possible that in Yolanda's memory a blend was made between stone monkeys bought in 1983 and stuffed monkeys bought as a replacement 10 years later? Is it possible that she identified the monkeys so intensely with her two lost children that when the stone monkeys were lost, she bought new ones and deleted the act of the replacement from her memory? Belli and Loftus (this volume) suggest that blends of two memories can occur even in normal people who are confronted with conflicting information. Why not in a traumatized victim confronted with two sets of monkeys, both representing her murdered children? Or is the whole story a fantasy that Yolanda created as evidence for a murder that could not be proved or never occurred? Traditional police work, which traced the stuffed monkeys to a date in 1993, did not contribute any useful insight into this matter. If the monkeys are not genuine, there is still a possibility that Yolanda's memories are genuine. A better understanding of the working of memory might have helped us to make the distinction between a true and a false story. As it stands now, we can only say that replacement of the stone monkeys by stuffed ones might have been lost in autobiographical memory.

Table 7.1

Date	Address
15 Sept 1981 – 26 May 1982	M. L. King Weg
26 May 1982 – 1 July 1982	Reformatory
1 July 1982 – 1 Sept 1983	M. L. King Weg
1 Sept 1983 – 1 Nov 1983	Campground
1 Nov 1983 – 25 Aug 1984	M. L. King Weg
25 Aug 1984 – 12 April 1985	Campground
12 April 1985 – 23 Dec 1985	M. L. King Weg

Remembering places

The literature on autobiographical memory generally shows that the recall of places is more accurate than the recall of dates (cf. Wagenaar, 1986). Yolanda moved a considerable number of times, so the recall of the house in which an event happened may provide a useful indication of time. Unfortunately, some of these addresses were not found in the official documents because she lived for a while in a reformatory and on two different campgrounds. In the period that is relevant for the story about the murders of Sjon and Sanne she lived at the addresses given in Table 7.1.

Yolanda remembered that the murders of Sjon and Sanne occurred at the Martin Luther King Weg, which is not really helpful, because that leaves a period between 1981 and 1985. In her diary she only mentioned that during the pregnancy she moved twice with her husband, and that "every time they returned to the Martin Luther King Weg." If she refers to the short stay on the campground in Epe the year 1983 would be confirmed, but it is not clear why she said "every time," because she returned to the Martin Luther King Weg only once. The owner of the campground remembered that Yolanda and her husband arrived in September and left the next May or June; she did not remember a particular year. There were no documents to support her statement, presumably because she did not want to report the rent to the tax inspector. Yolanda's parents seemed to remember that the mobile home was too cold for the winter, so that Yolanda and her husband lived with them in the Martin Luther King Weg during the winter months. The relationship with the campground in Epe is important because the (female) owner stated explicitly that Yolanda did not go to school and had no visible pregnancy during the whole period.

Again, a good way of dating events by means of documents went wrong because the documents are not precise and derive their meaning only from memories that appear to be imprecise.

Witnesses

Several witnesses closely related to Yolanda have tried to specify a period for the murders on Sjon and Sanne. Yolanda's older sister Evelyn was already married at the time, and had broken off every contact with her family. But when she was pregnant with her daughter Antoinette in the spring of 1985, she saw Yolanda at a bus station. She noted that her sister was also pregnant. Later her mother had told her that the pregnancy had resulted in the birth of "kids." That might mean the birth of Sjon and Sanne, since Yolanda claimed no other twins in that period. On the basis of this account we should situate the murders in 1985, as was also supposed by police officer Deelman. However, this conclusion is based upon the memories and interpretations of two people. Evelyn associated the meeting at the bus station with her own pregnancy in 1985, and her mother's remark to the pregnancy that ended with the birth of twins. In fact, Yolanda claimed three more pregnancies for the period 1984–1985. Yolanda's mother may have made an incorrect link between Evelyn's story about the meeting in the bus station and the delivery of twins. Yolanda's mother is illiterate and has an IQ below 60. Does this mean that her memory for dates is unreliable? Surprisingly, she was able to give the exact birthdates of her many brothers and sisters. We do not know much about Evelyn's intelligence, but Yolanda says that Evelyn is just like her mother. These are good reasons to doubt the precision of Evelyn's autobiographical memory.

Annette, a close friend of Yolanda, who was also at that time the girlfriend of Yolanda's brother, claimed that she had been in the house when the murders of Sjon and Sanne occurred. She was locked in a room, because she was not allowed to witness the events. But she heard the screaming and later saw the kitchen covered in blood. Annette said that she and Yolanda were 12 or 13 years old, which places the event in 1980 or 1981. At the same time she remembered that she and Yolanda were in their last school year, which was in 1984. She overheard a conversation between her parents and Yolanda's parents about the pregnancy and that it should be terminated. In her memory this happened when Yolanda was about to return from the reformatory, in June 1982. Annette remembered that Yolanda's parents had arrived in the night; the streets were covered with snow. That is not likely in June. The source of all this confusion is possibly that Yolanda had told her friend about another set of murdered twins, by the names of Jaimy and Melany. These twins were supposedly born in 1982, when Yolanda was 14.

The interview with Annette was recorded on tape. When she was confronted with the recording in the office of the examining judge and heard the vivid description of the murders of Sjon and Sanne, she was visibly shocked, and claimed that "another Annette" had told these stories. Apparently her therapist had given her the idea that she suffered from a multiple personality disorder, which was caused by being a victim of sexual abuse. This raises the interesting legal question whether testimony can be accepted when the witness attributes it to another personality inside her who is not available for further questioning.

The testimony by both women, Evelyn and Annette, who were closely related to Yolanda, cannot be used because their autobiographical memories are clearly not precise enough. Specifically, it appeared extremely difficult to distinguish between what the two women had seen themselves and what they had heard from Yolanda or from other sources.

Order of events

One theory of how events are dated in memory (Neisser, 1981) states that our memory contains some benchmarks for which the dates are known, such as when we graduated, when we got married, when we made that trip into the Himalayas. Other events are situated on a time line, relative to such benchmarks, so that dates can be inferred. A logical consequence of such a process is that the *order* of events is recalled more accurately than the exact date of events. Hence, when witnesses make statements about the order of events, we may with some confidence infer the time periods in which these events took place. Several people, among these Yolanda and her parents, made statements in which the order of events was mentioned. With respect to the murders of Sjon and Sanne, Yolanda produced this kind of partial ordering:

- Stay in the reformatory
- Back home
- Legal abortion
- Leaves school
- Murder of Sjon and Sanne
- Marriage

- Annette stays with Yolanda's family
- Murder of Sjon and Sanne
- Annette placed in reformatory

- Dr. Polders establishes pregnancy of twins
- Visit to Apeldoorn Zoo
- Santaklaus (December 5)
- Murders of Sjon and Sanne

Finally, Yolanda produced a time line, with four columns: address, year, number of event, description. Here is an example:

Address	Year	Number of event	Description
M. L. King Weg	1982	1	Murders of Jaimy and Melany
Reformatory		2	
M. L. King Weg	1983	1	Abortion with soap
Hospital		2	Legal abortion
M. L. King Weg		3	Abortion with vibrator
M. L. King Weg	1984	1	Murders of Sjon and Sanne
M. L. King Weg		2	Abortion with poker
In the woods	1985	1	Abortion by being dragged behind car
M. L. King Weg		2	Abortion with barbecue pins
Elburg	1986	1	Birth of son
Berkenlaan		2	Abortion with hot poker

The time line is remarkable for several reasons. It contains only one legal abortion, whereas in her deposition she described two. The time line has 20 abortions after Jaimy and Melany; the earlier deposition mentioned only 14. The time line has Jaimy and Melamy as the third pregnancy, whereas a deposition 1 week before had it as the first pregnancy. In the same deposition Jaimy and Melany was not situated in the Martin Luther King Weg, but at a previous address. An address in Wissel, and the abortion that she claimed occurred there, is missing in the time line. The stay at two different campgrounds, that were confirmed and lasted many months, are missing. Some of the abortions appear for the first time in this representation, others were described differently in earlier reports. All such discrepancies can easily be attributed to the weaknesses of autobiographical memory, and cause no problems with respect to Yolanda's credibility. Still, one may wonder why she did not base this account, and other accounts, on the diaries that she claims existed. Why did she attempt to reconstruct a past of 10 years ago on the basis of autobiographical memory, while she had full access to her diaries?

From the approach through partial orderings, the picture emerged that the murders of Sjon and Sanne, if it occurred at all, must have happened after the legal abortion in 1983, after quitting school, while the family lived in the Martin Luther King Weg, while Annette lived for a short while with the family before being sent to a reformatory, and before Yolanda's engagement. This places the event within the period mentioned in the charge, but allows no conclusion about the duration of the pregnancy.

Psychotherapists

Psychotherapists of all sorts engaged in the treatment and support of the major characters in this case. Yolanda was treated by an unknown number of therapists, among whom is the hypnotherapist Dori King. She was emotionally supported by police officer Deelman. Psychotherapy interferes with memory (cf. Loftus, 1993). Maybe this is for good therapeutic reasons, but the process of discovery of the truth is not always helped by it. A rather innocent type of therapy reconciles people with their memories without changing them; still the change of perspective can have an effect on what people will testify about and how. A more worrysome type of therapy helps people to change their memories, either by showing that some memories are only imagined, or the other way around, that some vague recollections came from very real experiences. The most dangerous type of therapy engages in the re-creation of memories to which the patient has no access. "Repressed" or "recovered" memories fall in this category. Without expressing any judgment about the usefulness of such therapies, and even about the reality of the memories thus elicited, I want to stress that the possibility of creation of false memories is always present in the therapeutic situation. A court will find it extremely difficult to distinguish between false and true memories that result from such practices.

A useful example came from the case of Yolanda. The police had launched the idea to bring the sisters Yolanda and Evelyn together, "to see whether that would stimulate their memories." Apart from the fact that there are good reasons to keep witnesses separate during an investigation, the meeting did not result in detailed support for Yolanda's claims. Evelyn told the police about how Yolanda once lost some blood, or a blood clot; she took Yolanda to the shower and washed her thoroughly. After this meeting Evelyn was treated by a social worker engaging in psychotherapy with no specific training. Her technique was to let the client visualise the scenes and then describe in the third person what the "I-figure" did, saw, felt. We do not know whether this allows people to tell more truthfully about the horrors they have experienced, but the effect on Evelyn was that now she gave a totally different account of the same event. Her parents had gone to Yolanda's room. Evelyn heard Yolanda scream "stop it." She went to Yolanda's room and saw that mother was holding her while father was hitting her with a cane. Evelyn was sent away. After a while the screaming stopped; she went to Yolanda's room and helped her. The whole bed, the whole mattress was soaked with blood that seemed to flow from Yolanda's vagina. It was finally stopped with sanitary napkins.

The first account of the story does not involve any violence and is not related to a criminal act. The second story is highly incriminating, and suggests an illegal abortion committed by Yolanda's parents. It is quite possible that the second account is true, although it was not confirmed by Yolanda. But the real point is that such highly incriminating evidence should be collected in a controlled situation, that is, by the police. They may employ trained therapists to do the questioning, they may even be allowed to use the "third-person" technique. But such techniques should never be applied by outsiders in-between interrogations. Even less should the products be used as evidence. The worst aspect is, of course, that after such a therapeutic session the memory of the witness may be irreversibly changed, and the effects cannot be undone by a more traditional questioning in court. If essential sectors of autobiographical memory are not accessible in the context of a traditional police investigation, we might be forced to develop new methods for questioning witnesses. Therapeutic techniques are definitely among the candidates that deserve further study. But the role of a police investigator cannot be usurped by an unlicensed and uncontrolled psychotherapist using an unvalidated technique. The result of the involvement of psychotherapists in this case was that the status of accounts from autobiographical memory became less clear.

Medical records

There are detailed medical records of Yolanda, because she paid frequent visits to a number of doctors. The problem is, however, that she disqualified the records by stating that one or more of these medical doctors were among her worst abusers. In her view, the records are part of a cover up, and hence cannot be admitted as proof of anything. This argument is not unusual in such complicated abuse cases (cf. Wright, 1993).

In the case of the murders of Sjon and Sanne the records show the following. The gynecologist Dr. Meulenbelt saw Yolanda on July 4, 1983. He gave her a contraceptive injection. Yolanda stopped the injections on October 19, 1983. This makes it unlikely that she had become pregnant through October. She saw Dr. Meulenbelt again on January 9, 1984. Then he prescribed her an oral contraceptive, which makes it almost impossible that she was visibly pregnant at that time. A pregnancy was also unlikely because apparently she did not tell the doctor about it. According to her own story, however, she was fully aware of the pregnancy, as she had already bought the monkeys. It should also be assumed that the gynecologist did not notice the pregnancy during his examination. On May 1 and May 11, 1984, Yolanda was seen by her physician Dr. Polders. Supposedly, she carried twins on May 1, and had lost them on May 11. Dr. Polders only made notes about some trivial medical details, nothing about a pregnancy, twins, or a delivery. These facts seem to exclude a pregnancy of any substantial length in 1983–1984. Yet some staunch defenders of Yolanda started discussions about the reliability of contraceptives, the validity of pregnancy tests, the accuracy of medical records, and the honesty of the two medical doctors. Thus the autobiographical memory of Yolanda is pitted against two sets of medical records, with sensible arguments from both sides.

For the period 1984–1985 in which the murders of Sjon and Sanne were first situated, Dr. Polders' records show that on April 3, 1985, a pregnancy test gave a negative result. The entry is made in the handwriting of an assistant. Fraud can only be believed if the assistant was part of the conspiracy, which is quite unlikely. Yet, again, the reliability of pregnancy tests was brought into the discussion, even though 1 month before the delivery of twins Yolanda should have been visibly pregnant. Remember that she claimed to have left school because she did not fit into the school desks anymore.

The medical records were available to the public prosecutor, Mrs. De Weerd, in June 1993, seven months before the trial. The inclusion of Sjon and Sanne in the charge means that the prosecutor did not expect that the medical evidence would severely undermine the belief in Yolanda's memory. Her reaction was to stretch the period from January 1, 1984, to December 31, 1985. Possibly her supposition was that the medical evidence allows a pregnancy somewhere in that period, and that Yolanda's precise account, both in her deposition and in her diary, of associations to other events in November, December, April, and May can be discarded as false and irrelevant products of autobiographical memory without destroying the belief in Yolanda's global story. Is that what psychologists' sustained testimony about the fallibility of memory has led to: that lawyers feel free to accept or reject memories at discretion?

Incremental production

Yolanda's story has grown over the years and has not yet reached its end. For instance, in the book that she published on the day of the verdict in the second trial, she wrote that she had her first pregnancy at the age of 9, much earlier than was ever mentioned in her time line. Two days later, she said on television that there had been an even earlier pregnancy, at the age of 8. Again, some defenders argued that such early pregnancies may occur in rare cases. But that is not the issue; the real question is why the story keeps changing all the time. There are at least six explanantions.

1. Investigation methodology. This explanantion argues that the witness is guided by the questions asked by the police. Since the police organized their investigations in an incremental way, this is reflected in Yolanda's testimony.

2. Minimal involvement. Since Yolanda's memories were traumatic, she tried to win her case with the smallest possible degree of involvement. Only when the process of a criminal prosecution demanded more facts was she able to bring herself to more extensive reporting.

3. Repressed memories. The memories were repressed because of their traumatic nature. They were recovered only because they were prompted by the investigative process.

4. Fantasy. The testimony is the product of an ever-growing fantasy.

5. Pressure by the police. Yolanda was pressed by the police to incriminate the defendants. Because the pressure continued, the stories became more and more extravagant.

6. Revenge. Yolanda was inspired by feelings of revenge. Since it appeared in 1991 that many of her purported assailants were not convicted on the charges then made, she decided to produce worse stories. The same experience in 1994 has led her to increase the horror in her stories again.

It is impossible to decide which of these explanations is correct. Possibly none is entirely correct, possibly some are working simultaneously. It is quite possible that the later report of some of the abortions was inspired by reason 2, whereas the accusation of rape, brought against four police officers, stemmed from a need to take revenge for their failure to stop the abuse when she came to them in 1981. Accounts 1, 2, and 3 explain the incremental nature of Yolanda's stories, but not the inconsistencies. Accounts 4, 5, and 6 do a better job in this respect.

The major difference between the six explanations is, of course, that 1, 2, and 3 assume that Yolanda's stories are true, while 4, 5, and 6 assume that they are false. The distinction between true and false memories cannot be made through an analysis of their contents. Some suggestions were made that statement reality analysis (cf. Undeutsch, 1989) allows us to make the distinction between true and false reports of children who claim to have been abused, but a careful analysis showed that the validity of the technique is negligable (Wagenaar et al., 1993). Some studies on true and false memories of adults are underway in our group in Leiden (Wagenaar, Jackson, Otten, and Penrod, 1995), but the preliminary results do not allow the conclusion that true and false memories can be reliably distinguished.

The incremental nature of Yolanda's stories do not point to either truth or falsehood. But the fact that the stories keep changing, even after the verdict, suggests that the version given to the court was probably not correct. It would be an unlikely coincidence that the version of January 1994 was more correct than the various versions in the 10 previous years, or more correct than the later versions that have appeared since Yolanda's deposition. We may decide to accept only the elements that are common to all versions, assuming that autobiographical memory is accurate with respect to the "gist" of stories (cf. Neisser, 1981), even when the details are wrong. But then we are left with a very general and aspecific story that contains not enough detail to warrant a conviction unless it is corroborated by other more precise evidence.

Confessions

Of the six defendants in the trial, only three were charged with the murders of Sjon and Sanne: both parents of Yolanda and her former husband. According to Yolanda's description of the event, other people had also been present, like Yolanda's brother, Dr. Polders, both parents of Annette, another man by the name of Vierhouter, and maybe more, but charges were brought against only three. It is not clear why the other accusations of Yolanda were taken less seriously. Did the prosecutor believe that Yolanda's memories could not be accepted as accurate, even though there are detailed descriptions of what all the others did?

   Murders in general were confessed by both parents and one of the others. The specific murders of Sjon and Sanne were confessed by the mother only, but her confession was confused and changing. The problem with all the confessions was that the suspects were imprisoned for many months. In this period they were questioned 20 to 30 times; the questioning was the main contact they had with people. Questioning periods were often long, up to 5 hours or more. We have only a faint idea of what happened during the interrogations, because in the Dutch legal system it is sufficient for police officers to write a short affidavit about what the defendant said. On the average, every hour of interrogation resulted in one page of written text, which means a reduction of about 20 to 1. From the few interviews of which verbatim protocols were made, we concluded that the police used a number of methods, described by White (1989) as police trickery. One example is a letter dictated by Yolanda to the police in which she threatened to commit suicide if her father did not confess to the murders. This was no empty threat, as she had attempted suicide before. The police showed this letter to Yolanda's father during one of the interrogations.

   It is easy to imagine what long confinement, frequent and long interrogations, and police trickery may do to uneducated and quite simple-minded defendants. A telling signal is that the confessions change over time. First, most defendants denied any involvement, but after some months they confessed to the most brutal murders. There is little agreement among these extreme confessions, and the stories do not match Yolanda's descriptions.

   The central question with respect to confessions is, of course, whether interrogation methods may induce people to produce untrue statements, or even may help to implant new memories that are later recalled as genuine. The extensive literature on this topic (see Gudjonsson, 1992) demonstrates that these dangers are very real. Should the amount of conflict between the various confessions in Yolanda's case, and between confessions and Yolanda's stories, be interpreted as normal failure of autobiographical memory, or as the result of flawed interrogation methods? In our report we took the second option, because the methods, for what we know about them, were likely to produce false confessions. We will see that the court decided otherwise: they believed that the methods were acceptable, to the extent that some of the confessions were accepted as legal proof.

The trial and the verdict

A few days before the trial started, the public prosecutor decided not to argue the murder charges. Later the Procureur-Generaal, who is in charge of the office of the public prosecutor in a whole region, told Soppe and me that this decision was based upon our demonstration that the autobiographical memories of the witnesses and the accused were not reliable. There was no other evidence for the murder charges. There were no bodies, no missing persons, no blood stains, only stories. This decision did not mean that the charges were withdrawn, so the court was still obliged to investigate them and to pronounce a sentence.

The court in the provincial town of Zutphen decided to acquit the six defendants of all murder charges. The verdict used quite strong terms, given the cautious phrases that are usually encountered. Most acquittals are formulated in terms of "was not proven" or "the evidence did not convince the court." It is almost never said that the charge was wrong and that the defendant was innocent. In this case the court said about the murders of Sjon and Sanne (Van Baak v. State of The Netherlands, 1994):

From the medical information in the criminal file, produced by the physicians and medical specialists of the purported victim -from here on: the medical information- it appears that a pregnancy of at least 24 weeks in or around May 1984/1985 is out of the question.

On the basis of the contents of Article 82a of the Penal Code, there can be no question of a child (or children) or a fetus (or fetuses) who could be expected to remain alive outside the body of the mother. The alternative and more alternative charge of abortion or grievous bodily harm is also not legally and convincingly proven. These facts are incompatible with the deposition and other statements of Yolanda, that 'Sjon and Sanne' were born after a completed pregnancy and after a natural delivery that was not elicited by others.

Rejection of the other murder charges was in almost identical terms. The reasoning in the verdict is mainly based upon the medical reports, which apparently were accepted as truthful, and next on the conflict between the alternative charge and Yolanda's recall of the spontaneous delivery. But it is more interesting to realize that the murders were described in much detail by Yolanda, and were confessed to by three out of six defendants. The verdict means logically, although the issue was not mentioned, that Yolanda's complaint and the confessions were partly false. On some of the other charges the defendants were convicted on the basis of evidence that came from the same sources: statements by Yolanda and confessions from the defendants. Thus, implicitly the court revealed that it made a distinction between the true and false memories of Yolanda and the true and false memories of the defendants. The reasons given for the convictions simply quote the statements from Yolanda and the defendants as far as they support the charge. It is not explained why these statements can be accepted as more reliable than the ones that were rejected. The report by Soppe and me attempted to provide a basis for such a decision, with the help of criteria that were partly derived from the domain of memory research. The court did not explicitly mention these criteria as their basis, probably because Dutch courts rarely explain *why* they reject or accept evidence, only *which* evidence they accept.

Conclusion

In the end, we do not know how much consideration the court gave to the issue of the reliability of autobiographical memory, even though the case depended entirely on the acceptance of memory accounts. But at the same time, it is clear that the memories produced in this case were vague, unstable, uncertain, and conflicting. Nothing abnormal, then, but this is not the type of evidence that a court is seeking. The lesson to be learned is that in complicated cases, involving long delay periods, reports from autobiographical memory tend to be imprecise. If the law requires precise answers, witness testimony is not the most promising source.

References

Gudjonsson, G. H. (1992). *The Psychology of Interrogation, Confessions, and Testimony*. Chichester, UK: Wiley.

Loftus, E. F. (1993). The reality of repressed memories. *American Psychologist*, 48, 518–537.

Neisser, U. (1981). John Dean's memory: A case study. *Cognition*, 9, 1–22.

—— (1982). Snapshots or benchmarks? In U.Neisser (ed). *Memory Observed: Remembering in Natural Contexts*. San Francisco, CA: Freeman.

Rubin, D. C., & Baddeley, A. D. (1989). Telescoping is not time compression: A model of dating autobiographical events. *Memory and Cognition*, 17, 653–661.

Undeutsch, U. (1989). The development of statement reality analysis. In J. C. Yuille (Ed.), *Credibility Assessment*. Dordrecht, The Netherlands: Kluwer Academic.

Van Baak v. the State of The Netherlands, No. 06/007512-93, District Court Zutphen, 1994.

Van Bavel, C. J. & Verbunt, R. P. G. L. M. (1990). Slachtoffer/getuige in zedenzaken en verhoor ter zitting. *Nederlands Juristenblad*, 65, 1399–1404.

Wagenaar, W. A.(1986). My memory: A study of autobiographical memory over six years. *Cognitive Psychology*, 18, 225–252.

Wagenaar, W. A., Koppen, P. J. van, & Crombag, H. F. M. (1993). *Anchored Narratives, The Psychology of Criminal Evidence*. Hemel Hampstead: Harvester Wheatsheaf.

Wagenaar, W. A., & Loftus, E. F. (1990). Ten cases of eyewitness identification: Logical and procedural problems. *Journal of Criminal Justice*, 18, 291–319.

Wagenaar, W. A. & Schrier, J. Van der. (1994). Face recognition as a function of distance and illumination: A practical tool for use in the courtroom. Paper presented at the Fourth European Conference of Law and Psychology in Barcelona, Spain. Submitted for publication.

Wagenaar, W. A., Jackson, J., Otten, D., & Penrod, S. (1995). True and false testimony by pairs of witnesses (In preparation).

White, W. S. (1989) Police trickery in inducing confessions. *University of Pennsylvania Law Review*, 127, 581–629.

Wright, L. (1993). Remembering Satan, Parts I and II. *The New Yorker*, May 17 p. 60–81; May 24, p. 54–76.

Part III
Emotions

8   Perspective, meaning, and remembering

John A. Robinson

> Historical truth does not founder chiefly on the unreliability of memory or the arbitrariness of an interpreter's reconstructive attempts, but on the reflective mutability of meanings themselves.
>
>   Rosenwald and Ochberg (1992)

An essential premise of cognitive psychology is that people selectively process the information available to them in their world. Attention is limited and tends to be guided by goals, expectancies, or prior knowledge. Because we categorize situations and events according to features abstracted and generalized from experience, we may overlook or misinterpret information when a familiar pattern can be easily read into a situation. Although processing is selective, it has a coherence that derives from the distinctive organization of knowledge and feeling that characterizes each person. Thus, experiencing is inevitably an expression of a perspective or point of view. Perspective is an ill-defined concept, but Novak's characterization of *standpoint* provides a working definition of the term:

A standpoint . . . is a complex of all those things that compose an inquiring *who*. It is the complex of past experience, a range of sensibility, accumulated images and imaginative patterns, interests, bodies of insights already appropriated, purposes, structured and unstructured passions, criteria of evidence and relevance, the repertoire of already affirmed concrete judgments, values, goals, decisions. (1978, p. 55)

In effect perspective is the integrated operation of both stable and transient factors that shape a person's state of mind moment by moment. Research on memory and on social cognition has amply demonstrated that events can be experienced in qualitatively different ways. Situational and task factors can be manipulated so that they are the dominant influence on perception and memory, but when allowed to operate, individual differences in interests, goals, abilities, or personality influence every aspect of information processing (cf. Fiske & Taylor, 1991; Jenkins, 1979; Kihlstrom, 1981; McAdams, 1982).

Cognitive psychology can be viewed as the science of perspectives, that is, the study of processes by which experience is rendered intelligible and meaningful (cf. Bruner, 1990). Autobiographical memory is a particular facet of this broader discipline of perspectives. It is the study of how perspectives function in linking past, present, and future. The central importance of the individual's perspective has been acknowledged in various formulations of the nature of memory. Bartlett (1932) claimed that the person's

199

"attitude" guided remembering. Attitude was an inclusive term covering motivation, emotion, and interests. Klein's (1970) synthesis of experimental psychology and ego psychology proposed a framework for relating individual emotional and cognitive styles to account for perception and memory. Among contemporary theorists, Jenkins (1979) and Tulving (1983) have argued that a person's cognitive state is an important determinant of memory encoding and retrieval. Finally, the diverse theories of the self share at least one assumption in common: that cognitive processing is guided by the interests and goals of the individual. The focus on perspectives places personal meaning at the center of inquiry. Accuracy and completeness have been the conventional standards for assessing memory. In the world of cognitive research, the criteria for accuracy and completeness are usually defined from a third-person point of view. The investigator knows what really happened and can specify exactly how any person's account deviates from some canonical reality. But these discrepancies are neither absolute nor unambiguous. The observer/experimenter brings one of potentially many perspectives to a situation (Edwards, Potter, & Middleton, 1992). A third-person or observer perspective provides indispensable information, and societies may decide that for certain purposes it should be privileged, but it needs to be joined to a thorough analysis of first-person perspectives. The relative weighting of first-person and third-person perspectives has become a matter of concern in many areas of psychological study. Riessman's (1991) critique of research on causes of divorce, and Duck, Pond, and Leatham's (1991) critique of research on personal relationships illustrate the limitations of relying on a third-person approach to human experience.

Accepting the need to include the personal in our science does not leave us stranded in relativism. We can objectively characterize first-person perspectives as consistent or inconsistent with (1) those of other participants and observers, (2) each person's established ways of experiencing, and (3) their previous reports of events. This leads to two questions for memory studies. First, how does one person's experience (or account of that experience) diverge from others and what do those divergences signify? Second, how does a person's account of an event at one time diverge from that person's account at a later time, and what do those divergences signify? The main concern of this chapter is the relationship between original and remembered meanings. People can agree about referential details but disagree about what they mean. A person's perspective is most clearly expressed in the goals and feelings they attribute to themselves and others. Those attributions express the central core of the current meaning of experience. In subsequent sections I discuss studies of memory for feelings and of explanations of significant life events. My interest is in understanding when and why meaning changes or remains stable over time.

Four propositions about meaning

The multiplicity of potential meanings

The concept of meaning has been discussed and debated periodically in the study of cognition, but usually with limited impact on theory or research (cf. the exchange between Conway [1993] and Crowder [1993]). One reason is that many investigators have tended to regard meaning as an attribute of stimuli rather than as a relation between person, task, and environment (cf. Jacoby & Craik, 1979). A normative theory of processing is encouraged when meaning is treated as an attribute. For example, words have many normative features, for example, statistical structure, frequency, association patterns, and these features are plainly involved in perceiving and remembering words. However, the characteristics of the person and the choices they make are equally influential. Words that refer to personally salient domains have lower perceptual thresholds than normatively comparable words that refer to less salient domains (Postman, Bruner, & McGinnies, 1948). Many words have several meanings. If the situation permits choice between meanings, two subjects could experience the "same" information differently.

Like words, the identification of objects and of activities is open to multiple construals. An inflated cube could be a toy or a doorstop depending upon context and intended use. Intentions are a major determinant of behavior and meaning, but often cannot be unambiguously identified from behavior alone (cf. Humphrey, 1986; MacIntyre, 1981). For example, two people may appear to be arguing but they might reject that description. They may regard their interaction as normal, intense, or a disagreement, but not an argument. If your definition of arguing includes pushing or punching then verbal dispute alone may not constitute an argument. A person can have several distinct goals or intentions motivating any activity. A man working in his garden may be trying to tidy up before his wife returns from a trip because he knows how much pleasure she gets from the garden. At the same time gardening may also be a distraction from other worries or a pleasurable type of exercise. Or it could be a step in a long-range plan to replant and restore the garden for his grandchildren. Behavior can be embedded in several plans operating over varied time spans and relationships. Thus, the same behavior can be appropriately described in several ways, for example, working in the garden, trying to please my wife, replanting the garden. Without further information an observer would not know which descriptions are valid or most salient. In practice the mix of observation and inference required even for a neutral observer limits the utility of agreement as the sole basis for determining what happened, and especially for understanding feelings and goals.

Deferred meaning

Meaning is not always fully explicated when events occur. The development of meaning has two routes: through categorization and recategorization, and by elaboration. Sometimes an aspect of experience that we barely noticed may become salient later on. Other times it may not be clear what has happened. We may be puzzled about some episode. Was that a slight, a rebuke, or just a case of irritability? If you do not understand the point of a person's behavior, you might not be comfortable assigning it significance or meaning and may suspend labeling or categorizing the event. Later you may learn that the person's marriage is breaking up and categorize the event as an understandable instance of generalized anger. It was not to be taken personally. But suppose you also learn that that same person was under consideration for a promotion that you received. Then the episode acquires additional potential significance. You could recategorize the event as an instance of office politics. If you are inclined to thoughtfulness you might maintain your previous view and augment it with an additional perspective. In that case meaning has been elaborated by embedding the same event in more than one category. Elaboration can take other forms than embedding. For example, an accountant may have consistently explained his occupational choice by saying he wanted to make a lot of money. Lately he has begun to add that the intellectual challenge of accounting was also one of the reasons he chose that career. He has not rejected an earlier understanding, only extended it to include other factors that do not fundamentally contradict each other.

Changing meaning

The meaning of any experience can change over time. New information or an altered perspective can prompt us to reinterpret specific experiences or entire segments of our personal history. Jobs we hated or people we regarded as authoritarian may, in hindsight, be seen differently. The work was hard, but good experience; the teacher was demanding, but prepared you for the competitiveness of the workplace. Some individuals, when they first learn that they were adopted by the people they have regarded as their natural parents, readily assimilate this surprise into their life story and seem to maintain their sense of identity unchanged. Others experience a crisis. They believe that there is a "truer self" that has been hidden from them and go through a difficult process of revising and reintegrating their sense of personal identity (Haimes, 1987). Their experiences, interests, accomplishments, and relationships may all be questioned. Through counseling, abused spouses may come to understand that they were not weak, but were skillfully manipulated, or women may conclude they were coerced into giving a child up to adoption rather than acting out of compassion. There is the urge to judge one meaning as "true" and others as mistaken or biased. Accuracy is the wrong category to use in these cases. Meanings should be judged by other criteria, such as authenticity and functional impact. Both prior and current meaning can be authentic. Each has been constructed within a perspective that reflects the person's preferred ways of organizing experience. When people change, their ways of interpreting the world may also change. The urge to treat one meaning as right or true and another as wrong or biased comes from the impact changing meaning has for the meaning of relationships not from epistemic edginess.

Negotiating meaning

We are all accountable to others for our actions and attitudes. We are expected to be able to describe and explain our lives. Perspectives have to be aligned to avoid sanctions or conflict. Aligning is a process of reciprocal persuasion (Edwards et al., 1992; Gergen & Gergen, 1988). Talking about experience requires various cognitive, linguistic, and social skills (cf. Fivush, Hirst & Manier, this volume). The reasons for talking are equally important. Robinson (1981a) proposed that personal narratives can be told to entertain, to argue or persuade, or to resolve uncertainty. Each function is associated with a mode of conversation that imposes constraints on the content and organization of a narrative and ascribes roles and privileges to teller and listener. Through these interactions meaning is shaped and constrained. Each of the aspects of meaning discussed above can be impacted by talking to others. New meanings can emerge, additional meanings can be brought out, and initial meanings can be revised.

These observations should prepare us to find that meaning can be quite dynamic and that remembered meaning may display a variety of changes and transformations (Barclay, this volume). I take up next memory for two aspects of first-person meaning: feelings and reasons. Feelings reflect a person's evaluation of the import of a situation for their current and future goals (Oatley, 1992; Singer & Salovey, 1993; Stein, Trabasso, & Liwag, in press). Reasons are accounts or explanations of behavior that specify plausible (and acceptable) goals. Reasons and feelings express salient features of a person's perspective on both present and past experience. It is likely that the goal structures that shape feelings and reasons are utilized in memory representations of personal experience (Conway, 1990, this volume; Singer & Salovey, 1993). However, like other information represented in memory, goals can be modified or reinterpreted. How we remember previous feelings and intentions depends upon the fit between our current view of things and the perspective that directed the encoding of that experience in memory. Current perspective is affected by situational and systemic factors. Situational aspects such as mood and setting are changeable. This means that recollection can also be changeable, apparently stable and consistent under some conditions but unstable or inconsistent under others. Systemic factors are ones that have produced a reorganiztion of central psychological structures such as beliefs and personal values. Remembering is always embedded in a developmental history (Fitzgerald, 1986, this volume). Changes of this magnitude do not inevitably produce a rewriting of personal history. The important factor is the extent to which the rememberer can construct a perspective on the past that approximates the one that prevailed originally.

Remembering feelings

As we think and talk about the meaningful experiences in our lives, we quickly confront feelings. Sometimes they emerge as apparent facts ("I was angry at him."; "It was the most fun I'd had in years."); sometimes as questions posed to oneself or by others ("Did you love her?"; "Were you afraid?"). Until very recently, most of the research by experimental psychologists on memory and feelings was concerned with forgetting. Debates about the impact of pleasantness or of affect intensity revolved around the probablility and accuracy of event recall. Affect was regarded as an amplifier or a distorter that could "stamp in" event details or produce biased perception and recollection. Far less attention was given to memory for feelings per se. But the issue of whether we can directly remember feelings has been debated since the turn of the century (B. M. Ross, 1990). One position is that feelings can be re-created but cannot be revived. In this view feelings are transient states that are encoded in cognitive form as part of the event representation in memory. Information about feelings could be explicitly represented in verbal descriptions or implicitly represented in perceptual representations of behavior. A person could "report" their original feelings by accessing either of those forms of information, or through inferences from the pattern of activities represented in the memory record. If the event is sufficiently salient, reporting about it may initiate arousal and behavioral reactions, and the person may experience feeling as she/he remembers. Thus, according to this view, memories start out phenomenologically "cold," but can become "hot" through cognitive reconstruction.

A contrasting view emphasizes that feelings are complex states consisting of physiological arousal, perceptual and sensory qualities, active knowledge, and a variety of appraisal procedures, and proposes distinct representational systems in memory for many of these aspects (e.g., Christianson, 1992; Johnson & Multhaup, 1992). One implication of the multiple systems view is that there are several different ways we can remember feelings. A person may know how she/he felt but not reexperience that emotion. The strong cognitive view of affect memory summarized above provides only one account of this outcome, but a multiple systems view provides several possibilities. Recall may be confined to knowing because other kinds of information related to the experience have been forgotten, or are inhibited from expression, or are otherwise inaccessible to recall. Memory of feelings can occur in three other forms: as spontaneous affect, as cognitively generated affect, and as implicit memory. A multiple systems view provides a more plausible account of spontaneous feelings accompanying recall than a reconstructive theory, but accounts for cases of reconstruction in essentially the same way as the strong cognitive position. A strong cognitive view of remembered affect has no place for implicit memory, but from a multiple systems view, it should be possible to experience feelings without a concomitant conscious recollection of the associated event (cf. Tobias, Kihlstrom, & Schacter, 1992).

There have been several demonstrations of apparent dissociations between affective and cognitive memory. Korsakoff's patients show normal preference effects though memory for the stimuli is impaired (Johnson, Kim, & Risse, 1985). Christianson and Nilsson (1989) reported that a rape victim returned to the scene of the assault was greatly agitated, but she did not consciously recognize it as the location where she had been raped. Dissociated affective reactions are a common feature of patients with functional amnesia and have been experimentally induced through hypnosis (Tobias, Kihlstrom, & Schacter, 1992). In many cases of trauma emotions reoccur spontaneously when the event is recollected, even when recall is involuntary. Dissociated reactions and involuntary recall provide strong evidence that affect may be directly encoded and authentically reexperienced.

At present the theoretical debate about constructed versus revived emotions is unresolved, but a multiple systems theory provides the scope and flexibility required to account for the various forms of remembered affect. It is clear that people can remember ordinary events very well and not experience much, if any feeling. For other more affecting events, the extent to which feelings are experienced during remembering may depend upon the nature of the event, subsequent experience, conditions at the time of recall, the reasons for remembering, and the manner in which remembering is organized (cf. Christianson and Safer [this volume] for a similar argument). Feelings are one indication of the personal significance of experience. Experiences that continue to be meaningful tend to evoke stronger feelings when recalled than those that are not. For example, Singer (1990) asked college students to rate the desirability of various goals derived from Murray's theory of needs and personality. Each goal was then used to cue autobiographical memories. Subjects' ratings of their current feeling about remembered events were positively correlated with goal desirability. There is a large body of literature on affect and memory, but a surprisingly small portion of it examines recall of feelings per se. In the following discussion my interest is in determining how a person's current perspective or state of mind influences how they remember prior feelings. I discuss three different circumstances: mood-based influences on recall of prior feelings; cognitive control of affect during recall; and schema-guided reconstructions of feelings.

Mood and remembered feelings

Current moods and emotions have strong effects on perception and thought (Forgas & Bower, 1987; Forgas, Bower, & Moylan, 1990). Common experience suggests that present feelings also affect how past experiences are appraised. There is considerable evidence that current mood can produce selective retrieval of mood-congruent memories (Blaney, 1986; Eich, 1989). The question posed here is whether the quality or intensity of present moods prompts people to either over- or underestimate characteristics of the previously experienced mood or emotion. Williams (1992) described a depressed woman who revised her feelings about a pleasant experience after a subsequent unpleasant episode. He suggested that her revisionist account was due to hindsight bias, that is, that in order to account for the recent unpleasant event she altered her account of the prior one so that it now could be seen as forecasting more unpleasantness. Retrospective bias may be partly mood dependent. There are several ways this type of lability could arise. One is that current mood may channel attention to certain aspects or details of an event. Details may have differential salience depending upon recall mood, or vary in the degree to which they can be used as warrants in an interpretation organized by current mood. Williams' patient, for example, retrospectively fastened on things she disliked about herself, such as her weight and her appearance in a swimsuit, that evidently did not bother her much at the time of the swimming party. People viewing a videotape of a prior interaction identified more negative social behaviors when they were in a sad mood, but more positive behaviors when they were in a good mood though neutral observers saw no difference in the number of positive and negative behaviors (Forgas, Bower, & Krantz, 1984).

Current mood or arousal level may serve as a temporary judgment standard for remembered feelings. Bower (1981) found that ratings of current intensity of feelings associated with prior experiences shifted in the direction of present mood. It is likely that the same result would have been found if subjects had rated their original feelings under contrasting moods. Another finding of the Forgas et al. (1984) study cited above is consistent with this assumption: participants who were in a positive mood for the retrospective tests said they had been more comfortable, relaxed, and interested than participants who were in a negative mood. There is some evidence that both contrast and assimilation effects can occur for retrospective judgments of feelings. Robinson (1981b) found that arousal level and the affective valence of a context set of life experiences interacted, elevating retrospective ratings of unrelated experiences in one condition and depressing them in another. A potentially important factor that has not been studied in relation to mood is the outcome or aftermath of events. Outcomes must be a salient aspect of one's perspective. The anxiety associated with the first test in a course may be regarded differently after several more tests have been taken, or after a final grade has been received. The pleasure of a romantic episode may be remembered in contrasting ways depending upon the subsequent course of the relationship. And experience in other courses and other relationships can provide a new basis of comparison. Though conjectural, it seems plausible that mood can affect the choice of events used for comparison and the way outcome information gets factored into retrospective judgments of feelings.

Cognitive control of emotions during recall

Whether feelings are experienced during recall can be subject to cognitive control. The success of varied therapies such as systematic desensitization as a treatment for phobias and anxiety disorders and cognitive therapies for depression, indicates that people can control their emotions as they recall or reflect on disturbing experiences. Studies of the phenomenology of memory provide evidence of another way emotionality is regulated when a person is remembering. Nigro and Neisser (1983) drew attention to the fact that remembering can be organized from differing perspectives or points of view. Subjectively, the rememberer may reexperience the event as a participant or as a spectator. With the participant or field perspective, the rememberer "sees" the event from his perspective as in normal perception. With the spectator point of view, the rememberer "sees" the self engaged in the event as an observer would. In one study Nigro and Neisser instructed subjects to remember specified events and to focus either on their feelings or on the physical context (the "objective circumstances") of the event. The observer perspective was reported more often when subjects focused on the context, whereas the field perspective was reported more often when they focused on their feelings. The interesting implication of that result is that altering recall focus (perspective) may alter the emotional content of recollections. Neisser (personal communication) has suggested that memory perspectives may regulate the affect experienced in remembering. A recent set of studies by Robinson and Swanson (1993) provides support for his view. They compared ratings of experienced affect for events recalled initially from one perspective and then a few weeks later from either the same or the other perspective. Two findings indicated that the affect experienced while remembering was associated with perspective. First, field memories of recent events were accompanied by more intense feelings when initially recalled than observer memories of recent events. Second, changing from a field to an observer perspective was associated with a significant reduction in both the affect experienced while remembering and the judgments of affect experienced when the event originally occurred. When the same perspective was adopted for both recalls experienced affect was more stable.

Robinson and Swanson (1993) proposed that perspectives function as retrieval descriptions and each accesses or guides construction of different components of affect-related information. Cognitive representations of goals and beliefs can be accessed by either perspective, but arousal records can only be accessed by the field perspective. Adopting an observer perspective functionally inhibits retrieval of arousal information. The observer perspective also becomes the default perspective when arousal information cannot be accessed or has been eliminated from memory. People can experience affect with either memory perspective, but it will be cognitively constructed and diminished in intensity when the observer orientation prevails. Memory perspective appears to function as a control process. It may influence other features of remembering than affect, but that remains to be studied.

Research on modes of remembering has been confined to ordinary events and memories, but phenomenal aspects of recollection are also important clues to the dynamics of coping with memories of traumatic experiences. The descriptions of "flashbacks" associated with posttraumatic stress disorder and other traumas suggest that such memory episodes always occur as field memories and are very hard to restructure. Expressive writing has been shown to be a powerful therapeutic tool for resolving the intense affects engendered by traumatic experiences (e.g., Harber & Pennebaker, 1992). One reason is that people can construct meaning through writing and attain some sense of control of the experience. One participant in such a program remarked that writing "helped me to look at myself from the outside" (Harber & Pennebaker, 1992, p. 376). The wording suggests that the person may have adopted an observer perspective at least some of the time, which, according to Robinson and Swanson, would have regulated the affect experienced while thinking about the event and moderated arousal enough to permit more cognitively based coping reactions. Williams (this volume) reviews a program of research that indicates that other memory processes are implicated in the maintenance of affective disturbances such as clinical depression. That research has shown that clinically depressed individuals have difficulty recalling specific experiences. The memory deficit he has documented has one quality in common with perspective: both the observer mode and the summarizing style distance the individual from strong affect in recall.

Schema-guided reconstruction of feelings

Many theorists have argued that feelings guide memory construction, that is, the recollected details of events are shaped to fit how the person currently feels about the experience. Contemporary theories of memory have elaborated on this assumption in two important ways. First, the cognitive organization of event knowledge has been clarified and shown to constrain constructive processing in recall. Second, feelings have been subsumed within a diverse class of evaluative processes and incorporated into memory representations of experience. The upshot is that remembered feelings can be subject to schematic bias as much as any other aspect of experience. The rapidly developing area of research on personal relationships is providing vital information about the dynamics of affect and memory. Most daily events involve other people. The feelings experienced in a shared event or reported after the fact may be constructed, in part, from cognitive schemas that represent attitudes and feelings towards the person(s) involved in the experience. Holmberg and Holmes (in press) had recently married couples record for several weeks daily events that impacted their feelings for their partners. A short time later each spouse was tested for recall of selected events. Retrospective reports of feelings towards partners for the day in question were significantly correlated with original ratings. However, regression analyses of discrepancies between the two reports showed that attitude toward the relationship was more important than general mood at the time of the test, and was as important as original feelings in predicting the pattern of discrepancies. The judgments of people who perceived their relationship as secure closely matched their original ratings for both positive and negative feelings. People who were insecure were less positive about positive states and more negative in their recall of negative states. Duck et al. (1991) obtained a similar result in their study of friends. The way a conversation about first getting acquainted was remembered depended, in part, on the level of satisfaction with the relationship. Those who were dissatisfied evaluated the remembered conversation more negatively than they had at the time of its occurrence even though the level of satisfaction itself had not changed.

Holmberg and Holmes (in press) proposed that both secure and insecure couples were reconstructing their earlier feelings from their current cognitive models of the relationship. Like schemas for other experience domains, person-relationship models are a source of stability in experience, but they can also be altered by experience. In the case of relationships, people may rehearse prior interactions and integrate them into their model, altering or maintaining the affective dimensions. Insecure spouses may be reminded more often of prior unpleasant interactions as another occurs, and regard that as evidence that reinforces their negative stance. Partners who feel lonely in a friendship probably find regular confirmation of their feeling with similar cognitive consequences. This could produce gradual polarization or affective drift in the model that would lead to greater negative bias in retrospective reports.

Holmberg and Holmes (In press) also showed that changes in a relationship can lead to retrospective revisions. They analyzed narrative accounts of the relationship, from the courtship phase through the wedding and honeymoon, obtained shortly after couples married and again 2 years later. Two groups of couples were compared: for one group marital satisfaction remained stable over the period, for the other there had been a substantial decline in marital satisfaction. The narratives of "stable" couples portrayed the history of the relationship and their marital partner in terms that matched their initial accounts. Male spouses of "decline" couples described the history of the relationship and their partner in more negative terms than they had 2 years previously. Female spouses of "decline" couples did not show the same bias. Selective retrieval and self-presentational strategies may be partly responsible for the gender difference, but the results strongly imply that current affective stance can bias summarizing judgments about an earlier period of a relationship. How that bias is generated is less certain. It may be based on reconstructions guided by a current relationship schema, but it may also be reflect a discrepancy between expected and actual status. People have conceptual models of ideal relationships and of what partners must do to sustain them (e.g., Baxter, 1992). Retrospective exaggerations of distress in a relationship may be a measure of disappointment based on discrepancies between expectations and experience.

Many of the significant events in people's lives, such as jobs and relationships, are spread out over months and years. There are times when we try to characterize them in a summary way. Did you have a happy childhood, a happy marriage, a satisfying career? The research reviewed by Christianson and Safer (this volume) indicates that people are poor judges of the relative frequency and intensity of their feelings. However, I surmise that not only our answers but the way we go about trying to answer may differ from one time to the next. Consider Field's (1981) findings about changes over time in judgments of happiness of childhood. Parents of children studied in the longitudinal Berkeley Guidance Study were interviewed about various aspects of family life at several intervals, for example, within the year when their children first entered the Study, when their children were 17, and when the children were grown adults (age 40) and the parents elderly. Field studied the consistency of responses to the interview questions across the periods. Overall, retrospective judgments grew more positive across the 40-year period. However, more respondents judged their childhood as generally unhappy at the time their children were 17 than at any other period. It appears that the relationship with their own children may have colored their judgments about the relationship they had as children with their parents. Several factors may be at work. Adolescence often strains parent-child relationships. Following Holmberg and Holmes' (in press) reasoning, parents' person-relationship models pertaining to their current relations with their children may act as a frame of reference for judging their own experience as children. Selective retrieval may also be an influential factor. A person-relationship model in which distress is currently elaborated could provide more retrieval cues for affectively related childhood memories.

Feelings are central to the meaning of experience because they are one expression of the way a person understands an experience. Theorists since Bartlett (1932) have argued that remembering, like perceiving, is guided by present ways of understanding. Thus, we would expect that anything that alters the way a past experience is interpreted would alter what a person remembers about that experience. The research on memory for feelings strongly supports this view. Some factors such as current mood and recall perspective are temporary influences. Others, such as cognitive models of self and others, vary in their span of stability. Memory processes such as retrieval and reconstruction are either controlled by the aforementioned states and structures or interact with them to determine recollective experience and memory judgments.

Remembering reasons

People need explanations of important events in their lives. Explanations are accounts that identify causes and consequences (Harvey, Weber, & Orbuch, 1990). Good explanations help people sustain their belief in an orderly, predictable world, and reinforce a coherent sense of personal identity and feelings of personal efficacy (Thompson & Janigan, 1988). People's explanations for their behavior are usually limited, selective, and biased: that is, they do not take into account all of the relevant influences and may distort or give disproportionate weight to some factors (Fiske & Taylor, 1991; Gilovich, 1991; Nisbett & Wilson, 1977). It is valuable to know whether a person's account is true to the facts from an external perspective, but that should not be the only concern in autobiographical memory research. Of equal interest is the roles explanations play in personal histories and whether or how those accounts may change over time. Explanations of everyday actions may not become an explicit part of one's personal history. They can be readily reconstructed from personal knowledge and self-schemata. Explanations of behavior and experiences that alter one's life do become an explicit part of one's personal history. Choosing a career, a mate, or to divorce have irreversible consequences, and the reasons for making those choices impact one's sense of identity and the coherence of one's life story.

Schema-guided memory for explanations

As already noted, explanations are constructed from a perspective. They may incorporate the views of others but always have a residual first-person aspect. This is particularly important to the recall of explanations for events. If we can understand a past episode in the same way we did then, our memory of it will appear to be stable. If we cannot, our memory will be seem to be unstable. Blackburne-Stover, Belenky, & Gilligan (1982) studied a group of women who were trying to cope with an unplanned pregnancy and had been referred to counseling services. Many of them subsequently decided to have an abortion. Blackburne-Stover et al. compared responses from an initial interview conducted at the counseling service with those given in a retrospective interview conducted about a year later. The initial interview was constructed to elicit each woman's thoughts and feelings about the pregnancy and to determine their moral perspective in terms of Kohlberg's stages of moral thinking. The same questions were posed in the follow-up interview but were rephrased in the past tense. For some women, retrospective accounts were essentially unchanged. For others, changes were noted. More changes were found for women who responded to the Kohlberg dilemmas at a "higher" level of moral reasoning a year later than those who did not advance. Spontaneous remarks about not remembering were also more frequent in the change group. Blackburne-Stover et al. interpret these results in a way that is quite similar to Ross' (1989) analysis of the role of implicit theories in remembering. Recall is guided by a conceptual framework, in this instance moral beliefs. One's current beliefs are more salient than any others and set the terms of memory reconstructions. When beliefs change, the bases of understanding both present and past also change. The study has several limitations, but is important because it focuses attention on a possible causal relation between memory and standpoint for an emotionally and morally complex situation.

Reinterpreting explanantions

Memory may be most unstable for experiences that involve unresolved conflicts. Explanations are stories. They specify causes and reasons to account for the details of an experience (cf. Robinson & Hawpe, 1986). Even ordinary events are open to alternative interpretations, but situations that evoke strong emotional conflicts are especially liable to reinterpretation. Eakin (1985) describes a striking instance of this process in his study of the autobiographical writings of Mary McCarthy. In her book *Memories of a Catholic Girlhood*, McCarthy (1957) explains how she got the nickname C.Y.E. while attending a convent school. The account given in *Memories* is quite different from one given in a story McCarthy published many years earlier. In her school advanced students bestowed nicknames on junior students but never explained what the names meant. The secrecy seems to have amplified McCarthy's insecurity. In the early story she describes being convinced that the nickname somehow mocked her, and the intense shame she experienced. The story is a cathartic drama, however, as it recounts a moment of insight years later when she is convinced that it stood for "Clever Young Egg" and was actually a sign of admiration if not acceptance.

In her memoirs, written more than a decade after the story, McCarthy approaches the nickname issue from a different perspective. Now it is embedded in an almost picaresque story about lies and impostures. She was stuck with a name she disliked but could not disown because it would mean disclosing how she had misled the nuns and students. McCarthy's reformulation was deliberate: in an interview she reports her dislike of the early story and the decision to recast the entire episode (see Eakin, 1985, pp. 32–33). It is interesting, however, that she chose not to comment on the matter in the reflective chapters she appended to each autobiographical sketch in *Memories* where she typically explored doubts about her recollections. The portrayal of her younger self in the short story has many of the qualities associated with a victim perspective (cf. Baumeister, Stillwell, & Wotman, 1990). The moment of revelation released her from that view and converted the experience to something less hurtful. As Eakin notes, however, the conversion seems not to have resolved McCarthy's feelings. The ending of the story is vengeful, the victim retaliates. The subsequent account in *Memories* continues the victim theme but now as a self-imposed condition. This narrative move seems to have helped McCarthy deal with a lingering if unconscious resentment by making herself the agent of her distress. She was in control, not her classmates.

Control, meaning, and consistency

While some explanations may be ad hoc and undermotivated, studies of account making are finding that typically they have some form of coherent structure. Riessman (1990) describes several narrative patterns in divorce accounts. The common cognitive task divorcing couples face is to construct a persuasive and plausible scenario that identifies conditions of the marriage that warrant their decision to divorce. This task can be accomplished in a variety of ways. The narrative genres Riessman identified illustrate the variety of explanatory patterns in use. How stable are such stories? Common experience suggests that it depends upon several factors. It would be very interesting to explore this matter by studying people who remarry and who stay married or divorce again. An explanation is more than a persuasive story, it is also a commitment to view experience in a particular way. There is likely to be strong pressure to be consistent, that is, to retain the explanatory perspective. This would predispose people to selective rehearsal of events or experiential themes that support their explanation, and enhance the accessibility of information organized by the explanation relative to other information that has not been incorporated. How do divorced couples respond to events in their marriage that contradict their explanations? For example, coming across photographs or unexpectedly meeting one's ex-spouse some years later may be reminders of aspects that had been suppressed in the interests of the divorce account. Do such familiar judgment rules such as salience, representativeness, or ease of scenario modification come into play to sustain or repair the canonical account? Do people tend to favor different types of accounts at different ages? Implicit theories of personal stability and change (Ross, 1989) could be a factor in stability of accounts. A 50-year-old man or woman who has had a satisfying second marriage after divorcing at age 20 might give a different account of that decision than he or she did originally, and it might differ from what they would have said at 35.

Explanations serve several functions. They provide individuals with justifications for their feelings and actions. They can reduce anxiety and a sense of powerlessness. And they help maintain or repair relationships with others. The terms of our accounts must balance personal and interpersonal conditions of utility and appropriateness (Gergen & Gergen, 1988). I surmise that the development of explanations over time resembles hypothesis testing. The "data" are remembrances, the "truth conditions" are explicit and implicit representations of personal and social goals and beliefs. A final account is adopted through selective testing of its elements for fit with personal need and social necessity. Acceptable explanations can change but must always satisfy personal and social criteria. Personal needs, social pressure for consistency, and tacit norms of continuity in self-identity constrain the ways explanations can change in retrospect. "I went into accounting for the money, but now I realize that I enjoy it, it's really challenging. I must have been drawn to it for that too, but money was more important to me and I just didn't think about other reasons for becoming an accountant." This kind of explanation is completely consonant with folk psychological beliefs about age-based goals, multiple motives, and degrees of insight. It meets the two criteria of adequate causality and continuity for career choice proposed by Linde (1993). Social norms are not just constraints, they can also be heuristic models for self-exploration (Robinson, 1992). We are expected to be able to explain our behavior but often need help in "clarifying" our motives and goals (cf. Robinson, 1981a). Linde's discussion of strategies for handling discontinuity between career choice and preceding or subsequent experience indicates how the stock of socially available explanations can help people construct coherent accounts of this important turning point.

There can be significant differences between public and private accounts. In many cases those differences may reflect impression management. For example, Baumeister and Stillwell (1992) report that people will credit other people more when recounting a recent, major success if they know their account will be shared with a group, than if they believe it will remain anonymous. But in other cases, especially those that involve strong emotions and risks, private accounts could be radically different from public accounts. People may feel they are not permitted to speak authentically about their experience, or that the risks of candor are too great. Explanations can change dramatically when people are judged to be more receptive than previously. We are naturally suspicious of dramatic changes and test the credibility of the new account by criteria of coherence, plausibility, and consistency with behavior. However, there may not be a definitive way of determining the authenticity of such revisions.

This survey shows that discrepancies between explanations from different periods in a person's life can be due to many factors including changes of perspective, meaning elaborations, selective retrieval and reconstruction, availability of social support, and changes in the perceived risk of disclosure. Changes are not de facto indications of revisionism, of egocentric rewriting of personal history. Because explanations organize experience in relation to intentions and self-appraisal their truth is never just a matter of conforming to a documentary record of behavior (Bruner, 1986; 1992). Rather, changes should also be evaluated in terms of the problems they create or the problems they solve for the person and those implicated in the history of the events involved. Changes may amplify or elaborate prior accounts but retain the previous elements, as in the hypothetical example about career choice given above. Incremental changes of this kind are typical of the insight (or hindsight) folk models attribute to aging. These elaborations preserve continuity of perspective, personal identity, and the meaning of relationships. Changes can be categorical, replacing a previous view with a different one. This tends to occur when there have been substantial changes in personal outlook, or when the need to reconcile private and public accounts becomes an urgent concern. Categorical changes disrupt continuity and create uncertainties about the meaning of relationships, as well as the trustworthiness of the individual. They typically create a crisis. Changes like those seen in Mary McCarthy's (1957) accounts of her nickname preserve important thematic aspects but exchange roles and alter other elements, a mnemonic equivalent of figure-ground reorganization. This type of change steers a middle ground: it stakes out a personal view of events and relationships but in a way that largely leaves the field open for others to maintain whatever view they may have of the situation.[1]

---

[1] In some types of psychotherapy the primary goal is to develop an explanation of the client's entire life history. This process usually leads to new interpretations of experience through a process of heuristic conarration of the events of the client's personal history. Therapist and client negotiate jointly acceptable meanings, and it is likely that the new meanings reflect categorical changes more often than elaborative changes. Bach (1952) reports the results of memory tests at the end of treatment with a few of the individuals he had treated in group therapy. His clients were quite poor at identifying statements they had made early in therapy relating to attitudes and experiences with parents and siblings. They rejected almost a quarter of them as entirely unlike their experience. Bach indicated that the rejected items were usually related to areas where significant improvement had occurred in the course of therapy. One interpretation of these results is that clients developed radically new perspectives on themselves and their life history and could not recover or reconstruct their prior perspectives. Bach advocated an interpersonal approach to remembering and disavowed the metaphor of fixed traces or memories. Thus, he would not label misidentifications as errors. Rather, they index attitudes that are no longer psychologically necessary or valid.

Conclusion

In many respects the past is a moving target. Sometimes we get lucky and hit it, many times we miss but have the illusion of having hit it. Establishing whether a memory is a hit or miss crucially depends upon the definition or choice of targets. I have argued that in autobiographical memory research we need to examine memory from both third-person and first-person perspectives. We need to know in greater detail how each participant perceived and encoded a situation before we can determine the status of what each person remembers. In this framework, accuracy is replaced by agreement among participants, and forgetting is replaced by stability or consistency between reports at different times. For some aspects of experience agreement (between experimenter and subject, or among participants) or conformity with some documentary information may be given priority. For the interpretive aspects of experience the first-person perspective has priority.

Remembering, like perceiving, is guided by present ways of understanding. Memory will be most stable when we construe events in the same way we did originally. In those instances it seems that remembering is mainly a process of successful retrieval. Whether (or under what conditions) correct or stable recall is the result of retrieval of unmodified traces or the result of reconstruction that is guided by an appropriate implicit model (Ross & Conway, 1986; Ross, 1989) is an open question. Some theorists describe retrieval as a process of reunderstanding (e.g., Reiser, Black, & Kalamarides, 1986). They propose that retrieval is mediated by descriptions that are used to search long-term memory. In this approach understanding refers to the active use of extant knowledge structures to generate retrieval cues. This approach is compatible with a perspectival theory and can account for some kinds of stability and instability in event recall (cf. Conway, this volume), but it underestimates the transformative effects of subsequent experience on information in memory, and of changes in the person. Memory for aspects of meaning can be affected by many factors. Some are situation specific and transient, others reflect significant changes in personal outlook and social utility. It is a conceptually restricted view that lumps all changes together as forgetting or bias. Instead, we should try to discriminate changes that reflect natural and productive developmental processes from those that are strategic practices designed to manipulate others. There is no absolute virtue in stability, and no necessary stigma in change.

References

Bach, G. R. (1952). Some diadic functions of childhood memories. *Journal of Psychology, 33,* 87–98.
Bartlett, F.C. (1932). *Remembering: A study in experimental and social psychology.* Cambridge, UK: Cambridge University Press.
Baumeister, R. F., & Stillwell, A. M. (1992). Autobiographical accounts, situational roles, and motivated biases: When stories don't match up. In J. H. Harvey, T. L. Orbuch, & A. L. Weber (Eds.), *Attributions, accounts, and close relationships* (pp. 52–70). New York: Springer-Verlag.
Baumeister, R. F., Stillwell, A., & Wotman, S. R. (1990). Victim and perpetrator accounts of interpersonal conflict: Autobiographical narratives about anger. *Journal of Personality and Social Psychology, 59,* 994–1005.
Baxter, L. A. (1992). Root metaphors in accounts of developing romantic relationships. *Journal of Social and Personal Relationships, 9,* 253–275.

Blackburne-Stover, G., Belenky, M. F., & Gilligan, C. (1982). Moral development and reconstructive memory: Recalling a decision to terminate an unplanned pregnancy. *Developmental Psychology, 18*, 862–870.

Blaney, P. H. (1986). Affect and memory: A review. *Psychological Bulletin, 99*, 229–246.

Bower, G. (1981). Mood and memory. *American Psychologist, 36*, 129–148.

Bruner, J. (1986). *Actual minds, possible worlds.* Cambridge, MA: Harvard University Press.

—— (1990). *Acts of meaning.* Cambridge, MA: Harvard University Press.

Bruner, J. (1992). The narrative construction of reality. In H. Beilin & P. Puffal (Eds.), *Piaget's theory: Prospects and possibilities* (pp. 229–248). Hillsdale, NJ: Lawrence Erlbaum.

Christianson. S.-A. (1992). Remembering emotional events: Potential mechanisms. In S.-A. Christianson (Ed), *The handbook of emotion and memory: Research and theory* (pp. 307- 340). Hillsdale, NJ: Lawrence Erlbaum.

Christianson, S.-A., & Nilsson, L.-G. (1989). Hysterical amnesia: A case of aversively motivated isolation of memory. In T. Archer & L.-G. Nilsson (Eds.), *Aversion, avoidance, and anxiety: Perspectives on aversively motivated behavior* (pp. 289–310). Hillsdale, NJ: Lawrence Erlbaum.

Conway, M. A. (1990). Associations between autobiographical memories and concepts. *Journal of Experimental Psychology: Learning, Memory, and Cognition, 16*, 799–812.

—— (1993). Method and meaning in memory research. In G. M. Davies & R. H. Logie (Eds.), *Memory in everyday life* (pp. 499–524). Amsterdam: North-Holland.

Crowder, R. G. (1993). Holy war or wholly unnecessary? Some thoughts on the 'conflict' between laboratory studies and everyday memory. In G. M. Davies & R. H. Logie (Eds.), *Memory in everyday life* (pp. 525–531). Amsterdam: North-Holland.

Duck, S., Pond, K., & Leatham, G. (1991). *Remembering as a context for being in relationships: Different perspectives on the same interaction.* Paper presented at the Third Conference of the International Network on Personal Relationships, Normal/Bloomington, IL.

Eakin, P. J. (1985). *Fictions in autobiography: Studies in the art of self-invention.* Princeton: Princeton University Press.

Edwards, D., Potter, J., & Middleton, D. (1992). Toward a discursive psychology of remembering. *The Psychologist, 5*, 441- 453.

Eich, J. E. (1989). Theoretical issues in state-dependent memory. In H. L. Roediger & F. I. M. Craik (Eds.), *Varieties of memory and consciousness* (pp. 331–354.) Hillsdale, NJ: Lawrence Erlbaum.

Field, D. (1981). Retrospective reports by healthy intelligent elderly people of personal events of their adult lives. *International Journal of Behavioral Development, 4*, 77–97.

Fiske S. T., & Taylor, S. E. (1991). *Social cognition* (2nd ed.). New York: McGraw-Hill.

Fitzgerald, J. M. (1986). Autobiographical memory: A developmental perspective. In D.C. Rubin (Ed.), *Autobiographical Memory* (pp. 122–133). New York: Cambridge University Press.

Forgas, J. P., & Bower, G. H. (1987). Mood effects on person-perception judgments. *Journal of Personality and Social Psychology, 53*, 53–60.

Forgas, J. P., Bower, G. H., & Krantz, S. E. (1984). The influence of mood on perceptions of social interactions. *Journal of Experimental Social Psychology, 20*, 497–513.

Forgas, J. P., Bower, G. H., & Moylan, S. J. (1990). Praise or blame? Affective influences on attributions for achievement. *Journal of Personality and Social Psychology, 59*, 809–819.

Gergen, K. J., & Gergen, M. M. (1988). Narrative and the self as relationship. In L. Berkowitz (Ed.), *Advances in experimental psychology.* New York: Academic Press.

Gilovich, T. (1991). *How we know what isn't so: The fallability of reason in everyday life.* New York: The Free Press.

Haimes, E. (1987). "Now I know who I really am": Identity change and redefinitions of the self in adoption. In T. Honess & K. Yardley (Eds.), *Self and identity* (pp. 359–371). London: Routledge & Kegan Paul.

Harber, K. D., & Pennebaker, J. W. (1992). Overcoming traumatic memories. In S.-A. Christianson (Ed.), *The handbook of emotion and memory: Research and theory* (pp. 359–387). Hillsdale, NJ: Lawrence Erlbaum.

Harvey, J. L., Weber, A. L., & Orbuch, T. L. (1990). *Interpersonal accounts: A social psychological perspective.* Cambridge, MA: Basil Blackwell.

Holmberg, D., & Holmes, J. G. (In press). Reconstruction of relationship memories: A mental models approach. In N. Schwarz & S. Sudman (Eds.), *Autobiographical memory and the validity of retrospective reports*. New York: Springer-Verlag.

Humphrey, N. (1986). *The inner eye*. London: Faber & Faber.

Jacoby, L. L., & Craik, F. I. M. (1979). Effects of elaboration of processing at encoding and retrieval: Trace distinctiveness and recovery of initial context. In L. S. Cermak & F. I. M. Craik (Eds.), *Levels of processing in human memory* (pp. 1–22). New York: Lawrence Erlbaum.

Jenkins, J. J. (1979). Four points to remember: A tetrahedal model of memory experiments. In L. S. Cermak & F. I. M. Craik (Eds.), *Levels of processing in human memory* (pp. 429–446). Hillsdale, NJ: Lawrence Erlbaum.

Johnson, M. K., Kim, J. K., & Risse, G. (1985). Do alcoholic Korsakoff's patients acquire affective reactions? *Journal of Experimental Psychology: Learning, Memory, and Cognition, 11*, 22–36.

Johnson, M. K. & Multhaup, K. S. (1992). Emotion and MEM. In S. -A. Christianson (Ed.), *The handbook of emotion and memory: Research and theory* (pp. 33–66). Hillsdale, NJ: Lawrence Erlbaum.

Kihlstrom, J. F. (1981). Personality and memory. In N. Cantor & J. F. Kihlstrom (Eds.), *Personality, cognition, and social interaction* (pp. 123–149). Hillsdale, NJ: Lawrence Erlbaum.

Klein, G. S. (1970). *Perception, motives, and personality*. New York: Alfred A. Knopf.

Linde, C. (1993). *Life stories: The creation of coherence*. New York: Oxford University Press.

McAdams, D. P. (1982). Experiences of intimacy and power: Relationships among social motives and autobiographical memory. *Journal of Personality and Social Psychology, 42*, 292–302.

MacIntyre, A. (1981). *After virtue*. Notre Dame, IN: University of Notre Dame Press.

McCarthy, M. (1957). *Memories of a Catholic girlhood*. New York: Harcourt.

Nigro, G., & Neisser, U. (1983). Point of view in personal memories. *Cognitive Psychology, 15*, 467–482.

Nisbett, R. E., & Wilson, T. D. (1977). Telling more than we can know: Verbal reports on mental processes. *Psychological Review, 84*, 231–259.

Novak, M. (1978). *Ascent of the mountain, flight of the dove* (rev. ed.). San Francisco: Harper & Row.

Oatley, K. (1992). *Best laid schemes: The psychology of emotions*. New York: Cambridge University Press.

Postman, L., Bruner, J. S., & McGinnies, E. (1948). Personal values as selective factors in perception. *Journal of Abnormal and Social Psychology, 43*, 142–154.

Reiser, B. J., Black, J. B., & Kalamarides, P. (1986). Strategic memory search processes. In D. C. Rubin (Ed.), *Autobiographical memory* (pp. 100–21). Cambridge, UK: Cambridge University Press.

Riessman, C. K. (1991). Beyond reductionism: Narrative genres in divorce accounts. *Journal of Narrative and Life History, 1*, 41–68.

Robinson, J. A. (1981a). Personal narratives reconsidered. *Journal of American Folklore, 94*, 58 – 85.

—— (1981b). Context effects in retrospective judgments of personal experiences. *Bulletin of the Psychonomic Society, 17*, 147–150.

—— (1992). First experience memories: Contexts and functions in personal histories. In M. A. Conway, D. C. Rubin, H. Spinnler, & W. A. Wagenaar (Eds.), *Theoretical perspectives on autobiographical memory* (pp. 223–239). Dordrecht, The Netherlands: Kluwer Academic.

Robinson, J. A., & Hawpe, L. (1986). Narrative thinking as a heuristic process. In T. R. Sarbin (Ed.), *Narrative psychology: The storied nature of human conduct*. New York: Praeger.

Robinson, J. A., & Swanson, K. L. (1993). Field and observer modes of remembering. *Memory, 1*, 169–184.

Rosenwald, G. C., & Ochberg, R. L. (1992). Introduction: Life stories, cultural politics, and self-understanding. In G. C. Rosenwald & R. L. Ochberg (Eds.), *Storied lives*. New Haven, CT: Yale University Press.

Ross, B. M. (1990). *Remembering the personal past: Descriptions of autobiographical memory*. New York: Oxford University Press.

Ross, M. (1989). Relation of implicit theories to construction of personal histories. *Psychological Review, 96*, 341–357.

Ross, M., & Conway, M. (1986). Remembering one's own past: The construction of personal histories. In R. M. Sorrentino & E. T. Higgins (Eds.), *Handbook of motivation and cognition* (pp. 122–144). New York: Guilford Press.

Singer, J. A. (1990). Affective responses to autobiographical memories and their relationship to long-term goals. *Journal of Personality, 58*, 534–563.

Singer, J. A., & Salovey, P. (1993). *The remembered self*. New York: Free Press.

Stein, N, Trabasso, T., & Liwag, M. (In press). The representation and organization of emotional experience: Unfolding the emotional episode. In M. L. Lewis & J. Haviland (Eds.), *The handbook of emotions*. New York: Guilford Publications.

Thompson, S. C., & Janigan, A. S. (1988). Life schemes: A framework for understanding the search for meaning. *Journal of Social and Clinical Psychology, 7*, 260–280.

Tobias, B. A., Kihlstrom, J. F., & Schacter, D. L. (1992). Emotion and implicit memory. In S.-A. Christianson (Ed.), *The handbook of emotion and memory: Research and theory* (pp. 67–92). Hillsdale, NJ: Lawrence Erlbaum.

Tulving, E. (1983). *Elements of episodic memory*. New York: Oxford University Press.

Williams, J. M. G. (1992). *The psychological treatment of depression: A guide to the theory and practice of cognitive behavior therapy*. London: Routledge.

9   Emotional events and emotions in autobiographical memories

Sven-Åke Christianson and Martin A. Safer

"And the question which I have for you (Professor Anita Hill) is how reliable is your testimony in October of 1991 on events that occurred 8, 10 years ago, when you are adding new factors, explaining them by saying you have repressed a lot?," asked Senator Specter. (Republicans and Democrats alternate in questioning, 1991). It is October 11, 1991, and the U.S. Senate Judiciary Committee is considering the controversial nomination to the Supreme Court of Judge Clarence Thomas. Toward the end of the nomination process, there is a surprise witness. An attorney, Anita Hill, who used to work for Thomas, claims he sexually harassed her a decade earlier. Hill, now a University of Oklahoma law professor, reluctantly agrees to testify in front of the Senate Judiciary Committee, and much of the nation watches spellbound as she testifies on television. "My working relationship became even more strained when Judge Thomas began to use work situations to discuss sex. . . . His conversations were very vivid. He spoke about acts that he had seen in pornographic films involving such matters as women having sex with animals and films showing group sex or rape scenes. . . . One of the oddest episodes I remember was an occasion in which Thomas was drinking a Coke in his office. He got up from the table at which we were working, went over to his desk to get the Coke, looked at the can and asked, "Who has put pubic hair on my Coke?" Anita Hill remembers specific incidents and phrases (Thomas, Hill make statements, 1991), whereas Judge Thomas refuses to acknowledge any harassment. "I have been racking my brains and eating my insides out trying to think of what I could have said or done to Anita Hill to lead her to allege that I was interested in her in more than a professional way and that I talked with her about pornographic or X-rated films" (p. 23-E). The Senators and the public wanted to know whose memory should be trusted. Was Anita Hill remembering facts or fantasies? Did she remember the *events* as they occurred or did she remember her *feelings* about the events and then justify

The preparation of this chapter was an equal collaborative effort and was supported by Grant F. 693/92 from the Swedish Council for Research in the Humanities and Social Sciences to Sven-Åke Christianson.

218

these feelings with some of the details? How accurately could she remember such information after 10 years? How could she remember the details such as the names of specific pornographic characters from the movies? Could she accurately remember her feelings of harassment and turmoil but perhaps inaccurately remember the details of the events themselves? Does Thomas not remember the events because they never occurred, because they did not occur as Hill described them, or because the events had no impact on Thomas at the time, whereas they caused Hill to be hospitalized and eventually to leave her job?

The above questions exemplify the issues to be discussed in this chapter. We will present a brief review of studies on autobiographical memories for emotional events, and some laboratory research that is relevant to this issue. We will also discuss the role of emotion as such in autobiographical memories, and whether emotions per se can be recalled. The chapter also discusses some practical implications of research on autobiographical memory for emotions in clinical settings.

Importance of emotion for autobiographical memory

Individuals are more likely to remember emotion-arousing events than neutral, everyday events. Indeed, they may even claim near-perfect memories for the circumstances surrounding unique emotionally charged events (Brown & Kulik, 1977). The superior memory for emotional events occurs even when recalling words in a list; words judged by others as being emotional are more likely to be recalled than are nonemotional words (Rubin & Friendly, 1986). The same superior memory for emotional events occurs for recall of one's daily activities. For example, Wagenaar (1986) recorded one or more events daily for 6 years. He recorded who, what, where, and when information about the events, as well as rated the events for saliency, emotional involvement, and pleasantness. Wagenaar found that he was particularly likely to recall pleasant events, in contrast to neutral and unpleasant events. Similarly, Linton (1982) tested memory for events from her own life (she recorded at least two events every day during an extended time period), and found that her recall was best for pleasant events. However, she notes an event's salience or emotionality may change over time. For example, events that were rated as neutral when they occurred (e.g., meeting a shy young professor) may become important emotionally over time (when she began to date him and eventually married him).

There are cases where emotional events, especially negative and unpleasant ones, are retained poorly. For example, victims of crimes may show a temporary inability to remember a traumatic event. There are also reports of early traumatic childhood experiences that are blocked until adulthood or never recovered, but which have profound effects on developing anxiety, depression, and dissociative symptoms in later life (Brewin, Andrews, & Gotlib, 1993). Various studies also indicate that the accuracy in recollection of emotional events is a matter of the type of detail information asked for, the amount of retrieval information provided, and the time of retrieval. Thus, although it is clear that emotional events are remembered differently than neutral or ordinary events, there is no simple relationship between emotion and memory such that emotion or stress impairs memory (Deffenbacher, 1983; Kassin, Ellsworth, & Smith, 1989; Loftus, 1979), or the opposite, that emotion leads to generally detailed, accurate, and persistent memory (Bohannon & Symons, 1992; Brown & Kulik, 1977; Heuer & Reisberg, 1990; Yuille & Cutshall, 1989). In fact, recent research in this field, independent of the approach used, shows that the way emotion and memory interact is a rather complex matter.

Autobiographical memory for emotional events

In discussing memory for emotional events, it is important to differentiate between situations where the to-be-remembered (TBR) event is accompanied by emotional arousal that is evoked by the TBR material proper, and situations where the source of the arousal is dissociated from the TBR event, as may occur in laboratory studies on emotional arousal and memory. In autobiographical studies of emotional events, it is natural that the emotional arousal is evoked by the TBR event, and that the source of the emotion and the emotional feelings are congruent. Thus, this research concerns how well subjects remember an eliciting negative emotional event and the emotions associated with this event.

Our discussion focuses primarily on autobiographical memory for negative emotional events and emotions. Perhaps this is the result of the clinical psychologist's interest in eliciting memories of unhappy patients or the forensic psychologist's efforts to try to obtain information about a crime from a witness or victim. There are several reasons why it is easier to study memories for negative events in controlled experiments. Normally, individuals experience negative emotional events more intensely and distinctly than positive events (Christianson, 1986). People vary less in their evaluation of negative events than of positive events. Also, it is easier to induce intense negative experiences in a laboratory experiment than an intense positive experience. Thus, there is a much more intense, immediate, and uniform reaction to negatively valenced stimuli, such as pictures of violent injuries and crimes, than to positively valenced stimuli, such as sensual motives, jokes, or cartoons. What may be positive for some people, such as mildly erotic pictures, might be viewed quite negatively by others. Finally, from an evolutionary perspective it may be important to identify and have an immediate reaction to threatening stimuli.

Real-life studies

In the clinical literature, there are many examples where traumatized victims show posttraumatic symptoms such as hysterical neuroses. These hysterical neuroses could be expressed either as dissociative reactions, where the patient shows transient inability to recall events associated with a life trauma and/or self-referential information (cf. psychogenic amnesia or fugue states and multiple personality disorder), or conversion reactions, where the patient exhibits physiological/sensorimotor symptoms (e.g., paralysis, numbness) without any organic basis for the symptoms. Generally these conversion symptoms have been interpreted as an unconscious indirect recall of aspects that are central to the original traumatic event.

An early theoretical interpretation of hysteric symptoms was offered through the repression hypothesis by Sigmund Freud (Breuer & Freud, 1895/1955; Freud, 1915/1957; see also Singer [1990] for a review). The essence of this view is that a highly emotional or traumatic experience can be repressed from a conscious state by the person in order to avoid and to cope with an overwhelming psychological pain. The intense negative emotional reaction is hereby seen as the inciting cause of the repressed state. According to this view, the emotional events are properly registered and retained but cannot be recalled until associations or ideas make contact with the emotional response appropriate to the repressed information. There are also several clinical reports showing that patients with hysterical amnesia or hysterical conversion symptoms manage to remember the previously inaccessible episode (Erdelyi & Goldberg, 1979). Although there is a desire to exclude threatening, anxiety-provoking memories from consciousness to avoid emotional confrontation, over time the unpleasant events will be less threatening, and thus will become more accessible for conscious remembering.

Another method to study autobiographical memories of emotional events is to study police reports and interview victims and witnesses of actual crimes. In a study by Yuille and Cutshall (1986), 13 witnesses to a murder were interviewed within 2 days after the crime and again 4 to 5 months later. The results showed a high degree of accuracy of memory and little decline over time. For example, color of clothing was found to be the most difficult feature to retain, yet the accuracy level for colors of clothing of the central character was quite high, varying between 66% and 83% correct. Furthermore, subjects who reported the highest amount of stress showed a mean accuracy of 93% in the initial police interview and a mean accuracy of 88% 4 to 5 months later. On the basis of the results from this study and similar studies using the same approach (Fisher, Geiselman, & Amador, 1989; Yuille & Cutshall, 1989), Yuille and Tollestrup (1992) conclude that a high stress level at the time of a traumatic event does not appear to affect memory for actions and details negatively. In terms of forensic situations, however, this might not apply to facial recognition. As noted by Cutshall and Yuille (1989, p. 117) in their discussion of eyewitness memory of actual crimes, the high rate of accuracy for actions and details might not apply to identifying a suspect's face, "The level of false identification was higher than has been reported in laboratory studies of eyewitness memory."

Using a similar approach as that of Yuille and Cutshall (1986), Christianson and Hübinette (1993) examined witnesses' memory and emotional reactions from 22 post office robberies. Witnesses who had observed a post office robbery, either as a victim (a teller under gunpoint) or as a bystander (fellow employee or customer), filled out a questionnaire concerning their emotional reactions during the robbery and their memory for specific event information. The consistency of the witnesses' accounts was measured by a comparison of the information in the police reports and the recollections given in the written research interview between 4 and 15 months after the robberies. Results showed that the witnesses' recollections of detail information concerning the actual robbery (e.g., action, weapon, clothing) were consistent with what was reported in the police reports. Recollections of the specific circumstances (e.g., date, time, other people) were, however, less consistent than other details. Furthermore, the accuracy rates among the victims were found to be significantly higher than the accuracy rates among the bystanders. This latter result seems not, however, to be related to differences in arousal during the robbery, since ratings of emotional reactions indicated that victims were not more emotionally aroused than bystanders (see also Hosch & Bothwell, 1990). Taken together, the results of the Christianson and Hübinette's study indicate that highly emotional real-life events are well retained over time with respect to details directly associated with the emotion-arousing event, but less so with respect to details of the concomitant circumstances of the event.

Another variation on the witness interview approach involves simply asking people about their memories for very negative emotional events. In a survey of people's autobiographical memories, Reisberg, Heuer, McLean, and O'Shaughnessy (1988) found that the more intense the emotional event, the more confident one was of the memory. In a similar interview study by Christianson and Loftus (1990), over 400 subjects were asked to report their "most traumatic memory" and to answer questions about their chosen memory. A major finding was a significant relationship between rated degree of emotion and the number of "central" details, but not "peripheral" details, the subjects believed that they remembered. Thus, according to these two survey studies, there seems to be a significant correlation between affect strength and rated memory vividness, at least for the central and critical details of the emotional events.

One way to verify the consistency of real-life memories is to compare the similarity between the recollections reported on two occasions. In such a double assessment method people are asked a series of questions about details and circumstances in which they first experienced the emotional event, and then asked the same questions again later in order to compare the consistency between the recollections reported on the two occasions. For example, in a study of extremely emotional experiences, such as being a victim of a Nazi concentration camp, Wagenaar and Groeneweg (1990) compared testimonies from 78 former prisoners of Camp Erika, collected in the periods 1943–1947 and 1984–1987. A comparison between testimonies from these two periods revealed that almost all victims remembered the concentration camp experiences in great detail even after 40 years. Although errors did occur, Wagenaar and Groeneweg found recall of the conditions in the camp and smaller details to be remarkably consistent and accurate (but see Barclay [this volume] for other effects).

A domain of studies that also supports the view that highly emotional events are well preserved in memory is research of so-called flashbulb memories. A number of studies have shown an impressive concordance in subjects' remembering of shocking national events, such as assassinations, etc. (see e.g., Bohannon, 1988; Brewer, this volume; Brown & Kulik, 1977; Christianson, 1989; Colgrove, 1899; Pillemer, 1984; Rubin & Kozin, 1984; Winograd & Killinger, 1983). Not only is the newsworthy event itself well retained (e.g., the assassination of one's president), but also the subjects' memories of the specific circumstances under which they heard the news (the informant, the location, the time, any ongoing activity, the subject's own affect, etc). Flashbulb memories have also been observed in children, and in line with studies on adults (Bohannon,

1988). Warren and Swartwood (1992) have found that children who reported higher emotional responses to the flashbulb event are more consistent over a 2-year period than those who reported lower emotional responses.[1]

A problem with flashbulb studies, as in most other studies of real-life events, is that these studies do not include a baseline measure; that is, a comparable salient everyday event. In an attempt to include such a control event Christianson (1989) found a higher recall performance for the flashbulb event as compared with the salient control event. In a study by Larsen (1992), news events and everyday personal experiences were collected in a diary over 9 months. In this study, both extremely upsetting and ordinary news events and personal events were included, and Larsen was able to provide a most appropriate baseline against which to evaluate flashbulb memories. Larsen found that as the surprise and importance of the news increased, memory of the reception context deteriorated (that is actually the opposite of flashbulb memories!), while memory for the news itself improved.

Using a double assessment technique, several researchers (Bohannon & Symons, 1992; Christianson, 1989; McCloskey, Wible, & Cohen, 1988; Pillemer, 1984) have found a fairly good consistency over longer retention intervals. This is not, however, to say that flashbulb memories are immune to deterioration with respect to all of the specific circumstances of the flashbulb event. It seems that the core information (i.e., informant, time, place, accompanying person) is less vulnerable to memory loss, whereas some specific detail information (i.e., own clothing, first thought) show a substantially decreased accuracy over a year (Christianson, 1989). Furthermore, although subjects' confidence in their own memories decreased somewhat over 1 year, subjects were still fairly sure that they remembered correctly the specific circumstantial details.

One problem with the double assessment technique is that we cannot tell how accurate people really are in their initial descriptions of the flashbulb event and its concomitant circumstances (this applies, of course, also to other real-life events). The initial recollections may not have been truthful or accurate observations of the original situation. They may very well be reconstructive, and presumably contain some erroneous information, as do most other types of memories. It is likely that a second recall to remember an event and its concomitant circumstances produces the same memory for some core elements, while many plausible details may be added (see work by Loftus [1979]; Winograd & Killinger [1983] for a discussion of influences on people's original recollections).

Although flashbulb memories may very well be partly a reconstructive process and may contain some erroneous information (see e.g., Christianson, 1989; McCloskey et al., 1988; Neisser, 1982; Neisser & Harsch, 1992), it is clear that people remember these sorts of public negative emotional events better than ordinary events that occurred equally long ago. However, the "flashbulb" or "video-camera" metaphors are misleading in suggesting the potential for perfect accuracy in remembering emotional events. In sum, the results from flashbulb studies and other autobiographical studies of emo-

[1] Other studies on children's autobiographical memories for stressful/traumatic events, for example by Terr (1983, 1990), indicate that traumatic experiences are remembered in great detail.

tional/shocking/traumatic experiences suggest that these events are very well retained over time, especially with respect to detail information directly associated with the traumatic event.

Laboratory studies

Studying the impact of emotion on memory from natural traumatic events has some obvious limitations. We usually do not know for sure what the original circumstances were, but only what the individual claims them to be. Furthermore, the level of emotional stress is difficult, if not impossible, to measure objectively. There is only a single stressful event, and no "neutral" event with which to compare it. Even when witnesses are grouped based on self-reports as to who was more or less emotionally aroused by this evocative event, the level of emotional stress remains confounded with other variables, such as vantage point, motivations for cooperation, etc. To circumvent these validation problems, a simulation approach can be used to study memory for emotional events. Although witnessing a genuine trauma is far more emotionally arousing than witnessing a simulated accident in a laboratory setting, recent research indicates that laboratory settings do not necessarily produce qualitatively different memories than does witnessing real-life events. On the contrary, recent laboratory findings in many ways mimic various phenomena observed from real-life settings.

However, whereas most autobiographical studies show that details of emotional events are retained quite well, laboratory simulation studies show many striking interactions (Christianson, 1992a). Such interactions are seen between type of event (emotional/nonemotional) and type of detail information (central/peripheral; e.g., Burke, Heuer, & Reisberg, 1992; Christianson & Loftus, 1987, 1991; Goodman, Hepps, & Reed, 1986), type of test (free recall, cued recall, recognition; e.g., Christianson & Nilsson, 1984; Davis, 1990; Wagenaar, 1986), or time of test (immediate/delayed; e.g., Burke et al., 1992; Christianson, 1984; Levonian, 1967). For example, in a study by Christianson and Nilsson (1984), a memory impairment was demonstrated in free recall of verbal TBR information presented along with "traumatic" pictures (grotesque forensic pathology photographs of facial injuries), as well as for TBR information succeeding these horrible pictures (i.e., demonstrating an anterograde amnesia). When memory for the TBR information was tested in a subsequent recognition test, the anterograde amnesia effect receded completely.

Hypermnesia (net gain in memory) is also seen in studies where memory for certain information is tested repeatedly (see Payne, 1987, for a review). In a study by Scrivner and Safer (1988), subjects watched a videotape that portrayed a burglar breaking into a house and shooting three people. Subjects were tested for detail memory about the violent event in four consecutive recall tests within 48 hours. The Scrivner and Safer study shows that subjects become more accurate over tests for details presented preceding, during, and succeeding the violent event, and the authors conclude, "the apparent amnesia for some details on the initial recall trial represented temporary, not permanent, failures of memory" (p. 375). Similarly, Davis (1990) reports hypermnesia effects for negative emotional experiences, especially in individuals who initially recalled very few negative emotional memories. She concludes that the overall pattern of results observed in her studies (mainly concerning repression) indicates that an initial difficulty in remembering certain kinds of negative emotional experiences reflects a limited accessibility, rather than a limited availability, to these experiences.

Perhaps the most striking interaction is that between type of event (emotional versus neutral) and type of detail information (central versus peripheral). A series of laboratory studies has shown that central details of emotional events are retained better than corresponding details in nonemotional events, whereas the reverse pattern is seen for peripheral details. Christianson (1984) found that subjects who had watched an emotional version of a slide sequence recalled the main features and the theme of the pictures better than subjects who watched a neutral version. However, when subjects were given a recognition test in which the main features of each picture were held constant and only the peripheral, surrounding information was varied, no difference was obtained between groups. In a subsequent study by Christianson and Loftus (1987), using the same type of stimulus material, the subjects were instructed to select and write down the most distinguishing detail of each slide. It was found that subjects were better able to recall central features selected from the emotional pictures than from the neutral pictures; however, they were less able to recognize the specific pictures that they had seen. This pattern of results was obtained both after a short (20 min) and a long (2 weeks) test interval.

Kebeck and Lohaus (1986) showed that subjects presented with either an emotional or a nonemotional version of a film recalled the central details of the film equally well. However, subjects who had seen the emotional version were less able to remember peripheral information. In a study by Goodman et al. (1986), three 7-year-old children's memories for a stressful event – having a blood test at a medical clinic – were compared with children in a control condition who were brought to the same clinic, but had a design placed on their arm instead of having their blood drawn. After a delay of 3 to 4 days, Goodman et al. found that the more highly stressed children remembered more of the central information than did the control children, whereas the control children remembered more of the peripheral information than did the highly stressed children. Furthermore, research by Heuer and Reisberg (Burke et al. 1992; Heuer & Reisberg, 1990) has replicated earlier findings on adults in showing that subjects presented with an emotional version of the story remembered more of the central information (i.e., information associated with the central characters in the slides and the gist of the event) than subjects who had seen a neutral version, and that this beneficial effect for emotional detail increases over time. However, they have also shown that the disadvantage for the peripheral details in the emotional condition decreases at delayed testing (Burke et al., 1992).

Also pertinent to the issue of memory for central and peripheral information in emotional versus neutral events is research related to the phenomenon of "weapon focusing," that normally demonstrates that certain critical stressful objects, such as a gun or a knife being used in a crime, can capture people's attention, and thus promote memory for the weapon at the expense of other details in memory (Cutler, Penrod, & Martens,

1987; Kramer, Buckhout, & Eugenio, 1990; Loftus, Loftus, & Messo, 1987; Maass & Kohnken, 1989). In a review article, Steblay (1992) states that "[t]he weapen effect does reliably occur, particularly in crimes of short duration in which a threatening weapon is visible" (p. 421). Steblay concludes that a weapon presence situation might lead to a reduced memory for faces in measures of lineup identification.

The issue of memory for central and peripheral detail in emotional versus neutral events was further explored in two studies by Christianson and Loftus (1991) and Christianson, Loftus, Hoffman, and Loftus (1991). In these studies, subjects presented with either emotional or nonemotional slides were equated with respect to (1) the critical TBR detail information of the event, and (2) the number of eye fixations on the critical TBR information. It was found that even when subjects were asked about the same TBR details and equated with respect to the number of eye fixations on these critical details, subjects in the emotional condition remembered the detail information associated with the central part of the picture better than subjects in the neutral condition.

In sum, both autobiographical studies and laboratory studies, suggest that highly negative emotional events are relatively well retained, both with respect to the emotional event itself and the central, critical detail information of the emotion-eliciting event, that is, the information that elicits the emotional reaction. It also seems that certain critical detail information of emotionally arousing events and some circumstantial information is less susceptible to forgetting compared with detail information in neutral counterparts over time. However, memory for information associated with unpleasant emotional events, that is, information preceding and succeeding such events, or peripheral, noncentral information within an emotional scenario, seem to be less accurately retained – especially when tested after short retention intervals. This relative decrement in memory may recede, however, with strong retrieval support, if delayed testing is employed, or after repeated memory testing.[2]

Tunnel memory

The following processes may contribute to memory for emotional events, and especially the interaction seen between type of event (emotional versus neutral) and type of detail information (central versus peripheral). First, there are preattentive processes activated for certain stimuli, such as blood, that trigger an orienting response so that this emotion-eliciting information becomes the focus of the subject's attention (cf. Öhman, 1991). If this narrowing of attention was simply a perceptional phenomenon, we would call it "tunnel vision" (cf. Easterbrook, 1959). However, it may be that a second stage mediates this tunneling effect. In this second stage, the subject engages in an emotional mode of processing where "controlled" mechanisms, such as poststimulus elaboration, are allocated to the emotion-provoking information. The process of elaboration, such

---

[2] Severe cases of traumatic experiences can produce dissociative reactions such as hysterical amnesia fugue state, or multiple personality disorder. Although such reactions may show an initial forgetting of the traumatic experience as well as a loss of self-referential information (i.e., no memory of their primary identity [Putnam, 1989]), recovery effects of the previously forgotten information are commonly observed in these cases (see e.g., Christianson & Nilsson, 1984).

as thinking about and reacting empathically to the emotion-provoking information, limits access to the information in the mental periphery. In cases of very strong emotions, the individual is occupied by intrusive thoughts about the threatening event. We describe the outcome of this narrowed attention and heightened psychological focusing on those critical details that were the source of the emotional arousal as "tunnel memory" (see Safer, Christianson, Autry, & Österlund, 1993). This mode of processing would promote memory for central detail information, that is, details of the gist of the emotional event, but actively inhibit processing of peripheral details, that is, details that are irrelevant and/or spatially peripheral to the emotion-eliciting event or the source of the emotional arousal (cf. results by Christianson & Loftus, 1991; Christianson et al., 1991). At this stage the emotional reaction may act as a cue for the emotion-provoking event information (i.e, a negative emotional reaction like fear, disgust, and anger, would cue a person to remember that there was something negative or upsetting in what he/she just saw). Thus, in an emotion-arousing situation there is a natural correspondence between what a person is feeling and the emotion-eliciting information. Neutral detail information does not normally elicit specific feelings that are intrinsic in the TBR information.

One observable consequence of tunnel memory is that individuals will remember a traumatic scene, at least temporarily, as more focused spatially than the actual stimulus input and more focused spatially than a comparable neutral scene (Safer et al., 1993). These tunnel memories may become less focused over time. In contrast, subjects remember neutral scenes as more wide-angled than the actual stimulus input (Intraub, Bender, & Mangels, 1992).

The initial effect of tunnel memory for traumatic event information (i.e., the second stage), along with the attentional widening in remembering neutral visual information, may explain why subjects recognize central details better for an emotion-arousing event and peripheral details better for a neutral event. This description would be consistent with the findings by Burke et al. (1992). They reported that detail information that was spatially and temporally associated with the central characters in an event was better retained in the emotional condition than in the neutral condition. Moreover, with a 1 week delay in testing, the favorable effects for central details at immediate testing increased, compared to the neutral condition, whereas the disadvantage for the peripheral details in the emotional condition decreased. Thus, emotional arousal may inhibit initial retrieval of background information, or the whole event in cases of traumatic amnesia, but helps long-term remembering of emotion-laden events. This gain over time in recall of actions and details is consistent with hypermnesia effects that are particularly strong for emotion-arousing events (Dunning & Stern, 1992, Erdelyi & Goldberg, 1979; Scrivner & Safer, 1988).

Mood states and autobiographical memory

There has been considerable research on how one's emotional feelings affect what is stored in or retrieved from memory. There are two phenomena related to this issue that have been studied in depth. One is the mood state-dependent effect and the other is the mood congruence effect (Blaney, 1986; Ellis & Ashbrook, 1989; see also Robinson, this volume, and Williams, this volume).

State-dependent effects (state-dependent learning or state-dependent retrieval) refer to an impairment in performance when there is a mismatch between physical or mental states at learning and at retrieval. The state-dependent effect assumes that mood acts as a critical context cue, no matter what the nature is of the information being learned and retrieved. The state-dependent effect is similar to a dissociative effect, wherein existing memories may, under certain circumstances, be unavailable to consciousness. A comic example is the drunk who hides money, and then can remember where he hid it only when he is drunk, not when he is sober.

There is some evidence that certain drug states are encoded along with the TBR material, such that being in a different drug state at learning and retrieval impairs recall of TBR information. Eich (1980) concluded that drug state-dependent effects occur reliably in humans when memory is tested using recall, but not with recognition. The drug state can effectively cue recall, but its potency is apparently overwhelmed when there are already strong mnemonic cues available, such as when recognition is tested. It is primarily mood-altering drugs, such as antidepressants and alcohol, that produce drug state-dependent effects (Eich, 1980; Overton, 1978, 1982).

Another type of state-dependent phenomena is context-dependent effects. Information learned in one context may be difficult to remember in another context. In the movies, as well as in real life, returning victims to the scene of the crime helps them remember details that they could not otherwise remember (Fisher & Geiselman, 1992). Godden and Baddeley (1975) demonstrated strong context-dependent memory effects in underwater divers. The divers learned lists of words either on land or underwater, and then were tested for recall either on land or underwater. The results are consistent with the typical findings for drug state-dependency. Recall was best when the divers learned and recalled words on land, followed by words learned and recalled underwater. Recall for the two mismatch situations, learned on land and tested underwater or learned underwater and tested on land, was about 37% less than the land/land and 25% less than the water/water conditions. Thus, divers recalled far less when tested in a different environment than the one in which they first learned the words. In line with Eich's findings, context-dependent effects did not occur when the divers were tested using recognition memory (Godden & Baddeley, 1980).

One reason why the drug state-dependent and context-dependent effects occur may be that the drug or the context alter the person's emotional state, and it is this alteration in the emotional state that is crucial for the state-dependent effects. The underwater divers may show context-dependent effects because the dangerous underwater environment arouses feelings such as excitement, anxiety, and fear.

Bower (1981) demonstrated mood state-dependent effects in a series of experiments with normal subjects. Subjects were hypnotized to experience a happy mood before learning a list of words. They were then hypnotized to experience sadness and to learn another list of words. For half the subjects, the order of the moods was reversed. Finally, the subjects were tested for recall while experiencing either a happy or a sad mood. The results clearly indicated a mood state-dependent effect, as subjects who were tested in a happy mood were less likely to recall words learned when they were sad than words learned when they were happy; similarly sad subjects were less likely to recall words learned when they were happy than when they were sad. Thus, a mismatch between the internal mood cue at learning and at testing led to impaired recall.

There have been a number of replications (see Blaney, 1986; Bower, 1981; Ellis & Ashbrook, 1989; Kuiken, 1989; Ucros, 1989, for reviews) as well as a number of failures to replicate mood state-dependent effect (Bower & Mayer, 1985, 1989), such as those described above. It seems that mood is a relatively weak cue for learning and retrieving neutral information, but may be a potent cue for learning and retrieving emotion-laden information. Mood state effects should be more likely when the mood is integrated with the TBR information (Gage & Safer, 1985; Bower, 1987, 1992; Eich & Metcalfe, 1989). This is normally the case in autobiographical memories where the TBR event naturally causes the rememberer to feel a pleasant or unpleasant emotion, as may be the case when state-dependent and mood congruent effects are combined (cf. the "causal belonging hypothesis" Bower, 1987).

In contrast to the small and sometimes unreliable mood state-dependent effects, there is considerable support for mood congruent effects. Mood congruence effects occur when stimuli agreeing in affective valence with one's mood are learned and retrieved better than stimuli of different affective valence (Blaney, 1986). The strongest effects are when current mood is affectively congruent with stimuli at learning (Singer & Salovey, 1988).

Mood congruence effects have been observed for both induced and naturally occurring moods and in both normal and depressed populations (Matt, Vazquez, & Campbell, 1992). In a typical experiment, subjects are asked to learn information containing equal numbers of positive and negative stimuli. The stimuli can be adjectives, sentences, or ideas. Based on their meta-analysis, Matt et al. concluded that normal, nondepressed subjects recall about 8% more positive than negative stimuli, subclinically depressed subjects recall positive and negative stimuli equally, and clinically depressed subjects recall about 10% more negative than positive stimuli. When normal subjects are induced to feel sad before learning the TBR information they recall about 6% more negative than positive stimuli, and when they are induced to feel happy, they recall about 4% more positive than negative stimuli. Mood congruence effects also occur when subjects are asked to recall recent autobiographical memories. The typical result is that subjects who are induced to feel happy tended to recall more happy than sad memories, as rated by objective judges, whereas the reverse is true for subjects who are led to feel sad (see Blaney, 1986; Singer & Salovey, 1988, for reviews).

In most studies of mood congruence effects, subjects are led to experience happy or sad moods and it is clear that they are expected to try to maintain those mood states throughout the experiment. In a recent series of studies, Parrott and Sabini (1990) investigated the effects of naturally occurring moods on autobiographical memory and obtained evidence for mood incongruent effects. In one study, they asked students who had just received an examination grade to briefly describe three memories from high school. The first memory recalled by students who did well on the exam was rated by outside judges as more sad and less happy than the first memory recalled by students who did poorly on the exam. This occurred even though the students who did well on the exam rated themselves as happier than the students who did poorly. A similar result occurred for students who were asked to recall three high school memories as they entered the university library. Some students were asked on a sunny day and some on a cloudy day; the former rated themselves as happier and less sad than did the latter. Nonetheless, the students entering the library on a sunny day recalled a memory that was rated as sadder and less happy than the first memory of students who entered on a cloudy day. Two additional laboratory studies also found that when students were unaware that their mood was being manipulated, via background music, their initial autobiographical memories were relatively incongruent with their mood. On the basis of these studies, Parrott and Sabini (1990) concluded that with naturally occurring fluctuations in mood, subjects attempt to maintain an affective balance by recalling mood incongruent memories. Parrott (1993) describes how mood incongruent recall may serve antihedonic motives in circumstances where one wants to inhibit good moods or maintain bad moods. Clearly there is a need for more research to specify when mood facilitates or hinders recall of affectively valenced information. Nonetheless, even mood incongruent effects indicate the effects of mood on memory. (See also Williams [this volume] on emotional disorders and autobiographical memory.)

Memories for emotions

Most research has examined whether emotions influence the content of what is recalled, rather than whether emotional feelings per se can be recalled. In discussing the latter aspect, one may ask whether we retain unique direct memories for emotion, or do we simply recapture a previous emotion by imagining and dwelling on the circumstances under which we experienced it?

Ross (1991) notes that William James and most contemporary academic psychologists would argue that emotions are retained in some cognitive representation, rather than as distinct entities. When asked to recall emotions, one recalls the cognitive circumstances and then experiences a similar, but new emotion. Thus, James (1890/1918, p. 474) wrote: "The revivability in memory of the emotions, like that of all the feelings of the lower senses, is very small. We can remember that we underwent grief or rapture, but not just how the grief or rapture felt. This difficult ideal revivability is, however, more than compensated in the case of emotions by a very easy actual revivability. That is, we can produce, not remembrances of the old grief or rapture, but new griefs and raptures, by summing up a lively thought of their exciting cause. The cause is now only an idea, but this idea produces the same organic irradiations, or almost the same, that were produced by its original, so that the emotion is again a reality. We have 'recaptured' it." Note that the revivability is for James a highly cognitive method of reviving a memory, but it may be possible to revive the memory using other methods of emotional arousal (see e.g., Izard, 1993).

There is some empirical support for James's argument that it is difficult to retain actual emotions. Strongman and Kemp (1991) asked 83 respondents to remember a time when he or she had experienced 12 different emotions. For example, they were asked to remember experiencing "disgust," and indeed respondents described incidents in which they felt disgusted. Respondents overwhelming provided objective descriptions of the events, rather than descriptions of their own physical feelings and reactions. Thus, subjects appeared to recall the circumstances associated with an emotion, rather than separate memories for emotions. However, by recalling the circumstances, one can presumably reinstate the emotional feelings. According to Strongman and Kemp, any discrepancy between what was originally experienced emotionally and what was recalled about those emotional feelings would be due to discrepancies in remembering the circumstances.

Nonetheless, some psychologists have argued for a unique memory for emotions, separate from a memory for the emotion-arousing event. The turn-of-the-century French psychologist Ribot not only claimed separate distinguishable memories for emotions, but that emotional memories had their own unique affective logic that was different from cognitive memories (Ross, 1991). Isen (1984), in a more modern guise, argues that memory organization may be different for emotional information versus purely cognitive information, specifically when one's current mood acts as a category or organizing unit in memory and so can influence what comes to mind in evaluating information. Isen has shown that mood influences judgments and evaluation of information, decision making, expectations, behavior, as well as memory. Thus, depending on how one is feeling, one is likely to solve problems differently, make different decisions about risky options, evaluate oneself and others differently, help or not help someone in need, and so on. It also seems that positive and negative mood states function differently. Positive material may be more elaborated and interconnected than negative material, perhaps because individuals actively try to escape from negative moods, whereas they automatically attempt to maintain positive moods.

Zajonc (1980) similarly makes a claim for the independence, indeed the primacy, of affective memory over cognitive memory. If you try to recall a movie you saw or a book you read a few years ago, you will probably forget most of the details, but may remember whether or not you liked it. Zajonc argued that an affective memory is necessary for speedy judgments that can allow an organism to survive in a hostile environment. Along the same line of thinking, Johnson argues that unconscious remembering for affective components of emotional events are mediated by evolutionary early perceptual subsystems (Johnson & Multhaup, 1992). Similarly, Tobias, Kihlstrom, and Schacter (1992) discuss how the emotional component of a memory can be dissociated and accessed implicitly by unconscious retrieval mechanisms in cases of strong emotional memories. Affective processing could also be accomplished in parallel with more conscious processing (Leventhal, 1984). Indeed, Christianson (1992b) proposed that nonconscious, preattentive mechanisms are involved in processing and remembering emotional experiences, and that affective components of an emotional event may in some situations be retained separately from the specific details of the event. Thus, it is conceivable that one could remember the affect without remembering the precipitating event, or conversely, remember the event without remembering the accompanying affect.

There are several findings in the literature indicating that retrieval of emotional information does not necessarily require the subject to remember the specific emotional episode itself. A frequently cited example is that by Claparede (1911/1951), who pricked the hand of a densely amnesic patient, and the patient thereafter refused to shake his hand, even though the patient could not remember him. In a study by Johnson, Kim, and Risse (1985), Korsakoff amnesics were presented with two pictures of faces and fictional biographical information depicting the person of the picture as either a "good guy" or a "bad guy." After a 20-day interval, the amnesics could recognize the faces, but not the biographical information. However, in emotion-evaluative ratings made by the amnesics, almost 80% of the patients showed a preference for the "good guy" over the "bad guy." Thus, these preferences were obtained even though the amnesics did not have voluntary access to the biographical information on which the preferences were based. According to Johnson and Multhaup (1992) this finding, along with similar observations, indicates that we do not necessarily have to depend on conscious or reflective memories to access emotionally related information.

Sometimes traumatic experiences are preserved through the emotions attached to the trauma, without having access to the traumatic event information. This condition may be seen in cases of hysterical amnesia. Christianson and Nilsson (1989) describe a rape victim who developed an amnesia for the assault and her life prior to the assault. When she was found, she could not explain what had happened to her, who she was, where she lived, etc. Later, when the woman was escorted by the police through the area of the assault, she felt very uncomfortable at specific places and she only recalled two things – bricks and path – but was not able to explain why these details crossed her mind. When she passed some crumbled bricks on another small path, she expressed an unbearable anxiety and claimed that she associated the unpleasant feelings with the pieces of brick on the track she was walking on. She strongly felt that something must have happened to her at this place. From a confession by the rapist a few days earlier, the policemen knew that this was the place where she had been attacked and from which she was forced out onto a small meadow where the rape occurred.

Her amnesia lasted for 16 weeks and started to recede when she was out running again for the first time after the assault. It is conceivable that the same internal context she experienced at the time of the attack was reinstated when she was running again (e.g., increased motor activity, heightened body temperature, hyperventilation, increased cardiac activity). At this time she was also exposed to external cues that strongly reminded her of the place of the attack (a bushy environment, a gravel track with pieces of brick, and a pile of bricks). This case is a good illustration of the state-/context-dependent effects discussed earlier in this chapter, and the type of dissociation between memory for one's emotions and memory for emotion-eliciting information as noted by Johnson, Zajonc, and others.

There have been a number of attempts to specify a neurological basis for an emotion memory (e.g., the role of subcortical and cortical brain structures in mediating emotional memories). LeDoux (1992) argues that different neural circuits underlie the memory for emotional significance of an event and the memory of the event itself. According to LeDoux, the amygdala is the critical structure of the brain that computes the affective meaning of an experience as separate from the cognitive aspects. Others have also argued for the amygdala as a critical structure for establishing affective valence in emotional memories (e.g., McGaugh, 1992; Mishkin, 1978). There are also indications of laterality effects. Several neuropsychological studies suggest that the right (nondominant) hemisphere is more important for emotional behavior than the left, speech-dominant, hemisphere (see Buck, 1984; Kolb & Whishaw, 1989; Perceman, 1983; Safer, 1981; Young, 1983, for reviews), and indeed, autobiographical memories recalled by right hemisphere damaged patients in response to cue words are less emotional than memories recalled by comparable control patients (Cimino, Verfaellie, Bowers, & Heilman, 1991). Van Lanecker (1991) has proposed that the right hemisphere plays a special role in processing and maintaining personally relevant aspects of an individual's identity. It is also suggested that the frontal lobe of the nondominant hemisphere is more critical for processing of emotional information than other neocortical areas of the brain (e.g., Kolb & Milner, 1981). However, there is also evidence of left hemisphere involvement in emotional behavior (Gainotti, Caltagirone, & Zoccolotti, 1993). In an effort to integrate the subcortical/cortical and left/right dichotomies in the study of emotions, Gainotti et al. (1993, pp. 71–72) argue that the "right hemisphere superiority for emotional functions concerns more basic ('subcortical') levels of emotional arousal and of autonomic response to emotional stimuli than the 'cortical' (cognitive and communicative) aspects of emotions." The left hemisphere emotional processing is seen by Gainotti et al. to play an important role in "cortical" functions such as inhibition and intentional control of the emotional ("subcortical") expressive mechanisms. Gainotti el al. also refer to Luria and discuss the possibility that the progressive importance of left hemisphere-level emotional processing "may be due to the emergence of language within this hemisphere and the role played by language in the intentional orientation and direction of human behavior" (p. 87).

The issue of separate memories for emotion and cognition is part of a broader argument about whether emotion and cognition are separate entities, and if so, whether one is primary and the other secondary. Zajonc (1980) has argued for the primacy of affect, whereas Lazarus (1984) has argued for the primacy of cognition. A number of attempts have been made to reconcile these opposing views (Izard, 1993; Leventhal & Scherer, 1987), but there has been no resolution about whether there is an independent emotion memory.

Izard (1993) provides a reconciliation of the various approaches to the arousing of emotion. Since emotion has a significant role in evolution and adaptation, cognitive processes can, according to Izard, hardly be the sole, primary mechanism for generating emotions. Izard argues that emotions can be aroused in four ways: neurologically, through sensory motor processes, through motivational processes, and cognitively. One could arouse emotion through direct stimulation of the brain (activating certain neurotransmitters, neural circuits, or network of structures), through certain expressions and motor actions (e.g., contracting facial muscles, vocal expressions, body postures, etc), through motivation such as pain, and cognitively. For example, pain brings about certain feeling states, certain facial and postural expressions, and it is possible that pain elicits emotions directly via subcortical mechanisms, and without cognitive mediation. Thus, it may be that memories for emotion differ as a function of the mode of arousal, and that memories of cognitively aroused emotions are more likely to be recalled than are other types of emotional memories.

Are emotions accurately recalled?

A few studies have examined whether subjects can recall the frequency and intensity of their affects. (See Robinson [this volume] for an insightful analysis of the different meanings of "accuracy.") It is often the case in therapeutic assessments that one must ask the client to estimate the frequency with which they experience certain emotions. Thus, on the Beck Inventory for diagnosing depression, one is asked to estimate how frequently one feels "blue" or how frequently one feels happy. How do we make such judgements? Fitzgerald, Slade, and Lawrence (1988) asked a nonclinical sample of subjects (students) to judge the frequency with which they experienced different affective states. They then presented the same adjectives, one at a time, to the subjects and asked for recall of a personal memory associated with the adjective. It was found that ease of recall, as measured by the time taken to remember an appropriate incident, was negatively correlated with the judged frequency of the event. Hence one remembers an appropriate event faster for affective states that one believes occur frequently. Also, nondepressed (nondysphoric) individuals, as classified by the Beck inventory, report positive memories faster than do depressed (dysphoric) individuals. However, the nondepressed and depressed individuals did not differ in the average event age for positive and negative affects. One would have expected nondepressed individuals to remember positive events as occurring more recently, if indeed they experienced positive emotions more frequently, and depressed individuals to remember negative events as occurring more recently. These results suggest that judgments about the frequency of affects may reflect something other than the actual occurrence of those affects.

Thomas and Diener (1990) reported two studies in which they asked undergraduates to keep mood diaries. In one study, the students recorded their mood at random times, four times a day, for 3 weeks. In the other, students made end-of-day ratings for 6 weeks. In both studies, students rated their moods, using 7-point scales, on four positive and five negative emotions. At the end of the recording period, subjects were asked to estimate the percentage of time in which their positive affect predominated over their negative affect, and to estimate the intensity of the positive affect when it was predominate. Corresponding estimations were also made when the negative affect was predominate. The results indicated that retrospective reports of emotional experiences are not particularly accurate. Subjects underestimated the frequency of their positive affect versus negative affect; that is, they more readily recalled times when their negative affect predominated. They also tended to overestimate the intensity of both their positive and negative emotions. An important conclusion of this study is, as pointed out by the authors, that people cannot accurately recall the intensity of their unpleasant emotions. This finding will then have some obvious implications for how one assesses emotions clinically.

Two studies have examined whether students can recall accurately how anxious they were before an examination. Devito and Kubis (1983) asked students to recall how anxious they were just before the exam, that they had taken 2 weeks earlier. They were also asked to rate their anxiety just before their final exam. In both cases, students rated anxiety on the Spielberger state anxiety scale. Students' recalled level of anxiety for a previous exam was greater than their actual anxiety just before a new exam. While this result is suggestive, it would be much more informative to compare actual and recalled anxiety ratings for the same exam. An unpublished pilot study (Keuler & Safer, 1993) asked graduate students who were about to take comprehensive exams to complete scales that measured anxiety specific to the exam (e.g., "After my performance on this exam, I will find it hard to face the professor"). About 1 month later, the students were asked to fill out the anxiety scales exactly as they had the first time. The students consistently overestimated how much anxiety they had reported on the morning of the exam 1 month earlier. Clearly, students' reports of test anxiety may be quite inaccurate. These results are important theoretically because anxiety is generally not associated with memory biases (Eysenck & Mogg, 1992; Mineka, 1992).

There have been relatively few studies that have examined recall of emotions in psychiatric populations. Two studies that examined patients' recall of depression did find that patients misremembered the intensity of their depression. Zimmerman and Coryell (1986) had patients rate their depressive symptoms soon after their discharge from a hospital, and then 6 months later they were asked to recall this initial report. Patients recalled more depressive symptoms than what they had actually recorded at the time of discharge. Similarly, Schrader, Davis, Stefanovic, and Christie (1990) found that psychiatric in-patients significantly overestimated the intensity of their depression on the Zung self-rating depression scale when they were asked to recall how depressed they had been 1 week earlier.

Thus, there are apparently no published studies in which a group of subjects has accurately recalled the intensity and/or the frequency of their previously recorded emotions. It may be that recall of emotions relies more on implicit memory as exemplified in the previously described studies. In a discussion of memory bias in clinically anxious patients, Eysenck and Mogg (1992) present evidence that these patients display an implicit negative memory bias. Thus, it may be that emotional reactions are remembered, but not in a way that makes them totally amenable to verbal judgments of frequency and duration. Indeed, in clinical situations, one may ascertain if a memory is emotional for a patient by observing the patient's reaction, not what is said or remembered.

Recall of pain

An important practical problem closely related to memory for emotions is memory for pain. What patients recall of their pain influences diagnoses and treatment. Moreover, pain consists of sensory and affective components (Fernandez & Turk, 1992), so that factors that influence recall of pain may be quite similar to those that influence recall of emotions.

One similarity is that how one remembers chronic pain seems to be influenced strongly by one's current pain, in much the same way that one's recall of emotions is influenced by one's current emotional state. This "pain congruent" memory was first observed in a study by Eich, Reeves, Jaeger, and Graf-Radford (1985). They had head-ache patients keep daily diaries of their feelings of pain. At each session they asked patients to recall how much pain they had experienced over the previous week. They found that patients who were experiencing a personally high level of pain were more likely to overestimate their average pain level for the previous week, whereas those who were experiencing personally low levels of pain at the time of recall remembered their average pain for the previous week as less than what they had actually recorded.

Smith and Safer (1993) provide an experimental demonstration of the effects of pre-sent pain on recall of past pain. They asked 30 chronic pain patients to record every change in their pain level for 1 week on a pocket-sized electronic diary. They recorded the change by moving a pain lever on a scale marked minimum to maximum pain. Pa-tients also recorded whenever they took pain medication. After 1 week, patients re-called their minimum, average, and maximum pain for the previous day and the pre-vious week, as well as their medication use for the previous day and previous week. Half the patients (the control group) were asked to recall before they received a session of physical therapy, consisting of heat and massage, whereas the other half recalled just after their physical therapy session. The results were quite straightforward. As expected, the patients who had just received the physical therapy reported much less current pain than those who had not yet had their physical therapy. Moreover, immediately after re-ceiving physical therapy, the patients recalled their previous day and previous week pain as significantly less than what they had recorded at the time, and significantly less than the control subjects who had not yet received their physical therapy. Indeed, the control patients recalled their previous day's and previous week's pain as significantly greater than what they had reported at the time. Immediately after receiving physical therapy, the patients also underestimated how much pain medication they had con-sumed. In contrast, the control group significantly overestimated how much medication they had consumed. Thus, patients who had their pain temporarily relieved recalled their previous pain as much less severe than a group who continued to experience pain. The implication is that current pain, like current affect, distorts how one recalls the past.

Episodes of acute pain are often recalled in a flashbulb memory matter; that is, what subjects recall are the circumstances (the pain event information). In a study of memory for "everyday" pains, Morley (1993) reported that 41% of the subjects were able to recall the pain experience (i.e., recalled intensity, distress, and sensory quality), but none of the subjects actually reexperienced the sensations themselves. That is, the in-dividual can recall the accident, the circumstances, but not feel (reexperience) the pain.

Clinical and other practical implications

What are the implications if people cannot recall their emotions accurately? One obvi-ous problem is in assessing personality and mental health. Items on a typical personality assessment may ask subjects to recall their frequency, intensity, or duration of emotions. For example, on the MMPI-2 (Hathaway & McKinley, 1989) subjects are asked to answer true or false to questions such as, "I am happy most of the time" or "At times I think I am no good at all." Clearly such questions ask subjects to recall the frequency and duration of past emotions in a way whose accuracy is unsupported by the data. The tests may still be valid predictors, but they may be based on inaccurate information. Patient assessment of mental health using the DSM III-R manual (American Psychiatric Association, 1987) indicates an even more critical problem with the lack of accurate recall of emotions. The problem is particularly important in assessing a patient for affective disorders. For example, the patient may be asked, "In the last month, has there been a period of time when you were feeling depressed or down most of the day nearly every day? If yes, how long did that last?" They will be asked to make similar judgments about loss of interest or pleasure. They will be asked to report how many separate times they have had episodes of depression of at least 2 weeks duration, their age at the first episode, and in diagnosing dysthymia, whether they have been bothered by depressed mood, "So that you have been depressed for most of the day more days than not."

Important diagnostic and treatment decisions are being made, at least in theory, on the basis of patient's self-reports of the frequency, duration, and intensity of depressive mood. Based on the few studies of self-reported affect described above, it is unlikely that patients can accurately report on their moods to the questions asked in these assessments. Indeed, it is unlikely that individuals can recall accurately the occurrence of psychiatric symptoms for more than a few months (Rogler, Malgady, & Tryon, 1992). There is likely to be both underreporting and fabrication of psychiatric symptoms, events, and "spells" with distortions to the current emotional state. It is also likely that individuals will have great difficulty dating the occurrence of psychiatric symptoms. More generally, there is little research into how mental health patients remember their emotional feelings and whether therapy in any way changes what they remember. Curiously, von Benedek (1992) reported that psychoanalysts were unable to recall, or recalled incorrectly, their initial assessments and treatment plans for patients who began in therapy 1 year earlier. The clinicians themselves were quite surprised when told of their initial treatment plans.

Conclusions

Ross (1991) notes that there are three "big" questions that have historically intrigued psychologists, philosophers, sociologists, and other students of autobiographical memory. These questions are whether everything that is personally experienced is capable of being remembered, whether memory could be improved, and whether emotional memories result from the retention of emotions as such. In this chapter we have examined these questions on the permanence, recovery, and representation of events in memory with a particular focus on the role of emotions on memory and in memory.

We conclude that emotional events in real-life situations are retained well, both with respect to the emotional event itself and the central, critical detail information of the emotion-eliciting event, that is, the information that elicits the emotional reaction. It also seems that certain critical detail information of emotion-arousing events and some circumstantial information is less susceptible to forgetting compared with neutral detail information over time. However, memory for information associated with unpleasant emotional events, that is, information preceding and succeeding such events, or peripheral, noncentral information within an emotional scenario, seem to be less accurately retained. This detrimental memory effect may recede as a function of retrieval support (e.g., reinstating emotional cues), as a function of time, or if repeated memory testing is employed. A theoretical assumption that focusing on certain detail information of emotional events occurs as a result of psychological processes in memory (i.e., tunnel memory), not in visual perception, can help clarify some of the differences seen between memory for emotional and nonemotional events.

Whereas memory for central emotional event information is relatively accurate, memory for emotions seems to be quite inaccurate (e.g., the intensity and frequency with which we experience emotions). This finding may have serious implications for diagnostic and treatment decisions in clinical settings, and should therefore be explored at further length in future research on emotion and memory. Finally, evidence is presented for separate memories for emotions.

References

American Psychiatric Association. (1987). *Diagnostic and Statistical Manual of Mental Disorders* (3rd ed.). Washington, DC: American Psychiatric Association.

Blaney, P. H. (1986). Affect and memory: A review. *Psychological Bulletin, 99,* 229–246.

Bohannon, J. N. (1988). Flashbulb memories for the space shuttle disaster: A tale of two stories. *Cognition, 29,* 179–196.

Bohannon, J. N., & Symons, V. L. (1992). Flashbulb memories: Confidence, consistency, and quantity. In E. Winograd and U. Neisser (Eds.), *Affect and accuracy in recall: Studies of "flashbulb" memories.* New York: Cambridge University Press.

Bower, G. H. (1981). Mood and memory. *American Psychologist, 36,* 129–148.

—— (1987). Invited essay: Commentary on mood and memory. *Behavioral Research and Therapy, 25,* 443–455.

—— (1992). How might emotions affect learning? In S.-Å. Christianson (Ed.), *The handbook of emotion and memory: Research and theory* (pp. 3–31). Hillsdale, NJ: Lawrence Erlbaum.

Bower, G. H., & Mayer, J. D. (1985). Failure to replicate mood-dependent retrieval. *Bulletin of Psychonomic Society, 23,* 39–42.

Bower, G. H., & Mayer, J. D. (1989). In search of mood-dependent retrieval. In D. Kuiken (Ed.), *Mood and memory: Theory, research, and applications.* Special issue of *Journal of Social Behavior and Personality, 4,* 121–156.

Bower, G. H., Monterio, K. P., & Gilligan, S. G. (1978). Emotional mood as a context for learning and recall. *Journal of Verbal Learning and Verbal Behavior, 17,* 573–585.

Breuer, J., & Freud, S. (1895/1955). Studies on hysteria. In J. Strachey (Ed.), *The standard edition of the complete psychological works of Sigmund Freud* (Vol. 2). London: Hogarth Press.

Brewin, C. R., Andrews, B., & Gotlib, I. H. (1993). Psychopathology and early experience: A reappraisal of retrospective reports. *Psychological Bulletin, 113,* 82–98.

Brown, R., & Kulik, J. (1977). Flashbulb memories. *Cognition, 5,* 73–99.

Buck, R. (1984). *The communication of emotion.* New York: Guilford Press.

Burke, A., Heuer, F., & Reisberg. (1992). Remembering emotional events. *Memory and Cognition, 20,* 277–290.

Christianson, S.-Å. (1984). The relationship between induced emotional arousal and amnesia. *Scandinavian Journal of Psychology, 25,* 147–160.

—— (1986). Effects of positive emotional events on memory. *Scandinavian Journal of Psychology, 27,* 289–301.

—— (1989). Flashbulb memories: Special, but not so special. *Memory & Cognition, 17,* 435–443.

—— (1992a). Emotional stress and eyewitness memory: A critical review. *Psychological Bulletin, 112,* 284–309.

—— (1992b). Remembering emotional events: Potential mechanisms. In S.-Å. Christianson (Ed.), *The handbook of emotion and memory: Research and theory.* Hillsdale, NJ: Lawrence Erlbaum.

Christianson, S.-Å., & Hübinette, B. (1993). Hands up! A study of witnesses' emotional reactions and memories associated with bank robberies. *Applied Cognitive Psychology, 7,* 365–379.

Christianson, S.-Å., & Loftus, E. F. (1987). Memory for traumatic events. *Applied Cognitive Psychology, 1,* 225–239.

—— (1990). Some characteristics of people's traumatic memories. *Bulletin of the Psychonomic Society, 28,* 195–198.

—— (1991). Remembering emotional events: The fate of detailed information. *Cognition & Emotion, 5,* 81–108.

Christianson, S.-Å., Loftus, E. F., Hoffman, H., & Loftus, G. R. (1991). Eye fixations and memory for emotional events. *Journal of Experimental Psychology: Learning, Memory, and Cognition, 17,* 693–701.

Christianson, S.-Å., & Nilsson, L.-G. (1984). Functional amnesia as induced by a psychological trauma. *Memory & Cognition, 12,* 142–155.

—— (1989). Hysterical amnesia: A case of aversively motivated isolation of memory. In T. Archer & L.-G. Nilsson (Eds.), *Aversion, avoidance, and anxiety: Perspectives on aversively motivated behavior* (pp. 289–310). Hillsdale, NJ: Lawrence Erlbaum.

Cimino, C. R., Verfaellie, M., Bowers, D., & Heilman, K. M. (1991). Autobiographical memory: Influence of right hemisphere damage on emotionality and specificity. *Brain and Cognition, 15,* 106–118.

Claparede, E. (1911/1951). [Recognition and 'me'ness.] In D. Rapaport (Ed.), *Organization and pathology of thought* (pp. 58–75). New York: Columbia University Press. (Reprinted from *Archives de Psychologies,* 1911, *11,* 79–90.)

Colgrove, F. W. (1899). Individual memories. *American Journal of Psychology, 10,* 228–255.

Cutler, B., Penrod, S., & Martens, T. (1987). The reliability of eyewitness identification. *Law and Human Behavior, 11,* 233–258.

Cutshall, J. L., & Yuille, J. C. (1989). Field studies of eyewitness memory of actual crimes. In D. C. Raskin (Ed.), *Psychological methods in criminal investigation and evidence* (pp. 97–124). New York: Springer-Verlag.

Davis, P. J. (1990). Repression and the inaccessibility of emotional memories. In J. L. Singer (Ed.), *Repression and dissociation: Implications for personality theory, psychopathology, and health* (pp. 387–403). Chicago: University of Chicago Press.

Deffenbacher, K. A. (1983) The influence of arousal on reliability of testimony. In S. M. A. Lloyd-Bostock & B. R. Clifford (Eds.), *Evaluating witness evidence* (pp. 235–251). Chichester, UK: Wiley.

Devito, A. J., & Kubis, J. F. (1983). Actual and recalled test anxiety and flexibility, rigidity, and self-control. *Journal of Clinical Psychology, 29,* 970–975.

Dunning, D., & Stern, L. B. (1992). Examining the generality of eyewitness hypermnesia: A close look at time delay and question type. *Applied Cognitive Psychology, 6,* 643–657.

Easterbrook, J. A. (1959). The effect of emotion on cue utilization and the organization of behavior. *Psychological Review, 66,* 183–201.

Eich, E. (1980). The cue-dependent nature of state-dependent retrieval. *Memory and Cognition, 8,* 157–173.

Eich, E., & Metcalfe, J. (1989). Mood dependent memory for internal versus external events. *Journal of Experimental Psychology: Learning, Memory, and Cognition, 15,* 443–456.

Eich, E., Reeves, J. L., Jaeger, B., & Graf-Radford, S.B. (1985). Memory for pain: Relation between past and present pain intensity. *Pain, 23,* 375–379.

Ellis, H. C., & Ashbrook, P. W. (1989). The "state" of mood and memory research: A selective review. In D. Kuiken (Ed.), Mood and memory: Theory, research, and applications in a special issue of the *Journal of Social Behavior and Personality, 4,* 1–21.

Erdelyi, M. H., & Goldberg, B. (1979). Let's not sweep repression under the rug: Toward a cognitive psychology of repression. In J. F. Kihlstrom & F. J. Evans (Eds.), *Functional disorders of memory* (pp. 355–402). Hillsdale, NJ: Lawrence Erlbaum.

Eysenck, M. W., & Mogg, K. (1992). Clinical anxiety, trait anxiety, and memory bias. In S.-Å. Christianson (Ed.), *The handbook of emotion and memory: Research and theory* (pp. 429–450). Hillsdale, NJ: Lawrence Erlbaum.

Fernandez, E., & Turk, D. C. (1992). Sensory and affective components of pain: Separation and synthesis. *Psychological Bulletin, 112,* 205–217.

Fisher, R. P., & Geiselman, R. E. (1992). *Memory-enhancing techniques for investigative interviewing.* Springfield, IL: Charles C. Thomas.

Fisher, R. P., Geiselman, R. E., & Amador, M. (1989). Field test of the cognitive interview: Enhancing the recollection of actual victims and witnesses of crime. *Journal of Applied Psychology, 74,* 722–727.

Fitzgerald, J. M., Slade, S., & Lawrence, R. H. (1988). Memory availability and judged frequency of affect. *Cognitive Therapy and Research, 12,* 379–390.

Freud, S. (1915/1957). Repression. In J. Strachey (Ed.), *The standard edition of the complete psychological works of Sigmund Freud* (Vol. 14, pp. 146–158). London: Hogarth Press.

Gage, D. F., & Safer, M. A. (1985). Hemisphere differences in the mood state-dependent effect for recognition of emotional faces. *Journal of Experimental Psychology: Learning, Memory, and Cognition, 11,* 752–763.

Gainotti, G., Caltagirone, C., & Zoccolotti, P. (1993). Left/right and cortical/subcortical dichotomies in the neuropsychological study of human emotions. *Cognition and Emotion, 7,* 71–93.

Godden, D.R., & Baddeley, A. D. (1975). Context-dependent memory in two natural environments: On land and underwater. *British Journal of Psychology, 66,* 325–331.

—— (1980). When does context influence recognition memory? *British Journal of Psychology, 71,* 99–104.

Goodman, G. S., Hepps, D. H., & Reed, R. S. (1986). The child victim's testimony. In A. Haralamic (Ed.), *New issues for child advocates.* Phoenix, AZ: Arizona Council of Attorneys for Children.

Hathaway, S. R., & McKinley, J. C. (1989). *Minnesota Multiphasic Personality Inventory-2.* University of Minnesota.

Heuer, F., & Reisberg, D. (1990) Vivid memories of emotional events: The accuracy of remembered minutiae. *Memory & Cognition, 18,* 496–506.

Hosch, H. M., & Bothwell, R. K. (1990). Arousal, description, and identification accuracy of victims and bystanders. *Journal of Social Behavior and Personality, 5,* 481–488.

Intraub, H., Bender, R., & Mangels, J. (1992). Looking at pictures but remembering scenes. *Journal of Experimental Psychology: Learning, Memory, and Cognition, 18,* 180–191.

Isen, A. M. (1984). Toward understanding the role of affect in cognition. In R. S. Wyer & T. K. Srull (Eds.), *Handbook of social cognition* (Vol. 3, pp. 179–236). Hillsdale, NJ: Lawrence Erlbaum.

Izard, C. E. (1993). Four systems for emotion activation: Cognitive and noncognitive processes. *Psychological Review, 100,* 68–90.

James, W. (1890/1918). *The principles of psychology* (Vol. II). New York: Henry Holt.

Johnson, M. K., Kim, J. K., & Risse, G. (1985). Do alcoholic Korsakoff's syndrome patients acquire affective reactions? *Journal of Experimental Psychology: Learning, Memory, and Cognition, 11,* 22–36.

Johnson, M. K., & Multhaup, K. S. (1992). Emotion and MEM. In S.-Å. Christianson (Ed.), *The handbook of emotion and memory: Research and theory.* Hillsdale, NJ: Lawrence Erlbaum.

Kassin, S. M., Ellsworth, P. C., & Smith, V. L. (1989). The "general acceptance" of psychological research on eyewitness testimony: A survey of the experts. *American Psychologist, 44,* 1089–1098.

Kebeck, G., & Lohaus, A. (1986). Effects of emotional arousal on free recall of complex material. *Perceptual and Motor Skills, 63,* 461–462.

Keuler, D., & Safer, M. A. (1993). Memory bias in the recall of anxiety. Manuscript in preparation. Catholic University of America, Washington, DC.

Kolb, B., & Milner, B. (1981). Observations on spontaneous facial expression after focal cerebral excisions and after intracarotid injection of sodium amytal. *Neuropsychologia, 19*, 505–514.

Kolb, B., & Whishaw, I. Q. (1989). *Fundamentals of human neuropsychology* (3rd ed.). New York: W. H. Freeman.

Kramer, T. H., Buckhout, R., & Eugenio, P. (1990). Weapon focus, arousal, and eyewitness memory: Attention must be paid. *Law and Human Behavior, 14*, 167–184.

Kuiken, D. (Ed.). (1989). Mood and memory: Theory, research, and applications. *Journal of Social Behavior and Personality, 4*, (2).

Larsen, S. F. (1992). Potential flashbulbs: Memories of ordinary news as the baseline. In E. Winograd & U. Neisser (Eds.), *Affect and accuracy in recall: Studies of "flashbulb memories."* New York: Cambridge University Press.

Lazarus, R. S. (1984). On the primacy of cognition. *American Psychologist, 39*, 124–129.

LeDoux, J. E. (1992). Emotion as memory: Anatomical systems underlying indelible neural traces. In S.-Å. Christianson (Ed.), *The handbook of emotion and memory: Research and theory* (pp. 269–288). Hillsdale, NJ: Lawrence Erlbaum.

Leventhal, H. (1984). A perceptual-motor theory of emotion. In K. R. Scherer & P. Ekman (Eds.), *Approaches to emotion* (pp. 271–291). Hillsdale, NJ: Lawrence Erlbaum.

Leventhal, H., & Scherer, K. R. (1987). The relationship of emotion to cognition: A functional approach to a semantic controversy. *Cognition and Emotion, 1*, 3–28.

Levonian, E. (1967). Retention of information in relation to arousal during continuously presented material. *American Educational Research Journal, 4*, 103–116.

Linton, M. (1982). Transformations of memory in everyday life. In U. Neisser (Ed.), *Memory observed: Remembering in natural contexts* (pp. 77–91). San Francisco: W. H. Freeman.

Loftus, E. F. (1979). *Eyewitness testimony.* London: Harvard University Press.

Loftus, E. F., Loftus, G. R., Messo, J. (1987). Some facts about "weapon focus." *Law and Human Behavior, 11*, 55–62.

Maass, A., & Kohnken, G. (1989). Eyewitness identification: Simulating the "weapon effect." *Law and Human Behavior, 13*, 397–408.

Matt, G. E., Vazquez, C., & Campbell, W. K. (1992). Mood-congruent recall of affectively toned stimuli: A meta-analytic review. *Clinical Psychology Review, 12*, 227–255.

McCloskey, M., Wible, C. G., & Cohen, N. J. (1988). Is there a special flashbulb-memory mechanism? *Journal of Experimental Psychology: General, 117*, 171–181.

McGaugh, J. L. (1992). Affect, neuromodulatory systems and memory storage. In S.-Å. Christianson (Ed.), *The handbook of emotion and memory: Research and theory.* Hillsdale, NJ: Lawrence Erlbaum.

Mineka, S. (1992). Evolutionary memories, emotional processing, and the emotional disorders. In G. H. Bower (Ed.), *The psychology of learning and motivation* (Vol. 28, pp. 161–206). New York: Academic Press.

Mishkin, M. (1978). Memory in monkeys severely impaired by combined but not by separate removal of amygdala and hippocampus. *Nature, 273*, 297–298.

Morley, S. (1993). Vivid memories. *Pain, 55*, 55–62.

Neisser, U. (1982). Snapshots or benchmarks? In U. Neisser (Ed.), *Memory observed* (pp. 43–48). San Francisco: W. H. Freeman.

Neisser, U., & Harsch, N. (1992). Phantom flashbulbs: False recollections of hearing the news about *Challenger*. In E. Winograd & U. Neisser (Eds.), *Affect and accuracy in recall. Studies of "flashbulb memories."* New York: Cambridge University Press.

Öhman, A. (1991). Orienting and attention: Preferred preattentive processing of potentially phobic stimuli. In B. A. Campbell, R. Richardson, & H. Hayne (Eds.), *Attention and information processing in infants and adults: Perspectives from human and animal research* (pp. 263–295). Hillsdale, NJ: Lawrence Erlbaum.

Overton, D. A. (1978). Major theories of state dependent learning. In B. T. Ho, D. W. Richards III, & D. L. Chute (Eds.), *Drug discrimination and state dependent learning* (pp. 283-318). New York: Academic Press.

—— (1982). Memory retrieval failures produced by changes in drug state. In R. L. Isaacson & N. E. Spear (Eds.), *The expression of knowledge: Neurobehavioral transformations of information into action* (pp. 113–139). New York: Plenum Press.

Parrott, W. G. (1993). Beyond hedonism: Motives for inhibiting good moods and for maintaining bad moods. In D. M. Wegner & J. W. Pennebaker (Eds.), *Handbook of mental control* (pp. 278–305). Englewood Cliffs, NJ: Prentice Hall.

Parrott, W. G., & Sabini, J. (1990). Mood and memory under natural conditions: Evidence for mood incongruent recall. *Journal of Personality and Social Psychology, 59*, 321–336.

Payne, D. G. (1987). Hypermnesia and reminiscence in recall: A historical and empirical review. *Psychological Bulletin, 101*, 5–27.

Perceman, E. (Ed.). (1983). *Cognitive processing in the right hemisphere.* New York: Academic Press.

Pillemer, D. B. (1984). Flashbulb memories of the assassination attempt on President Reagan. *Cognition, 16*, 63–80.

Putnam, F. W. (1989). *Diagnosis and treatment of multiple personality disorder.* New York: Guilford Press.

Reisberg, D., Heuer, F., McLean, J., & O'Shaughnessy, M. (1988). The quantity, not the quality, of affect predicts memory vividness. *Bulletin of the Psychonomic Society, 26*, 100–103.

Republicans and Democrats alternate in questioning. (1991, October 12). *New York Times* (National edition), L13.

Rogler, L. H., Malgady, R. G., & Tryon, W. W. (1992). Evaluation of mental health: Issues of memory in the diagnostic interview schedule. *Journal of Nervous and Mental Disease, 180*, 215–222.

Ross, B. M. (1991). *Remembering the personal past.* New York: Oxford University Press.

Rubin, D.C., & Friendly, M. (1986). Predicting which words get recalled: Measures of free recall, availability, goodness, emotionality, and pronounceability for 925 nouns. *Memory & Cognition, 14*, 79–94.

Rubin, D. C., & Kozin, M. (1984). Vivid memories. *Cognition, 16*, 81–95.

Safer, M. A. (1981). Sex and hemisphere differences in access to codes for processing emotional expressions and faces. *Journal of Experimental Psychology: General, 110*, 86–100.

Safer, M. A., Christianson, S.-Å., Autry, M, & Österlund, K. (1993). Tunnel memory for traumatic events. Manuscript submitted for publication.

Schrader, G., Davis, A., Stefanovic, S., & Christie, P. (1990). The recollection of affect. *Psychological Medicine, 20*, 105–109.

Scrivner, E., & Safer, M. A. (1988). Eyewitnesses show hypermnesia for details about a violent event. *Journal of Applied Psychology, 73*, 371–377.

Singer, J. A., & Salovey, P. (1988). Mood and memory: Evaluating the network theory of affect. *Clinical Psychology Review, 8*, 211–251.

Singer, J. L. (Ed.). (1990). *Repression and dissociation: Implications for personality theory, psychopathology, and health.* Chicago: University of Chicago Press.

Smith, W. B., & Safer, M. A. (1993). Effects of present pain level on recall of chronic pain and medication use. *Pain, 55*, 355–361.

Steblay, N. M. (1992). A meta-analytic review of the weapon focus effect. *Law and Human Behavior, 16*, 413–424.

Strongman, K. T., & Kemp, S. (1991). Autobiographical memory for emotion. *Bulletin of the Psychonomic Society, 29*, 195–198.

Terr, L. (1983). Chowchilla revisited: The effects of psychic trauma four years after a schoolbus kidnapping. *American Journal of Psychiatry, 140*, 1543–1550.

—— (1990). *Too scared to cry: Psychic trauma in childhood.* New York: Harper & Row.

Thomas, D. L., & Diener, E. (1990). Memory accuracy in the recall of emotions. *Journal of Personality and Social Psychology, 59*, 291–297.

Thomas, Hill make statements as panel begins hearings. (1991). *Congressional Quarterly Almanac, 47*, 23-E–26-E.

Tobias, B. A., Kihlstrom, J. F., & Schacter, D. L. (1992). Emotion and implicit memory. In S.-Å. Christianson (Ed.), *The handbook of emotion and memory: Research and theory.* Hillsdale, NJ: Lawrence Erlbaum.

Ucros, C. G. (1989). Mood state-dependent memory: A meta-analysis. *Cognition and Emotion, 3*, 139–167.

Van Lancker, D. (1991). Personal relevance and the human right hemisphere. *Brain and Cognition, 17*, 64–92.

von Benedek, L. (1992). The mental activity of the psychoanalyst. *Psychotherapy Research, 2*, 63–72.

Wagenaar, W. A. (1986). My memory: A study of autobiographical memory over six years. *Cognitive Psychology, 18*, 225–252.

Wagenaar, W. A., & Groeneweg, J. (1990). The memory of concentration camp survivors. *Applied Cognitive Psychology, 4*, 77–87.

Warren, A. R., & Swartwood, J. N. (1992). Developmental issues in flashbulb memory research: Children recall the Challenger event. In E. Winograd & U. Neisser (Eds.)., *Affect and accuracy in recall: Studies of "flashbulb" memories.* New York: Cambridge University Press.

Winograd, E., & Killinger, W. A., Jr. (1983). Relating age at encoding in early childhood to adult recall: Development of flashbulb memories. *Journal of Experimental Psychology: General, 112*, 413–422.

Young, A. W. (Ed.). (1983). *Functions of the right cerebral hemisphere.* New York: Academic Press.

Yuille, J. C., & Cutshall, J. L. (1986). A case study of eyewitness memory of a crime. *Journal of Applied Psychology, 71*, 291–301.

—— (1989). Analysis of the statements of victims, witnesses and suspects. In J. C. Yuille (Ed.), *Credibility assessment.* Dordrecht, The Netherlands: Kluwer Academic.

Yuille, J. C., & Tollestrup, P. A. (1992). A model of the diverse effects of emotion on eyewitness memory. In S.-Å. Christianson (Ed.), *The handbook of emotion and memory: Research and theory.* Hillsdale, NJ: Lawrence Erlbaum.

Zajonc, R. B. (1980). Feeling and thinking: Preferences need no inferences. *American Psychologist, 35*, 151–175.

Zimmerman, M., & Coryell, W. (1986). Reliability of follow-up assessments of depressed in-patients. *Archives of General Psychiatry, 43*, 468–470.

10   Depression and the specificity of autobiographical memory

J. M. G. Williams

There are many ways to become depressed, and many ways in which recovery from depression is impaired. This chapter outlines how a person's memory can play a role in both. Past research has shown how depression affects and is affected by the type of events a person remembers. Negative mood promotes the recall of unpleasant events, either by making their activation more easy, or by impeding retrieval of alternative, more positive events. But I am not concerned here with the connection between depression and the preferential access to negative episodic memory, important though it is. This has been reviewed before many times (see Blaney, 1986; Christianson & Safer, this volume; Teasdale & Barnard, 1993; Williams, Watts, Macleod, & Mathews, 1988). Most of the research investigating mood congruent memory uses word or story learning paradigms rather than autobiographical memory. When autobiographical memory is the subject of study, the questions asked of it naturally focus on the reasons why some memories are faster or more probable to retrieve than others. The predominant paradigm within which explanations are sought is associative network theory, a framework that has been increasingly found not to account for the complexity of the data (Teasdale & Barnard, 1993; Williams et al., 1988). Instead, in this chapter I am concerned with exploring the connection between depression and the quality of the memory that is retrieved, a topic of inquiry for which network theory was not designed. In particular, I am interested in whether a person retrieves a specific event or a summary of events.

First, I shall review evidence suggesting that depressed people use an overgeneral mode of retrieval, itself a clinically important phenomenon. The person is not aware that they have this tendency, yet it undermines their ability to use memory in imagining the future and in solving current interpersonal problems. Second, I shall examine possible causes of the phenomenon. I will suggest that part of the answer may be found in the parallels between the functional deficits observed in depression and the structural deficits that result from brain damage (Baddeley & Wilson 1986; Cimino, Verfaellie, Bowers, & Heilman, 1991; della Sala, Laiacona, Spinnler, & Trivelli, 1992) and aging (Winthorpe & Rabbitt, 1988). However, there is also evidence that the overgeneral style of memory retrieval may also be acquired during development. I will suggest that a

244

person may persist in using an early retrieval mode, that occurs naturally during cognitive development (Morton, 1990; Nelson, 1988), as a way of controlling affect. In this way, recall of specific aspects of past events are avoided. However, the result is that new events are encoded in a more schematic, less distinctive form. The more disrupted the early experience, the greater these tendencies – and I shall review evidence that people who have experienced trauma have greater difficulty in specific retrieval even for events unrelated to the trauma.

Third, I will examine the mechanisms that underlie overgeneral memory. Previously I have suggested that overgeneral memory represents a truncated search through hierarchically organized "descriptions." However, we now know that this is too general an explanation. For there are two different types of hierarchies in which events (or the search for them) can be organized (see Barsalou, 1988; Conway & Bekerian, 1987). First, events may be nested by lifetime periods or "extended event time lines." Second, events may be nested into categories such as people, places and activities. A truncated search through either or both hierarchies that led to retrieval being aborted at too early a stage would yield responses that were overgeneral, both by being extended memories (e.g., the time I lived near Oxford) and categoric memories (e.g., times I have stood at bus stops). Yet only categoric memories are abnormally high in depressed people. Instead, I suggest that retrieval becomes deadlocked only following the category description stage, because of the tendency for an initial self-referent categoric description to elicit other highly activated self-descriptions, so that retrieval moves across the hierarchy rather than down to more specific levels. I coin the term "mnemonic interlock" to describe this process. Mnemonic interlock can only be overridden at a high cost of effort, so that individuals who have reduced working memory or supervisory attentional capacity, either by virtue of structural damage to the brain or by virtue of preoccupation or distraction, find it particularly difficult to break the deadlock and access specific memories.

The phenomenon of overgeneral retrieval

Consider the following sample transcript from a psychotherapy interview.

Therapist	When you were young, what sort of things made you happy?
Patient	Well, things used to be alright then; I mean, better than they are now, I think.When my dad was there, he used to take me for walks on the Common sometimes after lunch on a Sunday.
Therapist	Can you tell me about one such a walk?
Patient	Well, we used to go out after lunch, sometimes we would take a ball and play around. Afterwards, we might go and see my granny who lived on the other side of the Common.
Therapist	When you think back, now, can you remember any particular time? I want you to try and recall any one of these

	times. Any time will do, it doesn't have to be particularly important or special.
Patient	I remember there used to be other children on the Common sometimes. Sometimes they would be friends of mine and I would stop and chat to them for a while.
Therapist	Can you remember any particular time when you met any of your friends?
Patient	If it was winter, there weren't usually many people about.

This transcript illustrates a frequent aspect of the interchange between a therapist and a patient. Note the apparent reluctance or inability of the patient to recollect specific memories as the therapist appears to require. Perhaps the therapist was not being specific enough in his or her questions. Perhaps there were simply too many memories to choose from, and there was nothing distinctive to help recall any one of them. Perhaps the patient did not want to recall potentially painful memories despite the fact that they knew they were there. However, the transcript is very similar to Baddeley and Wilson's (1986) transcripts of interviews with some of their frontal amnesic patients. The similarity of the memory deficit may exist only at this surface level, and need not be reflected in the mechanisms underlying it. Nevertheless, it suggests that the depressed patient's difficulty in being specific should not be dismissed as merely a deliberate attempt to frustrate the therapeutic process.

The observation that people who were suffering an emotional disturbance had difficulty in being specific in their memory was made during an experiment on mood-memory bias. We were interested in examining mood congruent memory in people who had recently attempted suicide in order to understand more about the psychological processes underlying suicidal feelings and actions. In pilot work using a sample of the cue words that Robinson (1976) had used (five negative: clumsy, hurt, angry, lonely and sorry; and five positive: happy, surprised, interested, successful and safe), we found that patients were not readily able to give the specific memories for which we had asked (see Table 10.1 for examples of typical responses for patients and controls).

Changing the instructions to make the task more clear did not help; neither did practice items. Yet the pattern of responses suggested that they were genuinely trying to retrieve specific memories. Keith Broadbent and I decided to examine the phenomenon more systematically (Williams & Broadbent, 1986). We compared 25 patients who had recently taken an overdose and were still depressed with the same number of control patients recruited from the same wards of Addenbrooke's Hospital, Cambridge. A further 25 controls were recruited from the subject panel of the Applied Psychology Unit. The groups were matched for age and educational level. We administered the same cue words, asking subjects to recall an event that the word reminded them of. The event could be important or trivial, recent or distant. They were then given additional instructions that the event should be specific – something that happened at a particular place and time and took no longer than a day. An example was given to illustrate what would and what would not count as such a specific event. Practice words were then used, and

Table 10.1 *Patterns of autobiographical recall in suicidally depressed patients and matched controls*

Cue word	Control subject's response	Patient's response (a = first response; b & c = response after prompting)
Happy	The day we left to go on holiday	a) When I'm playing squash b) When I beat my policeman friend 3 weeks ago*
Sorry	When I dropped something and my flatmate got annoyed	a) When I've had to do something b) When I lie to my mum
Safe	Down in London last weekend getting off the bus at 4 A.M.	a) When I'm at home in my week-end house b) When Stuart's around
Angry	With my supervisor on Monday	a) When I've had a row b) A month ago I stormed off in a car*
Clumsy	I spilt some milk on holiday	a) I fall down stairs b) It happens so often c) A month ago when the Jehovah's Witnesses came to the door*

Notes: (a) Items marked * are specific memories retrieved following prompting by the experimenter.
(b) Reliability of the allocation of memories to general/specific categories was checked after completion of the experiment by having two independent judges categorize a random sample of the 750 responses obtained. This yielded 87% and 93% agreement with the experimenter's categories.

the experiment did not start until the subject had retrieved a specific memory. During the autobiographical testing, subjects were allowed 60 seconds to retrieve a memory. If their response was inappropriately general, they were prompted with the words, "Can you think of a specific time – one particular event?" We recorded the latency to the first word of each separate response. The latencies to retrieve specific memories are shown in Figure 10.1.

The latency results confirmed what others investigators had found: that emotionally disturbed people show a mood congruent memory bias in that they have difficulty retrieving positive events. However, our pilot work had suggested that this latency effect might be the result of the tendency to retrieve overgeneral memories, and to then require further prompting. Should there have been a tendency to be nonspecific more in response to positive words than to negative words, this might explain the latency differences that were found. When we examined the transcripts of our patients and controls, we found just such a pattern.

The suicidal subjects were less likely to respond with a specific memory when first given a cue, and required prompting. Figure 10.2 shows the proportion of first responses that were specific autobiographical memories.

The results showed two significant effects. First, there was a group main effect (F(2,67) = 11.73; p < .001) due to the suicidal patients' tendency to be overgeneral in

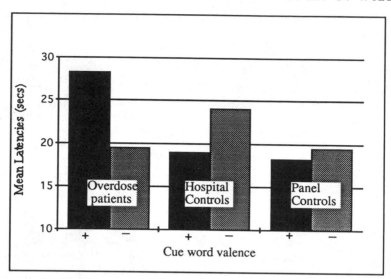

Figure 10.1 Mean latencies to retrieve specific autobiographical memories (Williams & Broadbent, 1986).

their first response to both positive and negative cues. However, this was modified by a significant group by cue valence interaction (F(2,67) = 4.24; p < .025) due to the suicidal patients finding it particularly difficult to retrieve specific memories in response to positive cue words.

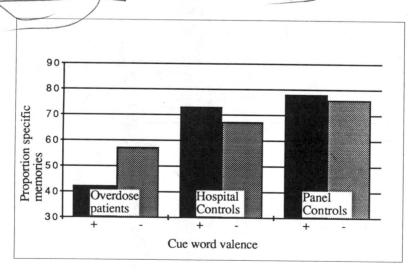

Figure 10.2 Mean proportion of first responses that were specific autobiographical memories (Williams & Broadbent, 1986).

It could be that the overgeneral responding was due to the aftereffects of the drug overdose. All patients had been seen between 36 and 96 hours postoverdose, after the clinical signs of the drugs had gone, but we needed to take account of the possibility that the cognitive effects of them would remain. We had therefore tested the subjects with the semantic processing speed test ("silly sentences") that had been found to be sensitive to drug effects (Baddeley, Emslie, & Nimmo-Smith, 1992). In this test, the subject is required to decide whether sentences are true or false. In the version that we used there were 50 sentences (such as "pork chops are meat" and "doctors are always sold in pairs"), and subjects were instructed to make the decisions as fast as possible, making as few errors as possible. There was a significant difference between the subject panel controls (M = 77.2 s) and the two other groups (overdose and hospital controls) that did not differ from each other (M's = 116.3 s and 112.2 s, respectively). Thus it appeared that the two patient groups were equally cognitively "sluggish" as each other, as compared to the nonpatient controls. Yet this was very different from the pattern of autobiographical memory results, where the hospital and panel control groups had similar responses, with the overdose group alone showing a distinct pattern of overgenerality. Subsequent work in our own and other laboratories has confirmed the robustness of these findings. Although a detailed review of these are beyond the scope of this chapter, the results may be summarized in the following way.

1. Overgeneral memories can be found using a variety of cueing techniques.
Williams and Dritschel (1988) added activity cues to emotionally valent nouns (e.g., "happiness – going for a walk"). The aim had been to see if providing an activity cue would assist the retrieval process. They found no difference at all in the pattern of results, with suicidal patients again giving more overgeneral memories. Moore, Watts, and Williams (1988) sampled autobiographical memories as part of a study of depressed subjects' perceptions of how much emotional and instrumental support they receive. Eight positive and eight negative scenarios (e.g., "a neighbor helped me with some practical problem"; "my partner criticized me") were presented to depressed subjects and matched controls. Subjects were asked to have a particular person in mind, and the task was to recall specific instances in each case. The results showed that cueing with vignettes in this way still revealed the depressed subjects' tendency to be overgeneral. The percentage of first responses that were inappropriately overgeneral was 40% for the depressed group and 19% for the control group (F(1,32) = 11.07; p < 0.01).

2. Overgeneral memory is found in people with a diagnosis of primary major depression even if not suicidal. Our early work had been on people who had recently taken an overdose. Although we had found that the drugs taken in the overdose did not appear to be a factor in the results, the very recency of the crisis itself might have affected memory processes. Moore et al.'s (1988) results suggested that the phenomenon might generalize to other clinical groups. This was found to be the case in a parallel study conducted in Newcastle upon Tyne (Williams & Scott, 1988). Twenty inpatients with a diagnosis of primary major depression were matched with 20 subject panel controls for age, educational level, and for their performance on Baddeley's semantic processing speed test. The depressed patients retrieved specific memories, on average, 40% of the time, compared to the control subjects' 70%. In a repeat of this experiment in a research clinic in Belgium, Puffet, Jehin-Marchot, Timsit-Berthier, and Timsit (1991) examined autobiographical memory performance in 20 clinically depressed patients and 20 matched controls. They replicated the earlier results of Williams and Scott (1988), finding greater overgenerality in the depressed patients, especially in response to positive cue words.

Finally, Kuyken and Brewin (in preparation), in a study to be reported in greater detail below, compared memory performance in 58 women meeting the criteria for major depressive disorder on the DSM-III-R (American Psychiatric Association, 1987) with 33 matched nonpsychiatric controls from the subject panel of the Institute of Psychiatry in London. Once again, they found greater overgenerality in the depressed group. It is clear from these results that overgeneral memory is a robust phenomenon in both suicidal and depressed groups.

3. Overgeneral memory is not associated with all forms of emotional disturbance; it is not found in anxious subjects. Two studies have examined the specificity of autobiographical memory in anxiety. Richards and Whittaker (1990) studied 40 subjects (ages 19 to 54) and compared high and low anxious subjects on a measure of trait autobiographical memory. Although anxious subjects were faster in retrieving events to threat-related cues (versus happy cues), whereas the low anxious subjects showed no difference, there was no evidence that high anxious subjects were more overgeneral in their memory. Although this null result might have been due to the fact that the subjects were not clinically anxious, another study that used patients diagnosed as having General Anxiety Disorder (DSM IIIR) also failed to find a generality effect. Burke and Mathews (1992) compared 12 such patients with 12 controls and gave subjects neutral cue words for which they had to retrieve either anxious or nonanxious memories. Little evidence for generality was found despite finding, once again, a mood congruent effect on the latency to retrieve the events. This pattern of inconsistency in memory biases in anxiety is also shown for laboratory episodic memory tasks (see Christianson & Safer, this volume; Williams et al., 1988, in press)

4. Overgenerality is not state-dependent: it does not disappear when the depression has remitted. Williams and Dritschel (1988) tested 16 recovered patients who had taken an overdose between 3 and 14 months prior. Ten positive and 10 negative words were given as cues, and the responses compared both to those of patients with a current suicidal crisis and to those of subject panel controls. Results showed that the proportion of responses that were specific in ex-patients (54%) was not significantly different from current patients (46%), but both of these groups were significantly different from the controls (71%). Although some of these ex-patients were still depressed, such people could not be distinguished at all, in level of generality, from those whose mood had recovered completely. Williams and Dritschel concluded that overgenerality seemed to be a cognitive style, perhaps a lifelong style of such patients that might render them more vulnerable for depressive moods. However, this study was cross-sectional, and no strong inferences could be drawn.

A later longitudinal study interviewed depressed patients on three occasions during recovery, so it was possible to see how autobiographical memory altered as depression lifted. Brittlebank, Scott, Williams, and Ferrier (1993) tested patients on admission, 3 months later, and 7 months later. There was no reliable fall in overgeneral memory in response to emotional cue words over this period. Overgenerality to neutral cue words did, however, fall as depression remitted, but even patients in remission remained impaired in their memory compared with levels that are found in normal or hospital control groups.

Another indication of the independence of overgeneral memory from current mood state is that in none of our studies have we found a significant correlation between extent to which memory is overgeneral and current depressed mood. Similarly Kuyken and Brewin (in preparation) found that the correlation between the level of depression (measured with the Beck depression inventory) and overgeneral memory in their 58 depressed patients was low and nonsignificant ($\rho = -0.01$).

5. Overgeneral memory is associated with poor problem solving. Evans, Williams, O'Loughlin, and Howells (1992) examined the relation between memory and performance on a test of interpersonal problem solving – the means-ends problem solving (MEPS) test (Platt & Spivack, 1975). This measure is based on the theory that problem solving involves several steps: problem orientation and definition (realizing that a problem exists and defining its nature); generating alternative solutions; evaluating the possible outcome of these solutions; implementing the most promising; and evaluating the outcome and starting over again if necessary. The test gives problem scenarios together with a positive ending to the story (e.g., moving to a new neighborhood and having few friends; the story ends with the person having successfully made some friends). It asks the subject to supply the middle of the story. There is little doubt that depressed and suicidal patients find such problem solving difficult (Marx, Williams, & Claridge, 1992). Evans et al. predicted that overgeneral memory would impair problem solving, because both the definition of a problem and the generation of alternative solutions demands an ability to address adequately the memory "database."

They gave both the MEPS test and a cue-word autobiographical memory test to 12 patients who had recently taken an overdose (within 15 to 36 hours of admission) and compared their performance with 12 carefully matched control patients who were in hospital for surgery. The alternative problem solutions produced by the subjects were independently rated for how effective they were, since this statistic has been found to differentiate depressed from other clinical groups (Marx et al., 1992). There was a significant correlation between the effectiveness of the problems produced and the specificity of autobiographical memory for the entire sample ($r(22) = 0.57$; $p = 0.002$) and for the overdose group ($r(10) = 0.67$; $p = 0.008$). In order to check the possibility that these correlations might have resulted from general unresponsiveness, the correlation between effectiveness of solutions and latency to respond on the memory task was computed. This correlation was not significant ($r = .25$). The partial correlation coefficient between problem solving effectiveness and specificity of memory, partialling out memory latency, was 0.69. This suggests that the association between generality and problem solving was not the result of general sluggishness to respond to the tasks. Williams (1992) suggested that this problem solving becomes inhibited because depressed people attempt to use the intermediate descriptions that they have retrieved as a database to try and generate solutions. The database is restricted because of the lack of specific information.

Note that this contrasts with the notion that generic memories are actually beneficial for problem solving. For example, Nelson (1991) in overviewing the significance of her findings of generic memories in young children, argues that any system of learning and memory conserves information about the environment, enabling the organism to act concerning its goals under specific conditions which may vary. This involves directing action in the present and predicting future outcomes. Generic scripts, she says, do this very well. However, this statement should be qualified. Generic scripts are useful in situations where there is a large amount of redundancy, where the solution of the problem merely requires a "read-out" of an average of previous similar situations and little new insight is necessary. However, many problems, particularly interpersonal ones such as "being alone on a Friday night at college," are more open-ended. They do not have one ready-scripted solution. Unlike the ubiquitous "restaurant script," such problems require a person to generate alternatives, then choose the most likely. Some aspects of this sort of task may require generic scripts, but the generation of adequate alternatives is likely to depend on having access to specific autobiographical event memory. If, when alone on a Friday night, the unhappy student tries to think of what sorts of things make her happy, then past specific situations are clearly relevant.

. . . however, if the only memory they retrieve is the generic description (e.g., when I'm with my boyfriend) then that in itself will not contain enough specific information to cue different coping strategies for dealing with the current situation. By contrast, if a nondepressed person is feeling unhappy and tries to think to themselves "what can I do to make myself better?", they are more likely to remember a specific event. Such a memory offers more cues for problem solving. Although "the boyfriend" may be part of this memory, there will be other details as well (e.g., "a walk with my boyfriend last Friday when we met his friends and went to have a drink"). This specific event offers a far greater range of cues. As well as "the boyfriend," there are also "the walk," "the meeting," "the other friends," "the pub" and "last Friday," each of which may cue other potential coping strategies. (Williams, 1992, p. 262).

I suggest that whether a generic script helps problem solving depends on the context. As far as the depressed patient is concerned, general memories are associated with difficulties in solving some of the most important problems, on which their recovery may depend. Depressed patients do not have problems knowing what to do in a restaurant (using the generic script governing general actions such as "wait to be seated," "look at the menu," "order food," etc.). They do have problems, however, with such aspects as how to keep the conversation going once they are in the restaurant (an open-ended problem requiring specific retrieval). In such cases, stopping short of retrieving a specific memory is clearly detrimental. Further research will be needed to determine what sort of problems are likely to benefit from which type of specificity (see also Pillemer, this volume).

6. Overgeneral memory is associated with poorer long-term outcome in emotionally disturbed people. Wahler and Afton (1980) studied women who had relationship problems with their children for which they had sought help. They found that these women, particularly those who had multiple problems, had difficulty in telling the therapist the details about what the children did to annoy them. They concluded that these mothers were having difficulty encoding the specifics about these stressful times in their daily lives. The women all participated in a parent training program. As treatment progressed, the mothers were able to produce more and more detailed pictures about the stressful situations. However, only those mothers whose descriptions had changed to become more detailed were found to improve in their relationships with their children using various independent measures of outcome.

The longitudinal study by Brittlebank et al. (1993), referred to above, gave a similar opportunity to examine whether overgenerality in autobiographical memory predicted subsequent resistance to psychiatric (mostly antidepressant) treatment. Twenty-two patients, all of whom met DSM-III-R criteria for major depressive disorder, were assessed at admission, at 3 months (all), and again at 7 months (N = 19). The correlation between overgeneral responses to positive cue words at Time 1 and depression severity at Time 2 and Time 3 was 0.56 and 0.59, respectively. Multiple regression analysis found that positive overgenerality (Time 1) predicted outcome and accounted for 33% of the variance of the final depression level. Dividing patients at initial testing into high and low overgenerality and examining the 7-month outcome for each subgroup revealed that only 1 out of 9 patients who were "highly overgeneral to positive cues" had recovered from their depression, whereas 8 out of the 10 patients who were "specific to positive cues" had recovered. Brittlebank et al. speculated that the nonresponsiveness of this group may be linked to the problem solving deficit discussed above. If they experience greater difficulty solving daily problems, negative experiences will appear more pervasive and durable, and the result is greater helplessness and less motivation to engage in activities that might otherwise have lifted their mood.

The possible causes of overgeneral memory: Not a frequency effect

In order to understand better what might be responsible for overgeneral retrieval in depression, we need first to ask under what circumstances people use generic memory normally. Clearly, the ability to summarize large numbers of individual episodes into a generic memory is efficient. General memories give quick access to a large amount of information that is necessary for many conversational purposes. Much of the time, people do not need to describe specific examples, the general gist of a number of memories is sufficient. The greater the frequency of an event, the more likely it is that time, place, and other contextual information will be lost. The result is that such information becomes an autobiographical "fact" rather than an autobiographical "event." Conway (1987) found that such memories for frequently repeated experiences (the most extreme example being hearing one's own name) appeared to follow a similar pattern of retrieval (e.g., in their sensitivity to being primed by semantic categories) as other, nonpersonal semantic knowledge. This was different from the pattern of results for the priming of autobiographical events, where semantic primes had no facilitatory effect (Conway & Bekerian, 1987). A related pattern of results from the mood congruent memory literature has been found. Teasdale and Barnard (1993) cite evidence to show that there is no facilitatory priming between retrieval of autobiographical event information and time taken to process trait adjectives describing the self.

From these sorts of results one might suggest that there exists a continuum, with unique episodic events at one end and generic knowledge schemas at the other (see Barsalou, 1988). Generic memory would occupy a position midway between the extremes of autobiographical event memory and autobiographical facts. They would reflect an as yet incomplete transformation from one status to another. However, there are a number of reasons to think that such a frequency effect is not a complete explanation of overgeneral memories. First, there are reliable individual differences in the extent to which people give overgeneral responses on an autobiographical memory test. It is not plausible to suppose that this reflects the increased frequency, across the board, of all events recalled. Second, the research on depressed groups has shown that they are as likely (and in some studies more likely) to retrieve overgeneral memories to positive as to negative cue words, and yet there is abundant evidence that such individuals have had many more negative experiences than nondepressed people. On a frequency basis, they should show a greater tendency to be overgeneral to negative cues, but this does not happen.

Third, studies of brain damaged people have found that they show nonspecificity in autobiographical recall. Baddeley and Wilson (1986) give details of transcripts from a series of frontal patients, and in a further study using the same word cues, Cimino et al. (1991) studied nine right hemisphere damaged patients and nine controls, giving them unlimited time to respond with a specific memory. Both studies found that the patients gave less specific responses. Further, Winthorpe and Rabbitt (1988) found that elderly people who scored low on a working memory test (the sentence span) had difficulty in generating specific memories when given a 10-minute free recall period. Each of these studies raise questions in their own right that are beyond the scope of this chapter. However, for the present discussion they are important in that they show that nonspecificity can arise from structural damage affecting retrieval processes operating on memories for events that we can assume were normally encoded and could have been specifically retrieved were it not for the brain damage. It raises the possibility that emotional disturbance might be a functional analogue of this structural disturbance. At the least it shows that nonspecificity need not merely reflect the frequency of the to-be-recalled event.

The final piece of evidence that generic retrieval is not dependent on the frequency of events comes from studies of normal people. It may, in fact, be quite common for people to retrieve events in generic form without having multiple experiences of the event. When I first moved to Cambridge, I once (and only once!) attended my local village's annual meeting. The details of the meeting I cannot now remember, except for the intervention from the floor of an elderly lady with an authoritative voice, who I later discovered was a senior member of an important local family, who quizzed the elected officials on several points. A few days later, someone was asking me about the meeting, and I found myself saying, "Mrs L. goes to them." I had created a generic memory out of a single, novel experience. So although generic memories might sometimes result from the attempt to recall events that have been frequently experienced, or frequently rehearsed, this does not account for all of them. Indeed, when Barbara Dritschel and I examined subjects' ratings of the frequency of events recalled in a cued autobiographical memory experiment (Williams & Dritschel, 1992), we found that there was only a modest correlation between the tendency for events to be recalled in generic form and the frequency of the event ($r(58) = .24$; $p = .06$). This suggested that I was not alone in retrieving, in generic form, events that occur relatively infrequently. Rather, an event may give rise to generic retrieval if it is seen as paradigmatic, or representative. Attending a Girton village meeting for the first time made me take that single experience as paradigmatic of such events. The retrieval system appears to have a strategy that delivers, as output, that which is seen as typical or paradigmatic independently of the frequency of the underlying event. A similar typicality strategy may account for the fact that young children find it hard to tell adults about specific things seen and heard prior to the development of adult-type autobiographical memory (Morton, 1990; Nelson, 1991), and it is to this research that I now turn.

Evidence from developmental studies

We have seen that overgeneral retrieval may be partly due to a more long-term cognitive style. This is consistent with the idea that some individuals may learn to use overgeneral encoding and retrieval styles as a means to control affect, and more specifically to minimize negative affect (Singer, 1984). In an early study of this question, Hanawalt and Gebhart (1965) examined childhood memories, asking subjects to give pleasantness ratings for both single events and recurrent events. They found single event memories of early childhood to be rated as more unpleasant than memories that summarized a number of events. The fact that such a result could arise from the inherent lower frequency of negative events does not lessen the possibility that some people may learn to selectively recall summarized events if they are naturally less likely to be negative.

In fact, a summary style of memory retrieval naturally occurs during cognitive development (see Fivush, this volume). Nelson and Gruendel (1981) found that 3 year olds gave a good response to the generic question, "What happens when you have dinner?," but produced less detail when asked the specific question, "What happened when you had dinner yesterday?" Even with specific questions, a mix of generic and specific information was produced, such as "we have orange juice." The conclusion drawn from this early research (see Nelson, 1988, for a summary) was that children of this age have no memory for individual episodes, only general event representations (GERs), and it seemed that a possible explanation for infant amnesia had been found. However, further research on young children (Fivush & Hamond, 1989; Fivush & Reese, 1991; Morton,

1990; Tessler, 1986) has found that they can retrieve specific events if given a great deal of very specific cueing. Fivush and colleagues further showed that if $2\frac{1}{2}$ year olds are reminded of events after an interval of 2 weeks, then they have good recall of these events 3 months later (as good a recollection as they had at 2 weeks). Nelson (1991) has revised her earlier theory to suggest instead that new memories are kept in a separate, temporary store. This episodic memory store is a holding operation, and the event representation will be lost if a similar event is not repeated within a certain time frame (that appears to be about 2 weeks). After a repetition the novel event is known to be the first in a series, and a new generic script is set up. As the child gradually shares his or her experiences with adults, an autobiographical memory system develops in which events are retained for longer, especially if they are distinctive.

Despite these findings that young children can retrieve specific memories under certain conditions, all of these researchers agree that for a long period the young child's preferential response to questions about the past is to give a generic answer. This is so even when an event is arranged that is quite distinctive, such as a person dressed as a witch visiting a nursery school at teatime (Morton, 1990). The day after, in answer to the question, "What happened yesterday at teatime?," only four out of eleven 3.5- to 4.9-year-old children answered appropriately. Other similar studies reported by Morton confirmed that young children's memory is poor in response to nondirective questioning of this sort. Specific event representations do exist, but they need specific cueing. It takes time for infants to translate adults' inquiries into recollection cues that they find helpful. The fact that children's memory requires such specific probing to elicit memory for particular events is important. It shows that GERs occur prior to the emergence of specific autobiographical memory as it is usually understood, and is, for some time during development, the preferred mode of recollection.

I suggest that children who suffer negative events continue to retrieve in generic form, as a means of controlling their affect. (The same may be true of those children who are particularly sensitive to negative events or have temperamental difficulty in controlling affect, a pattern associated with borderline personality disorder; Linehan, 1993). If so, there should be found, within depressed patients, a relation between those who have suffered particularly intense negative experiences and later tendencies to retrieve in generic form. I referred earlier to the research by Willem Kuyken and Chris Brewin (in preparation) who replicated our own findings that depressed patients retrieve generically. They had also asked the women in their study about the occurrence of child sexual or physical abuse, as part of a family relations interview. Thirty-seven of the 58 women in the study reported such abuse. When they compared those who had experienced sexual abuse with those who had not, the patients with the history of abuse retrieved more general memories. This is consistent with the hypothesis that negative events occurring in childhood might lead to the adoption of a particular style of encoding and retrieval as a means of minimizing the negative affect.

Kuyken and Brewin (in preparation) also examined the impact of these events on current functioning using the impact of events scale (IES). This is a 15-item scale consisting of two subscales, including questions about the impact (during the past 7 days) of a traumatic event: intrusion (seven items, such as "pictures about it popped into my mind") and avoidance (eight items, such as "I tried not to think about it"). They divided their patients into those who had experienced sexual and physical abuse and who had a high IES score (i.e., those for whom images were still intruding, and who were still attempting to avoid thinking about it); those who had experienced such abuse but had a low IES score; and a third group of those who had not experienced abuse. Results showed that those with a high IES score were significantly more likely to retrieve generic memories than the other two groups. This result permits two possible explanations. The fact that more generic memories were found in those with the greatest frequency of current preoccupation is consistent with the hypothesis that memory is less specific if there is significant distraction at retrieval (Williams & Dritschel, 1992). However, if the patients with higher IES scores had experienced more intense stress, then the effect could be a further example of defensive encoding and retrieval strategies in the face of trauma. In fact, Kuyken and Brewin (in preparation) report that those who score highly on the IES are indeed more likely to have suffered more intensely negative experience: more frequent abuse, abuse involving intercourse, and abuse by a caregiver. This research gives important information about the impact of real unpleasant events on other aspects of retrieval of autobiographical memory in general, but leaves open the possibility that these events have their effects either by affecting early encoding and retrieval styles, or by reducing the available capacity for later retrieval, or by a combination of the two.

However, abuse cases are special in that the children may have been told not to tell about the specific event. Although this might explain avoidance of recall of abuse memories, it would not explain generic memory for other events. In addition, there is other evidence that trauma is involved as a cause of generic memory. McNally, Litz, Prassar, Shin, and Weathers (1994) have found that Vietnam veterans with posttraumatic stress disorder (PTSD) tend to have more generic memories than veterans without PTSD (matched for amount of combat exposure). The question again arises whether it is the intrusiveness of the PTSD symptoms themselves that blocks retrieval of specific memories, or whether difficulties in memory are themselves a marker for an earlier trauma, that predated Vietnam. In fact, data from other sources indicates that some individuals are more prone than others to develop PTSD following combat exposure. These vulnerability factors include having been subjected to earlier physical abuse and a father's negative parenting behaviors (e.g., inconsistent love) (McCranie, Hyer, Boudewyns, & Woods, 1992). Thus, generality might come about in PTSD patients as the result of a cognitive style acquired early in life or as the result of later retrieval being impaired by intrusive thoughts. For the moment, we need to assume that it might be a combination of the two processes.

The mechanisms underlying overgeneral retrieval

Earlier accounts of overgenerality in memory (e.g., Williams & Dritschel, 1988) used descriptions theory as an explanatory framework (Norman & Bobrow, 1979; Williams & Hollan, 1981). According to this theory, retrieval is characterized as "a process in which some information about a target item is used to construct a description of the item and this description is used in attempts to recover new fragments of information" (Williams & Hollan, 1981, p. 87) Descriptions theory assumes that a person encodes only a limited amount of possible information (an incomplete list of properties or a partial image). To encode or retrieve any packet of information, a partial description is formed that provides an initial entry point into the memory, the description acting as an index for the memory packet. The major stages in such a retrieval process are "find a context," "search," and "verify." Reiser, Black, and Abelson (1985) made use of the same framework in studies looking at the priming of autobiographical events using activities or general actions. In their context-plus-index model, experiences are retrieved by accessing the knowledge structure used to encode the event and then specifying features that discriminate an event with the target features from others indexed within that context. The retrieval query is then elaborated using information contained in the knowledge structures to predict and further direct the search using additional features of the to-be-retrieved event. In describing the results of research with depressed patients, it has been useful to conceive of these "organizing contexts" or "descriptions" used in the encoding and retrieval of personal memories because they have clear implications for how the system might be affected and, in turn, might affect levels of depression. We assumed that our patients were accessing an "intermediate description" but stopping short of a specific example, and it was this "truncated search" that was responsible for overgeneral memory responses (Williams & Dritschel, 1988).

Problems with descriptions theory: Distinguishing categoric from extended intermediate descriptions

While the general notion of a hierarchical search strategy using intermediate description remains useful, the theory makes no distinction between the different types of hierarchy a person might use. Just as previous research has found it fruitful to examine subjects' retrieval errors to infer the properties of the memory system (Reiser et al., 1985; Williams & Hollan, 1981) so we turned to our samples of normal autobiographical memory to examine the types of overgenerality errors made. Williams and Dritschel (1992) studied the responses of 24 subjects each of whom attempted to retrieve specific autobiographical events to 20 positive and negative cue words selected from Paivio, Yuille, and Madigan's (1968) list of 925 nouns. Results showed that of the total number of 480 possible responses, 352 (73.3%) were specific. There were a further 45 occasions (9.4%) where subjects failed to retrieve any memory at all. There remained 17.3% "errors," and these responses (N = 83) were examined in more detail. Table 10.2 shows the frequency of error by category.

By far the largest number of "errors" fell into one of two categories. Either subjects responded with a summary or category of repeated memories (we called these "categoric memories") or they responded with an event that was longer than the time interval (1 day) specified by the instruction (we called these "extended memories"). It appears that there are at least these two different sorts of intermediate description available as retrieval strategies. Subjects might access activity contexts prior to searching for spe-

Table 10.2 *Types of "error" in cued autobiographical memory task (Williams &*
Dritschel, 1992)

	N	% of errors	% of total
Nonautobiographical	1	1.2%	0.2%
Person/Object only	8	9.6%	1.8%
Location only	0	0	0
Categoric description	40	48.2%	9.2%
Extended description	34	41.0%	7.8%

cific episodes (as Reiser et al., 1985, might suggest) or they might access "extended event time lines" before making a specific search (as Barsalou, 1988, has suggested).

What is the relation between these two types of superordinate memory? There has, in the past, been some confusion as to how they should be defined. Linton (1986) coined the term "extendure" for fairly long periods of time (for example, "the time I was at university"). This takes no account of memories that cover smaller intervals, such as a 3-week holiday, in which many shorter-term events will be nested. Neisser (1986) uses the term "extendure" more widely than Linton to refer not only to time periods but also to repetitions of an action, that is, to categoric memories (e.g., "all the airplane trips I have been on"). Brewer (1986) used the term "generic" memory to refer to a composite memory of an entire event (hiking up a mountain) to distinguish it from memories of specific details of the hike. It is clear, however, that he does not mean to refer to a series of mountain climbs when using the term generic. In fact, the hike itself should be seen as a shorter form of extended memory in which more microevents are nested, just as a 3-week holiday is an extended memory in which smaller events are nested. (The decision to use 1 day as a cutoff for single event memories is, of course, quite arbitrary.) However, the point remains that the distinction between different types of superordinate memory, that might fill the role of the initial description, have only recently been clarified (Barsalou, 1988; Conway & Bekerian, 1987; Williams & Dritschel, 1992). Conway and Bekerian compared lifetime period primes (e.g., "schooldays") with semantic primes. They found that the lifetime period primes were faster to elicit memories, and that the events thus cued were rated as more important, had been more frequently rehearsed, and were more specific than those retrieved to semantic cues. Williams and Dritschel confirmed that categoric and extended memories were functionally independent of each other. People who tend to respond with categoric memories do not also tend to give extended memories; cues that tend to elicit more categoric memories do not also produce more extended memories; and categoric and extended memories have significantly different associations with a range of memory variables such as the period from which events are recalled, the frequency, the emotionality, and the valence of the events.

If, then, there are two types of superordinate memory that can be used to form intermediate descriptions for memory retrieval, the question arises, what causes more problems for the emotionally disturbed patient? We therefore looked back at data from our previous clinical study. Williams and Dritschel (1988) found that their normal control group made 15% overgenerality errors compared to the suicidal patients' 25.5%. Looking first at the control group, we found that the errors were equally divided between categoric and extended errors (there being 8% and 7% of the total number of responses, respectively). Looking then at the clinical group, the proportion of extended errors was almost identical to that of the control group (7.5%). The increased overgenerality in the clinical group was wholly attributable to the excess of categoric errors (18%).

It seems then that the descriptions theory we have used in the past to explain overgeneral memory is itself too general. Simply assuming that retrieval is aborted too early in a hierarchy is not sufficient. For if overgeneral memory were simply "stopping short" then we ought to find depressed patients' errors being equally distributed between categoric and extended memories. We need to explain why, when patients use a categoric search strategy, they are more likely to get into difficulty. Why is it that if recollection involves a categoric intermediate description, it is vulnerable to becoming blocked?

If retrieval of specific episodes is to succeed, the categoric description process needs, at some point, to be inhibited so that contextual (time and place) information can be introduced in the mnemonic search. It is the ability to inhibit these relatively automatic categoric description processes that develops during the third and fourth years of life, and allows the child greater strategic control over the recollection process. It is this ability that is affected by reduced working memory capacity in aging and by brain damage. I have suggested that chronic stress in childhood may also affect the ability to learn fully to control these processes. Since it is generic memory due to emotional disturbance that is the main focus in this chapter, I shall indicate the most likely way in which adverse early experience brings about generic memory. I shall then briefly indicate the implication for studies of neurological impairment.

Further developmental research will be necessary to specify the variables influencing specificity and generality in autobiographical memory, but I suggest that there are two main factors that interact to produce the overgeneral memories that are observed later. First, the person growing up in such an environment may learn that specific episodic information is too negative, so the person passively avoids this punishing consequence of recollection. Figure 10.3 and 10.4 illustrate how, after some experience of negative affect as the result of retrieving a specific negative event, retrieval is likely to revert to the developmentally earlier GER. Whenever a mnemonic cue activates categoric intermediate descriptions that begin to retrieve fragments of a negative specific episode, the search is aborted. But, second, the retrieval process now attempts to do what it normally would if no event is accessed, that is, to make another iteration with other intermediate descriptions. After a number of such iterations, a more highly elaborated network of categoric intermediate descriptions will exist. Figure 10.4 shows the state of the system after such iterations. Whereas on the first iteration, the cue "unhappy" elicited the single description "I've always failed," that might normally have helped retrieve the event "re-

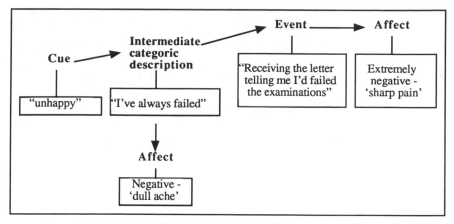

Figure 10.3 Effects on affect of retrieving specific event versus intermediate categoric description.

ceived the letter telling me I had failed the exams," the search is aborted, and an alternative description is derived, "I was never good at sport." Several such iterations produces a network of negative categoric descriptions including references to lack of friends, letting down parents, the impossibility of being happy, and being a worthless person.

The result is an overelaboration of categories, encouraged by and itself encouraging ruminative self-focus. In future attempts at retrieval, an initial cue is likely to activate an intermediate description that simply activates other self-descriptions. I coin the term "mnemonic interlock" for this phenomenon, reminiscent of the more general "depres-

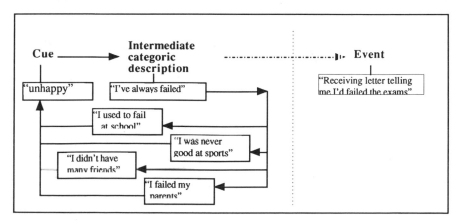

Figure 10.4 Aborting search for specific memory results in many iterations of intermediate stage ending in overelaborated categoric descriptions.

sive interlock" described by Teasdale and Barnard (1993) to explain the maintenance of entire ruminative cycles in depression.

The result of the tendency for negative early experience to affect retrieval processes in this way is that the child will come to have a range of self-descriptions in a chronically activated state, so that new emotionally valent events will be encoded along with many general trait self-descriptors. These overgeneric encoding-retrieval cycles constitute the cognitive style that we later find in our depressed and suicidal patients. The exact extent of later difficulties will depend on the existence of facilitatory or inhibitory factors existing in the retrieval context. For example, if another negative life event has recently occurred, there may be very few positive mnemonic cues in the environment to help the retrieval process. The result will be that the patient will have greater difficulty in retrieving specific positive events, a trend that has been found in some studies (Williams & Broadbent, 1986; Williams & Dritschel, 1988), though not others (Evans et al., 1992; Kuyken & Brewin, in preparation).

How is this effect similar or different from Freud's concept of repression? According to Freudian theory (1900/1953) memories of trauma may be repressed using psychological mechanisms that are also used to deal with infantile wishes contrary to the child's developing sense of right and wrong. However, it is difficult to know precisely what Freud's theory of repression was. It evolved throughout his writings. Starting from a narrow definition of repression as motivated forgetting, an intentional failure to access information stored in memory, the theory developed along with other theories about mechanisms of defense. Eventually, repression came to be a superordinate concept denoting a set of mechanisms involving any systematic avoidance of potentially threatening material. According to Erdelyi (1990), Freud left unspecified in most of his early writings whether repression was a conscious or unconscious process. Even in his later writings, it is clear that both conscious and unconscious processes would count as repression. In each case, however, the theories imply that the motivation for repression is anxiety, signaling that a great danger of traumatic intensity might happen. This danger appears to be the expectancy that the traumatic states experienced in infancy will recur.

The surface similarities between repression and mnemonic interlock arise because they are both, in the most general sense, an aftereffect of negative events. Both appear to be concerned with avoidance. However, there are important differences. First, repression is associated with the failure to retrieve the negative event that is at its core. The purpose of repression is to defend against memory of trauma. Yet as we have seen, more generic memories are found in those who are aware of their trauma and have intrusive thoughts about it (McNally et al., in press). Further, mnemonic interlock affects retrieval of neutral and positive events (Brittlebank et al., 1993), but repression makes no such prediction. Finally, repression theory explains failure to recall events in relation only to their emotional significance. This leaves retrieval failures associated with brain damage or aging outside the range of relevance of the theory. By contrast, mnemonic interlock and its interaction with working memory capacity provides an explanatory framework that can account for the effects of both structural (neurological damage) and functional (affective disturbance) limitations of the memory system. This allows the theory to make predictions about how such deficits may come about even when emotional disturbance is not involved; predictions that could not be made from repression theory. Here are three examples.

1. The inhibition of categoric descriptions will be particularly poor if the person does not have sufficient central executive capacity to override them. The evidence from neuropsychological studies suggest that disexecutive syndrome often results in nonspecific memory (see Conway, this volume, for a similar view). For example, in a study of 16 frontal patients, della Sala et al. (1992) found associations between autobiographical memory performance and tests of executive function (word fluency, digit cancellation, and Elithorn perceptual maze performance correlating 0.57, 0.65, and 0.66, respectively). However, that study did not report which aspect of autobiographical memory was most affected by reduced executive capacity. However, Williams and Dritschel (1992) were able to examine the association between fluency tasks and both categoric and extended memory errors. They found that people who were poor at semantic fluency tasks (naming animals, UK prime ministers, and US presidents) were more likely to make categoric memory errors. Such individuals were no more likely to make extended memory errors, however. This is consistent with the hypothesis that executive capacity is normally needed to inhibit the relatively automatic (and developmentally older) categoric stage of recollection.

2. Contextual cues that are distinctive (highly imageable or concrete) will be more successful at interrupting the categoric retrieval cycle. To examine this question, I returned to the data of Williams and Dritschel (1988). I examined the probability that each of the 20 cue words in the experiment would elicit a specific memory (mean for all 24 suicidal patients and 24 control subjects). There was a positive correlation between the imageability of the cue word and the mean specificity for both the overdose patients and the control subjects ($r = .50$ and $.67$, respectively).

3. In attempting to retrieve events, the more self-focused the retrieval query, the more likely it is that mnemonic interlock will occur and an overgeneral memory will be retrieved. Singer and Moffitt (1992) sampled the autobiographical memory of groups of students, asking them to retrieve a specific memory. However, in two of the experiments, some were told to recall a specific memory that typified them in some way, that "helps you understand yourself as an individual," the "real you." Of the 109 subjects given these "self-defining" instructions, 27% retrieved a generic memory, compared to only 8% of the 118 subjects given the usual instructions. In a further modified experiment incorporating the same contrast, of the subjects asked to recall a specific self-defining event 38% produced an inappropriately general memory compared to 22% given the normal instructions. These results are consistent with the hypothesis that self-focus promotes mnemonic interlock by causing the initial categoric description simply to activate other self-related generic information, making it harder to inhibit further iterations of the categoric search.

These data suggest that elderly or brain damaged people will find it particularly difficult to override generic descriptions to retrieve specific events if they conceive the task as characterizing themselves. Yet this may be precisely what many such individuals are attempting to use their memory for. Further, the association between low imageability of cues and poor specificity of memory suggests both a way in which such people find it effortful to retrieve specific events and a possible focus for remedial work.

Concluding remarks

Early research in the field of autobiographical memory was concerned with basic questions concerning the properties of such memories: what determines memorability?; how is such memory organized?; what determines forgetting? In this research (reviewed in Rubin, 1986, and Conway, 1990) investigators, wanting to gain as much control over the variable under study, focused on specific events as the unit of memory to be investigated. They looked at questions concerning how vivid or detailed the memory was; how old or veridical, how pleasant or unpleasant; and how each of these aspects of specific memory would be affected by different types of cues and primes. Later studies have taken more account of individual differences in autobiographical memory performance, differences between people due to aging or brain damage, and differences due to variations in the retrieval context or cueing conditions. The research reviewed here is consistent with this greater interest in individual differences. Although it had its roots in earlier mood congruent memory research conducted within associative network theory, I have shown how the focus moved away from an interest in the probability and latency of positive or negative memories (that had always been assumed to be specific event representations), away from an interest in which sort of memory would win the "accessibility race." Instead, the investigation has shifted towards the quality of the memory response itself, particularly the tendency of some individuals to recall overgeneral memories.

The research has shown that the difficulty arises from attempts to retrieve events using categoric intermediate descriptions. This chapter has suggested that one origin of the difficulty may be in the young child's exposure to negative early experiences affecting the development away from the use of GERs that the child normally uses before the third and fourth year. Retrieval of GER's after this age is used as an affect regulation strategy, but the end result is the overelaboration of self-focused intermediate descriptions, such that any subsequent self-focused mnemonic cue is likely to activate other intermediate descriptions – mnemonic interlock. Consistent with this, if subjects are given instructions to retrieve a specific memory that emphasizes the self-focus element, their memories are more generic. Further, there is evidence to support the predictions that mnemonic interlock is easier to overcome if individuals are given more imageable cues, or if they have more central executive capacity. Later changes associated with aging or neurological impairment may mimic this effect, reducing cognitive capacity and thereby affecting the person's ability to inhibit the production of categoric descriptions.

The significance of this research is that it builds bridges between experimental cognitive psychology and applied clinical psychology. The fact that such memory deficits are associated with poor problem solving, and that they predict how long a person will stay depressed, gives greater urgency to the search for the mechanisms underlying the deficits. Already there is enough prima facie evidence to support the case for specific anamnestic strategies to be built into the next generation of cognitive psychotherapies for treatment-resistant depressed patients, and this clinical work promises both to inform and to be informed by the current research on autobiographical memory.

References

American Psychiatric Association. (1987). *Diagnostic and statistical manual of mental disorders* (DSM-III-R). (3rd ed. revised) Washington, DC: American Psychiatric Association.

Baddeley, A.D., Emslie, H., & Nimmo-Smith, I. (1992). *The speed and capacity of language processing (SCOLP) test.* Bury St. Edmunds, Suffolk: Thames Valley Test Company.

Baddeley , A. D., & Wilson B. (1986). Amnesia, autobiographical memory, and confabulation. In D.C. Rubin (Ed.), *Autobiographical memory,* pp. 225–252. Cambridge, UK: Cambridge University Press.

Barsalou, L.W. (1988). The content and organization of autobiographical memories. In U. Neisser & C. E. Winograd (eds.), *Remembering reconsidered: Ecological and traditional approaches to the study of memory,* pp. 193–243. Cambridge, UK: Cambridge University Press.

Blaney, P. H. (1986). Affect and memory: A review. *Psychological Bulletin, 99,* 229–246.

Brewer, W. F. (1986). What is autobiographical memory? In D. C. Rubin (Ed.), *Autobiographical memory.* pp. 25–49. Cambridge, UK: Cambridge University Press.

Brittlebank, A. D., Scott, J., Williams, J. M. G., & Ferrier, I. N. (1993). Autobiographical memory in depression; Sate or trait marker? *British Journal of Psychiatry, 162,* 118–121.

Burke, M., & Mathews, A. (1992). Autobiographical memory and clinical anxiety. *Cognition and Emotion, 6,* 23–35.

Cimino, C. R., Verfaellie, M., Bowers, D., & Heilman, K. M. (1991). Autobiographical memory: Influence of right hemishere damage on emotionality and specificity. *Brain and Cognition, 15,* 106–118.

Conway, M. A. (1987). Verifying autobiographical facts. *Cognition, 26,* 39–58

—— (1990). *Autobiographical memory.* Milton Keynes: Open University Press.

Conway, M. A., & Bekerian, D. A. (1987). Organization in autobiographical memory. *Memory and Cognition, 15,* 119–132

della Sala, S., Laiacona, M., Spinnler, H., & Trivelli, C. (1992). Is autobiographical impairment due to a deficit of recollection? An overview of studies on Alzheimer dements, frontal and global amnesic patients. In M. A. Conway, D. C. Rubin, H. Spinnler, and W. A. Wagenaar (Eds.), *Theoretical perspectives on autobiographical memory.* (pp. 451–472). Dordrecht, The Netherlands: Kluwer Academic.

Erdelyi, M. H. (1990). Repression, reconstruction, and defense: History and integration of the psychoanalytic and experimental frameworks. In J. L. Singer (Ed.) Repression and dissociation. pp. 1–32. Chicago: University of Chicago Press.

Evans, J., Williams, J. M. G., O'Loughlin, S., & Howells, K. (1992). Autobiographical memory and problem solving strategies of parasuicide patients. *Psychological Medicine, 22,* 399–405.

Fivush, R., & Hammond, N. R. (1989). Time and again: Effects of repetition and retention interval on two-year-olds' event recall. *Journal of Experimental Child Psychology, 47,* 259–273.

Fivush, R., & Reese, E. (1991). *Parental styles for talking about the past.* Paper presented at the International Conference on Memory, Lancaster, UK.

Freud, S. (1900/1953). In J. Strachey (Ed.) *The standard edition of the complete works of Sigmund Freud* (Vol. 14) pp. 146–158, London: Hogarth Press.

Hanawalt, N. G., & Gebhart, L. J. (1965). Childhood memories of single and recurrent incidents. *Journal of Genetic Psychology, 107,* 85–89.

Kuyken, W., & Brewin, C.R. (In preparation). Autobiographical memory functioning in depression: The role of early adverse experiences.

Linehan, M. M. (1993). Cognitive behavioral treatment of borderline personality disorder. New York: Guilford Press.

Linton, M. (1986). Ways of searching and the contents of memory. In D. C. Rubin (Ed.), *Autobiographical memory*, pp. 50–70. Cambridge, UK: Cambridge University Press.

Marx, E. M., Williams, J. M. G., & Claridge, G. S. (1992). Depression and social problem solving. *Journal of Abnormal Psychology, 101*, 78–86.

McCranie, E. W., Hyer, L. A., Boudewyns, P. A., & Woods, M. G. (1992). Negative parenting behavior, combat exposure, and PTSD symptom severity. *Journal of Nervous and Mental Diseases, 180*, 431–438.

McNally, R. J., Litz, B. T., Prassas, A., Shin, L. M., & Weathers, F. W. (1994). Emotional priming of autobiographical memory in post-traumatic stress disorder. *Cognition and Emotion, 8*, 351–367.

Moore, R. G., Watts, F. N., & Williams, J. M. G. (1988). The specificity of personal memories in depression. *British Journal of Clinical Psychology, 27*, 275–276.

Morton, J. (1990). The development of event memory. *The Psychologist, 1*, 3–10.

Neisser, U. (1986). Nested structure in autobiographical memory. In D. C. Rubin (Ed.), *Autobiographical memory*, pp. 71–81. Cambridge, UK: Cambridge University Press.

Nelson, K. (1988). The ontogeny of memory for real events. In U. Neisser & C. E. Winograd (Eds.), *Remembering reconsidered: Ecological and traditional approaches to the study of memory*. pp. 244–276. Cambridge, UK: Cambridge University Press.

—— (1991). *Toward an explanation of the development of autobiographical memory*. Keynote address given to International Conference on Memory, Lancaster, UK.

Nelson, K., & Gruendel, J. (1981). General event representations: Basic building blocks of cognitive development. In *Advances in developmental psychology*, (Vol. 1), New York: Academic Press.

Norman, D. A., & Bobrow, D. G. (1979). Descriptions: An intermediate stage in memory retrieval. *Cognitive Psychology, 11*, 107–123.

Paivio, A., Yuille, J.C., & Madigan, S. A. (1968). Concreteness, imagery and meaningfulness values for 925 nouns. *Journal of Experimental Psychology, 76 (1)*, Monograph Supplement, Pt. 2.

Platt, J. J., & Spivack, G. (1975). *Manual for the means-ends problem solving test (MEPS): A measure of interpersonal problem solving skill*. Philadelphia: Hahnemann Medical College and Hospital.

Puffet, A., Jehin-Marchot, D., Timsit-Berthier, M., & Timsit, M. (1991). Autobiographical memory and major depressive states. *European Psychiatry, 6*, 141–145

Reiser, B. J., Black, J. B., & Abelson, R. P. (1985). Knowledge structures in the organization and retrieval of autobiographical memories. *Cognitive Psychology, 17*, 89–137.

Richards, A., & Whittaker, T. M. (1990). Effects of anxiety and mood manipulation in autobiographical memory. *British Journal of Clinical Psychology, 29*, 145–154

Robinson, J. A. (1976). Sampling autobiographical memory. *Cognitive Psychology, 8*, 578–595

Rubin, D.C. (1986). *Autobiographical memory*. Cambridge, UK: Cambridge University Press.

Singer, J. L. (1984). The private personality. *Personality and Social Psychology Bulletin, 10*, 7–30.

Singer, J. A., & Moffitt, K. H. (1992). An experimental investigation of specificity and generality in memory narratives. *Imagination, Cognition and Personality, 11*, 233–257

Teasdale, J. D., & Barnard, P. J. (1993). Affect, cognition and change. London: Lawrence Erlbaum.

Tessler, M. (1986). *Mother-child talk in a museum: The socialization of a memory*. New York: City University of New York Graduate Center.

Wahler, R. G., & Afton, A. D. (1980). Attentional processes in insular and noninsular mothers: Some differences in their summary reports about child problem behaviors. *Child Behavior Therapy, 2*, 25–41.

Williams, J. M. G. (1992). *The psychological treatment of depression: A guide to the theory and practice of cognitive behavior therapy*. London: Routledge.

Williams, J. M. G., & Broadbent, K. (1986). Autobiographical memory in attempted suicide patients. *Journal of Abnormal Psychology, 95*, 144–149.

Williams, J. M. G., & Dritschel, B. H. (1988). Emotional disturbance and the specificity of autobiographical memory. *Cognition and Emotion, 2*, 221–234.

—— (1992). Categoric and extended autobiographical memories. In M. A. Conway, D. C. Rubin, H. Spinnler, and W. A. Wagenaar (Eds.), *Theoretical perspectives on autobiographical memory.* (pp. 391–412). Dordrecht, The Netherlands: Kluwer Academic.

Williams, M. D., & Hollan, J. D. (1981). Processes of retrieval from very long-term memory. *Cognitive Science, 5,* 87–119.

Williams, J. M. G., & Scott, J. (1988). Autobiographical memory in depression. *Psychological Medicine, 18,* 689–695 .

Williams, J. M. G., Watts, F. N., Macleod, C., & Mathews, A. (1988). *Cognitive psychology and emotional disorders.* Chichester, UK: John Wiley & Sons.

—— (In press). *Cognitive psychology and emotional disorders* (2nd. ed.). Chichester, UK: John Wiley & Sons.

Winthorpe, C., & Rabbitt, P. A. (1988). Working memory capacity, IQ, age, and the ability to recount autobiographical events. In M. M. Gruneberg, P. E. Morris, & R. N. Sykes (Eds.) *Practical aspects of memory: Current research and issues II* (pp. 175–179). Chichester, UK: John Wiley & Sons.

Part IV
Social functions

11   Remembering as communication: A family recounts its past

William Hirst and David Manier

Remembering can be viewed as an act of communication. People remember their life stories by writing autobiographies, conversing with relatives, friends, and strangers, or even by talking to themselves. Their autobiographical memories emerge out of these varying forms of discourse. We cannot divorce the act of remembering from the act of communicating, nor can we treat an autobiographical memory as something distinct from the discourse itself. Recollections arise not from the depths of a storehouse in the head, but from a desire to communicate with others about the personal past. What is remembered and how it is remembered are functions of the resulting discourse. People remember the same episode differently when writing an autobiography, speaking to a group of strangers, reminiscing with a close friend, or conducting an internal dialogue (see Barclay, this volume; Pillemer, Krensky, Kleinman, Goldsmith, & White, 1991; Pillemer, Rhinehart, & White, 1986; Robinson, this volume; Tenney, 1989). The social conventions of autobiographical writing or speaking, the role of the audience, ordinary language assumptions, the embeddedness of meaning in context, the social interactions between speaker and audience – all shape the form and as well as the content of re-membering. Othello reports that Desdemona's father "questioned me the story of my life," but the story Othello remembered and told to the father was surely not so "passing strange" and "wondrous pitiful" as the tale that provoked in Desdemona a "world of sighs."

We are interested here in conversational remembering. There are many different forms of conversation. We focus on clearly purposeful conversations, ones with a well-defined goal (see Tracy, 1991, for a discussion of issues related to the importance of goals in conversation). A purposeful conversation might have the goal of providing a lost person with directions, determining a price for an art object, offering the comfort

We would like to acknowledge the support of NIMH grant #RO1–1MH50131, and a grant from the McDonnell Foundation. We have benefited greatly from both the assistance and the intellectual contributions of Stephen Hartman, Nimali Jayasinghe, and Elizabeth Pinner.

and love a child needs to fall gently asleep, or the present case of interest, jointly reconstructing a shared past experience. As Grice (1978) has pointed out, conversations are governed by a principle of cooperation that states that those conversing agree to cooperate with each other in their joint effort to communicate. In instances of conversational remembering, those conversing cooperate in their joint effort to reconstruct the past. We claim that they adopt various conversational roles as a means of achieving their goal. Conversational roles should be thought of in terms of identifiable patterns of speech taken on by participants in a conversation in order to facilitate (or hinder) the task at hand. They provide for each participant a function and place vis à vis other participants. This function or place can be held either for the entire conversation or for some fragment of it.

Consider the situation in which a single subject recounts to an experimenter or interviewer an autobiographical episode. The role of the experimenter or interviewer is defined in the one-on-one interview context as being relatively passive (although nonetheless complex), while the subject or interviewee is assigned in this context a particular type of active role: He or she alone must narrate the story (cf. Edwards & Middleton, 1986). When the group gets larger, the roles participants occupy will vary as a function of culture, the personal histories of the participants, the history of their interactions, personality variables, and the communicative setting, among other factors. Nevertheless, we can specify at least some of the possibilities.

In the dialectical drama of group recounting, where the goal is to remember the shared past, at least one participant should accept the primary responsibility of *narrating* the story. Another participant might aid in the reconstruction by *monitoring* the story, assessing its validity or falsity. Other participants might cooperate in the reconstruction by *mentoring,* guiding others to tell the story rather than telling it themselves. In many instances of joint reconstruction, parents adopt the role of mentor with young children (cf. Nelson, 1993; Rogoff, 1990), helping the young child to remember rather than supplying the story themselves (cf. Fivush & Hudson, 1990; see also Fivush, Haden, & Reese's chapter in this volume). We suspect that mentors may be found in acts of conversational remembering other than those involving young children. Participants in an act of recounting, then, could assist in reaching the conversational goal in at least three ways: by acting as a narrator, a monitor, or a mentor.

We want to investigate in this paper whether we can identify the roles adopted by participants in group efforts at reconstruction of the past and specify how roles can shape a recounting. We contrast the situation in which one person alone must "tell the story" with the situation in which several people contribute to the telling of the story, presumably by occupying differing roles. We concentrate here on the recountings of a family; our investigation focuses on an analysis of the conversation itself and the roles adopted in the conversation. Clearly we could have chosen a different group – one consisting, for instance, of only friends, strangers, or professionals. We chose a family because families figure centrally in most people's autobiographical recollections (see Reiss, 1981, for a discussion of how the family processes information and develops "family paradigms"). We intend this study of family recounting to provide the starting point for a broader ranging investigation of how the family as a social unit shapes the life stories of its members.

There has been little work on family recounting or the function of conversational roles in shaping family recounting (see Bruner, 1990, for an exception). In general, scholars who have looked at issues related to group remembering leave out of their analysis exactly what we are interested in – the conversations members of the groups engage in and the roles they adopt. Of course, this is not by accident, in that they have had different theoretical concerns than we do: the decisions scholars make about what data to encode and analyze and what data to ignore spring from a host of theoretical presuppositions (cf. Hirst & Manier, 1994; Mishler, 1986a, 1986b).

Yet many researchers have emphasized the social character of memory. They have shown that people, particularly married couples, distribute their memories when memorizing (Wegener, 1986; Wegener, Erber, & Raymond, 1991; for a more general discussion of the distributed nature of cognition, see also Cole, 1991; Lave, 1988; Pea, 1988; Salomon, 1993), that the discursive style a mother adopts with her child during their joint reconstruction of the past affects the development of the child's narrative skills (Fivush, 1991; Fivush & Fromhoff, 1988; Fivush & Hudson, 1990; Reese & Fivush, 1993), and that "consensus" memories – collective memories accepted by all participants – are more richly recollected than are memories constructed by individuals outside the group. Other researchers have analyzed the formal structural characteristics of narratives arising in conversations among friends, in the workplace, in physician's offices, and in psychotherapy (Frankel, 1984; Goodwin & Goodwin, 1987; Krainer, 1988; Labov & Fanshel, 1977; Linde, 1988; Polyani, 1989; Tannen, 1984), studied how autobiographies shape the construction of the self (Bruner, 1990; Schafer, 1992; Spence, 1982), and explored the structure of conversations without explicitly examining the conversation as an act of remembering (Garfinkel, 1967; Goodwin & Heritage, 1990; Heritage, 1984; Sachs, Schegloff, & Jefferson, 1974).

The work of Middleton and Edwards (1990; Edwards & Middleton, 1986, 1988; see also Eisenberg, 1985) is quite close to our present concerns. These researchers analyzed the conversation of young people jointly recounting their shared past. They had schoolmates talk about, for instance, a movie they had all seen, *E.T.* In their analysis of the conversations, they noted various linguistic devices that could structure the recountings the young people offered, including tags that signal or invite ratification ("doesn't he?"), overt requests for assistance in the joint task, overt agreements, and metamemory statements about the process of remembering itself. They did not, however, consider the importance of conversational roles (see Manier & Hirst, 1995).

The recountings of a family

General methodology

With the assistance of Stephen Hartman and Elizabeth Pinner, we obtained examples of conversational remembering from a family of four. We decided to concentrate our efforts on the conversational remembering of a single family because we felt that every family differs in the way that they remember conversationally. Other researchers have offered similar justifications for undertaking case studies (Caramazza, 1986; Marshall & Newcombe, 1984; Seidman, 1990). We wanted to develop a general approach to the study of family remembering, although we realized that generalization is difficult on the basis of a single case study. In accepting the possibility that conversational roles may shape autobiographical memories in many diverse ways, we saw as our chief aim the exploration of only a subset of these diverse ways, the ones exemplified by our sample family. Of course, we hoped that we could offer several tentative generalizations, even within the context of a case study, but our initial aim was to understand how conversational roles in our sample family shaped their autobiographical memory.

The family we studied, that we will call the Patels, immigrated to New York from India 2 years prior to our study. The father, 44 years old, was studying for a Ph.D. in engineering; the 36-year-old mother worked as an administrative assistant to support the family. There was a 17-year-old son, who had just graduated from a Catholic high school and was planning to start college soon, and a 15-year-old daughter, who had just finished her sophomore year in high school. Everyone in the family was thoroughly bilingual, with both Telegu and English spoken at home.

In our study, we solicited recollections from the family. Some studies of conversations have relied on spontaneously produced speech (e.g., Polyani, 1989, or Tannen, 1984). We decided to solicit narratives because we wanted to compare individual recollections with group recountings. It would have been unlikely that we would have obtained the needed data from spontaneous speech. Nevertheless, we feel that the conversations we solicited were relatively "natural." Families do discuss their shared past (Miller & Moore, 1989). To be sure, by soliciting the recollection, we may have imposed task demands not present in more naturally occurring conversations. For example, recollections in naturally occurring conversations may never be "completed," inasmuch as the conversational topic may switch before the narrative is done, whereas solicited narrative will usually be "completed," inasmuch as the group is told to "tell a story." Although the difference between solicited conversational remembering and naturally occurring conversational remembering needs to be carefully considered, the conversations that we obtained are enough like naturally occurring conversations to make their analysis worthwhile.

A week prior to the group recall, we collected individual recollections of eight different shared family experiences (the shared nature of these experiences had previously been established through a questionnaire given to all family members). For these individual recollections, that were videotaped in the family's home, an experimenter unknown to the family asked each family member (separately from each other) to recall an event all had taken part in: for example, "Tell me everything you can remember about the family outing to Coney Island." The experimenter was instructed not to interrupt the family member's narrative. After the story had ended, the experimenter requested more information – "Can you tell me anything else about what happened?" – until the family member reported that there was nothing more to say. The experimenter then probed for the next event.

The group recounting followed the same format, and was also videotaped. This time the entire family was assembled in a single room and allowed to sit anywhere they wanted. A new experimenter, again unknown to the family, asked the same questions raised in the individual (pregroup) recall and again followed up the recollections with a query for more information. The experimenter addressed her queries to the entire family and instructed that all family members should feel free to join in the discussion. The videotapes from both the pregroup and the group recountings were subsequently transcribed.

Are there discernible conversational roles in this family's group recountings?

In order to answer this question, we developed a coding scheme that broke the transcript into narrative and nonnarrative units, and each of these categories into structural units. A narrative unit consisted of a subject (perhaps implicit) and predicate and described a single "state," "action," or "event." It could include temporal tags and other descriptive phrases, but these phrases could not describe an additional state, action, or event. The sentences "I enjoyed the amusement rides" and "We saw the polar bear," that describe respectively a state and an event, are narrative units. The sentence "We went to Coney Island the year we came to the United States" also constitutes a single narrative unit, whereas the sentence "We went to the amusement park and to the beach" contains two narrative units because it describes two actions. The structural subunits we coded for, as well as examples of nonnarrative units, are listed in Table 11.1.

The following is a passage divided into structural units:

Father: [Facilitating remark] no, but talk about, talk about here, what, what did you spend. [Facilitating remark] What did you, what else do you remember?

Son: [Metamemory statement] Oh yeah! [Narrative telling] I got a jacket, yeah.

[. . .]

Daughter: [Contextualizing statement] we, usually in India we don't give each other gifts and everything. [. . .] [Affective-evaluative remark] I mean it wasn't such a big deal for us, you know, getting gifts or giving gifts.

We defined a "conversation" as the response to a single probe (e.g., everything said about the trip to Coney Island). We initially confined our analysis to two conversations: one about a family outing to Coney Island, another about the preceding Christmas the family spent together. We defined three conversational roles – narrator, monitor, and mentor – as follows:

Narrators: assume the function of telling the story. Their utterances are meant in some fashion to "further the narrative." Generally speaking, a narrator's utterances will preserve "narrative continuity" (cf. Middleton & Edward's, 1990, "default continuity"). That is, any given narrative telling will be interlinked (either causally, spatially, temporally, or thematically) with narrative tellings that precede or follow it. By definition, a family member is identified as a narrator in a conversation when

(1) narrative tellings are the most preponderant structural unit in his or her contributions to the conversation, *and*

(2) her or his share of all narrative tellings uttered in the conversation is greater than would be expected from chance (e.g., for a family of four, the narrator contributes more than 25% of the narrative tellings in the conversation).

Characteristically, narrators might be expected to contribute a greater share of the total number of words in the conversation than would be expected from chance; utter a large share of the group's metanarrative statements (e.g., "I'm getting off the point"); seek outside confirmation, perhaps by making overt requests for assistance; and endeavor to "contextualize" the narrative (see Table 11.1).

Mentors: assume the function of prompting narrators to further their narratives and provide more details. They encourage narrators to adhere to standards of narrative form and content, spurring narrators on by providing criticisms, directions, helpful remarks, substantial queries, and memory probes. Rather than furthering the narrative directly through their own utterances, mentors guide the narrative telling, often by providing retrieval cues to narrators in order to elicit further recollections from them. By definition, a family member is identified as a mentor when

(1) facilitating remarks are among the two most preponderant structural categories in her or his contributions to the conversation, *and*

(2) he or she contributes a greater share of the total number of the facilitating remarks uttered in the conversation than would be expected from chance.

Characteristically, mentors utter a relatively small share of the words, structural units, and narrative units – especially the narrative tellings – in the conversation.

Monitors: assume the function of explicitly agreeing or disagreeing with the utterances of the narrator, without taking personal responsibility for constructing the narrative. They evaluate whether the narrative, as told by the narrator, correctly and completely describes the episode, as remembered by the monitor. They assume a relatively passive role within the collective remembering. By definition, a family member is identified as a monitor when

(1) assessing statements are among the two most preponderant structural categories in her or his contribution to the conversation, *and*

(2) he or she contributes a greater share of the total number of assessing statements uttered in the conversation than would be expected from chance.

Characteristically, monitors make responses to overt requests for assistance, laugh more than the others (particularly in response to something a narrator has said), and utter a relatively small share of the words, structural units, and narrative units – especially the narrative tellings – in the conversation.

Others: Conversational participants who do not meet the criteria for any of the three conversational roles defined above will be classified as "other."

Conversational roles, then, are specified by two defining criteria and possess additional characteristic features. It is possible that roles could shift within a family's response to a mnemonic probe (our definition of a "conversation"), but for the present

Table 11.1 *Classification of utterances*

Structural Units	Definitions and Examples
NARRATIVE UNITS	
Narrative Tellings	Describe states or events that are linked together (causally, temporally, or spatially) and that relate to a central topic or theme. *Examples:* "We went to all these other places and then we went to Coney Island, and we went to the aquarium. We went to th-um, amusement park and we went to the beach."
Contextualizing Statements	Relate narrative telling(s) to events outside the spatial-temporal context of the central theme or topic of the current narrative. *Examples:* "We usually make a crib in India, like, we, put the crib and everything, but here we didn't." "We did that even before."
Affective-Evaluative Remarks	Provide editorial judgments or express emotional reactions to narrative tellings. *Examples:* "A very boring Christmas." "They had fun."
NONNARRATIVE UNITS	
Metamemory Statements	Evaluate one's own ability to remember; comment on the requirements for remembering successfully. *Examples:* "I'm very poor in remembering things." "I'm not sure whether [. . . .]" "Yeah, I remember."
Metanarrative Statements	Evaluate one's own narratives with (implicit or explicit) reference to standards of narrative structure. *Examples:* "But, uh, that's a different thing." "I'm getting off the point."
Overt Requests for Assistance	Ask for help on matters related to narrative telling(s). *Examples:* "Was last Christmas uh the one that we spent home?" "Was it last year?"
Responses to Overt Requests	Attempt to give help in reaction to overt requests for assistance. *Examples:* "Yeah, home." "Nah, the year before."
Facilitating Remarks	Attempt to spur someone else to further the narrative, provide more details, or "search their memory." Also, may evaluate someone else's narrative with (implicit or explicit) reference to standards of narrative structure. *Examples:* "What did we eat there?" "What did you, what else do you remember?" "Keep to the point." "That's irrelevant."
Assessing Statements	Agree, disagree, or in some other way judge the validity of a previous statement that is not an overt request for assistance. Includes a repetition of a phrase just spoken by someone else, as well as responsive utterances like, "oh," "okay," and "sure" (but not responses to overt questions). *Examples:* "Yeah, that's right." "No, you're wrong."
Laughter	Each separate instance of laughter was noted.

we define them in terms of the entire conversation. The defining criteria for the role of narrator differ somewhat from those of mentor and monitor. For a narrator, narrative tellings must be the most preponderant structural unit, but for a mentor and monitor the critical structural units need be only the second most preponderant unit. We imposed a weaker standard for mentors and monitors because we expected that there could be instances in which narrative tellings would preponderate in the utterances of all members of the conversation, including mentors and monitors. After all, our instructions were for the family members to tell narratives.

According to our definitions, in both conversations (the one about Christmas and the one about Coney Island) the daughter served as the narrator and the father as the mentor. The son and mother both served as monitors in the Coney Island conversation, and both had an undefined "other" role in the Christmas conversation (see Manier & Hirst, 1995, for details). The daughter produced substantially more narrative tellings in her contributions to both conversations than any other structural unit, uttered more narrative tellings than did anyone else in both conversations, and contributed a majority of the words spoken in both cases. Facilitating remarks were one of the two most preponderant structural units in the father's contributions to both conversations. Moreover, he contributed a greater share of facilitating remarks to the conversations than would be expected from chance, and hence served as mentor. Finally, for both the mother and son, assessing statements were one of the two most preponderant structural units in their contribution to the Coney Island conversation. Additionally, they each contributed more assessing statements to this conversation than would be expected from chance, and hence served as monitors. In the Christmas conversation, the mother and son each contributed fewer than 100 words, and failed to occupy any definite conversational role.

It should be noted that the mother appeared to have an additional role. She offered more affective-evaluative remarks than anyone else, in both the Christmas and the Coney Island conversation, and such remarks figured prominently in her utterances. The mother may have been inclined to put an emotional cast on the events, providing editorial judgments that imbued a general affective tone into the recollections. For example, she stated regarding the previous Christmas: "But it was very new to us, I mean we were trying to copy something, which . . . people did here, but we, I, I literally did not enjoy it."

Within a conversation, a family member may hold a conversational role with greater or less consistency. The concept of the strength of a conversational role captures this variability. We defined the strength for the three conversational roles under discussion as

Narrator: $N_s = (n + n')/2$, where
$\quad\quad\quad\quad N_s = $ strength of narrator's role,
$\quad\quad\quad\quad n = $ percentage of narrator's narrative tellings out of the total number of structural units he or she contributed, and
$\quad\quad\quad\quad n' = $ percentage of narrator's narrative tellings out of the total from all participants in the conversation.

Mentor: ME_s = $(f + f')/2$, where
ME_s = strength of mentor's role,
f = percentage of mentor's facilitating remarks out of the total number of structural units he or she contributed, and
f' = percentage of mentor's facilitating remarks out of the total from all participants in the conversation.

Monitor: MO_s = $(a + a')/2$, where
MO_s = strength of monitor's role,
a = percentage of monitor's assessing statements out of the total number of structural units he or she contributed, and
a' = percentage of mentor's assessing statements out of the total from all participants in the conversation.

Table 11.2 contains the strengths of conversational roles of family members for the two conversations we have considered. Since with a family of four 25% is chance level for most of the criteria involved in the definition of the strength of conversational roles, scores higher than 25 can be taken to be indications of a strong role. Consistent with the pattern described above, the daughter shows a strong narrator role and the father shows a strong mentor role in both conversations. The mother and son both show some strength in occupying monitor roles in the Coney Island conversation. Beyond this, the son also shows some strength as narrator in the Coney Island conversation (though not nearly as much as his sister), the mother shows some strength in the role of monitor in the Christmas conversation, and the father shows some strength as narrator in the Coney Island conversation (again, not nearly as much as the daughter). Thus, the results from an analysis of role strength is more nuanced, but consistent with our prior analysis of roles.

How do the different conversational roles shape conversational remembering?

We began our investigation of this question by comparing the narrative units produced in the pregroup recountings across individuals. We called *shared pregroup narrative*

Table 11.2 *Strengths of conversational roles (Christmas and Coney Island conversations)*

	Daughter	Father	Mother	Son
Christmas				
Narrator	70	11	10	14
Monitor	11	25	27	—
Mentor	—	57	11	—
Coney Island				
Narrator	50	27	14	32
Monitor	23	19	39	30
Mentor	14	44	9	—

units those narrative units the meaning of which (as agreed upon by two judges) was expressed in the utterances of more than one participant in the pregroup recountings, that is, those narrative units the meaning of which was "shared" by more than one participant. We called *unshared pregroup narrative units* those narrative units the meaning of which appeared in the utterances of one and only one participant in the pregroup recounting. For instance, in their pregroup recountings, family members gave different versions of the time of day they attended Christmas service. The son said: "uh, it's like just we went to a Christmas mass, like th- the night mass." The daughter made two separate statements: "uum, last Christmas was, um, we went for an, uh, late mass?" and later, "We went, I think, at eleven thirty or something to church" (further comments made it clear she was referring to the night mass). The mother recalled: "So we wanted to experience the night mass, in, uh, the church. So we went, um, all decked up in Indian clothes?" The father's account was quite different from those of the other family members: "Uh, the only thing I can remember is we all went together to church in the, m-, morning, I don't know, it is nine o'clock or ten o'clock." In these differing versions, there is only one shared narrative unit, that we might express as "We went to the night mass." This narrative unit was "shared" because it was expressed (albeit in somewhat different words) by the son, the daughter, and the mother. The daughter expressed an unshared pregroup narrative unit specifying the time as eleven thirty; the mother stated two unshared pregroup narrative units relating to what the family wore to church and what they "wanted to experience"; and the father offered only unshared pregroup narrative units, since his recollection was that the family had gone to a morning mass.

The narratives that the family members produced in their pregroup recountings differed greatly from each other. Of the pregroup narrative units expressed by the four family members, 45% occurred in the pregroup recounting of only one family member, while only 2% were recounted by all four family members (for details see Manier & Hirst, 1995). In other words, each family member told a rather different story, although a few basic facts (such as "we went to the amusement park, the aquarium, and the beach") were expressed by all four.

What determines what gets into the group recollection? Can we predict what will appear in the group narrative by considering what was said in the pregroup recollections and the conversational roles of the participants? At least in the present instances of conversational remembering, almost half of the narrative units in the group recall did not appear in any of the pregroup recollections. This interesting fact means that the story told in the group differed substantially from that told by the separate individuals, presumably because the group recollection was influenced in some manner by interpersonal dynamics. But what of the other half, that is, what of those narrative units in the group recall that captured the meaning of a narrative unit expressed in at least one of the pregroup recollections? Specifically, how effective were family members at introducing unshared narrative units from their pregroup recall, that is, their "unique recollections," into the group recollection? Conversational role plays an important part in answering this question.

Table 11.3. *Distribution among family members of new, unshared, and shared group narrative units, in percentage of the total for each type of narrative unit (Coney Island and Christmas conversations)*

| | Types of narrative units | | | |
	New	Unshared	Shared	All
Daughter	51	76	51	58
Father	25	8	24	20
Mother	11	8	14	11
Son	13	8	11	11

As the narrator, the daughter presumably accepted the main responsibility of telling the story. In doing so, she may have acquired an advantage over the others in injecting her version of the past into the family's collective recounting. She may, for instance, have had an advantage in introducing her unshared pregroup narrative units into the group recollection. This proved to be the case. The daughter introduced into the group recollection 33% of her unshared pregroup recollections, whereas the father inserted 25% of his unshared pregroup narrative units into the group recollection. The son and the mother both contributed to the group recounting less than 10% of their unshared pregroup narrative units.

Table 11.3 looks at this result from a slightly different perspective. It divides the narrative units into three categories: (1) narrative units that did not appear in any pregroup recollection (new units); (2) narrative units in the group recall that captured the gist of an unshared narrative unit in the the pregroup recall (unshared group narrative units); and (3) narrative units in the group recall that captured the gist of a shared narrative unit in the pregroup recall (shared group narrative units). The finding above suggests that the narrator does not simply narrate more than anyone else, but she narrates in a way that imposes her version of the story onto the family recounting. Thus, we would expect that the narrator should have a disproportionate number of unshared group narrative units, that is, she should contribute more of the unshared group narrative units than one would expect from her overall predominance in the conversation. This is what we found. The daughter contributed over 75% of the unshared group narrative units, but only 58% of all narrative units. She was more likely to introduce into the group recounting an unshared pregroup recollection than anyone else, even if we account for the fact that she dominated the conversation. As narrator, she got to tell the story she had told in her pregroup recollection to an extent that other family members did not. In other words, the group recounting reflected her "unique recollections" to a degree that substantially exceeded her overall contribution to the conversation. This advantage of the narrator does not follow tautologically from the definition of the narrator; it is a consequence of adopting the role, not a definitional characteristic of the role.

Are conversational roles fixed?

The conversational roles the family members held structured what the family remembered as a group. In the two instances that we looked at, the daughter profoundly influenced what was remembered because she occupied the role of narrator. But does the daughter shape all the family's recountings to the same extent? This privilege would only exist if the daughter's role was fixed – if she always or mostly served as narrator. But there are many instances in which another family member could conceivably assume the role of narrator. For instance, the daughter may act as narrator only when the family is recounting events in which all members shared equally, with no one member playing a central role in the events (like Christmas and the trip to Coney Island). In this case, we would say that she had the "default" role of narrator, but deferred to other family members under "extenuating" circumstances. Specifically, when the family is recounting an event in which one member played a central role, the member playing the central role in the event also would take a central (narrator) role in the recounting.

We explored this issue by expanding our sample of recountings to include two episodes in which someone other than the daughter played a central role. The first involved the events surrounding the son's graduation from high school. The second involved a family disagreement over the proposed purchase of a stereo set for the son. In this second episode, the son felt that the father had reneged on a promise to purchase a stereo for him. In the recountings of these events, in which the son played a more central role than the daughter, we predicted that the son would be more likely to occupy the role of narrator.

The results were more complicated than expected. As Tables 11.4 and 11.5 indicate, in the recounting of the graduation, narrative tellings were the most preponderant structural unit of the mother's contribution to the conversation. Moreover, the mother uttered more of the narrative tellings in the conversation than might be expected from chance. According to our definition, she clearly assumed the role of narrator. It also is worth noting that she uttered 282 words out of a conversational total of 644, or 44% of the words, displaying one of the characteristic features of a narrator. Interestingly, she also continued to offer more affective-evaluative remarks than any other family member, and these remarks were the second most preponderant structural units in her contributions.

The son contributed more than twice as many narrative tellings as either the sister or the father; narrative tellings clearly predominated in his utterances. Thus, he also meets our criteria for playing the role of narrator in this conversation. Not surprisingly, he also spoke almost as much as his mother, uttering 204 words.

The father played the role of monitor, with assessing statements being among the two most preponderant structural units in his utterances, and with his assessing statements taking up a greater share of all the assessing statements uttered in the conversation than would be predicted by chance. (The father also uttered a great many facilitating remarks, but they were the third most preponderant structural units in his contributions, so he did not meet our criteria for the role of mentor.) As for the daughter, she spoke so little that her role in this conversation was unclear. She is therefore classified here as "other."

Table 11.4 *Percentage of participant's contribution of a structural unit out of the total uttered by everyone in the conversation*

	Daughter	Father	Mother	Son
Graduation				
Narrative Tellings	13	13	42	33
Facilitating Remarks	*	100	*	*
Assessing Statements	29	29	36	7
Stereo				
Narrative Tellings	15	18	8	58
Facilitating Remarks	*	*	*	*
Assessing Statements	15	8	23	54

* – No examples of this kind.

In hindsight, it is not surprising that the mother, to an even greater degree than the son, served the role of narrator in this story. The graduation loomed large in the mother's plans. For instance, she arranged for her parents to come from India for her son's graduation, at considerable expense. The presence of the grandparents made the event as significant for the mother as for the son. The mother spoke of the elaborate preparations she undertook so that her parents could attend the graduation.

So it was something very new to us and we had watched previously the pe – I mean other students graduating so, we started planning to get, uh, the grandparents over for his graduation. So there was a lot of discussion before, uh, his, uh, graduation, you know, to bring them, and what type of visa, uh, whether they would give it or not, and we were planning on that way and then afterwards, uh, finally they came. [. . .] It was, uh, they really felt, uh, very nice, and they really felt that their coming was very important for that.

Table 11.5 *Percentage of a structural unit out of all units uttered by a participant*

	Daughter	Father	Mother	Son
Graduation				
Narrative Tellings	54	40	52	47
Facilitating Remarks	*	20	*	*
Assessing Statements	9	33	11	12
Stereo				
Narrative Tellings	55	56	30	59
Facilitating Remarks	*	*	*	*
Assessing Statements	20	9	30	20

* – No examples of this kind

The mother's predominance in this conversation very likely reflected the effort she expended to bring her parents over from India, as well as the pride both she and her parents took in the son's achievement.

In the conversation about the proposed purchase of the stereo, the son took an even more active role than he did in the graduation recounting. He spoke more than anyone else (uttering 558 out of a conversational total of 1,227 words, or 45%), and his narrative tellings dominated the conversation, with his contribution being not only greater than chance, but also greater than anyone else's. Narrative tellings also preponderated among his contributions to the conversation. He clearly had adopted the role of narrator. The son also served as a monitor in this conversation. He offered more assessing statements than anyone else, and such statements were among the two most preponderant elements in his contributions to the conversation. The son appeared to want to tell his story and also make sure that everyone else's tellings conformed to his version. There were clear reasons for this. The son strongly felt that the father had broken a promise to him, and he was not willing to let anyone dispute his view of what had happened.

In this conversation, the mother acted as a monitor. She said little (only 7% of the words were hers), but when she spoke, she offered more assessing statements than predicted by chance. Moreover, these structural units figured as one of the two most preponderant structural units in her contributions to the conversation. She appeared to be mediating between the father and the son by trying to get the facts "right." The father and the daughter did not meet the criteria for any of the three specified roles in this conversation, perhaps because the son dominated the conversation to such a great extent. We define their roles to be that of "other."

Using the criteria we established earlier, it will be interesting to look at the strength of the various conversational roles for each participant (see Table 11.6). In the conversation about the son's graduation, the role of narrator was strong for both the son and the mother, with the mother's role being somewhat stronger than the son's. The father's strength was as a mentor. He also achieved considerable strength in the role of monitor, although he did not meet our definitional criteria: his assessing remarks were not among the two most preponderant structural units in his contributions to the conversation. The

Table 11.6 *Strengths of conversational roles (Graduation and Stereo conversations)*

	Daughter	Father	Mother	Son
Graduation				
Narrator	34	27	47	40
Monitor	19	31	24	10
Mentor	*	60	*	*
Stereo				
Narrator	35	37	19	59
Monitor	18	9	27	37
Mentor	*	*	*	*

Table 11.7 *Strengths of conversational roles (Mean of All Four Stories)*

	Daughter	Father	Mother	Son
Narrator	47	26	23	36
Monitor	18	21	29	26
Mentor	14	54	10	–

daughter was more a narrator than anything else, although her strength in this role did not match that of the mother or the son. Turning to the conversation about the purchase of the stereo, the son strongly occupied the role of narrator in this conversation, and with less strength also occupied the role of monitor. The daughter and the father achieved some strength as narrators in this conversation, but to a substantially lesser extent than the son. The mother did not occupy any role with any great strength. No one served as mentor in this conversation, since no one offered facilitating remarks.

Clearly, family members do not adhere to a single conversational role in all cases, but do they have "default" roles? Given the limited and skewed sample that we have so far, it is difficult to answer this question definitively. However, one way to get a feel for whether family members have preferred roles is to look at the average strength of the roles across stories (confining our analysis only to those instances in which the relevant structural units are present). The average strength of the "default" role should be quite high across a wide range of stories, even if the role is occasionally not adopted. As can be clearly seen in Table 11.7, the daughter's strength as a narrator far exceeds that of any other family member, even though half of the sample was specifically chosen with the aim of limiting her role as narrator. Similarly, the father's strength as mentor dramatically exceeded that of the other family members. No one clearly dominated in the role of monitors. Thus, the daughter appeared to serve as narrator when everyone participated equally in the events described – as was the case in the Coney Island and Christmas recountings – but this default role did not hold when someone other than the daughter was the central focus of the conversation. When the son was a central figure in the recounted events, especially in the proposed stereo purchase, he clearly narrated more than he did in either the Coney Island or the Christmas recountings. The father, on the other hand, served as mentor in each conversation that included a mentor. These trends no doubt reflected both personality traits and general family roles (e.g., a parent is more likely than a child to serve as mentor).

Concluding remarks

In our analysis of the recountings of the Patels, we were able to discern three conversational roles – narrator, monitor, and mentor – and chart how these roles shaped the recountings. The narrator went beyond the functions specified in the definition – offering narrative tellings – by providing the recounting with a voice as well as much of its content. Although the four family members were capable of telling a story in the pregroup recountings, the narrator did most of the storytelling in the group recounting. More importantly, the resulting tale reflected her perspectives on the past more than one might expect given her overall generally high level of contribution. Thus, the narrator's unshared pregroup narrative units were more likely to appear in the group recounting than were the unshared pregroup narrative units of the other family members, even if we take into account her proclivity to talk more than anyone else.

The narrator is not the only character to play a role in the Patel's recountings, however. Although the issue needs to be investigated more thoroughly, monitors in our sample of recountings appear to impose their perspectives by providing assurance and confirmation to the narrator (or another family member), or by questioning certain statements in the recounting. When contradicted, the person telling the story can revise his or her account. The subsequent recollection becomes an interplay between the perspective of the monitor, who simply questions a statement, and the perspective of the person telling the story, who articulates the revised narrative.

A similar interaction appears to arise when the mentor offers facilitating remarks. The perspective or internalized schema of the mentor no doubt partially motivates his or her facilitating remarks, but the perspective of the narrator (or other family member currently telling the story) shapes the narrative response to these probes.

The interplay between narrator, monitor, and mentor changes from recounting to recounting, in part because the roles family members adopt are not fixed. Yet as noted, some family members may have "default" roles. For instance, the daughter appears to have held the default role of narrator, and the father the default role of mentor. This does not mean that the Patels as a family demonstrated a rigidity in role selection. The daughter, for instance, appeared to adopt her default role of narrator when no particular family member was central to the story – as was the case for the Coney Island and Christmas narratives. She yielded her default role to another family member when that member figured more centrally to the story than she did.

Our examination of the Patel's recountings uncovered several characteristics of role selection. For instance, family members adopted more than one conversational role at a time on occasion, failed to occupy any discernible conversational role on other occasions, and in some situations, shared the same role with another family member. Thus, the son occupied the roles of narrator and monitor in the stereo story, presumably because he not only wanted to tell his story, but also wanted to make sure that no one else told a story with which he disagreed. The daughter failed to occupy any discernible role in the stereo and graduation stories, yielding her "default" role of narrator to her brother and mother. In the graduation story, the mother and son shared the role of narrator.

Our study, then, demonstrated the importance of conversational roles as a theoretical construct in the investigation of family remembering and explored analytically the parameters constraining the adoption of a role. Our results showed that conversational roles shape family recountings. We suspect that they may even have an indirect effect on what family members remember in subsequent acts of recounting. Although we have not explicitly explored this latter claim here, it has at least been partially demonstrated in research establishing that prior conversation can change the subsequent recollection of such items as visual depictions of traffic accidents, previously heard stories, or ambiguous objects (Loftus, 1979; Pinner & Hirst, 1994; Weldon & Bellinger, 1993; Wilkes-Gibbs & Kim, 1991).

But as we made clear in the introduction, our interest here reaches beyond consideration of the effect different conversational roles have on recounting. Our present investigation is motivated by a strong claim: that autobiographical remembering is a communicative act, or to put it more forcefully, that one cannot divorce the act of remembering from the act of communicating (cf. Barclay, this volume). Our findings concerning the importance of conversational roles in understanding family recounting underline for us the need to treat remembering as a communicative act, but we realize that we can at best offer only a promissory note in support of our strong claim. Indeed, some people may feel that we have not subjected it to a rigorous test. For them, autobiographical remembering may involve communicating, but it is not only communicating. They would argue that we ignored the noncommunicative aspects of autobiographical remembering by focusing on what family members actually say in the conversation. In conversations, people also bring to mind information that they do not communicate. For instance, those conversing may bring to mind details about the target recollection, but hesitate to mention them because they think that someone else will (a situation similar to the bystander effect – cf. Latane, Williams, & Harkins, 1979). There also may be social strictures that prevent family members from saying something they clearly have in mind. In describing for us a family celebration of Divali, an Indian holiday, both Patel children told in their pregroup recountings of playing with firecrackers and setting a neighbor's sari on fire. Needless to say, they did not mention this memorable event in front of their parents.

We doubt, however, that we could be inclined to treat remembering as less bound together with communicating if we studied people recollecting the past in the solitary confinement of a cognitive science laboratory, or in their own room at home. Autobiographical memory – or what we might, following James (1983), call autobiographical memory proper – is always conscious. This conscious expression of the past can take many forms: verbal, visual, olfactory, and so on. We are mostly concerned with those instances in which memories are represented verbally, although we believe that our comments would apply equally to other modes of representation. When people remember in the privacy of their room a verbally represented past event, they are not only constructing a memory, but also discourse. They are, in essence, telling a story to themselves. As communication theorists have noted, such private speech can properly be viewed as communicative. Like more public versions of speech, the discourse is constructed with an audience in mind. In many cases, it is hard to specify who the audience is: it could be a specific person, as when someone rehearses what they are going to say to their therapist, or a generalized audience, as when someone muses in general terms about the depressing events of the day. But whoever the audience is, the private speech is responsive to an audience, and the structure and content of the speech changes as the audience changes.

The more we reflect on our memories, and the more we shape them into narratives, and the more we draw them into the socially textured realm of communication and discourse. Both public and private autobiographical recollections are constructed through discourse, with the structure and context of the discourse shaping the memory (Bruner & Feldman, this volume). From this perspective, private and public acts of remembering are acts of communication (cf. Halbwachs, 1980; Moscovici, 1983). Of course, we need to understand better the character of private remembering and how it differs from public remembering, just as we need to understand better the character of private speech and how it differs from public speech. But we can discern no reason in principle to divorce remembering from communicating simply because some acts of remembering are private affairs.

Remembering, then, has a dialogical quality that makes it subject to principles of discourse, especially the importance of context and meaning (cf. Bakhtin, 1981; Wertsch, 1991). Beyond this, recollections are made known to others only through acts of communication. These acts may be yes/no responses to a recognition test or may be subtle and complex autobiographical narratives. Either way, the remembering is the product of a socially complex interaction. Even in a cognitive science laboratory, remembering requires that a conversation take place between the experimenter and the subject, though many elements of this conversation may never be recorded or analyzed (cf. Mishler, 1986a, 1986b). One might, of course, try to eliminate conversation in the laboratory and strip away the effects of context, content, meaning, and social interaction. But this would be a futile endeavor: There is no stimulus entirely free of meaning, no context so pure as to have no effect on subjects, no social interaction so innocuous as to leave a subject absolutely untouched. It may be better to study how communication shapes remembering than to chase the ever-elusive will-o'-the-wisp of the "raw material" of memory (cf. Banaji & Crowder, 1989; Ebbinghaus, 1964; Hirst & Manier, 1995; Loftus, 1991; Neisser, 1978).

Treating remembering as an act of communication, as we have in this chapter, leads to the exploration of previously neglected topics in the field of autobiographical memory. Autobiographical memories are expressed in and shaped by conversations. Principles of communication, such as the importance of context and meaning, affect both how and what we remember, both to ourselves and to others. Conversational roles play an important part in this process. Only by analyzing remembering as an act of communication can we begin to understand in all its complexity autobiographical memory – how humans tell the stories of their lives to themselves and to others.

References

Bakhtin, M. M. (1981). *The dialogical imagination: Four essays by M. M. Bakhtin.* M. Holquist (Ed.), C. Emerson & M. Holquist (Trans.). Austin: University of Texas Press.

Banaji, M., & Crowder, R. (1989). The bankruptcy of everyday memory research. *American Psychologist, 44,* 1185–93.

Benjamin, K. (1992). *Group versus individual memory for dynamic and static stimuli.* Ph.D. dissertation, Graduate Faculty for Political and Social Science, New School for Social Research.

Bruner, J. (1990). *Acts of meaning.* Cambridge, MA: Harvard University Press.

Caramazza, A. (1986). On drawing inferences about the structure of normal cognitive systems from the analysis of patterns of impaired performance: The case for single-patient studies. *Brain and Cognition, 5,* 41–66.

Cole, M. (1991). On socially shared cognitions. In L. Resnick, J. Levine, & S. Behrend (Eds.), *Socially shared cognitions* (pp. 398–417). Hillsdale, NJ: Lawrence Erlbaum.

Ebbinghaus, H. (1964). *Memory: A contribution to experimental psychology.* New York: Dover.

Edwards, D., & Middleton, D. (1986). Joint remembering: Constructing an account of shared experience through conversational discourse. *Discourse Processes, 9,* 423–459.

—— (1988). Conversational remembering and family relationships: How children learn to remember. *Journal of Social and Personal Relationships, 5,* 3–25.

Eisenberg, A. R. (1985). Learning to describe past experiences in conversation. *Discourse Processes, 8,* 177–204.

Fivush, R. (1991). The social construction of personal narratives. *Merrill-Palmer Quarterly, 37,* 59–82.

Fivush, R., & Fromhoff, F. A. (1988). Style and structure in mother-child conversations about the past. *Discourse Processes, 11,* 337–355.

Fivush, R., & Hudson, J. A. (Eds.). (1990). *Knowing and remembering in young children.* New York: Cambridge University Press.

Frankel, R. (1984). From sentence to sequence: Exploring the medical encounter using microinteractional analysis. *Discourse Processes, 7,* 135–170.

Garfinkel, H. (1967). *Studies in ethnomethodology.* Englewood Cliffs, NJ: Prentice-Hall.

Grice, H. P. (1978). Further notes on logic and conversation. In P. Cole (Ed.), *Syntax and semantics.* New York: Academic Press.

Goodwin, C., & Goodwin, M. H. (1987). Concurrent operations on talk: Notes on the interactive organization of assessments. *IPRA Papers in Pragmatics, 11,* 1–54.

Goodwin, C., & Heritage, J. (1990). Conversational analysis. *Annual Review of Anthropology, 19,* 283–307.

Halbwachs, M. (1980). *Collective memory.* New York: Harper & Row.

Heritage, J. (1984). *Garfinkel and ethnomethodology.* Cambridge, MA: Basil Blackwell.

Hirst, W., & Manier, D. (1995). Opening vistas for cognitive psychology. In L. Martin, K. Nelson, & E. Tobach (Eds.), *Sociocultural Psychology.* New York: Cambridge University Press.

James, W. (1983). *The principles of psychology.* Cambridge, MA: Harvard University Press.

Krainer, E. (1988). Challenges in a psychotherapy group. *Proceedings of the Berkeley Linguistics Society, 14,* 100–113.

Labov, W., & Fanshel, D. (1977). *Therapeutic discourse: Psychotherapy as conversation.* New York: Academic Press.

Latane, B., Williams, K., & Harkins, S. (1979). "Many hands light the work": The causes and consequences of social loafing. *Journal of Personality and Social Psychology, 37,* 822–832.

Lave, J. (1988). *Cognition in practice.* New York: Cambridge University Press.

Linde, C. (1988). Who's in charge here? Cooperative work and authority negotiation in police helicopter missions. In *CSCW 88: Proceedings of the Conference on Computer-Supported Cooperative Work* (pp. 52–64). Association for Computing Machinery.

Loftus, E. (1979). *Eyewitness testimony.* Cambridge, MA: Harvard University Press.

—— (1991). The glitter of everyday memory . . . and the gold. *American Psychologist, 46(1),* 16–18.

Manier, D., & Hirst, W. (1995). The brain doesn't tell the whole story. In E. Manier (Ed.), *Neurobiology and narrative.* Notre Dame, IN: University of Notre Dame Press.

Marshall, J. C., & Newcombe, F. (1984). Putative problems and pure progress in neuropsychological single-case studies. *Journal of Clinical Neuropsychology, 6,* 65–70.

Middleton, D., & Edwards, D. (1990). Conversational remembering: A social psychological approach. In D. Middleton & D. Edwards (Eds.), *Collective remembering.* (pp. 23–45). London: Sage.

Miller, P. J., & Moore, B. B. (1989). Narrative conjunctions of caregiver and child: A comparative perspective on socialization through stories. *Ethos, 17,* 428449.

Mishler, E. G. (1986a). *Research interviewing: Context and narrative.* Cambridge, MA: Harvard University Press.

—— (1986b). The analysis of interview-narratives. In T. R. Sarbin, (Ed.), *Narrative psychology: The storied nature of human conduct*. New York: Praeger.

Moscovici, S. (1983). The phenomenon of social representations. In R. Farr & S. Moscovici (Eds.), *Social representations*. Cambridge, UK: Cambridge University Press.

Neisser, U. (Ed.). (1978). Memory: What are the important questions? In M. M. Gruneberg, P. E. Morris, and R. N. Sykes (Eds.), *Practical aspects of memory*. London: Academic Press.

Nelson, K. (1993). The psychological and social origins of autobiographical memory. *Psychological Science, 4,* 7–14.

Pea, R. (1988). *Distributed intelligence and education*. Palo Alto, CA: Institute for Research on Learning.

Pillemer, D. B., Krensky, L., Kleinman, S. N., Goldsmith, L. R., & White, S. H. (1991). Chapters in narratives: Evidence from oral histories of the first year in college. *Journal of Narrative and Life History, 1,* 3–14.

Pillemer, D. B., Rhinehart, E. D., & White, S. H. (1986). Memories of life transitions: The first year of college. *Human Learning, 5,* 109–123.

Pinner, E., & Hirst, W. (1994). *Effects of group recounting on subsequent individual memories*. Paper presented at the Third Conference on Practical Aspects of Memory, College Park, MD.

Polyani, L. (1989). *Telling an American story: A structural and cultural analysis of storytelling*. Cambridge, MA: MIT Press.

Reese, E., & Fivush, R. (1993). Parental styles of talking about the past. *Developmental Psychology, 29,* 596–606.

Reiss, D. (1981). *The family's construction of reality*. Cambridge, MA: Harvard University Press.

Rogoff, B. (1990). *Apprenticeship in thinking: Cognitive development in social context*. New York: Oxford University Press.

Sachs, H., Schegloff, E., & Jefferson, G. (1974). A simplest systematics of the organization of conversational turn-taking. *Language, 50,* 696–735.

Salomon, G., (Ed.). (1993). *Distributed cognitions: Psychological and educational considerations*. New York: Cambridge University Press.

Schafer, R. (1992). *Retelling a life*. New York: Basic Books.

Seidman, L. J. (1990). The neuropsychology of schizophrenia: A neurodevelopmental and case study approach. *Journal of Neuropsychology, 2(3),* 301–312.

Spence, D. (1982). *Narrative truth and historical truth*. New York: Norton.

Tannen, D. (1984). *Conversational style: Analyzing talk among friends*. Newark, NJ: Ablex.

Tenney, Y. J. (1989). Predicting conversational reports of personal events. *Cognitive Science, 13,* 213–233.

Tracy, K. (Ed.). (1991). *Understanding face-to-face interaction: Issues linking goals and discourse*. Hillsdale, NJ: Lawrence Erlbaum.

Wegener, D. (1986). Transactive memory: A contemporary analysis of the group mind. In B. Mullen & G. Goethals (Eds.), *Theories of group behavior.* (pp. 185–208). New York: Springer-Verlag.

Wegener, D., Erber, R., & Raymond, P. (1991). Transactive memory in close relationships. *Journal of Personality and Social Psychology, 61(6),* 923–929.

Weldon, M. S., & Bellinger, K. D. (1993). *Collective memory: How does group remembering affect recollection?* Paper presented at the Annual Meeting of the Psychonomic Society, Washington, DC.

Wertsch, J. (1991). *Voices of the mind: A sociocultural approach to mediated action*. Cambridge, MA: Harvard University Press.

Wilkes-Gibbs, D., & Kim, P. H. (1991). *Discourse influences on memory for visual forms*. Paper presented at the meeting of the Psychonomic Society, San Francisco, CA.

12 Group narrative as a cultural context of autobiography

Jerome Bruner and Carol Fleisher Feldman

The narration of a life history provides a special intersect where two richly elaborated psychological systems meet. The first involves the processes used in recounting or interpreting narrative itself; the second concerns processes involved in retrieving memories. To understand how a life history is told or how it is being interpreted is virtually impossible without a grasp of narrative structure. We have discussed narrative processes elsewhere (Feldman, 1991b; Bruner, 1990, 1991), and need only note two points here. The first is that in autobiography, as in all narrative, the product is a highly constructed one. The second is that how a narrative is constructed, its form or pattern, provides us with a basis for understanding or interpreting it – whether the interpretation is accurate or not, in whatever sense it may be accurate. Put bluntly, this is to say that narrative patterning does not "get in the way" of accurate autobiographic reporting or interpreting, but rather, provides a framework for both telling and understanding (Rubin, in press). This creates an anomaly similar to the one Bartlett (1932) introduced into the study of memory years ago, and we shall return to it presently. It is an anomaly that still plagues cognitive science today when it attempts to deal with such notions as frames and scripts (e.g., Bransford & Johnson, 1972; Pichert & Anderson, 1977).

The research reported in this paper was supported by a Spencer Grant to Carol Feldman, "Genres as Mental Models," 1990–1991. The present analysis was supported by a current Spencer Grant to Jerome Bruner, "Explorations in Cultural Psychology." We are indebted to Bobbi Renderer, who gave us access to the groups interviewed, conducted the interviews, and helped us understand the significance of events in the actors' lives. The data also formed the basis of her 1993 dissertation in Clinical Psychology at CUNY, where the groups are described in more detail and in other ways. We are indebted to David Kalmar for his development of the software that made these statistical group comparisons possible; he actually did the analyses as well. We also thank him for solving some new analytic problems that arose here in making the pronoun usage contrasts clear.

Students of memory have become increasingly interested in autobiographical memory in the last decade.[1] By autobiographical memory some mean any situated, real-life memory; others mean only personal memories, things in which, somehow, self was engaged (Rubin, 1986, introduction). All would agree, though, that while strictly autobiographical memory of this latter type is the prototype of this category, it is not all of it. Still, there has been a good deal of interest in it even in its narrower and precise definition. Particularly noteworthy expressions are the work of Linton (1986) and Barclay (1986), and in the developmental domain, Nelson (1989). These studies have described the patterning of personal memory and the manner in which such patterning compresses, deletes, expands, and even selects specific information for retention, all indicating the work of "construction" (Goodman, 1978). Whether such a construction is a "reconstruction" that imposes losses or distortions on "real events" or on the "true chronology" of those events need not concern us yet.

What is crucial and defining for strictly autobiographical memory is that it is dominated by a pattern that is not just a generalized narrative pattern, but one with special form – it seems under the control of a "self schema" that itself undergoes evolution as time passes. As Linton (1986, p. 64) says, over 12 years of diary writing, "one can see the internal historian begin to exercise its prerogative – rewriting has begun to occur." Not only is history being rewritten, but the historian is also being transformed by the very process of doing so. For the rewritten history, as it were, changes the perspective of the historian who rewrote it. In like manner, the self who constructs the past is changed by the outcome of its own construction. In this sense, the self schema differs from nearly all other interpretive schemata in its reflexivity. It is not a "free-standing" or self-contained procedure for interpreting text, but is itself constituted by those acts of interpretation. For the self schema is, in a sense, the (interpretive) person as constituted by (prior, schematized) interpretations of life events. Because autobiographical memory is, as it were, maximally situated in culturally meaningful life, it is perhaps the most interesting form of memory a psychologist interested in naturalistic processes can find. But, for the same reasons, it also poses special problems. Since the construction that we, as psychologists, are trying to understand here is actually the product of real people getting on in the world, our available store of psychological mechanisms is seriously understocked. Is the account of memory given in our current literature sufficiently rich to get us all the way to the reflexively constructed self just described?

The greatest difficulty is that many of the proposed procedures by which selves are constructed must yield selves that would be solipsistic with respect to one another. Each autobiographer necessarily creates a life story centered around a self under particularistic constraints that are shared with no one else. In part, this problem is exacerbated by

---

[1] This increased interest is due in no small measure to the influence of Rubin's (1986) volume. That book and Neisser (1982) brought narrative aspects of memory back into contemporary focus.

the (to our minds, at least) misguided emphasis in the current literature on accuracy of reference as a criterion of "good autobiography."[2]

Preserving the facts, in some systematic manner, is obviously essential to any narrated report of events. But these facts do not supply the patterning or schematic structure of narrated reports. Rather, this patterning comes from such narrative features as genre and plot type. In writing an autobiography, there is a wide choice of genres: most event sequences can be retold in several equally accurate renditions, differing chiefly in the meaning they give to reported events. Choice of genre is not dictated by the facts, but in response to other considerations – in particular, to the overall meaning or message that the narrator imposes on the life as a whole. Even in the humble folktale, individual events, as Vladimir Propp (1968) notes, become "functions of" the plot. In autobiography with its wide range of possible genres, event selection is driven by genre type as well as by plot function, not by life events as lived (whatever that last expression may mean ontologically!). Events are shaped for narrative purposes with a view toward meaning and signification, not toward the end of somehow "preserving" the facts themselves. To see it otherwise is to view narration as a mere (verbalized) copy of the (nonnarrated) things of the presymbolic world, responding only to the structural constraints inherent in the world or in cognitive, copylike representations of it.

So let us return to autobiographical memory. One way that autobiographical selves become public is by being based on narrative properties like genre and plot type that are widely shared within a culture, shared in a way that permits others to construe meaning as the narrator has. In this way private experiences (including experience of the self) are constituted meaningfully into a public and communicable form. Note that the means employed is to draw on shared instruments of the culture for patterning one's own meaningful events. This is about as universal a practice as one can find, which may be one reason why its singular exception, autism, has been of such rivetting interest. For precisely what an autistic person cannot do is to tell his, or any, story in a patterned form that guides consensual construal (Bruner & Feldman, 1993; Sacks, 1993–1994). Autobiographical memory, to be communicable, must be constructed of cultural materials.[3]

While virtually any culturally shared narrative form that can be used to interpret stories can be used for constructing a communicable social self, there is another constraint that cuts down on the possibilities. That constraint stems from the need of "sharing"

---

[2] Wagenaar (this volume) discusses some of the legal reasons why "accuracy of reference" looms so large in discussing autobiographical memory. Virtually all legal systems, and certainly our own, privilege personal or "eyewitness" memory over either inference or hearsay, and thereby encumber autobiographical memory with a "presumption of accuracy" that it may not merit and that may not be apposite outside the domain of the law.

[3] Fitzgerald (this volume) makes a similar point. He laments that "psychology remains oddly bereft of an understanding or even a description of how memory behavior fits into the daily commerce of human behavior." On our account, it is crucial to take into account the culturally canonical forms (narrative plot, agentivity, etc.) for framing autobiographical "self-related" memories. For it is in terms of these forms that one construes the "daily commerce of human behavior."

one's autobiography with the groups one interacts with on a face-to-face basis. The story of a life, when all is said and done, must be shared with one's "miniculture," with the proximal group(s) on which one's cultural existence depends. This was very clear in our studies, to be reported presently, of three New York theater groups, whose members all provided "autobiographies" of their groups. What is plain is that the accounts given by individuals constitute, in some important sense, the group's identity. Yet at the same time, a group's identity also constitutes the identities of its members. A self account is used for interpreting shared events of its group members' lives, and contributes to constituting each of them as a social self *within the group*.[4] To see how this interaction works, it helps to look at it in a culture different from our own, one that uses genres and practices that are unfamiliar.

We take for our example d'Azevedo's (1962) study of orally narrated history among the Gola. The Gola have a special status for members of a family or group of families who know the genealogy of their ancestors. These special family members can narrate stories that align presently living members of the family and derive them from ancestors in a historical line of descent. The stories do not simply enumerate ancestors but are organized to give historical meaning or significance to what is told. Among the Gola, the general idea is that "no person can know his place in society or *appreciate fully the kind of person he is* (our italics) unless he is familiar with the genealogy of his family" (p. 16). It is, to paraphrase d'Azevedo, not only that one learns about a large number of living kin, and so has the security of being from a large family, but also that one comes "of a family that can offer its younger members a sense of pride and security in a clearly defined tradition" (p. 16). D'Azevedo recounts how Gola genealogy oration provides a group building exercise, with the group constituting itself by its stories about itself. Once constituted by these stories, members can then draw on them to give meaning to their individual lives as members of the group. The family stories provide the cultural toolkit for individuals interpreting and giving meaning to their own lives. Family members share not only a stock of stories but a set of interpretive procedures for negotiating meanings. D'Azevedo gives one example of a Gola story, one made up to instruct *him* in the necessity of respecting the truth of multiple versions when each comes from a proper authority:

There was a great man with many slaves and followers. He was the brother of King Gaya of Mana, and my father's uncle. One day he found that much rice was gone from his kitchen. He called all his slaves together and said, 'One of you has taken rice from me.' Not one of them would agree. Then the man said to his old slave who had been with him for life, 'You have been eating rice I have not given you.' Though the old slave knew nothing of the rice, he

---

[4] Fivush and Haden (this volume) are similarly concerned with the question of "shared memory," though they emphasize a different side of it – the sharing of memories between child and caretakers. Obviously this form of sharing is essential to the forming of the microculture of the family, so important an aspect of self-formation and of one's entry into the culture generally. Work groups or friendship groups also serve to provide ways of extending self beyond the family, and it is this extension that provides opportunity for wider cultural identifications.

agreed. He was taken and whipped by the great man's sons. Now this *kabande* shows what respect is. The old slave respected his master and would not disagree with him. . . . [H]e thought, 'I do not know my master's mind in this thing. Maybe there is some reason for it which I will find out in time. Maybe I took the rice in my dreams, or maybe my master is testing me in some way.' This is how a country man is wise, and though that old slave was not of the Gola tribe, his wisdom is Gola wisdom. (pp. 27–28)

Many oral cultures have "literary" forms and genres that differ from discourse of everyday language in a way that marks them as art forms (Feldman, 1991a). These art forms virtually invite interpretation from their oral hearers. It is as if the drive to interpret meaning were so much a part of our universal human endowment that cultural means were created everywhere to exercise, support, and even challenge this interpretive drive. And just as universally, a culture's "literary" heritage is also seen by its members as somehow constituting the identity of the group. But though they may not be used directly as models for the constructing of a self, the stories at least make possible the negotiation of highly personal meanings with others. They seem to provide a means for transcending both the adaptive necessities of everyday life and the mundane talk devoted to those necessities.

It would seem that any group that wants to constitute itself as a lasting or important one has to develop shared stories that not only define the group's identity, but also provide a means whereby individual members can guide their own discovery of meaning in their own lives. If people are to go beyond what merely happened to what it meant to them, they need to share stylized genres of story, poetry, oratory, and history to mark their shared meanings off from the quotidian banalities of everyday life and talk.

With that much said, we turn now to the three theater groups. For it is among them that we hope to find analogues in local Western dress of those exotic cultures we have been discussing.

Theater groups as minicultures

The three theater groups had many things in common. They had all been students at New York University during the same period; they formed within a few years of leaving school; they were all interested in experimental theater; they were all rather idealistic and intellectual about what theater should be. In this they differed from many actors. The conditions of their lives, moreover, were in many important ways alike. They all shared the difficult struggle of finding a space in which to work, and of finding audiences to play to, not easy in the New York of the 1980s at the start of their existence. As groups, they were all about equally successful. A demographic description of the three groups is given in Table 12.1. Their similarities provide a well-controlled naturalistic experiment, particularly in light of their different group stories. For in that regard they could not be more different. Each group constituted its story along the lines of a particular genre, as we shall see below.

Group members were interviewed individually for 2 or 3 hours by a graduate student who was also the wife of an actor and known to many of them. Since she had a great deal of background theater knowledge, that interviewees recognized, they could quickly focus on their own distinctive experiences in their own lives and the lives of

Table 12.1 *Description of Theater Companies and Subjects*

Characteristics	Group		
	1 Club	2 Seminarians	3 Apprentices
	Theater Companies		
Year founded	1984	1983	1981
# of members	28	20	50+
# of nonfounding members	5	2	N.A.
Membership policy	Strict	Closed	Open
	Subjects		
Age at founding	21–25	20–22	19–35
Age at interview	27–32	27–28	27–44
Founding/nonfounding	6/2	6/2	2/6
Gender	5M/3F	5M/3F	4M/4F
Role in company[a]	1 leader	1 leader	2 leaders
	1 producer/ administrator	1 producer/ administrator	1 administrator
			1 producer/ fundraiser
	2 directors	3 directors	3 directors
	2 writers	0 writers	0 writers

[a] Seven of eight subjects in groups 1 and 2 are also actors. Five subjects in group 3 are actors.

their group. They simply (and rightly) presupposed that she was acquainted with the general conditions of young idealistic actors in New York. This doubtless helped in eliciting differentiated stories rather than potted actor tales. The interview schedule is given in appendix A. Not surprising, given all this, that the first question sufficed to trigger the great bulk of the interview.

We have provided pseudonyms for the three groups with the intention that they be both emblematic and disguising. They were the Seminarians, the Apprentices, and the Club.

The Seminarians were purists who shared a set of principles about acting, principles that they were taught by a shared (and famous) teacher who taught the class that got them started, and around which the group was defined. The group closed itself from the beginning. Newcomers could not be counted on to share their training and principles. The Seminarians performed a number of plays in New York, and then made a series of moves – from New York to Boston and back, to and from Maine. They had the pleasure and the terrors of a very early success that was not immediately repeated, one often noted in their stories. Seminarians are bound not only by a common origin and history, but by a shared theater technique at once demanding and disciplined, a technique that perhaps works against the cult of the individual.

The Apprentices were a loose group with two strong leaders, one of whom had been a disappointing last-minute novice substitute teacher in the original NYU class that members had attended. For all that, they liked the kind of acting he encouraged, found it deep, honest, and challenging, to use their words. The original class at first encouraged him to form a workshop group. He did, with the idea that as a for-profit company they would develop plays for playwrights in workshop that would then be farmed out to producing companies. The plan was that the Apprentices would live on the royalties they received from the ensuing productions. When this idea didn't bear fruit, they formed a not-for-profit production company. But when the Apprentices perform a play, they often recruit "name" outsiders for some parts. We call them Apprentices because though they are busy and work hard, very little of what they do (workshops, weekend marathons) is for an audience. Membership in this company means having a place where you can do things that interest you, rather than actually having a job – performing in plays for an audience. Members who have stayed on report that the group has helped them grow and stretch their personal boundaries in a supportive setting. The Apprentices have always welcomed new members and they are a much larger group than the other two.

The Club formed a year or two later than the others, really as a group of friends from NYU who had been individually quite successful in getting paid "commercial" work. They began their early meetings in a particular New York bar, and then met informally at each others' houses. Members of the Club shared the feeling that their commercial work was trivial, that it lacked meaning. They wanted to do theater they themselves had chosen, to do it with friends, for fun as well as for a living, artistically to push the envelope of acceptable theater toward the outrageous. After first performing for each other, they then produced their own plays in public, that were well received. An important turning point in the group's life came when they nearly lost their space. This was due to a management crisis in which the codirector, whose uncle had lent them their space, was voted out of the Club. Subsequently, the new director who had been voted in to take his place quit, the original codirector was restored, and with this their space and stability. The Club is lively and full of fun. Throughout its history, many other actors and writers have wanted to join, and some have been let in.

Lexical analysis

Recall that our interest is in the way that a story, common to members of each group, not only gives the group an identity by creating a shared cultural framework, but also provides a narrative convention by which individual members can give meaning to events in their own lives. One way to objectify the narrative pattern distinctive to each group would be to discover the language that is uniquely distinctive to the members of each group. More precisely, one would want to find the words that most sharply distinguish each group from the others – distinctive Seminarian talk, Apprentice talk, Club talk. And that is what we have undertaken to do – with the aid of a high capacity, highly

Table 12.2 *Type and token statistics for each group.*

Group	Type	Token	Ratio
Seminarians	4,178	80,831	0.05170
Apprentices	4,202	78,646	0.05343
The Club	4,332	81,012	0.05347

patient computer and an appropriate program (see Feldman, Bruner, Kalmar, & Renderer, 1993).

But before we could proceed with such a distinctive word frequency analysis, we had to see first whether our three groups had the same quantity, variety, and redundancy in their talk, something we could investigate with a machine run type/token count. Good fortune (and perhaps the theater tradition) were with us. A type/token count showed our three groups to be virtually identical with respect to number of words and number of word types (see Table 12.2).

So we may turn to each group's distinctive, defining words. The criteria for such distinctive words were (1) the word had to be used significantly more often by one group than by either of the other two at a high level of statistical reliability (an *F*-test comparing the three groups yielding a value at the $p < .01$ level, and two significant post hoc contrasts at $p < .05$), and (2) the word had to be used by at least five members (a majority) of the group for which it was distinctive. Note that this dual procedure permits us to find not the most frequently used words for a group, but the words that most strongly differentiate it from the other two – something like the most idiosyncratic components of the group pattern. There were 42 group-distinctive words for the Seminarians, 29 for the Apprentices, and 20 for the Club. The large differences in quantity relate to the different kinds of stories they tell, as well as to the cohesiveness of the group, as we will see. The distinctive words associated with each group are given in Table 12.3.

Right off it is evident that the Seminarians have a larger number of shared distinctive words than the other groups. Theirs is a kind of adventure tale, one that recruits a lot of words of place and time. They tell their story sequentially, moving from a defining origin through a great many specific places where they have been over time. Their words of time and place account for their whole surplus of distinctive lexemes. Indeed, they are the only group with any distinctive words of motion (came, go, back), or place names (4), or words that are part of names of specific theaters (3), or durative time, whether nature's seasons or the theater's (*December, fall, summer*; as well as *season* and *weeks*). The distinctively time-place chronological patterning of their narrative is further emphasized by two other verbs of manner, *haven't* and *will*. These words suggest that for them the present is essentially a point on a time line extending backward into the past and forward into the future. The word *haven't* is used to talk about what we should have but haven't done yet, and *will* to talk about future plans.

But theirs is an adventure tale in search of the holy grail, something of a mission, as we will see later. The effect of their group identity around a mission is to give members

Table 12.3[*] *Counts of the types of words that are distinctive to each group.*

	Group		
	Seminarians	Apprentices	The Club
TOTAL WORDS:	42	29	20
Proper nouns that refer to:[**]			
people	9	6	5
cities	4	0	0
theaters	3	0	0
play names	7	5	3
their group	1	3	2
SUBTOTAL	24	14	10
Common words			
time	5 December fall summer season weeks	0	0
motion	3 came go back	0	0
manner	2 haven't will	0	0
space	0	2 above 40th	2 space bar/cafe
projects	0	5 lab one-act studio marathon weekend	0
SUBTOTAL	10	7	2
Key words	8 common ensemble formed joined managing principles taught technique	8 artist arts auditioned development executive percentage playwright playwrights	8 fun group other people quit talented vote written

[*] Index words were used significantly more by each group than by the other two groups. Index words were selected on the basis of their having (1) an overall F with $p<.01$, and (2) the largest mean frequency in the particular group of which it was characteristic was reliably greater than the means for the other two groups at $p<.05$ level, as determined by post hoc t-tests.

[**] For the sake of preserving the subjects' anonymity, only counts are given here. When proper nouns are given in the text, they have been changed.

a more highly shared story than in the other groups. It is this common sense of the meaning of the group experience that accounts for their large number of shared words, an outgrowth of the fact that this group's members all tell a more nearly identical story – they share a single kind of experience and they speak about it with one voice (see appendix B for the short versions of the group history). It may follow from this that both individual autobiographies and group histories are more closely linked among Seminarians than in the other groups. For them, the story of the self and the story of the group become less distinguishable. But we will say more about this when we discuss the pronominal lexical analyses later in the chapter.

For the other two groups, though "place" is neither a named locus nor is it salient, they do speak of the more local and more deictic rehearsal space. Apprentices use *above* (referring deictically to their studio) and *40th* (meaning the New York street of that number). Members of the Club literally use *space* as a word to refer to that performance place they nearly lost. And there is another composite space word they use, *bar+cafe*, interchangeable words used to describe where they habitually met when the Club started. Interestingly, just as there were no "rigid descriptor" place words, there are no distinctive words in the time, motion, or manner categories for either the Apprentices or the Club members. Their stories do not have a pattern of motion through time, nor are they anchored in geographic space.

Not surprisingly, all three groups have distinctive words referring to their group names, and to people important to them. But consistent with their "landmarked" way of talking, Seminarians also use play names somewhat more than the others, while correspondingly, the Apprentices refer more to the informal work products that constitute their life in the group (lab, one-act, studio, marathon, weekend).

The remaining distinctive words, eight from each group, provide a collage of meanings characteristic of each of them, almost group defining – they are "key words." Take, first, the thus far undescribed Club. Their words are revealing: fun, group, other, people, quit, talented, written, vote. The words *quit* and *vote* refer back, of course, to that difficult turning point when a vote was taken to oust their old director, which nearly lost them their space, only to have the new director *quit*. *Vote* also appears in other contexts, most often emphasizing the free-for-all democracy of the Club. The rest of their distinctive words tell their story nearly as well as their interviews! A *group* of *talented people* (who first got together in a *bar/cafe*, and nearly lost their *space* at one point) had a lot of *fun* doing *projects* with each *other*, working on things that they themselves had *written*. In a word, talented people at play as much as artists at work. This was how they saw their group. Since the basic view of the group that emerges is of a gang that supports the individual expression of its members, the key words also tell us about how they formed an image of themselves individually in the context of that group.

Let us return to the Apprentices, for they make the sharpest contrast. Their remaining eight words are down to earth (or work) by comparison: artist, arts, auditioned, development, executive (director/s), percentage, playwright, playwrights. The last three refer, of course, to the original work plan of the group – that it would get playwrights to pay them a percentage of commercial production for trying their plays out in workshop. The central story is conveyed by the remaining words. It is a story of a group where individual members involved with the *arts* are enabled to undergo personal *development* as *artists* under the shelter of the two group leaders (*executive* directors), and sometimes *audition* to get into plays. The genre type here is a *bildungsroman* about serious work on the self, undertaken in order to bring about development of a higher level suitable for entry into society – in this case, the specialized society of the group. The group is defined by its common leaders, and the shared experience of personal development under them, rather than by its horizontal connections among members. The group leaders frame and permit individual effort to grow within its facilities. The individual meaning of experiences must, in the culture of this group, be given in terms of the artistic development of the person having them. Each autobiography is different, and none of them would read the same as the group's story.

Finally, the Seminarians, with their richly locative landscape and their time line and chronology. Their style is conveyed rather neatly by their remaining eight distinctive words: common, ensemble, formed, joined, managing (director), principles, taught, technique. There is a story in these words. We are a closed group of actors (an *ensemble*) who share a *common* theater *technique taught* by our founder and also our *managing* director. We have remained faithful to our *common principles* ever since we *formed*. This is an interpretive framework in which the action adventure is in the service of a personal calling shared by all members of the group. Taken in conjunction with the Seminarians' rich narrative patterning of events in space and time, this narrative of dedication has, as we commented before, an almost medieval monkish quality, hence our earlier allusion to a group traveling in search of the holy grail. Their story is told in the genre of a "quest."

This way of going about characterizing the groups, based upon distinctive lexical differences between them, may seem to some observers to be scientistic, reductionist, or even as leading to statistical artifacts (Olson & Salter, 1993). It always needs supplementation. And generally, in order to attach interpretations of meaning to such distinctive lexemes, we need a careful reading of how they are used in context by members of the group for which the lexemes are distinctive. We give some examples of such contextualizing in appendix B, where summary group histories and their morals (obtained in response to Questions 15 and 16, see appendix A) are presented. We ask the reader, in consulting these examples, to consider how much less we would have known from reading text alone without any knowledge of group-distinctive lexemes.

The three groups, as we commented earlier, could not be more divergent in constructing their respective group identities, even to using different genres, or, we believe, in constructing selves in reference to those groups. Up to now our emphasis has been upon the first of those, on group identity. Now we must turn to the issue of self-identity and its construction in relationship to different group construction processes.

Group related self-identity

How does one make good empirically on a claim as abstract as the one we have been setting forth: that the processes involved in constructing a group's identity are kindred to those that form group member's concept of self? Taken philosophically, it is by no means a new claim. It has its near ancestry in George Herbert Mead's (1934) *Mind, Self, and Society*. One can sharpen the focus of such a general claim by concentrating on the actual discourse processes jointly involved in creating both group identity and self identity by looking in a comparative context where different patterns of group formation will make themselves evident. It is in the context of the three different minicultures, each with its distinctive lexical patterning, that we can ask how individual lives are revealed. One needs to get beneath "culture in general" to the intimate miniculture of the face-to-face groups with which an individual engages to see something of the variety of ways that people make their autobiographies in relation to the way they make the story of their community. Specifically we have sought to detail the distinctive patterns of discourse that individual members of such groups use in outlining both their group's history and their own "self history."

How do we know, the skeptic might ask, that the distinctive discourse patterns that each group uses in establishing its own identity are also being used individually in the "making of self" by members of our three groups – by the Seminarians, the Apprentices, and the Club? Obviously there is no "ultimate" empirical answer to such a question. But we can at least take some steps toward pinning our claim down in more empirical detail. One obvious way to do so is to see whether the group-distinctive discourse terms discussed before are used *personally* as well as to characterize "what the group did." Do group members use these distinctive terms in self-referring expressions? Or to use a rather old-fashioned expression, are the terms "ego involving" or "self-formative"? If so, then we have a useful hint for answering our more general question, even though it would leave us short of an "ultimate" answer. It is a little like the old political joke about Charles de Gaulle, that it was impossible to tell from his remarks whether he was talking about himself or about France. Yet even that ambiguity told something about DeGaulle's self.

In pursuit of this question, we have subjected each group member's interview to a linguistic analysis that might reveal how they used their group's distinctive lexical terms – whether personally or impersonally. Admittedly this is difficult to do on the basis of content, precisely because of the "DeGaulle dilemma." So rather than using content (reflected in the subjects' key-word usage), we have relied upon form (reflected in the subjects' pronoun usage). Specifically, we inquire whether these group distinctive terms occur only in impersonal sentences, bare of personal pronouns, or whether they also occur in utterances containing such personal pronouns as I, we, he/she, they, and you, and their accusative and genitive derivatives such as me, mine, and myself. We can look at this association as a sign of the "personalness" of group identity.

The rationale for this procedure, though it may not be as psychologically subtle as a psychoanalyst might demand, has the virtue, at least, of being empirically viable. It is based upon rather obvious hypotheses about pronominalization. The first is simply that pronominalization indicates a personal connection. An example will help the point. A sample of Oxonians, say, is asked to tell about the Oxford that they knew when they were there. Another sample from, say, the University of East Anglia, is asked to do the same thing for their time at that university. We now extract the distinctive terms used by each group – say *ancient* and *distinguished* are the distinctive terms for the Oxonian, and *young* and *egalitarian* are the counterparts for the East Anglians. Compare the sentences:

> We all felt we were in a very *distinguished* (*egalitarian*) place.
>
> Oxford (East Anglia) was a very *distinguished* (*egalitarian*) place.

The first is more self-referential, presumably more ego-related than the second. Perhaps group distinctive terms (since they tend to relate to collective and institutional matters) might not be as likely to occur with accompanying personal pronouns in their sentences as might, say, more individually idiosyncratic terms chosen at random from the interviews. But even so, one would expect there would be more than a few such associations if the group distinctive terms were really "getting to" their users personally.

The results of this analysis are contained in Table 12.4. Key group distinctive terms are indeed used in the company of personal pronouns in most sentences where they occur: from two-thirds to three-quarters of sentences containing key words also contain personal pronouns. Nevertheless, group distinctive key words are pronominally personalized in this way somewhat less frequently than random control words. These control words appear with pronouns about three-quarters to seven-eighths of the time.

In fact, comparing the main pronoun groups across the three acting groups reveals group distinctive patterns consistent with what we saw in the lexical analysis above, as we shall see. They also provide a first step toward seeing different autobiographical

Table 12.4 *For each group, percentage key-word or random-word sentences that contain personal pronominals.*[*]

	Key-word sentences	Random-word sentences
Group		
Seminarians	66%	83%
Apprentices	76%	82%
The Club	72%	78%
# of sentences with pronouns	341	425
# of sentences without pronouns	141	97
Total # of sentences	482	522

[*] To look at usage, we had to isolate each group's sentences containing their 8 key words. We found a tremendous imbalance: the Club group yielded 1,266 sentences, whereas the Seminarians yielded 237, and the Apprentices 181. An examination of the number of sentences generated by each word revealed that the Club words "group," "other," and "people" were responsible for the imbalanced distribution. When these three words were removed from the analysis, the distribution was better balanced (Club = 121 sentences; Seminarians = 237; Apprentices = 181). A further step removed all but one case of each sentence that appeared twice or more (because it contained two or more key words), leaving Club = 113, Seminarians = 201, and Apprentices = 168 as sentence totals for all analyses reported below. All key-word pronominal analyses therefore were based on the remaining 21 terms, 5 for the Club, and 8 for each of the other two groups.

styles, for they will let us see the pattern with which group members make their own identity in the context of the group. Each group, when talking about its group defining ideas, has a distinctive pattern of pronoun use, different from the others. We found this by first finding all the sentences in each group that contain at least one of that group's key terms. Then we looked at pronoun usage in those sentences for group distinctive patterns. They are reported in Table 12.5. We analyzed this first in a rough and ready way by focusing on dominant pronoun usage.

In Table 12.5, we tallied the usage of each pronoun class separately. Sentences were counted that had any first-person singular pronouns, whether or not they contained other pronoun classes; sentences were counted that had any first-person plural pronouns, ignoring other classes; etc. The dominant usage patterns being reported here concern intragroup pronoun configurations as they appear to the naked eye – what is implied is a qualitative, not a quantitative, claim.

Seminarians' distinctive pronoun is *we*, consistent with the way each member speaks for all members, as part of a shared commitment to common principles. But also individual meaning and identity comes for them from being one, not very distinguishable member, of the shared reality. In this group, personal autobiography is not made alone, hence their correspondingly low usage of *I*: autobiography is made with *we*.

In contrast, the Apprentices' dominant pronouns are *I* and *they* (their third-person usage is dominated by *they*, which appears 10.1 times per 1000 words, in contrast with *he* at 3.3, and *she* at 1.3). As we have already seen, Apprentices feel that their group membership involves principally being well supported by powerful leaders (*they*) who create a context that will permit them to develop as much as they can, if they make proper use of it. Everything's all laid on. It's up to them to make the most of it. There is an emphasis on solitary effort (*I*) under a powerful umbrella (*they*). Their other fellow strivers are not central to this story, and the corresponding use of *we* is not central to their usage. If in the Seminarians the autobiography was nearly the same as the group story, here each autobiography is distinct up to a point (what effort made, what growth attained), but the nature of the activity (effort and development) and the enabling conditions are the same in all the individual stories. It is this shared matter – the leaders, the experience of living inside a support system for effort and growth, and the historical vicissitudes (or adaptive survival) of the support system the individuals share, that constitutes the group story – that is, the *they* and the relationship of all the *I*'s to *they*.

The Club shows another pattern. Members are a group of rugged individualists slugging it out in combat as each tries to make something work for which he needs the help of the others. Consistent with this picture is the dominance of the pronoun *I* in their usage. Their group story is made from individual autobiographies, as it were. Other members, and the group, enter in as resources for expressing individually distinctive ideas, goals, visions, and projects; the group is a collection of individuals. If in the Seminarians, the group story constituted each autobiography, here it is the collection of autobiographies that constitute the group story.

We turn now to the random-word sentences. It is a matter of great interest that the group-distinctive patterns of pronoun usage that accompany key words are also ob-

Table 12.5 *All pronoun classes. For each group, percentage of key-word, random-word, and other group's words sentences that contain one or more members of each class of pronominals. Percentages do not sum to 100 because sentences may contain more than one kind of pronoun.*

	Key-word sentences		
	Group		
	Seminarians	Apprentices	The Club
Pronoun class			
1st-person singular	25	41	36
1st-person plural	35	20	27
3rd person	28	32	25
2nd person	17	27	19
Total # of sentences	201	168	113

	Random-word sentences		
	Group		
	Seminarians	Apprentices	The Club
Pronoun class			
1st-person singular	36	47	44
1st-person plural	34	17	30
3rd person	21	30	19
2nd person	28	35	19
Total # of sentences	232	175	115

	Other groups' word sentences		
	Group		
	Seminarians	Apprentices	The Club
Pronoun class			
1st-person singular	28	44	59
1st-person plural	33	6	18
3rd person	12	28	26
2nd person	18	11	21
Total # of sentences	60	36	34

tained in sentences containing any words at all – the random-word sentences. The form or style of talk about the self – whether as part of a "we," or as in dialectical relationship with another who are "they," or as an independent ego aggregated with others for creative purposes, seems to be a pervasive and general matter. The individual relates in this group-distinctive fashion to everything the group does, and not just to the group-distinctive activities reflected in key words. The pronoun patterns seem, therefore, to reflect a pervasive style of relating to group activities and even, perhaps, a way of thinking about them.

This suggests that the key-word patterns and the pronoun-usage patterns are two separate systems, reflecting different aspects of group identity. If the key words tell us about shared content that defines the group itself, the distinctive pronoun-usage patterns seem to tell us about the way that individuals construct themselves in relation to their group – one system for the group identity, the other for individual identity. Note, however, that key words define the group in a fashion all the individual members share, and that pronoun usage consititutes an individual way of looking that is distinctive to the group. Thus, though these two systems have differing foci, each one captures a two term relationship between individual and group identity.

We wondered whether our random-word sentences were playing tricks on us. We therefore constructed a second, and more precise, test of the pervasiveness of the group distinctive pronoun-usage patterns observed for key words. This time we looked at pronoun usage when group members were talking about concepts that were, by definition (and statistical test), of *no* importance to their group – namely, the key terms of the other two groups, called "other groups' words" in Table 12.5. If anything, the observed key-word pattern is more evident here than for random words. Evidently, group distinctive-pronoun usage is adopted by individuals as a pervasive way of relating to life in the group, even to aspects of group life that are not important to the identity of the group itself. That is why it seems to constitute a separate, second system, seemingly one about the making of the self.

Since this matter is so consequential, the qualitiative characterizations of pronoun patterns so far given cry out for some statistical confirmation. By means of chi square, we compared the groups with one another (pairwise) for their distributions across the three pronoun types that have entered the picture – first-person singular (e.g., *I*), first-person plural (e.g., *we*), and third-person (mostly *they*). The second person (e.g., *you*) was omitted, it having played no role in our present understanding. We examined all three sentence groups – key, random, and other groups' words. For the key-word sentences, Seminarians' pronominal pattern differs from Apprentices' (chi-square = 8.10, $p < .02$). The other two pairs of groups were not significantly different for the key-word sentences. For the random-word sentences, Seminarians differ from Apprentices (chi-square = 8.67, $p < .02$), and now Apprentices also differ from the Club (chi-square = 6.16, $p < .05$). But for the sentences containing other groups' key words, Seminarians differ dramatically from the Apprentices (chi-square = 28.51, $p < .0001$) and from the Club (chi-square = 15.97, $p < .0003$). There is also a marginal difference between Apprentices and the Club (chi-square = 4.90, $p < .09$). There is no question that the pronoun-usage patterns observed in the qualitative data are at their strongest in the personally idiosyncratic matters that have to do with creating individual autobiography and self, rather than with constructing group identity. And there is no question either that,

Table 12.6 *First person pronouns: I versus we. For each group, percentage of key-word and random-word sentences containing only singular or only plural first-person pronominals, without regard to any other class of pronoun present.*

	Key-word sentences		
	Group		
	Seminarians	Apprentices	The Club
Pronoun class			
1st-person singular	17	35	27
1st-person plural	27	13	18
Total # of sentences	201	168	113
	Random-word sentences		
	Group		
	Seminarians	Apprentices	The Club
Pronoun class			
1st-person singular	28	40	35
1st-person plural	27	10	22
Total # of sentences	232	175	115
	Other groups' words sentences		
	Group		
	Seminarians	Apprentices	The Club
Pronoun class			
1st-person singular	22	44	53
1st-person plural	25	6	12
Total # of sentences	60	36	34

with respect to such personally idiosyncratic material, the three theater groups use pronouns in patterns that differ from one another.

We claim then that these distinctive patterns of pronoun usage are a way of making the self in a cultural context. When they are viewed as being about the making of self, one might have a special interest in the subset of data consisting of first-person pronouns. Do the acting groups differ in their use of the singular and plural first-person pronouns when these pronouns alone are considered? In Table 12.6, this contrast is displayed by comparing the percentage of sentences containing singular (and no plural) first-person pronouns with sentences containing plural (and no singular) first-person pronouns. To do this, we exclude sentences containing both or neither.[5]

The Seminarians, strikingly more so than either of the other groups, use *we* words in preference to *I* words in sentences containing their key words. This is in sharp contrast to the Apprentices and to Club members, who favor *I* over *we* in key-word talk about their groups. Chi-square comparisons of the Seminarians with the other two groups yields 10.98 with the Apprentices ($p < .001$), and 4.06 with the Club ($p < .05$). The Seminarians' preference when compared to the Apprentices for *we* words in the key-word sentences is still present in random-word sentences (chi-square = 9.71, $p < .002$), while the contrast with the Club disappears in the random-word sentences (chi-square = 1.25, p = n.s.). Finally, for sentences containing other groups' key words, Seminarians differ from Apprentices (chi-square = 18.90, $p < .0001$) and from the Club (chi-square = 14.87, $p < .0001$); the Apprentice–Club comparison is not significant. As before, the effect is not tied to key terms, but is pervasive. But, with respect to the first-person pronouns, all of the significant effects show a difference between the Seminarians and the other groups.

Recall that the Seminarians are the ones with the highest sense of internal coherence and dedication. We think this dedication and their almost religious seriousness about theater predisposes them toward a slightly monkish identification, or fusion, with their group – that is reflected, of course, in the *we* talk, and its tie to key terms. The two other groups (whose *I*–*we* balances are statistically indistinguishable one from the other) favor *I* words over *we* for different reasons – or at least one gets that impression from looking at transcripts. The Apprentices tend to use first-person singular language in a more functional way in connection with their group membership, emphasizing their relationship to group projects and enterprises in which they are engaged. Club members seem, rather, to be using *I* language more agentively, with a good deal of emphasis upon the fun they are getting out of group membership. Half in jest, then, we can speak of fusion, function, and fun as providing a psychological "conduit" between self-identity

---

[5] Table 12.5 and Table 12.6 both contain entries for first-person singular and first-person plural pronouns. Yet the percentages entered into the table differ. Both percentages are based upon the same number of key-word sentences – for example, for the Seminarians, 201.

Of the 201 sentences, 51 of them contain one or more first-person singular pronouns. Some of these 51 may also contain first-person plural pronouns; some may also contain third-person pronouns; some may also contain second-person pronouns. The presence of other pronouns is ignored in computing the tally of 51 used in Table 12.5. Thus, Table 12.5 represents independent tallies of whether or not sentences contain given types of pronouns. This 51 constitutes 25% of the 201 sentences.

Table 12.6 is concerned with the relative distribution of first-person singular versus first-person plural pronouns. Of the 51 sentences Table 12.5 reports as containing first-person singular pronouns, only 34 are relevant for Table 12.6. This is because, in fact, of the 51 sentences, 17 also contain first-person plural pronouns. Thus, actually only 34 sentences contain first-person singular pronouns without any first-person plural pronouns at all. These 34 sentences make up 17% of the total 201 sentences. Thus, 17% is entered in Table 12.6.

and group-identity. These are linguistic patterns that characterize both distinctive talk of group identity and talk implicating self.

We would want to urge, finally, that it is principally when one examines the intimate bonds between individuals and their culturally specific, activity-focused groups (their minicultures) that such links as these can be discerned. Granted that these three mini-cultural groups operate in a broader cultural-historical setting – what could be more such a setting than New York theater – the broader culture achieves its effects not "at a distance" but through local participation in its institutions. This fact, though generally true, is probably more exquisitely a fact of life for actors than for many other people. One of us happened recently to describe this study to a gifted and famously intellectual actress at a house warming given by a mutual friend. Did we realize, she asked, how dependent actors were on being in a group, the right group – "It can't be done alone." Indeed, when one reflects on the matter, few things can. And if they go badly when done together, then (as in the Sartre play), "l'enfer, ce sont les autres." Our general thesis, then, is simply that "the culture," however wide or general, is always encountered as local culture – constituted of local knowledge achieved in local praxis (Geertz, 1983). And by that same token – and this is the point of the present paper – we are also proposing that autobiography and an autobiographical self are products of that same local culture of participation.

We admire the bold effort of Hirst and Manier (this volume) to deal with memory as remembering and, as such, to treat it as a communicative activity rather than exclusively as a matter of "storage and retrieval." If acts of remembering are considered as communicative acts, then one is compelled to consider the roles of those participating in joint remembering, as Hirst and Manier have in their chapter. The roles that they adopt in recall – narrating, monitoring, and mentoring – are particularly apt in describing the interactions that occur in "family remembering." We did not have the kind of data necessary for studying how members of our three groups went about recalling events when they were jointly involved in reminiscing about the past. (It would have taken a quite different kind of study to have gathered such data.) But there still remains the question, how our subjects told (or "remembered") their stories in interaction with an interviewer. Surely the nature of the relationship between "subject" and "interviewer" in our own study affected how subjects gave their accounts. One could well imagine, to make a contrast, that if the interviewer had been seen not as, say, "the knowledgeable and sympathetic wife of an actor" but as a stereotypically "clinical" kind of psychologist "digging" for "unconscious" material, that a different mode of storytelling might have emerged. This is, of course, an issue of lively interest, but it will have to await further inquiry.

We must return finally to a methodological note. Our heavy use of lexical analysis in the foregoing discussions has not been intended as a substitute for interpretation in the usual hermeneutic sense. There is no substitute for interpretation when dealing with the such essentially "textual" matters as self accounting, or characterizing a group "history." We believe that lexical analysis can sharpen the focus of interpretation, though it remains the servant of interpretation. For all that, linguistic analysis, of whatever kind, remains a "discovery procedure" not a "proof procedure." It provides more discerning methods for use in interpretation. In the end and after all our lexical analysis, we are still left to speculate interpretively about the ways that group identity and self-identity become related – sometimes fused, sometimes with one instrumental to or merely a source of fun for the other, sometimes even at war. And ours was only one among many forms of lexical analysis that could have been applied – some finer-grained, some more discursive, some even tropologic. None would ever "prove the case." But they might surely make it more plausible and, we suspect, more interesting as well.

Appendix A interview schedule

Q1   First, I'd like you to tell me the story of the _____ company from your point of view. And I don't mean a summary of the story, but more like you would tell it to someone who didn't know anything about it, who really cared and who had all the time in the world.

Q2   Have the goals or purposes of the company changed over the years?

Q3   Could you identify any particular turning point for the company?

Q4   And have there been any turning points in your own thinking or feelings about the company?

Q5   What are the directions the future could take for the company?

Q6   If you had to predict, which way do you think it will go?

Q7   What have been the most important things that have kept the group going all this time?

Q8   Can you tell me about the most difficult situation that you and the company have faced?

Q9   And what is the story of the most satisfying experience?

Q10 Can you think of anything that has happened that surprised you, in the sense that it seemed out of character with what you would expect from the group?

Q11 What *kind* of company is this? How would you compare and contrast it to others in the city?

Q12 Could you talk about New York as a context for the group? What is it like to work in this environment?

Q13 What does the company mean to you personally?

Q14 What made you happen to go into theater?

Q15 Okay, for these last few questions, I'd like you to reflect back on what you've talked about so far, so that these are shorter answers that summarize your thinking about these things. And the first thing I'd like is for you to tell me the short version of the story of the group.

Q16 What would you say is the moral of this story?

Q17 And what is the most important idea that one could take away from the story, the gist of it?

Q18 Where does the story go from here?

Q19 And why do you see it going that way?

Q20 Age?
Q21 Highest grade completed?
Q22 Years with company?
Q23 On a scale of 1 to 10, how would you rate your life right now?
Q24 How would you have rated it 5 years ago?
Q25 How do you expect to rate it 5 years from now?
Q26 And how would you rate your feelings about your relationship with the company?

Appendix B answers to Q15: "Tell me the one-page version of the story," and Q16: "What's the moral of the story?"

The Club

1. Right. A group of us, um, mostly guys, one girl, get together. Want – want autonomy. Feeling frustrated. We find a place to meet. We meet once a week. We do readings. We do improvs. Uh, we fight like dogs. Um, we – we start to grow in size. And, um, and people start to appreciate the consistency of the place, a club environment where you can go once a week. And, um, eventually we get a space. Um, and start to produce our own work from within the company. Um, which gives the actors a chance to work, but doesn't really fulfill – doesn't really please an audience. And then, um, realize that we – if we're going to do anything worthwhile, we've got to – we've got to bring in people that are talented in writing and directing and merge our talents as actors. Because we were 95 percent actors. And, uh, once we did that, we – we emerged – we started to become a legitimate company. Um, and with our home, which is someplace that's become this really special place that we built. Um, we started to, uh, to do worthwhile theater, you know, in – in a bigger world.

I was going to say, you know, there's something about being supportive. But then, you know, there's plenty of times where we weren't supportive. Or I guess there's something – the moral is, um, is in trying, you know. As long as people try, as long as we're trying, it's a good thing. As long as there's motion, it's a good thing. It doesn't matter.

2. Mm-hmm. Okay. A bunch of people who wanted to get together for some nurturing relationships, because it's a mean world out there in the business of Hollywood and acting, and everybody wanted a home base and a sense of family so they wouldn't have to feel so isolated. And that's what we've all been creating since then.

Um, attention to individual needs serves the group.

3. Ooh. The story is a group of people who wanted to come together and act and read. Not necessarily to act, but just to find a home outside of the theater. Uh, developed into a group of people sharing artistic ideas in a variety of venues. Uh, became a producing organization. Was given a large gift at a very, um, early age. Wasn't quite sure how to handle it yet. Fumbled it, almost dropped it. Recovered. Learned from the experience. Grew as artists and as individuals. Harnessed the power that is around us and are now, uh, looking towards a positive future.

Invest in yourself. Invest in your friends. Invest in those around you. Uh, the importance of trust. The importance of simple things in life: trust, honesty, hard work. Um, compassion. It sounds so cheesy, but it's really true. Those are really the lessons. Uh –

4. The short version of the story of the company? Uh, it was – the company started – was started by and for a bunch of working actors, basically, who really needed something to do while they were not working. And kind of a reason for being here. And, uh, we got together and started doing play readings. And as an extension of that, uh, started writing and producing themselves. Uh, so a bunch of actors who got together that started writing and – and, uh, acting and – and producing, you know, theater pretty much of, by and for themselves since. That's the story, pretty much.

Uh, the moral, unfortunately – and it's – as – really, uh, sort of glib and superficial as it might sound, I think, is that it is actually possible to – to do, uh, whatever you want, as long as you have people who are dedicated to – to what they are doing and have some sense of – of that community. You know, we – we're lucky that we have people who are professionals. Because every once in a while people would say, "This – this doesn't cut it in professional place." You know.

5. Okay. Uh, a group of us who had been friends and, uh, classmates at NYU and/or friends, uh, had been talking about, uh, starting up, uh, a group to work on stuff that we couldn't do, uh, in the commercial theater. We got together. We started doing readings. And then readings led to, uh, small productions. Then small productions led to bigger productions. And then that led to space. And once we found a space, we were just sort of off and running. And the company grew in size and sort of solidified. Then we picked the name. And then – and then we – then we came to the space. Um, that's a brief outline.

Oh, I think it's – I think it has something to do with the fact that creativity – uh. Metaphorically speaking, creativity can move mountains. And we've moved some mountains to get where we are. And, uh, it's because of the power of that, of creativity. And that, uh, it can bind and bound and push and contrive and – and overcome and inspire.

6. Um, a group of people, mostly actors, uh, got together and wanted to start a theater company. Uh, and various spaces and various stages have, uh, gradual stages, getting to the point of, uh, getting a name, producing original works. Which is where we are now. You know. A large group of actors, I would say, cum director, cum writer. A lot of people have changed.

Is there a moral to this story? Uh, I think THE CLUB is a story of luck. And it continues. But so far I think we've been blessed, you know. And we've been very lucky. Extremely lucky. Uh, and I think we've worked hard too. But I think it's a story of luck. So the moral is, you know, try some – try your luck. To anyone.

7. Um, I – I think, uh, THE CLUB is a group that has come together to do quality theater, which is something that is a primal need in New York and probably everywhere. Um, I think we are committed to – to – to that kind of work, that kind of quality work. And we will continue to do so as long as we get support from – from very

wealthy people. I think that – that our work keeps getting better, too. I think we're just, like, a big group of talented people that have come together. That's what I think.

God. Um, the moral of this story is, is you have to stay with that little seed of desire that you have as a young person. And you have to take a risk. Because no matter how difficult it gets, that little voice inside of you that says there's something to share, there is something to strive for, you have to pursue that. And I think that along the way it gets very cloudy. And it – and it can get very sad and sort of – there's a lot up against it, you know. There's the financial end of – of the production. There's the – there's just a lot of crap in the way. And I think that you have to persevere. Um, and I think that that's what THE CLUB does. I think that it overcomes a lot of obstacles.

The Apprentices

1. Oh my God. Um, well, it started out as a group of people who wanted to, uh, sort of set up a, uh, a – a, uh, a process like a factory to develop plays. Um, uh, they went through various incarnations. Different theaters where they tried things out. Um, the group changed and grew. Um, then production entered into the picture with a one-act festival started by actors. Um, yeah. The role of the actors was always important, um, in the process – progress of THE APPRENTICES. Um, and then with, uh, production came a little bit of recognition. And, uh, the original developmental process shifted. Um, it wasn't the main focus any longer. And, uh, then it went through some hard times financially, so it couldn't produce. And I think, uh, it still is in a little bit of a situation of limbo as to how to – what the next step is.

Hmm. The moral of the story. Well, maybe the moral of the story is that if you're going to venture into something like this, if you have any inkling of how hard it's going to be or what it's going to take, you should really know exactly, uh, specifically why you want it. And just be clear on what you – be more clear on what – what you want.

2. OUR TEACHER got hired to do an acting class. Um, he did what he usually does. He got fired from the job for, uh, having too much fun. And so did the kids. So they formed a theater company. They put together a couple of shows. And HIS FRIEND and OUR TEACHER became partners. And, uh, formed a theater company which waited – waited, uh, with bad ideas and good feelings for, uh, someone like, uh, like me and MEMBER A and MEMBER B to come along and bring it in the direction of good ideas. And HIS FRIEND and OUR TEACHER and the rest of us have been running with it ever since.

Always listen to me. No. Um, invest in people.

3. Well, OUR TEACHER was a teacher. And he got kicked out by the, uh, school authorities. And the students revolted. And they decided to con – continue the class. And so they found a space, and they continued to have meetings, and that became THE APPRENTICES.

[Uh, could you continue it a little further on into the – towards the present.]

Until the present? Okay. Um, the students, on their own right, they developed and they began doing things and became more and more professional. And that evolved. And as they grew, they brought in more artists. And that became the family of THE APPRENTICES.

"You can do anything you want. At Alice's restaurant." I mean, I don't – I don't know. I mean, um, I don't know. Uh, the moral of the story. Um, I think we're still in the middle of it. So I – in the development of it. So I don't think there is a moral. But I think it's all going to work out fine.

4. The short. Okay. Um, THE APPRENTICES began with a group of kids who went to school together and who didn't want to stop doing what they were doing and they wanted to keep going. And so they, uh, graduated and they – they stayed together. And they, uh, kept on challenging each other and formed a theater company and did whatever was in front of them. And found a home and a space, then got another space and kept going. And through the years of being together, um, they attracted more actors and more playwrights and more directors and – and they got a name for themselves. And, um, and they're still beginning. I mean, they're still here. And they're 8 years now. So that's what it's about.

Um, never give up on yourself, no matter what you want.

5. Uh, short version. Um, OUR TEACHER is a teacher. Met up with a group – group of excited and exciting students. And as far as I know, they just wanted to keep working and did.

Um, that even in New York if you believe in your work you can make it happen. You don't have to be a victim to – to the conventional system of auditioning, classes. You can make what you want happen.

The Seminarians

1. Okay. Um, THE SEMINARIANS came together as an acting/training program in 1983 organized by OUR FOUNDER and OUR OTHER LEADER. Um, they taught us a new system of acting that OUR FOUNDER had devised based on the later writings of Stanislavsky, based on the writings of Joseph Campbell, Bruno Bettelheim, William James, uh, stoic philosophy, uh, _____, who was a student of Stanislavsky's. It was, uh, a technique of acting that deemphasizes character and emphasizes telling the story of the play according to the writer's intentions and living truthfully under the imaginary circumstances of the play. After studying with OUR FOUNDER and OUR OTHER LEADER for 2 years, we formed a theater company, produced in Maine, produced in Boston, come back to New York. Um, had a big success in New York with PLAY A, which was done at THEATER A. Which raised the visibility of the company and made it an Equity company. Um, continued to seek out good new American plays to do. Uh, in '89 finally branched into classics by doing Shakespeare and now doing Chekhov and later – in the future doing Ionesco. Um, that would be it.

Gosh, I don't know. I'd like to be cooperative and give you one, but I don't know if the moral – if the moral has revealed itself yet. Um, all right. I'll qualify it. I'll say I don't think I know the moral of the story yet, because I don't think the story is over. But if I had to say what the moral of the story was right now, I would say the moral of the story is the – the best way to realize anything – any goal or any vision – is to form – to – to identify a vision, to identify a group of people that share that vision and to work as a group towards the vision. That none of us as individuals would be anywhere, finally. We might have wherever our various careers would be, um, but the – THE SEMINARI-ANS – is a group of individuals with a shared vision or a shared idea of what theater can do, and that keeps us together. And having a group of people who believe in the same thing gives us an oasis from the rest of the community, gives us a strength to produce work that we otherwise probably couldn't do as individuals. I think the moral of the story is find a bunch of people you want to spent a lot of time with.

3. Hmm. Well, it's a group of people that, you know, basically followed the same mentor for all these years. And, um, and want a common, um, somewhat common, uh, goal in – in their lives at this point. Which is to – to have a company that they can kind of come and go from. And also, I think, have their own careers outside of the company. And, um, we'll see if it can – can work. I mean, I – you know, there's a lot of – of, um, um, examples of things that didn't work. And not that many that did. So, especially in New York. I mean, that's not the history, but –

I think the moral is that you should – that, um, that what this group can teach is that, um, you should try, you know, it's not what you want isn't that far away for you not to try to do it. Because, um, you know, people think that – that, "Oh, well, you know, that's impossible to do." And this group has done a lot of those things. And it's not so far away from, you know, from the from just sitting down with some common sense and thinking it through.

4. The story of the group. Um, okay. Well, the story of the group is it is a group of students that studied with OUR FOUNDER a specific technique of acting which they found more accessible and more practical than the other techniques they had been studying. They started out as a theater company in, uh, 1983 and since then have been embracing HIS TECHNIQUE, which is what OUR FOUNDER's technique is, and have been trying to strive to embrace the technique and embrace this, uh, philosophy of theater and life to a certain extent in their work. Um, we've been – we've done most – mainly new plays. And, as I said before, I got involved in 1987. And I'm one of the only people who didn't go to NYU. Uh, and it's – it's been a company about doing new work and striving for this technique and showing this technique and this philosophy of acting. And, uh, challenging ourselves. And I would say that would – that would be about it.

The moral of the story? Uh, the moral of the story is have a clear goal and work for it. Commit yourself to it, and you'll see the results.

5. Okay. Uh, we – we were founded by OUR FOUNDER, um, after two summer workshops that he conducted in Maine, uh, and OUR OTHER LEADER, who's our resident

director. They founded the company, uh, based on this acting technique that they taught us. And, uh, we started producing plays, putting on plays in 1985. We went to Boston for a year, 1986, before we decided to tackle New York. We came back. Um, we did some productions of one-acts to raise money. We went to Maine again to workshop new productions and bring them back to New York. We rented different spaces until, uh, we were eventually produced by THEATER A, PLAY A. Which kind of put us on the map. Um, and then we, uh, continued to dedicate ourselves to working with new playwrights and doing new works. And, uh, gained over the years more and more momentum, until we were able to hire a managing director and – and – and a staff, uh, which consists of managing director and the artistic director and a production manager. And got to the point where we could afford our own space and we bought our own theater. And that's where we are now.

Um, to go out and create your own theater. You know, don't wait for it to happen to you. Because your life will pass you by. And, um, really assess the reason why you are an actor or a director or a writer. Um, well, writers probably just do it anyway. But I mean, as an actor, um, it's really important to just work and that's the thing, create it yourself.

6. One-page version of the story of the group. Here's a group of people that basically didn't know each other, thrown together, studied together. Uh, ended up with a quick common history and decided to form a company out of it. That took themselves away, sort of went into exile to Boston for a while. Um, which really solidified the bonds of the company. Um, and came back to keep itself together over time. Um, to produce – with goals of producing great theater. Not with really the goals of becoming famous. I mean I think that the really true goals, and we were also younger at the time, true goals of the company were really to produce great theater and still are, uh, above everything else. Uh, so, uh, and now it's just got its own home and is trying to recreate – refind ourselves and – and start to now, with a chance – with easier – with an easier way of producing that theater, uh, now its going to become.

What would I say is the moral of this story? The moral of the story is that if you put enough energy into something, you're doomed to be stuck with it. And doomed to love it, you know. I think that's the moral of the story, really. If you – if you close your eyes and kind of step out into the void, you're going to end up in the void and have to deal with it. And so – and so that's – that's what – that's the moral. No, I guess perseverance also, you know.

7. Uh-huh. Um, the company is a group of actors, directors and writers who – who came together, um, studying a technique taught by OUR FOUNDER called HIS TECH-NIQUE. The group, uh, decided to f – to form a company based on this – this technique and these principles, um, applied to theater. That's how the company got together. And, um, we've stayed together because we have this common goal and this common tech-nique.

Oh _____. I don't know. Oh, yeah I do. I think that the moral of the story for me personally is that – that I was given a gift by OUR FOUNDER, which is: one, the technique, and two, the freedom of having this person that we respected so much say create your own work. Do your own thing. That that's going to make it happen for you. Rather than getting out of school and going, "Where do I start in this big wide world?" So we were given that thing. And what's come out of it would be, um, a great part of my life experience. You know, even if it – even if it's only 10 years of my life. Uh, I have learned so much. Even if I don't continue acting. The moral is that I think that we've all grown personally in a very specific way because of that.

References

Barclay, C. (1986). Schematization of autobiographical memory. In D. C. Rubin (Ed.) *Autobiographical memory*. Cambridge, UK: Cambridge University Press.

Bartlett, F. C. (1932). *Remembering*. Cambridge, UK: Cambridge University Press.

Bransford, J., & Johnson, M. (1972). Contextual prerequisites for understanding. *Journal of Verbal Learning and Verbal Behavior, 11,* 717–726.

Bruner, J. (1990). *Acts of meaning*. Cambridge, MA: Harvard University Press.

—— (1991). The narrative construction of reality. *Critical Inquiry*, Autumn, 1–21.

Bruner, J., & Feldman, C. (1993). Theories of mind and the problem of autism. In S. Baron-Cohen, H. Tager-Flusberg, & D. Cohen (Eds.). *Understanding other minds: The perspective from autism*. Cambridge, UK: Cambridge University Press.

d'Azevedo, W. (1962). Uses of the past in Gola discourse. *Journal of African History, 3*(1), 11–34. Partly reprinted in Neisser (1982) as "Tribal history in Liberia."

Feldman, C. (1991a). Oral metalanguage. In D. Olson & N. Torrance (Eds.) *Literacy and orality* (pp. 47–65). Cambridge, UK: Cambridge University Press.

—— (1991b). Genres as mental models. In M. Ammaniti & D. Stern (Eds.), *Rappresentazioni and narrazioni*, Rome-Bari: Laterza (in Italian). English translation (1994). New York University Press.

Feldman, C., Bruner, J., Kalmar, D., & Renderer, B. (1993). Plot, plight, and dramatism: Interpretation at three ages. *Human development, 36*(6), 327–342, with a Reply to Olson and Salter, 346–349. Also, with a methodological appendix, in W. F. Overton & D. S. Palermo (Eds.) (1994) *The nature and ontogenesis of meaning*. Hillsdale, NJ: Lawrence Erlbaum.

Geertz, C. (1983). *Local knowledge*. New York: Basic Books.

Goodman, N. (1978). *Ways of worldmaking*. Hassocks, Sussex: Harvester.

Linton, M. (1986). Ways of searching and the contents of memory. In D. C. Rubin (Ed.), *Autobiographical memory* (pp. 50–67). Cambridge, UK: Cambridge University Press.

Mead, G. H. (1934). *Mind, self, and society*. Chicago: University of Chicago Press.

Neisser, U. (Ed.) (1982). *Memory observed*. San Francisco: W. H. Freeman.

Nelson, K. (Ed.) (1989). *Narratives from the crib*. Cambridge, MA: Harvard University Press.

Olson, D., & Salter, D. (1993). Commentary on Bruner, Feldman, Kalmar, & Renderer, "Plot, plight, and dramatism: Interpretation at three ages." *Human development, 36*(6), 343–345.

Pichert, J., & Anderson, R. (1977). Taking different perspectives on a story. *Journal of Educational Psychology, 69,* 309–315.

Propp, V. (1968). *Morphology of the folktale* (2nd ed.). Austin: University of Texas Press.

Rubin, D. C. (Ed.). (1986). *Autobiographical memory*. Cambridge, UK: Cambridge University Press.

—— (In press). Stories about stories. In T. K. Srull & R. S. Wyer, Jr. (Eds.). *Knowledge and memory: The real story*. Hillsdale, NJ: Lawrence Erlbaum.

Sacks, O. (1993–1994). An anthropologist on Mars. (1993, December 27/1994, January 3). *The New Yorker*.

13   Memories of college: The importance of specific educational episodes

David B. Pillemer, Martha L. Picariello,
Anneliesa Beebe Law, and Jill S. Reichman

This chapter addresses the issue of how specific educational events are remembered, and how they influence the lives of college students and alumni. Mainstream psychological and educational researchers have rarely looked at the impact of specific college events on students. Rather, research has focused on learning and retention of course content, as assessed by exams, written assignments, standardized tests, and graduation rates. Acquiring general knowledge is seen as paramount, not remembering the specifics of how or when the knowledge was acquired. Endel Tulving (1983, p. 51), perhaps the world's leading authority on episodic memory, stated that "children and people of all ages go to school in order to learn skills and knowledges that they need for life. They do not go to school in order to acquire a storehouse of temporally dated personal memories."

Educational psychologists are not alone in their neglect of the specific. The primary focus in educational research on general rather than episodic learning is consistent with dominant research strategies in cognitive psychology. Tulving (1983) commented that episodic memory "has received little direct attention from psychologists or other scientists" (p. 1), and that "experiments done in the past *can* be interpreted as episodic- rather than semantic-memory experiments . . . but they were not designed as part of a grand plan to understand how people remember personal experiences" (p. 129). This situation is changing. Once one accepts the idea that people's subjective experience of memory, and the belief systems associated with memory, are topics worthy of study in their own right, then research can address areas of personal experience for which controlled experimentation is not possible. In the years following Neisser's (1982) advocation of research on memory in natural contexts, psychologists have increasingly turned their attention to personal memories. For example, "flashbulb" memories of learning about

The research described in this chapter was supported by a grant from the Spencer Foundation and by the Class of 1932 Social Science Research Fund of Wellesley College. A summary of the research was presented at the American Psychological Society Convention, San Diego, CA, 1992. Lisa Haueisen provided research assistance, and Richard Light and David Rubin provided valuable comments on an earlier draft.

shocking newsworthy events have been examined extensively and systematically (Winograd & Neisser, 1992).

In this chapter, we identify a potentially rich but relatively unexplored source of information about the form and function of personal event memories: educational experiences. Our focus is squarely on the specific. One potentially important influence on students' lives is the *educational episode* – a pinpointed, one-moment-in-time event that occurs in an educational context. Teachers do much more than transmit general knowledge. They also present information in idiosyncratic and potentially memorable ways, they have pivotal conversations with individual students, they write detailed and personalized comments on student assignments, and they interact closely with students on an informal as well as a formal basis. An autobiographical statement written by the distinguished child psychologist Jerome Kagan provides one clear example:

My commitment to chemistry was also weakened by a psychology professor's idle comment in the introductory psychology course. He had posed a question I cannot remember, but to which I apparently gave a good answer. He asked me to stay and as we walked across the campus he said I had an apperceptive feeling for psychology and added, "You would probably be a good psychologist." The sentence rings as clearly now as it did that afternoon 22 years ago. I began to think about psychology more seriously. (1972, p. 140)

Dale Marshall, President of Wheaton College and former Dean of Wellesley College, reported a similarly influential encounter with a professor:

I still remember vividly how lonely I felt when I walked into my dorm room at Cornell University for the first time. . . . Two conversations with experienced Cornellians also helped tremendously in making me feel at home. The first was with a professor in an introductory Political Science class. Knowing that it is hard to adjust to new academic expectations, he took special care after the first mid-term to talk about writing essay exams. Then he read portions of student answers as examples of how to write good answers. Mine was one of the anonymous examples used. That gave me the courage to talk with him after class, and the ensuing friendly informal conversation ended my reticence about talking to professors (and probably started me on the path to becoming a Political Science professor myself). (Marshall, 1986, p. 11)

Comments made by a former student of Harvard historian Simon Schama suggest that seemingly idiosyncratic episodes such as these may not be uncommon:

The ebullience, attentiveness, structure, and entertainer's flair . . . that Schama brought to each lecture was unsurpassed in this former student's experience, and the personal investment and accessibility that characterized his relations with freshmen and Ph.D. candidates alike belied any critic berating the supposed inattentiveness of Harvard's senior faculty. . . . Had [the author of an article on Schama] consulted yet more of those legions of students who have enjoyed Professor Schama's incisive intellect and ever-expansive grasp of material, he would have found not one but hundreds of memorable anecdotes – and not a few students whose lives (intellectual and otherwise) were changed in the process. (Ariev, 1992, p. 12)

Autobiographical anecdotes such as these suggest that specific interactions with professors can have lasting consequences, but there is a need for more systematic and comprehensive analysis. Are influential educational episodes commonly remembered? What is the structure and content of the memories? How are they distributed in time? How do specific, idiosyncratic experiences influence students' attitudes and behaviors, including the choice of a major, postgraduate plans, and, more generally, how students plan to live their lives? What types of student-faculty interactions are especially influential? How can the quality of these interactions be improved? This chapter begins to address these questions.

Previous research on the college experience

Previous analyses of memorable encounters during college have been largely anecdotal and descriptive. For example, Beidler (1986) questioned finalists for the Professor of the Year Award of the Council for Advancement and Support of Education. The respondents identified specific teachers, courses, and experiences from their undergraduate years that had had a profound impact on their academic careers. Meier (1986) provided case examples of the "small moments" of learning: "They are the odd and quirky moments that spin off from a teacher's love of the moment and willingness to improvise, go on a hunch, to take a risk, to deviate a little. . . . For the student, such moments are like morals to fables. . . . They can be hidden in the cracks and crevices of one's education and brought out for reference as one needs them" (p. 300). Although suggestive, studies such as these do not provide a systematic account of memorable episodes occurring in educational contexts.

Larger-scale quantitative analyses of the effects of a college education on students have not directly assessed the impact of specific educational episodes. For example, although prior research has examined the relation between the quantity of student-faculty contact and educational outcomes, little systematic information exists about what actually happens in influential interchanges between students and professors. Astin (1993) recently attempted to answer the question, "What matters in college?," with an impressively large-scale multivariate study. He concluded that frequent interaction between faculty and students was of "critical importance to student development" (p. 384). Pascarella and Terenzini's *How College Affects Students* (1991) is an extraordinarily thorough review of the quantitative research literature within traditional educational psychology. The reviewed studies indicated that "faculty members' impact . . . is enhanced when student-faculty interactions extend beyond the formal classroom setting" (p. 393). For example, interactions with professors can influence students' academic interests and career choices. Yet neither Astin's study nor Pascarella and Terenzini's review provides a direct analysis of the structure and content of memories of influential encounters between professors and students. As a result, we do not know why and how such interactions are influential, and the precise circumstances that promote influential interactions have not been identified.

Our previous research addressed the issue of educational episodes more directly and systematically. In a series of questionnaire studies, undergraduates attending Harvard and Wellesley recounted memories of their first year in college (Pillemer, Rhinehart, & White, 1986). Respondents described the first four memories that came to mind, with no restrictions on content, and then answered a series of direct questions about the remembered events. Specific episodes were commonly reported; most of the memories described one moment-in-time events (such as a conversation with a roommate or a particular final exam) rather than more general occurrences (such as the quality of the relationship with a roommate or general reactions to exams during first year). Memory content was by no means limited to academic themes; in fact, a majority of memories focused on other topics such as recreation or housing. Respondents' ratings of the remembered events identified elevated emotional reactions as a common characteristic of memorable episodes, whereas mean ratings of life impact were at or below the moderate level.

The temporal distribution of memories across the academic year showed a marked peak at the point of transition into college, with about 30% of all first-year memories occurring in the month of September. The pronounced clustering of memories in September was not simply a result of students starting their memory search at the beginning of the specified time interval; clustering in September occurred whether the students were asked to provide memories of events occurring during the traditional 9-month academic year (September to May) or during an alternative 9-month interval (February of senior year in high school to October of freshman year in college).

This general pattern of results was confirmed in a follow-up study of memories of the first year in college provided by Wellesley alumnae (Pillemer, Goldsmith, Panter, & White, 1988). Questionnaires were sent to alumnae who had graduated from college 2, 12, or 22 years earlier. A majority of memories described specific episodes rather than general or repeated occurrences, although the proportion of specific memories decreased as the number of years since graduation increased. Memories focused more often on nonacademic than on academic themes. The temporal distribution of memories across the 9-month academic year showed a sharp clustering in September, with about 40% of memories occurring in September for all three alumnae groups. Most of the remembered events were rated as at least moderately emotional, whereas mean ratings of life impact were below the moderate level.

Perhaps the most striking finding of these studies is the pronounced and consistent overrepresentation of memories at the point of transition into college. We have also found memory clustering at the beginning of the first academic year using other study designs. Panter and Pillemer (1987) examined first year students' memories of a particular college course at Wellesley. Professor's statements spoken during the first week of class were overrepresented in memory relative to statements spoken at other time periods. Pillemer, Krensky, Kleinman, Goldsmith, and White (1991) analyzed Harvard undergraduates' oral histories of the first year in college. Students frequently opened their oral accounts with a discussion of activities that had occurred at the beginning of the school year. Robinson (1986) also examined memories reported by college students and found a clustering of memories in August, which for students in the location studied (Kentucky) marked the end of summer and the start of the academic year.

The clustering of memories at points of life transition suggests that the memories serve a directive function (Pillemer, 1992; Pillemer, Koff, Rhinehart, & Rierdan, 1987; Pillemer, Rhinehart, & White, 1986). At transition points, events are novel and distinctive. Entering students are unaccustomed to college routines and college scripts are not yet fully formed; as a result students may be particularly attentive to early episodes that convey information about how to live and act in the new environment. In this sense, the time interval encompassing a life transition may be a "critical period" for the encoding of vivid episodic memories. These early events may be frequently revisited in memory and may continue to influence attitudes and behaviors long after the original moment of occurrence.

Memories of influential college events: Two new questionnaire studies

Our earlier questionnaire studies demonstrated that college students and alumnae can readily access vivid memories of specific educational episodes, and that transitional and emotional events are especially likely to persist in memory. Respondents were not asked to report particularly influential memories; rather, they simply described the first college experiences that came to mind. Our initial follow-up study, to be reported here, extended the scope of earlier work to include the issue of influence: What is the structure, content, and temporal distribution of freshman year memories when college students are asked explicitly about influential events? A second limitation of earlier studies is the exclusive focus on the first college year. It could be argued that much of what is truly influential about college happens later on, after this initial period of transition and flux. Unable to identify freshman year events that have proven to be of lasting influence, respondents may simply describe their memorable initial encounters with the new environment. In a second follow-up study, also described below, Wellesley alumnae recounted memories of influential events that had occurred at any point in their 4 years of college. This study provides a broader and richer look at the form and function of influential college experiences.

Students' memories of influential events from the first year in college

This study provided a replication of earlier questionnaire studies, with one procedural change: students were asked to describe influential events from the first year in college.

Respondents. Participants were 43 Wellesley College students (11 juniors and 32 seniors) who responded to notices posted on campus. Students were paid $4.00 for their participation. Because Wellesley is a women's college, all participants were female.

Questionnaire. Students completed a two-part questionnaire. Part 1 first asked for a description of an influential freshman year experience:

We are exploring peoples' memories of influential experiences while in college. In the space below, please describe a memory of an *influential* experience that occurred during your *freshman year in college*. The memory can focus on *any* topic. Your description can be as long or as short as you deem necessary. Please be as *precise* as possible; include any remembered details even if they do not seem particularly important now. Write on the back of this page if necessary.

Students were then asked for a second, third, and fourth memory of an influential experience from their freshman year in college, and they provided some personal information (e.g., their age and year in college). Part 2 of the questionnaire contained additional questions about the four memories that had been described in Part 1. Respondents rated on a 5-point scale the intensity of emotion experienced, the level of surprise that they felt, the impact of the experience on their lives at the time of the event and in retrospect, and the clarity of the memory. They also estimated when during freshman year the experience had occurred, described the emotions they felt, estimated the number of times that they had previously recounted the memory, and commented on how the experience had influenced their lives. Finally, students answered some general questions about the quality of their adjustment to college.

Temporal distribution of memories. Most (83%) memories were assigned a single month of occurrence. The distribution of these datable memories across the 9-month academic year is presented in Figure 13.1. The memories show a pronounced peak at the beginning of the academic year, with 32% of the remembered events occurring in the month of September. The temporal distribution of influential events is strikingly similar to distributions based on the first memories of freshman year to come to mind (Pillemer, Rhinehart, & White, 1986; Pillemer, Goldsmith, Panter, & White, 1988).

Memory structure. As in previous studies (e.g., Pillemer, Goldsmith, Panter, & White, 1988), memories were assigned to one of three structural categories: specific, general, or mixed. (Williams, this volume, uses a similar distinction between specific and general memories to analyze memories reported by depressed individuals.) Specific memories contained an explicit description of a one-moment-in-time event; the event was the focus of the memory. For example:

During one of my French classes, my professor corrected another student in a very harsh manner. The student had made a mistake regarding the reading for the class and the professor yelled and embarrassed the student because she had not done the homework. This might have been a scare tactic since it occurred early in the semester, but I thought it was needless.

General memories consisted of a nonspecific discussion of events, or they summarized repeated events. For example:

Being involved in House Council: I became involved in House Council in my dorm because I had been feeling somewhat isolated to the people in my dorm. By so doing I got to know a lot of other students and I am now good friends with some of them. From the House Council experience – I learnt a lot of things about how student activities were organized at Wellesley College and who was responsible for what. In a way this experience gave me a broad overview of the residential student life.

Mixed memories clearly contained both specific and general components. Two individuals coded all of the memories and intercoder agreement was 81%. Disagreements were resolved by discussion.

Consistent with previous questionnaire studies, specific memories of influential freshman year events were frequently recounted: a majority (60%) of memories were categorized as specific, whereas 22% were general, and 18% were mixed.

Characteristics of the remembered events. Memories were assigned by two coders to one of several content categories: academics, recreation and leisure, housing, romance, or miscellaneous. Intercoder agreement was 76%. The request for memories of influen-

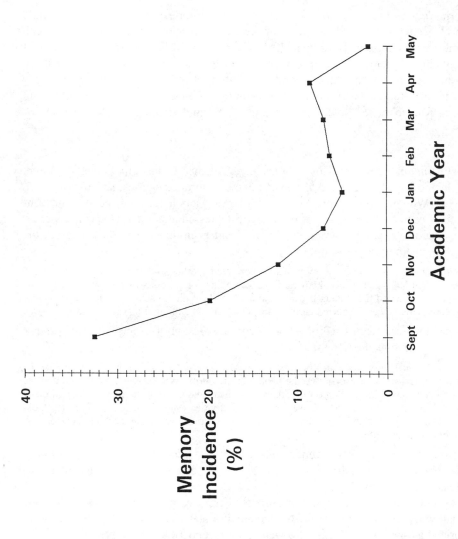

Figure 13.1 Temporal distribution of freshman year memories. (Respondents were current Wellesley juniors and seniors.)

tial events did not increase the proportion of academic memories compared to previous studies in which students reported the first memories that came to mind; only 17% of memories focused on academic activities.

Memory ratings indicated that the remembered events were perceived as being strongly emotional ($M = 3.83$ on a 5-point scale), moderately surprising ($M = 3.12$), having moderate life impact at the time of the event ($M = 3.25$), and having moderate to strong life impact in retrospect ($M = 3.40$). Ratings of emotion and life impact are slightly higher in the present study than in past studies (Pillemer, Rhinehart, & White, 1986) where the focus was on the first events to come to mind rather than on influential events. Ratings of the emotional quality of the remembered events captured the difficulties new students often experience while making the transition to college life: Only 26% of influential first-year happenings were rated as positive, 30% were rated as negative, 39% were rated as mixed, and 6% were rated as neutral.

Alumnae memories of influential college experiences

In this study, Wellesley College alumnae recounted memories of influential experiences that had happened at any time during their 4 years of college.

Respondents. In 1989, 600 questionnaires were sent to Wellesley College alumnae representing the graduating classes of 1968, 1978, and 1988; 200 randomly selected alumnae from each graduating class were included in the sample. Usable questionnaires were returned by 164 alumnae ($n = 64, 51$, and 49 for the classes of 1968, 1978, and 1988, respectively).

Questionnaire. Respondents completed a two-part questionnaire. For Part 1, they described three separate influential college experiences and provided personal background information. For Part 2, they answered direct questions about the experiences that they had recounted in Part 1. They rated on ordered 5-point scales the intensity of emotion experienced, the perceived life impact at the time of the event and in retrospect, and the clarity of the memory. They also estimated when the event had occurred, identified the type of emotion felt, estimated the number of times they had previously recounted the memory, described situations in which the memory came to mind, and indicated how the event had been influential. Finally, respondents provided information about their transition to college, the quality of their college experience, and their activities following graduation from Wellesley.

Temporal distribution of memories. Because the three alumnae groups produced similar temporal distributions of memories, the data were combined. About one-half (47%) of memories were assigned a specific month and year of occurrence; other college experiences spanned more than 1 month or year, or were not precisely datable. Precisely datable memories are clearly overrepresented during the transitional first college year: 37% of remembered events occurred during freshman year, whereas 22%, 14%, and 26% of remembered events fell in sophomore, junior, and senior years, respectively. Including events datable to a specific year but not a specific month resulted in a similar, but flatter, distribution. The very low incidence of junior year memories is probably attributable in part to the relatively large proportion of students who spend junior year away from Wellesley; these alumnae may have been reluctant to report nonWellesley events. Nevertheless, the same overall pattern of results is still evident when students who spent junior year away are omitted from the analysis.

Figure 13.2 shows the distribution of memories across the 9-month academic year for each year in college separately; entries represent the proportion of all datable memories that occurred during the specified month and year. Memories clearly cluster at the beginning of freshman year, with 25% of influential events from the entire pool of datable memories, representing all 4 college years, occurring during the first 3 months of freshman year. A second, smaller peak exists at the other obvious transition point, the end of senior year; 10% of all datable influential events occurred in April or May of senior year.

Memory structure. Two coders assigned memories to one of three structural categories used in previous studies: specific, general, or mixed. Intercoder agreement was 74%, and disagreements were resolved by discussion. Many of the disagreements involved conflicts between the specific and mixed categories. In their description of a specific influential event, some respondents provided extensive background information and context, and added interpretative conclusions; when categorizing these memories, one coder favored the specific category and the other coder favored the mixed category.

Because structural characteristics of the memories were similar across the three alumnae groups, the data were combined. Specific episodic memories were prominently represented among alumnae recollections of influential college experiences: a majority (51%) of memories focused on a specific event, 28% were general, and 20% were mixed.

Characteristics of the remembered events. Memories were assigned to one of two content categories: academic or nonacademic; intercoder agreement was 91%. The proportion of academic memories was 43%, approximately twice the proportion observed in previous studies of memories of freshman year only. The lower proportion of academic than nonacademic influential memories (43% versus 57%) may be attributable in part to the fact that all respondents were female; when asked to report a college incident that was especially important to them, Light (1990) found that Harvard women were far more likely than men to recount nonacademic events.

Memory ratings indicated that the remembered events were perceived as being strongly emotional ($M = 3.96$), having moderate life impact at the time of the event ($M = 3.08$), and having moderate to strong life impact in retrospect ($M = 3.60$). Year of graduation comparisons revealed that mean ratings of life impact in retrospect decreased with increasing years since graduation. Ratings of the emotional quality of the experiences again demonstrated a diversity of emotional reactions to influential college events: 37% were rated as positive, 30% were negative, 29% were mixed, and 3% were neutral.

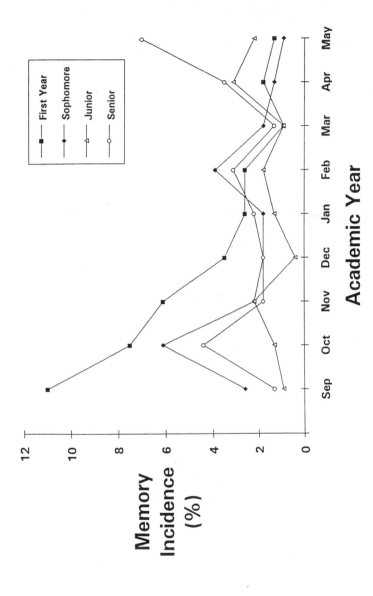

Figure 13.2 Temporal distribution of academic year memories for each year in college separately. (Respondents were Wellesley alumnae.)

327

Summary of quantitative patterns revealed by questionnaire studies

The two new questionnaire studies of influential college experiences described above, taken together with previous studies exploring the first college memories to come to mind, present a highly consistent pattern of results. The pattern holds for Harvard and Wellesley students, and for current students and alumnae up to 22 years after graduation. Although academic educational psychology has been primarily concerned with general learning, specific college events are commonly remembered in vivid detail. In these episodes, the influence is perceived to have been transmitted through particular comments or actions by a peer or professor, or some other identifiable and datable occurrence, rather than by entire courses, broad readings, or the general curriculum. Many of the remembered events focus on nonacademic themes, and they are often described as highly emotional. The memories are not evenly distributed throughout the college experience; instead, they demonstrate a marked temporal clustering at transition points: the beginning of college and, to a lesser extent, the end of senior year.

This brief summary leaves many questions unanswered. Why do specific educational episodes persist in memory for years? What is the functional significance of memory clustering at transition points? What lessons do the the memories hold for educators and for memory researchers? These questions are addressed in the following section.

Analysis of memory function

Following Bruce (1989), we use the term *memory function* to refer to "the real-world usefulness or adaptive significance of memory mechanisms" (p. 45). Two different senses of function are implied in Bruce's definition. An analysis of college memories that illuminates the "adaptive significance of memory mechanisms" would explore basic theoretical issues about how memory operates, such as how and why transitional episodes come to have a privileged status in autobiographical memory. An analysis that illuminates "the real-world usefulness" of college memories would focus on the ways that recollection influences students' or graduates' life decisions, feelings and attitudes, and also on the ways that the memories can inform educational practice.

In this section we explore both senses of Bruce's definition of memory function. The first topic to be addressed – directive functions – illustrates potential adaptive advantages of remembering specific educational episodes. The other topics focus on aspects of faculty-student interaction, revealed by analyses of memory content, that are potentially relevant to educational practice – including emotional quality, timing, and personal connection. To illustrate these aspects of memory function, we broaden our perspective to include qualitative analysis of individual memories in addition to inspection of broader quantitative patterns in the data.

Directive functions

Why are specific educational episodes remembered in vivid detail years later? From the perspective of memory theory, there are several possible causal mechanisms. One candidate is the strong emotion experienced at the time of the events, as reflected by the respondents' elevated ratings of emotional intensity (Pillemer, Rhinehart, & White, 1986). Another possibility is event novelty or distinctiveness; some of the remembered events involved unique, transitional, or first-time happenings, that are unlikely to be absorbed readily into college scripts (Pillemer, Goldsmith, Panter, & White, 1988).

From a functional perspective, educational episodes may persist in memory and continue to be perceived as influential because of the valuable messages that they contain. This directive function of episodic memories has been described in detail elsewhere (Pillemer, 1992). Although behaviors are often directed by generalized expectations or scripts, periods of life transition are characterized by uncertainty and require profound emotional and cognitive adaptations (Stewart, Sokol, Healy, Chester, & Weinstock-Savoy, 1982). During critical transitions "the perturbation to the person-in-environment system is experienced as so potent that the ongoing modes of transacting with the physical, interpersonal, and socio-cultural features of the environment no longer suffice" (Wapner, 1981, p. 223). At these times of life transition, the individual may be especially attentive to environmental cues. Unarmed with an established college script with which to organize one's activities, the student attends closely to salient events that occur in the new environment. Memories of specific transitional events often are capable of fulfilling a predictive or directive function. For example, Tulving (1983) commented that there is a scripted protocol that one acquires for attending dinner at old Oxford colleges, but that "if you have only been to one such dinner, you may still be able to answer many of the same questions [about dinner protocol] on the basis of your recollection of the particular event" (p. 64).

The marked clustering of memories at the beginning of the first year in college is consistent with the idea that the memories provide directives for behaviors and attitudes. Although it may not be possible to anticipate which particular events will be influential and memorable, there may be identifiable life periods during which specific episodes command special attention and take on heightened importance: "A science of psychology does not have much to say about the occurrence of fortuitous intersects. . . . However, psychological knowledge can provide the basis for predicting the nature, scope, and strength of the impact they will have on human lives" (Bandura, 1982, p. 749). Bandura (1982) analyzed the effects of chance encounters on life paths and concluded that it is at times of uncertainty that "fortuitous influences more easily hold sway" (p. 751).

Some of the directives contained in college memories are explicit and obvious to the reader. For example:

I remember a late night chat with neighboring sophomores shortly after arriving to Wellesley my first year. These older and wiser women were telling me and my roomies that we did *not* go to a "girls' school"; we attend a *Women's College* and be sure to correct anyone who says otherwise. I also remember that we discussed male/female roles. . . . We specifically talked about how men and women act when passing each other on the streets – the woman will look at the man only briefly and then will look away whereas a man will simply continue to stare at a woman. . . . Someone said we should be able to stare down any man particularly here on our own turf. I distinctly remember trying it when passing an MIT exchange student on campus and realized *he* was completely shocked/surprised by my "boldness."

The student reported that her attitudes and behaviors were altered by this salient late-night encounter. In describing how the event influenced her life, this alumna stated that she "became instantly aware of the male/female aspect of society; realized much role playing would (or should) be absent from Wellesley society; I felt much more powerful when I realized I could act contrary to society's expectation which didn't make sense anyway." The alumna also commented on a longer-term "directive": "Later on in my career in banking, I think I was a much better negotiator knowing that it was OK to act like a Banker (professional) and not be forced to take a 'female' role."

In many other memories, the directive is not explicit but is implied by the memory content. For example:

My first Shakespeare class . . . would have to rank as one of my most influential experiences, since it started me on the life I'm following now (graduate school in Elizabethan literature). But the memory I have from that class is very small and tight. Oh well. Although I have good feelings and good memories about the entire class (1st semester of sophomore year) I remember the first day best. I was fascinated by the easy way [the professor] roamed through Shakespeare, by just the amount of knowledge he had. He seemed to know everything. In fact, after class, I asked him if he could identify a quote I had found about fencing "Keep up your bright swords, for the dew will rust them." Immediately he said "*Othello*, Act 1, Scene 2 I believe." Which turned out to be exactly right. I wanted know a body of literature that well. I'm still working on it.

In this instance, the perceived directive – pursue literature until you achieve a level of excellence – is not spoken directly; rather, it is modeled by the professor.

The Shakespeare example suggests that specific, apparently casual encounters can take on a symbolic, almost mythical quality. Some students and alumnae traced the beginning of a career path, or a belief about themselves or the world, to one particular originating event. The author of the Shakespeare memory is an alumna who was a Ph.D. student in English when she completed the questionnaire. She described the event's influence as follows: "Well, it made me an English major with a concentration in Shakespeare and a desire to teach undergraduates." Another example of this phenomenon is provided by the statement spoken to Jerome Kagan by his introductory psychology professor described earlier – "You would probably be a good psychologist" – that prompted Kagan's switch from chemistry to psychology.

In these examples, the initiating event cannot be accepted at face value as a direct "cause" of the chosen life path. Erikson (1969, 1975) and Runyan (1982) have cautioned against what Erikson called the "originological fallacy," in which life outcomes are causally linked to early events only retrospectively. But the psychological power of the memories cannot be questioned; the connection between originating events and present activities is psychologically real to the rememberer. As Bruner (1987) has argued, "we *become* the autobiographical narratives by which we 'tell about' our lives" (p. 15), so that "a life is not 'how it was' but how it is interpreted and reinterpreted, told and retold" (p. 31). The psychological reality of the event and its active connection to the rememberer's present activities is important regardless of its absolute truth value.

In the preceding examples, there is a direct connection between the specific content of the remembered episode and the chosen life path: interaction with a professor of

English or psychology encouraged the student to pursue a similar career. In other instances, educational episodes exert their influence through analogy rather than direct suggestion or modeling. The memory contains a general lesson about how to live one's life. For example:

A second influential experience that I can recall involved an Art History paper. I wrote about a sculpture from a picture I had, rather than going to the museum to view it as we had been instructed. When I received the paper back it had no grade, but instead a note which said "see me." Upon meeting with the instructor I was informed that the piece about which I wrote was currently being restored. Since I had not followed instructions and written about a piece I had seen, I was required to write another paper. In addition to being extremely embarrassed, I learned a valuable lesson about not taking shortcuts.

The alumna rated the retrospective impact of this event on her life as strong, and wrote that this memory comes to mind "when the temptation to take a shortcut is present." The directive has transcended the particular area of scholarship and type of behavioral transgression.

Another way that the directive function manifests itself is the anchoring event. The pinpointed event anchors a belief system and is frequently revisited in memory. The memory can provide reassurance, direction, or validation, especially in contexts where one's skills or values are questioned. For example:

[A professor] said to us that the most talented people he'd ever known in his life he had seen come through his classrooms at Wellesley, and the obvious high esteem in which he held Wellesley students was an added boost to me. My self-esteem and self-awareness of my own abilities has not ever been low, but in moments since my Wellesley years when my own doubts, or the doubts of others as to my ability to do something have bothered me, I hear this man's words and know I can give it as good a try as *anyone* else could.

In a second example, a professor's statement foretold an unsettling truth about the world outside of Wellesley. The statement anchored a continuing and troubling belief:

I had a professor . . . in my senior year . . . One day in class he said, "The most wasted resource in this country is female brain power." . . . He was not impressed with me or my work particularly. I remember telling myself that he was crazy when he made this remark. I hadn't been out of Wellesley and working for more than 6 months before I found for myself that what he had said was true. Wellesley was an ivory tower in terms of the regard in which women were held; but wider society was far less respectful, and the women in it held themselves in lower esteem. I guess this was an influential experience because I thought about it 1,000 times after I graduated. In fact, when I started writing this I remembered the thinking about the incident better than the incident itself.

This alumna described the incident's influence as follows: "It made me realize that I was a bit out of step with contemporary life and that I held myself to a higher standard of capability than most other women. It made me more aggressive and determined to achieve and this has gotten me into trouble at times."

Current students' memories of the first days of college – arriving at Wellesley, meeting one's roommate, moving into the dorm, attending the first class – may serve an anchoring function of a less dramatic form. Memories of initial college events could serve as mental anchor points much the same way that the entering student's initial place of residence serves as an anchor point for spatial representations of the college environment, and thereby forms a stable base for the organization of behavior in the new environment. Wapner (1981) summarized research demonstrating that college freshmen's spatial maps of the college environment use "a salient anchor-point or base of operations as the organizational principle" (p. 230). The anchor point "continues to maintain its function as a basis for organization, as the new setting becomes cognitively more differentiated and complex with increased exposure to the locale" (p. 230). Research discussed by Wapner also suggests that people make use of social as well as spatial anchor points in their dealings with the interpersonal aspects of a new environment; for example, the social anchor for adjustment to college may be a roommate. Similarly, vivid memories of early college episodes may serve as relatively stable points of comparison and reorientation as the student continues to confront a flood of new and disequilibrating events.

Although the analysis of adaptive significance in this chapter has focused exclusively on various forms of memory directives, the act of remembering specific episodes undoubtedly serves other purposes, such as communicative and emotional functions (Pillemer, 1992). Many college memories do not cluster at critical transition points, and do not serve an obvious prescriptive, originating, or anchoring function. By illustrating the potential value of functional analysis in one limited domain, we hope to encourage similar efforts across a broad spectrum of event types and functional goals.

Educational applications

In this section we provide several concrete examples of how college students' and graduates' memories may provide useful information for educators. The goal is not to lay out a comprehensive plan for improving classroom teaching, but rather to illustrate the potential practical value of examining specific memories. Educational researchers often eschew qualitative analyses of personal experience in favor of quantitative abstractions extracted from multiple cases. Sarason (1993) recently argued that eliminating personal experience from analyses of educational policy is counterproductive: "In fact, in the entire literature, reference to personal experience is very rare. I'm quite aware of the arguments against using personal experience to prove anything or as a basis for a policy recommendation. But what if there are certain types of personal experiences that are so general, so illuminating, so important that they should not be dismissed on grounds of subjectivity?" (p. 10). Similarly, Lampert (1985) has called for an integration of case study and quantitative approaches to educational issues: "Efforts to build generalized theories of instruction, curriculum, or classroom management based on careful empirical research have much to contribute to the improvement of teaching, but they do not sufficiently describe the work of teaching. Such theories and research are limited in their capacity to help teachers know what to do about particular problems" (p. 179).

The approach that we advocate is similar in some respects to the case method of instruction used at Harvard and elsewhere to train teachers and business students. Like college students' written recollections of influential encounters, cases used in training teachers "provide a slice of life, written in an engaging narrative" (McCarthy, 1987,

p. 11). Some educators have been willing to sacrifice quantitative rigor for the practical insights contained in teachers' stories: "These stories capture, more than scores or mathematical formulae ever can, the richness and indeterminacy of our experiences as teachers and the complexity of our understandings of what teaching is and how others can be prepared to engage in this profession" (Carter, 1993, p. 5). For example, most would agree with the general observation that a professor's use of sarcasm can have a devastating effect on some students (Riesman, 1985), but the immediacy, emotionality, and drama of a specific instance recounted by a wounded student is especially persuasive; the concrete and vivid details may enable other educators to clearly identify and avoid similarly damaging situations.

To illustrate several practical lessons for educators contained in students' memories of college, our analysis will focus on memories involving specific influential encounters with professors. The examples are taken primarily from the questionnaire study of influential college memories recounted by Wellesley alumnae described above. Such illustrations are plentiful; although many college memories were about nonacademic topics, most (84%) respondents described at least one academic memory, and almost one-half of these alumnae mentioned a specific interaction with a professor.

Emotional quality. Academic events recounted by Wellesley alumnae were almost evenly assigned to positive, negative, and mixed categories. Positive feedback from professors was almost always viewed retrospectively in a positive light. For example:

My orals for my thesis were a terrifying proposition. I knew I wanted honors *so* I knew I needed to go through the interrogative hell, but that didn't help me calm down any-more . . . one of my most proud moments came after the grueling hour and a half. I was waiting in the Political Science lounge for the judgment of my committee. [A student] started speaking with me . . . when my advisor arrived with the good news. I had passed! I was so proud. Leaving [the building], I ran into my major advisor and a professor of mine whom I idolized. . . . We stood and talked as they heaped praise upon me. I felt so proud about my academic efforts as well as my personal achievements. I had finally accomplished what I came to Wellesley to achieve: self-confidence in my abilities and my self.

Reactions to negative feedback were more complex. In some instances, harsh criticism was devastating emotionally and either resulted in lowered self-esteem or prompted the student to distance herself from what the professor appeared to "stand for." For example:

In my sophomore year, I took an English literature course. I loved the course material, enjoyed writing papers, and felt pretty good about it until. . . . I wrote an essay on my interpretation of a poem. I felt I had great insight into a special meaning within the verse. When the paper was returned, the teacher told me I didn't have any understanding of the material and she hoped I wasn't going to be an English major. I remember her pinched face and small, tight mouth as she said these things to me. I thought no way do I want to be like her. So I changed my major from English to Sociology.

In other instances, the professor gave what the student viewed as strong criticism, but also offered a face-saving way out or means to rectify the situation. In these cases, the student often described the event as having a motivating and ultimately positive

impact on her life, even though the initial experience had been painful. Two examples
follow:

After a terrible 1st year academically, my second year I really began to apply myself. Still,
even though I wanted to do well I had this feeling that I didn't belong at Wellesley; I felt like I
was not "smart enough" to be there and compete. Then, after studying for my [politics] exam
for days, I did terribly on it. My self-confidence was virtually nonexistent. My professor had
written a note on my exam to go talk to him about my grade and I did. He spent an hour going over my exam, showing me how to take an essay exam, and in the end he let me take my
exam over. After a string of C's, I never never received one again. In fact my G.P.A. went
from 2.2 my first semester to a 3.89 my last. That one hour in my [politics] professor's office
had to be [my] most influential experience at Wellesley.

Early in senior year when I was doing honors research and had been working at a comfortable
pace (but probably responding to the immediate deadlines of regular course work) my advisor
called me in to say that things weren't progressing as quickly as they should. She suggested
that perhaps I would be more comfortable with the less demanding requirements of independent research. The "threat" (although it wasn't couched in those terms) of losing my honors status galvanized me and drove me to work at the pace required. . . . I learned that I could
do it, and that independent work had to be scheduled by me and attended to with the same immediacy of externally imposed deadlines. Since then my career has continued to involve both
kinds of deadlines and the lesson learned senior year has served to assure a very successful career as well as personal life.

Timing. In addition to the emotional tone of the feedback, the timing of the interaction
between professor and student is an important consideration. For example, some students appeared to be particularly vulnerable to the negative effects of harsh criticism
during the initial transition to college. For example:

My first writing assignment – freshman year – a description. I described the autumn foliage.
The comment I got back – "too kodachrome" – puzzled me. The colors *were* kodachrome, to
me. There must be something wrong with the way I saw them. Perhaps I remember this because it was part of the process of jettisoning hope and trust and opting for survival which
characterized my first months there.

This memory demonstrates the extreme sensitivity and shaky self-confidence of a beginning student. Had the relatively innocuous comment – "too kodachrome" – come in
a later course or even later in the semester, the student may have been better able to
take it in stride. Entering students lack established routines or scripts to guide thought
and behavior in the college setting, and they may be particularly receptive to external
sources of evaluation and guidance at these times. As was discussed earlier, even casual
input from a highly valued or powerful source, such as a faculty member or parent, may
become an originating event or anchor for a student's subsequent adaptation to the college environment.

Personal connection. On occasion, college professors intentionally or unintentionally
step out of the impersonal professor mold and make a more intimate intellectual or affective connection with a student. The professor may reveal details about his or her own
values, emotions, or private life, or the professor may encourage the student to share
such information about herself. These moments of personal connection can make a last-

ing impression. The student may be especially likely to emulate values, attitudes, or behaviors revealed at these times. For example:

My teacher was . . . something of a tyrant. She would occasionally stand on her desk to make a point, and I was so terrified of not measuring up that I would occasionally be learning vocabulary while brushing my teeth in the cold bathrooms. Nonetheless, [the professor] and I got along fine. She gave me B's; I worked my tail off for them. When I came back from my summer abroad, she took me out to lunch with her, off-campus. I believe we went to the dining room of a small hotel on the edge of town. . . . I was no longer [her] student, yet she desired to know everything about my summer. . . . Wellesley – in my years there – were difficult ones for me, for many reasons, only some of which have to do with the college itself. [The professor] may or may not have sensed this, but the fact that she found my off campus life – my summer – of great interest and import meant a lot to me, and I've not forgotten our lunch. I went on to major in [her area of study], partly because of her attention to me.

Interacting with professors in more intimate or comfortable circumstances may stimulate intellectual growth and insight as well as social and emotional well-being. For example:

Another influential experience involved an outstanding professor . . . [the professor] encouraged me to think beyond the words on the page, and to draw upon other pieces I had read, as well as upon my own experience, to gather the meaning of what I was reading. . . . I do remember that near the end of this class, we were assigned an interpretation of a rather short, but rhythmic piece of poetry. I remember reading it over and over without really understanding what the poet was trying to convey. I left it aside for awhile, and visited [the professor] at her home. . . . We were discussing something completely different from the poem (by this point in the semester, she had become a personal friend), when it "dawned" on me what the poem was about. . . . My face must have shown that I had stumbled upon the answer, because [the professor] asked me what I was thinking about. I replied that I had figured it out! That I had been stumped before this point, and that it was all clear now! I proceeded to explain, without even looking at the poem, what the poet's message was. After I was finished, [the professor] just looked at me, and said "You're absolutely right. I knew you would get it. I'm not sure anyone else will." I was thrilled. And, no one else did get it.

Sometimes the personal contact is fleeting, but is influential nevertheless. In a recent pilot interview, a current Wellesley student attributed her decision to major in biochemistry rather than biology in part to what appeared to be a superficial personal connection with her chemistry professor: "I didn't go to any bio office hours, but I went to her [chemistry professor's] office hours, not very much, more like twice and she knew my name. But it was an intro class and I didn't really expect that, so that was like, you know, an encouraging sign . . . and just very enthusiastic about chemistry."

The detailed memories recounted by Wellesley graduates underscore the potential impact of specific moments of interpersonal connection with faculty members. These vignettes provide concrete illustrations of the general conclusion that "faculty members' impact . . . is enhanced when student-faculty interactions extend beyond the formal classroom setting" (Pascarella and Terenzini, 1991, p. 393).

Conclusions

The primary goal of this chapter has been to demonstrate the pervasiveness and potential importance of memories of educational episodes. Most college students and alumnae readily recounted specific events and encounters that they perceived to have influenced their lives. Quantitative analyses demonstrated that the memories are not entirely idiosyncratic with respect to their structure and content. The remembered events tended to be highly emotional; they represented a balance of positive, negative, and mixed emotional categories; and they tended to cluster at transition points, especially the beginning of the first year of college. A majority of the memories focused on nonacademic topics, although academic memories also were reported by most alumnae.

The value of this descriptive assessment is enriched when supplemented by qualitative analyses of memory content. The adaptive significance of remembering college episodes, and educational applications, were illustrated through a combination of quantitative summaries and qualitative case examples. Although memory clustering at transition points suggested that the memories serve a directive function, content analyses of individual memories were necessary to identify the form of memory directives – including explicit and implicit prescriptions for behavior, originating events, and anchoring events. In addition, descriptions of specific encounters between professors and students provide suggestions of what to emulate and what to avoid in educational settings. Quantitative summaries suggest that interactions between professors and students can be influential, but without a direct analysis of specific episodes, we will not discover why or how certain types of encounters with professors are beneficial or disabling. Specific incidents also evoke a sense of immediacy and emotionality on the part of the reader or listener, and they frequently are more engaging, instructive, and persuasive than a sterile quantitative summary (Pillemer, 1992).

We view our findings as compelling evidence for the potential importance of specific events and specific memories in education and many other domains. Formal analysis of memory structure and content can reveal quantitative regularities, such as the pervasive temporal patterns found in our studies of college memories. Detailed qualitative analyses can reveal the meanings the memories convey and the functions they appear to serve. Once identified, memory functions can be incorporated into more systematic analyses. One could explore whether particular situations or life periods are especially likely to give rise to memories that fulfill a particular function. For example, the college years may prove to be an especially rich source of originating events compared to other life stages. From an applied perspective, our understanding of undergraduate life is deepened by the inclusion of insights obtained by examining autobiographical memories. When addressing broad questions relevant to educational policy, such as which factors encourage or discourage women to pursue careers in science, or the value of interdisciplinary studies, the answers suggested by quantitative research will be enriched by systematic, detailed analysis of present and former students' personal event narratives.

References

Ariev, M. (1992, January-February). Schama the riveter [Letter to the editor]. *Harvard Magazine*, p. 12.

Astin, A. W. (1993). *What matters in college?* San Francisco: Jossey Bass.

Bandura, A. (1982). The psychology of chance encounters and life paths. *American Psychologist, 37,* 747–755.

Beidler, P. G. (Ed.). (1986). *Distinguished teachers on effective teaching.* San Francisco: Jossey-Bass.

Bruce, D. (1989). Functional explanations of memory. In L. W. Poon, D. C. Rubin, & B. A. Wilson (Eds.), *Everyday cognition in adulthood and late life* (pp. 44–58). New York: Cambridge University Press.

Bruner, J. S. (1987). Life as narrative. *Social Research, 54,* 11–32.

Carter, K. (1993). The place of story in the study of teaching and teacher education. *Educational Researcher, 22,* 5–12, 18.

Erikson, E. H. (1969). *Ghandi's truth.* New York: Norton.

——— (1975). *Life history and the historical moment.* New York: Norton.

Kagan, J. (1972). A psychologist's account at mid-career. In T. S. Krawiec (Ed.), *The psychologists* (Vol. 1, pp. 137–165). New York: Oxford University Press.

Lampert, M. (1985). How do teachers manage to teach? Perspectives on problems in practice. *Harvard Educational Review, 55,* 178–194.

Light, R. J. (1990). *The Harvard Assessment Seminars: Explorations with students and faculty about teaching, learning, and student life* (First Report). Harvard University.

Marshall, D. R. (1986, September 12). A Cornellian perspective. *The Wellesley News,* p. 11.

McCarthy, M. (1987, Fall/Winter). A slice of life: Training teachers through case studies. *Harvard Graduate School of Education Association Bulletin, 32,* 9–11.

Meier, D. (1986). Learning in small moments. *Harvard Educational Review, 56,* 298–300.

Neisser, U. (1982). *Memory observed.* San Francisco: W. H. Freeman.

Panter, A. T., & Pillemer, D. B. (1987, April). *What do students remember about a college course?: A naturalistic approach.* Paper presented at the American Educational Research Association convention, Washington, DC.

Pascarella, E. T., & Terenzini, P. T. (1991). *How college affects students.* San Francisco: Jossey-Bass.

Pillemer, D. B. (1992). Remembering personal circumstances: A functional analysis. In E. Winograd & U. Neisser (Eds.), *Affect and accuracy in recall: Studies of "flashbulb" memories.* New York: Cambridge University Press.

Pillemer, D. B., Goldsmith, L. R., Panter, A. T., & White, S. H. (1988). Very long-term memories of the first year in college. *Journal of Experimental Psychology: Learning, Memory, and Cognition, 14,* 709–715.

Pillemer, D. B., Koff, E., Rhinehart, E. D., & Rierdan, J. (1987). Flashbulb memories of menarche and adult menstrual distress. *Journal of Adolescence, 10,* 187–199.

Pillemer, D. B., Krensky, L., Kleinman, S. N., Goldsmith, L. R., & White, S. H. (1991). Chapters in narratives: Evidence from oral histories of the first year in college. *Journal of Narrative and Life History, 1,* 3–14.

Pillemer, D. B., Rhinehart, E. D., & White, S. H. (1986). Memories of life transitions: The first year in college. *Human Learning, 5,* 109–123.

Riesman, D. (1985). Academic colleagueship and teaching. *Antioch Review, 43,* 401–422.

Robinson, J. A. (1986). Temporal reference systems and autobiographical memory. In D. C. Rubin (Ed.), *Autobiographical memory* (pp. 159–188). New York: Cambridge University Press.

Runyan, W. M. (1982). *Life histories and psychobiography.* New York: Oxford University Press.

Sarason, S. B. (1993). *The case for change.* San Francisco: Jossey-Bass.

Stewart, A. J., Sokol, M., Healy, J. M., Jr., Chester, N. L., and Weinstock- Savoy, D. (1982). Adaptation to life changes in children and adults: Cross-sectional studies. *Journal of Personality and Social Psychology, 43,* 1270–1281.

Tulving, E. (1983). *Elements of episodic memory.* New York: Oxford University Press.

Wapner, S. (1981). Transactions of persons-in-environments: Some critical transitions. *Journal of Environmental Psychology, 1,* 223–239.

Winograd, E., & Neisser, U. (1992). *Affect and accuracy in recall: Studies of "flashbulb" memories.* New York: Cambridge University Press.

Part V

Development and disruption

14 Remembering, recounting, and reminiscing: The development of autobiographical memory in social context

Robyn Fivush, Catherine Haden, and Elaine Reese

Recounting our past experiences is a pervasive part of social interaction. Whether we are talking with old friends or new acquaintances, speaking with faraway relatives, or simply chatting with our family around the dinner table, we talk about the past. In fact, estimates based on spontaneous conversations among families indicate that conversations about past events occur as often as five to seven times an hour (Blum-Kulka & Snow, 1992; Miller, 1994). Why is talk about the past so prevalent? Clearly, when recounting an experience to someone who was not present, the narrative has an informative function. By telling someone about the kinds of events that we have experienced, we are both telling the listener something about the kind of person we are (e.g., Brewer, 1986; Bruner, 1987; Fitzgerald, this volume; Fivush, 1988), as well as imparting important or interesting information about events in the world.

But much of social interaction focuses on recounting events with others who shared these experiences with us. This kind of joint remembering, or reminiscing, serves a very special purpose, that of creating interpersonal bonds based on a sense of shared history. In the process of recounting, interpreting, and evaluating our experiences together, we are creating a shared understanding and representation of our world and the ways in which our lives are intertwined (see also Bruner & Feldman and Hirst & Manier, this volume). Somewhat surprisingly, reminiscing begins very early in development. Parents and children talk about shared past experiences almost as soon as children begin talking (Engel, 1986; Hudson, 1990; Nelson, 1988), and personal narratives are the earliest stories that children participate in telling (Miller & Sperry, 1988). Because remi-

The research reported in this chapter was funded by a grant from the Spencer Foundation to the first author. We would like to thank Liza Dondonan for her help in data collection and Laura Underwood, Marcella Eppen, and Marci Feldman for their help in data transcription and coding. We also appreciate comments by Janet Kuebli, Susan Butler, April Schwarzmueller, and Janine Przybylinski on an earlier draft of this chapter.

niscing is a fundamental process for establishing our sense of self and our relationships with others, the ways in which parents and children reminisce is critical for children's developing understanding of their past and themselves (e.g., Fivush & Reese, 1992).

In this chapter, we examine the development of reminiscing through a longitudinal investigation of mother-child conversations about the past. By studying mother-child conversations about the past across the preschool years, we can document the ways in which mothers help children structure their recounts of the past, and how children come to understand and value the activity of reminiscing.

The development of reminiscing

When parents and children first reminisce together, it is the parent who provides much of the structure and content of the conversations, and the child participates minimally, if at all (Eisenberg, 1985; Engel, 1986; Sachs, 1983). For example, in this excerpt, a mother and her 32-month old child are discussing a car trip to visit the child's grandparents (from Fivush & Fromhoff, 1988):

> MOTHER: Remember when Mommy and Daddy and Sam (baby brother) went in the car for a long time and we went to MaMaw's (Grandma's) house?
>
> CHILD: (shakes head yes)
>
> MOTHER: Yeah, and what did we see when we were in the car? Remember Daddy was showing you outside the car? What was it?
>
> CHILD: . . . I don't know
>
> MOTHER: Do you remember we saw some mountains and we went to that old house and what did we do. We took off our shoes and we walked on the rocks. What did we do? What was there?

This conversation continues for quite a while, but as can be seen, the child provides very little information about what occurred. The mother essentially tells the whole story while the child simply confirms or repeats what the mother says. As children grow older, however, they begin to participate more fully in these conversations, providing information about what occurred and even bringing up past events as a topic of conversation. By the time children are 3- to 4-years old, they are reasonably competent participants in conversations about the past, although clearly their memory and narrative skills continue to develop (Hudson & Shapiro, 1991; Peterson & McCabe, 1983).

The pattern of change over time suggests that the development of reminiscing might be best described by the "scaffolding" model (Wertsch, 1985; Wood, Bruner, & Ross, 1976). At first the child is unable to accomplish the task of recounting a past event, and so the adult performs the task for the child. By participating even minimally in this process, the child is beginning to learn the necessary skills and processes for accomplishing the task alone, and over time begins to take over more and more responsibility for performing the task. According to the scaffolding model, as the child becomes more competent, and is better able to perform, the adult withdraws the guiding structure and allows the child to perform the task independently. The endpoint of development is achieved when the child can perform the task completely alone, recounting coherent personal narratives without adult guidance.

The scaffolding model may help explain the ways in which children develop skills for recounting personal experiences to others who were not present (see, e.g., McNamee, 1987; Pratt, Robins, Kerig, & Cowan, 1989, for relevant data on fictional narratives). In this situation, the adult is trying to elicit information from the child that the child knows but the adult does not. Adults help children to recount this information by asking many questions and providing many prompts; as children develop and become better able to recount their experiences without this external help, adults ask fewer and fewer questions. But recounting past experiences with others who shared these experiences is quite different. In this kind of reminiscing, the function of the activity is to collaboratively recount the event, to share the experience again. Thus, for reminiscing, the more appropriate model may be a collaborative "spiral" rather than a scaffold. According to this model, it is still the adult who carries much of the task early on when the child is just learning to participate, but as the child becomes more and more competent in recounting past experiences, the adult and child begin to tell more and more elaborately detailed stories, embellishing and enriching each other's contributions to the recount.

Whereas in the scaffolding model the adult provides less information as the child provides more, in the spiral model both participants provide more information as the dyad becomes increasingly collaborative in the retelling. Essentially, in the scaffolding model of the development of reminiscing, the adult's underlying goals are to teach the child to recount their past experiences coherently and independently. In contrast, in a spiral model of the development of reminiscing, the adult's underlying goal is to share experiences and collaboratively recount richly embellished narratives about past experiences with the child. By examining change and consistency in how mothers and children talk about past experiences together over the preschool years, we can chart the developmental process and begin to understand how and why children come to reminisce.

It is important to make explicit several assumptions that underlie these developmental models. First, reminiscing is linguistically based. When adults and children share their past experiences together, they do so by talking about them. Although children as young as 1 and 2 years old are able to recall aspects of their past experiences as demonstrated through action (Nelson & Ross, 1980; Perris, Myers, & Clifton, 1990), language provides new ways of structuring and understanding these experiences. Thus, a major function of language in personal memories is organizational. More specifically, language helps to organize personal memories as canonical narratives (e.g., Bruner, 1987; Labov, 1982; Peterson & McCabe, 1983; but see Barclay, this volume, for a different perspective).

Janet (as cited in Ross, 1991) claims that personal memories are organized as narratives because the purpose of reminiscing is not simply to convey to another all of the elements of an event, but to re-create the event so that the listener can experience the event with the teller. A simple listing of people, places, and objects would not serve that purpose. By telling a past event in story form, the event is ordered in a way that maps onto experience and is coherent to listeners. Thus, an important part of the development of autobiographical memory is learning the culturally appropriate narrative forms for recounting the past. Children learn these narrative forms in early adult-guided conversations; thus, through engaging in reminiscing, children come to understand and organize their past experiences in fundamentally new ways (see Nelson, 1993, for related arguments).

Inseparable from language's organizational qualities are its social, communicative functions. We use language to serve the social purposes of re-creating an event for another person, or with another person. As Halbwachs (1992) argues, language is the social, communicative convention that allows us to experience shared memories. Through joint reminiscing children are not just learning to organize their past experiences; they are also learning to communicate effectively about these experiences both to others and to themselves. As children come to recount their past experiences to others in more narratively coherent ways, they also begin to represent their past experiences to themselves in more narratively coherent ways. In this way language becomes the medium both of recounting and of representing the past. Language is not a simple overlay on memory; language and memory are inextricably intertwined in experiencing, remembering and recounting events.

While language is critical in the development of autobiographical memory, we do not believe that children's developing autobiographical memories are completely constructed in linguistic interaction as Halbwachs (1992) and Gergen (1985, in press) have intimated. Instead, following Vygotsky (1978; see also Wertsch, 1985), we propose that the organizational and communicative functions of language are initially displayed and learned in social interaction; with development these functions are internalized, becoming the intrapsychological skills of the individual. Children are learning the skills of remembering and reminiscing, not the content of particular experiences. Certainly, children's memories may be shaped by the ways in which parents structure events for them, just as parents' memories are affected by what children choose to highlight in recall. Both parents and children accommodate their personal memories in light of their joint reminiscing, but these reconstructed memories are not complete fictions having no relationship to the original experience. Rather, they are *negotiated* memories – changed, but not reinvented (Barclay, this volume; Robinson, this volume).

Individual variation in parent-child conversations about the past

Given the role of language in children's developing autobiographical memories, it is significant that mothers (and fathers as well) display a great deal of variability in the way they structure conversations about the past with their children (Engel, 1986; Fivush & Fromhoff, 1988; Hudson, 1990; McCabe & Peterson, 1991; Reese & Fivush, 1993).

Some parents provide a great deal of event information for their children. They talk about past events in rich detail, recounting more and more information with each conversational turn. Importantly, parents who engage in this kind of highly elaborative recounting of the past do so whether or not their children are recalling any information (e.g., Fivush & Fromhoff, 1988). These parents pursue the conversations by continuing the story, recounting more and more about what occurred, even when their children are not contributing to the retelling. An example will help illustrate this conversational style (this and all subsequent examples are from Reese, Haden, & Fivush, 1993). In this excerpt from a conversation about going to a carnival, the mother and child are discussing a prize the mother won:

MOTHER: Do you remember what we got there?

CHILD: Unha.

MOTHER: What did we get?

CHILD: Um, I don't know.

MOTHER: Do you remember Mommy played a game, and I won something?

CHILD: Unha.

MOTHER: Do you remember what that was?

CHILD: What?

MOTHER: And we got to bring it home with us?

CHILD: A green crayon.

MOTHER: That's right, a green crayon! Do you remember how, the game that I played?

CHILD: Unha.

MOTHER: What did I throw?

CHILD: Um, a arrow.

MOTHER: Darts. That's right!

As can be seen in this example, the mother chooses to provide many details about what they won at the carnival, even though the child does not immediately recall any information. As the mother provides more and more details, the child does remember the green crayon. The mother works to continue the child's participation by asking related questions about the game they played, again weaving together a coherent story. Notice too, that the mother confirms and implicitly praises the child's memory responses, communicating to the child that his participation is encouraged and of interest. In this way, highly elaborative mothers work to elicit and maintain their children's contribution to the memory conversation.

In contrast, other parents are more likely to encourage children's independent recall by repeating their own questions about the event and by issuing empty prompts to children. These parents try to elicit their children's memory by coaxing them to remember, but do not seem interested in providing information or telling a story about what happened. Again, this style of interaction can be seen in the following example of a mother and child discussing an outing to see Sesame Street Live:

MOTHER: I think someone went with us. Who went with us?

CHILD: Cry baby.

MOTHER: Who went with us to see Sesame Street?

CHILD: (soundplay)

MOTHER: You remember. (pause) You remember who went with us. (pause)

When the child does not recall the information asked for, this mother simply repeats her question over and over. When the child still does not respond, the mother simply switches topic. Many studies have dichotomized parents into one of these two styles, variously labeled "high elaborative" versus "low elaborative" (Hudson, 1990), "elaborative" versus "repetitive" (Fivush & Fromhoff, 1988), "reminiscers" versus "practical rememberers" (Engel, 1986), and "topic-extending" versus "topic-switching" (McCabe & Peterson, 1991). But researchers agree that the styles can also be conceived of as a continuum. Most parents tend to be at least somewhat elaborative. Particularly when children recall some information, it is difficult for parents not to respond with additional new information. Yet some parents are much more elaborative relative to other parents, especially when children are not contributing much information to the joint recount.

Individual variation in the ways in which parents structure conversations about the past with their young children suggests that individual children may be learning different skills for recounting and reminiscing in these early adult-guided conversations. Some preliminary evidence supports this theoretical argument. Peterson and McCabe (1992) studied two children of highly elaborative mothers over an 18-month period, from when the children were 27 to 44 months of age. One mother emphasized context questions (e.g., who, where, when, and why), and her child came to incorporate a great deal of contextual orientation spontaneously in her independent narratives. The other mother, in contrast, elicited more temporally ordered descriptions of actions and occurrences comprising the experience; her child's narratives were better organized structurally but included less contextual information than the first child's. Similarly, Fivush (1991) examined the kinds of narrative structures mothers displayed in conversations with their 32- to 35-month-old children, and then assessed the children's independent narrative skills 14 months later. Mothers who placed past events in context by providing a great deal of orienting information for their children during the earlier conversations had children who provided a great deal of orienting information in their later independent narratives. Similarly, mothers who expressed more evaluative and emotional content about past events had children who subsequently included more of this kind of information in their independent narratives.

By examining maternal style at one point in time and then assessing children's personal narrative skills at a later point in time, these studies demonstrate that maternal style of talking about the past does facilitate specific aspects of children's developing abilities to recount their past. What has not been assessed to date, however, is how mother-child conversations about shared past events change over time. That is, what kind of consistency and/or change do we see in maternal style, and how does this relate to children's developing autobiographical memory skills? Moreover, no study has explicitly examined the development of joint reminiscing.

Whereas there is evidence of maternal facilitation of children's developing independent narrative skills, there are no data on how mothers and children talk together about shared past experiences over time. As we argued earlier, and will discuss in more detail later in the chapter, joint reminiscing is a special expression of autobiographical memory, in that it is closely linked with interpersonal bonding and self-concept. Thus the development of joint reminiscing plays an important role in the development of autobiographical memory; it is this process that we examined in a longitudinal study of mother-child talk about the past across the preschool years.

Relations of maternal style and children's memory over time

In an ongoing longitudinal study of parent-child narrative interactions, we are examining 19 white, middle-class families beginning when the target child is 40 months of age. In this chapter, we discuss conversations about past events between mothers and their children when children were 40, 46, 58, and 70 months old. Fathers also talked about past events with their children at the 40-month and 70-month time points; for the present discussion, we focus on the maternal data in order to provide more detailed information about parent-child relations over the preschool years. However, it should be noted that father-child conversations about the past are extremely similar to mother-child conversations (see Reese & Fivush, 1993, and Reese, Haden, & Fivush, 1994, for details).

Families were visited in their homes and mothers were asked to talk about two to three special, one-time or highly infrequent events with their children at each time point. The events the mothers chose, with the help of the researcher, were all events that the mother and child had experienced together, and ran the gamut from the child's first visit to the zoo, a visit to or from a special friend or relative, or experiencing the death of a pet. Note that we restricted mothers to discussing shared past experiences in order to examine the development of joint reminiscing. Once several events were selected, the mother and child sat comfortably in a quiet place in the home and discussed the events for as long as they wished while the researcher was out of the room. All conversations were audiotaped, transcribed verbatim, and coded reliably on several dimensions (see Reese et al., 1993, for details).

As found previously, it was again evident that some mothers were more elaborative in their conversations about past events than others. It is important to point out that it is not the case that some mothers are simply more "talkative" than other mothers. If this were true, then we would expect measures of maternal elaborativeness to extend to other conversational contexts. But, in fact, mothers who were highly elaborative when talking about the past in these conversations were no more or less likely to be elaborative in a free play situation with their child (Haden, 1992). Maternal level of elaboration, then, does not seem to be a general characteristic of maternal language style, but rather a context-specific expression of maternal conversational goals. We will return to this issue later in the chapter.

Most important, because we examined these conversations longitudinally, we were able to investigate two additional critical issues. First, we were able to document the patterns of mother-child talk about the past over time. As children became more competent participants in these conversations over this developmental period, we were sure that mothers would show some change in the ways in which they structure these conversations. But what kind of change might we see? Did mothers become less and less elaborative over time, as would be expected by a scaffolding model, or did they become more and more elaborative over time as would be predicted by a spiral model? Second, we were able to examine the relationships between individual variation in maternal talk about the past and children's developing autobiographical memory skills. Did more elaborative mothers facilitate the development of reminiscing in their children over time?

In order to address these questions, we examined the level of maternal elaborations and the level of children's memory responses over time. Elaborations are the provision of any new information about the event under discussion. For example, a mother who asks, "What did we do at Grandma's?," and continues with, "Did we bake special cookies?" is credited with an elaboration, because new information about the event is embedded in her second question. Similarly, if a child recalls having cake and the mother responds, "Yes, it was an ice cream cake," this too is an elaboration because the mother is embellishing on the information provided by the child. For mothers, level of elaboration has been the major factor differentiating the two maternal styles found in previous studies and therefore is a critical element in examining individual variation in maternal talk about the past.

For children, we used essentially the same measure; that is, the provision of new information about the event under discussion. But because most of children's memory information was recalled in response to the mother's questions, especially at the earlier time points, it seemed more appropriate to label the provided information as "memory responses." Again, if the mother asks, "Where did we go in that big airplane?" and the child responds, "Spain," the child is credited with a memory response. The mean number of maternal elaborations and children's memory responses at each time point are shown in Table 14.1. In order to examine relationships of maternal elaborations to children's memory responses over time, we conducted a series of concurrent and cross-lagged correlations, and all significant correlations are shown in Figure 14.1.

Importantly, as shown in Table 14.1, mothers significantly increased their level of elaboration over time, especially between the first two time points. And children clearly increased in their participation in these conversations over time, recalling almost twice as much information at the fourth time point, when they were 70 months of age, than they had at the first time point, when they were 40 months of age. Because, in general, mothers adopt the strategy of supplying more elaborations as children get older, coupled with children's increased recall with age, the conversations become more and more

Table 14.1 *Mean frequencies (and standard deviations) per event of maternal elaborations and children's memory responses across time*

Time Points	Maternal Elaborations	Children's Memory Responses
Time 1: 40 months	19.24 (7.00)	8.09 (3.85)
Time 2: 46 months	23.05 (8.93)	11.01 (5.23)
Time 3: 58 months	20.72 (10.56)	12.59 (10.32)
Time 4: 70 months	23.11 (11.19)	14.89 (10.32)

collaborative over time. It is not the case that as children recall more information, mothers provide less, as predicted by the scaffold model of the development of reminiscing. This pattern further indicates that mothers are not elaborating on their questions solely to cue their children's memories. If this were the case, then we would expect a decrease in maternal elaborations as children's memory responses increased. Rather, the data support the spiral model, in that as children are able to participate more fully by recounting what happened during these shared past experiences, mothers provide more embellishments and details. As children get older, mothers and children are jointly constructing richer, more detailed recounts about the past.

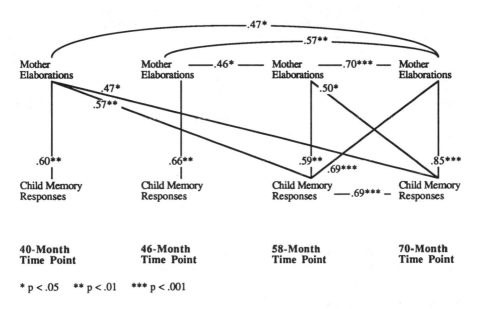

* p < .05   ** p < .01   *** p < .001

Figure 14.1 Concurrent and cross-lagged correlations between maternal elaborations and children's memory responses.

Yet equally important, those mothers who showed higher levels of elaboration early in their children's development, continued to show higher levels of elaboration later in development, as demonstrated by the correlations between maternal elaborations across the four time points displayed in Figure 14.1. While all mothers generally increased their levels of elaboration, more highly elaborative mothers still continued to show higher levels of elaboration over time than less elaborative mothers. Thus, although all mothers may adapt to children's increased skills over time, some mothers are consistently more elaborative in relation to other mothers across the preschool period.

A critical question is whether mothers who adopt a more elaborative style of conversing about the past do so simply in response to their children's better memory skills. That is, some children may be better able to recall information about the past for various cognitive or linguistic reasons, and these children may elicit a more elaborative strategy from their parents. While we believe that children play an important role in their own development, and must be influencing their parents to some extent, several aspects of the data suggest that the direction of influence is more from mother to child than from child to mother, especially during the early phases of the development of reminiscing.

First of all, children show little consistency in their ability to contribute memory information during these conversations early in development. Note in Figure 14.1 that there is no correlation between how much children are remembering between the first two time points, when children are 40 and 46 months of age, nor any relation between these time points and later participation when children are 58 and 70 months of age. The fact that children are inconsistent in their participation in these conversations over time, whereas mothers are quite consistent in their level of elaboration during this same period, indicates that maternal style is not a simple response to what children are doing. Children who are providing more memory responses early in development do not seem to be eliciting higher levels of maternal elaborations later in development.

Second, as we mentioned earlier, all mothers tend to elaborate when their children are recalling information. When children answer their mother's questions, mothers almost always follow this response with a confirmation and elaboration. For example:

> MOTHER: Did we have your party at home?
>
> CHILD: At the toy store.
>
> MOTHER: At the toy store, that's right! And what was the theme of your party?

As did most mothers, when this child recalls some information, the mother immediately confirms its accuracy and elaborates on that response in her next question. Differences between mothers emerge most strongly when children are not recalling information. As in the following example, more highly elaborative mothers are significantly more likely to continue prompting their children with more and more information, essentially keeping the story going, until their children recall some information or the whole story is told:

MOTHER: What did we do?

CHILD: I don't know.

MOTHER: Do you remember what we saw that you liked a whole lot?

CHILD: What?

MOTHER: Do you remember a helicopter?

In this case, when the child does not recall, this highly elaborative mother provides additional details in each of her subsequent questions, serving both to cue the child's memory and to elaborate on the event under discussion. Less elaborative mothers, in contrast, tend to respond to their children's lack of response by either repeating their previous question or using empty prompts that do not move the story forward:

MOTHER: Do you remember last Easter?

CHILD: Yeah.

MOTHER: What did we do at Easter?

CHILD: What.

MOTHER: What did we do at Easter?

CHILD: Yeah.

MOTHER: Can't remember?

Here, when the child is not recalling, the mother simply repeats the same question over and over, asking the child to recall a particular piece of information about the event without providing any additional details. The finding that maternal style differences emerge most clearly when children are not recalling any information suggests again that mothers are not adopting a more elaborative strategy solely in response to what their children are doing.

Most telling are the relationships between mothers and children. As expected from previous research (Fivush & Fromhoff, 1988; Hudson, 1990; Reese & Fivush, 1993), children's memory responses are highly concurrently related to maternal elaborations. The more elaborative mothers are, the more their children recall within that same conversation. Of course, concurrent relationships give us no information about direction of effect. The critical relationships are the longitudinal correlations between maternal elaborations and children's memory responses. Do mothers who are more elaborative early in the preschool period have children who recall more at a much later age? The answer to this question is yes, as demonstrated by the strong correlation between maternal elaborations at 40 months and children's provision of unique memory responses at 58 and 70 months. Moreover, there are no direct relationships between children's memory responses at the earlier time points and maternal elaborations at the later time points. Thus, the longitudinal relations strongly suggest that the direction of effect is from mother to child. Those mothers who, early in development, engage in highly elaborated discussions of past events with their young children seem to facilitate their children's developing ability to engage in these kinds of conversations.

It is intriguing that these relations emerge only after relatively long time delays. Mothers' use of elaborations at 40 months does not show any effect on children's memory responding at 46 months, but does show an effect $1\frac{1}{2}$ years later, at 58 months, as well as continuing to show an effect $2\frac{1}{2}$ years later, at 70 months. Of course, the argument is not that this one conversation assessed in our study is the critical event. Quite clearly, mothers and children are continuously engaging in conversations about past events across this time period. Our data suggest that the cumulative effects of engaging in these conversations emerges slowly over time. The development of reminiscing is a long and gradual process, and it may take years before the memory skills displayed by the mother early on become part of the child's own repertoire.

Yet it also seems to be the case that children come to exert a greater influence on the dyad's interactions later in development. At the last two time points, children are consistent in their memory responses; those children who are participating more fully in these conversations at 58 months of age are also participating more fully at 70 months of age. More interesting, children's participation at 58 months of age is related to maternal elaborations at 70 months of age, suggesting that by the end of the preschool years, the way in which the dyad converses about past events has become much more reciprocal. To put it simply, early in development, some mothers seem to adopt a more highly elaborative style of talking about the past than other mothers regardless of what their children are doing in these conversations. Highly elaborative mothers, in turn, facilitate their children's later participation in conversations about past events. And once children become fully engaged in these conversations, they begin to influence their mothers as well, such that highly elaborative mothers and children engage in richly detailed collaborative recounts of their shared past experiences.

The developmental patterns become clear by looking at some examples. The following two selections were taken from conversations between the same highly elaborative mother and child at the first, 40-month time point and at the last, 70-month time point of the study. As can be seen, at Time 1, the child does not provide much information about their trip to the aquarium. But even when the child's contribution is not correct ("Ducks!"), the mother chooses to provide the child with more and more details about the event:

> MOTHER: Remember when we first came in the aquarium? And we looked down and there were a whole bunch of birdies . . . in the water? Remember the names of the birdies?
>
> CHILD: Ducks!
>
> MOTHER: Nooo! They weren't ducks. They had on little suits. (pause) Penguins. (pause) Remember what did the penguins do?
>
> CHILD: I don't know.
>
> MOTHER: You don't remember?
>
> CHILD: No.

MOTHER: Remember them jumping off the rocks and swimming in the water.

CHILD: Yeah.

MOTHER: Real fast. You were watching them jump in the water, hum.

CHILD: Yeah.

Again, even though this child is not recalling, this mother continues to expand on her previous questions, providing more details about the event with each conversational turn. By doing so, the mother essentially tells the whole story. By Time 4, the child is contributing much more information to the recounting of a family excursion to see a puppet show. The highly elaborative mother encourages the child's contributions through many questions, and maintains the collaborative conversation through expansions on the child's utterances and asking related elaborative questions:

MOTHER: Let's talk about, remember that puppet show we went to last summer?

CHILD: You mean um with the boy and the little dog and the space dog?

MOTHER: Yeah.

CHILD: Oh yeah, I remember that! I liked those little um, brooms.

MOTHER: Those little funny brooms?

CHILD: Yeah.

MOTHER: Mm hm. . . What else do you remember about the puppet show?

CHILD: Um, um I remember when the boy was crying.

MOTHER: Why was the boy crying?

CHILD: Because, um, I don't remember that part.

MOTHER: The dog was dead or____?

CHILD: Maybe it was just sleeping or maybe it, maybe the dog um went to the end of space.

MOTHER: Oh, okay. Did the dog get lost?

CHILD: Yeah.

MOTHER: And then what happened? . . . Did the dog ever come back to life?

CHILD: Yeah.

MOTHER: Yeah.

As this excerpt demonstrates, by Time 4 there is truly a sense of a shared experience being jointly reconstructed by the mother and child. It must be emphasized again that all mothers become more elaborative over time. And all mother-child dyads become more collaborative in recounting their shared experiences over time. But some mothers are more highly elaborative than others throughout their children's preschool years, and these mothers seem to facilitate the development of highly collaborative, richly detailed recounts of the past with their children.

What develops in the development of reminiscing?

The data clearly indicate that the quantity and quality of mother-child conversations about the past show important individual variation, that is related to children's developing ability to participate in these conversations. But what exactly is it that children are learning by participating in conversations about the past? We argued earlier that children are learning how to recount and represent their personal past, but not necessarily learning the content of these memories. In this sample, we were able to examine this issue directly. At each of the four time points, a research assistant interviewed the child about several past events a few days after the mother-child conversations were recorded. One of the events asked about in the researcher-child interviews was an event the mother and child had discussed days earlier, and the content of these conversations was analyzed (Fivush, 1994).

All information provided by either the mother or the child during the mother-child interview was identified, as was all information provided by the child during the researcher-child interview at each of the time points. Then, all the information the child recalled at each time point with the researcher was categorized as (1) information the mother had provided on the previous interview; (2) information the child had recalled on the previous interview; or (3) new information not recalled by either participant on the previous interview. The overwhelming majority of information recalled with the researcher was new information. Overall, across the four time points, only about 10% of the information provided by the mother was subsequently recalled by the child.

Moreover, although only two other studies in the literature have examined this issue, they found essentially the same results (Fivush, Hamond, Harsch, Singer, & Wolf, 1991; Hudson, 1990). Children do not seem to incorporate information provided by the mother into their own recall of personally experienced events. Thus there is no evidence that children are learning what to recall. Rather, we believe that children are learning how to recall (see Hudson, 1990, for related arguments). Children of highly elaborative mothers are learning to recount their past in rich detail, although the details they recount will be based largely on their own memories of the events, and not what they have been told about.

Language, reminiscing, and the development of autobiographical memory

There is little doubt that through participating in conversations about the past, children are developing skills for recounting personal experiences. Most important, because individual mothers engage in this activity in different ways, children come to engage in this activity in different ways as well. Mothers who discuss past events in richly detailed and embellished ways have children who come to engage in these conversations more fully and more elaborately than children of less elaborative mothers. But what are the relationships between children's developing abilities to reminisce about past events and their ability to remember their personal past? That is, are some children simply learning more elaborated ways of recounting their past experiences than others, or do they actually come to understand and represent their past in more elaborated ways as well?

On the one hand, it is possible that the skills of reminiscing that children are learning through participating in adult-child conversations about the past are purely language skills. Children of highly elaborative mothers are learning more sophisticated ways of talking about their past, but their memories of these experiences are no different from the memories of children of less elaborative mothers. An extreme form of this argument assumes that language and memory are completely independent. There is a presumed underlying memory representation of an event based on experience and, when this event comes up in conversation, this memory representation is accessed and translated into language for purposes of social discourse. However, the ways in which the event is discussed do not change the memory representation at all; once the conversation is over, the memory is again stored in some form but the event representation has not changed as a function of talking about it. According to this view, the memory representation is stable; it may be strengthened through rehearsal or decay as a function of time, but it will not be transformed as a function of discussion (e.g., Brainerd, Reyna, Howe, & Kingma, 1990).

At the other end of the continuum is the view that memories are completely constructed through language. According to this view, there is not anything like a "memory representation." All that matters is how the event is talked about. Memories are constructed in the moment of social discourse and are dependent on the immediate context, the conversational partner, and the individual's motives and purposes for discussing the event. Memories do not exist outside of this discourse (see Barclay, this volume; Gergen, in press; and Middleton & Edwards, 1990, for arguments along these lines).

Most memory researchers take more of a middle position. In this view, the experience is represented in some underlying form, but the representation may be transformed in some way as a result of the way it is talked about, such that when it is now stored again, the memory representation is different. For children of more elaborative mothers, this would mean that by engaging in richly detailed conversations about past events, those events will come to be represented in more detailed ways. Although the original memory representation may be sparse, because mothers and children discuss the experience vividly, the memory representation will be embellished and children will have more vivid memories of these events.

What all these views share in common is a distinction between language and memory. This is clear in the first two views, where the memory is either assumed to be unaffected by language, or where language is assumed to be all that exists and there is no memory representation at all outside of language. But even in the third view outlined, the assumption is that there is an underlying memory trace that may be transformed in some way through language but is not isomorphic with language. In contrast to these views, we believe, as stated earlier, that language and memory become inextricably intertwined in the development of autobiographical memory; there is a memory representation, but this representation and the ways in which events are talked about are completely enmeshed.

If we assume that the memory representation and language remain somewhat separate throughout development, then we would expect children of more elaborative mothers to learn to talk about specific past events in more elaborative ways. That is, it is through talking about a past event in elaborated ways that children come to have a more elaborated representation of that event. But our data indicate that the skills that children are learning for recounting the past are not specific to the events they have already discussed with their mothers. It is quite clear that children are not learning either the content or the structure for recounting particular experiences. Rather, children are learning general skills of recounting past events in more vivid and detailed ways. Thus, it is not the case that specific memories become more detailed and elaborated through discussion of that event. Rather, talking about particular past experiences in more elaborated ways leads children to recount their past experiences in general in more elaborated ways.

What, then, is it about talking about some past events in more elaborated ways that leads to recounting the past in general more elaborately? Clearly, mothers are displaying important skills for recounting the past in early parent-child conversations. But just as important, by talking about the past in elaborated richly embellished ways, mothers are also implicitly communicating why these conversations are important. The mother's underlying beliefs about the functions of reminiscing are communicated in these early conversations about the past, and it is these functions that children are coming to understand and internalize in the process of development. Essentially, children are learning the value of reminiscing. As mothers ask more and more memory questions and provide much detailed information about past events, a clear interest in eliciting and maintaining their children's conversational participation is revealed.

Consistent with the spiral model of the development of reminiscing, the function of these conversations appears to be the sharing of past experiences through a collaborative recounting. Both before the child is able to fully participate in these conversations, and later when the child plays a more integral role, mothers emphasize the social aspects of talking about the past. Reminiscing is highlighted as an important way of interacting socially with others, as the mother works to involve her child in elaborated and embellished recountings of shared past events. And as the pair coconstruct their past experiences, these shared stories become ones where interpersonal bonds are emphasized and strengthened. In this way, reminiscing comes to be valued as a social-interactional activity, and as an important chance to emphasize interpersonal relatedness through construction of shared histories.

Thus, the development of reminiscing involves learning at two levels. At one level, children are learning the specific language skills for recounting the past. These include organizing recounts into canonical narratives and telling stories that are studded with rich detail and emotional evaluation. But equally important, by talking about past events in highly elaborated, richly textured ways, mothers are communicating to children the value of reminiscing. Sharing our past experiences with others is an important part of creating shared histories and interpersonal bonds. Children learn specific linguistic skills in the process of reminiscing, but they are also learning the value of talking about the past in general.

Notably, whereas all mothers and children become more elaborative over time, children of more highly elaborative mothers may come to especially value sharing past experiences with others in richly detailed ways as an important part of social interaction. Children of more highly elaborative mothers may become more interested in engaging in these conversations, and may do so more frequently than children of less elaborative mothers. Moreover, because through retelling shared stories, connections with people who shared in the experiences are continually reestablished, these conversations may become an important source of children's self-understanding and understanding of their relationships with others. In this way, children of highly elaborative mothers may come to have more elaborated, shared stories from which to draw on and interweave in understanding themselves and others than do children of less elaborative mothers.

Most important, we argue that because children of highly elaborative mothers talk about past events in more embellished ways, they also come to think about the past in more embellished ways. The linguistic skills that children learn for recounting the past are internalized, such that richly detailed narratives become the organizational form for understanding and representing experiences. It is not simply the case that some children come to recount their past experiences in more elaborated ways; rather, some children actually come to represent their past experiences in more elaborated ways. It may even be the case that these highly elaborated forms come to be used for encoding events as they occur. Recent research by Tessler and Nelson (1994) indicates that maternal style extends to the ways in which mothers talk about events with their children as they are experiencing them. And the more highly elaborated the discussion of the ongoing event is, the more highly elaborated is the child's subsequent recount. So children of highly elaborative mothers may actually come to encode experiences in more richly detailed ways than children of less elaborative mothers. This is an intriguing area for further research.

According to this argument, then, language is both the means for talking about past experiences and the medium for representing those experiences. As Nelson (1993) has argued, the autobiographical memory system is unique in that it is socially constructed through language. Although we may have episodic memories outside of language, autobiographical memories are those memories of personally experienced events that are socially sharable and linguistically based (see Pillemer & White, 1989, for related arguments). The ways in which events are talked about as they occur, and as they are remembered in social conversations, are integral to the memory representation.

Conclusions

The development of autobiographical memory is a gradual and complex process. It is not simply a matter of remembering personally experienced events; children must learn the appropriate ways of recounting those events. Importantly, parents who talk about the past in richly embellished ways facilitate their children's developing ability to recount their own personal past. Thus, the development of autobiographical memory is very much a social process. Children learn the linguistic forms of reminiscing through engaging in social interactions. Perhaps most intriguing, there is a great deal of individual variation in how elaboratively parents talk about past events with their young children, and those parents who talk in more elaborated ways come to engage in more collaboratively elaborated conversations with their children as they grow older. At the same time, by engaging in reminiscing, children are learning to value the activity of sharing their experiences with others, collaboratively creating a shared history and thereby strengthening interpersonal bonds. Thus the development of autobiographical memory, and especially the development of joint reminiscing, is an integral part of the developing sense of self and interpersonal relatedness.

References

Brainerd, C. J., Reyna, V. F., Howe, M. L., & Kingma, J. (1990). The development of forgetting and reminiscence. *Monographs of the Society for Research in Child Development, 55*. Serial No. 222.

Blum-Kulka, S., & Snow, C. E. (1992). Developing autonomy for tellers, tales, and telling in family narrative events. *Journal of Narrative and Life History*, 2(3), 187–217.

Brewer, W. F. (1986). What is autobiographical memory? In D. C. Rubin (Ed.), *Autobiographical memory* (pp. 25–49). New York: Cambridge University Press.

Bruner, J. (1987). Life as narrative. *Social Research, 54*, 11–32.

Eisenberg, A.R. (1985). Learning to describe past experience in conversation. *Discourse Processes, 8*, 177–204.

Engel, S. (1986). *Learning to reminisce: A developmental study of how young children talk about the past.* Unpublished doctoral dissertation, City University of New York.

Fivush, R. (1988). The functions of event memory: Some comments on Nelson and Barsalou. In U. Neisser & E. Winograd (Eds.), *Remembering reconsidered: Ecological and traditional approaches to memory* (pp. 277–282). New York: Cambridge University Press.

—— (1991). The social construction of personal narratives. *Merrill-Palmer Quarterly, 37*, 59–82.

—— (1994). Young children's event recall: Are memories constructed through discourse? *Consciousness and Cognition*, 3, 356–373.

Fivush, R., & Fromhoff, F. (1988). Style and structure in mother-child conversations about the past. *Discourse Processes, 11*, 337–355.

Fivush, R., Hamond, N. R., Harsch, N., Singer, N., & Wolf, A. (1991). Content and consistency of young children's autobiographical recall. *Discourse Processes, 14*, 373–388.

Fivush, R., & Reese, E. (1992). The social construction of autobiographical memory. In M. A. Conway, D. C. Rubin, H. Spinnler, & W. A. Wagenaar (Eds.), *Theoretical perspectives on autobiographical memory* (pp. 115–132). Dordrecht, The Netherlands: Kluwer Academic.

Gergen, K. J. (1985). The social constructionist movement in modern psychology. *American Psychologist, 40*, 266–275.

Gergen, K.J. (In press). Mind, text and society: Self-memory in social context. In U. Neisser & R. Fivush (Eds.), *The remembering self: Construction and accuracy in the life narrative*. New York: Cambridge University Press.

Haden, C. (1992, April). *Consistency and change in maternal styles in different contexts.* Paper presented at the Conference on Human Development, Atlanta, GA.

Halbwachs, M. (1992). *On collective memory*. L. A. Coser (Ed.). Chicago: University of Chicago Press.

Hudson, J. A. (1990). The emergence of autobiographic memory in mother-child conversations. In R. Fivush & J. A. Hudson (Eds.), *Knowing and remembering in young children* (pp. 166–196). New York: Cambridge University Press.

Hudson, J. A., & Shapiro, L. (1991). Effects of task and topic on children's narratives. In A. McCabe & C. Peterson (Eds.), *New directions in developing narrative structure* (pp. 89–136). Hillsdale, NJ: Lawrence Erlbaum.

Labov, W. (1982). Speech actions and reactions in personal narrative. In D. Tannen (Ed.), *Analyzing discourse: Text and talk* (pp. 219–247). Washington, DC: Georgetown University Press.

McCabe, A., & Peterson, C. (1991). Getting the story: A longitudinal study of parental styles in eliciting narratives and developing narrative skill. In A. McCabe & C. Peterson (Eds.), *Developing narrative structure* (pp. 217–253). Hillsdale, NJ: Lawrence Erlbaum.

McNamee, G. D. (1987). The social origins of narrative skills. In M. Hickmann (Ed.), *Social and functional approaches to language and thought* (pp. 287–304). New York: Academic Press.

Middleton, D., & Edwards, D. (1990). Conversational remembering: A social psychological approach. In D. Middleton & D. Edwards (Eds.), *Collective remembering* (pp. 23–45). London: Sage.

Miller, P. J. (1994). Narrative practices: Their role in socialization and self-construction. In U. Neisser & R. Fivush (Eds.), *The remembering self: Construction and accuracy in the life narrative* (pp. 158–179). New York: Cambridge University Press.

Miller, P. J., & Sperry, L. L. (1988). Early talk about the past: The origins of conversational stories of personal experience. *Journal of Child Language, 15*, 293–315.

Nelson, K. (1988). The ontogeny of memory for real world events. In U. Neisser & E. Winograd (Eds.), *Remembering reconsidered: Ecological and traditional approaches to memory* (pp. 277–282). New York: Cambridge University Press.

—— (1993). The psychological and social origins of autobiographical memory. *Psychological Science, 1*, 1–8.

Nelson, K., & Ross, G. (1980). The generalities and specifics of long-term memory in infants and young children. In M. Perlmutter (Ed.), *Children's memory* (New directions for child development, No. 10, pp. 87–101). San Francisco: Jossey-Bass.

Perris, E. E., Myers, N. A., & Clifton, R. K. (1990). Long-term memory for a single infancy experience. *Child Development, 61*, 1796–1807.

Peterson, C., & McCabe, A. (1983). *Developmental psycholinguistics: Three ways of looking at a child's narrative*. New York: Plenum Press.

—— (1992). Parental styles of narrative elicitation: Effect on children's narrative structure and content. *First Language, 12*, 299–321.

Pillemer, D. B., & White, S. H. (1989). Childhood events recalled by children and adults. *Advances in Child Development and Behavior, 21*, 297–340.

Pratt, M. W., Robins, S., Kerig, P., & Cowan, P. A. (1989, April). *Apprentice narrators: Parents as listeners and young children's acquisition of story telling skills*. Paper presented at the meetings of the Society for Research in Child Development, Kansas City, MO.

Reese, E., & Fivush, R. (1993). Parental styles of talking about the past. *Developmental Psychology, 29*, 596–606.

Reese, E., Haden, C., & Fivush, R. (1993). Mother-child conversations about the past: Relationships of style and memory over time. *Cognitive Development, 8*, 403–430.

—— (1994). *Mothers, fathers, daughters, sons: Gender differences in autobiographical reminiscing*. Submitted manuscript.

Ross, B. M. (1991). *Remembering the personal past: Descriptions of autobiographical memory*. New York: Oxford University Press.

Sachs, J. (1983). Talking about the there and then: The emergence of displaced reference in parent-child discourse. In K. Nelson (Ed.), *Children's language* (Vol. 4, pp. 1–28). Hillsdale, NJ: Lawrence Erlbaum.

Tessler, M., & Nelson, K. (1994). Making events memorable. *Consciousness and Cognition, 3*, 307–326.

Vygotsky, L. S. (1978). *Mind in society: The development of higher psychological processes*. M. Cole, V. John-Steiner, S. Scribner, & E. Souberman (Eds.). Cambridge, MA: Harvard University Press.

Wertsch, J. (1985). *Vygotsky and the social formation of mind*. Cambridge, MA: Harvard University Press.

Wood, D. J., Bruner, J. S., & Ross, G. (1976). The role of tutoring in problem solving. *Journal of Child Psychology and Psychiatry, 17*, 89–100.

15 Intersecting meanings of reminiscence in adult development and aging

Joseph M. Fitzgerald

The cognitive revolution that began in the late 1960s (Neisser, 1967) led to drastic changes in models for the acquisition, storage, and retrieval of information. For life-span developmental psychologists, the issues were particularly complex because developmentalists seek not only to specify models of how the mature organism accomplishes the various tasks of adaptation, but also to construct valid accounts of how systems develop over time, to identify how systems are maintained across the adult years, and to determine what happens to them as the organism ages.

Volumes of research have been generated in an effort to accomplish this agenda, but fairly early on in the process some developmentalists with interests at various stages of the life span perceived significant problems (Meacham, 1977; Riegel, 1976). Most developmental researchers viewed the memory system in the context of 19-year-old college freshman performing tasks designed to test the memory system under maximum load and independent of contextual supports. The very nature of tasks such as attempting to memorize a list of 40 words after one presentation seemed an unlikely yardstick for comparing individuals of varying developmental levels.

Similarly, many cognitive psychologists sensed that there were aspects of memory and cognition that might be overlooked if the field relied on traditional methodologies. Neisser (1978) urged psychologists to draw research problems from the real world so that their work would possess ecological validity. Landauer (1989) expressed the sentiment guiding many of these researchers when he wrote, "If the mind is studied in the laboratory, it will be very easy to miss some of the functions for which it was designed, some of the environmental and experiential support on which its function depends, and some of the obstacles with which it needs to contend" (pp. 118). The efforts of those who took these issues to heart is represented in collections such as Conway, Rubin, Spinnler, and Wagenaar (1992), Gruneberg, Morris, and Sykes (1978), Neisser (1982), Neisser and Winograd (1988), and Rubin (1986).

In the context of this search for alternative methodologies and paradigms, developmental psychologists must clarify their priorities. Much of the early memory research with both children and older adults seemed oriented to cataloging deficits in the performance of these groups relative to college students. There was little concern with establishing the nature of memory functions in children or older adults in developmentally appropriate contexts. Great theories of memory development and decline were built on the fact that one can construct a memory task on which children have average scores of nearly zero, or that by pacing the presentation of stimuli at a very fast rate one finds college students recalling five times as many words as older adults.

Thus emerged the view of both children and older adults as barely competent. Even a rudimentary ecological analysis of either group quickly reveals, however, that memory systems are quite functional across the life span. Further, a careful examination of memory functions at different points in development is likely to contribute to the development of more adequate models of memory in the mature adult. For example, Nelson, Perlmutter, Fivush, and others working with infants and toddlers (see Fivush, Haden, & Reese, this volume) have reported not only that infants and toddlers encode and retrieve episodic memories with some success, but their work has also helped to clarify the role of scripts, schema, and other hypothesized mechanisms of event memory. All this is not designed to create the impression that there are not important differences in levels of memory performance across the life span or that controlled experiments are not needed to clarify our understanding of memory phenomena. Rather, the point is that we need to look at each memory system in context in order to fully understand it.

The focus of the present chapter is on adult memory development, specifically the topics of the reminiscence effect in autobiographical retrieval and the nature of reminiscence behavior in adulthood. These two topics have been the object of two different research streams. The reminiscence effect was identified empirically in research on autobiographical memory. Rubin, Wetzler, and Nebes (1986, p. 208) define the reminiscence effect as "an increase in early memories above what would be expected by a monotonically decreasing retention function." Much of the research is quite recent and our understanding of the phenomenon is relatively limited.

Reminiscence behavior became the object of empirical research as a result of a theoretical article by Robert Butler (1963) on a process he termed as life review.

I conceive of life review as a naturally occurring, universal mental process characterized by the progressive return to consciousness of past experiences, and particularly the resurgence of unresolved conflicts; simultaneously, and normally, these reviewed experiences and conflicts can be surveyed and integrated. (p. 66)

As discussed below, gerontologists have attempted to verify his hypothesis in a variety of correlational and experimental studies with mixed results. Although there is somewhat more research on reminiscence behavior than the reminiscence effect, our understanding is similarly limited.

The topics of reminiscence behavior and the reminiscence effect have been linked by some researchers. For example, Rubin, Wetzler, and Nebes (1986) cite several papers on reminiscence behavior as containing possible explanations of the reminiscence effect. More recently, Webster and Cappeliez (1993) have reviewed many studies from both domains and have proposed that research simultaneously examining the two topics would be valuable. In this chapter, we build on their review and present more recent data. Although a true integration of the two areas of research meets with obstacles, cross-fertilization promises to enrich the conceptual development of both topics.

A developmental approach to autobiographical memory

One must begin any discussion of autobiographical memory with a definition of what one means by the term because there is consensus on neither its conceptual meaning nor the measurement rules to be followed in indexing it. A definition offered by Nelson (1992) (see Brewer, this volume, for an alternative formulation) provides a useful starting point:

From this perspective autobiographical memories are a type of episodic memory consisting of those memories that are retained and accessible to later recall, sometimes for a lifetime, and become part of one's life story. (p. 174)

For Nelson this definition allows her to distinguish between episodic memories of two sorts, autobiographical and nonautobiographical. This distinction forms the basis for her account of early childhood amnesia. It is her view that episodic memory is a general family of memories and that the species autobiographical memory emerges as a result of representational changes that Nelson hypothesizes are rooted in language development (Fivush et al., this volume, discuss the emergence of autobiographical memory in maternal-child dialogues).

This is the first definition of autobiographical memory that essentially describes it as a reminiscence phenomena. Nelson notes that the representation of episodic memories in language allows for (1) the reflection on, and (2) the exchange with others of representations. These two activities of reflection and exchange are at the core of any definition of the phenomena of private and social reminiscence. One could rephrase the portion of her definition that reads "those memories which are retained and accessible to later recall" to read "those memories which are retained and accessible for private and/or social reminiscence" and change the meaning very little. The only caveat needed would be to refer to unconscious recall, which is not excluded from Nelson's original definition, but would not be included in a explicitly reminiscence-based definition.

Nelson locates the origin of autobiographical memory in the interchanges of young children and their parents and caregivers. Other researchers have supported similar hypotheses by demonstrating that autobiographical memory behavior is influenced by maternal behavior (Fivush et al., this volume; Fivush & Reese, 1992). The clear implication is that the processes of forming, selecting, and exploring episodic memories in an autobiographical framework is learned and constructed over time through social interaction. This is a powerful idea requiring careful analysis. In essence, Nelson is proposing that humans can take their memory system and employ it for the very specific purpose of forming a life history. This life history has interesting properties that distinguish it from other aspects of episodic memory, but because it is constructed within episodic memory, some of its characteristics will overlap with episodic memory. How do we sort out what is common and what is distinctive? Or is there any merit to the attempt?

Consider, for example, a man who goes to the race track, places a wager, watches the race, collects his winnings, and goes directly home to go to sleep. Sometime later, he is asked what he did on that day. He correctly reports that he went to the race track, won his bet, but states he went out to celebrate. When asked what horse won the race and what he paid, he replies "I don't have the slightest idea but I know Pat Day was the rider, I always bet on his horses in big races." He adds correctly that "It paid $4.40 to win." In this example, we have an autobiographical report that is largely accurate but for the conclusion. There is also the nonautobiographical question of what horse won the race, for which the respondent reports a retrieval failure, but he manages a successful retrieval of the value of a winning wager. At this point, researchers need to identify the properties characteristic of each type of memory.

This example also suggests some of the difficulty of drawing a clear demarcation between autobiographical and nonautobiographical memories, even with the guidance of the taxonomies such as that provided by Brewer (1986, this volume). Episodic memories typically involve witnessing or being told of events. It might seem that witnessing an event makes it material for an autobiographical memory, but that is not the case, at least as Nelson (1992) defines an autobiographical memory. Clearly, witnessing a list of 40 nonsense syllables does not qualify them for the status of autobiographical memory unless by some cause the experience becomes part of the individual's life history. The difficulty for those wishing to argue that autobiographical memory is in some way(s) distinctive is in locating the causes responsible for some memories becoming autobiographical memories while others do not.

One approach to this question is provided by a developmental context. If the developmental histories of autobiographical and nonautobiographical memory performance differ, such differences may provide clues as to the nature of any systematic differences. For example, the finding that children exhibit very poor autobiographical memory performance before the age of four, even though episodic memory is evidenced in young infants, suggests that at some point children must gain either the means (linguistic representation) and/or motivation (being asked questions about the self and its activities) that allow and promote the development, maintenance, and utilization of a distinctive data base that we call autobiographical memory. This might be likened to the emergence of an "expert system" in which the substantive area is not chess, physics, or medicine, but rather is the self. Just as a chess expert displays enhanced memory, problem solving, and productive thinking within the domain of expertise, individuals may become experts about themselves. This "self-expertise" would not necessarily be uniform across individuals, but one would expect that normatively autobiographical memory performance would be enhanced relative to other forms of memory. Howes and Katz (1992) recently reported a greater decrease with age in recall for public events than for autobiographical memories, implying that the autobiographical system has some properties that favor long-term retention. This is consistent with the notion of an expert system view.

Although Nelson (1992) emphasizes the point that linguistic representation of memories is a key element in the emergence of autobiographical memory, she also acknowledges the role of noncognitive factors. I would hypothesize that the emergence of linguistic representation is valuable to the child because it allows him or her to answer some very pressing questions about the self. Erikson (1959) noted that at roughly 4 or 5 years of age the child is asking what kind of person am I? These self-oriented questions may arise from the fact that others ask the child such questions. He posits that the child is forming sexual, moral, and psychological identities. In contemporary cognitive terms these might be considered as self-representations. The development of such representations is an ongoing goal throughout the life span as we move through various life stages and behavioral contexts. To achieve these goals, children need data for both reflection and communication, processes that are greatly facilitated if the data are represented linguistically. Out of this process of forging the basic underpinnings of a sense of identity, the systems of autobiographical memory emerge. In the current context, identity is defined as a set of knowledge statements about the self that are notable for both their comprehensiveness, that is, they apply to a large variety of situations, and their enduring character, that is, they are not typically changed as the result of ordinary events. Some aspects of identity, however, do change as a function of significant contextual and developmental events. As noted below, identity statements may take either a paradigmatic "I am a doctor," or a narrative form "My life is a steady stream of conflicts that I win."

Developmental aspects of memory sampling

One of the striking characteristics of autobiographical memory is the sheer number of both possible memories and accessible memories. To begin to understand something about this phenomena, Crovitz and Schiffman (1974) modified a technique that Galton devised to study the nature of memory for everyday experiences. Crovitz and Schiffman used a prompt word technique in which subjects are presented with a word and asked to think of a specific memory they associate with that word. This task is conceived of as a sampling task in which the individual would be drawing a relatively random sample of memories from the available pool of memories. As such, the characteristics of this sample of memories were thought to reflect the characteristics of the underlying pool of memories. Crovitz and Schiffman reported that the results conformed quite closely to a power function in which the log of memory strength declined linearly as a function of the log of time since occurrence.

Their work has led directly or indirectly to much of the research reported in this volume. We are concerned here with the developmental research that has included some work on early childhood amnesia (Fitzgerald, 1991; Wetzler & Sweeney, 1986) and autobiographical sampling in adolescents (Fitzgerald, 1980; 1981), but most notably a series of studies on sampling patterns over the late adolescent and adulthood years. That later body of work has provided results that Conway and Rubin (1993) refer to as a "among the most fascinating in cognitive psychology because they are among the most regular and because they relate directly to so many theoretical issues" (p. 115).

Crovitz and Schiffman (1974) had studied college students, and the fact that the straightforward power function accounted for sampling patterns over a period of nearly

20 years was impressive. An obvious question was how well the power function would account for the data of subjects over the age of 20. The first study with a wider age range was reported by Franklin and Holding (1977). They reported results that were in "accordance" with Crovitz and Schiffman, that is, the log of the number of memories declines as a function of a logarithmic scale of elapsed time. Naturally, older adults had, on average, older memories, but Franklin and Holding make very explicit their main theme: older adults are not living in the past. Unfortunately, Franklin and Holding did not report their data in the same format as Crovitz and Schiffman, so direct comparison of power functions for each age group was not possible.

Fitzgerald and Lawrence (1984) reported the next set of life-span data using the prompt-word technique. Power functions for adolescents, college students, middle-aged adults, and older adults all were shown to closely fit the theoretical predictions of linear decline over time. The most notable exception was in the sampling pattern of the older adults. Although their data largely fit the pattern of linear decline, on close inspection it was found that older adults reported more memories from their late adolescence and early adulthood than predicted by the model. Shortly thereafter, Rubin, Wetzler, and Nebes (1986) combined the data of Franklin and Holding (1977), Zola-Morgan, Cohen, and Squire (1983), Fitzgerald and Lawrence (1984), and their own laboratory to make a more detailed examination of the phenomenon. A summary of some of those data are presented in Figure 15.1 from Rubin et al. (1986). Figure 15.1 is based on a total sample of 70 adults who were approximately 70 years old when tested using the prompt-word technique.

Most striking about Figure 15.1 is the fact that it omits nearly 50% of the memories reported by the subjects. Rubin et al. (1986) omitted memories recalled from the most recent year, because it would have rendered the remaining data more obscure. Combined with what is not presented, the data in Figure 15.1 further affirm the point that older adults are not living in the past; 30% of the memories included are from the past decade. Thus, a total of nearly 80% of reported memories are from the relatively recent past. While the reminiscence effect provides our current focus, the overwhelming trend to recall recent events should not be ignored. In addition to the recency effect, the pattern of results indicates that the oversampling of memories from the adolescent and early adulthood years reported by Fitzgerald and Lawrence (1984) was not a fluke. Several additional replications of the reminiscence effect appear in the literature, including studies by Hyland and Ackerman (1988), Rubin (1989), and Fromholt and Larsen (1991). Rubin's replication is particularly interesting for two reasons. First, he reports data for only two subjects, but each subject had been cued for 921 memories. Both subjects displayed a reminiscence hump, replicating the basic phenomenon. Second, there were dramatic differences in the magnitude of the effect, with one subject showing much more of a recency effect and the other sampling roughly 50% of his or her memories from the period starting with infancy and ending at age 30. These large individual differences invite further investigation in terms of both cognitive and noncognitive factors. Working with a much smaller sampling of memories, Sperbeck, Whitbourne, and Hoyer (1986) were able to find a modest ($r = -.29$) relationship between average age

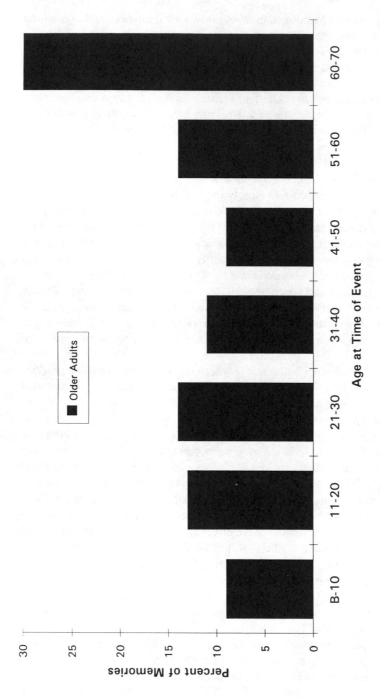

Figure 15.1 The distribution of autobiographical memories in prompt-word studies excluding the most recent year. (Adapted from Rubin, Wetzler, & Nebes, 1986.)

of memories and openness to experience, such that those more open to experience tended to report more recent memories.

Rubin et al. (1986) carefully reviewed possible explanations of the phenomenon. At that time, they concluded that it was most likely that some characteristic of the older individual who was being cued for memories was responsible for the outcome. They argue against three alternative explanations: differential encoding based on age at the time of the event, differential encoding based on calendar year of the event, and an increasing strength of resistance hypothesis. No evidence has emerged to support either the second and/or third of these hypotheses since Rubin et al. discussed them. However, a variant of the differential encoding hypothesis has been offered that we will discuss next.

Rubin et al. (1986) dismissed the differential encoding hypothesis based on a straightforward analysis of retention functions. Reviewing the literature, they found no evidence that individuals at ages 12, 20, and 30 were encoding more memories than older subjects. If they did, their retention functions would not be as steep as the power function, though such an analysis may be faulted for not being sufficiently sensitive. Fitzgerald (1988), however, approached the differential encoding hypothesis from a different tack. He asked not whether more memories were encoded, but rather whether the nature of encoding at this point in the development of the individual favored the long-term retention of memories from this era as opposed to other eras of the life span. This hypothesis was derived, in part, from the research on flashbulb or vivid memories by Brown and Kulik (1977) and Rubin and Kozin (1984). Those studies indicated that at least phenomenologically it makes sense to talk about a pool of memories that subjects regard as particularly vivid, important, and well rehearsed; such a pool of memories might, therefore, be more accessible which would produce the pattern of bias termed the reminiscence effect. It must be noted, however, that there is considerable disagreement that vivid memories are any more reliable than any other sort of memories.

Fitzgerald (1988) reported data from a sample of community older adults who were asked to report three flashbulb memories, defined as those for which the subject had a highly vivid image. They also completed a series of ratings on each memory that included frequency of rehearsal, degree of personal importance, and degree of national importance. Subjects reported most of the events in vivid detail and rated most memories highly on either personal or national importance, although the latter constituted only 5% of the memories recalled. The age distribution of these memories is represented in the unshaded bars of Figure 15.2. (This is a slightly different presentation than Fitzgerald (1988) in which the actual number of memories was reported.) The analysis clearly showed a much stronger reminiscence effect than had been reported in any of the cued-memory papers. Vivid memories did indeed have a tendency to cluster around the chronological age range of 15 to 25 with more than half the memories taking place before the individual was 30. A secondary "blip" clustered around the age of 48 reflects national history more than personal history. Many of the memories were for the assassination of President Kennedy or the urban violence of the 1960s.

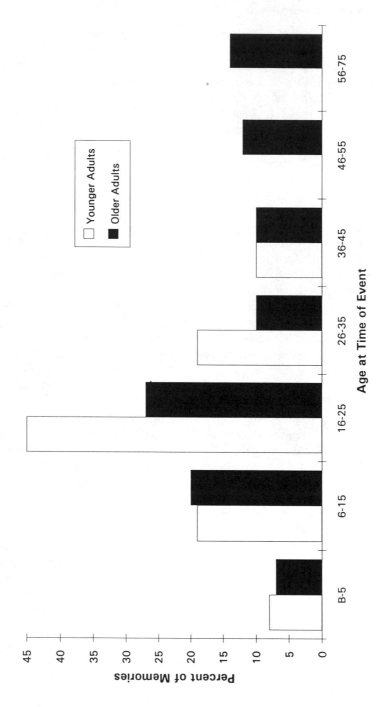

Figure 15.2 The distribution of flashbulb memories produced by younger and older adults. For the older adult sample, the last two decades have been combined because few subjects were older than 65.

Having identified the presence of this pool of highly vivid memories, the next task is to explain why it is there. Perhaps the reminiscence effect reflected the occurrence of a large number of life events such as marriages and graduations in the 15 to 25 age range. Fitzgerald conducted a categorical analysis to test this hypothesis and found no evidence to support it. Life events accounted for only 18% of the data, and for the reminiscence peak they only constituted 14%. There was no evidence that any other category of memory was particularly overrepresented in any time period except for the assassination effect noted above.

Fitzgerald (1988) considered several cognitive interpretations, but found no support in his data or in any of the available autobiographical memory studies. Rubin et al. (1986) had also dismissed the notion that there was anything about the memory system or the retention functions of different age groups to explain the phenomena. Instead, Fitzgerald presented a noncognitive hypothesis that centered on identity formation. The term *noncognitive* merits explanation. The intention is not to suggest that cognitive mechanisms are not involved, but rather that additional levels of explanation are necessary. For example, it might be that variables such as rehearsal, distinctiveness, or the like are the proximal mechanisms, but that the more distal or contextual causes are not part of the familiar domain of cognitive psychology. Examples of such noncognitive explanations include completing the normative developmental task of answering questions about the self ("What are you going to do with your life?"), or establishing organizing themes to make the experiences of adulthood more comprehensible.

The link between autobiographical memory and identity had been discussed earlier by Barclay (1986), but not in the context of explaining the reminiscence effect. Fitzgerald (1988) reasoned that the process of self-definition, that Erikson (1968) had highlighted as a particularly important developmental task for adolescents, might be related to the presence of this pool of memories. He broadened Erikson's concept of identity by emphasizing that identity contains not only the type of paradigmatic statements emphasized by trait theorists ("I am a person committed to helping others."), but also narrative knowledge of one's history ("When walking downtown last week I gave some poor people some money and then went back home and started working with my friends to collect blankets for the homeless."). The narrative mode of thinking has received renewed attention in psychology due to the work of scholars such as Bruner (1986), Robinson and Hawpe (1986), and Sarbin (1986). In this view, an essential part of identity formation is the development of a self-narrative that consists of a collection of stories and their themes that brings an understandable order to the course of a person's life. After this self-narrative is shaped in adolescence, there is less motivation to continuing performing the cognitive work involved in answering "Who am I?" sorts of questions. A person who constructs a self-narrative that provides an understandable order to his life with a clear central theme has little motivation to add new stories unless some form of feedback from the environment or self-evaluation indicates a need for change. Developmentalists would discuss a challenge to existing structures as a disturbance in equilibrium, a frequent source of developmental change.

Fitzgerald (1988, 1992) has discussed how the narrative form is used in literature to reveal the nature of characters without resorting to paradigmatic language. In fact, it sometimes seems that only the full narrative can express an author's conceptualization of the character, and when critics or commentators use paradigmatic language they either over- or underinterpret the nature of the character. In addition to communicative power, the narrative mode has advantages that relate to flexibility of interpretation. Many novels illustrate the point that a character's behavior can receive an entirely new interpretation in the light of a revelation at the end of the story. Similarly, an individual may experience a series of failures in some domain, perhaps the occupational, and from these construct a self-narrative centered on themes of personal incompetence. But if this individual developed new skills, was then hired for a new job and became successful, his or her self-narrative might center on themes of finding the right niche and perseverance. This type of revision of central themes of the self-narrative may then influence the recall and interpretations of events already present in memory (Fitzgerald, 1986). The recall of specific memories as representative of a set of events fits with the notion of "repisodes" put forward by Neisser (1981). The accuracy of recall for repisodes matters not so much as their ability to reflect what the individual believes is going on. Neisser's analysis of John Dean's testimony at the Watergate hearings is illustrative of this point. Dean made many mistakes of fact, but his testimony clearly reflected a pattern of behavior in the Nixon White House.

The narrative mode is also used extensively in the socialization process by which new members are taught the underlying themes and values of the group through "true" stories, fables, and allegories that take a narrative mode. Once individuals learn the "correct" stories that may communicate such themes as the power of a central authority or the power of the common people, leaders simply need to remind members of the group about these stories (repisodes) as they call upon the people to play out some new episode in the history of the group that demonstrates once again the "character of our people." As members of such cultures, children not only learn the content of the stories but the method of representing history in such forms. They are then able to take the method and use memory to construct their own histories.

Clearly the use of such modes of thinking may represent very specific cultural practices. Simply because western researchers find that members of modern Western cultures make extensive use of the narrative mode does not imply either that it is universal or in any way superior to other modes. Also note that personal identity is a culturally and historically specific notion. In fact, until the fifteenth century the aim of "self" examination and reflection was not to reveal the true self, but rather to reveal God's will. St. Augustine, for example, wrote his autobiography not to tell a story about himself, but to tell a story about God. But from the very first stories told or read in the nursery, members of modern Western society are taught both the value and the mechanics of narrative thinking as a means of knowing the self and others.

Forming the self-narrative requires extensive cognitive "work" or effort. Episodes are mulled over both privately and in social contexts. Not unlike the historian working in the archives, alternative meanings and outcomes may be considered. Entirely new versions of the basic story may emerge in response to distortions or attempts to construct forgotten details. Relatively minor incidents may take on importance by accident of spatial or temporal association. Such cognitive effort may be the proximal cause of the reminiscence effect, but the developmental context provides a more complete understanding of the phenomenon.

Thus, the larger than expected pool of vivid memories identified by Fitzgerald (1988) associated with the age range of roughly 15 to 25 is hypothesized to emerge as the result of interactions of the memory system, culturally defined developmental tasks, and culturally derived forms of representation. Defined as such, the self-narrative hypothesis is comfortable with both individual differences within a culture, such as those noted by Rubin (1989), and differences between cultures (Benson, 1992). Benson presents the only data set in which two cultures are examined with the same methodology. She asked subjects from Japan and rural midwestern America to report 10 vivid memories. She replicated the finding of an exaggerated reminiscence effect in both groups; but while the effect seemed associated with early adulthood in Japan, it was more apparent in adolescence for the American sample.

Two specific questions have been raised about the self-narrative hypothesis. First, Neisser (1988) suggested that if the link to identity was correct, then the observed memory distribution should be replicated if we asked people to, in some sense, tell their life stories. The second point is raised by Conway and Rubin (1993). They note that if the pool of memories is there, then using appropriate instructional conditions, researchers should be able to find it. Specifically, they propose that a group of 35 year olds should show the reminiscence effect if asked to provide a set of vivid memories. The importance of using 35 year olds is to observe whether the pool of memories is available as a function of properties of the era of their occurrence, or if the effect represents the product of life review or reminiscence behavior in later life. A bump in the number of memories is best seen in the context of a long period of declining memory strength. In the case of typical autobiographical memories, for a group of 35 year olds, the period of 25 to 35 is heavily populated with relatively recent autobiographical memories and our view of the bump is obscured. Normally we must wait until many of these memories fade over time in order to see a bump. However, if the hypothesis is correct, there should not be as many vivid memories in the 25 to 25 period. The bump, if present, should be observable. By extension, if the identity aspect of the hypothesis is correct, we should also see the effect if we ask 35 year olds to tell us their life stories.

Three sets of data have been collected that provide some answers to these questions. The first is a set of data collected at the same time as those presented in Fitzgerald (1988). In addition to the data on older adults, data was also collected on individuals ranging in age from 25 to 50. As part of the publication process, it was determined that, as originally organized, their inclusion did not add to the paper. However, some of the data allow for a response to Conway and Rubin's (1993) observation that we should able to find this pool of vivid memories in subjects over 30. In Figure 15.2, data for 31 individuals ranging in age from 31 to 46 are reported. The data are quite consistent with the notion that the pool of vivid memories sampled by the older adults is also available for sampling by the "thirty-something" sample. The overall pattern in both groups is one of a strong peak in the 16 to 25 age range, followed by a definite dip. In fact, the young adults report an even higher percentage of memories in the peak period than the older adults.

Second, Fitzgerald (1992) reported on the age distribution of memories elicited by instructing older adults to "Tell us three stories from your own life. We'd like you to select events that are important to you. Often these are vivid memories but they don't have to be. Think of these as three stories that belong in a book about your life." Subjects recalled these memories in long continuous monologues with minimal prompting from the interviewer. The subjects for that study were 25 adults over the age of 60. The results were very similar to the older adult data presented in Figure 15.2, thus supporting the link between the pool of vivid memories and the individual's selection of memories reflective of their life story.

The third set of data are reported here for the first time. The data were collected using a written format similar to that of Fitzgerald (1988) with the same life story instructions as Fitzgerald (1992). Subjects responded to a questionnaire that had been sent to them. It asked them to write a description of themselves and to then write four memories for stories they would want included in a book about their lives. After they wrote the memories, they were asked their age at the time of the event and to describe the frequency with which they had discussed it. There were 45 subjects aged 31 to 46, median age 36, and 45 subjects aged 60 to 76, median age 66. The distribution of memories over decade of occurrence is presented in Figure 15.3. Once again the reminiscence effect is clearly present, and it is present for both older adults and younger adults. The strength of the peak for the young adults suggests that the stories and themes formed in their adolescence and early adulthood are available for recall under the appropriate instructional conditions. For the older adult sample there is a small upswing in the proportion of memories for the most recent decades. This is partly due to the longer length of time, but most of the memories are from the 55 to 65 decade (note that the median age was 66). This phenomenon can be attributed to the high level of salience that a relatively recent important memory is likely to have. This recency effect is also likely to account for the relatively large number of memories reported by the younger adults for the 26 to 35 decade.

In summary, these three data sets are consistent with the notion that the distribution of memories that are regarded as highly vivid and important departs dramatically from the norm of a standard retention function. This set of memories appears to be relatively easy to access, and with proper instructional conditions it can be observed in adults over 30 years of age. Fromholt and Larsen (1991) have also reported on the recall of important memories for older normal and demented adults. The distributions of memories over the life span were very similar to those presented in Figures 15.2 and 15.3. The proximal causes of this unusual distribution are hypothesized to fall within the general rubric of cognitive effort. This cognitive effort is thought to reflect the intensity of the process of addressing issues of self-definition and identity formation during adolescence and early adulthood. At the moment, such explanations are neither precise nor

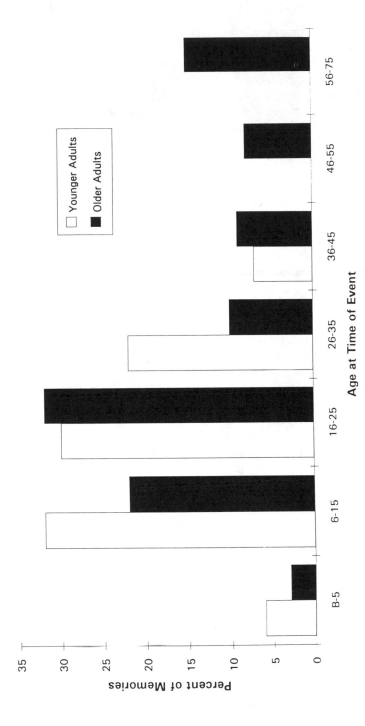

Figure 15.3 The distribution of memories to be included in a book about their lives. For the older adult sample, the last two decades have been combined because few subjects were older than 65.

373

readily testable. However, it may be that individual difference strategies in which identity variables, changes in context such as moving to a new job or life stage (such as becoming a parent), and autobiographical memory variables are studied within the same individuals will be productive.

When the reminiscence effect was first noted, it gave rise to two general questions: First, why does the reminiscence effect seem to be centered on the age period of 11 to 25? Second, why do we not see this effect until later in life? To some extent, we can say that the reason we haven't seen the phenomenon in younger adults is that the Galton technique is not the most appropriate way to sample important memories. The bump is best seen in the context of an extended period of declining memory strength, but in adults aged 31 to 46, the period between the present and the age range associated with the reminiscence effect is "filled" with relatively recent memories. As we have seen, when we examine the distribution of vivid and personally defining memories, the reminiscence phenomenon clearly stands out. In the future, it may be more accurate to term this the *identity effect*. To provide additional context for this phenomenon, however, we turn to the literature on reminiscence behavior.

Reminiscence behavior

Even in the context of folk psychology, reminiscence is a poorly defined term. The *Oxford English Dictionary* presents several definitions of *reminisce* and *reminiscence* that do not go much beyond the notion that to reminisce is to recollect or remember. The examples of usage in printed English date from 1589 with no apparent movement toward specification or clarity. Although there is what one might describe as a common nuance that the term involves recollection of something other than immediate context, there is no clear association of the term with a particular age group, nor is age a defining characteristic of reminiscent reports. Another connotation of the word appears to be a lack of trust in the validity of "mere" reminiscence in contrast to the products of more serious intellectual inquiry.

Psychologists prefer to deal with terms that are easily conceptualized and yield readily to measurement rules. Reminiscence does neither. Consider the following two sentences:

> The witness recalled that two women sat at the table eating lunch.
> Dorothy reminisced about her luncheon with a friend many years ago.

Although we may not totally understand how the witness recalled that two women sat at a table, it is fair to state that there is considerable agreement about what the term *recall* means and that we can readily develop measurement rules for certain characteristics of recall such as latency and accuracy. When we use the term *reminisce*, however, it is not at all clear what is meant. For example, some authors emphasize that reminiscence is characterized by some sort of free flow of randomly associated memories, whereas others emphasize the deliberate effort to recall memories of unresolved conflicts. Other writers suggest that a variety of motives or functions serves to define types of reminiscence. For example, Fivush et al. (this volume) use the term reminiscence in the context of individuals collaboratively reconstructing events. Still other discussions of reminiscence imply that the vintage of the memories is an issue, suggesting, for example, that only memories at least 5 years old qualify as objects of reminiscence, whereas others suggest that only memories from an individual's youth qualify for reminiscence. Finally, many researchers act as if reminiscence is in some way the special province of individuals of a certain age, most often older adults, although others have at least acknowledged that, in principle, reminiscence should be approached as a lifespan issue (Havighurst & Glasser, 1972).

Reminiscence research has been the subject of several reviews (e.g., Merriam, 1980; Molinari & Reichlin, 1984–1985; Webster & Cappeliez, 1993). As noted earlier, many of the studies find their origin in the work of Butler (1963) on the concept of life review. In the main, the reminiscence literature can be seen as attempting to affirm the inference that life review has some positive impact on the psychological adjustment of older adults. A small but growing literature has been more concerned with simply trying to develop adequate measures of some aspects of reminiscence or to provide basic data on such questions as how often does reminiscence occur. As Thornton and Brotchie (1987) have noted, the results of the first set of studies are equivocal at best, which is probably to be expected given the lack of conceptual clarity and the weaknesses of the available measures when those studies were conducted.

What is known about reminiscence behavior? The available literature suggests that over the age range from late adolescence to late adulthood, there is little if any change in frequency of simple reminiscence (Hyland & Ackerman, 1988; Merriam & Cross, 1982; Romaniuk & Romaniuk, 1983). But this literature has certain constraints. First, the available data consists entirely of subjective reports on Likert scales that are marked with the phrases "a great deal," "some," or "very little" reminiscence (Havighurst & Glasser, 1972). But do these phrases have the same behavioral meaning for individuals of every age group? If, for example, individuals are responding according to age group norms and those norms change, then the available data could be deceptive. As several investigators and reviewers have suggested, the ideal assessment technique would be some form of time or experience sampling method that would ask subjects whether they had engaged in reminiscence behavior within the past few minutes. A second limitation is that the definitions of reminiscence provided to subjects across studies have been deliberately vague, perhaps reflecting the conceptual confusion noted above, but often justified as casting the widest possible net. It would seem more profitable to investigate the relationship of age to the frequency of several well-defined behaviors proposed as constituents of reminiscence, as well as patterns of correlation among these constituents, as a means of developing both definitions and measures of reminiscence. For example, as it stands now the available literature does not speak to age differences or changes in various specific forms and contexts of reminiscence such as social conversations, dyadic interactions, simple private reminiscence, and the use of reminiscence in the context of life review. The situation is somewhat akin to asking what happens to the frequency of automobile accidents as people grow older. The answer that the number of accidents does not change very much masks a number of important phenomena regarding the nature and cause of such accidents, the rate of accidents per mile driven, and so forth.

Another research focus is possible age-related change in the function of reminiscence. To date this has been accomplished in one of two ways. The first is to ask individuals to make introspective judgments about the frequency with which they reminisce in the service of particular motives. This methodology offers the advantage of a high degree of face validity, but is subject to the criticism that such judgments may not be very accurate reflections of what takes place (Nisbett & Wilson, 1977). Webster (1993a) has recently developed a scale to measure such judgments about reminiscence frequency. In addition to face validity, the scale appears to possess at least modest levels of construct validity, as indicated by a factor analysis that led to the identification of a set of conceptually meaningful factors: boredom reduction, death preparation, identity/problem solving, conversation, intimacy maintenance, bitterness revival, and teach/inform. The items on the scales were generated by naive subjects who were asked why they reminisced. It is noteworthy that this procedure yielded a set of factors that relate to themes that had been discussed in the reminiscence literature even though the items were generated by naive subjects, suggesting that at this point the conceptualizations of reminiscence in popular culture (folk psychology) and scientific research are highly similar. In particular, the death preparation scale contains several items that relate to Butler's (1963) concept of life review, including this item: because it helps me to see that I've lived a full life and can therefore accept death more calmly. As evidence for the construct validity of his measure, Webster correlated scores on the reminiscence scales with scores on a measure of personality (Costa & McCrae, 1985). He reports, for example, that neuroticism correlates .42 with bitterness revival. This type of information helps to establish convergent validity. Unfortunately, not all the correlations are presented, so it is difficult to establish whether the data support divergent validity as well.

Webster (1993b) has also reported on the relationship between age and the seven scales of his inventory. His sample covered the age range of adolescence to later life. There are age differences on several scales, two of which are of particular interest in this context. First, identity/problem solving is reported as a frequent function of reminiscence across the life span, but it is most frequent in the first three decades of life. Second, death preparation shows a steady increase with age, an increase that accelerates in the 70s and 80s. Together these results support the notion that thinking about experiences/memories in terms of their meaning for the self may be a common feature of adolescence and later adulthood, distinguishing them from middle age. If the memories recalled in reminiscence related to death preparation or life review tend to be from the self-narrative established earlier in life, they may have more linkages to current representations of the self than is true of memories from midlife. Such linkages would help to explain why it is they are reported more often in autobiographical memory sampling studies (Fitzgerald & Lawrence, 1984; Rubin et al., 1986). Unfortunately, such data are not available.

An alternative methodology for the study of reminiscence functions involves a content analysis of memories produced in the context of reminiscence. A number of categorical schemes have been suggested in the past decades, but without the measurement rules needed to implement them. Recently, Wong and Watt (1991) presented a taxonomy that builds on earlier work and appears to be sufficiently well defined to allow for reliable analysis of verbal protocols. They identify six types of reminiscence: integrative (reflecting self-acceptance), instrumental (reflecting a focus on goals and problem solving), transmissive (reflecting on a focus of covering lessons learned), escapist (reflecting an exaggeration of past achievements), obsessive (reflected in statements of bitterness, guilt, and despair), and narrative (reflected in simple, uninterpreted accounts of past events and the absence of indicators of the other types). The perspective brought by this taxonomy only partly overlaps with that of Webster (1993a), who has criticized the Wong and Watt system because the categories appear to overlap in terms of function. He gives the example of how one particular memory might be integrative, instrumental, and transmissive. While that is true, it is also true that when subjects respond to an inventory such as his own reminiscence function scale, their responses probably reflect an attempt to express how often one particular function is dominant during reminiscence behavior. Thus, individuals might recognize that when they engage in instrumental reminiscence, they often are attempting to either teach/inform (Webster) or transmit some message (Wong & Watt). Methodological improvements may be gained by changing from an absolute taxonomic system to a graded system in which the relative role of each function is rated for each segment of the protocol. A potentially more serious problem for the Wong and Watt system is that it was developed in the context of a study of older adults. It may be that a life-span approach will identify other functions.

At this point, there is limited data available on the type of taxonomy developed by Wong and Watt (1991). Their data do suggest the construct validity of their system in that successful agers (designated as such by a multimodal assessment) engage in more integrative and more instrumental reminiscence. Unfortunately, Wong and Watt did not validate their system on a life-span sample. One earlier taxonomic study by Liebermann and Falk (1971) did compare older adults and middle-aged adults. They suggest that for middle-aged adults problem solving is the more frequent function of reminiscence, while in older adults "self-satisfaction" is a more dominant focus. Although their data clearly do not provide a comprehensive view of the life span, this last result is consistent with the notion of a focus on the self.

Finally, in discussing the functions of reminiscence, the topic of life review merits specific attention because many investigators have either equated reminiscence with life review or treated life review as a separate category. Butler (1963) describes life review as a normative process and claims that successful completion of a life review is most often beneficial to the older adult. In some cases, however, the life review may be difficult and may result in depression or anxiety. Clearly, data that supported the existence of life review as a normative process distinctive to later life would be consistent with the notion that focus on the self contributes to the emergence of the reminiscence phenomena in memory sampling by older adults. Similarly, experimental conditions in which adults 31 to 45 are asked to engage in life review tasks might induce a bias in memory sampling.

Unfortunately Butler (1963) attributes several characteristics to life review that make his hypotheses difficult to examine empirically. First, he asserts that life review may occur outside of the awareness of the individual. This would make self-reports regarding the frequency of life review suspect, if not meaningless. Second, he suggests that memory processes are involved, but so are other cognitive processes such as problem solving. The vagueness of his references to memory and the casual reference to other cognitive processes make it difficult to specify what differentiates life review process from other forms of memory behavior such as storytelling or simple reminiscence. This is a particular problem for those who attempt to institute life review therapies or interventions. The result has been a series of studies with largely inconclusive and frequently conflicting findings. As Merriam (1993) notes, however, life review continues to be viewed "optimistically" in the face of mixed results.

At this point, the life review literature really adds very little to our overall understanding of the relationship between reminiscence behavior and memory phenomena. It appears that as long as the primary mechanism for measuring life review are self-report instruments, several aspects of Butler's (1963) hypothesis cannot be adequately tested. For example, Merriam (1993) asked this question:

Some people review and evaluate their past in order to get an overall picture of their life. This is called life review. Have you reviewed, or are you currently reviewing your life?

She reports that 46.4% of her subjects aged 60 to 100 responded no. But since Butler implies that such review might occur outside of awareness, the meaning of these responses is ambiguous. Her data pose another problem for Butler's theory in that life satisfaction did not covary with self-reported life review activity. Of course, this failure could once again be excused by reference to the potential for unconscious life review.

Butler (1963) also proposes that some reorganization of experience will occur after life review. The only descriptive criterion he provides for this reorganization is that following life review, organization should be more integrated. How to measure such integration is not clear. Hypothetically, individuals would provide more integrative life themes following life review, but long-term longitudinal data is needed to differentiate those who provide integrative themes because they have completed life review from those who have shown such insights throughout life. Such studies would need to employ more qualitative analysis. The criterion that would guide such an analysis might emerge from a focus on the integrative power or scope of such themes, building on the work of Wong and Watt (1991).

In summary, the literature on reminiscence behavior provides very little clear-cut evidence that older adults reflect a higher level of self-focus in their reminiscence, or that they reminisce more often, or that they normatively engage in life review. Although several theorists hypothesize that such changes do take place, the lack of clear conceptualizations, clear measurement rules, and adequate research designs prevent the evaluation of these hypotheses. Progress in the development of measurement techniques is seen in the work of Webster (1993a) and Wong and Watt (1991), giving rise to optimism for the future study of reminiscence behavior.

Moving forward

Memory behavior, including reminiscence, generally remains very poorly understood. For all of its attempts to understand the mechanisms and/or structures of memory, psychology remains oddly bereft of an understanding or even a description of how memory behavior fits into the daily commerce of human behavior. Even those of us who study autobiographical memory, more often than not find ourselves drawn to classical questions in the study of memory such as accuracy, structural organization, and retention. These efforts are not altogether inappropriate and have led and will continue to lead to enrichments of laboratory-based models. But as of yet, autobiographical research has not moved beyond these traditional questions to develop a perspective on memory behavior in such contexts as the developmental tasks of the individual, the maintenance of dyadic relationships, or the playing out of social roles. In contrast, the questions posed by reminiscence researchers require that we regard autobiographical memory in a functional perspective, but to date researchers have not made frequent use of actual memories.

With few exceptions autobiographical memory researchers have centered their attention on the individual independent of contextual factors. Although some have extolled the power of a functional approach to memory (Bruce, 1989), the power of this approach has yet to be exploited. By asking the "What's memory used for?" question, the reminiscence researcher is led to explore various contexts for answers, nominating internal contexts such as life review (Butler, 1963), but other functions for reminiscence, such as conversation and teaching, highlight the variety of contexts that may shape memory behavior.

In discussing the self-narrative, I attempted to broaden the framework of personal identity by highlighting the origins of identity questions in the social environment. Even the simple question of "What's your name?" places a focus on the individual identity. The role of autobiographical memory in representation of the self may vary across cultures. In a culture in which the questions of identity are not primarily personal ("Who are you?") but rather are social ("Who are your people?" or "Which is your clan?"), repisodes may symbolize collective behavior. The study of diverse implementations of similar functions may lead to a better understanding of the memory mechanisms utilized.

Future reminiscence research needs to explore variation in reminiscence behavior across contexts and across the life span. Contexts can be defined by setting (storytelling, intimate conversation, private reflection) or purpose (problem-solving, entertainment). Variability in the properties of memories/memory reports could be examined in such research. As Bruce (1989) notes, variation is an essential feature of studies of function. Although some of these questions may be addressed using the quantitative approaches employed over the past two decades of autobiographical memory research, qualitative methodologies may also be needed. One strategy might involve contrasting the properties of memories produced in response to an instructional set emphasizing identity issues to those of memories produced for instructions that emphasize the transmission of valuable lessons. Although there may be much to be learned from the study of naturally occurring examples of such memories, a cognitive anthropology of reminiscence, interview or laboratory techniques may also emerge. As Neisser (1984) noted, the hallmark of the ecological approach is not an aversion to the laboratory but preserving "the integrity of variables that matter in natural settings" (p. 25) in laboratory studies.

At this point, one may fairly ask whether enough is known about variables that matter to continue relying upon them to guide theory and research. I suspect that the bases for many sound hypotheses are available but that knowledge base is not collected in one place, or more properly, one discipline. Such disciplines as communications, linguistics, sociology, neurobiology, and philosophy, all can inform a scientific approach to memory behavior. In fact, it is worth noting that the interdisciplinary nature of gerontology is probably one reason why so many different viewpoints on reminiscence have been developed. Furthermore, although many cognitive psychologists subscribe to constructivist views of memory, very little research has been conducted on how such factors as the goals, affective states, or social status influence the constructive process (See Conway, this volume). Although there have been demonstrations of such effects (Blackburn-Stover, Belenky, & Gilligan, 1982), the issue of how process and form follow function is largely unexplored.

Lest experimentalists be put off by reference to qualitative variables, there is clearly a role for their rigor and their creativity. It has already been shown, for example, that raters can reliably differentiate memory reports on the basis of function (integrative, instrumental, and transmissive). At the moment, this is achieved by providing raters with sets of exemplars of each type that they employ in making their ratings. But what are the essential cues for making these distinctions. Are they linguistic? Rhetorical? Sociolinguistic? Psychodynamic? This sort of problem can yield to controlled experimental investigation. By clarifying which variables influence the perceptions of everyday observers of memory, we are likely to learn something about the variables that matter to ecologically valid theories of memory. If one considers the importance and frequency of reminiscence functions in daily life, the systematic exploration of their impact on memory behavior will provide the base for an exciting research effort in the coming years.

References

Barclay, C. R. (1986). Schematization of autobiographical memory. In D. C. Rubin (Ed.), *Autobiographical memory*. New York: Cambridge University Press.

Benson, K. A., et al. (1992). Socio-historical context and autobiographical memories: Variations in the reminiscence phenomenon. In M. A. Conway, D. C. Rubin, H. Spinnler, & W. A. Wagenaar (Eds.), *Theoretical perspectives on autobiographical memory*. (pp. 313–322). Boston: Kluwer Academic.

Blackburn-Stover, G., Belenky, M., & Gilligan, C. (1982). Moral development and reconstructive memory: Recalling a decision to terminate an unplanned pregnancy. *Developmental Psychology, 18,* 862–870.

Brewer, W. F. (1986). What is autobiographical memory. In D. C. Rubin (Ed.), *Autobiogrphical memory* (pp. 25–49). New York: Cambridge University Press.

Brown, R., & Kulik, J. (1977). Flashbulb memories. *Cognition, 5,* 73–99.

Bruce, D. (1989). The functional explanation of memory. In L. W. Poon, D. C. Rubin, & B. A. Wilson (Eds.) *Everyday cognition in adulthood and late life* (pp. 44–58). New York: Cambridge University Press.

Bruner, J. (1986). *Actual minds, possible worlds.* Cambridge, MA: Harvard University Press.

Butler, R. (1963). The life review: An interpretation of reminiscence in the aged. *Psychiatry, 26,* 65–76.

Conway, M. A., Rubin, D. C., Spinnler, H., & Wagenaar, W. A. (Eds.) (1992). *Theoretical perspectives on autobiographical memory.* Boston: Kluwer Academic.

—— (1993). The structure of autobiographical memory. In A. C. Collins, S. E. Gathescote, M. A. Conway, & P. E. M. Morris (Eds.), *Theories of memory* (pp. 103–137). Sussex: Lawrence Erlbaum.

Costa, P. T. Jr., & McCrae, R. R. (1985). *The NEO Personality Inventory* (Manual). Odessa, FL: Psychological Assessment Resources.

Crovitz, H. F., & Schiffman, H. (1974) Frequency of episodic memories as a function of their age. *Bulletin of the Psychonomic Society, 4,* 517–518.

Erikson, E. (1959). *Identity and the life cycle.* New York: International Universities Press.

—— (1968). *Identity: Youth and crisis.* New York: W. W. Norton.

Fitzgerald, J. M. (1980). Sampling autobiographical memory reports in adolescence. *Developmental Psychology, 16.* 675–676.

—— (1981). Autobiographical memory reports in adolescence. *Canadian Journal of Psychology, 16,* 69–73.

—— (1986). Autobiographical memory: A developmental perspective. In D. C. Rubin (Ed.), *Autobiographical memory* (pp. 122–133). New York: Cambridge University Press.

—— (1988). Vivid memories and the reminiscence phenomenon: The role of a self narrative. *Human Development, 31,* 261–273.

—— (1991). A developmental account of early childhood amnesia. *Journal of Genetic Psychology, 152,* 159–171.

—— (1992). Autobiographical memory and conceptualizations of the self. In M. A. Conway, D. C. Rubin, H. Spinnler, & W. A. Wagenaar (Eds.), *Theoretical perspectives on autobiographical memory.* (pp. 99–114). Boston: Kluwer Academic.

Fitzgerald, J. M., & Lawrence, R. (1984). Autobiographical memory across the life-span. *Journal of Gerontology, 39,* 692–699.

Fivush, R., & Reese, E. (1992). The social construction of autobiographical memory. In M. A. Conway, D. C. Rubin, H. Spinnler, & W. A. Wagenaar (Eds.), *Theoretical perspectives on autobiographical memory.* (pp. 115–134). Boston: Kluwer Academic.

Franklin, H. C. M, & Holding, D. H. (1977). Personal memories at different ages. *Quarterly Journal of Experimental Psychology, 29,* 527–532.

Fromholt, P., & Larsen, S. F. (1991). Autobiographical memory in normal aging and primary degenerative dementia (Dementia of Alzheimer Type). *Journal of Gerontology: Psychological Sciences, 46,* 85–91.

Gruneberg, M. M., Morris, P. E., & R. N. Sykes (Eds.), *Practical aspects of memory: Current research and issues.* New York: Wiley.

Havighurst, R. J., & Glasser, R. (1972). An exploratory study of reminiscence. *Journal of Gerontology, 27,* 245–253.

Howes, J. L., & Katz, A. N. (1992). Remote memory: Recalling autobiographical and public events from across the lifespan. *Canadian Journal of Psychology, 46,* 92–116.

Hyland, D. T., & Ackerman, A. M. (1988). Reminiscence and autobiographical memory in the study of the personal past. *Journal of Gerontology: Psychological Sciences, 43,* 35–39.

Landauer, T. K. (1989). Some bad and some good reasons for studying memory and cognition in the wild. In L. W. Poon, D. C. Rubin, & B. A. Wilson (Eds.), *Everyday cognition in adulthood and late life* (pp. 116–125). New York: Cambridge University Press.

Liebermann, M. A., & Falk, J. (1971). The remembered past as a source of data for research on the life cycle. *Human Development, 14,* 132–141.

Meacham, J. (1977). A transactional model of memory. In H. W. Reese & N. Datan (Ed.), *Life-span developmental psychology: Dialectical perspectives on experimental research* (pp. 253–283). New York: Academic Press.

Merriam, S. B. (1980). The concept and function of reminiscence: A review of the research. *Gerontologist, 20,* 604–608.

Merriam, S. B. (1993). Butler's life review: How universal is it? *International Journal of Aging and Human Development, 37, 163–175.*

Merriam, S. B., & Cross, L. (1982). Adulthood and reminiscence: A descriptive study. *Educational Gerontology, 8,* 275–290.

Molinari, V., & Reichlin, R. (1984–1985). Life review and reminiscence in the elderly: A review of the literature. *International Journal of Aging and Human Development, 20,* 81–92.

Neisser, U. (1967). *Cognitive psychology.* New York: Appleton-Century-Crofts.

—— (1976). *Cognition and reality.* San Francisco: W. H. Freeman.

—— (1978). What are the important questions? In M. M. Gruneberg, P. E. Morris, & R. N. Sykes (Eds.), *Practical aspects of memory* (pp. 3–24). London: Academic Press.

—— (1981). John Dean's memory: A case study. *Cognition, 9,* 1–22.

—— (1982). Snapshots or benchmarks? In U. Neisser (Ed.), *Memory observed: Remembering in natural contexts* (pp. 43–48). San Francisco: W.H. Freeman.

—— (1984). Toward an ecologically oriented cognitive science. In T. M. Schlecter & Toglia, M. P. (Eds.), *New directions in cognitive science* (pp. 17–32). Norwood, NJ: Ablex.

—— (1988). Commentary. *Human Development, 31,* 271–273.

Neisser, U., & Winograd, E. (1988). *Remembering reconsidered: Ecological and traditional approaches to the study of memory* (pp. 244–276). New York: Cambridge University Press.

Nelson, K. (1992). The emergence of autobiographical memory at age four. *Human Development, 35,* 172–177.

Nisbett, R. E., & Wilson, T. D. (1977). Telling more than we can know: Verbal reports on mental processes. *Psychological Review, 84,* 231–259.

Riegel, K. (1976). *The psychology of development and history.* New York: Plenum.

Robinson, J. R., & Hawpe, L. (1986). Narrative thinking as a heuristic process. In T. R. Sarbin (Ed.) *Narrative psychology: The storied nature of human conduct* (pp. 111–125). New York: Praeger.

Romaniuk, M., & Romaniuk, J. G. (1983). Life events and reminiscence: A comparison of the memories of young and old adults. *Imagination, Cognition, and Personality, 2,* 125–136.

Rubin, D. C. (Ed.), (1986). *Autobiographical memory.* New York: Cambridge University Press.

—— (1989). Issues of regularity and control: Confessions of a regularity freak. In L. W. Poon, D. C. Rubin, & B. A. Wilson (Eds.) *Everyday cognition in adulthood and late life* (pp. 116–125). New York: Cambridge University Press.

Rubin, D. C., & Kozin, M. (1984). Vivid memories. *Cognition, 16,* 81–95.

Rubin, D. C., Wetzler, S. E., & Nebes, R. D. (1986). Autobiographical memory across the adult life span. In D. C. Rubin (Ed.), *Autobiographical memory.* New York: Cambridge University Press.

Sarbin, T. (Ed.) (1986). *Narrative psychology: The storied nature of human conduct.* New York: Praeger.

Sperbeck, D., Whitbourne, S., & Hoyer, W. (1986). Age and openness to experience in autobiographical memory. *Experimental Aging Research, 12,* 169–172.

Thornton, S., & Brotchie, J. (1987). Reminiscence: A critical review of the empirical literature. *British Journal of Clinical Psychology, 26,* 93–111.

Webster, J. D. (1993a). Construction and validation of the reminiscence functions scale. *Journal of Gerontology: Psychological Sciences, 48,* P256-P262.

—— (1993b). Adult age differences in reminiscence functions. Paper presented at the 46th Annual Scientific Meeting of the Gerontological Society of America, New Orleans, LA.

Webster, J. D., & Cappeliez, P. (1993). Reminiscence and autobiographical memory: Complementary contexts for cognitive aging research. *Developmental Review, 13,* 54–91.

Wetzler, S. E., & Sweeney, J. A. (1986). Childhood amnesia: An empirical demonstration. In D. C. Rubin (Ed.), *Autobiographical memory* (pp. 202–221). New York: Cambridge University Press.

Wong, P. T. P., & Watt, L. M. (1991). What types of reminiscence are associated with successful aging? *Psychology and Aging, 6,* 272–279.

Zola-Morgan, S., Cohen, N. J., & Squire, L. R. (1983). Recall of remote episodic memory in amnesia. *Neuropsychologia, 21,* 487–500.

16   Schizophrenic delusions and the construction of autobiographical memory

Alan Baddeley, Andrew Thornton, Siew Eng Chua, and Peter McKenna

In recent years, the study of normal cognitive function has gained substantially from the study of patients with cognitive deficits. Research on autobiographical memory is no exception, and research on retrograde amnesia and on confabulation in patients suffering from brain damage featured prominently in an earlier volume on this topic (Rubin, 1986). However, while the contribution of neuropsychology to the understanding of normal function is well established, neuropsychiatry has so far been less influential. One of the reasons is that psychiatry itself has been far from unanimous in its approach to the most appropriate conceptualization of its subject matter. There has, for example, been prolonged controversy as to whether schizophrenia should be regarded as a physical disorder resulting from some form of dysfunction of the brain, or as others would claim, a psychological response to psychosocial stress.

While there is still little agreement as to what, if any, physical changes in the brain are associated with schizophrenia (see Waddington, 1993, for an overview), the application of neuropsychological techniques to the study of schizophrenic patients makes it clear that cognitive deficits are characteristic, and in particular tend to produce an impairment in memory (see McKenna, Clare, & Baddeley, 1995, for a review), and in executive functions (see Frith, 1992). These deficits do not appear to be a result of drug treatment, nor can they readily be explained in terms of problems of motivation, or disruption by positive symptoms such as hallucinations and delusions. In the case of the memory deficit, it has some similarities to the classic amnesic syndrome, in showing preserved digit span and recency in free recall, together with impaired long-term learning for both verbal and visual material (McKenna, Tamlyn, Lund, Mortimer, Hammond, & Baddeley, 1990; Tamlyn, McKenna, Mortimer, Lund, Hammond, & Baddeley, 1992). As with the amnesic syndrome, there is also evidence for the preservation of implicit and procedural learning (Clare, McKenna, Mortimer, & Baddeley, 1993). In addition, however, schizophrenic patients typically show impaired semantic memory performance (Clare et al., 1993), together with a tendency for the executive processes of working memory to be disrupted (Morice & Delahunty, 1994).

It is, of course, important in discussing the cognitive impairments shown in schizophrenic patients, to bear in mind that these are only part of the pattern of the illness. A crucial aspect of schizophrenia is the presence of symptoms such as hallucinations and delusions. Such symptoms, that are a crucial hallmark of schizophrenia, do not, of course, occur frequently or prominently in the population of brain damaged patients that are encountered by the neuropsychologist. For that reason, hallucinations and delusions have been comparatively little studied using cognitive or neuropsychological methods. They nevertheless present a fascinating challenge to the understanding of normal function. How can hallucinations be related to "normal" veridical perception, and the issue that concerns us here, how can delusions – false beliefs that invariably refer to the patient's own experience – be related to normal autobiographical memory?

In an earlier volume on this topic, Baddeley and Wilson (1986) studied the breakdown of autobiographical memory in a small sample of brain damaged patients. The approach taken was very much that of the natural historian, describing the patients and subsequently attempting to make sense of the pattern observed. It led to a taxonomy of autobiographical memory that, in turn, suggested two lines of development. The first consisted of the observation of marked differences in autobiographical memory in patients who superficially appeared to have similar amnesic deficits. This finding suggested the need for better clinical measures of autobiographical memory, and led to the development by Kopelman, Wilson, and Baddeley (1989, 1990) of the autobiographical memory inventory, a clinical instrument that measures the patient's capacity to remember autobiographical facts and autobiographical episodes across the life span.

The second line of development was concerned with the observation of confabulation in two of the patients who were suffering from bilateral damage to the frontal lobes, resulting in a deficit in executive processes. This finding led to the hypothesis that confabulation demands the combination of impaired memory and defective operation of the executive component of working memory; subsequent research does seem to support the view that confabulation is typically accompanied by both these deficits (Shallice, 1988). From the viewpoint of understanding normal memory, the fact that pure amnesia does not lead to confabulation emphasizes the importance of executive processes in retrieving and interpreting autobiographical memories.

What might the study of confabulation in dysexecutive patients tell us about the nature of delusions? And what might delusions tell us about normal autobiographical memory? We should begin by differentiating between these two types of cognitive distortion. A confabulation is a nonveridical recollection. Confabulations can be divided into two classes (Kopelman, 1987), one of which represents a relatively normal tendency to go beyond the mnemonic evidence by producing a plausible guess. The other that is much more pathological, represents the invention of episodes that not only did not happen, but may on occasion be quite bizarre, such as writing a letter about the death of a brother who is still alive. It is this latter type of confabulation that is associated with the combination of amnesia and the dysexecutive syndrome. Our evidence suggested that such confabulations tended to be highly unstable, and were denied and replaced by other confabulations when the patient was retested on a later occasion (Baddeley & Wilson, 1988). In contrast, a delusion is typically considered to reflect a relatively coherent account by the subject that is nonveridical; it may be quite bizarre, but differs from the typical confabulation in that it persists over time. Phenomena similar to delusions are observed in dysexecutive patients, although in our experience they tend to be much less florid than is typically found in schizophrenia. For example, one dysexecutive patient with a memory problem, when tested, would frequently remark that as a nurse tutor, she had given the same tests to student nurses, while the patient, Clive Wearing, who is so densely amnesic that he believes he has only just recovered consciousness (Wilson & Wearing, in press), often comments that he had worked in hospitals extensively during his vacations as a student (he had, in fact, worked in hotels). In both cases, it seems likely that the patients find the situation strangely familiar and have developed a consistent way of explaining its familiarity.

Is it plausible to assume that schizophrenic patients who show evidence of delusions might demonstrate a similar pattern of cognitive deficits to our confabulating neuropsychological cases? While they are clearly not the same, since, as we shall see, the extent and quality of the delusions differs, nevertheless, as mentioned earlier, there is evidence that schizophrenic patients tend to have both memory deficits and to show dysexecutive symptoms. We therefore decided to take a somewhat similar approach to that taken by Baddeley and Wilson in studying confabulation, namely to begin with natural history. Of the authors, one (PMcK) had many years of experience of working with schizophrenic patients, while another, (AB) had encountered relatively few patients. We decided on the following strategy: PMcK would select a sample of patients who were characterized principally by the presence of marked delusions. These would each be interviewed on two occasions by AB, who would simply try to characterize the nature of their delusions, possibly formulating some general hypotheses. This would be followed by a second phase in which these patients and an equivalent number of schizophrenic patients, who were not deluded but were matched for age and premorbid intelligence, would be tested on a range of neuropsychological tests, in particular concentrating on memory and executive functions. These results would then be used to test a range of possible hypotheses. Finally, the implications of the results for understanding both delusions and normal distortions of autobiographical memory will be discussed.

The nature of schizophrenia

The essential feature of schizophrenia is the development, usually in early adult life, of a range of severe disturbances in the realms of thought, perception, emotion, and behavior. These disturbances fall into two main groups: florid or positive symptoms and negative or deterioration symptoms. One important class of positive symptoms is delusions, which are the subject matter of this chapter. Delusions are beliefs that are abnormal by virtue of being inherently unlikely; in many cases, as will be seen below, they are patently absurd and sometimes they can be quite fantastic in nature. Nevertheless, the beliefs are held with complete conviction and seem impervious to counterargument. Other positive symptoms include hallucinations. These are most commonly auditory –

the symptom of hearing voices – but hallucinations may occur in any sensory modality: visual, tactile, smell, or taste. Additionally, some schizophrenic patients exhibit so-called formal thought disorder, a breakdown in the normal coherent pattern of thinking and communication so that what they say becomes difficult to follow. In extreme cases speech may become totally incomprehensible (see Frith, 1992, for a discussion of this).

Positive symptoms typically wax and wane over time, but alongside these a large majority of patients with schizophrenia develop negative symptoms that tend to be permanent. Important symptoms of this type include lack of volition, a state of apathy that impairs the ability to work and carry on leisure activities, and affective flattening, a loss of emotional responsiveness that may manifest itself in coldness, indifference or extreme withdrawal from social contact.

Although no two patients with schizophrenia show exactly the same symptoms, the overall picture tends to be characteristic and easily recognizable. The typical patient with established schizophrenia presents as an individual who is obviously odd in manner, and who may also be withdrawn, unkempt, or rather taciturn. He or she may or may not experience continuing positive symptoms like delusions and hallucinations, and peculiarities of speech may be noticeable. The patient will probably be living an isolated and rather empty life, getting up late, going to bed early, with little productive activity in between. Unemployment is the rule in schizophrenia, and the more severely affected patients have difficulties with basic activities like washing, changing clothes, and providing for themselves. A sizable proportion are unable to live independently and only manage in the community with supervision and support; some require indefinite inpatient care.

The patients

We believe that it is important to give a relatively detailed account of the patients and their delusions, since we feel that the qualitative character of delusions represents an important component of what must be explained. However, since each patient was interviewed for up to an hour on two occasions, a full transcript would be prohibitively long. We have therefore opted to give a summary of each interview, concentrating in the second interview on any new information or discrepancies with the first. In order to give a flavor of the interview, quotations will be used extensively. As will become clear, while some patients converse relatively normally, others show a degree of formal thought disorder. We attempt to include quotes that are sufficiently lengthy to give an overall impression of each patient's style of communication. For each of the five patients selected, the account of the interview (by AB) is preceded by a brief case history, provided by PMcK. The nature of the interview was essentially unstructured, with the interviewer trying to obtain as straightforward an account as possible of the experience and beliefs of each patient. Since the principal concern was with delusions, there was, of course, a consistent aim to follow up any reference to delusional beliefs, and to probe their origins and reason for retention. If similar delusions were not mentioned on the second occasion, then the interviewer would attempt to probe, while being careful to avoid any direct suggestion. We will begin with patient SD, who is the most articulate in talking about his illness and his delusions.

1. SD: Master chess player and pop star?

SD is a 31-year-old man who, following the typical schizophrenic pattern, first became ill in young adult life. At about the age of 21 his family noticed that he was increasingly moody and lethargic. Two years later he rather abruptly began to express ideas that he was going to be sexually tortured and castrated. He had three admissions to hospital over the next 2 years during which he showed delusions and various other positive symptoms, but he made a good recovery with treatment each time. He then moved to Cambridge to attend college but found himself unable to keep up. Shortly afterwards his delusions recurred and he had a further prolonged admission to hospital. During this admission, schizophrenic negative symptoms became clearly evident, in particular lack of volition. This time improvement was slow, but eventually he became well enough to move to a hostel for psychiatric patients where he has lived for the last 2 years.

SD continues to show a mild degree of lack of motivation. Many of his florid symptoms have subsided and not recurred since his last hospital admission. However, he remains continuously deluded. He believes that he is really a rock star, but that doctors have removed his memories of this part of his life by a process of hypnosis. As a result, he only has occasional experiences to remind him of his other life, for instance recognizing himself in photographs of rock groups or occasionally recalling isolated memories such as walking in the park with a man who looked like Mick Jagger. SD also believes that he is a chess master, these memories having been once again removed. Otherwise, he appears normal in every way, and is able to give a lucid account of his symptoms without any trace of formal thought disorder.

Interview 1. SD described how he had been a college student in the north of England and in Cambridge before dropping out and taking a job as a hospital porter, that he enjoyed until he was sacked because of mental illness.

> AB: What's the nature of your mental illness?
> SD: Well originally I was diagnosed as paranoid schizophrenic. I ended up in hospital, say February 1985.
> AB: What are the symptoms of that?
> SD: I thought I was going to be got by people, castrated or sexually tortured.
> AB: Do you feel that now?
> SD: No it's gone away now. It did go away immediately I'd taken the injections in hospital.

He is currently afraid of socializing in case he says or does something wrong and feels stupid. When asked to elaborate he reports:

> SD: Well I have this idea that I am a rock star chess player.
> AB: Both at the same time?
> SD: Yes.

AB: When you say you have the idea, do you believe it, or do you say you have the idea?

SD: I sort of jockey between the two things, believing and disbelieving.

AB: And at the moment?

SD: Well usually I tend to believe it in a sort of hopeful, – just to hope that I've done something with my life.

When asked about the evidence for his belief, he mentions having seen himself on TV, and having a friend who is a rock star.

AB: Can you remember being a rock star?

SD: No. I've had some flashback type things, like remembering I was in this studio with these particular people. These American New York. . . .

It then emerged that SD thinks he is a guitar player, but cannot actually play the guitar.

AB: You can't play the guitar?

SD: No.

AB: And at the moment what do you think? Do you think you're a rock star?

SD: I think so, yes.

AB: Why do you think that, if you can't play the guitar?

SD: Well I think there's a . . . look to playing the guitar, and they all play guitar when it's like really needed, or perhaps I sort of conserve energy to play guitar very well. There's a thing that Eric Clapton never practices, I think it's something like that really.

Moving on to his chess playing skills,

AB: You say you're also a chess player?

SD: (Laughs) Yes, originally when I came to hospital I thought I was a Grand Master at chess.

It is clear from talking to him that he does know something about chess and reports having an ELO grade of 170, quite strong but by no means Grand Master class.

AB: What sort of competitions did you play in?

SD: I can't remember. I had an idea that I was a player called Z . . . , he's a Russian player, for some reason when I came to hospital I – there's no chance that I could be Russian, so I thought I might be German because I speak a bit of German.

AB: So you think you might be a Russian?

SD: Half Russian, I was hoping to, if you want to play for something you want to play for Russia really, at chess.

AB: But, if you don't speak Russian, isn't that rather odd for a Russian chess player?

SD: Yes, well I don't speak Russian, but I think it's possible that I've been hypnotized to forget things like the fact that I can speak Russian. I've no memory of ever living in Russia, but I think it's possible that when

I go to Russia I'd go out, which is to go into another state of mind, another state of consciousness that's cut off from the one that lives in England. Because another thing about that is that I think I've got a mate called Sonny, and I've got this idea that he's a Russian Grand Master and all he speaks is Welsh and English, he doesn't speak Russian so far as I know. I asked him if he was this Russian chess player and he said "No." So he's no sense of ever having been a Russian chess player, but I think he probably was. Quite a good player actually, one of the top Russian players.

SD comments that other people "don't really care, or perhaps don't see why it's such a vital thing for me . . . "

AB: Maybe they don't believe you really were?

SD: Yes, I understand that, but I think they could be deluded as well as I can be deluded because if I am a rock star or chess player I didn't have any inkling of it until I was about 28.

AB: Right, when you say you didn't have any inkling of it until you were 28, do you mean that you weren't a rock star until you were 28?

SD: No, I am saying that I went out to be a rock star, I went into this different consciousness that's cut off from my everyday existence. That's clear isn't it?

AB: Yes. Can you move into this other consciousness?

SD: No, I've no idea how I get there, I imagine it's some kind of hypnotic say, semblance of words that leads into this other state of mind, but I don't really know these things.

Interview 2. This comprised further discussion of the belief that he is a Russian chess Grand Master, together with the belief that a number of his friends are also Grand Masters, and a further attempt to explain his belief as follows:

SD: Well I have this idea that most of the time I am in a thing called a *calm*, which is a state of forgetfulness, you forget all the things that you've done . . . and so it gives you a very good sort of rest . . . which is sort of essential for people who are full of mental exaggerations, and who have mental demands made upon them.

AB: And you have a lot made on you do you think?

SD: Well if I'm a chess Master and a rock star, probably yes. So I'd need that kind of sleep I suppose.

He referred to a brief mention in the previous interview that he might also be a writer, in this case he thinks he would have written books like those of Axel Munthe.

Returning to the rock star theme,

SD: I had this idea that I might be three rock stars, which is like different kind of cosmetic changes in my face perhaps, different nose, different eyes, different mouth.

When pressed as to how this would happen, SD was rather vague, but explained

> SD: . . . I've got a mate called Jake, when I knew him he had a really small face, when I first met him, and then later on getting to know him a bit better, his face sort of puffed up a bit and he looked like a rock star – so I was very excited by that when I sort of discovered he was my friend, I thought he was Don Fagin [a member of the rock group Steely Dan].
>
> AB: Why should Don Fagin suddenly appear here under a different name with no evidence of being a rock star?
>
> SD: Everybody . . . Elton John is really Reg Dwight, so everybody's got their own names – what do you call that, the opposite of a stage name? I didn't know for certain that he was Donald Fagin, I just hoped. I confronted him in a pub once.
>
> AB: And what did he say?
>
> SD: I said "I keep thinking you're somebody else," and he said "Who?," and I said "Donald Fagin," and he said "Who the f's he?" I said "He's a musician/composer" and then he said "I compose women" which was quite an interesting thing to say. He was, he is a very good-looking guy really.

The remainder of the interview was chiefly notable because of the account he gave of what it felt like during the early stages of his illness.

> SD: Things like tidal waves of sort of panic. Or just tidal waves that weren't panicky, just feeling slightly queasy and dizzy.

He later referred to what he described as "mental seizure."

> SD: Well say I was . . . , I wouldn't be able to understand what somebody was talking about at the other end, because my brain would just sort of go like that . . . , squeeze together sort of in a way and not . . . up, if you know what I mean. And it made it very difficult to understand. I remember I had this problem, I was trying to find out whose these keys were, of where the keys were or what, and I couldn't think straight. I was trying to talk to one of the staff, and I just couldn't grasp what I was trying to think about.

SD also explained his earlier statement that he had been afraid that people were trying to castrate him. He had written a letter to one of his teachers, "A really stupid letter, not a threatening letter, it wasn't very nice, but it wasn't really horrible . . . it wasn't really a love letter, and she was married as well. I had sort of these guilt feelings, that I was going to be castrated because I'd sort of offended her I suppose." He went on to explain that he had never had a girlfriend, but had almost had one, but he had heard her say to someone "It's alright I'll give him cancer . . . so I thought she might have tried or was thinking of giving me AIDS."

AB: Do you think you might have misheard, it does seem a strange thing to
    say?

SD: Well I have had a lot of these things where I've heard somebody say-
    ing something a bit strange, especially when I'm drunk.

Discussion. Perhaps the most striking feature of SD is the contrast between the
strangeness and implausibility of his beliefs, coupled with his ability to talk about them
rationally and relatively analytically. Given their implausibility, and the apparent flim-
siness of the evidence, why does he hold to them so firmly? We will return to this issue
later. The next patient, RS, is considerably more florid in his delusions, and in the distortions in his language behavior, which include a number of neologisms.

2. RS: An interplanetary traveler?

RS's illness dates back to his adolescence, when he started truanting from school and
lost all interest in his work. After 2 years of this behavior he was referred to a psychia-
trist where he was noted to be depressed and withdrawn. After several more years
where by all accounts he remained withdrawn and eccentric but managed to obtain a
job as a warehouseman, at the age of 24 he suddenly started behaving bizarrely and
voicing many delusions. These symptoms settled over a few weeks with treatment, but
it was clear that they did not recede completely.

Over the next few years RS had a number of relapses and gradually his illness transformed into a state characterized principally by multiple florid delusions. He shows the
phenomenon of fantastic delusions, beliefs that are so bizarre that they violate common
sense at its most elementary. RS's delusions are expressed against a background of considerable incoherence of thinking, but he currently shows a lack of other symptoms
such as auditory hallucinations. He lives in a hostel adjacent to the hospital site.

Interview 1. This began with RS declaring that "I don't want to be a nut, I'd rather be
more of a turgit." This was followed by a rather unsuccessful attempt by AB to understand these terms, eventually leading on to the suggestion by RS that he was ill because
his "chemicals had been exchanged with those of a black man." When pressed for further details, he eventually declared it to be a secret. When asked about the symptoms,

RS: My body is all weak and willy-nilly, do you know what I mean?

AB: Yes, has it always been this weak?

RS: Well I've got the strength, but I haven't the energy – I'm six or seven
    z-forces in strength.

AB: Sorry, what's z-force?

RS: Strength – so I'll probably be one z-force I suppose in Geneva's terms.

AB: What are Geneva's terms?

RS: Well I'd say one would be seven of mine, if I had seven z-forces it
    would be one z-force.

AB: Sorry?

RS: I suppose the measurement's gone up.

When asked if there were any further problems,

> RS: Right now someone – I haven't got my own mind in my head at the moment. I don't know if there's any lines of blood going from my head to somebody else's.
>
> AB: Lines of blood?
>
> RS: I don't know if someone switched minds with me or whether I've got my own mind back now. . . . . It can cause a lot of hassle because they might be swindling you. Well you see, you never know if you're owed money by somebody and, well, they switch minds to swindle you.
>
> AB: It seems a complicated way of swindling somebody, switching minds.
>
> RS: Well it's easy isn't it, 'cause you just see the – they recognize the person to be the person whose mind it belongs to, as the person who's got it.

After a number of attempts to sort out the meaning of this particular sentence,

> RS: I've had it done on me when I was younger. From birth 'til I was 25 years old. Someone switched minds with me. Some man called George Hurding – Hurding, who I believe is Adolf Hitler.
>
> AB: You think he's really Adolf Hitler?
>
> RS: I think he is yes, because I remember blowing the regime up. I blew the regime up on a certain planet you see once. – A planet called Judacy . . . we blew it up. Germans . . . and gas . . . that was a long time ago that was . . . that was a separate war from what you know. It was in between two world wars. I'm talking about some time before, it's like as if I was some man called Agapon Bond once . . . that was the commander of M19.

RS went on to explain that he had flown to the planet on a "jecalaysia" from Saturn, where he had been born. Hitler was "getting up to wicked things, causing the Jewish race so much harm, that we couldn't stand it any longer, so we just flew out to gas them."

> AB: How did Hitler get on to this planet?
>
> RS: I can't disclose that, that's an official secret.
>
> AB: And you're sure about this, you couldn't be wrong? It couldn't be something you just read about?
>
> RS: I know it happened because there was a war in Germany against the Jews.
>
> AB: That's true but. . . .
>
> RS: That wasn't in 1945, it was in between the First and Second World Wars.
>
> AB: But wasn't Hitler at that time in Germany, not on this planet?
>
> RS: Mm.
>
> AB: So how did he? . . .
>
> RS: Dropped gelignite down the bunker.

AB: Right, but how, he seems to have been in two places at once?

RS: Well it's like as if there's a Hitler everywhere. I can't tell you, I'm not allowed to tell you, it's a secret. . . . It's like if there's someone of some description is a Hitler, relatively a Hitler somewhere by some other name or other.

RS goes on to refer to being "booked for a case job, on four or five different planets by someone living at a place called Samosa Jorna. I got booked for it and I got skinned for it, tortured for 17 years." The torture is described as "Some person who looks what I used to look like, before I went snap. My look's all wrong at the moment."

RS: Well I went snap see and my bone structure changed in my face. So probably Michael did.

AB: Sorry, Michael is who?

RS: Michael who was sitting here [an earlier patient]. I think he went snap as well. You go snap you see, and if you haven't repaired special like, like I know how to mend snap people, like they can with beans and chips, I don't know if you knew that.

AB: No.

RS: A pound of chips and five ounces of baked beans, an odd sausage twice a day.

AB: For how long?

RS: For 3 weeks and then a week on one meal of it for a week.

AB: And when you snap, what does it mean?

RS: Like your world can go, your mind can break, mine broke see. We went on to discuss the symptoms.

RS: 'cause I'm blind you see.

AB: You can see me though can't you?

RS: I'm not sure if I can. I can see colors. I'm not seeing the colors that you're wearing, it's the opposite. . . . I purchase the opposite, when I purchase clothes.

When asked to name the colors I was wearing, however, he was quite accurate.

RS: I want to save the world you see, if I can.

He explained that this would be achieved through the "Dems, short for Democrat Fegelanians and the Fegelanian Rights Act that says that 'If you see funny things or hear funny things, that it's treason against a person, according to the Law'."

RS: I've been searching Jesus, and that's all. He's around somewhere. Unless it's 'cause I believe that I see other people, I see Jesus everywhere, in people. Yourself included.

He then went on to talk about his earlier life and job as a warehouseman, although in a somewhat disjointed and disconnected way.

Interview 2. On this occasion, RS explained that his illness had happened shortly after trying unsuccessfully to make love to a girl he was in love with, "I went snap, 2 days after I tried to make love to her. I tried with all my heart and soul." He goes on to mention problems of having his mind switched, referring to the Bible, "Well, it's in the Bible you see, on those pages. Back eight pages or back twenty pages." However he denied that the mind-switching caused a problem with his girlfriend, although it "caused problems with me wife though, the magic I had done on me when I was . . . someone was up to black magic with me. That girl that I went out with before I got married."

When asked about any current problems, he refers to not having any socks on because "they're in the wash," and to what he terms "a love illness," referring to a separation from his wife. He goes on to refer to "finding a weakness in his arms" that interferes with his saving the world. He talks about voices and again refers to "Democrats," followed by a rather convoluted definition, and the remark "I'm not saying anything really am I?"

> AB: Well you're saying something but I don't entirely understand.
> RS: I'm not allowed to say it you see, it's treason.
> AB: What would happen if you did?
> RS: I'd probably get butchered.
> AB: Who by?
> RS: By the police.

There followed a long and rambling conversation about music and the guitar and how you can commit treason on a guitar "If you squeeze a guitar . . . the notes are, and they cross over, and if they cross over it's an infinity treason . . . "

> RS: Would you like a cigarette?
> AB: No I don't smoke thanks.
> RS: I don't blame you. Please don't start will you 'cause it does your life in.

Discussion. It is clear that RS has much more florid and bizarre delusions than did the previous patient, combining paranoia and grandiosity, and expressed in a rather characteristic schizophrenic style that is difficult to follow, both in terms of its syntax and in terms of the content and vocabulary that contains, in the first interview, a number of neologisms. The second interview is substantially less florid, with the suggestion that RS is being intentionally obscure because he will be killed or imprisoned by the police if he gives away crucial information. Unfortunately this makes it difficult to be sure, on the present evidence, that the delusion is a consistent one. However, PMcK who knows the patient well can confirm that the delusion of interplanetary travel and warfare is a persistent feature of RS, who in addition has many other delusions.

3. EN: A wicked sister?

EN is a 34-year-old woman who had an uneventful childhood, and was an outgoing and sociable, if somewhat wayward, young woman until she became ill at the age of 22.

Over a few days she became behaviorally disturbed and was admitted to hospital in a trancelike state. This hospital admission was the first of 10, the most recent of which lasted 4 years. EN's illness has always featured marked delusions, among other symptoms. Early on she expressed a variety of beliefs, for example that her mother was a witch and was sucking fluid from her brain and that she had been taken over by a poltergeist. Approximately 5 years ago she began to talk of having a (nonexistent) identical twin sister, who had the same Christian name as she did.

EN seemed destined for long-stay hospital care until treatment with a new drug, clozapine, brought her symptoms and behavioral disturbance under control and allowed her to leave hospital and move into a hostel. Currently she is superficially well, has a good grasp of the fact that she has been ill and is now much better, and has managed to find part-time work. She does not spontaneously discuss her delusions, but if they are inquired about it is clear that they are all still present.

Interview 1.

> AB: Can you tell me what your name is please?
> EN: I was christened Lady Dorothy Lake, but my stepparents call me E – the same as my sister.
> AB: Were you just given that name, or were you actually a titled person?
> EN: Yes I am, yes yes, the Queen Mother's got my birth certificate.
> AB: Why the Queen Mother?
> EN: I don't know, because my family, my dad's name was Sir Grace Darling,[1] and when I was a little girl I saw Douglas Bader walk up the street with my dad – the pilot with no legs. And I can remember when I was a little girl, this is true, I can remember, I went to Buckingham Palace and the Queen took me to the toilet, when I was a little girl.

EN went on to explain that the Royal Family keep in touch by letter, and that she had had "a very pleasant letter from Margaret Thatcher 2 years ago. It was helping me get my flat organized." EN then explained that she was adopted, given the same name as her sister, who was born in Suffolk (where EN was), and later moved to Cambridgeshire. This was followed by an account of a terrible accident when she was a little girl.

> EN: Someone hit me on the back of the head with a brick. So I had to go away and the Queen Mother arranged for me to go to a special hospital to see if I can have anything done. Because I've got a big hole in the back of my skull.
> AB: Has that healed up now?
> EN: No it hasn't no.
> AB: Is that a problem?
> EN: Yes. It hurts sometimes.

---

[1] Grace Darling was a famous Victorian heroine who rescued shipwrecked sailors during a storm.

AB: And your sister, is she your real sister or your stepsister?

EN: She is my stepsister, yes. She's a bit of a nutcase, when she was 13, she wrote to Prince Charles and said would Prince Charles marry her 'cause she's the Princess of Wales. She's a bit funny in the head.

AB: Do you still see her?

EN: No I haven't seen her for 10 years. I only saw her for a week, I was sunbathing in the garden, and a car pulled up and she walked in the gate with her suitcase, she only stayed a week. And when she was 18 she started to smoke cannabis, and she was living with a hippie in Burwell [a local village]. I know for a fact that she was mainlining with sulphate – speed.

AB: And that was 10 years ago?

EN: Yes. I haven't seen her since. I don't take no injections like that, I'm a coward having blood taken. People get us mixed up you know, and I don't know why.

AB: Does she look like you?

EN: No she doesn't, nothing like me at all. She's got big hips, bigger hips than me, she's got a beauty mole on the side of her mouth.

AB: Is she a nice person?

EN: If you're a man she is, yes. Nobody likes her, she's such a bitch, no wonder they won't take any notice of her, they don't like her.

AB: And does she attract men?

EN: Yes she does. She doesn't get anywhere. I heard her boyfriend said to me, a lot of 'em were saying she's nothing but a tease.

When asked how she was at the moment she said:

EN: I'm fine, I'm fine, I've had a lot of headaches, a lot of headaches, and my eyes are getting worse, it's getting slowly darker. I've lost the light. I lost the light 10 years ago.

AB: In what way did you lose the light?

EN: The light, you know the light all around you, not sunlight, the light after 5 o'clock, I don't see that no more, where I am now it's exactly the same wherever I am at night, morning whatever – everything was clear and bright. My mum taught, she taught me at. But I can't go it no more 'cause something got me from inside my head. A tendon, I've got stitches in the back of my head, where something was removed.

AB: But you're not blind now so. . . .

EN: Yes I am. It's very dark, the carpet is dark gray.

When asked about the color of my sweater and curtains she was quite accurate in naming them.

Interview 2. Again EN began by saying that her first name was Lady Dorothy Lake, but called E – by her stepparents.

When asked about her sister:

> EN: I don't want to know, everybody said they're trying to find my sister, for God's sake, what has she done? . . . People, different doctors and people like you all along the way, people who get to know me, they say "Where's your sister?" But there, it's not directed at me in any way, it's my sister. I don't know what she's done, why men are looking for her, I ain't got a clue.
>
> AB: Yes, alright, let's forget about your sister. Tell me a bit about your . . .
>
> EN: If you want to know about her you'd better ask her mother hadn't you? . . . Because just before Christmas I phoned up my brother, I said, "Hello Kevin," I said, "It's Dorothy here." He said "I know it's Dorothy, E – said you were Dorothy." So this proves that she's somewhere you see.

She went on to talk about her birth certificate having been sent to the Queen Mother, and being hit on the head with a brick, and then being sent to Russia to be treated, where presumably she learnt Russian. "Why Russia?" "The surgeons were better in Russia than they were here."

When asked about her eyes again she said that she had got new glasses that make things a little bit better. When asked about the symptoms she suggested that her eye problem came from a small cyst on her jaw that could also be the cause of her mental illness because it's near the temple. She again, however, said that things looked dark and the colors were duller.

Discussion. EN has a delusional alter-ego, in the sense that she seems to assume that a person called EN is, in fact, her rather disreputable sister, and that she herself is Lady Dorothy Lake, somehow related to the Royal Family. She acknowledges an illness that creates headaches and visual symptoms, and that led to her having an operation in Russia and learning Russian. In general, her delusional system remains consistent over the two sessions. Her language and capacity for communication was much better than the previous patient, although a problem did arise at one point as a result of the interviewer assuming that her name, EN, referred to the patient, while the patient indignantly maintained that this was the name of her wicked missing sister. It was also striking the extent to which the imaginary sister dominated the first interview, while in the second, EN complained bitterly that everybody seemed to be more interested in her sister than in her.

4. JH: Financier and politician?

JH is a 56-year-old man who has been continuously ill for about 15 years. The onset of his illness was at the age of 40, rather late for schizophrenia but by no means exceptional. His symptoms started at the time of the break up of his marriage and the failure of his joinery business, events that may, of course, have been a result of emerging illness rather than precipitating it.

For virtually the whole period of his illness, JH has shown a vast, highly complex system of persecutory and grandiose delusions. Many of these delusions are fantastic and some of them shift and change while others – for example, that he is being persecuted by the Mafia and that he is related to royalty – form consistent themes around which other ideas are embroidered. JH regularly acts on his delusions, ringing the police, visiting army bases, and on one occasion attempting to break into Buckingham Palace to see the Queen. He shows other symptoms, notably auditory hallucinations, and he exhibits a minor degree of formal thought disorder, but apart from these he shows little if any evidence of deterioration and he is able to live within the community with only minimal support. A notable feature of JH's presentation is his ability to talk completely rationally for long periods, giving the appearance of complete normality, until his delusions are touched upon, whereupon he launches into the kind of account detailed below.

Interview 1. JH began by explaining that he did not know who his real parents were, claiming that his stepfather had procured a birth certificate when he was 10 years old. He talks volubly and in a mildly disordered way as in the following reply to a question of whether the certificate presented a problem:

> JH: It is a problem because I've got a family tree. I'm the eldest son according to them in a booklet that I could have brought up to you today if I'd thought about it. [This is true – he responded to an advertisement that offered to trace anyone's family tree and to provide a 'coat of arms'.] It's got a coat of arms, a lovely coat of arms which I'm proud to wear, it's got a Knight in the family, of medieval times and it calls itself out of mural crown, I don't understand this. It's got a crown on the emblem, on the coat of arms. It talks of a Saxon king giving this order like, you know. So it dates back to Saxon times, the family of H, if I'm an H. But my penis was cut underneath and stitched up when I was a boy, and I don't know the reason for that, why they done that, over money or something that was taken from me in life. I couldn't keep a penny of my money, I had people thieving it from me all over.

This feeling of paranoia cropped up again when he was talking about his treatment when he commented, "I've got people watching me, the police, and I think they've ordered no drugs, that's what I believe."

> AB: Why do you think the police might want to influence your drugs?
> JH: Because I've given policies for the government in a letter, and phoned them up when I've thought about policies, phoned them up on the telephone. And they've said to me they've proved that my mother and father was King George and the Queen Mother – I was taken away from them, that's what the police told me. They phoned up the Queen

Mother some time ago, I wouldn't tell the doctor anything about it.
But they phoned up for me the Queen Mother and she said she was
my mother, and she wanted to see me. And when the Queen Mother
came here to open the Trumpington Road memorial museum . . . she
looked at me on the road, I was on the corner, as she turned round the
corner . . . she looked at me all the time and wouldn't take her eyes off
me.

He also claimed to have been recognized by her at race meetings and similar occasions.
When asked about his job:

JH: Carpentry and joinery, painting.
AB: Do you still do any of it?
JH: No, I've been ordered not to.
AB: So what other things are you interested in?
JH: Poetry, writing, politics. I've got a new range of politics for the world.
    I want to change it to paradise, I think I can get it. The first thing, I
    would commandeer the banks, I want the banks, I want the Stock Ex-
    change, I want the firms to be either government or me handling them
    – as King, as permanent King. Now, I've got enough money which
    I've won.
AB: How did you win it?
JH: Well I won it on horses, a lot of money has been on horses.
AB: It must have been a big bet?
JH: Yes, big bets – 10 million at a time. My policies are, that, let me think
    if I can think about them – all buildings go onto the banks as Stock Ex-
    changes, as money – hospitals, the value of the hospital going into
    banks as money, police.
AB: I'm not sure that I understand, when you say all buildings go to the
    banks, do you mean we sell them?
JH: No, as money orders, as vouchers of so much money, invested in the
    bank, never losing it. Just paying the staff off from profits, what you
    get, make profits on the profits what are invested on in the bank.

JH claimed to have originally tried to influence the Labour party, and then to have
moved to the Conservatives, where Mrs. Thatcher wanted him in her Cabinet for his
advice.

JH: . . . and brief them like, you know, brief them about politics. And
    I briefed them about politics, I've given them all money, not money,
    I've given them all word for their conferences – been my word,
    striking the other governments and what they've done and every-
    thing, that's me. They never paid me out, and I'm holding the word
    all up secret, so that I can have it in court, to get money which I've
    never had.

When asked about an earlier reference to voices, JH described them starting when he was 17.

> JH: Yes they came to me when a girl came to me, she was a dream of mine, when I was 17. It wasn't possible for me to dream of her, but I dreamt of this girl and she came one night as this girl, and I loved her. Not sex, but loved that girl for her being. That was my dream girl that I wanted before I had a girlfriend. And I wanted this girl so much to come in my life, in my dream as a young man. I was a decent young man, no wrong, and wanted a girlfriend very much. And she came into my life and I was married and I told her I couldn't do nothing without I'd have to get separated.
>
> I never married her. No she's got my children, she's held up from coming to me, I've seen her at Epsom with the Queen. Straight afterwards with me they oo'ed at the sight of her, she's a very voluptuous girl, luxurious girl, a very good girl.

He does however have other voices.

> JH: Voices – they're boys and girls and Mafia and book company and police and everyone talking to me.
>
> It's a nuisance, I'm fed up with it. I'll hit them for not giving me a letter to prove that they're talking to me like, you know. . . . .They think I'm Jesus, that's what they think. . . . They ask me on church, when I watch the church service, what beliefs shall we given, and I say something and next week it comes out.
>
> AB: Appears in a church service here?
>
> JH: Not here, no, on television. They listen to me on television.

When asked what other voices were talking to him, JH claimed that it was "because I was a Sir above, the Mafia wanted to watch me." Going on, he claimed that there was a statue of him in Edinburgh named Bonnie Prince Charles, but with JH's face. When asked for more detail about the voices:

> JH: Some are bad with pain, they talk to me about giving me pain, 'cause I'm a rotten sod to 'em. They swear at times, call me a bastard. I'm used to that word being used, I don't use it myself. But they do condemn me for writing the book, with my girl. . . . And I reckon they hit her, my daughter.
>
> AB: What, the voices?
>
> JH: Well, the Mafia can make you do things. If they want me bald and shave my head off, they'll do it, I'd have to do it, I tell you.
>
> AB: How do they make you do that?
>
> JH: They make your arm, grab hold of things and do it, cut it. Yes, you can't stop 'em.

He claims to have threatened to kill them off by reading the Bible, but that they now know that it's all over as there is a court case coming out against them, with the police working for him, in exchange for his help in picking up drug barons.

Interview 2.

    AB: How have you been?

    JH: Reasonable. I've had reasonable voices. No complaints about them. You know, they explain the reason for me being held up is that my father was Edward VIII. I was taken from him by the Mafia.

    AB: Last time you were telling me you thought the Queen Mother was your mum?

    JH: That's what I did think, they've made 'em think this. They've got a way of swaying the brain, by computer, it travels through the air like a wave to a wireless or something like that, television . . . and she did tell me in my head, spoke to me, said, "I am your mother, I know the full story." And I stopped her. 'Cause I said to the Queen when she spoke to me, she said, "You're my brother I think," and I said, "No I'm your cousin." This was years ago.

He goes on at a later point to explain that his real mother was Mrs. Simpson, the divorcee for whom Edward VIII abdicated in 1937. He went on to describe various financial transactions, and again gave a complex and detailed account of his political plans for running the world.

This was followed by a rather strange section on his having had a bent penis when young, and been laughed at, followed by further references to circumcision and sex, but no suggestion on this occasion that the voices were nasty to him or caused him to do things he didn't want.

Discussion. The same broad theme emerges in both interviews, of royal birth, although the suggested mother and father have changed. The elaborate parody of Thatcherite economics again comes through, together with clear overtones of paranoia featuring the Mafia, and the police who are regarded as allies. All this is presented in a rather earnest tone and somewhat convoluted style.

5. MH: *Good and bad angels*

MH is a 50-year-old man who was first admitted to hospital at the age of 21 when he was working as an assistant in a butcher's shop. At this time he showed typical schizophrenic symptoms – social withdrawal, auditory hallucinations, and various delusions. Subsequently MH has had around 20 admissions that culminated in his becoming chronically hospitalized 5 years ago. Recently he has become resettled and lives in the same hostel as patient RS.

In the past MH has shown a wide range of symptoms, both positive and negative. For several years, however, his clinical picture has been dominated by hypochondriacal delusions, bizarre ideas concerning bodily change and malfunction that he attributes to the work of good and bad angels. These delusions are extremely florid and incorporate delusional memories and bizarre delusional explanations. Of all the patients described, MH shows the most obvious evidence of negative symptoms. His schizophrenic deterioration is also associated with a degree of overall intellectual decline (see later).

Interview 1. MH began by describing the onset of his illness, with a disturbance of sleep and waking patterns, up for 2 days and 2 nights, with subsequent periods of difficulty in getting up in the morning that caused him to lose his job as a butcher. The critical event that led to his being brought to hospital was an occasion when he put a saucepan of milk on the stove and fell asleep, causing it to burn and almost setting fire to the house. When asked why he was so sleepy he said that he thought it might have resulted from a brain operation:

> MH: I just said I'll have the operation one day, and they took me down to the place, drew all the curtains, make it pitch black, and then this light came towards me, and that's all I know about it until after it's . . . I was told that I only had, somebody told me that I only had a square inch of brain to live on.

He reports now having a new brain that has been reprogrammed to be very similar to the old one, and "God keeps doing things to me to program it." He goes on to claim that he knows about God because of what a special female angel tells him, adding, "I am still getting damaged by other angels you see."

> AB: What sort of angels?
> MH: I don't know, I can't see them, I only know 'cause when they're inside me they talk to me.
> AB: And the female angel, is she always on your side?
> MH: Well she tests me out sometimes, she makes out she's somebody else. Just to make sure she knew how my brain worked, was working, 'cause God's going to make me a free man, that's what it amounts to. He's going to make me a free man.
> AB: What will she do to make you free?
> MH: When she's operating on me, the other angels come and puts bugs in the mess, and try and play me up, and she undoes all that when the angels are caught and . . . I mean, everyday of the week I'm getting this, more or less every day of the week, getting angels come in and do damage to me, and then it's repaired.
> AB: What sort of damage would they do?
> MH: Cut me insides and that – the whole lot's been replaced.
> AB: Has it? So why would it be replaced?
> MH: 'Cause God promised to replace anything that got damaged. He's protecting me. He's saved my life several times.
> AB: Can you tell me about it?

MH: When I was on Elm Ward, something or somebody took my spinal cord and I was walking around, and I feel a bit stiff, wondering why I was feeling so rough, and he came and mended that, he put a new heart in me.

AB: How would you know if your spinal cord was. . . . I would imagine that without a spinal cord you wouldn't be able to stand up or move your legs or anything, could you do that?

MH: I could do that, yeah.

AB: So why do you think it was the spinal cord? I mean, couldn't it just have been that you felt a bit rough that day?

MH: 'Cause God told me. All this time I've been in hospital, I've suffered more than I've ever suffered before in my whole life. It's no joke, and that R – , he gets on my bloody nerves. [R is patient RS.]

MH: He keeps on about he knows the whole Bible and he doesn't. . . . I told him, if he wanted to feel better he ought to get somebody to take the radio out of him, that's playing him up, 'cause he's talking to himself half the time, and giggling. I shouldn't talk about him, but I mean, he gets on my pip.

When questioned further about the reality of the radio inside RS, MH insisted that it was a real radio made by "holy people." Returning to the theme of angels, the question cropped up as to whether MH knew what they looked like:

MH: No I don't. . . . I saw one partially, it was only a glimpse.

AB: And what did she look like?

MH: I was messing about with one of my fridges, in my flat . . . and there was miniature men and women flying about after that. . . . They were living in the gas chamber in the fridge. I think they were trapped in there by somebody – it's a bit like genie and the magic lamp isn't it?

AB: What did they look like?

MH: I can't explain it, they were just four individuals . . . they had different colored clothes on.

AB: And could they fly?

MH: They could fly, yeah.

AB: With wings?

MH: I don't know, I couldn't notice that.

AB: And do you think that the ones that are inside your head are the same sort of angels?

MH: No, God's angels are different.

When asked if the nasty angels were also God's angels:

MH: Some of them make out they are. They're really doing me malicious damage, after they say that they're from God, and my angel takes their lives.

AB: I see, your angel kills them?

MH: Mm. Not all the time. God, he makes them operate on me and do operations inside me, instead of them doing damage all the time, he makes them do operations.

AB: And are these good operations?

MH: I don't know, it's something to do with me being a free man. The truth is I think I am working for God.

He suggests that God orders the operations to protect him, but that the bad angels do bad operations, all over his body.

MH: My legs have been sawn through, my head's been sawn through. Sawn through on the bone.

AB: Is there blood and things when that happens?

MH: No.

AB: So how do they manage to do it without blood?

MH: Well it might be blood inside. They don't damage your flesh.

AB: Have you ever talked to someone when this was happening? You know, so that they could see? Do you think if they were to take X-rays that you would see the angels?

MH: I doubt it, 'cause they're invisible to me to see.

AB: How do you know that they are angels though, and it's not just a way of thinking about pain?

MH: I talk in my head, and that's how God likes it 'cause he can communicate with the angels, tell me what's what.

MH goes on to explain that he thinks he has been chosen by God and is "a bit immortal."

MH: I contacted God on another planet, with a record player. I wired it up a special way. God just told me he came from space on another planet and that he was coming back quite soon.

When questioned further about the other planet he pointed out that he had never been there, but that the record player was the one in his room, and that God spoke to him when he was playing a holy record, not a hymn but a "Negro record" that had been lost in his flat. He goes on to explain that the reason for God's interest is that:

MH: They done lots and lots and lots of tests, just to make sure that I was his son, he said, "You are my son," and he was glad that he found me.

AB: So do you think you're Jesus Christ?

MH: Could be.

AB: But you're not sure?

MH: I've never been told that. I mean larking about in the house, they talk about things like that, they mentioned it the other night. Me and June sitting . . . , Edmund did, he was being funny, he's got a nasty nature.

AB: And this was about you being Jesus?

MH: Jesus Christ yes. We've got two Jesus Christs, pointing at June and at me.

AB: Who's the other Jesus Christ then?

MH: Me and June, he meant.

AB: But wasn't Jesus a man?

MH: Yes he was.

AB: So how come June is Jesus?

MH: Jesus *was* a man, but I believe he could change to woman.

AB: I suppose he could, yes. So if June is Jesus, and you're Jesus, doesn't that mean that you and June are the same?

MH: I don't know. I think we've got a similar blood count.

AB: Right, but you're not the same person are you?

MH: No.

AB: So how can you both be Jesus? I'm not sure I understand.

MH: That was his idea, it weren't my idea.

Interview 2. MH greeted me on this second occasion by telling me he had some news.

AB: What's the news?

MH: I had an angel, I think it was a foreign angel, operate on me, got in my head and operated on me, and then left me, and there was all electrical shorts and fire, and I beared it out most of the afternoon, then I got in town and I thought my angel came back and I told her to earth it, and she earthed it, and I'm OK again. And God's been operating on me today.

He went on to explain that the foreign angel took advantage of his angel being off doing another job for God. When asked about the start of his illness he again gave an account of his work as a butcher and the difficulty he had in getting up and being called to the main office where he was told, "We could sack you," and he said, "Well why don't you?," and they did. He goes on to give an account again of the various operations:

MH: Well God's given me a new brain. He's give me a new heart, he's give me new kidneys, he's give me new liver. He cut off my sperm so I wouldn't be masturbating too much. He told me I was spoken for, but I don't know who I'm spoken for yet, but I'm sure he's quite a good judge.

Discussion. MH talks reasonably clearly and coherently about the early stages of his illness, and his problem with coping with his job as a butcher. He talks in a surprisingly matter-of-fact way about his angels, and the way in which they remove his internal organs, and shows no embarrassment at the apparent bizarreness of this belief. His response to the question of evidence is to refer to what the angels say. Similarly, he seems quite happy to accept that both he and a female patient could be Jesus Christ, but perhaps understandably has rather less willingness to defend her claim. In general his language is relatively normal, and it is not at all difficult to carry on a reasoned discussion, apart from the occasional odd change of topic when he comments on other patients.

Making sense of the delusions

Taken as a whole, the five patients appear to produce a farrago of bizarre experiences and beliefs that are difficult if not impossible to make into a single coherent pattern. When considered individually, however, the striking thing was how reasonable many of the patients were, given that one was prepared to accept that they had had the very strange experiences they report. In general, the delusions were consistent across the two sessions, and represented a coherent way of interpreting the world.

This was particularly true of SD, who believes that he is both a Russian chess Grand Master and one or possibly more pop stars. He entirely accepts the strangeness of his not being able to speak Russian or play the guitar, but suggests that he may actually be different people at different times, with the necessary skills such as speaking Russian lying dormant when he is not functioning in that mode. While this is a bizarre view, it is reasonably coherent, and there have, of course, been cultures in which it was felt that the soul did go out of the body, for example during sleep. Furthermore, if one had seen oneself being interviewed on television as a rock star, as SD believed, it might give cause for reflection. Perhaps a further clue is given by the patient's response to the observation that he seems to imagine himself to have been some rather famous people, that "Well it's better than just being on the dole for 10 years."

While SD could be regarded as showing a pattern that is a rather exaggerated form of Walter Mitty daydreams, RS's delusions are clearly much more extreme, involving interplanetary wars, persecution, and delusions of grandeur, all presented in an odd and rather garbled style, complete with neologisms. The failure to note the same delusions on the following week, possibly due to paranoia makes it a little more difficult to decide how much was a consistent delusion and how much a set of spontaneous confabulations. Information from other sources suggests that RS has such a wealth of delusions that one can never be sure what is consistent and what is not. The main themes persist, although they evolve and change over the years.

It is clearly the case that a good deal of the content has been transferred from knowledge of the World War II and the behavior of the Nazis. The idea of mind switching and "bloodlines" and possession features strongly, while the idea of the mind "snapping" sounds like the popular concept of a "nervous breakdown," although the treatment by sausage, beans, and chips is somewhat unconventional. The neologisms often seem to have some association with the meaning. For example, the planet on which the Jews are being persecuted is called "Judacy," while the commander of M19 is called "Agapon Bond," presumably a reference to the fictional James Bond, although why another planet should be "Samosa Jorna" or Adolf Hitler "George Hurling" is not clear.

Whereas SD imagined himself as a number of people who lead more interesting, exciting, and successful lives than he does, EN seems to have taken aspects of her own life and passed them on to an imaginary sister, leaving herself as someone of noble birth who happens to have been adopted by a lowly family. Again there is a strong element

Table 16.1 *Characteristics of the delusions of the five patients studied*

Patient	Control	Voices	Paranoia	Grandeur	Visual Symptoms	Physical Symptoms	Sexual Content
SD: The chess master		X	X	X	X	X	X
RS: The interplanetary traveller	X	X	X	X	X	X	X
EN: Lady Dorothy			X	X	X		X
JH: The economist		X	X	X	X		X
MH: The man full of angels	X	X	X	X	X		

of wish fulfillment, together with a willingness to accept evidence that a normal person would regard as quite unconvincing.

JH also has a strong conviction of his royal birth, although the question of whether the Queen is his sister or cousin varied from one interview to the next. Like RS, he has delusions of grandeur, imagining himself to be a great financier and someone of considerable political weight who can sort out the world. This, together with the mystery of his royal birth, is used as an explanation for a paranoia, that was particularly marked during the second interview when he claims that he will be butchered by police if he tells too much.

Finally, MH is quite clear and lucid in talking about the way in which his illness interfered with his job, and he has a very coherent and persistent set of beliefs about the nature of his internal symptoms, in which the good and bad angels provide an account of both his headaches, somatic symptoms, and the hallucinatory voices. These seem to be much the strongest feature of his delusion, although there is also an underlying feeling that he has been "chosen" and that he may actually be Christ.

Table 16.1 lists some of the features that appear to crop up with some frequency and indicates their occurrence for each of the five patients. All of them show a degree of paranoia, coupled with grandiosity, with the two often linked; the patient is threatened because he is so important and hence is a threat to the established order. All but EN mentioned hallucinatory voices as an important component of their symptoms, and most refer to visual symptoms of one kind or another. In some cases these are hallucinations such as seeing angels emerging from a refrigerator, while others are rather less dramatic, a change in the brightness or perceived color of the world (EN and RS), or some form of facial distortion, as when SD's friend came to look like a pop musician or when JH reported that the statue of Bonnie Prince Charlie had his own face.

Another striking feature in virtually all cases is the presence of overt sexual content, often associated with guilt and reports of the failure of sexual relationships. Finally, the presence of painful physical symptoms, notably headaches and general malaise, together with reports of a feeling of being controlled from outside crops up in a number of cases.

How might one explain this pattern of findings? In psychiatry it has become customary to distinguish two phenomenological attributes of delusions, their *form*, or structural characteristics, and their *content*. In terms of form, all the patients show the classical features of delusions: they freely express beliefs that are patently untrue, that are idiosyncratic and not shared by others, that incline to the bizarre or even fantastic, and that are justified in an entirely illogical way – that sometimes amounts to little more than explaining delusions with more delusions. In addition, the beliefs are held onto with an extraordinary, matter-of-fact conviction, being expressed as though they were everyday happenings to be taken for granted (SD is something of an exception, in that some of his ideas are expressed with a degree of doubt, but this phenomenon of "partially held" delusions is well recognized). Another feature of the patients' delusions, that is particularly characteristic of delusions in schizophrenia, is their lack of systematization. Even the coherently expressed beliefs of SD and MH are not completely internally consistent. Some of those of the other patients are clearly contradictory, and in RS there is a chaos of widely differing beliefs. It is these formal aspects of delusions that, above all, give them their unique "ununderstandable" quality: normal individuals may hold outlandish beliefs, but when these are probed, it is clear that their mode of development and the ways in which they are justified and supported are quite different from the patients described here.

The content of our five patients' beliefs also makes them instantly recognizable as delusions. This is clearly at variance with the way in which our society assumes that the world operates and the mind works. People are not simultaneously pop singers and chess players; people do not regularly transport themselves to other planets, and are rather rarely the secret offspring of royalty. The content of delusions, however, is less opaque to understanding than their form. To some extent, many of the beliefs can be construed as explanations, albeit pathological explanations, of other experiences. The themes of grandeur and persecution could possibly represent exaggerated responses to normal feelings of elation, suspicion, and guilt. If such emotions occurred for no reason, it is reasonable to expect that the patient might try to come up with explanations for them. The same sort of process might well apply to feelings of not being in control of one's thoughts and actions, that then become attributed to influence by machines, X-rays, or telepathy. Even somatic symptoms, such as headache, dizziness, or anxiety could provide the stimulus for claims like MH's of having one's internal organs operated on by angels. Finally, auditory hallucinations should be able to provide a fertile source for delusional elaboration. In fact, this is recognized as the phenomenon of delusional explanation. Thus, for example, a patient who hears voices comes to believe that he has a radio transmitter in his head. Logically, this idea does not bear close scrutiny and it shows the typical delusional characteristics of fixity, absurdity, and so on; nevertheless the link between the experience and the belief is plain.

Given that we provisionally accept this rather simple-minded view of delusions as ways of making sense of some extraordinary experiences, how should we explain those experiences? The next section will be concerned with a brief discussion of existing accounts of delusional behavior, after which we will consider the neuropsychological evidence from our own patients and their controls.

Current explanations of delusions

As described, for example, by Frith (1992), historically there have been two main approaches to the explanation of delusions. One of these assumes that deluded patients apply normal logic to abnormal experiences, and the other assumes that the processes of logic are themselves disturbed.

The first view has a long tradition, but its only contemporary version is the theory proposed by Maher (1974). It can be illustrated by a quote from Evelyn Waugh's semi-autobiographical novel, *The Ordeal of Gilbert Pinfold*. Gilbert Pinfold is on a cruise, when he begins to hear voices: "For a long time, two hours perhaps, Mr Pinfold lay in his bunk listening. He was able to hear quite distinctly not only what was said in his immediate vicinity, but elsewhere. He had the light on, now, in his cabin, and as he gazed at the complex of tubes and wires that ran across his ceiling, he realized that they must form some sort of general junction in the system of communication. Through some trick or fault or wartime survival everything spoken in the executive quarters of the ship was transmitted to him" (Waugh, 1957).

Frith (1992) agrees that the assumption of normal reasoning coupled with abnormal experiences provides a good explanation where the primary symptom, for example auditory hallucinations, is clear, but argues that the theory is rather unsatisfactory when delusions are present in the absence of any obvious perceptual abnormality. (To explain delusions in these circumstances Maher (1974) invoked the idea of a "central neuropathology" that gives rise to an inchoate feeling of significance that is then in turn elaborated on.) The theory faces other difficulties, notably that it fails to explain why patients choose explanations for their experiences that are bizarre and fantastic rather than mundane. As Frith points out, the theory also predicts that normal individuals should develop delusions if subjected to abnormal experiences. However, patients with various abnormal perceptions such as tinnitus, epilepsy, and the phantom limb syndrome, do not generally become deluded. We will return to this point later.

The second traditional explanation proposes that delusions arise as a failure of judgment and intellect. Early versions suggested that delusions arise in a setting of poor general intellectual function that renders the patient unable to assess the evidence on which he forms beliefs adequately. This approach remains popular as an explanation of the ideas concerning theft and persecution that are seen in patients with dementia. However, it cannot be simply applied to schizophrenia, where it is well recognized that delusions are by no means restricted to patients who are of low intelligence or in whom general intellectual impairment has supervened. A recent version of this theory has been proposed by Hemsley and Garety (1986) and Garety, Hemsley, and Wessely (1991), who found evidence that deluded patients show a particular form of cognitive impairment – a tendency to be overconfident and jump to conclusions from limited information. Such an explanation, though postulating a specific deficit, still implies that delusions would be found particularly in patients whose illnesses are associated with widespread cognitive impairments.

A third possibility has recently been advocated by Frith (1992). He argues that delusions are a result of failure in central monitoring. Frith gives an account of attentional control based on that proposed by Shallice (1988) in which the attentional control of action depends upon two sources. The first involves the operation of well-learned schemata in response to control from environmental stimuli. The second comprises a supervisory attentional system that is responsible for willed intentions and that is capable of overriding the more habitual schema-based control processes. Frith proposes a monitoring system that is analogous to the feedback provided by corollary discharge in eye movements, and that informs the system both what was intended and what actually happened. Frith suggests that it is this monitoring process that is principally defective in schizophrenic patients leading to a dissociation between what the patient actually does and what they are aware of trying to do. This can account for certain types of delusion, particularly the important schizophrenic symptom of delusions of control – when willed behavior is dissociated from feedback, indicating that such activities had been initiated, the patient might understandably come to the conclusion that someone else is controlling his actions.

What might these three types of explanation predict in the way of neuropsychological deficits in patients demonstrating delusions? The explanation offered by Maher (1974) does not necessarily imply any particular neuropsychological impairment, though it would, of course, have to provide an explanation for the abnormal experiences.

The second class of hypothesis might predict that delusions should be most prominent in schizophrenic patients who show the most marked degrees of overall cognitive impairment. It is now well established that schizophrenia is associated with a general tendency to poor cognitive test performance, and in some, perhaps a majority of cases, this becomes translated into an IQ decline or more pronounced deficits that can occasionally approach the levels seen in dementia (see McKenna et al., in press, for a discussion of this).

In the case of the Frith hypothesis, one would expect delusions in schizophrenia to be associated with deficits on tests of executive function. Executive deficits are well documented in schizophrenia (e.g., see Frith, 1992; Shallice, Burgess, & Frith, 1991), but their association with symptoms has not been investigated to any great extent. Additionally, in light of the earlier discussion about the possible relationship between confabulation and delusions, one might also predict that deluded patients would be those who combine memory deficits with deficits in executive control. The next section therefore examines the neuropsychological characteristics of our patients, comparing them with five individually matched patients who were not deluded.

Table 16.2 *Psychiatric rating of the five deluded patients and their IQ matched control patients who were not currently deluded*

Patient	Delusions (range 0–45)	Hallucinations (range 0–30)	Formal Thought Disorder (range 0–45)	Negative Symptoms (range 0–24)
SD: The chess master (a)	15	5	1	10
Control patient (1)	2	5	3	13
RS: The interplanetary traveler (b)	27	0	12	4
Control patient (2)	1	7	1	12
EN: Lady Dorothy (c)	13	0	7	10
Control patient (3)	0	8	0	4
JH: The economist (d)	25	17	7	3
Control patient (4)	0	0	0	2
MH: The man full of angels (e)	25	11	1	12
Control patient (5)	3	6	0	16

Neuropsychological characteristics of patients with delusions

Although delusions are a prominent feature of schizophrenia, they are by no means universal in chronic patients; the five patients described were selected on the basis of having florid and persistent delusions as their leading symptom. For each of these patients a control patient was identified who was approximately matched in age, estimated premorbid IQ, and current level of intellectual functioning. These patients were not currently deluded, although, as with most patients with schizophrenia, most had shown some delusions at some earlier stage of their illnesses. Table 16.2 shows the characteristics of the five patients and their five matched controls on standardized ratings of schizophrenic symptoms. While there is, of course, a clear distinction in the delusional rating between each patient and his or her control, the two groups do not separate clearly on either hallucinations or negative symptoms, although four of the five show more evidence of formal thought disorder than their controls. This suggests the need for a closer examination of their neuropsychological performance.

Figure 16.1 shows four measures of overall cognitive performance. The National Adult Reading Test (NART) is an estimate of premorbid intelligence based on the capacity to read and correctly pronounce a series of irregular words varying in frequency. Current IQ was measured using the Wechsler Adult Intelligence Scale (WAIS), while two measures of dementia are included, the Mini Mental State Examination (MMSE), a dementia screening test developed by Folstein, Folstein, and McHugh (1975), and the Middlesex Elderly Assessment of Mental State (MEAMS), a neuropsychological screening test developed by Golding (1989). The pattern from all these measures is broadly consistent in suggesting that while the two groups are somewhat below average, they would not be categorized as suffering from dementia, and more importantly that there is no suggestion that those patients experiencing delusions were any lower in overall cognitive performance than the patients without delusions.

Figure 16.2 shows performance on a range of long-term memory measures. The Rivermead Behavioral Memory Test (Wilson, Cockburn, Baddeley, & Hiorns, 1989) provides an estimate of probable memory performance outside the clinic, with subtests assessing visual and verbal memory, together with memory for a route, prospective memory, and an estimation of orientation in time and place. Three subjects in each group show a moderate degree of impairment, while two were more severely impaired in memory performance. Overall, however, the two groups do not differ. No clear difference is shown on the two semantic memory tests that contribute to the Speed and Capacity of Language Processing Test (Baddeley, Emslie, & Nimmo-Smith, 1992). The spot-the-word test is a lexical decision task requiring the subject to decide which of a series of pairs of items constitutes a real word and which a pseudoword. The test is unspeeded and provides a measure of vocabulary and, indirectly, an estimate of probable premorbid intelligence. The two groups do not differ on this, nor do they differ in either speed or accuracy on the semantic processing test that involves verification of sentences that are either obviously true (e.g., "Slippers are sold in pairs"), or obviously false (e.g., "US Presidents have feathers"). As the cutoff points for normal performance indicate, with the exception of patient MH (the man full of angels), accuracy of lexical decision is within the normal limits and approximately equal for the two groups. Speed of semantic processing is again rather slow, with patient MH being abnormally so; in general, however, the two groups are approximately comparable both in speed and accuracy.

We next considered the performance of the two groups on tests that are assumed to be sensitive to deficits in executive function, or to frontal lobe damage. The results of these are shown in Figure 16.3. One of the most frequently used measures of executive function is the Wisconsin card sorting test, in which subjects are required to sort cards according to a series of different cues such as color, size, border, etc. Once the subject has learned to sort on a given dimension, then the dimension is switched. Performance is measured in terms of how many of the six successive sorting dimensions can be achieved, and on the number of perseverative errors in which the subject goes on making a response according to the previously correct dimension. For the present series of patients the simplified version of the test developed by Nelson (1976) was employed. It is clear from Figure 16.3 that if anything, the patients with delusions perform rather better than the controls, with all of the deluded patients acquiring the maximum of six categories and tending to show, if anything, less evidence of perseveration than the control subjects.

The next classic measure of executive function is the verbal fluency task, in which the subject is asked to generate as many items as possible from either a semantic category, in this case animals, or from words beginning with an initial letter, in this case *S*. Sixty seconds were allowed, and the results are shown in Figure 16.3, together with the cutoff point for normal performance. There is no doubt that performance is rather poor

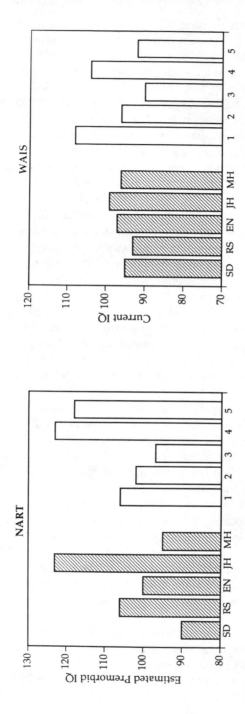

Figure 16.1 Overall performance of deluded patients and nondeluded control patients on the National Adult Reading Test (NART), Wechsler Adult Intelligence Test (WAIT), Mini Mental State Examination (MMSE), and Middlesex Elderly Assessment of Mental State (MEAMS) (continued next page).

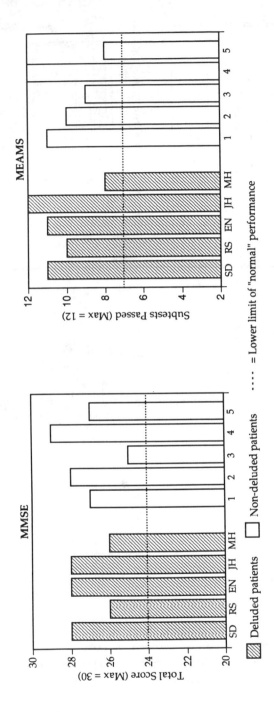

Figure 16.1 (continued).

415

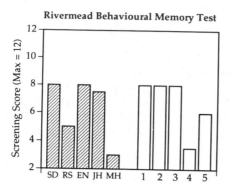

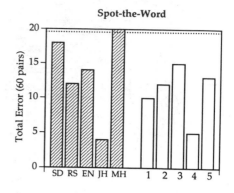

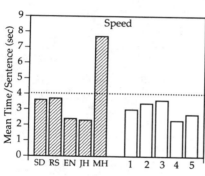

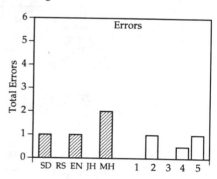

Figure 16.2 Performance of deluded and nondeluded patients on test of episodic memory, the Rivermead Behavioral Memory Test, and on two tests of semantic memory, one involving accuracy of lexical decision (spot-the-word), and the other speed and accuracy of sentence verification (semantic processing).

on both fluency tasks, a result that is characteristic of the performance of schizophrenic patients (Clare et al., 1993). There is, once again, however, no clear evidence of a difference between the two groups; the patients with delusions seem to do slightly worse on category fluency, but this is not the case for letter fluency. The absence of a clear difference between groups also holds for the final dysexecutive task, that involving cognitive estimates, in which subjects are asked to answer a series of questions for

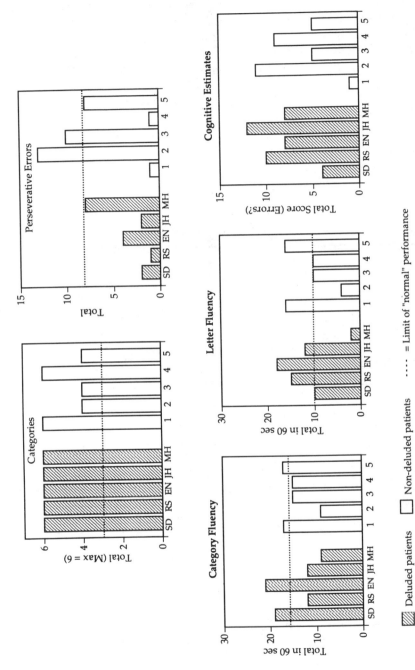

Figure 16.3 Performance of deluded and nondeluded patients on tests of frontal lobe or executive function, the Wisconsin Card Sorting Test, Category and Letter Fluency, and the Cognitive Estimates Test.

417

which they need to work out the answer using general knowledge. Examples include, "What is the average length of a man's spine?," or "How high is the Post Office Tower in London?" Certain patients with the dysexecutive syndrome tend to make a large number of errors on these questions, by typically coming up with fantastic or bizarre results rather than working out something that is broadly sensible (Shallice & Evans, 1978).

Autobiographical memory and patients with delusions

Our final comparison concerned the performance of the two groups on the Autobiographical Memory Inventory (Kopelman et al., 1990), in which subjects are tested for both "personal semantic memory," that is, knowledge of facts about their early life such as the names of teachers and the addresses of schools, and also about personal episodes, with memory in each case being probed for early life, midlife, and for recent memories (see Figure 16.4). Mean performance on the recall of autobiographical facts was reasonably good in both groups, with the exception once again of patient MH, a deluded patient who also scored poorly on tests of both episodic and semantic memory.

The second panel of Figure 16.4 shows performance for the two groups on recollecting three episodes from each of three different periods of life. A score of 3 is given for each incident recalled from a specific time and place, 2 for a specific personal memory with unspecified time and place, 1 for a vague personal memory, and 0 for a response

Autobiographical Memory Inventory

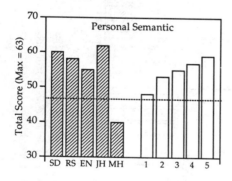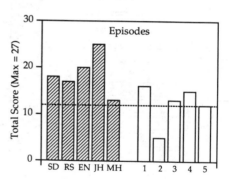

☒ Deluded patients   ☐ Non-deluded patients

- - - - = Lower limit of "normal" performance

Figure 16.4 Performance of the two patient groups on the Autobiographical Memory Inventory. The left panel represents performance on test of "personal semantic memory" such as the recall of names of teachers or school friends, while the right panel represents the capacity to recollect specific episodes.

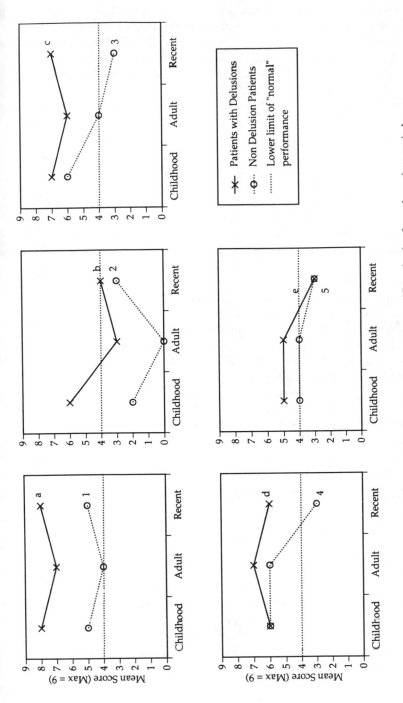

Figure 16.5 Capacity of deluded and nondeluded patients to recollect specific episodes from three time periods.

419

based on general semantic information. There is on this autobiographical incident score a suggestion that the two groups might differ, with the patients without delusions, somewhat unexpectedly, performing more poorly than the deluded group. Figure 16.5 gives a more detailed analysis of performance on this aspect of the test, comparing each patient with his or her control across the three periods of the life span. There is no evidence of a consistent temporal gradient over time such as is typically shown by Korsakoff patients (Kopelman, 1985), but the tendency for poorer performance in the nondeluded subjects occurs for each of the five pairs of subjects studied. On this measure therefore, the deluded patients are comparatively normal, whereas the nondeluded tend to show impairment.

Failure to produce autobiographical memories can be reflected in either of two ways. One is the failure to produce any recollection from the relevant time period, while the second is the production of generic memories rather than specific episodes. Examples of the latter include, "My parents take me to the pub every Wednesday," or "I nearly had a girlfriend. I used to go to visit her, but she didn't want anything to do with me. My mum drove me there." Figure 16.6 shows the distribution of these three types of responses, illustrating the tendency of the nondeluded patients to produce both generic memories, and in three cases a failure to recollect any personal incident. However, although the rate of production of personal recollections among deluded patients was relatively normal, their content was less so. While they were typically not obviously delusional, they did tend to be somewhat odd, such as, "When I was a child I was dressed up in girls' clothes," or "My friend GM had cut her throat in the bath," or "I burnt a bush down near a well and got into serious trouble."

While it would be unwise to place too much weight on a single unexpected difference between the two groups in autobiographical memory, this aspect of our results would certainly seem worth further investigation. Such a view is reinforced by a study that reached us during the revision of the present paper in which David and Howard (in press) applied the measures of experimental phenomenology developed by Johnson and Raye (1981) to the evaluation of delusional and nondelusional memories by schizophrenic patients. They observed that delusional memories tended to be rated as clearer and having a more sensory character than "real" memories; they suggest that this may play an important role in their acceptance as veridical by the patients. David and Howard note that the factual knowledge of their patients is intact, and propose an interpretation of the origin of delusions that is not dissimilar to our own.

To summarize the neuropsychological results, our deluded patients who were matched on overall intellectual performance show no evidence for poorer executive functioning then the nondeluded group. Memory performance also seems approximately the same, although there is a difference in pattern of performance on the Autobiographical Memory Inventory. Here, the two groups appear to be equivalent and comparatively normal in their capacity to recall autobiographical facts from their earlier life, but differ in their capacity to produce specific autobiographical memories. The control subjects appear to be more limited in their capacity to recall such memories than

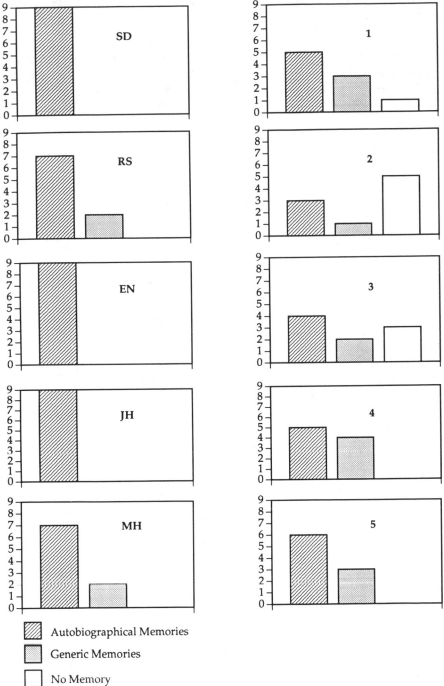

Autobiographical Memories

Generic Memories

No Memory

Figure 16.6 Responses from deluded patients (a–e) and control patients (1–5) to the request to produce a total of nine autobiographical recollections.

the deluded patients, who seem to produce rather a high proportion of "odd" memories, that may or may not be delusional in origin.

Discussion

The pattern of performance on the Autobiographical Memory Inventory is the most unexpected feature of the neuropsychological investigation. This is because the most abnormal pattern of behavior has come from the control patients, who are schizophrenic, but who do not report delusions. The deluded patients, for the most part, show reasonably good autobiographical memory, particularly when measured in terms of the personal semantic component. Their episodic recollections are perhaps slightly impaired, and do seem to contain a rather high proportion of rather odd recollections. These may be confabulatory, or they simply may reflect either the somewhat odd lives that patients have often led, or perhaps a rather idiosyncratic choice of memory.

On the other hand, the pattern of performance for the nondeluded patients is distinctly unusual in that their autobiographical recollection appears to be relatively normal, while their capacity for recalling personal incidents is very poor. The typical pattern is for performance on these two aspects of autobiographical memory to be highly correlated (Kopelman et al., 1989), and although there are starting to appear one or two individual cases of the isolated impairment of either the semantic component (e.g., De Renzi, Liotti, & Nichelli, 1987) or the episodic component (Hodges, personal communication, 1994), to the best of our knowledge, this is the first time that a group has shown this differential disruption of capacity to recollect personal experiences, although Williams and Broadbent (1986) reported a tendency for patients who have attempted suicide to show a lack of richness and detail in their autobiographical recollections. This issue is discussed in more detail by Williams (in press; this volume).

Of the three explanations of delusions discussed earlier, the impaired reasoning hypothesis would predict an association between delusions and dementia or impaired general intellectual functioning. Such a link was not observed. Frith's (1992) interpretation, in terms of impaired executive processes, might seem to predict that the deluded patients would perform more poorly on executive or frontal lobe tests, which again was certainly not the case. On the present evidence, it seems unlikely that delusions arise because of a general intellectual executive deficit. The possibility remains, of course, that the relevant executive deficit is one that is not reflected in any of the conventional frontal lobe tests that we used, but until a more suitable measure is proposed and evaluated, our data lend little support to Frith's position. The remaining hypothesis is Maher's (1974) suggestion that delusions represent an attempt to come to terms with extraordinary experiences; this was not tested.

While it thus seems unlikely that delusions will yield to any simple neuropsychological interpretation, it might be possible to use some of the above theory and experiment to lay the groundwork for a more detailed account of the phenomenon. The approach we take makes the assumption that the pathological process affecting cognitive function in schizophrenia is relatively nonspecific and affects multiple cognitive subsystems. It also draws on the classical phenomenological division between the form and content of delusions, proposing that insights as to the former might be sought by reference to processes occurring within memory, whereas understanding of the latter is likely to require understanding how experience itself is integrated.

Attempts to account for the symptoms of schizophrenia tend to have assumed that the disorder results from a single deficit, specified either in terms of a cognitive function (e.g., selective attention or executive function) or in terms of a particular anatomical region (usually the frontal or temporal lobes). Another possibility, of course, is that the cause may be less anatomically and functionally specific than this. One possibility, for example, might be a deficit in a neurotransmitter system that plays an important role in a number of different cognitive and emotional subsystems. Such a deficit would be expected to have rather diffuse and diverse effects. An analogy might be with the effect of reducing the oil supply on the economic activity of a Western state. Some of the effects would be direct and obvious, but many would be complex and indirect, such as changing preferred residential patterns away from those involving lengthy travel to work.

Picking up a complex pattern of cognitive and other deficits resulting from the disruption of several anatomically separate systems that happen to use a common neurotransmitter would be likely to prove difficult. It is possible that there may be a clear common function, such as the reduction in inhibition across a range of systems, that could have a common signature. Cohen and Servan-Schreiber (1992) present a model of this kind, supported by PDP simulation; while the range of evidence they attempt to explain is disappointingly narrow and selective, this type of approach would seem to have considerable potential for offering explanations of diseases such as schizophrenia and Alzheimer's disease. Furthermore, if the assumption is made that the distribution of the neurochemical imbalance is not uniform across patients, then it becomes possible in principle to explain the marked individual differences in the pattern of deficit reflected in diseases such as schizophrenia (McKenna et al., 1990) and Alzheimer's disease (Baddeley, Della Sala, & Spinnler, 1991).

The form of delusions

As noted at the beginning of this chapter, there are certainly structural similarities between confabulation and delusions. Both consist of the production of false factual information, both are held with firm conviction, and both may be fantastic in nature. In addition, both are concerned solely with the individual's own personal experience. The two phenomena also show differences. Confabulations are false episodic memories, whereas delusions seem to involve personal semantic information. Confabulations characteristically shift and change, whereas delusions tend to be relatively fixed. However, it is apparent from the five schizophrenic patients' delusions presented earlier that these differences are relative rather than absolute – EN showed delusional memories and some of RS's and JH's delusions gave the impression of being less than completely stable.

Although we found no support for the idea that delusions are associated with a deficit in executive function, either by itself or in association with memory impairment as in confabulation, our examination of schizophrenic patients did throw up the finding that those with and without delusions show different patterns of autobiographical recollection. This parallels a pattern seen in frontal lobe patients with and without confabulation (Baddeley & Wilson, 1986). One group of patients produced fluent and extensive recollections inconsistent from one test to another, while the other group produced very few memories, but did so consistently. This suggests that a common factor linking confabulation and delusion lies not in executive function but in memory. It could be that when memory impairment is coupled with executive impairment, confabulation is the result, whereas for delusions to be the outcome, memory impairment needs to interact with some other unknown factor or factors. There is plenty of scope for such unknown factors, if it is assumed that the pathological process of schizophrenia has a number of effects, both direct and indirect, on different cognitive systems.

The content of delusions

Historically there is considerable controversy as to whether the experiences of schizophrenics are unique and uncommunicable as Jaspers (1959) suggests, or could perhaps be considered as a distortion of normal experience. Evidence for a possible continuum comes from questionnaires in which samples of normal subjects have been asked about their experience of such apparently abnormal phenomena as hallucinations. The results of such studies suggest that hallucinations are by no means limited to schizophrenic patients. One area of overlap between hallucination and normal experience is represented by the phenomenon of hypnogogic and hypnopompic imagery studied a few years ago by McKellar (1957). Hypnogogic images are visual or auditory sensory experiences that occur just as one is falling asleep. They are phenomenologically similar to experiences resulting from a genuine external stimulus, but occur in the absence of a stimulus. They can include such things as voices saying a phrase, or in the case of a colleague who had been driving too long one night, of the sensation that he was just about to drive into a ballroom full of dancers.

Dreams also represent a situation in which we appear to hear and see things, often as part of an elaborate and complex scenario, that may be bizarre, but nevertheless tends to be accepted as veridical during the time that we are experiencing the dream. In the case of one of us at least (AB), a dream has occasionally fused into a semiwaking state. A street lamp shines a shaft of light across the ceiling of the bedroom overlooking a route that revelers often take when returning from the pub. On being awakened on one occasion, AB became convinced that the ray of light had some sinister and supernatural function. The possibility that it came from a street lamp was considered carefully, but rejected for now-forgotten reasons. One feature of the experience was the apparent inability to bring "common sense" to bear on the problem, together with a combination of, on the one hand, a substantial superstitious fear and, on the other, the response, "Well never mind, let's go back to sleep."

While not everyone has these strange nocturnal experiences, everyone dreams, and presumably has bizarre experiences during these dreams, that may well be accompanied by emotions such as fear or suspicion or joy. Why do we have these when asleep and not awake? And if schizophrenic patients do have such experiences when awake, why do they not subsequently dismiss them in the same way as normal people deal with their dreams?

There are, of course, a number of theories of experience that suggest more than one state of consciousness: the Freudian concept of the unconscious, for example, or some of the popular extrapolations from interhemispheric differences that suggest that we have two minds – an analytic, controlled, left-hemisphere mind, and an emotional, intuitive, right-hemisphere mind. While not finding either of these particularly attractive, we suggest that it is likely to be necessary to assume a system that operates at more than one level of awareness. One recent model that makes such a distinction is the interacting cognitive subsystems (ICS) model proposed by Barnard (1985) in order to explain a range of psycholinguistic data, and more recently developed by Teasdale and Barnard (1993) into a model for handling the interaction between cognition and emotion. In addition to a series of relatively peripheral cognitive systems that could be broadly mapped onto the phonological and visuospatial slave systems of working memory, there lie two more central systems, namely the propositional and the implicational systems.

Figure 16.7 shows the structure of interacting cognitive subsystems proposed by Barnard and Teasdale (1991). The acoustic morpholexical and articulatory subsystems are concerned with language processing, and the visual, object, and limb subsystems with vision and motor behavior. The propositional and implicational subsystems comprise what Teasdale and Barnard refer to as "the central engine" of cognition. The propositional system is concerned with semantic entities and relationships; "knowing that" something is the case depends on this subsystem. It is, of course, linked with both the visual object processing system and with the morpholexical language system, and is one of the major ways of interacting with the implicational subsystem. The type of information in the implicational subsystem is the most difficult to describe because it represents "an abstract description of human existential space itself." It is concerned with both ideational and emotional information, as well as somatic information regarding bodily feelings such as pain, muscle tension, or gastric discomfort. The implicational system contains schematic models of experience, but these are represented in a holistic rather than analytic sense.

Barnard (personal communication, 1993) has suggested that schizophrenia may reflect a disruption of communication between the propositional and implicational components of the central engine of cognition, resulting in a mismatch between the feelings experienced, including bodily sensations, as represented in the implicational system, and their transformation into a propositional code. This could produce an incorrect attribution of self-generated inner speech, leading to experiences such as auditory hallucination, which, in turn, may result in delusional explanations. By a similar process, the misattribution of willed or motor behavior may result in delusions of mind control. This aspect of the explanation does, of course, have much in common with that proposed by Frith (1992), but has the advantage that it is embedded in a rather broader theoretical framework. It is notable that the implicational subsystem is also accessed directly by

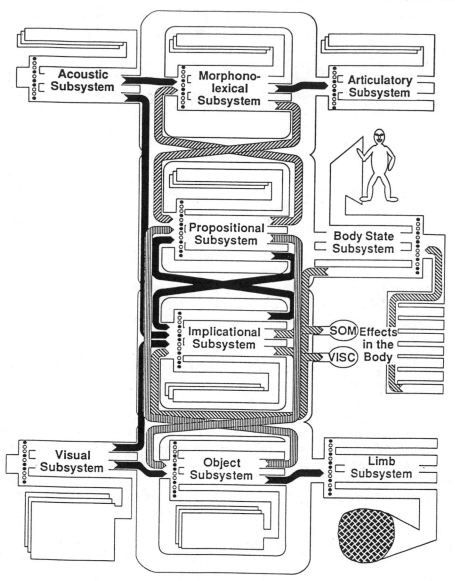

Figure 16.7 Barnard's interacting cognitive subsystems model. It can be broadly divided into three components, an audition-language-speech system, a vision-object recognition-motor response system, and a core system that stores and manipulates semantic and experiential data, and is accessed by emotional and body-state information. (Adapted from Teasdale and Barnard, 1993.)

the body state subsystem that produces somatic sensations, and these, of course, also feature strongly in the delusions reported by our patients. While the model has been developed and applied to the analysis of depression (Teasdale & Barnard, 1993), its application to schizophrenia is still at an embryonic stage. However, given its impressive scope and success in dealing with the interaction between cognition and emotion, the model would seem to have considerable promise in the area of schizophrenia.

In conclusion, while the delusional beliefs of schizophrenic patients are often bizarre, our results suggest that they do not simply reflect the breakdown of autobiographical memory as a result of cognitive deficit. The patients studied on the whole are much less impaired than many neuropsychological cases who show no evidence of either delusional or confabulatory behavior. In general, the delusions are coherent and seem more readily interpretable on the assumption that the patient is attempting to rationalize some extraordinary experiences. In doing so, the patient typically abandons the generally held social norms as to what is and what is not plausible. It is important to bear in mind, however, that such norms are a social construction, and that other cultures, and indeed our own culture in earlier times, are quite happy to accept beliefs in witchcraft, mind control, and magic. Studying the way in which the schizophrenic patient reconstructs reality may well have important lessons to teach us about the way in which the rest of us construct our autobiographical memories.

References

Baddeley, A. D., Della Sala, S., & Spinnler, H. (1991). The two-component hypothesis of memory deficit in Alzheimer's disease. *Journal of Clinical and Experimental Neuropsychology, 13,* 372–380.

Baddeley, A. D., Emslie, H., & Nimmo-Smith, I. (1992). *The Speed and Capacity of Language Processing (SCOLP) Test.* Bury St. Edmunds, Suffolk: Thames Valley Test Company.

Baddeley, A. D., & Wilson, B. (1986). Amnesia, autobiographical memory and confabulation. In D. C. Rubin (Ed.), *Autobiographical memory* (pp. 225–252). New York: Cambridge University Press.

—— (1988). Frontal amnesia and the dysexecutive syndrome. *Brain and Cognition, 7,* 212–230.

Barnard, P. (1985). Interacting cognitive subsystems: A psycholinguistic approach to short-term memory. In A. Ellis (Ed.), *Progress in the psychology of language* (Vol. 2, pp. 197–258). London: Lawrence Erlbaum.

—— (1993). Personal communication.

Barnard, P. J., & Teasdale, J. D. (1991). Interacting cognitive subsystems: A systemic approach to cognitive-affective interaction and change. *Cognition and Emotion, 5,* 1–39.

Clare, L., McKenna, P. J., Mortimer, A. M., & Baddeley, A. D. (1993). Memory in schizophrenia: What is impaired and what is preserved? *Neuropsychologia, 31,* 1225–1241.

Cohen, J. D., & Servan-Schreiber, D. (1992). Context, cortex and dopamine: A connectionist approach to behaviour and biology in schizophrenia. *Psychological Review, 99,* 45–77.

David, A. S., & Howard, R. (In press). An experimental phenomenological approach to delusional memory in schizophrenia and late paraphrenia. *Psychological Medicine.*

De Renzi, E., Liotti, M., & Nichelli, N. (1987). Semantic amnesia with preservation of autobiographic memory. A case report. *Cortex, 23,* 575–597.

Folstein, M. F., Folstein, S. E., & McHugh, P. R. (1975). 'Mini-Mental State': A practical method for grading the cognitive state of patients for the clinician. *Journal of Psychiatric Research, 12,* 189–198.

Frith, C. D. (1992). The cognitive neuropsychology of schizophrenia. Hove: Lawrence Erlbaum.

Garety, P. A., Hemsley, D. R., & Wessely, S. (1991). Reasoning in deluded schizophrenic and paranoid patients: Biases in performance on a probabilistic inference task. *Journal of Nervous and Mental Disease, 179,* 194–201.

Golding, E. (1989). *The Middlesex Elderly Assessment of Mental State.* Bury St. Edmunds, Suffolk: Thames Valley Test Company.

Hemsley, D. R., & Garety, P. A. (1986). The formation and maintenance of delusions: A Bayesian analysis. *British Journal of Psychiatry, 149,* 51–56.

Hodges, J. (1994). Personal communication.

Jaspers, K. (1959). General psychopathology. In J. Joenig and M. W. Hamilton (Trans.), 1963. Manchester, UK: Manchester University Press.

Johnson, M. K., & Raye, C. L. (1981). Reality monitoring. *Psychological Review, 88,* 67–85.

Kopelman, M. D. (1985). Rates of forgetting in Alzheimer-type dementia and Korsakoff's syndrome. *Neuropsychologia, 23,* 623–638.

—— (1987). Two types of confabulation. *Journal of Neurology, Neurosurgery and Psychiatry, 50,* 1482–1487.

Kopelman, M. D., Wilson, B. A., & Baddeley, A. D. (1989). The autobiographical memory interview: A new assessment of autobiographical and personal semantic memory in amnesic patients. *Journal of Clinical and Experimental Neuropsychology, 11,* 724–744.

—— (1990). *The Autobiographical memory interview.* Bury St. Edmunds, Suffolk: Thames Valley Test Company.

Maher, B. A. (1974). Delusional thinking and perceptual disorder. *Journal of Individual Psychology, 30,* 98–113.

McKellar, P. (1957). *Imagination and thinking: A psychological analysis.* London: Cohen and West.

McKenna, P. J., Clare, L., & Baddeley, A. D. (1995). Schizophrenia. In A. D. Baddeley, B. A. Wilson, & F. N. Watts (Eds.), *Handbook of memory disorders.* Chichester, UK: John Wiley.

McKenna, P. J., Tamlyn, D., Lund, C. E., Mortimer, A. M., Hammond, S., & Baddeley, A. D. (1990). Amnesic syndrome in schizophrenia. *Psychological Medicine, 20,* 967–972.

Morice, R., & Delahunty, A. (1994). Working memory impairment in schizophrenia. Personal communication.

Nelson, H. E. (1976). A modified card sorting test sensitive to frontal lobe defects. *Cortex, 12,* 313–324.

Rubin, D. C. (Ed.). (1986). *Autobiographical memory.* Cambridge, UK: Cambridge University Press.

Shallice, T. (1988). *From neuropsychology to mental structure.* New York: Cambridge University Press.

Shallice, T., Burgess, P. W., & Frith, C. D. (1991). Can the neuropsychological case-study approach be applied to schizophrenia? *Psychological Medicine, 21,* 661–673.

Shallice, T., & Evans, M. E. (1978). The involvement of the frontal lobes in cognitive estimation. *Cortex, 14,* 294–303.

Tamlyn, D., McKenna, P. J., Mortimer, A. M., Lund, C. E., Hammond, S., & Baddeley, A. D. (1992). Memory impairment in schizophrenia: Its extent, affiliations and neuropsychological character. *Psychological Medicine, 22,* 101–115.

Teasdale, J. D., & Barnard, P. J. (1993). *Affect, cognition and change.* Hove, Sussex: Lawrence Erlbaum.

Waddington, J. L. (1993). Neurodynamics of abnormalities of cerebral metabolism and structure in schizophrenia. *Schizophrenia Bulletin, 19,* 55–69.

Waugh, E. (1957). *The ordeal of Gilbert Pinfold.* London: Chapman and Hall.

Williams, J. M. G. (1995). Depression and the specificity of autobiographical memory. In D. Rubin (Ed.), *Constructing our past: Autobiographical memory.* New York: Cambridge University Press.

Williams, J. M. G., & Broadbent, K. (1986). Autobiographical memory in suicide attempters. *Journal of Abnormal Psychology, 95,* 144–149.

Wilson, B., Cockburn, J., Baddeley, A., & Hiorns, R. (1989). The development and validation of a test battery for detecting and monitoring everyday memory problems. *Journal of Clinical and Experimental Neuropsychology, 11,* 855–870.

Wilson, B. A. & Wearing, D. (In press). A permanent state of just awakening. In R. Campbell & M. Conway (Eds.), *Broken Memories: Neuropsychological case studies.* Oxford, UK: Blackwell.

Subject index

accessibility principle, of memory dating, 132
accuracy, 39, 45, 70, 223
   confidence in, 4, 25, 26, 47–9
   of dating, 130, 134–5, 143, 144, 152, 153
   for details, 44, 221
   of recall, 7–8, 9, 219, 235
   related to imagery, 35–6, 43
   of victims compared to bystanders, 222
action sequences, 87
activity contexts, 258
affect intensity, 203
affective components of emotional events,
   231
affective-evaluative remarks, 278, 282
affective memory, 204, 231, 233
age distribution, of memories, 372
Alzheimer's disease, 1, 153, 423
amnesia, 5, 74, 153
   anterograde, 85–6, 224
   functional, 95, 204
   hysterical, 221, 232
   infant/childhood, 255, 362, 364
   retrograde, 71–2, 82, 83, 88, 89
amnesic deficits, 385
amnesics, 6, 232, 246
amnesic syndrome, 384
anchoring point, 331, 332, 334
anxiety, 206, 219, 262
arousal, emotional, 220
autobiographical facts, 19, 31, 38, 253, 254
   recall of, 385, 418, 420
autobiographical knowledge, 67, 69, 76, 80,
   81, 88
avoidance, 257, 262

Beck inventory for diagnosing depression,
   234
behaviorist, 22, 56
behavior, multiple construals of, 201
benchmarks, 189. *See also* landmark events
bias, retrospective, 205
biological memory mechanism, 32, 37
blends, of memories, 186
blocking hypothesis, 169–70, 171
boundaries, 131, 143, 144
brain damaged patients, 254, 264, 385
brain injury, 82
breakfast questionnaire, 34, 35
British Empiricists, 27

Challenger explosion, memories of, 42, 43,
   45, 48, 158
Chernobyl nuclear power disaster, 133
childhood, 26, 209
   abuse, 172, 173, 257
   memories of, 255–6
   stress, 260
   trauma, 219
children's memories, 361, 363
   of emotional events, 222–3, 225
   generic nature of, 252, 256
   recounting skills and, 346, 354
children's memory responses, 348, 351, 352
   and maternal elaborations, 349, 350
children's personal narratives, 343, 346
chronological organization theory, 133
chronological recall, 141
coding, of event succession in memory, 133
cognition and emotion interaction, 425, 427

429

Author index

448